Windows Forms in Action

Windows Forms in Action

Second Edition of
Windows Forms Programming with C#

ERIK BROWN

MANNING

Greenwich
(74° w. long.)

For online information and ordering of this and other Manning books, go to www.manning.com. The publisher offers discounts on this book when ordered in quantity. For more information, please contact:

Special Sales Department
Manning Publications Co.
209 Bruce Park Avenue
Greenwich, CT 06830
Fax: (203) 661-9018
email: orders@manning.com

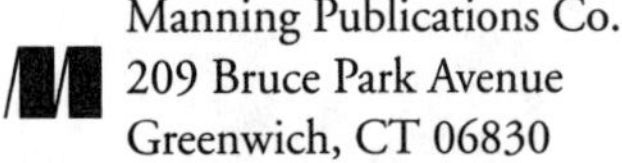

Manning Publications Co.
209 Bruce Park Avenue
Greenwich, CT 06830

Copyeditor: Liz Welch
Typesetter: Dottie Marsico
Cover designer: Leslie Haimes

ISBN 1932394-65-6

Printed in the United States of America
1 2 3 4 5 6 7 8 9 10 – VHG – 10 09 08 07 06

In memory of Thelma Rose Wilson,
and for her beautiful daughter, whom I still love

brief contents

contents

preface

In my younger days at school and later working with various startup companies, I thought Unix ruled the world and never expected to find myself working with "the dark side" of the computer industry: that is, Microsoft Corporation. So I find it amusing that here I am publishing not a first but a second book in support of Microsoft technologies. I guess you go where the road leads, and my paths have carried me fully into the depths of Windows-based development. Fortunately, I am happy with my conversion, which I suppose is the way of the dark side.

As to this publishing idea, it is a very curious thing. The excitement of writing wears off after a while, and you realize that you not only want to write a book, you want to write a good book. This changes your approach and mentality, in that you put in the extra effort and time to make it "good." Then one day you have another revelation: you not only want to write a good book, you want to write a book people actually like and are willing to purchase.

Such was my journey for both the first and the second editions of this book. The first edition was reasonably well received, and a second edition for .NET 2.0 seemed apparent. Unfortunately, those clever folks at Microsoft added and changed so much of the Windows Forms namespace that I found myself rewriting pretty much the entire book.

While you might think the journey involved for a second edition is easier than the first, don't kid yourself. It is true that I knew how to approach the text and the basic format is the same, but as a "seasoned author" I wanted to create a better design for both the book and the sample application built throughout. The chapters are more concise and I attempted to apply my experience with .NET enterprise application development at Unisys Corporation to generate a better program design. I added more diversions from the main MyPhotos application to cover additional material and to present code samples for alternate or interesting topics.

Another curious fact was that while writing the first edition of this book I was a consultant, and it was fairly easy to take weeks off here and there to devote to writing. As a full-time program manager these days, finding such time for the second edition was not easy. My family and friends were equally supportive for both editions, for which I am very thankful.

In the end, I find myself quite happy with this second edition of the book. Some key concepts and classes, such as encryption, custom controls, and progress bars, found their way into the text. I like the chapter layout for the second edition, from 18 chapters in the first edition to 23 chapters in this book. I am also much happier with the index, which I'm sure you'll find easier to use than in the first edition.

Another big change between the first and second editions of this book is the title. This edition has been renamed *Windows Forms in Action* to differentiate it from other books and to work with Manning's new "in Action" titling theme. The Action-Result table format used throughout this book lends itself to our new name. New title, new cover, new chapters, and we appear to have a book.

Enjoy.

preface to the first edition

In early 2001 I began using Microsoft's .NET Framework for a project I was working on with a small startup company. Unfortunately, the winds changed and I found myself with more free time than I would normally hope for. So when Manning Publications asked me if I would contribute to a book on programming with the .NET Framework, I welcomed the idea.

As events unfolded, I found myself with some fairly strong opinions about how such a book should be organized, and offered up a proposal to write a solo book on programming Windows Forms applications. I have always enjoyed the book *Programming Windows 95 with MFC* by Jeff Prosise, so a book about developing Windows-based applications with the .NET Framework seemed like an obvious subject.

The core idea behind my proposal was to build a single application over the course of the book. The application would evolve to introduce each topic, so that by the end of the manuscript readers would have a robust application they had built from scratch. Manning Publications seemed to like the idea as well, and thus I suddenly found myself writing this book.

In approaching the task, I set out to achieve two objectives. The first was to provide ample coverage of most of the classes in the namespace. I have been frustrated by many books that do not provide robust examples for a topic. So I try to provide detailed examples that demonstrate how Windows Forms classes can be used and manipulated in real applications.

A second objective was to present advanced user interface topics such as tree views and drag and drop. While the book spends a good deal of time on fundamental classes, such as menus and buttons, more than a cursory glance is given to some of the more complex controls available for Windows-based programming.

The result of my proposal, these objectives, and a number of late nights is the book you see before you. I take a tutorial approach to application development by creating a common application throughout the book, and provide summaries of relevant classes and other topics that might be of further interest. Hopefully, this approach provides enough detail to demonstrate how Windows-based applications are put together with the .NET Framework, and yet offers additional information that should prove helpful as you develop and expand your own .NET projects.

While the book is not specifically about C# and Visual Studio, the text does attempt to introduce and explain the syntax and usage of C# as well as the features and functionality of Visual Studio. These topics are presented "along-the-way" by introducing relevant concepts and features as they are used in the examples. An overview of C# is also provided in appendix A at the back of the book.

acknowledgments

It never ceases to amaze me how the tangled threads of our lives come together to produce a tangible result, in this case the book you are reading. While the front of this book bears my name, a number of people knowingly or unknowingly contributed to its conception and development. I would especially like to acknowledge Manning typesetter Sydney Brown, whose care and insight contributed greatly to the visual quality of the first edition. Sydney is no longer with us, but she is missed, and her echoes in this and other Manning books remain.

Thanks go to my family: to my wife Bridgett for her patience and love; to Katie and Sydney for the smiles and laughter they bring to my world; to Bianca, who really wishes she was the only animal in the house; and to Laura, who has become my faithful companion, stretching out in my office on a regular basis (much to Bianca's dismay).

I am also grateful for my parents, David and Janet, and teachers and others who have supported me throughout my life. Special recognition goes to Steve Cox and David Cobb, who first interested me in computer programming so long ago.

Thanks also to my many friends who provided support and encouragement in ways that only friends can do, most notably Jean Siegel, Tommy McCracken, Tony Mason, and Reggie Blue.

Many reviewers from all corners of the globe dedicated their time and energy to reading early versions of various chapters, and for them I am especially grateful. This book would not be the same without their assistance and efforts. This is especially true of Dave Corun for his exhaustive technical review of the entire text during final production. Also many thanks to Erick Ellis and other members of the Microsoft Windows Forms team, both for the early looks at the .NET 2.0 Framework and for the many constructive comments offered on the text. Other reviewers that offered insightful comments or thoughts on the text include Andrew Deren, Berndt Hamboeck, Jack Herrington, Shane Jervis, Joe Litton, Robert Marshall, Robert McGovern, Mark Monster, Alan Newson, Vipul Patel, Heath Stewart, Gary Udstrand, and Andrew Varner.

I would also like to recognize the reviewers of my original first edition outline way back in 2001, namely Steve Binney, Mark Boulter, Drew Marsh, Josh Mitts, and

Kunle Odutola. Their suggestions were critical to my thinking for the first edition that resulted in the focus and layout that carries forward into this edition.

Finally, I would like to acknowledge the many people I worked with from and through Manning Publications whom I have never met and yet who provided critical support throughout the writing process. This especially includes Susan Capparelle for seeing some merit in my original proposal; Marjan Bace for his ideas and guidance in the first edition and for his thoughts and support for a second edition; Karen Tegtmeyer for coordinating all the reviewers and their feedback; Leslie Haimes for designing the very cool cover; Mary Piergies for overseeing the project and answering my many questions; Ann Navarro, Susannah Pfalzer, and Lianna Wlasiuk for working with me on the structural elements of the book; Liz Welch for her very thorough copy edit of my final documents; Barbara Mirecki and especially Katie Tennant for their detailed wordsmithing of the final manuscript; Dottie Marsico for creating appendix C with page numbers and for the final typesetting of the book itself; Helen Trimes for coordinating the sales and marketing aspects; and finally Lee Fitzpatrick for continuing to sign my royalty checks.

about this book

The .NET Framework is composed of such a large range of topics that it is impossible to cover all of them in a single book of any depth. This section introduces the focus of this book, and provides an overview of the contents and conventions used in the text. The end of this section describes the online forum available for any questions or comments on the book, and explains how the source code used in the book can be downloaded from the Internet.

Introducing .NET

Microsoft has a history of reinventing itself. Originally strictly an operating systems company, it expanded into office applications with the likes of Word and Excel, and later took on the Internet with Internet Explorer. The push behind the creation of .NET was likely driven by the success of the Internet and Java as a general environment for large-scale computing solutions. The first version of the framework defined two rather important ideas. The first was a new language, C#, and the second was a standard framework for Windows-based solutions.

The easiest way to understand C# might be to imagine someone writing down all the annoying aspects of C++ and then designing a language to do away with each annoyance. In C++, for example, dealing with pointers can be painful; a number of coding errors are not caught by the compiler (such as `if (x = 5)`); manipulating strings can be difficult; and there is no good way to safely "downcast" an object to a derived type. The predecessors of C and C++, the B and BPCL languages, did not define a formal type system, which may well account for the rather free-wheeling nature of integers, pointers, and characters in these languages.

The C# language was redesigned from the ground up with the idea of retaining the flexibility of C and C++ while formalizing the type system and language syntax. Many common runtime errors in C++ are compiler errors in C#. Other distinct features include a built-in string type, lack of global variables, and integration of critical system and application errors into a common exception model. Appendix A of this book provides an overview of the syntax, keywords, and features of the C# language. The "What's new in 2.0" section later in this introduction summarizes the changes made for the 2.0 release of the .NET Framework.

The .NET Framework provides a common theme for most of Microsoft's development technologies and environments that have evolved over time. Aside from the various corporate benefits of rallying the company around the single brand called .NET, the .NET Framework has an important technical purpose as well. The framework is, essentially, an execution environment for applications running on Windows platforms. While the Java environment is, at its core, an environment for running programs written in a single language on any operating system; the .NET Framework is, at its core, an environment for running programs written in any language on a single operating system. This is not to say which is better or worse, just to point out that the fundamental goals of Java vs .NET are different.

The .NET Framework is organized into *namespaces*. This concept is discussed in chapter 1, but here simply know that namespaces define logical groupings of like-minded classes and other types. For a summary of the various namespaces supported by the .NET Framework, see appendix B at the back of this book.

Namespaces impose structure on the vast collection of objects supported by the .NET Framework, and in my case provide some direction and focus for writing a book. This book focuses on the `System.Windows.Forms` namespace, affectionately known as *Windows Forms*. Windows Forms applications are programs executed by the Windows operating system. Such programs employ the user interface features familiar to Windows desktop users everywhere.

The book attempts to provide a methodical approach to Windows Forms. Most types defined by this namespace are covered here. Appendix C provides a class diagram of the Windows Forms namespace, and includes a reference to the table or section where each class or other type is discussed.

ROADMAP

The book contains 23 chapters organized into three parts.

Part 1: Hello Windows Forms

The first part of the book introduces fundamental concepts behind C# in general and Windows Forms specifically. Chapter 1 creates an application similar to figure 1 using a text editor. We discuss some key C# terminology, how a Windows Forms application is executed by the .NET Framework, and the structure of a Windows Forms program in C#.

In chapter 2 we begin using Visual Studio, Microsoft's graphical development environment for creating applications in the .NET Framework. This chapter recreates the application constructed manually in chapter 1. We call this application MyPhotos.

Part 2: Basic Windows Forms

The next part takes a systematic approach to the classes in the Windows Forms namespace. The development of the MyPhotos application built in chapter 2 continues, shown in figure 2 as it appears in chapter 16. As you can see, part 2 covers

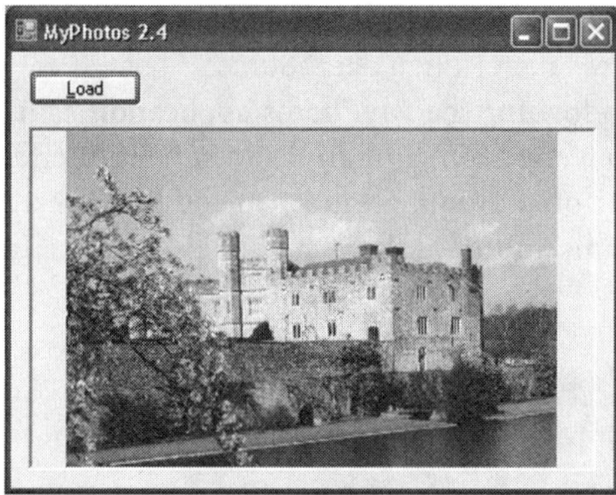

Figure 1
The MyPhotos application as it appears in part 1.

the core user interface components required to build Windows Forms applications, including menu and status strips, dialog windows, text boxes, and combo boxes.

The MyPhotos application displays the contents of a photo album consisting of one or more image files, or photographs. The application stores each photo album in a file, and permits the user to view the images one at a time and edit the properties of both albums and photographs.

Along the way various concepts important to Windows application development are covered. This includes reusable libraries, file streams, encryption, background processing, progress bars, and resource files. The introduction for part 2 gives a more detailed list of topics covered from chapters 3 through 16.

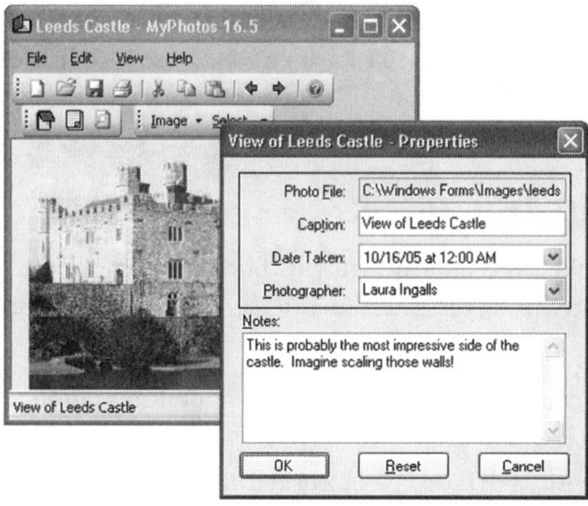

Figure 2
The MyPhotos application in chapter 16. This figure shows the main window and a dialog box for editing the properties of a specific photograph.

Part 3: Advanced Windows Forms

More advanced topics such as custom controls, list views, and drag and drop are covered in part 3 of the book. This part builds a few different applications using the photo album concept, including an application similar to Windows Explorer for browsing photo albums; and a data-driven application that binds the contents of Windows Forms controls to values taken from a data source.

Figure 3 shows the main window for the MyPhotos application as it appears in chapter 23. The application is converted into a multiple document interface that displays multiple albums. A number of additional features are added here as well, such as dragging photos between albums and displaying the book's web site from within the application.

Figure 3 The MyPhotos application in chapter 23. A parent window contains one or more MyPhotos windows from part 2 of the book.

WHO SHOULD READ THIS BOOK?

Like any author, I would like everyone to read this book. The more the merrier! In the interest of full disclosure, however, I wrote *Windows Forms in Action* with three sorts of readers in mind:

- Windows programmers interested in developing desktop applications with .NET
- Developers familiar with .NET or C# interested in learning more about Windows Forms classes and programming
- C++ programmers with little or no experience creating Windows applications

The first edition of this book was also found useful by Visual Basic and Java programmers interested in learning about Windows application programming with C#, so if you fall into these categories you may find the text useful as well.

Once again, I should point out that this book examines one portion of the .NET Framework: the `System.Windows.Forms` namespace. The book also provides a great deal of information about C# and Visual Studio, and in particular details the steps necessary to build each sample application using Visual Studio. For additional information, appendix D provides a list of resources for C# and .NET, and the bibliography at the back of the book references a number of other books that cover various aspects of application development.

CONVENTIONS

The following typographical conventions appear throughout the book:

- Technical terms are introduced in *italics*.
- Code examples and fragments appear in a `fixed-width` font.
- Namespaces, types, and their members appear in a `fixed-width` font.
- Portions of code that have changed when compared with a prior example appear in a **`bold fixed-width`** font.
- Many sections of code have numbered annotations ❶, which appear in the right margin. These numbered annotations are then discussed more fully in a subsequent list following the code.

Table Conventions

In addition to the prior typographical conventions, a number of graphical conventions are used to present information in the text. Starting in chapter 2, all modifications made to the sample applications are illustrated with Action-Result tables showing step-by-step instructions for making the change in Visual Studio. An example of this is shown here.

DESCRIPTION OF THE TASK DESCRIBED BY THESE STEPS		
	Action	**Result**
1	Description of the action to perform.	Description of the result of this action. This is a textual description, a graphic, or the resulting code.
2	The second action to perform. **How-to** a. Detailed steps required to perform the described action. b. More steps if necessary.	The second result. **Note:** A comment about or explanation of the result.

In addition to these tables, a number of classes and other types found in .NET are summarized using a .NET Table. These tables provide an overview of a class or other type discussed in a nearby section, and serve as a quick reference when referring back to these pages at a later time. Full details on these and any other members of the .NET Framework are available in the online documentation.

Of course, most of these .NET Tables describe members of the Windows Forms namespace. An example of this format is shown here as .NET Table 1 using the `PictureBox` class.

.NET Table 1 PictureBox class

The `PictureBox` class represents a control that can display an image. Scroll bars are not supported when the image is larger that the client area, so care must be taken to ensure that the image appears properly within the control. This class is part of the `System.Windows.Forms` namespace, and inherits from the `Control` class. See .NET Table 3.1 for members inherited from the base class.

Public Properties	BorderStyle	Gets or sets the style of border for the control
	ErrorImage	Gets or sets the image to display when an error occurs
	Image	Gets or sets the image for the picture box
	SizeMode	Gets or sets how the image is displayed
	WaitOnLoad	Gets or sets whether the image is loaded asynchronously
Public Methods	*CancelAsync*	Cancels an asynchronous image load
Public Events	SizeModeChanged	Occurs when the value of the `SizeMode` property changes

Note the following features of these tables:

- An initial paragraph defines the purpose of the class, the namespace that contains the class, and the base class. If the namespace containing the base class is not indicated, the described class and base class are in the same namespace. If the base class is not indicated, then the described class is derived from the `System.Object` class.
- The members of the class, namely the properties, methods, and events specific to this class[1] are summarized after the initial paragraph. The members inherited

[1]We define exactly what these terms mean in part 1 of the book.

from base classes are not shown in these tables. In .NET Table 1, there are seven members shown: five properties, one method, and one event.

- Members added for the .NET 2.0 release of the Framework are shown in *italics*. In .NET Table 1, the `ErrorImage` and `WaitOnLoad` properties as well as the `CancelAsync` method are all new as of the .NET 2.0 release.
- Classes and other types added for the .NET 2.0 release include a **New in 2.0** prefix at the start of their introduction. In addition, all members of these new types are shown in italics to stay consistent with how new members are indicated in other tables.

Try It! Suggestions

Another convention in the book is the use of special paragraphs to highlight topics for further exploration of Windows Forms and the .NET Framework.

TRY IT! These paragraphs provide suggestions or discussions of changes you can make to the sample application using the material discussed in the prior sections. TRY IT! paragraphs provide an opportunity to further your understanding of the related topic. The code for these sections is not provided in the book, but is available on the book's web site.

The TRY IT! paragraphs appear throughout the text, and occasionally discuss class members that were not directly used in the sample code.

Coding Conventions

A final convention worth mentioning is the various coding conventions followed throughout the book. Microsoft does define some standards for this, which you can see by searching for "design guidelines for class library developers" at www.google.com, or by visiting "http://msdn.microsoft.com/library/en-us/cpgenref/html/cpconnetframeworkdesignguidelines.asp." I generally follow most of these standards, with a couple exceptions and preferences I summarize here.

First, I treat variables in Visual Studio differently than in hand-written code. In Visual Studio I prefix variables with the type of control: *btn* for buttons, *txt* for text boxes, and so forth. In hand-written code I prefix private variables with an underscore to clearly indicate they are private. One of the main reasons is to make auto-generated event handlers more readable, with no underscores, and more accessible from the code window, since they line up alphabetically by type of control in the method drop-down list.

Because this is a book, where space is at a premium, I also take some shortcuts to keep the code more readable and reduce the width and number of code lines. I avoid use of the `this` keyword; do not use braces with single-statement `if` or `for` loop statements; and abbreviate variable names (such as "pwd" instead of "password") instead of using complete words. This makes the code easier to copy and read, and it certainly makes the book easier to typeset as these conventions reduce the length and width of code (which, as you'll see, there is quite a bit of!).

While I do my best to be consistent, I am certain I violate these and other conventions more than once. What can I say? I tend to buck conventions at times, even in my own book.

SOURCE CODE DOWNLOADS

All source code for the programs presented in *Windows Forms in Action* is available to purchasers of the book from the Manning web site. Visit the site at www.manning.com/eebrown2 for instructions on downloading this source code.

AUTHOR ONLINE

Free access to a private Internet forum, Author Online, is included with the purchase of this book. Visit the book's web site at www.manning.com/eebrown2 for detailed rules about the forum, to subscribe to or access the forum, to retrieve the code for each chapter and section, and to view updates and corrections to the material in the book. Make comments, good or bad, about the book; ask technical questions, and receive help from the author and other Windows Forms programmers.

Manning's commitment to readers is to provide a venue where a meaningful dialog among individual readers and among readers and the author can take place. It is not a commitment to any specific amount of participation on the part of the author, whose contribution remains voluntary (and unpaid).

what's new in 2.0

While the book title has changed, this really is the second edition of *Windows Forms Programming in C#*, based on the second edition of the .NET Framework. This section provides an overview of what is new in .NET 2.0 as well as new material covered in this edition.

In both .NET 2.0 and this book, changes appear all over the place. Let's start with C#. One of the biggest changes is the addition of generics, similar in spirit to C++ templates but not quite the same. The .NET Framework adds a number of generic collection classes as well. Both generics and generic collections are discussed in chapter 5.

Other C# 2.0 changes include partial classes, a class split across multiple files; static classes, a class with only static members; iterator support with the `yield` keyword; and anonymous methods, the ability to pass a block of code as a parameter. You can look up these topics in the index or the .NET documentation for more information.

Changes abound in the Windows Forms namespace as well. All classes now (finally!) support the useful `Tag` property, and the ability to perform custom drawing within controls, or owner draw, has been greatly expanded. Other features are more easily supported by the framework, such as double buffering, background processing, and sound file playback.

The support for menus, status bars, and tool bars has been rewritten in the `ToolStrip` and `ToolStripItem` classes. The old interfaces are still available, but the new classes are now recommended. Tool strips are a fairly big addition, and are discussed in chapters 3, 4, 16, and 20. Other new classes include the `MaskedTextBox`, `SplitContainer`, and `WebBrowser` controls, all of which are also discussed in the book.

More advanced form layout is provided in 2.0 using the `TableLayoutPanel` and `FlowLayoutPanel` classes. The display of data has been greatly improved with the `DataGridView` and related classes, discussed in detail in chapter 21. The `BindingSource` class, presented in chapter 22, simplifies data binding support for all controls compared with the support provided in the .NET 1.x releases.

Visual Studio has also been enhanced, with vastly improved layout assistance in the designer, the addition of smart tags, and automatic recognition of custom controls. Another useful feature is that generated code now appears in a separate file, using the

C# partial classes feature. These and other features of Visual Studio are presented as appropriate over the course of the text.

All these changes necessitated numerous changes to the book as well. While some material is the same as in the first edition, all of the text has been reviewed and most of it rewritten. The chapters are more concise, so some chapters in the first edition became two chapters in the second edition. There were 18 chapters in the first edition, and are 23 chapters in this second edition. A new book necessitates new topics as well. Areas presented in this edition that received little or no coverage in the prior edition include streams, encryption, user controls, progress bars, custom controls, and application deployment.

The overall approach to the book remains similar. This is still a tutorial best read front to back, and provides detailed instructions for duplicating every line of code in the sample application. I believe the overall design of the sample has greatly improved, with better separation of the logic and presentation portions of the code and better use of user and custom controls where applicable.

about the cover illustration

The cover for the first edition of this book, *Windows Forms Programming with C#*, was a "Pescador del Cabo de Buena Esperanza," a fisherman from the Cape of Good Hope in Africa. The illustration was taken from a late 18th century Spanish collection of drawings. The choice was especially appropriate for the first edition, since the author, Erik Brown, worked with the U.S. Peace Corps in Botswana, which is not too far from the Cape of Good Hope.

For the second edition, the cover has been updated, along with the title. The figure on the cover of *Windows Forms in Action* is a medieval foot soldier and crossbowman, "Pieton, Arbalètrier." The illustration is taken from a French compendium of historic and regional costumes assembled by Sylvain Maréchal. This four-volume compendium was first published in Paris in 1788, one year before the French Revolution. Each illustration is expertly drawn and colored by hand.

At a time when it is hard to tell one computer book from another, Manning celebrates the inventiveness and initiative of the computer business with book covers based on the rich history and diversity of dress customs of centuries past, brought back to life by the illustrations of unknown artists, who would no doubt be very surprised to see their artwork gracing the covers of computer books two hundred years later!

PART 1

Hello Windows Forms

It is common practice to write some sort of "Hello" program at the beginning of a book. This book is no different, and we begin our discussion on Windows Forms with the most basic of forms: an empty window. While this book is all about Windows Forms, Microsoft's interactive development environment, called Visual Studio, is an important part of creating .NET applications. To introduce both Windows Forms and Visual Studio, we create the same program in two subsequent chapters.

Chapter 1 is titled "Getting started with Windows Forms." This chapter introduces Windows Forms programming and covers some fundamentals of the C# language and .NET Framework. The C# command-line compiler is used so we can focus on a sample program and not get distracted by the graphical environment. While the remainder of the book uses Visual Studio for all examples, we provide some detail about the command-line tools in case you want to follow along using an alternate editor.

Chapter 2, titled "Getting started with Visual Studio," rebuilds the example from Chapter 1 within the Visual Studio IDE. This gives us a chance to cover additional subtleties of .NET and C#, and gives you, the reader, a second go at understanding any code you missed in chapter 1.

Part 2 of this book extends the program built in chapter 2 as it continues our investigation of Windows application development.

CHAPTER 1

Getting started with Windows Forms

With the introduction behind us, we can get down to business. We start with a basic application of the "Hello World" variety, adding some functionality to introduce several key features and concepts. This chapter takes a quick look at the following aspects of Windows Forms programming:

- The `Form` class: Creating a blank form
- Program execution: Understanding how the .NET Framework executes a program
- Controls: Exploring controls as distinct classes, and adding controls to a form
- C# classes: Reviewing and using the different kinds of class members
- Files: Opening an image file in C#
- Events: Handling events to process user actions

As you likely know, part of the .NET experience is the Visual Studio development environment. Within this environment, a set of command-line programs does the real work of compiling and linking applications and libraries. In this chapter, we use the same command-line tool employed by Visual Studio internally. This allows us to focus on C# and Windows Forms concepts, and not discuss Visual Studio until chapter 2.

If you have prior experience with Windows programming, you will see many similarities in the names of .NET controls. This chapter introduces some of these names, as well as some new terms and features. If you are new to Windows programming, this chapter should be a good foundation for the remainder of the book.

We take a bit of a wild ride through C# and .NET, so don't worry too much about the details here. The concepts and topics in this chapter should become clearer as we progress through the book. A more formal discussion of the C# language is given in appendix A, which you can read before this chapter if you prefer.

This discussion assumes you have successfully installed the Microsoft .NET Framework SDK 2.0 or later on your computer. The SDK is installed automatically when you install Visual Studio; if you are using Visual C# Express, the SDK must be installed first. The 2.0 framework is available at http://msdn.microsoft.com/netframework/downloads/updates/.

1.1 PROGRAMMING IN C#

Let's create a blank form in C# to see how a program compiles and runs in the .NET Framework. Such a form is shown in figure 1.1. This is the most basic of Windows applications that can be created in .NET.

Crank up your favorite editor and type in the code shown in listing 1.1. If you're not sure which editor to use, type this code into Notepad here and throughout the chapter. Save this file as "MyForm.cs" in a convenient directory. Note that, by convention, "cs" is the standard extension for C# files.

Figure 1.1
Our first Windows Forms program produces this skeleton form. The rest of the chapter builds on this program.

Listing 1.1 Your first form

```
[assembly: System.Reflection.AssemblyVersion("1.0")]
namespace MyNamespace
{
  public class MyForm : System.Windows.Forms.Form
  {
    public MyForm()
    {
      this.Text = "Hello Form";
    }
    [System.STAThread]
    public static void Main()
    {
      System.Windows.Forms.Application.EnableVisualStyles();
      System.Windows.Forms.Application.Run(new MyForm());
    }
  }
}
```

To compile this program, we use the C# compiler, called `csc` for C Sharp Compiler. This requires a command prompt with the `PATH` environment set to access the .NET Framework programs and libraries. You can define these settings by hand or via a batch program, or use the shortcut Microsoft provides to do this for you. This shortcut is available via the Start menu.

To reach this shortcut, click Start > Programs > Microsoft .NET Framework SDK v2.0 > SDK Command Prompt. A command window opens, a batch file executes, and the appropriate variables are assigned. With the default installation directories, this menu item executes the following command. This command is really a single line, but is broken into two lines to look pretty on this page.

```
cmd /k "C:\Program Files\Microsoft Visual Studio 8\
        SDK\v2.0\Bin\sdkvars.bat"
```

Open a .NET Framework SDK command prompt, change to the directory containing your MyForm.cs file, and compile this program using this command:

```
> csc MyForm.cs /reference:System.dll
      /reference:System.Windows.Forms.dll
```

The `/reference` switch specifies a library containing additional functionality for the program. In .NET, libraries as well as programs are referred to as *assemblies*. In our application, we reference the System assembly (`System.dll`) and the Windows Forms assembly (`System.Windows.Forms.dll`).[1]

[1] Strictly speaking, the `csc` compiler automatically references all major system DLLs. As a result, the `/reference` switches are not really needed. We use them here and throughout the chapter to be explicit about the libraries required by our program.

Once this command completes, you should see a MyForm.exe file in your directory. Run the program using the `myform` command to see the result.[2] You should see a window similar to figure 1.1.

```
> myform
```

While our program is not very useful yet, it only took a few lines of code to create a fully functional Windows application. Most of the work is done internally by the .NET Framework and Windows. This includes drawing the outer portion of the window such as the title bar and frame; handling the taskbar and standard windows interactions such as minimize, maximize, move, resize, and close; and redrawing the window when the application is behind, in front of, or obscured by other windows.

Stand up, stretch, stifle a yawn, and go tell your neighbor that you just wrote your first .NET Windows Forms application.

We add bells and whistles to this application, of course. Before we do, our fully functional program warrants some discussion. Let's break down the parts of our code to examine how the .NET Framework executes our program.

The first line of the program simply sets the version number for the program to 1.1, matching the section number of the book.

```
[assembly: System.Reflection.AssemblyVersion("1.0")]
```

You can verify this by right-clicking the myform.exe file, selecting Properties, and then clicking the Version tab. We look at version numbers more closely in chapter 2.

1.1.1 Namespaces and classes

A *namespace* defines a group, or *scope*, of related classes, structures, and other types. A namespace is a bit like a family: it defines a group of distinct members with a common name and some shared sense of purpose.

All objects in the .NET Framework, and indeed in C# itself, are organized into namespaces. The `System` namespace includes objects related to the framework itself, and most namespaces defined by .NET are nested within the `System` namespace. The `System.Windows` namespace defines types and namespaces related to the Windows operating system, while the `System.Web` namespace defines types and namespaces related to web pages and servers.

This organization into namespaces permits two objects with the same base name to be distinct—much as two people can both share the same first name. For example, the `Button` class in the `System.Web.UI.WebControls` namespace represents a button in a web application, while `Button` in the `System.Windows.Forms` namespace represents a button in a Windows application. An overview of the more commonly used namespaces in .NET is provided in appendix B.

---

[2] When you run this program, notice that the program waits for the application to exit. This is because the compiler creates a console application by default. We see how to create a Windows-based application using the `/target` switch in chapter 5.

In our program we use the `namespace` keyword to declare a new namespace called `MyNamespace`:

```
namespace MyNamespace
{
  . . .
}
```

A namespace contains one or more types, such as the class `MyForm` in our program. A *type* defines an abstraction for a particular concept or entity. The possible C# types, discussed throughout the book, are classes, structures, interfaces, enumerations, and delegates.

A *class* defines a new data abstraction, in that it defines a class name and a collection of members for representing and operating on the class. Classes in C# support *single inheritance*, as each class inherits from at most one other class. As you may know, inheritance allows one class to support, or inherit, the functionality of another class, called the *base* or *parent* class. A class that inherits from another class is called a *derived* class.

In our program, we define a class called `MyForm` that inherits from the `Form` class, which is found in the `System.Windows.Forms` namespace. The period notation is used to separate namespaces and classes, so that the complete, or *fully qualified*, name for the class is `System.Windows.Forms.Form`. We see how to abbreviate this name later in the chapter.

```
namespace MyNamespace
{
  public class MyForm : System.Windows.Forms.Form
  {
    . . .
  }
}
```

The `Form` class is a cornerstone of Windows-based applications in .NET. It represents any type of window in an application, from dialog boxes to Multiple Document Interface (MDI) client windows, and provides the ability to display, place controls within, and interact with an application window. We discuss this class in detail in chapter 7, with a discussion of MDI applications in chapter 20. For now, simply understand that the `Form` class represents the application's main window.

Classes in .NET contain one or more *members* that define the behavior and features of the class. Class members may be constants, fields, methods, properties, events, indexers, operators, constructors, and nested type declarations. Each of these members is discussed in subsequent chapters. Let's take a look at the two members employed by our program.

1.1.2 Constructors and methods

Take another look at the declaration of our MyForm class. Notice the two members defined by this class, namely the MyForm constructor and the Main method.

Both members are declared as public, as is the class MyForm. C# provides the accessibility levels public, protected, and private that C++ programmers should be familiar with. The accessibility levels internal and protected internal are also provided, which restrict access to types in the same assembly or derived types in the same assembly, respectively.

```
public class MyForm : System.Windows.Forms.Form
{
  public MyForm()
  {
    this.Text = "Hello Form";
  }
  public static void Main()
  {
    . . .
  }
}
```

The first member here is the *constructor*, which works much like a constructor in C++. This is an *instance constructor* since it initializes new instances of the MyForm class. An instance constructor with no parameters, such as our constructor, is called the *default constructor*. C# also supports *static constructors* to initialize the class itself.

In the constructor for our MyForm class, a single statement sets the Text property of the form to the string "Hello Form." We discuss exactly what a *property* is shortly. For now, know that this line places "Hello Form" on the title bar of the application window. As in C++, the this keyword refers to the current object.

The second member of our class is a *method*. A method is a member that performs an operation for the class. An *instance method* operates on a class instance, while a *static method* operates on the class type. Methods in C# work much like their C++ counterparts.

An instance constructor for a class is invoked when an object of that class is first created, typically with the new keyword. The Main method used here is the *entry point* for our program and is invoked by the .NET Framework itself, a topic we return to in a moment.

At this point, we have discussed how C# programs are composed of namespaces, which contain types, which in turn contain one or more members. A constructor is a special member used to initialize the type. There are, in fact, two distinct kinds of types in C#, which is our next topic.

1.1.3 C# types

The new keyword is used to initialize any type in C#. This includes classes and structures as well as simple types such as int and enumerations. In fact, a C# program cannot be compiled successfully if it uses an object before it has been initialized, as the compiler flags this as a fatal error. Any instance constructor provided for a given type, such as the `MyForm` constructor in our code, is invoked during initialization. In our case, we initialize the `MyForm` class with the following code:

```
public static void Main()
{
  System.Windows.Forms.Application.EnableVisualStyles();
  System.Windows.Forms.Application.Run(new MyForm());
}
```

There are two classifications of types in C#, with different initialization behavior for each. *Value types* contain the actual data for the type. These include built-in types such as `int`, `char`, and `bool` as well as all structures created with the `struct` keyword. Value types are typically small or short-lived, making it useful to have their value stored in place, either on the stack or within the object containing them, such as an integer declared as a member of a class.

Reference types contain a reference to the actual data for the type. This is much like an object reference in C++, or a pointer in C, except that in C# the reference is implicit. All classes in C# are reference types, as are the built-in `object` and `string` types. When a value type is passed into a method as an `object` instance, the compiler automatically converts the value type into a reference type as required, using a process called *boxing*.

As an example, consider the following code:

```
int x = new int();
x = 54;
string s = new string();
s = "Fifty-Four";
```

As you might guess, this can be abbreviated as:

```
int x = 54;
string s = "Fifty-Four";
```

The storage allocated as a result of this code is illustrated in figure 1.2. The variable `x` is a value type and contains the integer 54. The variable `s` is a reference type, and points to the string "Fifty-Four" somewhere else in memory. The variable `s` simply contains a reference to this memory.

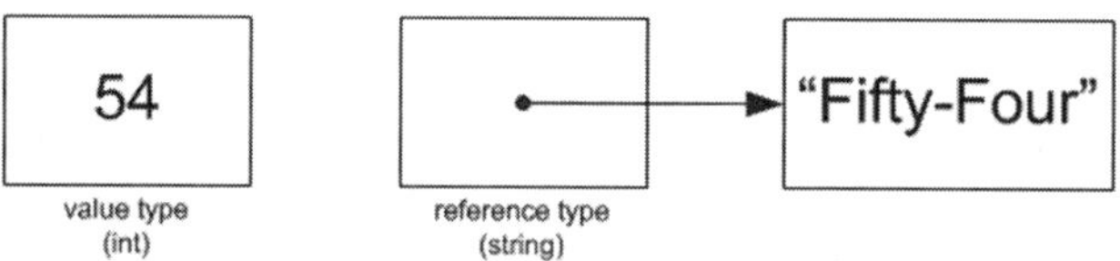

Figure 1.2 This graphic illustrates the two kinds of types in C#: value types, such as the integer 54; and reference types, such as a reference to the string "Fifty-Four."

The area of memory reserved for such reference data is called the *managed heap*, or just the *heap*. Memory allocated on the heap, such as the string in figure 1.2, is reclaimed using *automatic memory management*, or *garbage collection*. The *garbage collector*, or GC as it is called, automatically identifies blocks of memory that are no longer referenced and reclaims them when the program has extra processing time or requires more memory. Rather than the manual memory management required in classic C++ programs using the `new` and `delete` keywords, garbage collection manages memory behind the scenes so you can concentrate on writing your program. Of course, from a performance perspective, with garbage collection you still have to pay the piper sooner or later. Delaying such reclamation with the GC may allow an idle CPU cycle or two to be discovered and provide better overall performance.

There is no need to get knee-deep in this topic. For our purposes, garbage collection means no more pointers lying around leaking memory and resources. Of course, there are other ways to mismanage your memory and resources, and garbage collection creates its own set of problems, but more on that as we go along.

We know from this discussion that classes are reference types, and an instance of a class cannot be used until it is assigned to an actual object using the `new` keyword or an existing object. In the case where one reference type is assigned to an existing reference type, both objects refer, or point, to the same block of data on the heap, and both variables must go out of scope before the memory for this data can be reclaimed by the GC.

Back in our application, the `MyForm` class is a reference type, so we create a `MyForm` object using the `new` keyword.

TRY IT! Go ahead, break your code. Change your `Main` method to the following:

```
public static void Main()
{
  MyForm badForm;
  System.Windows.Forms.Application.EnableVisualStyles();
  System.Windows.Forms.Application.Run(badForm);
}
```

If you compile this change, you should receive an error as follows:

```
MyForm.cs(15,48): error CS0165: Use of unassigned
local variable 'badForm'
```

We could have implemented our `Main` method with a variable to represent the form:

```
public static void Main()
{
  MyForm goodForm = new MyForm();
  System.Windows.Forms.Application.EnableVisualStyles();
  System.Windows.Forms.Application.Run(goodForm);
}
```

However, this variable is not required, so we wrote the `Main` method without it.

1.1.4 The Main method

Every C# program starts execution in a `Main` method, just like it does in C, C++, and Java—although in C# it must begin with a capital M. This method is the starting point, or *entry point*, for our application. After the Windows operating system creates a new process, initializes various internal data structures, and loads the executable program into memory, our program is invoked by calling this entry point, optionally providing the command-line arguments specified by the user.

The entry point in C# is similar to the `main` method found in C and C++, except that in C# it must be a static member of a class. The `Main` method can be `void` or return an `int`, and it can optionally receive the command-line parameters as an array of strings. The four possible forms for this function are shown here:

```
public static void Main();
public static int Main();
public static void Main(string[] args);
public static int Main(string[] args);
```

The expression `string[]` specifies an array of `string` objects. Arrays in C# are zero-based, so the array `args` shown here has `string` values `args[0]`, `args[1]`, and so forth. Unlike C++, the first element in the array here, `args[0]`, is the first parameter for the program, and not the name of the executable.

The C# compiler locates the `Main` method and assigns it as the entry point for the program. If there are multiple `Main` methods in an assembly, the `/main` switch can be used to indicate which method should be used, or to specify an alternate method as the entry point.

```
[System.STAThread]
public static void Main()
{
  System.Windows.Forms.Application.EnableVisualStyles();
  System.Windows.Forms.Application.Run(new MyForm());
}
```

Our `Main` method is `void` and accepts no arguments. Note the `[System.STAThread]` line prior to this method. This line is required in Windows Forms applications, and indicates that the thread executing this method should use a single-threaded apartment (STA) threading model. Technically, the threading model is related to how the application interacts with COM libraries and controls. Even though we are not using COM explicitly, Windows Forms requires it to ensure that various interactions with the operating system perform as expected. Practically, you don't really need to understand this right now. Just make sure you include this line in all of your Windows Forms applications.

Our `Main` method invokes two methods in the `Application` class, which we discuss next.

1.1.5 The Application class

The `Application` class is used to manage applications, threads, and Windows messages. An overview of this class appears in .NET Table 1.1. If you skipped the introduction, these .NET Tables are included for reference and to indicate class members

.NET Table 1.1 Application class

The `Application` class encapsulates the static members necessary to manage and process forms, threads, and Windows messages on behalf of a program. This class is *sealed*, meaning that the class cannot be inherited. The `Application` class is part of the `System.Windows.Forms` namespace. You cannot create an instance of this class, as no accessible instance constructor is provided.

Public Static Properties	AllowQuit	Gets whether the caller can quit this application.
	CommonApp-DataRegistry	Gets the `RegistryKey` for application data shared among all users.
	CurrentCulture	Gets or sets the locale (for internationalization) for the current thread.
	OpenForms	Gets the collection of `Form` objects active in this application.
	ProductName	Gets the product name for the application.
	ProductVersion	Gets the product version for the application.
	StartupPath	Gets the path for the executable file that started the application.
	UserApp-DataRegistry	Gets the `RegistryKey` for application data specific to the current user.
Public Static Methods	AddMessage-Filter	Installs an `IMessageFilter` interface to monitor Windows messages on the current thread. This can be used to intercept incoming messages to a form.
	DoEvents	Processes any Windows messages currently in the message queue.
	EnableVisual-Styles	Enables visual styles for the application.
	Exit	Stops all running message loops and closes all windows in the application. Note that this may not force the application to exit.
	ExitThread	Stops the message loop and closes all windows on the current thread only.
	Run	Starts a standard message loop on the current thread. If a `Form` is given, also makes that form visible.
Public Static Events	ApplicationExit	Occurs when the application is about to shut down.
	Idle	Occurs when the application is about to enter the idle state.
	Thread-Exception	Occurs when an uncaught exception occurs in a thread.
	ThreadExit	Occurs when a thread in the application is about to shut down.

that may not be discussed explicitly in the text, with members new in .NET 2.0 shown in italics. Typically, such tables provide a summary of the class, since many classes have too many methods to fit conveniently on a single page.

The `Application` class is commonly used to display the initial form for a Windows Forms executable and wait for user actions to occur within this form. This is exactly how we use this class here:

```
public static void Main()
{
  System.Windows.Forms.Application.EnableVisualStyles();
  System.Windows.Forms.Application.Run(new MyForm());
}
```

The first line calls the `EnableVisualStyles` method, which causes controls to draw themselves consistent with the current operating system style. This method has no effect if the operating system does not support visual styles.

The `Run` method begins a message loop in the current thread to wait for operating system messages. If a `Form` object is provided, as is done in our program, then this form is displayed on the desktop and starts interacting with the user.

Internally, the `Run` method creates an `ApplicationContext` class instance to hold pertinent information about the new thread. We could write our code to use an explicit application context as follows:

```
[System.STAThread]
public static void Main()
{
  System.Windows.Forms.Application.EnableVisualStyles();
  System.Windows.Forms.Form f = new MyForm();
  System.Windows.Forms.ApplicationContext context
      = new System.Windows.Forms.ApplicationContext();
  context.MainForm = f;
  System.Windows.Forms.Application.Run(context);
}
```

The `Run` method encapsulates this logic for a given `Form`, simplifying our code.

1.1.6 Program execution

Before we leave this section, let's review what we've learned about how our program executes within the operating system. Run the MyForm.exe program again to see this in action. When you execute this program, the Windows operating system creates and initializes a process that initializes the .NET Framework with the `Main` method as the entry point for execution, which:

1. Invokes the `Application.EnableVisualStyles` method to allow visual styles in our application if the operating system supports them.
2. Instantiates an instance of the class `MyForm` using the `new` keyword, which:
   a. Invokes the instance constructor for `MyForm`, which assigns the string "Hello Form" to the title bar.

3 Back in our `Main` method, the `Application.Run` method is called with the newly created `MyForm` object as a parameter, which:
   a Displays `MyForm` as the application window.
   b Waits for and processes any messages or user interactions that occur on the form.
4 When the `MyForm` window closes:
   a The `Application.Run` method returns.
   b The `Main` method returns.
   c The program exits.

And that is how it is done in the world of .NET. Of course, our blank window, while fascinating, could use some decorating, so let's add some controls to the form.

1.2 WINDOWS FORMS CONTROLS

Let's make our program a little more interesting by adding some graphical controls. Throughout the course of the book, we build a photo-viewing application, so let's add a button for loading an image file, and a box where the image can be displayed. When we are done, our form will look like figure 1.3.

Revise your code as shown in listing 1.2. Changes from our previous code listing are shown in bold. In particular we changed the version number of our program to 1.2 to distinguish it from our original code and to match the current section.

Compile this program as before and run it to see our changes.

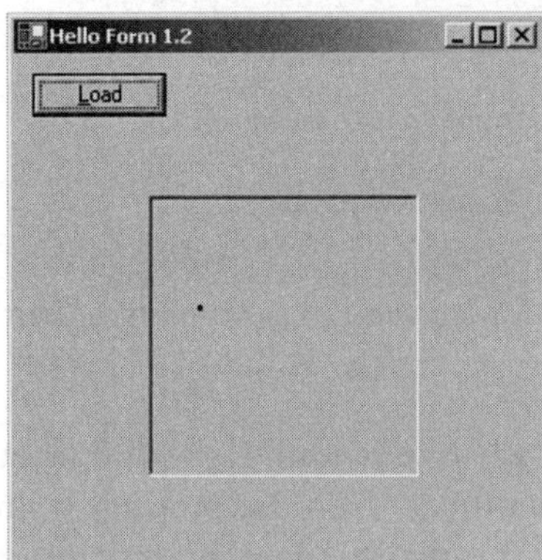

Figure 1.3
This form contains a Load button and a picture box control.

Listing 1.2 A Button and PictureBox control are added to the form.

```
using System;
using System.Windows.Forms;

[assembly: System.Reflection.AssemblyVersion("1.2")]
namespace MyNamespace
```

```
{
  public class MyForm : Form
  {
    private Button btnLoad;
    private PictureBox pbxPhoto;

    public MyForm()
    {
      this.Text = "Hello Form 1.2";

      // Create and configure a button
      btnLoad = new Button();
      btnLoad.Text = "&Load";
      btnLoad.Left = 10;
      btnLoad.Top = 10;

      // Create and configure a picture box
      pbxPhoto = new PictureBox();
      pbxPhoto.BorderStyle =
      System.Windows.Forms.BorderStyle.Fixed3D;
      pbxPhoto.Width = this.Width / 2;
      pbxPhoto.Height = this.Height / 2;
      pbxPhoto.Left = (this.Width - pbxPhoto.Width) / 2;
      pbxPhoto.Top = (this.Height - pbxPhoto.Height) / 2;

      // Add our new controls to the form
      this.Controls.Add(btnLoad);
      this.Controls.Add(pbxPhoto);
    }

    [STAThread]
    public static void Main()
    {
      Application.EnableVisualStyles();
      Application.Run(new MyForm());
    }
  }
}
```

1.2.1 The using directive

The first change you may notice in listing 1.2 is the `using` keyword:

```
using System;
using System.Windows.Forms;
```

Programmers are always looking for shortcuts, and older programmers—some would say more experienced programmers—often worry that their lines may be too long for the compiler or printer to handle. The programmers at Microsoft are no exception, so while one team probably agreed that fully qualified names are a good idea, another team probably sought a way to avoid typing them. The result is the `using` keyword.

The `using` keyword actually plays two roles in C#: the first as a directive for specifying a shortcut, and the second as a statement for ensuring that nonmemory resources are properly disposed of. We discuss the `using` keyword as a statement in chapter 7.

As a directive, `using` declares a namespace or alias to use in the current file. Do not confuse this with include files found in C and C++. Include files are not needed in C# since the assembly incorporates all of this information directly, making the `/reference` switch to the compiler sufficient in this regard. This really is just a shortcut mechanism.

In our original program in section 1.1, the `Main` method called the method `System.Windows.Forms.Application.Run`. In our new listing the `using` directive allows us to shorten this call to `Application.Run`. The long form is called the *fully qualified name* since the entire namespace is specified. Imagine if you had to use the fully qualified name throughout your code. Aside from tired fingers, you would have long, cluttered lines of code. Our new code is a bit easier to read than in listing 1.1:

```
public static void Main()
{
  Application.EnableVisualStyles();
  Application.Run(new MyForm());
}
```

Since `Application` is not a C# keyword or a globally available class, the compiler searches the `System` and `System.Windows.Forms` namespaces specified by the `using` directives in order to locate the `System.Windows.Forms.Application` class.

You can also specify an alias with the `using` keyword to create a more convenient representation of a namespace or class. For example,

```
using WFalias = System.Windows.Forms
using MyAppAlias = System.Windows.Forms.Application
```

With these defined, we could write our `Main` method as:

```
public static void Main()
{
  WFalias.Application.EnableVisualStyles();
  MyAppAlias.Run(new MyForm());
}
```

Typically, the `using` directive indicates a namespace employed by the program rather than an alias, and this is how we use this directive in our program and throughout the book. So rather than the fully qualified name `System.Windows.Forms.Button` in our code, we simply use the class name `Button` directly.

You may recall that there is a `Button` class in the `System.Web.UI.WebControls` namespace as well. The compiler uses the correct `System.Windows.Forms.Button` class because of the using keyword, and because the System.Web namespace is not referenced by our program.

1.2.2 The Control class

Let's go back to our use of the Button and PictureBox classes. The top of our class now defines two member variables, or *fields* in C#, to represent the button and picture box on our form. Here, Button and PictureBox are classes in the Windows Forms namespace that are used to create a button and picture box *control* on a Form. The Button and PictureBox classes are both derived from the Windows Forms Control class.[3] The Control class is the basis for all graphical components that display information to the user. The term *control* refers to any class that is derived from the Control class.

```
public class MyForm : Form
{
  private Button btnLoad;
  private PictureBox pbxPhoto;
```

Our controls, like all types in C#, must be initialized before they are used. This initialization occurs in the constructor for the MyForm class.

```
  public MyForm()
  {
    // Create and configure the Button
    btnLoad = new Button();
    btnLoad.Text = "&Load";
    btnLoad.Left = 10;
    btnLoad.Top = 10;

    // Create and configure the PictureBox
    pbxPhoto = new PictureBox();
    pbxPhoto.BorderStyle = BorderStyle.Fixed3D;
    pbxPhoto.Width = this.Width / 2;
    pbxPhoto.Height = this.Height / 2;
    pbxPhoto.Left = (this.Width - pbxPhoto.Width) / 2;
    pbxPhoto.Top = (this.Height - pbxPhoto.Height) / 2;
    . . .
```

Note the use of the new keyword to initialize both controls. Each control is then assigned an appropriate appearance and location. You might think that members such as Text, Left, BorderStyle, and so on are all public fields in the Button and PictureBox classes, but this is not the case. Public member variables in C++, as well as in C#, can be a dangerous thing, as these members can be manipulated directly by programmers without restrictions. A user might accidentally—or on purpose!—set such a variable to an invalid value and cause a program error. Typically, C++ programmers create class variables as protected or private members and then

[3] There is also a Control class in the System.Web.UI namespace.

provide public access methods to retrieve and assign these members. Such access methods ensure that the internal value never contains an invalid setting.

In C#, *properties* are designed especially for this purpose. Properties permit controlled access to class fields and other internal data by providing read, or `get`, and write, or `set`, access to data encapsulated by the class. Examples later in the book will show you how to create your own properties. Here we use common properties inherited from the `Control` class that are available to all Windows Forms controls.

We have already seen how the `Text` property is used to set the string to appear on a form's title bar. For `Button` objects, this same property name sets the string that appears on the button, in this case "&Load." As in previous Windows programming environments, the ampersand character, &, specifies a mnemonic or accelerator for the control using the Alt key. So typing Alt+L in the application performs a click of the Load button.

Windows Forms controls also provide `Left`, `Right`, `Top`, and `Bottom` properties to specify the location of each respective side of the control. Here, the button is placed 10 pixels from the top and left of the form, while the picture box is centered on the form.

The `Width` and `Height` properties specify the size of the control. Our code creates a picture box approximately one half the size of the form and roughly centered within it. This size is approximate because the `Width` and `Height` properties in the `Form` class actually represent the width and height of the outer form, from edge to edge.[4]

The `Control` class itself is rather vast and provides a wide range of functionality that is discussed throughout the book. A summary of this class appears in .NET Table 3.1 in chapter 3.

1.2.3 The Controls property

The final lines in the `MyForm` constructor make the button and picture box controls appear on the form. The `Controls` property returns an instance of the `Control.ControlCollection` class. This class defines an `Add` method that adds a control to the collection. As you would expect, the `Controls` property can be used to retrieve the controls on a form as well.

```
public MyForm()
{
  . . .
  // Add our new controls to the form
  this.Controls.Add(btnLoad);
  this.Controls.Add(pbxPhoto);
}
```

[4] The `ClientRectangle` property represents the size of the internal display area, and could be used here to truly center the picture box on the form.

When a control is added to a form, it is placed at the end of the *z-order* of the stack of controls on the form. The term z-order is used for both the set of forms in the application and the set of controls on a particular form, and indicates the order of windows stacked on the screen or controls stacked on a form, much like stacking dishes on a table.

The end of the z-order is the bottom of the stack. You can think of this as the view a chandelier has of a table. If the tabletop is the form, and a cup and saucer are controls, in your code you would first add the cup control to the table, then add the saucer control so that it appears underneath the cup. This can be a bit nonintuitive, so make sure you understand this point when programmatically adding controls to your forms.

The term *z-order* comes from the fact that the screen is two-dimensional, and is often treated as a two-axis coordinate system in the X and Y directions. The imaginary axis perpendicular to the screen is called the z-axis. This concept of z-order will be important later in the chapter when we have overlapping controls.

Now that our controls are placed on the form, we can use them to load and display an image file.

1.3 LOADING FILES

The next change to our little program will permit the user to click the Load button and display a selected image file in the picture box control. The result appears in figure 1.4.

Revise your program in accordance with listing 1.3. Once again the changes are shown in bold type, and the version number has been incremented, this time to 1.3.

Figure 1.4
The image here is scaled to correctly fit within the picture box control's display area.

Listing 1.3 The OpenFileDialog class is now used to load an image file.

```
using System;
using System.Drawing;
using System.Windows.Forms;

[assembly: System.Reflection.AssemblyVersion("1.3")]
namespace MyNamespace
{
  public class MyForm :Form
  {
    Button btnLoad;
    PictureBox pbxPhoto;

    public MyForm()
    {
      this.Text = "Hello Form 1.3";

      // Create and configure a button
      btnLoad = new Button();
      btnLoad.Text = "&Load";
      btnLoad.Left = 10;
      btnLoad.Top = 10;
      btnLoad.Click += new EventHandler(this.HandleLoadClick);

      // Create and configure a picture box
      pbxPhoto = new PictureBox();
      pbxPhoto.BorderStyle = BorderStyle.Fixed3D;
      pbxPhoto.Width = this.Width / 2;
      pbxPhoto.Height = this.Height / 2;
      pbxPhoto.Left = (this.Width - pbxPhoto.Width) / 2;
      pbxPhoto.Top = (this.Height - pbxPhoto.Height) / 2;
      pbxPhoto.SizeMode = PictureBoxSizeMode.Zoom;

      // Add our new controls to the form
      this.Controls.Add(btnLoad);
      this.Controls.Add(pbxPhoto);
    }

    private void HandleLoadClick(object sender, System.EventArgs e)
    {
      OpenFileDialog dlg = new OpenFileDialog();
      dlg.Title = "Open Photo";
      dlg.Filter = "jpg files (*.jpg)|*.jpg|All files (*.*)|*.*";

      if (dlg.ShowDialog() == DialogResult.OK)
      {
        pbxPhoto.Image = new Bitmap(dlg.OpenFile());
      }

      dlg.Dispose();
    }

    [STAThread]
    public static void Main()
```

```
        {
          Application.EnableVisualStyles();
          Application.Run(new MyForm());
        }
    }
}
```

Note that there is a new namespace reference here:

```
using System.Drawing;
```

This is required for the `Bitmap` class used to load the image file. As you'll recall, the using keyword allows us to shorten the fully qualified name `System.Drawing.Bitmap` to the more manageable class name `Bitmap`. To include the definition of the `Bitmap` class, the `System.Drawing.dll` assembly is required when the program is compiled. The new compiler command for our program is shown here. Note that we use the short form `/r` of the `/reference` switch discussed earlier in the chapter:

```
> csc MyForm.cs /r:System.dll /r:System.Windows.Forms.dll
  /r:System.Drawing.dll
```

Run the new program. Click the Load button and you will be prompted to locate a JPEG image file. If you do not have any such files, you can download some sample images from the book's website at www.manning.com/eebrown2. Select an image to display in the image window. Figure 1.4 shows the form with a selected image displayed.

As before, let's take a look at our changes in some detail.

1.3.1 Events

If you think about it, Windows applications spend a large amount of time doing nothing. In our example, once the window is initialized and controls drawn, the application waits for the user to click the Load button. This could happen immediately or hours later. How an application waits for such user interactions to occur is an important aspect of the environment in which it runs. There are really only two possible solutions: either the application has to check for such actions at regular intervals, or the application does nothing and the operating system kicks the program awake whenever such an action occurs.

Waiting for a user action can be compared to answering the phone. Imagine if there were no ringer and you had to pick up your phone and listen for a caller every couple of minutes to see if someone was calling. Even ignoring the extra time a caller might have to wait before you happened to pick up the receiver, it would be difficult to perform any other activities because you would constantly have to interrupt your work to check the phone. The ringer allows you to ignore the phone until it rings. You can fall asleep on the couch while reading this book (not that you would, of course) and rely on the phone to wake you up when someone calls (unless you turn off the ringer, but that is a separate discussion).

Similarly, Windows would grind to a halt if applications were actively looking for user actions all the time. Instead, applications wait quietly, and rely on the operating system to notify them when an action requires a response. This permits other applications to perform tasks such as checking for new email and playing music CDs between the time you run a program and the time you actually do something with it. The interval between running the program and using it may only be seconds, but to a computer every fraction of a second counts.

Internally, the Windows operating system passes messages around for this purpose. When the user clicks the Load button, a message occurs that indicates the button has been pressed and released. The `Application.Run` method arranges for the application to wait for such messages in an efficient manner.

The .NET Framework defines such actions as *events*. Events are predefined situations that may occur. Examples include the user clicking the mouse or typing on the keyboard, or an alarm going off for an internal timer. Events can also be triggered by external programs, such as a web server receiving a message, or the creation of a new file on disk. In C#, the concept of an event is built in, allowing classes to define events that may occur, and instances of that class to indicate functions that receive and process these events.

While this may seem complicated, the result is simply this: when the user clicks the mouse or types on the keyboard, your program can wake up and do something. In our code, for example, we want to do something when the user clicks the Load button. The `Button` class inherits an event called `Click` from the base `Control` class. Our program defines a method called `HandleLoadClick` to handle this event. We link these two together by registering our method as an *event handler* for the `Click` event.

```
btnLoad.Click += new EventHandler(this.HandleLoadClick);
```

Since it is possible to have more than one handler for an event, the += notation is used to add a new event handler without removing any existing handlers. When multiple event handlers are registered, the handlers are typically called sequentially in the same order in which they were added. The `System.EventHandler` is a *delegate* in C#, and specifies the signature required to process the event. In this case, `EventHandler` is defined internally by the .NET Framework as follows:

```
public delegate void EventHandler(object sender, EventArgs e);
```

The `object` parameter receives the source, or sender, of the event, while the `EventArgs` parameter receives any additional information, called *event data*, for the event. Typically, the `sender` parameter receives the control that raises the event. In our case, this is the actual `Button` instance. The `e` parameter receives an `EventArgs` instance, which by default does not contain any additional information.

A delegate is similar to a function pointer in C or C++, except that delegates are type-safe. The term *type-safe* means that code is specified in a well-defined manner that can be recognized by a compiler. That is, an incorrect use of a delegate is a compile-time error. This is quite different than in C++, where an incorrect use of a function pointer may not cause an error until the program is running.

As of .NET 2.0, C# allows the delegate to be omitted, since the compiler already knows that the `Button.Click` method accepts the `System.EventHandler` delegate. This permits the shortened form:

```
btnLoad.Click += this.HandleLoadClick;
```

We will discuss events and delegates in more detail later in the book, most notably in chapters 3 and 13. For now, simply recognize that `HandleLoadClick` is an event handler that is invoked whenever the user clicks the Load button.

The next section examines the `HandleLoadClick` method directly.

1.3.2 The OpenFileDialog class

Once our `HandleLoadClick` event handler is registered, we are ready to load a new image into the application. The signature of the `HandleLoadClick` method must match the signature of the `EventHandler` delegate by being a `void` function that accepts an `object` and `EventArgs` parameter. Note how this is a private method so that it is not available except within the `MyForm` class.

```
private void HandleLoadClick(object sender, System.EventArgs e)
{
  OpenFileDialog dlg = new OpenFileDialog();
  dlg.Title = "Open Photo";
  dlg.Filter = "jpg files (*.jpg)|*.jpg|All files (*.*)|*.*" ;

  if (dlg.ShowDialog() == DialogResult.OK)
  {
    pbxPhoto.Image = new Bitmap(dlg.OpenFile());
  }

  dlg.Dispose();
}
```

The `OpenFileDialog` class is used to prompt the user for an image to display. This class inherits from the more generic `FileDialog` class, which provides a standard framework for reading and writing files. A summary of this class is given in .NET Table 1.2.

```
OpenFileDialog dlg = new OpenFileDialog();
dlg.Title = "Open Photo";
dlg.Filter = "jpg files (*.jpg)|*.jpg|All files (*.*)|*.*" ;
```

The `Title` property sets the string displayed in the title bar of the dialog box, while the `Filter` property defines the list of file types that can be seen in the dialog box. The format of the `Filter` property matches the one used for file dialog boxes in previous Microsoft environments: the vertical bar character, |, is placed between each part of the string. Each pair of values in the string represents the string to display in the dialog box and the regular expression to use when displaying files, respectively. In our example, the dialog box presents two options for the type of file to select. This first is "jpg files (*.jpg)"—which matches all files with the format `*.jpg`—and the second is "All files (*.*)"—which matches all files with the format `*.*`.

Once the `OpenFileDialog` object is created and initialized, the `ShowDialog` method displays the dialog box and waits for the user to select a file. This method returns a member of the `DialogResult` enumeration, which identifies the button selected by the user.

```
if (dlg.ShowDialog() == DialogResult.OK)
{
  pbxPhoto.Image = new Bitmap(dlg.OpenFile());
}
```

If the user clicks the Open button, the `ShowDialog` method returns the value `DialogResult.OK`. If the user clicks the Cancel button, the value `DialogResult.Cancel` is returned. When the Open button has been clicked, the selected file is loaded as a `Bitmap` object, which is our next topic.

TRY IT! Note that no error handling is performed by our code. Try selecting a non-image file in the dialog box to see how the program crashes and burns. We talk about handling such errors in the next chapter.

Before we move on, note the final line of our `HandleLoadClick` event handler:

```
dlg.Dispose();
```

While the garbage collector frees us from worrying about memory cleanup, nonmemory resources are still an issue. In this case, our `OpenFileDialog` object allocates operating system resources to display the dialog box and file system resources to open the file via the `OpenFile` method. While the garbage collector recovers these eventually, such resources may be limited by the operating system and should always be reclaimed manually by calling the `Dispose` method.

The `Dispose` method is the standard mechanism for cleaning up such resources. We discuss this method in detail in chapter 7.

.NET Table 1.2 FileDialog class

The `FileDialog` class is a common dialog box that allows a user to select a file. This class is *abstract*, meaning you cannot create an instance of it, and serves as the base class for the `OpenFileDialog` and `SaveFileDialog` classes. The `FileDialog` class is part of the `System.Windows.Forms` namespace and inherits from the `CommonDialog` class.

Public Properties	AddExtension	Gets or sets whether the file dialog box automatically adds the file extension if omitted by the user.
	CheckFileExists	Gets or sets whether the dialog box displays a warning if the specified file does not exist.
	DefaultExt	Gets or sets the default filename extension.
	FileName	Gets or sets the string containing the selected filename.
	FileNames	Gets an array of strings containing the set of files selected.
	Filter	Gets or sets the filename filter string, which determines the file type choices in the file dialog box.
	InitialDirectory	Gets or sets the initial directory displayed by the file dialog box.
	RestoreDirectory	Gets or sets whether the dialog box restores the current directory to its original value before closing.
	ShowHelp	Gets or sets whether the Help button appears in the file dialog box.
	Title	Gets or sets the title bar string for the dialog box.
Public Methods	Dispose (inherited from Component)	Releases any resources used by the dialog box.
	Reset	Resets all properties in the dialog box to their default values.
	ShowDialog (inherited from CommonDialog)	Displays a common dialog box and returns the `DialogResult` enumeration value of the button selected by the user.
	FileOk	Occurs when the Open or Save button is clicked.
Public Events	HelpRequest (inherited from CommonDialog)	Occurs when the Help button is clicked.

1.3.3 Bitmap images

So far we have discussed how our application responds to a click of the Load button and enables the user to select an image file. When the user clicks the Open button in the open file dialog box, the `HandleLoadClick` method loads an image into the `PictureBox` control. It does this by creating a new `Bitmap` object for the selected file and assigning it to the `Image` property of the `PictureBox` control:

```
if (dlg.ShowDialog() == DialogResult.OK)
{
  pbxPhoto.Image = new Bitmap(dlg.OpenFile());
}
```

The Windows Forms namespace defines the `PictureBox` control to display an image in an application. All we have to do is set the `Image` property to a bitmap object and the class takes care of the rest.

The `OpenFileDialog` class provides a couple of ways to access the selected file. The `FileName` property retrieves the path to the selected file. In our code, we opt for the `OpenFile` method to open this file with read-only permission. The open file is passed to the `Bitmap` constructor via our friend the `new` keyword to load the image.

The constructed bitmap is assigned to the `Image` property of our `pbxPhoto` variable. This property can hold any object based on the `Image` class, including bitmaps, icons, and cursors.

How this image appears within the picture box control depends on the `PictureBox.SizeMode` property setting. In our case, we set this property so that the image is entirely displayed within the `PictureBox` control without altering the relative size of objects within the image:

```
pbxPhoto.SizeMode = PictureBoxSizeMode.Zoom;
```

TRY IT! If you're feeling slightly adventurous, you should now be able to add a second `Button` and second `PictureBox` to the form. Label the second button "Load2" and implement a `HandleLoad2Click` event handler that loads a second image into the second `PictureBox` control.

As an alternate modification, change the `Main` method to receive the array of command-line arguments passed to the program in an `args` variable. Load the first parameter in `args[0]` as a `Bitmap` object and assign it to the `PictureBox` control for the `MyForm` class. To make this change, add a new constructor to the `MyForm` class that receives the name of an image file to display.

1.4 RESIZING FORMS

The final topic in this chapter is resizing forms. For readers familiar with the Microsoft Foundation Classes (MFC) in Visual C++ 6.0, you will know that it can take some work to properly resize a complicated form. The folks at Microsoft were likely aware of this when they sought to simplify this task in .NET.

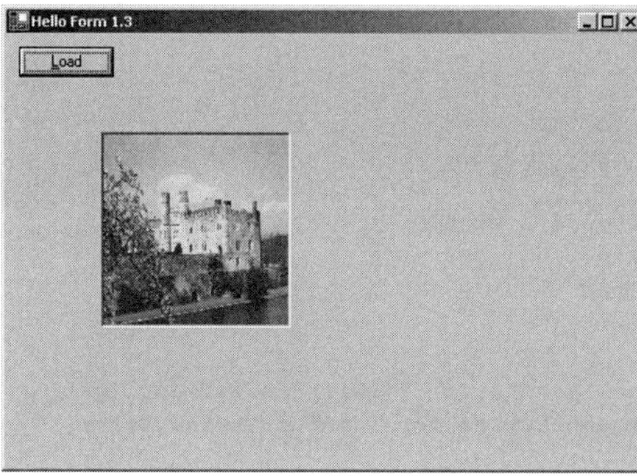

Figure 1.5
Version 1.3 of the application uses the default resize behavior, with both controls anchored to the top and left of the window.

Before looking at our new code listing, try resizing our existing program to see what happens. The position of each control is fixed relative to the top-left corner of the form, as shown in figure 1.5.

We would prefer the `PictureBox` control to resize automatically along with the window, as shown in figure 1.6. Fortunately, the base `Control` class provides some properties to gracefully resize a form.

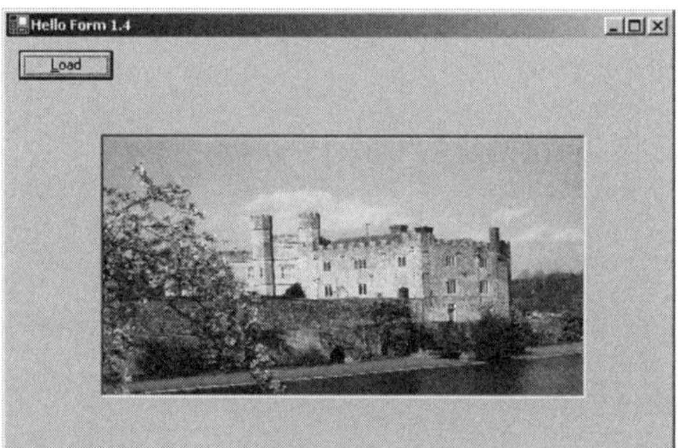

Figure 1.6
Version 1.4 resizes the picture box automatically whenever the window is resized, as the picture box is anchored to all sides of the form.

Revise your code so that it matches listing 1.4. This new code sets the `Anchor` property for each control.

Listing 1.4 The picture box resizes based on the Anchor property setting.

```
using System;
using System.Drawing;
using System.Windows.Forms;

[assembly: System.Reflection.AssemblyVersion("1.4")]
namespace MyNamespace
{
  public class MyForm :Form
  {
```

```
        Button btnLoad;
        PictureBox pbxPhoto;

        public MyForm()
        {
          this.Text = "Hello Form 1.4";

          // Create and configure a button
          btnLoad = new Button();
          btnLoad.Text = "&Load";
          btnLoad.Left = 10;
          btnLoad.Top = 10;
          btnLoad.Click += new EventHandler(this.HandleLoadClick);
          btnLoad.Anchor = AnchorStyles.Top | AnchorStyles.Left;

          // Create and configure a picture box
          pbxPhoto = new PictureBox();
          pbxPhoto.BorderStyle = BorderStyle.Fixed3D;
          pbxPhoto.Width = this.Width / 2;
          pbxPhoto.Height = this.Height / 2;
          pbxPhoto.Left = (this.Width - pbxPhoto.Width) / 2;
          pbxPhoto.Top = (this.Height - pbxPhoto.Height) / 2;
          pbxPhoto.SizeMode = PictureBoxSizeMode.Zoom;
          pbxPhoto.Anchor = AnchorStyles.Top | AnchorStyles.Bottom
            | AnchorStyles.Left | AnchorStyles.Right;

          // Add our new controls to the form
          this.Controls.Add(btnLoad);
          this.Controls.Add(pbxPhoto);
        }

        private void HandleLoadClick(object sender, System.EventArgs e)
        {
          OpenFileDialog dlg = new OpenFileDialog();
          dlg.Title = "Open Photo";
          dlg.Filter = "jpg files (*.jpg)|*.jpg|All files (*.*)|*.*";

          if (dlg.ShowDialog() == DialogResult.OK)
          {
            pbxPhoto.Image = new Bitmap(dlg.OpenFile());
          }

          dlg.Dispose();
        }

        [System.STAThread]
        public static void Main()
        {
          Application.EnableVisualStyles();
          Application.Run(new MyForm());
        }
      }
    }
```

As an aside, note in figures 1.5 and 1.6 how the image only fills a portion of the picture box. This `PictureBoxSizeMode.Zoom` setting preserves the *aspect ratio* of the contained image. The aspect ratio is the ratio of the height of an image to its width. A standard 4-inch by 6-inch photograph, for example, has an aspect ratio of two-thirds (4 divided by 6). As the form is resized the image is scaled such that the aspect ratio is maintained. If you modify the code to use the `PictureBoxSizeMode.StretchImage` instead, the image will always fit the entire control, and will not preserve the aspect ratio.

While we have only added two new lines here, these are the only changes required to properly resize our form.

1.4.1 The Anchor property

The two lines added to our program use the `Anchor` property to fix the control on the form in relation to the form's edges:

```
// Create and configure a button
. . .
btnLoad.Anchor = AnchorStyles.Top | AnchorStyles.Left;

// Create and configure a picture box
. . .
pbxPhoto.Anchor = AnchorStyles.Top | AnchorStyles.Bottom
  | AnchorStyles.Left | AnchorStyles.Right;
```

All controls in the .NET Framework support the `Anchor` property for this purpose. The property is set using the `AnchorStyles` enumeration, as shown in .NET Table 1.3.

The `Anchor` property preserves the distance from the control to the anchored edge or edges of its container. Here, the container for the button and picture box controls is the `Form` itself. In chapters 7 and 8 we'll encounter other containers such as the `Panel` and `GroupBox` controls that can hold anchored controls as well.

.NET Table 1.3 AnchorStyles enumeration

The `AnchorStyles` enumeration defines the settings available for the `Anchor` property in the `Control` class, and by inheritance all controls in the .NET Framework. The enumeration is part of the `System.Windows.Forms` namespace. An `Anchor` property is set for a control object using a bitwise or (with the vertical bar operator, |) of the desired values.

Enumeration Values	Bottom	The control is anchored to the bottom edge of its container.
	Left	The control is anchored to the left edge of its container.
	None	The control is not anchored to its container. When an `Anchor` property is set to `None` on a control and its container resizes, the control moves half the distance that its container is resized in all directions.
	Right	The control is anchored to the right edge of its container.
	Top	The control is anchored to the top edge of its container.

You can think of an anchor as being much like a boat tethered to a floating pier at the edge of a lake. The lake is "resized" as the water level rises and falls, but the distance of the boat from the pier remains constant based on the length of the tether.

In our code, the `Button` is anchored to the top and left of the form, which is the default setting for the `Anchor` property. As a result our Load button remains in the upper-left corner of the display window as the form is resized. The `PictureBox` control is anchored to all four sides so that it expands as the application window expands and shrinks as the window shrinks.

TRY IT! Change the `Anchor` settings in your program to experiment with this property. In particular, set the button control's `Anchor` property to `AnchorStyles.None`. You will find that the control moves half the distance the form is resized in this case. Expand the form by 10 pixels horizontally, and the button will be 5 additional pixels from the left edge.

1.4.2 The Dock property

The use of `Anchor` is fine when you have a set of controls and need to define their resize behavior. In the case where you want to use as much of the form as possible, the `Anchor` property does not quite work. Although you could position the control at the edges of the form and anchor it to all sides, this is not the most elegant solution. Instead, the `Dock` property is provided for this purpose.

The `Dock` property is related to `Anchor` in that it also affects the resizing of controls on a form. In our previous analogy of the boat tethered to a floating pier, the boat itself is "docked" to the shore, in that it remains at the edge of the lake as the water rises and falls. Similarly, the `Dock` property establishes a location for a control within its container by fixing it flush against a side of the form.

Like `Anchor`, the `Dock` property takes its values from an enumeration, in this case the `DockStyle` enumeration. Note that the `AnchorStyles` enumeration is plural since a control can have multiple anchor settings, while the `DockStyle` enumeration is singular since a control can have a single docked value. More details on this enumeration appear in .NET Table 1.4.

We can see how the `Dock` property works by replacing the `pbxPhoto.Anchor` line in our program with a `Dock` setting that causes the `PictureBox` control to fill the entire form. Also change the version number in your program code to 1.5 (not shown here):

```
pbxPhoto.Top = (this.Height - pbxPhoto.Height) / 2;
pbxPhoto.SizeMode = PictureBoxSizeMode.Zoom;
pbxPhoto.Dock = DockStyle.Fill;

// Add our new controls to the form
this.Controls.Add(btnLoad);
this.Controls.Add(pbxPhoto);
```

.NET Table 1.4 DockStyle enumeration

The `DockStyle` enumeration defines the settings available for the `Dock` property in the `Control` class, and by inheritance all controls in the .NET Framework. This enumeration is part of the `System.Windows.Forms` namespace. If a `Dock` property other than `None` is set for a control, then the `Anchor` setting for that control is set to the top and left edges

Enumeration Values	Bottom	The control is positioned flush against the bottom edge of its container.
	Fill	The control is positioned flush against all sides of its container.
	Left	The control is positioned flush against the left edge of its container.
	None	The control is not docked to its container. This is the default, and indicates that the `Anchor` property is used to indicate the control's position within its container.
	Right	The control is positioned flush against the right edge of its container.
	Top	The control is positioned flush against the top edge of its container.

Compile and run the program again. After loading an image, your form should look something like figure 1.7. Note how the Load button is still visible since it is added to the form first and is therefore higher in the z-order stack than the image.

Note that if multiple controls are set to the same `Dock` value, the z-order of the controls determines the order in which the controls are docked. The top, or first, control in the z-order stack is placed flush against the docked edge. The next control is placed flush against the first control, and so on. The exception is the

Figure 1.7
The PictureBox control is docked to fill the entire client area of the form.

`DockStyle.Fill` value. In this case the controls appear on top of one another, and the z-order determines which control is visible.

TRY IT! Modify the order in which the controls are added to the form by adding the `PictureBox` first and the `Button` second to change the z-order of the button and picture box. This will cause the button to be hidden behind the image so that it no longer appears. The button is still present, however, and you can use the mnemonic Alt+L to load an image.

While you are at it, try setting the `Dock` property for the `Button` to `DockStyle.Top`. How does this affect the application window, and how does the z-order for these controls affect their placement on the form?

Of course, feel free to experiment with other Dock settings as well.

We use the `Dock` and `Anchor` properties throughout the book, so more examples with these properties are yet to come.

1.5 Recap

Before we move on, let's quickly review what we covered in this chapter. These chapter recaps will present a quick synopsis of what was covered and provide an introduction for the subsequent chapter.

In this chapter we did a whirlwind tour of the C# language, .NET Framework, and Windows Forms programming. We showed how to build and run an application containing a blank form, and added a Load button to select an image file and a picture box control to display this file. We discussed different members of C# classes such as constructors, methods, properties, and events, and saw how .NET executes a program. We also looked at the `OpenFileDialog` class to open a file, and the `Anchor` and `Dock` properties for setting the resize behavior of a control.

We intentionally ignored Visual Studio in this chapter. Instead, we edited code by hand and used the command-line compiler to build and link our program. In the next chapter, we examine how to build the identical program using Visual Studio, and use the opportunity to present some additional details about the world of .NET.

Many of the concepts presented here are discussed in more detail in later chapters. So if you missed something the first time, you may have a second chance to figure it out.

CHAPTER 2

Getting started with Visual Studio

This chapter looks at Microsoft's interactive development environment (IDE). This, of course, is Visual Studio, sometimes referred to as Visual Studio .NET or VS .NET. While the environment does consume a lot of resources, which may make it run a bit slowly on some older machines, it provides a number of advances over prior versions of Microsoft's IDE that make it worth a look. Some savvy developers may prefer a good text editor and a set of build files over Visual Studio as well.

Since Visual Studio is intended as the development environment of choice for .NET, the rest of this book uses Visual Studio in its examples. If you are comfortable using command-line programs and/or makefiles, you should be able to follow these examples and associated code excerpts to write the code in an alternate editor if you prefer.

Do not discount the use of Visual Studio, however. Even relatively modest Windows applications require a number of files and classes to create the resulting program. When working in a text editor, you the programmer must remember the required files, classes, member names, and other information. Visual Studio attempts to organize such information on your behalf and alleviates the need to track all of these pieces. In addition, Visual Studio provides some graphical shortcuts intended to ease the layout and programming of your applications. How much they actually help your efforts depends on your personal preferences. Take a look and make a conscious decision.

As this book is not specifically about Visual Studio, this is the only chapter that focuses solely on this new environment. So pay close attention to the procedures and discussion here. Additional information on Visual Studio is discussed as it arises. By the end of this chapter, you should know how to do the following tasks in Visual Studio:

- Create a new Windows Forms project.
- Add and place controls on a form.
- Modify the properties of a control, including the variable name for the control.
- Add a `Click` event handler to a `Button` control.
- View the z-order for controls on a form.

In order to concentrate on the environment, most of this chapter re-creates the photo application already presented in chapter 1. We call our new program "MyPhotos" and follow the sections from the previous chapter to create a similar application. This application will be used throughout the rest of the book as we add and refine the features and capabilities of the program.

Lest you get bored, some new topics are thrown in as well. In particular, we look more closely at two topics:

- Assembly attributes such as version numbers
- Exception handling in C#

2.1 PROGRAMMING WITH VISUAL STUDIO

Version 1.0 of the MyForm program was a blank form. A similar application is the default starting point in Visual Studio. In this section we create an initial MyPhotos application using Visual Studio instead of a text editor. Of course, we are still programming in C#, but we're using just the graphical tools provided by Visual Studio instead of the command-line tools used in chapter 1. In this section we create a program very similar to that shown in figure 1.1 in the first chapter.

This discussion assumes you have installed the .NET SDK 2.0 or later and the corresponding Visual Studio on your PC. It also assumes you have some knowledge of Windows, such as the ability to start and manipulate application windows in the environment. The initial window of Visual Studio 2005 is shown in figure 2.1. If you are using Visual C# Express or another edition of Visual Studio, you may see a slightly different screen. Visual C# Express is freely available from http://msdn.microsoft.com/vstudio/express/visualcsharp.

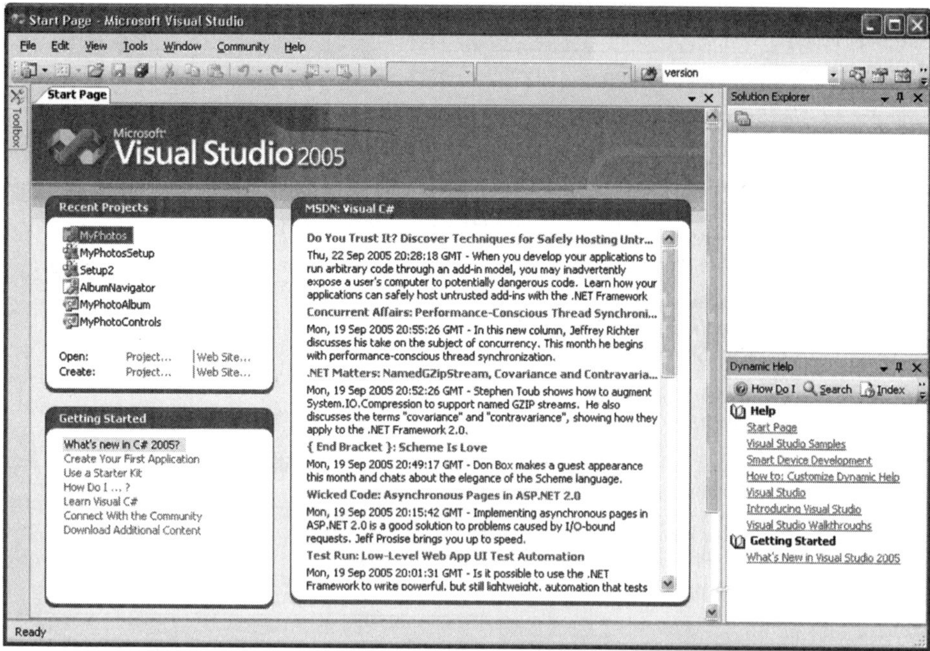

Figure 2.1 This figure shows Visual Studio 2005 configured for Visual C# programming. The configuration and placement of windows may vary depending on your local settings.

As a way to structure our discussion, this and subsequent chapters use the action-result table format described in the introduction. These tables provide numbered instructions for each task, including the actions to perform and result of each action.

In this section we create a Visual Studio project for our application, compile and run this application within Visual Studio, and look at the source code generated by Visual Studio in contrast to the program we wrote in section 1.1.

2.1.1 Creating a project

To begin, let's create a Visual Studio project called MyPhotos and duplicate the functionality presented in section 1.1. The following table enumerates the steps required. The term *project* and other aspects of the application are discussed following this table.

CREATE THE MYPHOTOS PROJECT

	Action	Result
1	Start Microsoft Visual Studio. **How-to** Locate the appropriate item in the Start menu.	The Microsoft Development Environment displays. **Note:** This window is illustrated in figure 2.1. You may want to consider closing the Dynamic Help window (by clicking the X in the upper-right corner of this window) while using this book. While quite useful in that it provides help related to your current activities, this window uses CPU and memory resources.

CREATE THE MYPHOTOS PROJECT *(CONTINUED)*

	Action	Result
2	Display the New Project dialog box. **How-to** Click the File menu, expand the New item, and select Project. **Alternately** Use the keyboard shortcut Ctrl+Shift+N.	The New Project dialog box appears. This figure illustrates the window after steps 3, 4, and 5 have been completed. 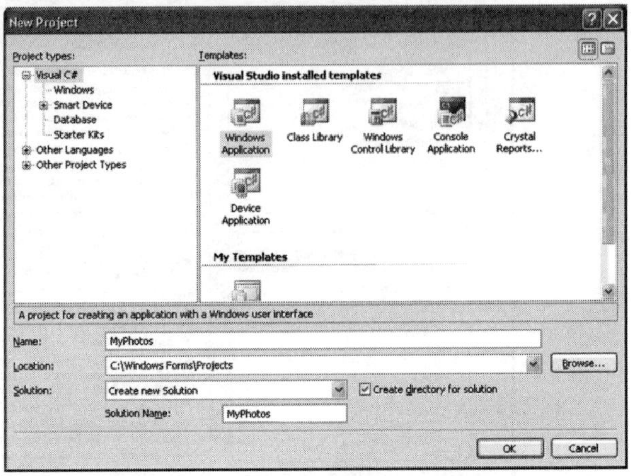 **Note:** The Location setting may vary depending on which version of Windows you are using. To avoid any confusion, this book uses the directory C:\Windows Forms\Projects. For your project, use the default setting provided by the environment. In Visual C# Express, a location is not required until the project is saved for the first time.
3	Under Project Types, select Visual C#.	
4	Under Templates, select Windows Application.	
5	In the Name field, enter "MyPhotos."	
6	Click the OK button.	The new MyPhotos project is created within a new MyPhotos solution. The Solution Explorer now displays the files in the solution, and the main window displays a blank form. 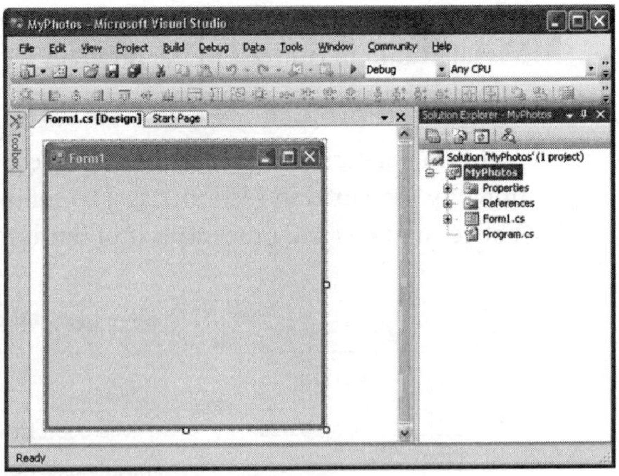

As you can see, Visual Studio presents a lot of information and a ton of features. We cover some of these features in this section, and others as we develop our application. The Solution Explorer window, typically but not always on the right side of the Visual Studio window area, shows the contents of the current solution—that is, the projects in the solution and the files in these projects.

Visual Studio uses projects and solutions to manage application development. Conceptually, a *project* is a collection of files that produce a .NET assembly, such as a library (.dll) or executable (.exe). A *solution* is a collection of projects that are grouped for development or deployment purposes. When a solution has only one project, the two words are somewhat equivalent. By default, Visual Studio creates a directory for the solution, and then creates a directory for each project within this solution directory.

The MyPhotos solution is stored on disk in a file called MyPhotos.sln. This solution holds a single project called MyPhotos, stored in the C# project file MyPhotos.csproj. The Solution Explorer window shows the MyPhotos solution containing the MyPhotos project. This project displays four items:

- *Properties*—The properties for the solution. If you expand this item, you will see the *AssemblyInfo.cs* file, which contains assembly information for the project; the *Resources.resx* file, which holds resource information; and the *Settings.settings* file, which holds projects. We talk about the assembly file in section 2.2.1 and resources files in chapter 15, section 15.2.
- *References*—The list of references for the project. These are provided to the compiler using the `/reference` switch we saw in chapter 1. You can expand this entry to see the default list of assemblies for the project, or wait until chapter 5 where we discuss how to add an assembly to this list.
- *Form1.cs*—A file containing the default `Form` class created for our application. If you expand this entry you will see the Form1.Designer.cs file. We look at both of these files in a moment.
- *Program.cs*—The `Program` class file, which contains the entry point `Main`.

We discuss the meaning and use of these items in this chapter and throughout the book.

2.1.2 Executing a program

Our MyPhotos project is in fact a fully functional application. To see this, let's compile and run the application from within Visual Studio, as shown in the following steps.

	COMPILE AND RUN THE MYPHOTOS APPLICATION	
	Action	**Result**
1	Compile the project. **How-to** Select the Build Solution item from the Build menu. **Alternately** Use the keyboard shortcut Ctrl+Shift+B.	This compiles the project and creates an executable file. **Note:** The default keyboard shortcut is Ctrl+Shift+B. Depending on your configuration, you may see a different shortcut in your application. Click the Options item under the Tools menu to view keyboard and other settings.
2	Run the application. **How-to** Select the Start Without Debugging item from the Debug menu. **Alternately** Use the keyboard shortcut Ctrl+F5.	The MyPhotos application executes, displaying our not-so-exciting blank form. **Note:** This window is similar to the original MyForm application written in chapter 1. Here and throughout the book, you can run applications with or without debugging. The result should be the same in either case.

We have not written any code to create this application; the code has been generated for us by Visual Studio. By default, Visual Studio displays the Windows Forms Designer window for the main `Form` class created in the project, which presents a graphical display of the form. We can also display the source code files for the `Form1` class, a topic we discuss next.

2.1.3 Viewing the source code

As in section 1.1, our application here is not all that glamorous. While a number of files are shown in Visual Studio, the actual source code for this form appears in the Form1.cs and Program.cs files. We take a look at these files here, and save the remaining files for later. The following table shows how to view the code in these two files.

	VIEW CODE GENERATED BY VISUAL STUDIO	
	Action	**Result**

1	View the Program.cs source file.
	How-to
	In the Solution Explorer window, double-click the Program.cs file.
	Solution Explorer - Solution 'MyPh...
	Solution 'MyPhotos' (1 project)
	MyPhotos
	Properties
	References
	Form1.cs
	Program.cs
		A Program.cs tab appears in the main window containing the C# code for the `Program` class.
		`using System;`
		`using System.Collections.Generic;`
		`using System.Windows.Forms;`
		
		`namespace MyPhotos`
		`{`
		`  static class Program`
		`  {`
		`    . . .`
		`  }`
		`}`

	VIEW CODE GENERATED BY VISUAL STUDIO (CONTINUED)	
	Action	**Result**

2	View the Form1.cs source file.
	How-to
	Right-click the Form.cs file in the Solution Explorer window and select the View Code item. 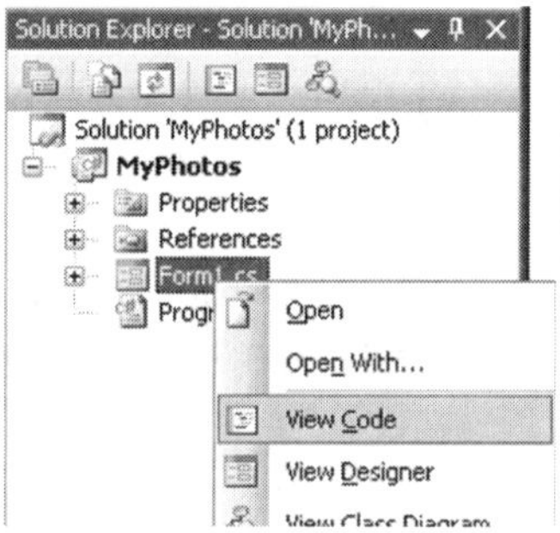
	Solution Explorer - Solution 'MyPh...
	Solution 'MyPhotos' (1 project)
	MyPhotos
	Properties
	References
	Form1.cs
	Progr
	Open
	Open With...
	View Code
	View Designer
		A Form1.cs tab appears in the main window containing C# code for the `Form1` class.
		`using System;`
		`using System.Collections.Generic;`
		`using System.ComponentModel;`
		`using System.Data;`
		`using System.Drawing;`
		`using System.Text;`
		`using System.Windows.Forms;`
		
		`namespace MyPhotos`
		`{`
		`  public partial class Form1 : Form`
		`  {`
		`    . . .`
		`  }`
		`}`

3	View the Form1.Designer.cs source file.
	How-to
	Click the plus sign next to the Form1.cs file in the Solution Explorer window and double-click the Form1.Designer.cs file.
		A Form1.Designer.cs tab appears in the main window containing C# code for the `Form1` class.
		`namespace MyPhotos`
		`{`
		`  partial class Form1`
		`  {`
		`    /// <summary>`
		`    /// Required designer variable.`
		`    . . .`
		`  }`

These three files make up the bulk of the code for our program. We discuss the code in each file separately.

Listing 2.1 The Program.cs file

```
using System;                                  ❶ Using directives
using System.Collections.Generic;
using System.Windows.Forms;

namespace MyPhotos
{                                        ❷ Static classes
  static class Program
  {
    /// <summary>                                    ❸ XML documentation
    /// The main entry point for the application.
    /// </summary>
    [STAThread]              ❹ Main entry point
    static void Main()
    {
      Application.EnableVisualStyles();
```

```
            Application.SetCompatibleTextRenderingDefault(false);
            Application.Run(new Form1());
        }
    }
}
```

The Program.cs file is shown in listing 2.1. This file defines the `Main` method, much like the `Main` method in our original MyForm application. The namespace `MyPhotos` is used, and a class `Form1` is created as part of a call to the `Application.Run` method. Some key differences from our original `Main` method are as follows. Note that the numbers here correspond to the numbered annotations in the code.

1. As discussed in chapter 1, the `using` directive allows members of the indicated namespace to be referenced directly in the code. We do not need the `System.Collections.Generic` namespace here, but it does not hurt to leave it in the code. We discuss generics in chapter 6.

2. The `Program` class is defined as a `static` class. This is a new feature in C# 2.0 that indicates the class cannot be instantiated and contains only static members. Both C++ and earlier C# versions allow classes with only static members, of course. The advantage here is that the compiler enforces this constraint, and generates an error if a static class defines any nonstatic members.

3. Visual Studio inserts comments for documenting your program and its methods. The C# language defines a standard for XML documentation style for code. Such lines must begin with three slashes and precede certain C# constructs such as classes, properties, and namespaces. Appendix A includes a section that summarizes the standard for what this documentation should look like. Check out the online documentation for complete details. The C# compiler `csc` accepts a `/doc` switch that gathers all such documentation lines and generates HTML reference pages. Visual Studio can do this as well if you set the appropriate output file setting in the project's properties.

4. This line defines the `Main` entry point for our application. We discussed the `EnableVisualStyles` and `Run` methods in chapter 1, where we also mentioned that the `[STAThread]` line is required in all Windows Forms applications. The `SetCompatibleTextRenderingDefault` method assigns whether text rending should be compatible with previous releases of Windows Forms. This is set to `false` by default.

The `Main` method in the `Program` class creates a new `Form1` object. The `Form1` class is partially defined by the Form1.cs file shown in listing 2.2. Let's discuss the notated sections of this code in more detail.

Listing 2.2 The Form1.cs file

```
using System;
using System.Collections.Generic;
using System.ComponentModel;
using System.Data;
using System.Drawing;
using System.Text;
using System.Windows.Forms;

namespace MyPhotos
{
  public partial class Form1 : Form      <-- 5 Indicates class is partially defined
  {
    public Form1()
    {
      InitializeComponent();      <-- 6 Calls designer-generated code
    }
  }
}
```

❺ The `partial` keyword declares that this file only contains a portion of the `Form1` class definition. This keyword allows other files to define additional members of the class. The full class is defined by the set of all partial definitions taken together, so it is an error if two partial definitions conflict with each other.

❻ The `InitializeComponent` method is the only statement in the `Form1` constructor. This special method holds the C# code generated by the Windows Forms Designer to represent the form within Visual Studio. We discuss this method in more detail in a moment.

If you compare the code in listings 2.1 and 2.2 with the code from listing 1.1, you will notice that additional code is still required. This, of course, is the code for the `InitializeComponent` method. The `partial` keyword in C# allows this code to exist in a separated file: the Form1.Designer.cs file. Listing 2.3 shows the Form1.Designer.cs file generated by Visual Studio.

Listing 2.3 The Form1.Designer.cs file

```
namespace MyPhotos
{
  partial class Form1
  {
    /// <summary>
    /// Required designer variable.                   Private components field 7
    /// </summary>
    private System.ComponentModel.IContainer components = null;   <--

    /// <summary>
    /// Clean up any resources being used.
```

```
    /// </summary>
    /// <param name="disposing">true if managed resources should be
    /// disposed; otherwise, false.</param>
    protected override void Dispose(bool disposing)
    {
      if (disposing && (components != null))
      {
        components.Dispose();
      }
      base.Dispose(disposing);
    }

    #region Windows Form Designer generated code
    /// <summary>
    /// Required method for Designer support - do not modify
    /// the contents of this method with the code editor.
    /// </summary>
    private void InitializeComponent()
    {
      this.components = new System.ComponentModel.Container();
      this.AutoScaleMode = System.Windows.Forms.AutoScaleMode.Font;
      this.Text = "Form1";
    }
    #endregion
  }
}
```

8 Dispose method

Form initialization code 9

Listing 2.3 defines additional members of the `Form1` class within the `MyPhotos` namespace. Note the use of the `partial` keyword and the documentation comments in this code. Points annotated in listing 2.3 are as follows:

7 The Windows Forms Designer requires this field in order to ensure that components are properly managed on the form at runtime, and specifically for components that are not also Windows Forms controls. We discuss this field in chapter 9 when we discuss the `ToolTip` component.

8 The use of garbage collection in .NET means that you have no idea when memory and other system resources will be freed for objects that are no longer in use. The `Dispose` method provides a way to control how certain resources are released and reclaimed by the system. We discuss this concept in chapter 5.

9 The `#region` and `#endregion` directives define a named section of code. Regions are simply a visual aid, and editors such as Visual Studio allow you to expand and collapse the region within the editor. This region defines the `InitializeComponent` method, used by the designer to create and initialize controls and other components on the form. This code is processed by the Windows Forms Designer window whenever the design window is displayed. As you can see, right now this method simply initializes the `components` field and assigns the `AutoScaleMode` and `Text` properties on the form. While Microsoft recommends that you do not edit this code manually, if you are careful, manual changes can be applied.

Congratulations once again for creating your first Windows Forms program in Visual Studio. Sit back in your chair to savor your accomplishment, and move on section 2.2 when ready to add some controls.

2.2 WINDOWS FORMS CONTROLS

In this section we add the `Button` and `PictureBox` controls to our form, similar to listing 1.2 in chapter 1. As you may recall, section 1.2 also modified the version number of the application, so let's begin by looking at how this is done in Visual Studio.

2.2.1 The AssemblyInfo file

When you create a C# Windows application project, Visual Studio includes an AssemblyInfo.cs file in the project. This file defines various attributes for the program assembly, such as the version number shown in the Version tab of a program's Properties dialog box in Windows Explorer. An *attribute* in C# is a declarative tag that affects the settings or behavior exhibited by an assembly, type (such as a class), or type member (such as a method or property). All attributes are based on the `System.Attribute` class defined in the .NET Framework as part of the `System` namespace.

The AssemblyInfo.cs file makes use of some assembly-related attributes defined by this namespace. These settings are defined using the standard format for attributes targeted at the assembly file:

```
[assembly: <attribute>(<setting>)]
```

The various attribute classes defined for this purpose include the `AssemblyVersionAttribute` class supporting the file version number settings. In C#, the `Attribute` portion of the class name can be omitted, resulting in a version number setting something like the following:

```
[assembly: AssemblyVersion("1.0")]
```

A summary of the attributes used by this file appears in table 2.1.

Table 2.1 Common attributes in the AssemblyInfo.cs file

Attribute	Description
AssemblyTitle	The title for this assembly
AssemblyDescription	A short description of the assembly
AssemblyCompany	The company name for the assembly
AssemblyProduct	The product name for the assembly
AssemblyCopyright	The copyright string for the assembly
AssemblyVersion	The version string for the assembly
AssemblyFileVersion	The version number for the Win32 file version resource

Most of these attributes accept a string that specifies the value for the attribute. One exception is the `AssemblyVersion` attribute. The version number is used internally for comparing expected and actual version numbers of other assemblies, namely programs or libraries, used by your application. The format for the version number is a string specified as follows:

```
Major.Minor.Build.Revision
```

These four values should all be integers. The first two values are for the major and minor version number used by most products these days. The third value, the build number, is for different compiles of the same minor version of an assembly. The final value, the revision number, is for bug fixes or other incidental updates. Of course, you can use these numbers to mean whatever you wish; these are just recommendations.

The build and revision number can be inserted automatically by the compiler each time an assembly is created. This is done by inserting an asterisk (*) in place of one or both of these numbers.

The automated build number in this case is the number of days since January 1, 2000, in local time, and the automated revision number is the number of seconds since the previous midnight, local time, divided by 2. These automated values ensure that new build and revision numbers are generated for each compile, that the build number always increases, and that the revision number increases within a generated build number. It should be noted that this scheme is good for thousands of years, and that the revision number will never be larger than a 32-bit integer.

In our application, as a way to link the code in the book with the downloadable code on the book's website, we set the version number equal to the current section number. The following steps set the version number for our application to 2.2. While we are here, we also assign values to other settings in the AssemblyInfo.cs file, and use the `ProductVersion` property of the `Application` class to include this version number in our title bar automatically.

SET THE VERSION NUMBER FOR THE MYPHOTOS PROJECT

	Action	Results
1	Display the project's AssemblyInfo.cs file. **How-to** Open the Properties folder and double-click the file name in the Solution Explorer window.	An AssemblyInfo.cs tab appears in the main window containing the source code for this file. **Note:** In a production application, the properties discussed here would normally be set project-wide and be approved by Marketing and other departments. These settings are visible to an end user of the application, so a process for assigning these values is important. Similarly, the version number should be tightly controlled, and the version settings should probably include a build and revision value to differentiate different builds of the code on a day-to-day basis.

<table>
<tr><th colspan="3">SET THE VERSION NUMBER FOR THE MYPHOTOS PROJECT (CONTINUED)</th></tr>
<tr><th></th><th>Action</th><th>Results</th></tr>
<tr><td>2</td><td>Find the version lines and change the version number to "2.2."</td><td><pre>[assembly: AssemblyVersion("2.2")]
[assembly: AssemblyFileVersion("2.2")]</pre></td></tr>
<tr><td>3</td><td>Set the other assembly attributes to reasonable values.</td><td>In my code, I used the following settings:<pre>[assembly: AssemblyTitle("MyPhotos")]
[assembly: AssemblyDescription("Sample application "
    + "for Windows Forms in Action")]
[assembly: AssemblyConfiguration("")]
[assembly: AssemblyCompany("Manning Publications Co.")]
[assembly: AssemblyProduct("MyPhotos")]
[assembly: AssemblyCopyright("Copyright "
    + "(C) Manning Publications")]
[assembly: AssemblyTrademark("")]
[assembly: AssemblyCulture("")]</pre></td></tr>
<tr><td>4</td><td>At the end of the <code>Form1</code> constructor in the <code>Form1.cs</code> file, call a <code>SetTitleBar</code> method to set the text on the title bar.</td><td><pre>public Form1
{
  InitializeComponent()
  SetTitleBar();
}</pre></td></tr>
<tr><td>5</td><td>Implement the <code>SetTitleBar</code> method to include the version number in the title bar.

Note: Minor point, but make sure this method appears within the <code>Form</code> class code block, right after the <code>Form1</code> constructor.</td><td><pre>private void SetTitleBar()
{
  Version ver
      = new Version(Application.ProductVersion);
  Text = String.Format("MyPhotos {0:0}.{1:0}",
    ver.Major, ver.Minor);
}</pre>Note: This code uses the <code>Version</code> class to decode the version string. The <code>Version</code> constructor used here accepts a string and provides access to the individual parts of the corresponding version number.</td></tr>
</table>

In your applications, you can set the build and revision numbers explicitly, or allow .NET to generate them automatically. We change the version number repeatedly throughout this book as a way to indicate which section of the book corresponds to the current application. You can change or not change the version number as you wish. In the downloadable code, these version numbers are used to identify the files associated with a specific section of the book.

The version number identifies a specific instance of a product that your customers or friends are using. This is useful for documentation and support reasons, and for indicating to your customers when new features and functionality are added to a product. Note that it is common practice to include the version number in a dialog box, often called an About box, that is available from a top-level Help menu in an application. We include this feature later in the book.

Of course, the class `Form1` is not the most descriptive name, so let's rename this class next.

2.2.2 Renaming a form

We should make one other change before we add controls to our form. Visual Studio created the class `Form1` in our project. Let's rename this file and associated class to `MainForm`, as per the following steps.

RENAME THE FORM1 CLASS AND FILE TO MAINFORM

	Action	Result
1	Rename the Form1.cs file in the Solution Explorer window to MainForm.cs. **How-to** a. Right-click the Form1.cs file in the Solution Explorer. b. Select the Rename item. c. Enter the name "MainForm.cs." d. Press the Enter key.	You are asked if you'd also like to rename all references to "Form1" as well. The graphic here is truncated intentionally to make the text more readable.
2	Indicate you wish to rename all references by clicking Yes.	The file is renamed, along with the designer and code windows. The `Form1` class name and constructor are also renamed to `MainForm`.
3	Compile and run the application.	The application displays a blank form, with the text "MyPhotos 2.2" shown in the title bar.

With these administrative tasks out of the way, we can get back to the topic of placing controls on our form.

2.2.3 The Toolbox window

In future chapters, we do not include the excruciating details of adding controls to forms and setting their properties in the Windows Forms Designer, so make sure you understand the process here. If you recall, in chapter 1 we inserted a `Button` and a `PictureBox` on our form. We do the same here in the subsequent steps using Visual Studio.

ADD THE CONTROLS TO OUR FORM

	Action	Result
1	Click the MainForm.cs [Design] tab.	The Windows Forms Designer appears, displaying our blank form.
2	Open the Toolbox window. **How-to** Click the Toolbox tab on the upper-left side of the window. **Note:** Your Toolbox may appear on the right or left, depending on your settings. If the Toolbox tab is not visible, select the Toolbox item from the View menu.	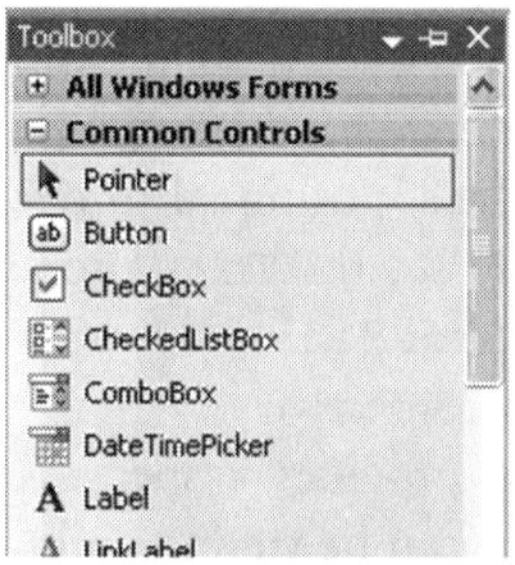 **Note:** The order of topics or controls in your window may be different from what you see here. The contents of this window can be customized, and new controls can be added. Look up "toolbox, customizing" in the online documentation for more details on this latter point.
3	Add a `Button` control to the form. **How-to** a. Click the Button item in the Toolbox window. b. Click the blank form.	A new `Button` control appears on the form. 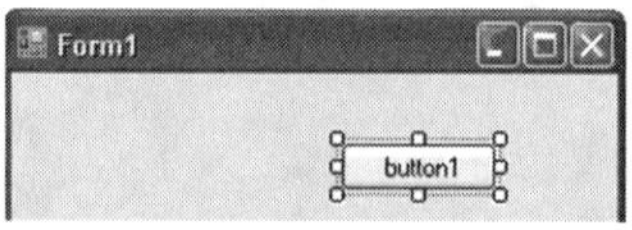
4	Similarly, add a `PictureBox` object to the form.	A new `PictureBox` control appears on the form. **Note:** The order in which controls are added establishes the tab order and the z-order for these controls. All controls support the `TabIndex` property for this purpose, which we discuss later in the chapter.
5	Arrange the controls so that the `Button` is at the top left and the `PictureBox` roughly in the middle. **How-to** Move each control by clicking and dragging it. You can also click and drag a control's corners or edges to resize the control.	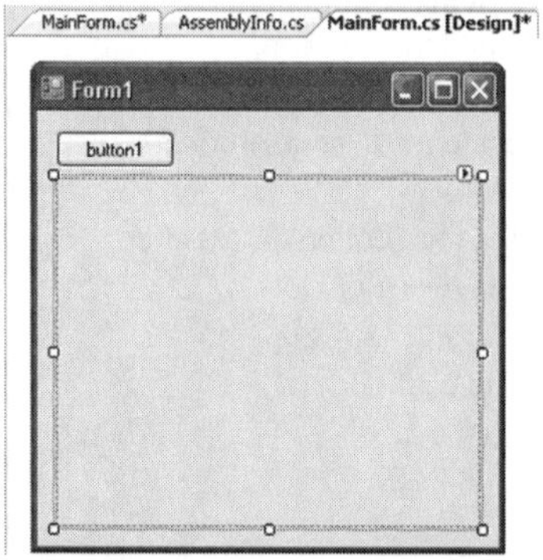 **Note:** A small asterisk (*) appears on the tabs related to the MainForm.cs file to indicate that changes to this file have not been saved.

Our controls are now on the form. By default, each control is named based on the type of control. The `Button` is called `button1`, while the `PictureBox` is called `pictureBox1`. Visual Studio automatically creates a name for a new control using the class name followed by a number. A second `Button` object added to the form would be called `button2`, and so forth. As for the `Form1` class earlier in this chapter, we would prefer more descriptive names for our controls, so we will rename these items.

In addition, we need to set the properties for our controls similar to the settings in chapter 1. Since we have set our control's position and size graphically, there is no need to assign the positional properties such as `Left` and `Height` here. In chapter 1, we also set the `Text` property of the button to "&Load" and the `BorderStyle` and `SizeMode` properties of the `PictureBox` control to the `Fixed3D` and `Zoom` values, respectively.

Visual Studio provides a special Properties window where the properties and name of a control can be viewed and modified. We use these to update our controls, as a continuation of our previous steps.

RENAME THE CONTROLS AND DEFINE THEIR PROPERTIES

	Action	Result
6	Display the properties for the `Button` control. **How-to** a. Right-click the `Button` control. b. Select the Properties item. c. If the controls are not shown alphabetically, click the A-Z button in the Properties window.	The Properties window appears with the properties for the `button1` control displayed. **Note:** On your PC, the Properties window may appear below or to the right of the main window. You can move it by dragging its tab, located below the window, to a new location. I prefer this window on the right side of Visual Studio to allow a longer list of properties to be displayed. Properties always are displayed alphabetically in the book, rather than by category. You can display the entries either way in your own application.
7	Rename the control from "button1" to "btnLoad." **How-to** a. Locate the (Name) entry at the top of the list. b. Click the "button1" text after this property.[a] c. Enter the new name "btnLoad."	The variable associated with the button is renamed. 

Rename the controls and define their properties *(continued)*		
	Action	**Result**
8	Modify the `Text` property for the button to be "&Load." **How-to** a. Locate the Text entry in the Properties window. b. Changes its value to "&Load."	As in chapter 1, the ampersand (&) is used to indicate the mnemonic for the button. Notice that the `TabIndex` property for this control is set to 0, since it was the first control added to the form.
9	Display the `PictureBox` control properties. **How-to** Right-click the control and select Properties. **Alternately** Select the `pictureBox1` entry from the drop-down list at the top of the Properties window.	
10	Set the `(Name)` property to "pbxPhoto."	
11	Set the `BorderStyle` property to `Fixed3D`, and the `SizeMode` property to `Zoom`.	In the Properties window, the assigned values are displayed in **bold**, to indicate that these values are not the default settings. **Note:** These properties are set via drop-down lists since they are based on a fixed set of enumeration values, in this case those taken from the `BorderStyle` and `PictureBoxSizeMode` enumerations.
12	Display the properties for our `MainForm` object. **How-to** Click the title bar of the form, or select the `MainForm` entry from the drop-down list.	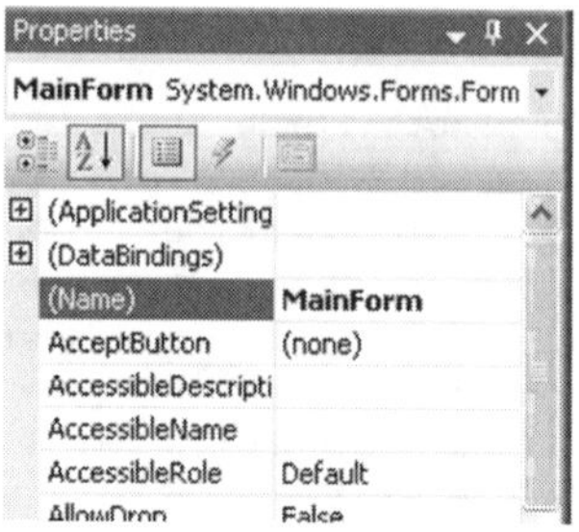
13	Set the `Text` property to "MyPhotos."	This setting immediately appears in the title bar of the form in the designer window. **Note:** We already added code to assign a new title bar in the constructor of our class, but it's nice to have a default title bar regardless.

a. Technically the (Name) entry is not a property, of course. It just refers to the name assigned to the variable in the code. Since it appears in the Properties window, we call it a property anyway, to simplify our discussions.

Before we compile and run this code, let's see how the source code generated by Visual Studio has changed in response to our actions. This is now in the MainForm.Designer.cs file, to match our renamed class file MainForm.cs. Listing 2.4 shows the region that defines the `InitializeComponent` method, which you might want to contrast with the prior code in listing 2.3. The numbered points are worth some additional discussion.

Listing 2.4 The Windows Form Designer region after adding controls

```
#region Windows Form Designer generated code
/// <summary>
/// Required method for Designer support - do not modify
/// the contents of this method with the code editor.
/// </summary>
private void InitializeComponent()
{                                                          Creates the controls ❶
  this.btnLoad = new System.Windows.Forms.Button();
  this.pbxPhoto = new System.Windows.Forms.PictureBox();
  ((System.ComponentModel.ISupportInitialize)
        (this.pbxPhoto)).BeginInit();
  this.SuspendLayout();
  //
  // btnLoad
  //
  this.btnLoad.Location = new System.Drawing.Point(12, 12);
  this.btnLoad.Name = "btnLoad";
  this.btnLoad.Size = new System.Drawing.Size(75, 23);        ❷ Sets standard control settings
  this.btnLoad.TabIndex = 0;
  this.btnLoad.Text = "&Load";
  this.btnLoad.UseVisualStyleBackColor = true;
  //
  // pbxPhoto
  //
  this.pbxPhoto.BorderStyle
      = System.Windows.Forms.BorderStyle.Fixed3D;
  this.pbxPhoto.Location = new System.Drawing.Point(12, 41);
  this.pbxPhoto.Name = "pbxPhoto";                            ❸ Sets control location and size
  this.pbxPhoto.Size = new System.Drawing.Size(268, 213);
  this.pbxPhoto.SizeMode
      = System.Windows.Forms.PictureBoxSizeMode.Zoom;
  this.pbxPhoto.TabIndex = 1;
  this.pbxPhoto.TabStop = false;
  //
  // MainForm
  //
  this.AutoScaleDimensions = new System.Drawing.SizeF(6F, 13F);
  this.AutoScaleMode = System.Windows.Forms.AutoScaleMode.Font;
  this.ClientSize = new System.Drawing.Size(292, 266);
  this.Controls.Add(this.pbxPhoto);           ❹ Adds controls
  this.Controls.Add(this.btnLoad);               to form
  this.Name = "MainForm";
```

```
    this.Text = "MyPhotos";
    ((System.ComponentModel.ISupportInitialize)
             (this.pbxPhoto)).EndInit();
    this.ResumeLayout(false);
  }
  #endregion

  private System.Windows.Forms.Button btnLoad;
  private System.Windows.Forms.PictureBox pbxPhoto;
```

5 Defines control variables

1 The `InitializeComponent` method creates the required class instances and prepares each object for initialization. As we discussed in chapter 1, all controls are classes. The `new` keyword creates the actual object for each control. All controls provide layout logic to render the control on the form. The `SuspendLayout` method defers this logic until the `ResumeLayout` method is called; otherwise the control might try to lay out a partially modified control. Some controls, including the `PictureBox` class, also support the `ISupportInitialize` interface,[1] allowing the control to optimize changes to multiple related properties. This typically prevents the control from recalculating complex or expensive display logic each time a property is modified.

2 Any properties set in the Windows Forms Designer are defined in a separate section for each control. The `Name` property is always set to the variable name of the control, while the `TabIndex` property is also assigned, starting with zero (0), to establish the tab order for the controls on the form. Other properties are assigned as required.

3 The size and location of each control are defined by the Windows Forms Designer as well. These settings are defined using structures such as `Point` and `Size` from the `System.Drawing` namespace. A structure, unlike a class, is a value type, so the `new` statement creates these objects on the stack and copies their value into the appropriate property.

4 After all controls on the form are created and initialized, the `InitializeComponent` method adds each control to the form itself using the `Add` method available to the `Form.Controls` property. As discussed in chapter 1, the `Form.Controls` property returns the collection of controls on the form, allowing controls to be added or removed from the collection. The order in which controls are added defines the initial z-order of the controls on the form. Also note that the initialization of the `PictureBox` control is ended, and the layout logic for the `Form` object is resumed. We discuss these points in more detail as we progress through the book.

5 At the bottom of the file, after the region for the `InitializeComponent` method, the variables for the control are defined. You may know that in C++ class variables must be defined before they are used. C# takes a somewhat holistic approach to this

---

[1] We discuss interfaces in chapter 5.

issue, allowing a class variable, or *field* in C#, to be defined before, after, or even in a separate partial file as long as it appears somewhere in the class.

When you have finished reviewing this code, compile and run the program as before. As in version 1.2 of the MyForm application in chapter 1, this version displays our controls but does not allow a user to do anything with them. Enabling the user to load an image is our next topic.

2.3 LOADING FILES

With our controls on the form, we can load an image into the `PictureBox` control using the `OpenFileDialog` class. Most of our changes up until this point have simply set values via Visual Studio and let the environment do the work on our behalf. In this section we need to write a bit more code. The result of our labors will allow a file to be selected, as shown in figure 2.2.

There are a couple of topics worth discussing here. We start with the dialog box shown in figure 2.2, and then discuss how to handle the case where the user selects an invalid file.

2.3.1 Handling events in Visual Studio

As we saw in the previous chapter, an event is a predefined action that a program can respond to, such as a user clicking a button or resizing a window. In chapter 1 we

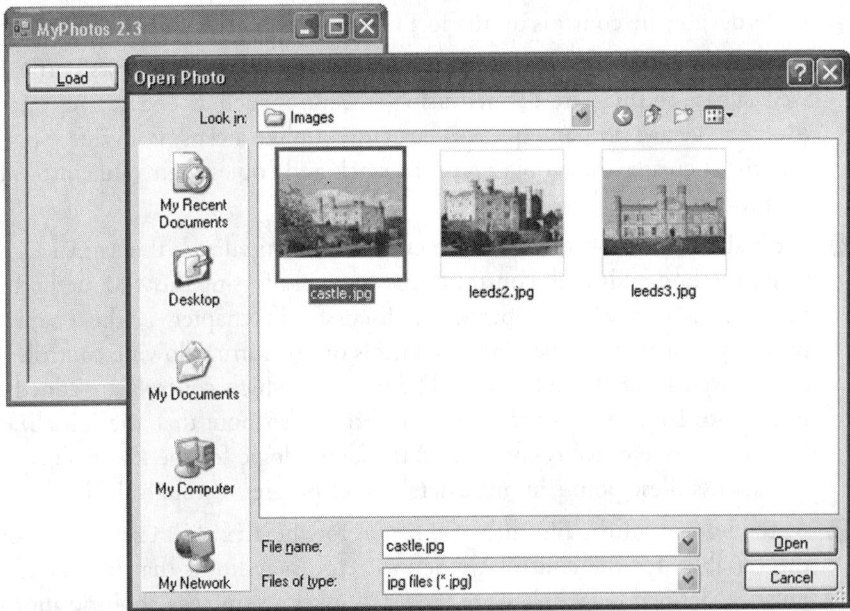

Figure 2.2 The dialog box used to select an image file in our application, created using the OpenFileDialog class

handled the event that occurs when the user clicks the Load button. Here we do the same using Visual Studio rather than a text editor.

As you may recall, the Load button handler allowed the user to select an image file and then assigned the `Bitmap` image in the file to our `PictureBox` control. This involved setting a `Click` event handler for the button and using the `OpenFileDialog` class to prompt the user for an image to load.

To duplicate this behavior in our MyPhotos application, the event handler code will be identical to that already shown and discussed. So if you skipped ahead and missed this discussion, go back to chapter 1.

To match the downloadable code for this section, set the version number of the application to 2.3. We do not remind you to do this in every section, but I thought a single reminder here might get past my editor.

IMPLEMENT A CLICK HANDLER FOR THE BTNLOAD BUTTON

	Action	Result

1	In the MainForm.cs [Design] window, add a `Click` event handler for the Load button.
	How-to
	Double-click the Load button.
		The MainForm.cs source code window is displayed with a new `btnLoad_Click` method added.
		`private void btnLoad_Click(object sender, System.EventArgs e)`
		`{`
		`}`
		Note: Visual Studio uses a naming convention for all event handlers consisting of the variable name, followed by an underscore, followed by the event name.

2	Add our code to handle the `Click` event.
	How-to
	Cut and paste your previous code into the window, or enter the code as shown here.
		`private void btnLoad_Click(object sender, System.EventArgs e)`
		`{`
		`  OpenFileDialog dlg = new OpenFileDialog();`
		
		`  dlg.Title = "Open Photo";`
		`  dlg.Filter = "jpg files (*.jpg)|*.jpg"`
		`      + "|All files (*.*)|*.*";`
		
		`  if (dlg.ShowDialog() == DialogResult.OK)`
		`  {`
		`    pbxPhoto.Image = new Bitmap(dlg.OpenFile());`
		`  }`
		
		`  dlg.Dispose();`
		`}`
		Note: Some of these lines do not fit the width of this table. The `dlg.Filter` line, in particular, should be a single string. Here and throughout the book, we reformat the code to fit the table in a way that is still valid C# code. If you are reading the electronic edition of the book, you can cut and paste these blocks of code directly into Visual Studio.

Before we discuss this code, it is worth calling attention to the statement completion feature of Visual Studio. If you typed in the code by hand, then you probably noticed

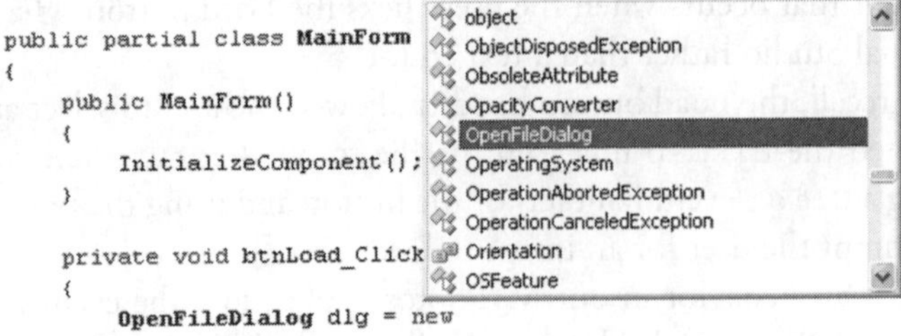

Figure 2.3 When enabled, the statement-completion feature in Visual Studio displays a scrollable list of possible completions for the current item.

how Visual Studio pops up with class member information as you type. Figure 2.3 shows what you might see after entering part of the first line of the `btnLoad_Click` method. After you type "new," Visual Studio pops up a list of possible classes, highlighting the `OpenFileDialog` class since the `dlg` variable is of this type. You can press Enter immediately to accept the highlighted class.

Visual Studio uses a different icon for different types. In the figure, most entries are classes, although `Orientation` is an enumeration type. You can scroll through the list to view the icons for alternate types.

The feature applies to variables and classes as well as the `new` keyword. When you begin typing the next line to set the `Title` property of the dialog box, you may see something like figure 2.4, where the class properties, methods, and events available to the `dlg` variable are displayed. These correspond to the members of the `OpenFile-Dialog` class.

Once again note how Visual Studio uses different icons for different items. In this figure, `ShowDialog` is a method and `Title` is a property. You can scroll through the dialog box to locate an event such as `Disposed` or `FileOk` in order to see its icon.

You will notice other statement-completion pop-ups as you type. One particularly nice feature is that signatures of methods are displayed as you type, and you can step through the various overloaded versions of a method using the arrow keys. As we see

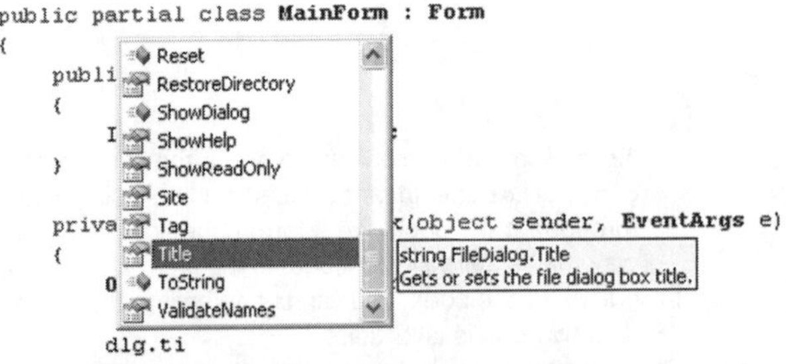

Figure 2.4 Statement completion applies to class members especially, allowing you to view the name and documentation for each class member. In this case the yellow pop-up shows that Title is declared as a string property in the FileDialog class.

in chapter 5, Visual Studio also picks up the classes and structures defined in your solution and incorporates them into these pop-up menus. Any documentation provided by <summary> tags within these classes is included as well, providing an automated forum for conveying important information about a particular member to other programmers.

Of course, like any feature, all these pop-up windows require a certain amount of CPU and system resources. If you are running Visual Studio on a slower machine, or do not want such windows to appear, you can turn statement completion off in the Options dialog box shown in figure 2.5. Choose Tools > Options to display this dialog box. Click the Text Editor settings in the list on the left, the C# item, and then select General.

As you see in the figure, you can disable the automatic listing of members, the display of parameter information, or both of these features. Feel free to look around and use the question mark (?) help button for additional details on any settings.

Back to our btnLoad_Click method, the code used here matches the code used for the MyForm program in chapter 1. Take another look at the InitializeComponent method in the hidden MainForm.Designer.cs file. Visual Studio has added the Click event handler for the btnLoad control.

```
this.btnLoad.Click += new System.EventHandler(
                            this.btnLoad_Click);
```

Compile and run the application to verify that the program can now load and display an image. If you recall, we noted in chapter 1 that this code presumes the selected file

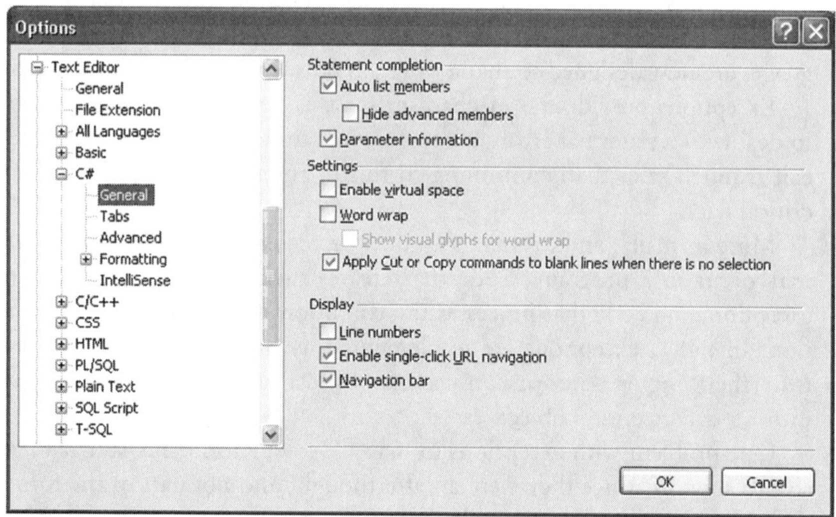

Figure 2.5 The Visual Studio Options dialog box can be used to enable or disable the statement-completion feature. Additional completion settings appear in the IntelliSense options.

can be turned into a `Bitmap` object. If you select a file that is not actually an image, the program exits in a most unfriendly manner. This is a fine opportunity to fix this problem, so we make it the subject of our next section.

2.3.2 Handling exceptions

You may well be familiar with exception handling, since a number of C++ development environments, including earlier Microsoft environments, support this feature. Newer languages such as Java also support exceptions. Exception handling came into existence as a common way to deal with unexpected errors in a program. In our application, we rely on the user to select a JPEG or other image file that can be opened as a `Bitmap` object. Most of the time, no error occurs. However, if a corrupted or invalid JPEG file is selected, or perhaps if the operating system is low on memory, then this creates an exceptional condition where it may not be possible to create our `Bitmap`. Since such situations will certainly occur, a way to recognize such errors is required.

Historically, C-based languages provided a number of alternatives for handling errors from a procedure or function. These included having an error parameter as part of the routine, returning an error value from a function, and updating a global error code within a module to indicate an error. The problem with these and similar approaches is that the programmer is required to do something in order to process errors. It is all too easy to ignore or forget this not-so-minor detail. In the production code of a Fortune 500 company, this can result in disastrous behavior or corruption of critical business data. Even worse, a programmer might get fired over such a problem.

To address this issue, computer language creators realized that programmers are generally lazy. Rather than allow a program to work when errors are ignored, languages are now designed so that a program fails when unexpected situations arise.

Exceptions provide the mechanism for this behavior. They force a programmer to deal with a potential error, or force a program to exit if they are ignored. A forced exit is much safer than continuing to run in an errant state and risk compromising critical data.

More formally, an *exception* is an unexpected error, or exceptional condition, that may occur in a program. Code that creates such a condition is said to *throw* the exception, and code that processes the condition is said to *catch* or *handle* the exception. In .NET, exceptions are implemented as classes. All .NET exceptions inherit from the `System.Exception` class, and most non-.NET exceptions are translated into a .NET exception object.

One problem with exceptions in many C++ environments is that they are expensive to support, since they were an afterthought and not part of the formal language definition. Modern languages like Java and C# have done away with this problem by designing exceptions into the language so that compilers are required to handle them cheaply and gracefully. As a result, the performance of exception blocks in C# is quite good, with extra processing only occurring when an exception actually occurs. This processing overhead also means that exceptions should only be used in truly exceptional situations.

The format used to process exceptions is the well-known `try-catch-finally` blocks employed in distributed computing interfaces and C++ development environments for many years. The code to monitor is enclosed in a `try` block, with exception-handling code enclosed in a `catch` block. Code to execute regardless of whether an exception occurs is placed in a `finally` block. We discuss this syntax in more detail in a moment. First, let's add such a block to the code where we create the `Bitmap` object. Here is our existing code:

```
if (dlg.ShowDialog() == DialogResult.OK)
{
  pbxPhoto.Image = new Bitmap(dlg.OpenFile());
}
```

The following steps detail how to catch exceptions in this code.

HANDLE EXCEPTIONS IN THE BTNLOAD_CLICK METHOD

	Action	Result

1	In the `btnLoad_Click` method of the MainForm.cs file, insert a `try` block around the `Bitmap` creation code.	The changes to the existing code are shown in bold.
		`if (dlg.ShowDialog() == DialogResult.OK)`
		`{`
		`try`
		`{`
		`pbxPhoto.Image = new Bitmap(dlg.OpenFile());`
		`}`

2	Add a `catch` block to catch the `ArgumentException` that occurs when an invalid image file is passed to the `Bitmap` constructor.	**`catch (ArgumentException ex)`** **`{`** **`// Handle exception`** **`}`** `}` **Note:** We use `ex` as a standard variable name for an `Exception` object, to avoid any confusion with the "`e`" parameter used by Visual Studio for the event argument in event handlers.

The C# `catch` clause takes an exception class name, and an optional variable to use when referring to this class. The block is executed if one of the statements in the `try` block throws this class as an exception. The `catch` clause can leave the class name out to catch any exception, and can leave out the variable name if the exception is never referenced.

It is common practice by some programmers to catch all exceptions that occur in their code. This is generally a bad idea, since you then mask or otherwise hide system problems such as out of memory or disk input/output (I/O) errors. Handling an exception indicates that the code recognizes that a problem may occur, and knows how to deal with it. As a result, only catch exceptions that you really do know how to handle.

Returning to our code, we catch the `ArgumentException` that occurs when the user selects a file that is not an image. When this occurs, a message is displayed to indicate the problem. The code uses the `MessageBox` class to do this, which is discussed in detail in chapter 7.

HANDLE EXCEPTIONS IN THE BTNLOAD_CLICK METHOD (CONTINUED)		
	Action	**Results and Comments**

3	Handle the exception by displaying a message to the user and clearing any image displayed in the picture box.	One way to do this is as follows:
		`catch (ArgumentException ex)`
		`{`
		`  // Handle exception`
		`  MessageBox.Show(`
		`    "Unable to load file: " + ex.Message);`
		`  pbxPhoto.Image = null;`
		`}`

The `Message` property is used in our dialog box to insert the exception message provided by the `ArgumentException` object. This and other members of the base `Exception` class are summarized in .NET Table 2.2.

We use exceptions throughout the book to handle errors in a similar manner. Other concepts associated with exceptions will be presented as they are required by our sample program.

We have one more task to perform to bring our application in line with the MyForm application from chapter 1. This is the topic of resizing a `Form` using the `Anchor` and `Dock` properties.

2.4 RESIZING FORMS

Our final task in this chapter is to set the behavior when resizing using the `Anchor` or `Dock` property for our controls. We discussed the meaning and use of these properties in chapter 1, so here we examine how these properties are assigned in Visual Studio.

2.4.1 Assigning the Anchor property

In chapter 1 we set the `Anchor` property for our `Button` control to `Top` and `Left`, and for our `PictureBox` control to `Top`, `Bottom`, `Left`, and `Right`. Since the default value for all controls is `Top` and `Left`, we only need to modify the property for the `pbxPhoto` control. The result of this change is shown in figure 2.6.

	Set the Anchor property for the pbxPhoto control	
	Action	**Result**
1	In the properties for the `pbxPhoto` control, use the `Anchor` property to anchor this control to all four sides of the form. **How-to** a. Click the down arrow for the Anchor item setting. b. Click the right and bottom areas as in the graphic to add Bottom and Right to the setting. c. Click outside the drop-down graphic to set the selected value.	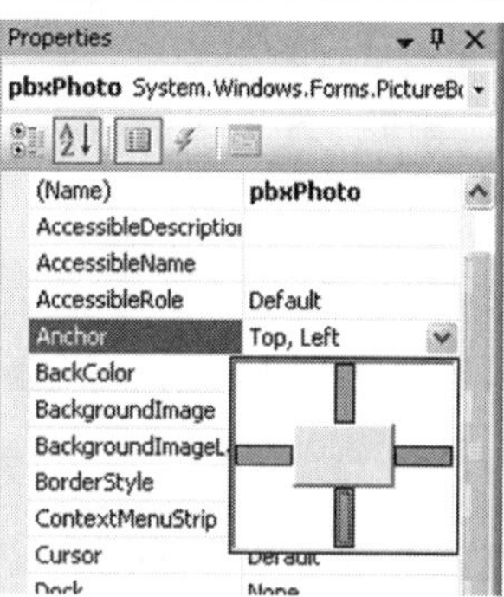

.NET Table 2.2 Exception class

The `Exception` class represents a generic exceptional condition, and serves as the base class for all exception classes in .NET. This class is part of the `System` namespace, and provides information required to raise (`throw`) and process (`catch`) exceptions. Note that it is possible for unmanaged code to throw exceptions that will not be seen as `Exception` objects. These exceptions can be caught using an empty `catch` clause.

Public Properties	*Data*	Gets a collection of user-defined data that provides additional information about this exception.
	HelpLink	Gets a link to help information associated with this exception.
	InnerException	Gets the inner (nested) exception associated with this object, if any.
	Message	Gets the message text assigned to the exception.
	Source	Gets or sets a string containing the source of the exception, such as the name of the application or object that generated the error.
	StackTrace	Gets the stack trace as a string. By default, the stack is captured just before the exception is thrown.
	TargetSite	Gets the `MethodBase` object for the method that threw this exception.
Public Methods	GetBaseException	Returns the original `Exception` that caused the current exception to be thrown. Useful when a chain of nested exceptions is received.
	ToString (overridden from Object)	Returns the fully qualified name of the exception, and typically other information such as the message text, a stack trace, and information about any inner exceptions.

Figure 2.6
The resized application here illustrates how the PictureBox control maintains the aspect ratio of the image when the SizeMode property is set to Zoom.

Windows Forms defines a special graphic for the `Anchor` property that is used by Visual Studio to modify its value. Since the `Anchor` property is defined as a set of flags, it also displays each value separately.[2] If you look in the `InitializeComponent` method generated by Visual Studio, you will notice that this value is set much like our code in chapter 1. Note that the `Anchor` property for the `Button` class is not set in this method since it uses the default value.

```
this.pbxPhoto.Anchor = ((System.Windows.Forms.AnchorStyles)
    ((((System.Windows.Forms.AnchorStyles.Top
        | System.Windows.Forms.AnchorStyles.Bottom)
        | System.Windows.Forms.AnchorStyles.Left)
        | System.Windows.Forms.AnchorStyles.Right)));
```

Compile and run the application to verify that the program resizes as in figure 2.6. Now that we have duplicated the MyForm program from chapter 1, you might take a look at the source code for our application and compare it to our final MyForm.cs code in listing 1.4. You should see that the code is much the same, except that Visual Studio splits the code into multiple files. These files are not required, but separate the generated from the written code, which in theory makes the code easier to manage and maintain.

2.4.2 Assigning the Dock property

One final topic we should discuss is the `Dock` property. This property was presented in chapter 1, so we leave the use of this property in Visual Studio as an exercise.

---

[2] This occurs because the `AnchorStyles` enumeration has the `FlagsAttribute` attribute assigned. An attribute defines a behavior or configuration setting for a type, in this case the fact that the enumeration allows a bitwise combination of its member values.

TRY IT! In the Properties window, you will notice a drop-down for the `Dock` property similar to the one shown for the `Anchor` property, as in figure 2.7. Here you select the section of the box to dock against, namely the `Top`, `Left`, `Right`, `Bottom`, `Fill` (in the middle), or `None`. Set the `pbxPhoto.Dock` property to `DockStyle.Fill`, which is selected in figure 2.7. If the picture box covers up the Load button, right-click the picture box and select the Send to Back option. Compile and run the program to see the new behavior.

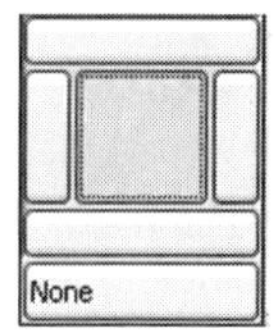

Figure 2.7 The Dock property drop-down

You can see the z-order for a form by displaying the Document Outline window while the Designer window is displayed. With the MainForm.cs [Design] window displayed, select View > Other Windows > Document Outline. This window shows a layout of the controls on the form, with the order indicating the z-order of each control within its container.

As a more adventurous change, try adding a second `Button` and `PictureBox` control to the application using Visual Studio, similar to the task suggested at the end of chapter 1. Name the button `btnLoad2` and set the text on the label to "Loa&d2" with a `Click` event handler that loads a second image and displays it in the second `PictureBox` named `pbxPhoto2`. You can use the `Anchor` property to position these controls, or set the `Dock` property for the first picture box to `DockStyle.Top`, and the second picture box to `DockStyle.Fill`.

2.5 RECAP

In this chapter we re-created the application from chapter 1 using Visual Studio. While much of the code was quite similar, we saw how Visual Studio generates the `InitializeComponent` method in a separate designer file to initialize the controls created in the Windows Forms Designer window. We discussed projects and solutions in Visual Studio, and the initial contents of a Windows application project. We examined the AssemblyInfo.cs file and looked at exception handling in C#.

This ends part 1 of the book. The MyPhotos application created in this chapter serves as the basis for many of the remaining chapters. Part 2 begins a systematic discussion of Windows Forms controls, beginning with menus and status bars.

PART 2

Basic Windows Forms

If you have read part 1 of this book, then you have a good idea where we are going here. Chapter 2 constructed a MyPhotos program using Visual Studio and extended the discussion of the .NET architecture and Windows Forms programming provided in chapter 1. Here we pick up where chapter 2 left off and provide a somewhat systematic discussion of basic Windows Forms development. The goal here is to cover the essential concepts and classes needed in most Windows Forms applications.

Following our practice in chapter 2, the complete steps required to create each example are provided. Typically, the MyPhotos application is extended in each chapter. In a couple of places we create alternate applications to provide variety and because I felt the topics were better presented separately.

For all applications, the code used for each section in the book is available on the book's website at www.manning.com/eebrown2. Follow the instructions and links to the version number corresponding to the desired section in order to retrieve the appropriate files.

We begin this part of the book with chapter 3, "Menus," and add various types of menus to the MyPhotos application. This chapter also presents the foundations of the Windows Forms class hierarchy.

Chapter 4 continues the discussion begun in chapter 3 to examine events and event handlers in more detail than shown in chapter 2. The chapter presents the classes for context menus and status bars. By the end of chapter 4, our application is able to load a photographic image from disk and display it in the main window, with information about the displayed image shown in a status bar.

Chapter 5, "Reusable libraries," steps out of Windows Forms momentarily to create a reusable photo album library, with classes to encapsulate a photograph and a photo album. This chapter examines collection classes, interfaces, and generics. A detailed discussion of the penultimate ancestor, the `object` class, is provided as well.

Chapter 6 integrates the library built in chapter 5 with the MyPhotos application during the course of presenting files and common dialog boxes. A new menu bar is created and standard dialog boxes are used to access, store, and load image and album data on disk. The `StreamReader` and `StreamWriter` classes in the `System.IO` namespace are used to read and write album data on disk.

Chapter 7 introduces dialog boxes, beginning with simple message boxes and moving on to `Form` classes as dialog boxes. The difference between modal and modeless is discussed, and an example of a modeless dialog box is created as part of the MyPhotos application. The `Label` and `Panel` classes are also introduced in this chapter.

Chapter 8 begins a review of the standard Windows Forms controls available in the .NET Framework. This chapter introduces text boxes, standard as well as masked. A modal dialog box to hold the properties of a photograph is created here to introduce both text boxes and the concept of form inheritance.

Chapter 9 covers buttons, from standard push buttons to radio and check box buttons. A modal dialog box to hold the properties of a photo album is created using the various types of buttons, and tool tips and error providers are introduced as examples of extender provider controls.

Chapter 10, "Handling user input and encryption," takes a break from the ongoing control discussion. Handling input from the keyboard and mouse is discussed, as are the basics of the cryptographic classes in the `System.Cryptography` namespace. We build an encrypted album file, using the `LinkLabel` class in place of buttons on a password dialog box.

Chapter 11, "List boxes," returns to our control discussion. This chapter builds a new MyAlbumEditor application to introduce both simple and multiline list boxes. Item selection and list reordering are also explored.

Chapter 12, "Combo boxes," covers another type of list control. This chapter presents both standard and editable combo boxes, as well as the features of automatic completion and item formatting. The MyAlbumEditor application is extended to demonstrate each class and concept discussed.

The classes for tab controls and pages are discussed in chapter 13. The fundamentals of both tab controls and pages are explained. This chapter also covers owner-drawn controls, with examples for both the `TabControl` and the `ListBox` classes.

Chapter 14 takes on the classes for dates, calendars, and progress bars. This includes the `DateTimePicker` control for display of a single date and the `MonthCalendar` control to display one or more months at a time. We review date and time formatting using the `DateTime` and `DateTimeFormatInfo` classes, and present the idea of deriving a set of controls from the `UserControl` class to encapsulate the layout required for a particular tab page. This chapter finishes with the `ProgressBar` and `BackgroundWorker` classes, and illustrates how to run operations in the background on behalf of a form.

"Bells and whistles," chapter 15, looks at various image-related classes such as `Bitmap`, `Icon`, and `Cursor`, and we see how to include custom bitmaps and icons within our MyPhotos application. We also explain how to embed resources and play sounds within an application. These features are included in a new slide show dialog box built using the `TrackBar` class to present a numeric value graphically, and the `Timer` class to perform a task after a scheduled interval.

Tools strips are the final topic in this part. The `ToolStrip` and `ToolStripItem` classes are briefly discussed in chapters 3 and 4, so chapter 16 rounds out the discussion with a review of the features and capabilities of these versatile classes. The various styles of tool strip buttons are discussed, along with the `ToolStripControlHost` class for hosting a Windows Forms control within a tool strip.

Part 3 of this book expands on these chapters to cover more advanced Windows Forms topics.

CHAPTER 3

Menus

Menu bars provide a good starting point for our discussion in part 2. Menus provide a convenient way to group similar or related commands in one place. Most users are familiar with the menu bar concept and expect standard menus such as File, Edit, and Help to appear in their applications. Even novice computer users quickly learn that clicking a menu on the menu bar displays a drop-down list of commands.

Menus became popular in Windows applications in the late 1980s, following their success on the Apple Macintosh. Prior to menus, users had to cope with a wide array of interfaces offered by desktop applications. The function keys still found at the top of computer keyboards were developed in part as a standard way to access common functions in an application, and some programs even provided a plastic template that sat on top of these function keys to help users remember the available commands.

Perhaps because of this history, many developers take the usefulness and popularity of menus for granted and do not spend sufficient time laying out a consistent, usable interface for their application. While graphical elements such as menus, toolbars, and other constructs make applications much friendlier, this is not an excuse to ignore good user design and rely on customers to become "experienced" to make effective use of the interface.

If that little lecture doesn't get your creative juices flowing, then nothing will. Back in .NET-land, Visual Studio provides a rather intuitive interface for the construction of menus that does away with some of the clunkiness found in earlier Windows development environments from Microsoft. No more dealing with menus in one place, the application in another place, and the processing code in a third place.

This chapter introduces some of the core classes used in Windows Forms in addition to discussing the menu interface in .NET. We cover the following aspects of Windows Forms and menu creation:

- The base classes for Windows Forms controls
- The different types of menus
- The classes required for Windows Forms menus
- How to create and modify menus and menu items

The examples in this chapter assume you have the code for MyPhotos version 2.4 available, as developed with Visual Studio in chapter 2. You can use this code with or without Visual Studio as a starting point for the tasks covered here. If you did not work through chapter 2, download the project from the book's website at http://www.manning.com/eebrown2. Follow the links and instructions on the site to retrieve version 2.4 of the application.

3.1 CONTROLS AND CONTAINERS

Before we plunge into menus, it is worth taking a look at the classes behind some of the .NET classes that support menus and other controls in Windows Forms, as shown in figure 3.1. This section walks through the class hierarchy behind Windows Forms controls and the `Form` class.

3.1.1 Control classes

All Windows Forms controls inherit from the `System.Windows.Forms.Control` class, or simply the `Control` class. The `System.Web.UI` namespace also contains a `Control` class for use in ASP.NET web pages, but since our focus is on Windows Forms, we use the terms control and `Control` class to mean the one in the `System.Windows.Forms` namespace.

So far we have seen the `Button` control and the `PictureBox` control classes. Figure 3.1 shows the class hierarchy for these classes. A *class hierarchy* is the set of classes from which a particular class is derived, and gives some indication of the purpose and capabilities behind the specific class. A brief discussion of the classes in figure 3.1 follows.

❶ All classes in C#, even internal types such as `int` and `char`, implicitly derive from the `object` class. In the .NET Framework, this class is equivalent to the `Object` class. We discuss this class in more detail in chapter 5.

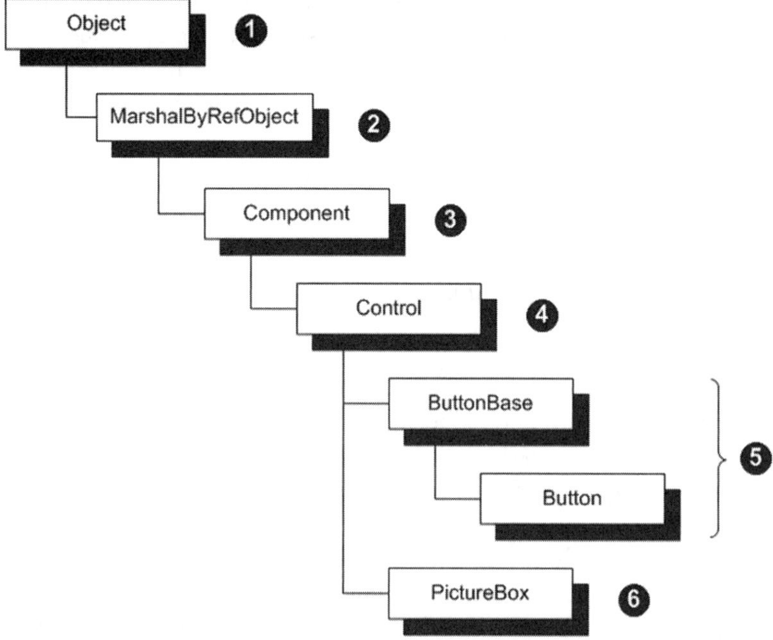

Figure 3.1 The class hierarchy for the Button and PictureBox controls is representative of the hierarchy for all Windows Forms controls.

❷ The `MarshalByRefObject` class is an object that must be marshaled by reference. *Marshaling* is a method of passing an item from one context so that it can be understood in another context. A typical use for marshaling is in remote procedure calls between two different machines, where each parameter of a function call must be converted into a common format (that is, marshaled) on the sending machine so that it may be interpreted on the receiving machine. In the .NET world, Windows controls are `MarshalByRefObject` objects since they are only valid in the process that creates them, and can be used outside this process only by reference.[1]

❸ The `Component` class is the base implementation of the `IComponent` interface for objects that marshal by reference. A *component* is an object that can exist within a container, and allows cleanup of system resources via the `Dispose` method. This class supports the `IDisposable` interface as well the `IComponent` interface. We cover interfaces in chapter 5, so don't get caught up in the terminology here. Since graphical controls exist within a `Form` window or other container control, all Windows Forms controls ultimately derive from this class.

---

[1] The details of marshaling are totally hidden for most Windows Forms applications, so you do not really need to know any of this. Hopefully, you find it somewhat interesting, if not useful.

❹ The Windows Forms `Control` class is a component with a visual representation on the Windows desktop. This class provides display functionality such as position and size, keyboard and mouse input, anchor and dock support, fonts, background images, and message routing. A summary of the members in this class is shown in .NET Table 3.1.

❺ The `ButtonBase` class is the base class for all buttons, including radio buttons and check box buttons in addition to the regular `Button` class we have already seen. Buttons are discussed in chapter 9.

❻ The `PictureBox` class is summarized in .NET Table 1 in the introduction.

3.1.2 Container classes

Controls that contain other controls are called *container controls*. The `Control` class itself provides support for containers, in members such as the `Controls` property or the `GetNextControl` method. Some container controls, such as the `GroupBox` control, inherit directly from the `Control` class. Group boxes are discussed in chapter 8. The `Form` class that we used in chapters 1 and 2 is also a container control. One of the unique features of this class is its ability to support scrolling for a contained set of controls. The `Form` class hierarchy supporting this and other functionality is shown in figure 3.2. Let's take a closer look at the numbered portions of this figure:

❶ You might think that all classes with scrolling inherit from the `ScrollableControl` class. In fact, this class is only for objects that support automated scrolling over a contained set of objects. Scrollable controls are discussed in chapter 13.

❷ The `ContainerControl` class is a control that provides focus management, providing a logical boundary for a contained set of controls. This class tracks the active control in a container even when the focus moves to an alternate container, and can manage the Tab key press for moving between the controls in the container.

❸ Almost all desktop windows in Windows Forms applications are represented by the `Form` class. This class is discussed throughout the book, of course, but especially in chapter 7.

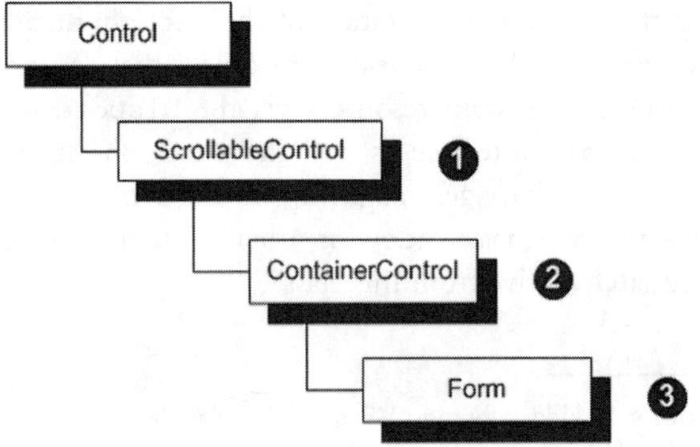

Figure 3.2
The class hierarchy for the Form class is similar to the hierarchy for many Windows Forms containers.

.NET Table 3.1 Control class

The `Control` class for Windows Forms is a component with a visual representation on the desktop. This class is part of the `System.Windows.Forms` namespace, and inherits from the `System.ComponentModel.Component` class. This class encapsulates the standard functionality used by all Windows Forms controls.

Public Properties	AllowDrop	Gets or sets whether to allow drag-and-drop operations in this control. Drag-and-drop is discussed in chapter 23.
	Anchor	Gets or sets the anchor setting for the control. The `Dock` property gets or sets the dock setting.
	BackColor	Gets or sets the background color of the control.
	ContextMenuStrip	Gets or sets the context menu for the control.
	Controls	Gets or sets the controls contained by this control.
	ClientRectangle	Gets the client area of the control. The `DisplayRectangle` property gets the display area.
	Cursor	Gets or sets the `Cursor` to display when the mouse is over the control.
	Enabled	Gets or sets whether the control is enabled.
	Location	Gets or sets the control's location. The `Top`, `Bottom`, `Left`, and `Right` properties gets the control's edges.
	Parent	Gets or sets the parent of this control.
	TabIndex	Gets or sets the tab index of the control.
	TabStop	Gets or sets whether the user can use the Tab key to give the focus to the control.
	Text	Gets or sets the text associated with this control.
	Visible	Gets or sets whether control is visible. This also affects any controls contained by this control.
Public Methods	BringToFront	Brings the control to the front of the z-order. A similar `SendToBack` method also exists.
	GetNextControl	Returns the next or previous control in the tab order.
	Invalidate	Forces all or part of the control to be redrawn.
	PointToClient	Converts a screen location to client coordinates.
Public Events	Click	Occurs when the control is clicked.
	KeyPress	Occurs when a key is pressed while the control has focus.
	MouseUp	Occurs when a mouse button is released within the control.
	Paint	Occurs when all or part of the control should be redrawn.

3.2 THE NATURE OF MENUS

Let's turn our attention now to menu classes. Menus in .NET, as we see in this section, are container controls that contain menu items. We begin by presenting the different kinds of menus generally, most importantly menu bars and context menus, and then turn our attention to how menus are defined in the .NET Framework.

3.2.1 Menu terminology

The traditional *menu bar*, sometimes called the *main menu* or an *anchored menu*, is a set of menus shown horizontally across the top of an application. The menus in a typical menu bar display a drop-down list of commands when they are activated with the mouse or by a keyboard accelerator. Figure 3.3 shows an example of a menu bar with the File menu exposed, and a submenu of the Image menu item is displayed as well.

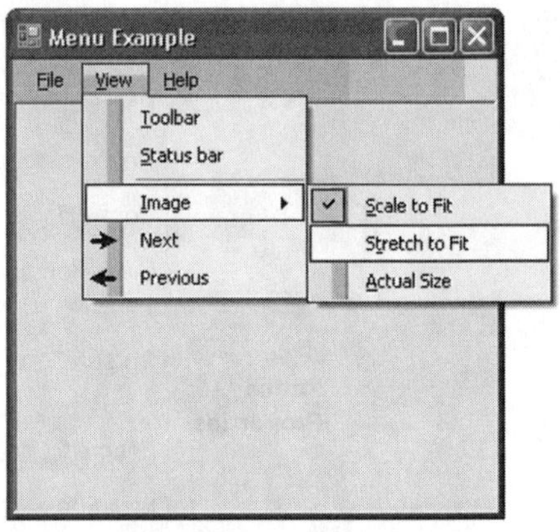

Figure 3.3 A traditional menu bar provides a set of menus across the top of an application.

Another type of menu is a *context menu*, also called a *pop-up menu* or *shortcut menu*. A context menu is a menu that appears in a particular situation, or context. Typically, a context menu contains a set of commands or menus related to a specific graphical element of the application. Such menus appear throughout the Windows environment at the right-click of the mouse. For example, right-click the Windows desktop, any program icon on your screen, or even the Windows Start menu, and a context menu appears with a set of commands related to the desktop display, the program, or the Start menu, respectively. Newer keyboards contain an accelerator key designed to simulate this behavior at the cursor's current location.

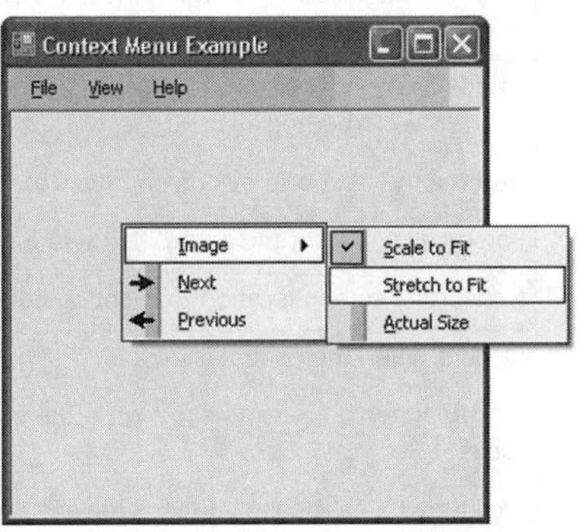

Figure 3.4 A context menu often provides quick access to items that also appear on the menu bar.

Context menus in .NET are typically associated with a specific control, the contents of which may change to reflect the condition of the control or type of item selected within the control. Figure 3.4 shows an example of a context menu associated with the main window of the application.

3.2.2 Menus in .NET

The menu classes provided by .NET received a complete rewrite for .NET 2.0. In .NET 1.*x*, the menu classes were based on the Win32 menu classes, and supported via the `Menu` class hierarchy. The `MainMenu`, `ContextMenu`, and `MenuItem` classes all derived from this `Menu` class, supporting Win32 menus and context menus within Windows Forms applications. These classes are still supported in .NET 2.0 for compatibility and use, but are no longer the preferred mechanism for menus in most applications.

The new and improved classes for menus are based on the `ToolStrip` and `ToolStripItem` classes, which are the base classes for all manner of toolbar objects and the items within them. A `MenuStrip` class derives from `ToolStrip` and represents a menu, while a `ToolStripMenuItem` class derives from `ToolStripItem` to represent an item within a menu. The `ToolStrip` class and associated derived classes are shown in figure 3.5. We look at the `ToolStripItem` classes later in the chapter.

Between this and our prior class hierarchies, there is a lot to take in. As we did in part 1 of the book, we lay some groundwork here for future discussion, and revisit

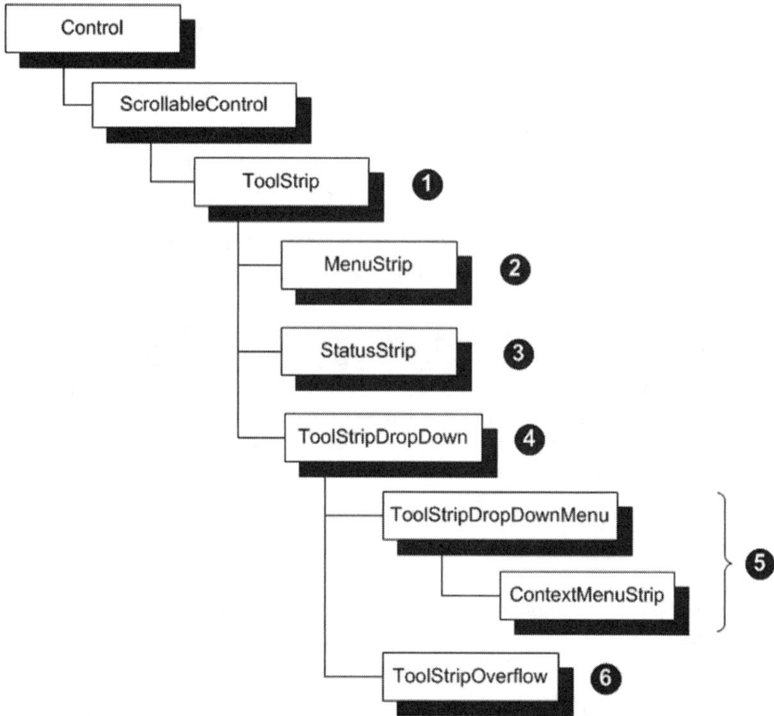

Figure 3.5 The ToolStrip classes replace the various *bar* classes available in prior versions of the .NET Framework, including the Menu, StatusBar, and ToolBar classes. These classes are still available to support Win32-style controls and for backward compatibility with existing applications.

the classes mentioned in passing here later in the book. Let's take a closer look at the classes in this hierarchy.

❶ The ToolStrip class is a scrollable control that contains a set of ToolStripItem objects. While tool strips do not scroll in the traditional sense, they allow controls to overflow into and out of the visible portion of the strip in a manner similar to scrolling. We discuss the details of tool strips in chapter 16.

❷ Menus are supported by the MenuStrip class. Menu strips behave like traditional menus and additionally support XP and Microsoft Office styles of appearance. The members of this class are shown in .NET Table 3.2.

❸ The StatusStrip control is a tool strip that acts as a traditional status bar, except that it additionally supports the functionality provided by tool strip objects. We discuss status strips in chapter 4.

❹ Tool strip objects that do not appear directly within a control are supported by the ToolStripDropDown class. This class is the generic base class for any drop-down strip, and is also discussed in chapter 4.

❺ The ContextMenuStrip class is specially designed to display menu item objects, or instances of the ToolStripMenuItem class, in a pop-up menu. This is the default drop-down created for drop-down items, instances of the ToolStripDropDownItem class. A context menu strip can be added to any Windows Forms control via the Control.ContextMenuStrip property. The ToolStripDropDownMenu class can be used to provide context-like functionality in a custom class, but it primarily serves as the base class for ContextMenuStrip objects.

❻ The final control in the figure, the ToolStripOverflow class, supports the overflow behavior of tool strip objects. This behavior is discussed in chapter 16.

.NET Table 3.2 MenuStrip class

New in 2.0 The MenuStrip class is a tool strip control that represents a menu bar on a form. Menu strips contain one or more menu items, as ToolStripMenuItem objects, that represent clickable menus within the menu bar. This class is part of the System.Windows.Forms namespace, and inherits from the ToolStrip class.

Public Properties	*MdiWindowListItem*	Gets or sets the menu item contained by this menu strip that displays a list of MDI child forms for the associated form object
Public Events	*MenuActivate*	Occurs whenever the menu is accessed via the keyboard or mouse

As you can see in .NET Table 3.2, most of the functionality for menu strips is contained in the ToolStrip class. In order to behave more like a traditional menu, the MenuStrip class also turns off various features of its parent class. By default, tool strips support item overflow functionality, a positioning grip, tooltips, and the ability to fit multiple strips in a single row on a form. Menu strips define these properties more appropriately for menus, so the `CanOverflow` property defaults to `false`, rather than `true` as in the `ToolStrip` class. Similarly, the `GripStyle` property defaults to `Hidden`; `ShowToolTips` to `false`; and `Stretch` to `true`. These and other properties in the `ToolStrip` class are discussed in chapter 16.

3.3 MENU BARS

So, let's do it. Looking at our MyPhotos application, it would be nice to replace the Load button with a menu option. This allows more space in our window for the displayed image, and permits additional commands to be added in the future related to loading images. As an added benefit, it provides a nice example for this book, which is, of course, our ultimate goal.

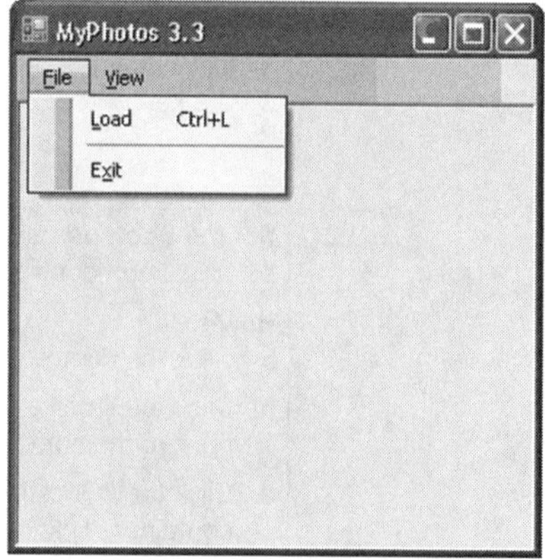

Figure 3.6 Notice in this File menu how the Load item displays Ctrl+L as its keyboard shortcut.

Our new application is shown in figure 3.6. Load and Exit menu items have been added to a File menu on the main menu bar. The Load menu item replaces our Load button from the previous chapter. The line separating these items is called a *menu separator*. A View menu is also shown, which is discussed later in this section.

As you may expect, the menu bar appears in our code as a `MenuStrip` object. Menus such as the File menu are represented as `ToolStripMenuItem` objects contained within the menu strip. The Load and Exit menu items underneath the File menu are also `ToolStripMenuItem` objects. The menu separator is a special `ToolStripSeparator` object.

3.3.1 Adding a menu strip

In this section, we show the steps for adding our main menu. As already mentioned, this book uses Visual Studio for all example programs. If you are writing the code by hand and using the C# compiler on the command line, read through the steps and use the code inside or follow the task description as a model for your own program. Note that the downloadable code from the book's website alters the version number for the program at the beginning of each section. This tracks our progress throughout the book. If you recall, the version number is modified in the AssemblyInfo.cs file of the project.

Before we add our menu, we need to remove the existing Load button from the form.

REMOVE THE LOAD BUTTON		
	Action	**Result**
1	Remove the Load button from the form. **How-to** a. Right-click the Load button in the MainForm.cs [Design] window. b. Select the Delete option. **Alternately** Simply select the button and press the Delete key.	Visual Studio automatically removes all generated code related to the button from the `InitializeComponent` method of the MainForm.cs file. **Note:** When a control is deleted, any assignments of event handlers to the control are removed as well. The actual event handling code, in this case our `btnLoad_Click` method, is still in the source file and must be removed manually. We leave this code in the MainForm.cs file for now, and deal with it later in the chapter.
2	Set the `Dock` property for the `PictureBox` control to `Fill`. **How-to** a. Click the control. b. Click the small arrow at the top right of the control. c. Click the "Dock in parent container" link. PictureBox Tasks Choose Image Size Mode Zoom Dock in parent container	The `PictureBox` control is docked within the form in the designer. **Note:** You can, of course, assign the `Dock` property as described at the end of chapter 2. The designer provides the small arrow, called a smart tag, for most controls to give quick access to common settings and tasks. We do not discuss the smart tags for every control, but you can look for them as we progress through the book.

With the Load button gone, our way is clear to move the Load functionality into a menu. To do this, we need to add a `MenuStrip` to our form, to act as a container for the menu items to display. The following table continues the above steps.

CREATE THE MENU BAR		
3	Drag a `MenuStrip` object from the Toolbox onto your form. This object appears in the Menus and Toolbars group within the toolbox.	A `MenuStrip` object called `menuStrip1` is added to your form. This object is shown within the form and in the *component tray*, located below the form as in the graphic. The component tray displays objects that may not have a physical presence in the window, such as timers, database connections, menu strips, and context menu strips. menuStrip1

Let's take a look at the source code generated by these actions in the MainForm.Designer.cs window. As you can see in listing 3.1, the Windows Forms Designer has replaced the button control with our menu strip. The overall structure of this code follows what we saw in chapter 2: controls are created, layout is suspended, controls are initialized, controls are added to the form, layout is resumed, and finally the control definitions appear at the end. The annotated points highlight the menu strip portion of this code.

Listing 3.1 The designer region after adding a MenuStrip

```
#region Windows Form Designer generated code
. . .
private void InitializeComponent()
{
  this.pbxPhoto = new System.Windows.Forms.PictureBox();
  this.menuStrip1 = new System.Windows.Forms.MenuStrip();
  ((System.ComponentModel.ISupportInitialize)
      (this.pbxPhoto)).BeginInit();
  this.SuspendLayout();
  //
  // pbxPhoto
  //
  this.pbxPhoto.BorderStyle
      = System.Windows.Forms.BorderStyle.Fixed3D;
  this.pbxPhoto.Dock = System.Windows.Forms.DockStyle.Fill;
  this.pbxPhoto.Location = new System.Drawing.Point(0, 24);
  this.pbxPhoto.Name = "pbxPhoto";
  this.pbxPhoto.Size = new System.Drawing.Size(292, 242);
  this.pbxPhoto.SizeMode
      = System.Windows.Forms.PictureBoxSizeMode.Zoom;
  this.pbxPhoto.TabIndex = 1;
  this.pbxPhoto.TabStop = false;
  //
  // menuStrip1                    ❶ Initializes menu strip
  //
  this.menuStrip1.Location = new System.Drawing.Point(0, 0);
  this.menuStrip1.Name = "menuStrip1";
  this.menuStrip1.Size = new System.Drawing.Size(292, 24);
  this.menuStrip1.TabIndex = 2;
  this.menuStrip1.Text = "menuStrip1";
  //
  // MainForm
  //
  this.AutoScaleDimensions = new System.Drawing.SizeF(6F, 13F);
  this.AutoScaleMode = System.Windows.Forms.AutoScaleMode.Font;
  this.ClientSize = new System.Drawing.Size(292, 266);
  this.Controls.Add(this.menuStrip1);    ❷ Adds menu
  this.Controls.Add(this.pbxPhoto);         strip to form
  this.MainMenuStrip = this.menuStrip1;
  this.Name = "MainForm";
```

```
    this.Text = "MyPhotos";
    ((System.ComponentModel.ISupportInitialize)
        (this.pbxPhoto)).EndInit();
    this.ResumeLayout(false);
    this.PerformLayout();
  }
  #endregion

  private System.Windows.Forms.PictureBox pbxPhoto;
  private System.Windows.Forms.MenuStrip menuStrip1;
```

❶ The `MenuStrip` control is initialized much like the `Button` and `PictureBox` controls in chapter 2. The `Dock` property for a menu strip control is set to `DockStyle.Top` by default, which is why this setting does not appear here.

❷ The strip is added to the control just like any other control, even though it really does not have much visual presence except through its contained menu items. As we see shortly, menu items are added to the menu strip control, rather than to the form itself.

3.3.2 Adding a menu item

With a `MenuStrip` on our form, we can now add menu items. You may have noticed that the menu strip represents the container rather than the actual menu items. Each menu item is created using the `ToolStripMenuItem` class. In this section we create a top-level File menu. In the next section we create the drop-down menu that appears when the user clicks on this menu.

CREATE THE FILE MENU

	Action	Result
1	Edit the menu strip in the MainMenu.cs [Design] window. **How-to** Click on the menuStrip1 item that appears below the form.	An empty menu bar appears at the top of the form. The space for the first top-level menu contains the words "Type Here."
2	Type in a top-level File menu as "&File."	A File menu appears on the form. MyPhotos / File / Type Here / Type Here **Note:** The ampersand (&) specifies the character, in this case F, to use as the mnemonic for this menu. Such mnemonics are used with the Alt key. In our application the File menu is displayed whenever the users clicks on it or when they enter Alt+F via the keyboard.

CREATE THE FILE MENU *(CONTINUED)*		
	Action	**Result**
3	Modify the `(Name)` property for this menu to be "menuFile." **How-to** Use the Properties window for the new File menu item, and modify the (Name) entry.	The variable name for the control is renamed to `menuFile` in the source code files. **Note:** The string "&File" we entered for the menu appears in the `Text` property for the item.

Your application now contains a File menu on the menu bar. The designer file has been updated to define and initialize the menu item. The relevant portions of this code are shown in listing 3.2. The `InitializeComponent` method now contains additional lines to initialize this menu item and add it to our `MenuStrip` object.

Listing 3.2 Designer code after portion of File menu is created

```
#region Windows Form Designer generated code
. . .
private void InitializeComponent()
{
  this.pbxPhoto = new System.Windows.Forms.PictureBox();
  this.menuStrip1 = new System.Windows.Forms.MenuStrip();
  this.menuFile = new System.Windows.Forms.ToolStripMenuItem();
  . . .
  this.menuStrip1.SuspendLayout();
  . . .
  //
  // menuStrip1
  //
  this.menuStrip1.Items.AddRange(new
      System.Windows.Forms.ToolStripItem[] {
          this.menuFile});
  this.menuStrip1.Location = new System.Drawing.Point(0, 0);
  this.menuStrip1.Name = "menuStrip1";
  this.menuStrip1.Size = new System.Drawing.Size(292, 24);
  this.menuStrip1.TabIndex = 2;
  this.menuStrip1.Text = "menuStrip1";
  //
  // menuFile
  //
  this.menuFile.Name = "menuFile";
  this.menuFile.Size = new System.Drawing.Size(35, 20);
```

```
  this.menuFile.Text = "&File";
  . . .
}
#endregion

private System.Windows.Forms.PictureBox pbxPhoto;
private System.Windows.Forms.MenuStrip menuStrip1;
private System.Windows.Forms.ToolStripMenuItem menuFile;
```

.NET Table 3.3 ToolStripMenuItem class

New in 2.0 The `ToolStripMenuItem` class represents a menu within a `MenuStrip` or `ContextMenuStrip` object, or a submenu of another `ToolStripMenuItem` object. `ToolStripMenuItem` objects are displayed to the user, while `MenuStrip` and `ContextMenuStrip` objects simply establish a container in which such menu items can appear. The `ToolStripMenuItem` class is part of the `System.Windows.Forms` namespace, and inherits from the `ToolStripDropDownItem` class. See .NET Table 4.2 for a list of members inherited from this base class.

Public Properties	*Checked*	Gets or sets whether a checkmark appears next to the text of the menu item.
	CheckState	Gets or sets a three-state value for the menu item, based on the `CheckState` enumeration. This is similar to `Checked`, but allows an indeterminate setting when the checked or unchecked state cannot be determined.
	Enabled (overridden from ToolStripItem)	Gets or sets whether the menu item is enabled. A disabled menu is displayed in a grayed-out color, cannot be selected, and does not display any child menu items.
	Overflow (overridden from ToolStripItem)	Gets or sets how the menu item interacts with an overflow button, based on the `ToolStripItemOverflow` enumeration.
	ShortcutKeyDisplayString	Gets or sets the string to display as the shortcut for the menu. If this is blank, the actual shortcut key setting is shown.
	ShortcutKeys	Gets or sets the shortcut keys for this menu item, using the `Keys` enumeration values.
	ShowShortcutKeys	Gets or sets whether to display the `ShortcutKeys` setting when displaying the menu.
Public Events	*CheckedChanged*	Occurs when the `Checked` property value changes.
	CheckStateChanged	Occurs when the `CheckState` property value changes.

This code follows the now familiar pattern of creating the control, initializing the control in its own section, and adding the control to a parent container. One difference here is that the File menu item is contained within the menu strip, rather than the `Form` itself. Note how the menu item is added to the `menuStrip1` control by creating an array of `ToolStripItem` objects with `menuFile` as the only entry. Arrays of objects in C# are created just like any other class, with the addition of square brackets, `[]`, to indicate that an array of objects should be created rather than a single object.

The File menu is listing 3.2 is defined as a `ToolStripMenuItem` object. An overview of this class appears in .NET Table 3.3. We discuss the class hierarchy for this class in a moment.

3.3.3 Adding drop-down menu items

So far, we have created a main menu with a single File menu item. Our next step is to create the drop-down menu, or submenu, that appears when this menu is clicked.

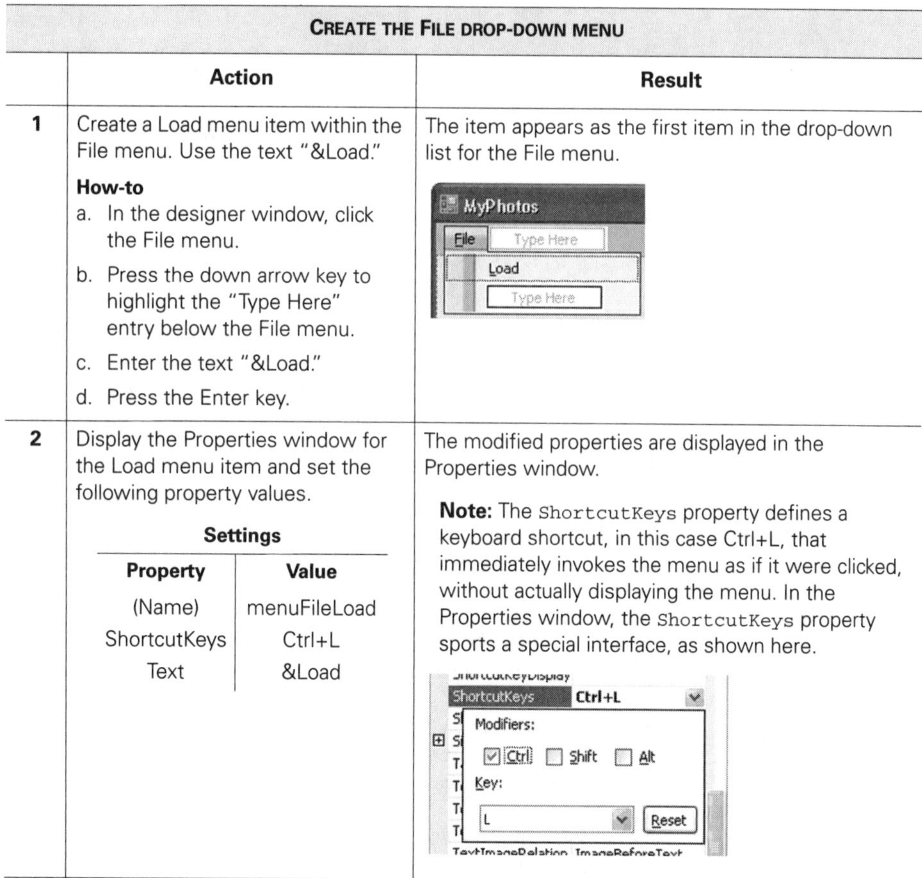

CREATE THE FILE DROP-DOWN MENU

	Action	Result
1	Create a Load menu item within the File menu. Use the text "&Load." **How-to** a. In the designer window, click the File menu. b. Press the down arrow key to highlight the "Type Here" entry below the File menu. c. Enter the text "&Load." d. Press the Enter key.	The item appears as the first item in the drop-down list for the File menu.
2	Display the Properties window for the Load menu item and set the following property values. **Settings** **Property** / **Value** (Name): menuFileLoad ShortcutKeys: Ctrl+L Text: &Load	The modified properties are displayed in the Properties window. **Note:** The `ShortcutKeys` property defines a keyboard shortcut, in this case Ctrl+L, that immediately invokes the menu as if it were clicked, without actually displaying the menu. In the Properties window, the `ShortcutKeys` property sports a special interface, as shown here.

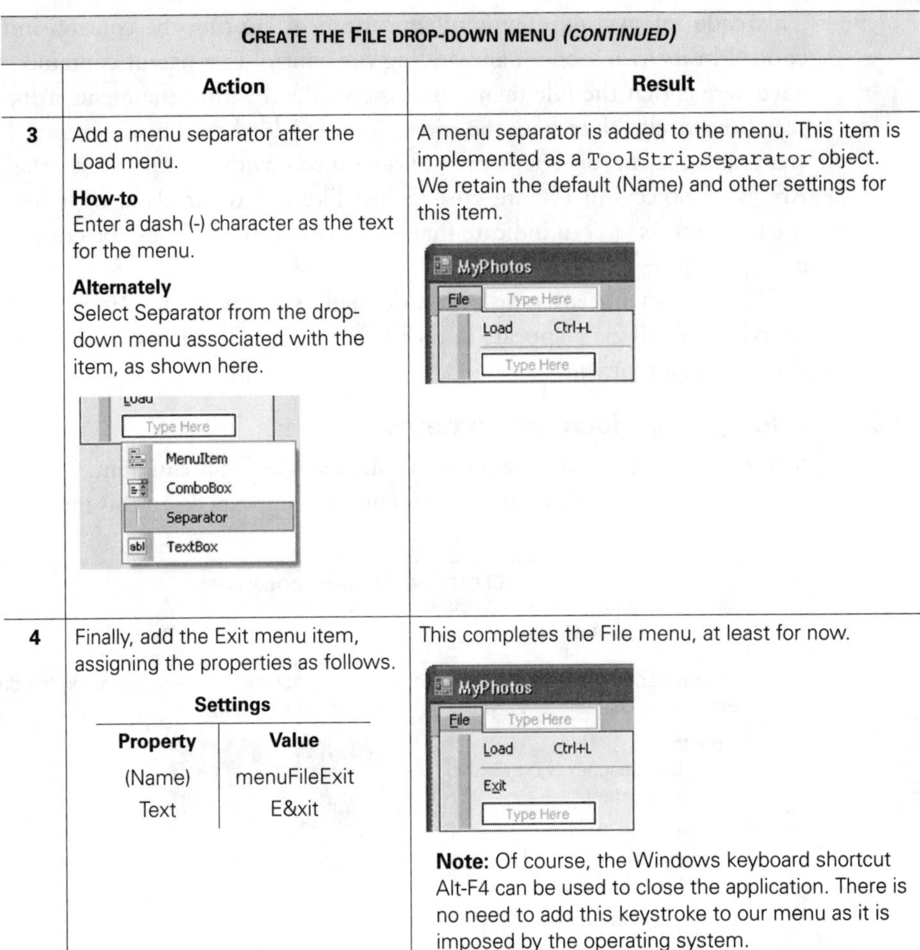

CREATE THE FILE DROP-DOWN MENU *(CONTINUED)*

	Action	Result
3	Add a menu separator after the Load menu. **How-to** Enter a dash (-) character as the text for the menu. **Alternately** Select Separator from the drop-down menu associated with the item, as shown here. Type Here MenuItem ComboBox Separator TextBox	A menu separator is added to the menu. This item is implemented as a `ToolStripSeparator` object. We retain the default (Name) and other settings for this item. MyPhotos File Type Here Load Ctrl+L Type Here
4	Finally, add the Exit menu item, assigning the properties as follows. **Settings** **Property** / **Value** (Name) / menuFileExit Text / E&xit	This completes the File menu, at least for now. MyPhotos File Type Here Load Ctrl+L Exit Type Here **Note:** Of course, the Windows keyboard shortcut Alt-F4 can be used to close the application. There is no need to add this keystroke to our menu as it is imposed by the operating system.

As you might expect, the code generated for the MainForm.cs file uses `ToolStripMenuItem` objects to construct the drop-down list for the File menu, with the objects initialized in the `InitializeComponent` method. The relevant code from the designer generated region is extracted in listing 3.3.

Listing 3.3 Designer code after complete File menu is created

```
private void InitializeComponent()
{
  this.pbxPhoto = new System.Windows.Forms.PictureBox();
  this.menuStrip1 = new System.Windows.Forms.MenuStrip();
  this.menuFile = new System.Windows.Forms.ToolStripMenuItem();
  this.menuFileLoad
          = new System.Windows.Forms.ToolStripMenuItem();
  this.toolStripMenuItem1
          = new System.Windows.Forms.ToolStripSeparator();
```

```
    this.menuFileExit = new . . .;
    . . .
    this.menuStrip1.Items.AddRange(
      new System.Windows.Forms.ToolStripItem[] {
      this.menuFile});
    . . .
    //
    // menuFile
    //
    this.menuFile.DropDownItems.AddRange(
      new System.Windows.Forms.ToolStripItem[] {
      this.menuFileLoad,|#1
      this. toolStripMenuItem1,|#1
      this.menuFileExit});|#1
    . . .
    //
    // menuFileLoad
    //
    this.menuFileLoad.Name = "menuFileLoad";
    this.menuFileLoad.ShortcutKeys = ((System.Windows.Forms.Keys)
        ((System.Windows.Forms.Keys.Control
            | System.Windows.Forms.Keys.L)));
    this.menuFileLoad.Size = new System.Drawing.Size(152, 22);
    this.menuFileLoad.Text = "&Load";
    //
    // toolStripMenuItem1
    //
    this.toolStripMenuItem1.Name = "toolStripSeparator1";
    this.toolStripMenuItem1.Size = new System.Drawing.Size(149, 6);
    //
    // menuFileExit
    //
    this.menuFileExit.Name = "menuFileExit";
    this.menuFileExit.Size = new System.Drawing.Size(152, 22);
    this.menuFileExit.Text = "E&xit";
    . . .
}
. . .
private System.Windows.Forms.MenuStrip menuStrip1;
private System.Windows.Forms.ToolStripMenuItem menuFile;
private System.Windows.Forms.ToolStripMenuItem menuFileLoad;
private System.Windows.Forms.ToolStripSeparator
        toolStripMenuItem1;
private System.Windows.Forms.ToolStripMenuItem menuFileExit;
```

❶ Creates File drop-down menu

❷ Defines keyboard shortcut

While much of this code is similar to what we have seen for other controls, a couple aspects are worth highlighting:

❶ The items to appear under the File menu are added by constructing an array of the desired objects and assigning them to the `menuFile.DropDownItems` property. The `ToolStripMenuItem` class derives from the `ToolStripDropDownItem` class.

This base class defines the `DropDownItems` property used here, which contains the collection of items to associate with the menu. The `AddRange` method on this collection adds a set of items to the menu. The order of objects in the array establishes the order in which these items appear within the File menu.

❷ The Ctrl+L shortcut for the Load menu item is defined through the use of the `System.Windows.Forms.Keys` enumeration. Note how the `Keys.Control` and `Keys.L` values are or'd together using the vertical bar (|) operator.

If you wish to see the application so far, compile and run the code to view the File menu. You may notice that our menus still do not actually do anything. To fix this, we need to handle the `Click` event on our menus, which is the subject of our final section.

The `ToolStripMenuItem` class used to define the Load and Exit menu items, as well as the File menu, is part of the `ToolStripItem` class hierarchy. This class is a component, and serves as the base class for the various tool strip items available in Windows Forms. Since this class is not a control, it defines a number of members similar to the `Control` class discussed earlier in the chapter to maintain consistency between control and tool strip item objects. We discuss the `StatusStrip` and `ContextMenuStrip` classes in the next chapter; and `ToolStrip` classes in general in chapter 16. Here, let's take a quick look at the rather large `ToolStripItem` class hierarchy, as shown in figure 3.7. Let's discuss the annotated areas:

❶ The `ToolStripItem` class is the basis for the hierarchy in the figure. Details on this class appear in .NET Table 3.4.

❷ A common use of tool strips is to display a button that responds to a click of the mouse, much like a normal button on a form. The `ToolStripButton` class encapsulates this functionality.

❸ One of the more interesting features of tool strips is their ability to host almost any Windows Forms control as an item within the strip. The `ToolStripControlHost` class encapsulates this functionality, with predefined classes for the `ComboBox`, `ProgressBar`, and `TextBox` controls. The base class can be used to host other controls as well, as we see in chapter 16.

❹ Some tool strip items support the ability to display additional items in an associated drop-down list, such as a menu item that displays a submenu. The `ToolStripDropDownItem` class is the base class for such items, and uses a `ToolStripDropDown` instance as a container for the set of drop-down items. We have already used the `ToolStripMenuItem` class for our menu items. The `ToolStripDropDownButton` item is a button that displays a drop-down list when clicked. The `ToolStripSplitButton` item is a normal button next to a drop-down button, such as a graphic with an associated drop-down arrow used in many applications. We discuss these and other tool strip items, including the overflow functionality supported by the `ToolStripOverflowButton` class, in chapter 16.

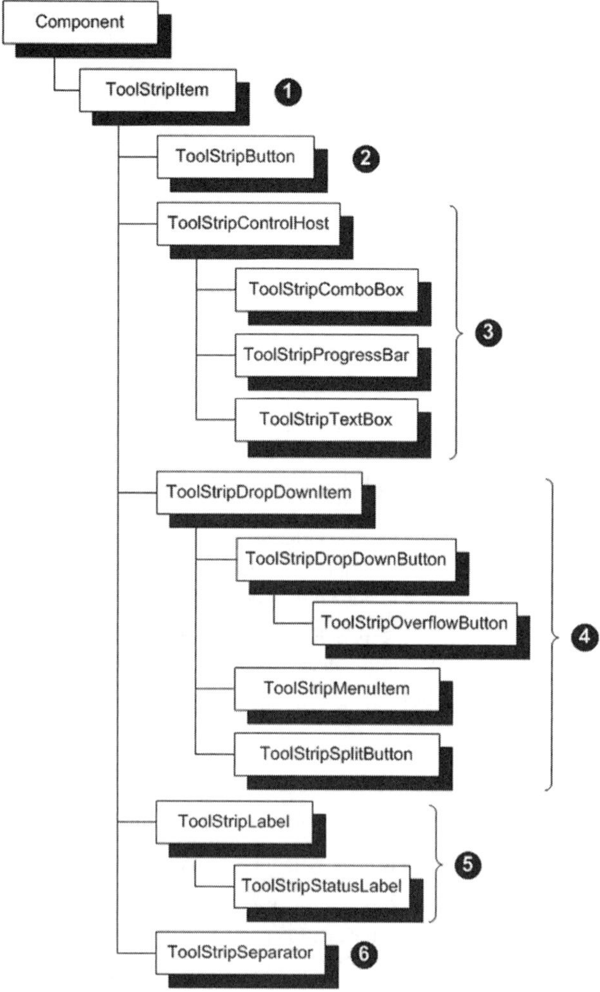

Figure 3.7 The classes derived from ToolStripItem are all components, and cannot exist on a form outside of a ToolStrip object.

❺ The `ToolStripLabel` class displays nonselectable text and graphics, or can link to other information by acting as a hyperlink. A special type of label is the text that appears in a status bar, represented by the `ToolStripStatusLabel` class discussed in the next chapter.

❻ When a large number of items appear in a single strip, whether buttons in a toolbar or menu items in a menu, there is a need to partition the strip into logical areas to make it easier for users to locate and understand the desired functionality. The `ToolStripSeparator` class encapsulates this functionality, as we saw for the separator between our Load and Exit menu items.

.NET Table 3.4 ToolStripItem class

New in 2.0 The `ToolStripItem` class is a component that represents an item on a `ToolStrip` object, and encapsulates the standard functionality used by all tool strip items. This class is part of the `System.Windows.Forms` namespace, and inherits from the `System.ComponentModel.Component` class.

Public Properties	*AllowDrop*	Gets or sets whether item reordering and drag-and-drop operations use the default (false) or custom behavior (true).
	Alignment	Gets or sets whether the item aligns toward the beginning or end of the containing tool strip.
	Anchor	Gets or sets how the item attaches to the edges of its container. A `Dock` property also exists.
	BackColor	Gets or sets the background color of the item.
	ClientRectangle	Gets the area where content can be drawn within the item without overwriting background borders.
	DisplayStyle	Gets or sets the `ToolStripItemDisplayStyle` enumeration value that defines whether text and images are displayed for the item.
	Enabled	Gets or sets whether this item can respond to user interaction.
	Image	Gets or sets the image displayed on the item.
	MergeAction	Gets or sets how the item merges into a target tool strip.
	Parent	Gets or sets the parent of this item.
	Text	Gets or sets the text associated with this item.
	ToolTipText	Gets or sets the tooltip text. If not set and `AutoToolTip` is `true`, the `Text` property is used as the tooltip.
	Visible	Gets or sets whether item and any subitems are visible.
Public Methods	*Invalidate*	Indicates that all or part of the item should be redrawn.
	PerformClick	Invokes the `Click` event behavior for this item.
Public Events	*Click*	Occurs when the item is clicked.
	DragDrop	Occurs when a drag-and-drop operation on the item is completed.
	MouseUp	Occurs when a mouse button is released within the bounds for the item.
	Paint	Occurs when all or part of the item should be repainted.

3.4 MENU HANDLING

A menu, of course, is not very useful if you can't make it do something. In this section we define some event handlers for our File menu items, and examine how event handlers work in more detail than we covered in prior chapters.

In part 1 we saw how an event was defined using the += syntax in C#, and how Visual Studio generates this code whenever an event is defined for a Windows Forms control. Events can be added from the Windows Forms Designer window directly, or via the Properties window. We discuss and demonstrate each method separately in the context of our File menu items.

3.4.1 Adding handlers via the designer window

As you may expect, Visual Studio adds a `Click` event handler whenever you double-click a menu item control in the Windows Forms Designer window. We saw this behavior for buttons in chapter 2, so let's use this feature to add a handler to the Load menu item here.

Since this code matches the handler we discussed in chapter 2 for the Load button, we will not discuss it again.

Compile the application to verify that the Load menu item works just like the Load button in chapter 2. You should be able to load a new image using the menu bar via the mouse, using the access keys Alt+F and then Alt+L to invoke the menu item from the keyboard, or using the keyboard shortcut Ctrl+L.

ADD CLICK HANDLER FOR THE LOAD MENU

	Action	Result

1	In the MainForm.cs [Design] window, add a `Click` handler for the Load menu item.
	How-to
	Double-click the Load menu item.
		A new event handler for the item is added and the cursor is placed in the code window within the newly added handler.
		`private void menuFileLoad_Click(`
		`  object sender, EventArgs e)`
		`{`
		`}`
		The new handler is also registered as a `Click` handler for the item in the `InitializeComponent` method of the MainForm.Designer.cs file.
		`menuFileLoad.Click += new System.EventHandler`
		`    (this.menuFileLoad_Click);`

	ADD CLICK HANDLER FOR THE LOAD MENU *(CONTINUED)*	
	Action	**Result**

2	Copy the code from the now defunct `btnLoad_Click` handler into our new method and delete the old method.
	
	Note: Unless you removed it, the code for `btnLoad_Click` should still be present in your MainForm.cs file.
		This code is identical to the code used with our Load button in chapter 2; it is just invoked via a menu item rather than a button.
		<pre>private void menuFileLoad_Click
		     (object sender, System.EventArgs e)
		  {
		    OpenFileDialog dlg = new OpenFileDialog();
		
		    dlg.Title = "Load Photo";
		    dlg.Filter = "jpg files (*.jpg)"
		        + "|*.jpg|All files (*.*)|*.*";
		
		    if (dlg.ShowDialog() == DialogResult.OK)
		    {
		      try
		      {
		        pbxPhoto.Image = new Bitmap(dlg.OpenFile());
		      }
		      catch (ArgumentException ex)
		      {
		        MessageBox.Show("Unable to load file: "
		                         + ex.Message);
		      }
		    }
		    dlg.Dispose();
		  }</pre>

3.4.2 Adding handlers via the properties window

Most controls in Windows Forms define a default event. Visual Studio adds an event handler for this event whenever a control is double-clicked in the designer window. As we have seen, the default event for button and menu controls is the `Click` event. We discuss default events for other controls throughout the book.

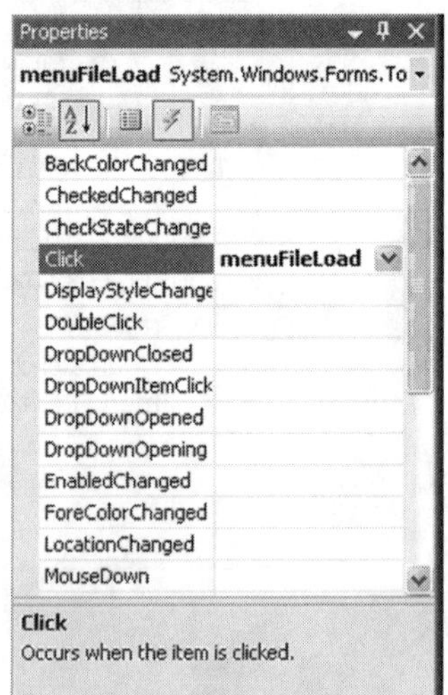

Figure 3.8 This Properties window shows the events for the Load menu item in our application, including the menuFileLoad _Click event handler.

The .NET classes provide a rich set of events for everything from key presses and mouse clicks to redrawing or resizing a control. To support these and other events, Visual Studio provides a generic way to add event handlers using the Properties window.

We have seen how the Properties window provides the list of properties associated with a specific control. It also provides the list of events and allows new event handlers to be added, as illustrated in figure 3.8. Note the small toolbar buttons between the object dropdown and the list of object members. Clicking the Properties button displays a list of properties for the current object. If you click the Events button, the lightning bolt icon, this window displays a list of events. The events for our menuFileLoad menu item are shown in the figure.

We can use this window to add an event handler for the Exit menu item. The following steps add a Click event handler for this menu that closes the application.

ADD A CLICK HANDLER FOR THE EXIT MENU ITEM		
	Action	**Result**
1	Display the Events for the Exit menu item in the Properties toolbar. **How-to** Display the Properties window for the item and click the Events button.	Properties menuFileLoad System.Windows.Forms.To BackColorChanged CheckedChanged CheckStateChanged Click DisplayStyleChanged DoubleClick

2	Double-click the Click item listed in the window.	A `Click` event handler is added to the `menuFileExit` object.
		`private void menuFileExit_Click(`
		`    object sender, EventArgs e)`
		`{`

3	Call the `Form.Close` method within this handler.	`Close();`
		`}`
		Note: The code for this event handler is split across steps 2 and 3. We do this throughout the book as a convenient way to discuss different portions of code for a single member of a class.

The Form.Close method is used to exit the application. This method closes the associated Form, or the entire application if the form was the startup window for the application.

As you may have noticed in chapter 1, the Application class provides an Exit method that we could use instead here. This call forces all message loops started by Application.Run methods to exit, and closes any forms associated with them as well.

In our existing code, either method would close the application. As we discuss in chapter 7, however, the Close method ensures that all resources associated with a form are disposed, and invokes various closing events to permit additional processing as required. As a result, use of the Close method is normally preferred to exit a Form rather than the Application.Exit method.

TRY IT! Compile and run the code to verify that the Load and Exit menu items now work. If you feel like experimenting, here are a couple areas worth exploring:

- Set the `ShowShortcutKeys` property for the Load menu item to `false` in order to prevent the Ctrl+L shortcut from appearing on the menu. Note that the keyboard shortcut still works, even though it is not displayed.
- Modify the `Enabled` and `Visible` properties for the Exit menu item to see how they change the behavior of this menu when the application runs.
- Create a new Clear item between the Load item and the subsequent separator that clears the picture box control by assigning `null` to the `Image` property.

Our handling of the File menu is now complete, and we have seen the two main ways to add event handlers in Visual Studio.

Sit back for a moment and think about what we have done here. If you have used Visual C++ with MFC, realize that the secret macros and magic interface files required by this environment are gone. In their place are well-designed objects that can quickly and easily be used to create arbitrarily complex menu structures. Also realize that we created these menus with very little explicit code. The designer interface handled much of the work required to define and arrange these menus within the application.

3.5 RECAP

In this chapter we modified our application to use a Load menu item, rather than a Load button to open and display an image in the `PictureBox` control. We looked at various kinds of menus, and examined the classes required to build and manipulate menus in Windows applications with the .NET Framework.

Along the way we took a quick tour through many of the foundational classes in the Windows Forms namespace. We discussed how the `Component` class is the basis for objects that can exist within a container, and the `Control` class is the basis for all Windows Forms controls. We also saw the class hierarchy for the `Form` class, including the `ScrollableControl` and `ContainerControl` classes.

We discussed the different types of menus, and the `MenuStrip` and `ToolStripMenuItem` classes used to create menus in Windows Forms. The `MenuStrip` class is part of the `ToolStrip` classes that are used to define menu bars, status bars, and all manner of tool bars in .NET. These classes display the `ToolStripItem` classes within their borders to represent various types of items. The `ToolStripMenuItem` class is one such item, and represents a menu item within a menu. We also saw the `ToolStripSeparator` class, used to create a separator line within a menu.

The Visual Studio interface for creating menus was also discussed, and we created some top-level menus for our sample MyPhotos application. We looked at the code generated for these menus, and how collections of menus are defined as arrays within the designer file.

In chapter 4 we discuss additional aspects of tool strips in Windows Forms by examining the classes for creating context menus and status bars.

CHAPTER 4

Context menu and status strips

We began chapter 3 with a quick tour through some of the Windows Forms classes and a discussion of menu objects in general, and saw how menus are part of the `ToolStrip` functionality provided by .NET. In this chapter we extend this discussion to cover context menus, as well as how to share a menu between a context menu and a menu bar.

The `StatusStrip` class is another kind of a tool strip, typically appearing at the bottom of a form to display various feedback to the user. This chapter looks at status bars in Windows Forms as well.

Figure 4.1 shows our application as it appears at the end of this discussion. In addition to our menus, you can see that the status bar contains two areas, called *panels* or *labels*. You can place any number of panels on a status bar, and display both textual and graphical information within each panel.

Continuing our tutorial approach, this chapter assumes you have the MyPhotos solution from section 3.4 available as the starting point for our discussion. You can also download this code from the book's website.

Figure 4.1
Our status bar includes the optional sizing grip graphic at the lower right of the control, which allows a user to resize the form.

Before we get to status strips, we need to finish our menu discussion. We begin with the `ContextMenuStrip` class.

4.1 CONTEXT MENU STRIPS

Although the creation of context menus requires some extra effort by a programmer, such menus improve the usability of an interface greatly and should be seriously considered in any application. The ability of a user to right-click a control and instantly see a list of commands is a powerful mechanism that experienced users especially appreciate. Context menus are typically associated with a specific graphical control, but can also be displayed programmatically. As a result, context menus provide quick access to commands immediately relevant to what the user is currently trying to accomplish or understand.

Most controls in the `System.Windows.Forms` namespace support the `ContextMenuStrip` property inherited from the `Control` class to specify a `ContextMenuStrip` object to associate with the control.[1] This setting can be changed dynamically to allow different context menus to display depending on the state of the control.

In this section we discuss context menus generally and add one to our `PictureBox` control. As shown in figure 4.2, this creates a shortcut for a user who wishes to alter how an image is displayed. We begin by adding a context menu to our application and populating its contents.

---

1 All controls also support a `ContextMenu` property that links in the Win32-based `ContextMenu` class. These are fully supported, but do not appear in Visual Studio by default to discourage use of the Win32-based classes.

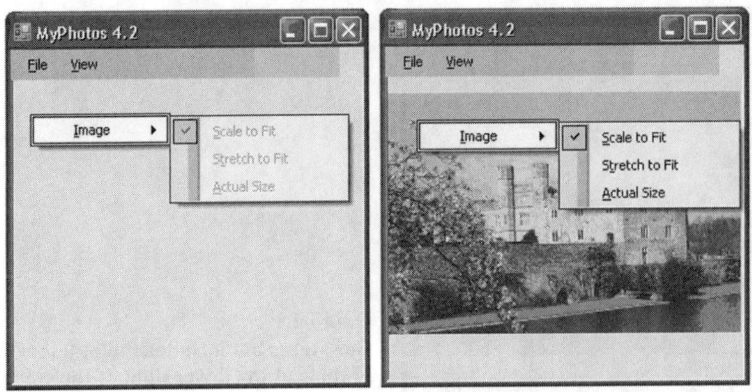

Figure 4.2 Our application disables the Image submenu when no image is loaded, and marks the current display mode whenever the submenu is shown.

4.1.1 Creating a context menu

We begin by simply adding a new context menu to our application and associating it with the `pbxPhoto` control. The classes behind a context menu in .NET are discussed following these changes. The next section explains how to populate this menu with some menu items.

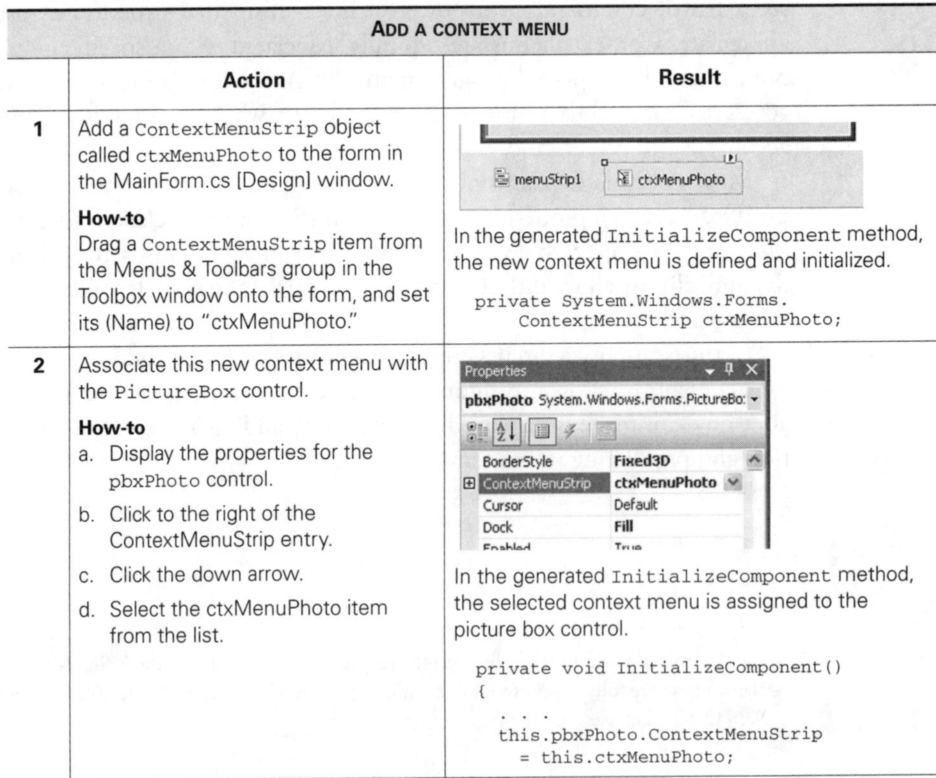

ADD A CONTEXT MENU

	Action	Result

1	Add a `ContextMenuStrip` object called `ctxMenuPhoto` to the form in the MainForm.cs [Design] window.
	How-to
	Drag a `ContextMenuStrip` item from the Menus & Toolbars group in the Toolbox window onto the form, and set its (Name) to "ctxMenuPhoto."
		menuStrip1 ctxMenuPhoto
		In the generated `InitializeComponent` method, the new context menu is defined and initialized.
		`private System.Windows.Forms.`
		`    ContextMenuStrip ctxMenuPhoto;`

2	Associate this new context menu with the `PictureBox` control.
	How-to
	a. Display the properties for the `pbxPhoto` control.
	b. Click to the right of the ContextMenuStrip entry.
	c. Click the down arrow.
	d. Select the ctxMenuPhoto item from the list.
		Properties
		pbxPhoto System.Windows.Forms.PictureBo:
		BorderStyle Fixed3D
		ContextMenuStrip ctxMenuPhoto
		Cursor Default
		Dock Fill
		In the generated `InitializeComponent` method, the selected context menu is assigned to the picture box control.
		`private void InitializeComponent()`
		`{`
		`  . . .`
		`  this.pbxPhoto.ContextMenuStrip`
		`    = this.ctxMenuPhoto;`

The `ContextMenuStrip` class is essentially a container for the `ToolStripItem` objects that appear within the menu. As we saw in figure 3.5, this class derives from the `ToolStripDropDownMenu` class, which in turn is based on the `ToolStrip-DropDown` class. While the core functionality for all of these controls comes from the `Control` and `ToolStrip` classes, of course, much of the drop-down functionality is defined by the `ToolStripDropDown` class. The key members of this class are shown in .NET Table 4.1.

.NET Table 4.1 ToolStripDropDown class

New in 2.0 The `ToolStripDropDown` class is a tool strip that displays a set of items from another tool strip item—for example, the drop-down list that appears when a `ToolStrip-DropDownButton` is clicked. This class is part of the `System.Windows.Forms` namespace, and inherits from the `ToolStrip` class. See .NET Table 16.1 for the members inherited from the `ToolStrip` class.

The `ToolStripDropDownMenu` class inherits from `ToolStripDropDown`, and is the base class for the `ContextMenuStrip` class.

Public Properties	*AutoClose*	Gets or sets whether the drop-down should automatically close when it loses focus.
	CanOverflow (overridden from ToolStrip)	Gets or sets whether items overflow. The default for drop-down strips is `false`.
	OwnerItem	Gets or sets the `ToolStripItem` that owns this drop-down strip.
Public Methods	*Close*	Closes the drop-down strip, optionally providing a reason as a `ToolStripDropDownClose-Reason` value.
	Show	Displays the drop-down strip at the specified coordinates.
Public Events	*Closed*	Occurs after the drop-down strip has closed.
	Closing	Occurs just before the drop-down strip closes.
	Opened	Occurs after the drop-down strip is shown.
	Opening	Occurs before the drop-down strip is shown.

4.1.2 Adding items to a context menu

We are now ready to add items to our context menu, as illustrated in figure 4.3. Our context menu will define three different display settings for an image, corresponding to three different `PictureBoxSizeMode` enumeration values. The user can use this menu to alter how the image is displayed in the `PictureBox` control.

The creation of context menu items within Visual Studio is much the same as what we saw for menu strips in chapter 3: click the `ctxMenuView` object in the designer window to display a "Type Here" message, and enter the new menus. Since this is already familiar to us, the following table simply summarizes the changes required to add some menu items to our context menu strip.

<table>
<tr><th colspan="3">POPULATE THE CONTEXT MENU STRIP</th></tr>
<tr><th></th><th>Action</th><th>Result</th></tr>
<tr><td>1</td><td>Add an Image menu item called "menuImage" to the context menu.</td><td>A new ToolStripMenuItem object called menuImage is added to the MainForm.Designer.cs source code, and defined as a drop-down item for the ctxMenuPhoto menu.
. . .
this.ctxMenuPhoto.Items.AddRange(
  new System.Windows.Forms
      .ToolStripItem[] {
    this.menuImage
  });</td></tr>
<tr><td>2</td><td>Add a "Scale to Fit" submenu item to the Image menu and assign its properties.
How-to
Enter this item to the right of the Image menu.
Settings<table><tr><th>Property</th><th>Value</th></tr><tr><td>(Name)</td><td>menuImageScale</td></tr><tr><td>Checked</td><td>True</td></tr><tr><td>Text</td><td>&Scale to Fit</td></tr></table></td><td>The new menu appears in Visual Studio as in figure 4.3. The menuImageScale menu item is created and initialized in the generated source code, and defined as a drop-down item for the menuImage menu.
//
// menuImage
//
this.menuImage.DropDownItems.AddRange(
      new System.Windows.Forms.
          ToolStripItem[] {
      this.menuImageScale});
. . .</td></tr>
<tr><td>3</td><td>Similarly, add the "Stretch to Fit" and "Actual Size" menus as submenus of the Image menu.
Settings<table><tr><th>Menu</th><th>Property</th><th>Value</th></tr><tr><td>Stretch to Fit</td><td>(Name)
Text</td><td>menuImageStretch
S&tretch to Fit</td></tr><tr><td>Actual Size</td><td>(Name)
Text</td><td>menuImageActual
&Actual Size</td></tr></table></td><td>The new menus appear in Visual Studio, and are reflected in the generated source code. In particular, an array of ToolStripItem objects is created and defined as the drop-down items for the menuImage menu.
this.menuImage.DropDownItems.AddRange(
      new System.Windows.Forms.
          ToolStripItem[] {
    this.menuImageScale,
    this.menuImageStretch,
    this.menuImageActual});</td></tr>
</table>

The code generated in MainForm.Designer.cs for our context menu is similar to the code we examined in chapter 3, so we do not review it again here. Realize that the menus here are all the same kind of control—a `ToolStripMenuItem` object—regardless of where they happen to appear in the interface. The Image menu item, as well as the three submenu items, are all objects of type `ToolStripMenuItem`.

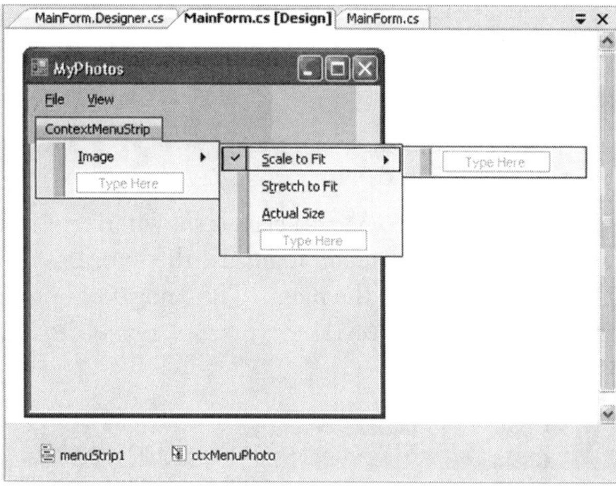

Figure 4.3 The "Type Here" in the menu editor indicates where new items can be added, and the area in front of each item holds an optional image or check mark.

Before we actually process our context menu, it would be useful to have the context menu items accessible from the menu strip in our application as well. The next section shows how these items can be shared so they appear in both a new View menu and our context menu strip.

4.1.3 Sharing a context menu

While it is certainly possible to re-create the Image menu within our menu strip, it does not seem like the most elegant solution. Having this menu in two places would require that we update one menu when we make any change to the other. Ideally, we would prefer to have a single menu, and find a way to share this menu between the two strip objects.

The solution is to implement the menus in our context menu and then reuse these menus as the drop-down for a new View menu in the application. This is possible since both the context menu and menu item classes can both contain a submenu collection. The `ContextMenuStrip` class is based on the `ToolStripDropDown` class and defines the `Items` property to hold a collection of `ToolStripItem` instances; the `ToolStripMenuItem` object is based on the `ToolStripDropDownItem` class, which defines a `DropDown` property that holds a `ToolStripDropDown` instance.

As we will see, this allows us to assign a context menu as the drop-down for a menu item. The following code illustrates this capability:

```
// Create a menu strip with a single top-level item
MenuStrip ms = new MenuStrip();
ToolStripMenuItem menuTop = new ToolStripMenuItem("Top");
ms.Items.Add(menuTop);

// Create a context menu with three menu items
```

```
ContextMenuStrip ctxMenu= new ContextMenuStrip();
ctxMenu.Items.Add("Item 1");
ctxMenu.Items.Add("Item 2");
ctxMenu.Items.Add("Item 3");

// Assign context menu as dropdown for the top-level item
menuTop.DropDown = ctxMenu;
```

An overview of the `ToolStripDropDownItem` class is shown in .NET Table 4.2. As we saw in chapter 3 with our File menu, menu items use the `DropDownItems` property to define the individual items within the menu. The `DropDown` property used in the prior code snippet allows an existing `ToolStripDropDown` object to be assigned as the drop-down list.

.NET Table 4.2 ToolStripDropDownItem class

New in 2.0 The `ToolStripDropDownItem` class is a tool strip item that displays a set of drop-down items when clicked. This class is the basis for the drop-down button item, menu item, and other tool strip items with drop-down functionality.

The `ToolStripDropDownItem` class is part of the `System.Windows.Forms` namespace, and inherits from the `ToolStripItem` class. Members inherited from `ToolStripItem` are shown in .NET Table 3.4.

Public Properties	*DropDown*	Gets or sets the `ToolStripDropDown` object that is displayed when the item is clicked
	DropDownItems	Gets the collection of items in the `ToolStripDropDown` class associated with this drop-down item
	DropDownDirection	Gets or sets a `ToolStripDropDownDirection` enumeration value that indicates where the drop-down control is displayed relative to its parent control
	HasDropDownItems	Gets whether the drop-down list contains any items
Public Methods	*HideDropDown*	Hides the drop-down associated with the item
	ShowDropDown	Displays the `ToolStripDropDown` control associated with this item
Public Events	*DropDownClosed*	Occurs when the `ToolStripDropDown` control associated with this item has closed
	DropDownItemClicked	Occurs when an item within the associated `ToolStripDropDown` control has been clicked
	DropDownOpened	Occurs when the `ToolStripDropDown` control associated with this item has opened
	DropDownOpening	Occurs when the `ToolStripDropDown` control associated with this item is about to open

The ToolStripDropDownItem class also provides properties to indicate where the drop-down list is displayed and whether it contains any items. It also defines methods to show or hide the list, and events that fire as the list is opened and closed.

In our application, we need to create the View menu to hold the contents of our context menu. As just discussed, we can assign the DropDown property of this menu to our context menu. The following steps illustrate this procedure.

ASSIGN THE CONTEXT MENU STRIP AS THE VIEW MENU DROP-DOWN

	Action	Result

1	In the MainForm.cs [Design] window, add a top-level View menu to the right of our existing File menu.
	Settings
	Property / **Value**
	(Name): menuView
	Text: &View
		`private void InitializeComponent()`
		`{`
		`  . . .`
		`  this.menuStrip1.Items.AddRange(`
		`      new System...ToolStripItem[] {`
		`        this.menuFile,`
		`        this.menuView});`
		`  . . .`
		`  //`
		`  // menuView`
		`  //`
		`  this.menuView.Name = "menuView";`
		`  . . .`
		`}`
		`. . .`
		`private System.Windows.`
		`    Forms.ToolStripMenuItem menuView;`

2	In the MainForm constructor, add a line that assigns the DropDown property for the View menu to the ctxMenuPhoto context menu.	`public MainForm()`
		`{`
		`  InitializeComponent();`
		`  SetTitleBar();`
		`  menuView.DropDown = ctxMenuPhoto;`
		`}`

This change allows both a right-click on the picture box and a click on the new View menu to display the same menu. Compile and run this code to see this in action.

With our menus defined, we are ready for some event handlers for the Image menu to alter how the image displays based on the selected setting.

4.2 DROP-DOWN EVENTS AND EVENT ARGUMENTS

The Load and Exit menu items in our File menu are fairly straightforward as menus go. Each item raises a Click event when selected, and the associated event handler performs the appropriate action. In our Image menu, we need to alter the PictureBox.SizeMode setting whenever an Image submenu item is selected. One obvious solution is to handle the Click event associated with each submenu item, and explicitly alter the SizeMode property to the appropriate setting.

While this would work just fine, it is not our approach. Instead, we would prefer to process all three submenu items in a single event handler. There are a couple of reasons for this. First, of course, it provides an alternate example for this fine book you are reading. More importantly, it encapsulates the logic for these menus in a single handler. If we later need to make a change or add a new submenu item, we only need to modify this one handler.

Another feature we'd like to add is the ability to check the submenu item associated with the current display setting. The `Click` event for the Image menu is still raised, so we could process a mouse click on the Image menu as the submenu is displayed, and update these menus accordingly.[2] Conceptually, the user is looking to display the submenu contents, not click the parent menu, so the `Click` event is not the right paradigm for this purpose.

Our Image menu is the parent menu for the Scale to Fit, Stretch to Fit, and Actual Size menu items. When the user clicks such a parent menu, they expect to see the submenu associated with the menu. The `ToolStripMenuItem` class supports various drop-down events before, during, and after such a submenu is displayed. This permits an event handler to modify the contents or appearance of the submenu as dictated by the application. An example of this concept can be found in the Windows operating system. Open the My Computer window and display the File menu. The contents of this menu change depending on the type of file currently selected.

For Windows Forms menu strips, the menu item drop-down events are inherited from the `ToolStripDropDownItem` class, shown in .NET Table 4.2. The drop-down events are activated when a user clicks the menu in order to display the collection of items in the associated drop-down object.

In this section we illustrate the `DropDownItemClicked` and `DropDownOpening` events to alter the appearance and behavior of the Image submenu items. The other drop-down events are handled in a similar manner.

4.2.1 Handling a submenu item click

The submenu for the Image menu item pops up whenever the Image menu is clicked. When the user clicks an Image submenu item, we want the image display to change accordingly. To do this, we will assign the `SizeMode` property of our `PictureBox` control depending on which menu is selected. The `SizeMode` values are taken from the `PictureBoxSizeMode` enumeration, as shown in .NET Table 4.3.

As mentioned in the section intro, we use the drop-down events to manage the behavior of the Image submenu. The drop-down events work well in cases like this where the submenu contains a set of values or other related items that are applied in a similar fashion. These handlers take advantage of the fact that our View menu and context menu share the same menu items.

To facilitate this amazing behavior, we begin by employing the `Tag` property in our menus to record the desired `SizeMode` value for each menu.

---

[2] This is a change in behavior from the Win32-based menus encapsulated in the `Menu` and `MenuItem` classes. In these classes, the `Click` event is only raised if the menu does not contain a submenu.

DEFINE THE SIZEMODE SETTINGS FOR THE IMAGE SUBMENU		
	Action	**Result**

1	From the MainForm.cs [Design] window, assign the `Tag` property for each item in the Image submenu to contain the desired `PictureBoxSizeMode` enumeration value.
	
	Settings
	Menu Item / **Tag Property**
	Scale to Fit / Zoom
	Stretch to Fit / StretchImage
	Actual Size / Normal
		The settings are assigned in the `InitializeComponent` method of the generated designer file.
		
		`this.menuImageScale.Tag = "Zoom";`
		`. . .`
		`this.menuImageStretch.Tag`
		`    = "StretchImage";`
		`. . .`
		`this.menuImageActual.Tag = "Normal";`

.NET Table 4.3 PictureBoxSizeMode enumeration

The `PictureBoxSizeMode` enumeration specifies the possible display modes for the `PictureBox` control, and is used with the `PictureBox.SizeMode` property. This enumeration is part of the `System.Windows.Forms` namespace.

Enumeration Values	AutoSize	The size of the `PictureBox` control adjusts automatically to the size of the contained image.
	CenterImage	The image is centered within the `PictureBox` control, clipping the outside edges of the image if necessary.
	Normal	The image is placed in the upper-left corner of the `PictureBox` control, clipping the right and bottom of the image as necessary.
	StretchImage	The image is stretched or shrunk to fit within the `PictureBox` control.
	Zoom	The image is scaled to fit within the `PictureBox` control, so that the aspect ratio of the image is preserved.

The `Tag` property is available in most Windows Forms components, including `ToolStripItem` objects, and allows pretty much anything to be associated with the component. The `Control` class defines this property for all Windows Forms controls. The property is of type `object`, so any class, structure, or other value can be assigned. In our code, we assign the string value of the enumeration setting we wish to associate with each item.

With these values set, we are ready to handle the events. The `DropDownItemClicked` event occurs when a child item is clicked. As mentioned in chapter 1, all .NET event handlers employ a common set of arguments. The first parameter is the object sending the event, while the second parameter is the event argument object.

For basic events like Click, as we have seen, the EventArgs class is a placeholder for this second parameter.

For more complex events, including the DropDownItemClicked event, more details are required to properly process the event. In such cases, a new class is derived from the base EventArgs class to hold this information. Let's see how this works by continuing our changes.

ADD DROP-DOWN EVENT HANDLERS FOR THE IMAGE SUBMENU

	Action	Result

2	Add a DropDownItemClicked event handler to the Image menu.
	How-to
	Display the events for the Image menu item and double-click the DropDownItemClicked event.
		A new method is registered for the menuImage object in the generated designer file.
		`this.menuImage.DropDownItemClicked`
		`  += new System.Windows.Forms`
		`    .ToolStripItemClickedEventHandler(`
		`        this.menuImage_DropDownItemClicked);`
		The MainForm.cs code window is shown with the cursor at the beginning of this new method.
		`private void menuImage_DropDownItemClicked(`
		`    object sender,`
		`    ToolStripItemClickedEventArgs e)`
		`{`

3	Within this handler, call a ProcessImageClick method with the given arguments.	`  ProcessImageClick(e);` `}`

4	Implement the ProcessImageClick method to modify the SizeMode property for the picture box control based on the selected item.	`private void ProcessImageClick(`
		`    ToolStripItemClickedEventArgs e)`
		`{`
		`  ToolStripItem item = e.ClickedItem;`
		`  string enumVal = item.Tag as string;`
		`  if (enumVal != null)`
		`  {`
		`    pbxPhoto.SizeMode = (PictureBoxSizeMode)`
		`      Enum.Parse(typeof(PictureBoxSizeMode),`
		`           enumVal);`
		`  }`
		`}`

There is a lot going on here, so let's break this down to see exactly what is happening. First, note in step 2 how the event handler is assigned to our Image menu. For the Click event, the base EventHandler class is used to define this handler. Events that define an event argument other than the EventArgs class require an alternate event handler class. By convention, the event handler and event argument class for such events utilize the same name with different suffixes. For the DropDownItemClicked event, the event argument is a ToolStripItemClickedEventArgs object and the event handler is a ToolStripItemClickedEventHandler object.

Listing 4.1 ProcessItemClick method

```
private void ProcessImageClick(ToolStripItemClickedEventArgs e)
{
  ToolStripItem item = e.ClickedItem;
  string enumVal = item.Tag as string;
  if (enumVal != null)
  {

   pbxPhoto.SizeMode = (PictureBoxSizeMode)
        Enum.Parse(typeof(PictureBoxSizeMode), enumVal);
  }
}
```

❶ Receives ItemClicked event argument

❷ Converts Tag value to string

❸ Converts string to SizeMode value

Listing 4.1 displays the code for the method that supports our new event handler. Let's look at the numbered points in this listing in more detail:

❶ The `DropDownItemClicked` event handler receives the sender parameter, much like our `Click` event handlers earlier in the chapter. It also receives some event data as a `ToolStripItemClickedEventArgs` instance, derived from the `EventArgs` class as shown in figure 4.4. This event argument class provides a `ClickedItem` property that retrieves the associated `ToolStripItem` object clicked by the user. Our code utilizes this property to alter its behavior depending on which drop-down item was clicked.

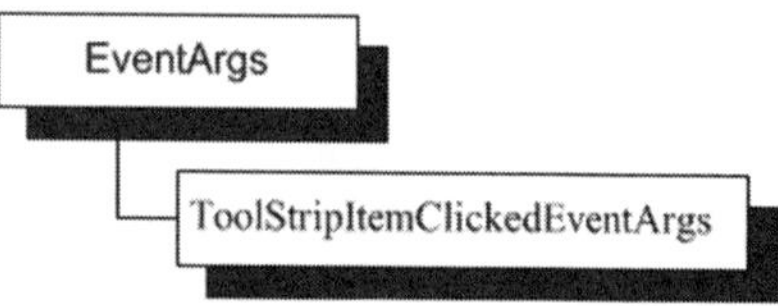

Figure 4.4 All event argument parameters inherit from the base EventArgs class.

❷ Once we determine the item clicked by the user, we make use of the `Tag` property containing the desired `SizeMode` string value. Since the `Tag` property is an `object`, we must convert its value to a `string` to obtain the assigned value. The C# `as` keyword converts a variable to a given reference type, in this case a string object. If the variable cannot be converted to the given type, then `null` is returned.[3] In our example, we know that the `Tag` property always contains a string value. Still, it is good practice to check for `null` anyway, since you never know how the program may evolve over time.

❸ The .NET Framework contains a special `Enum` structure that is the implicit base class for all enumerations. This class contains various static methods for manipulating enumeration values and their corresponding strings, and is summarized in .NET

[3] You can also cast the value directly to a string, using the code "string enumVal = (string)item.Tag;". This code throws an `InvalidCastException` object if the cast cannot be performed, as opposed to the `as` keyword, which simply assigns the `null` value.

Table 4.4. The code here includes a few new concepts, so let's break this line down a bit further to see what is happening.

.NET Table 4.4 Enum structure

The `Enum` structure is the implicit base class for all enumerations. This structure is part of the `System` namespace, and implements the `IComparable`, `IFormattable`, and `IConvertible` interfaces.

Public Methods	CompareTo	Returns whether a given object is less than, equal to, or greater than the enumeration value
	GetTypeCode	Returns the `TypeCode` enumeration value representing the underlying `Type` of values for this instance
	ToString (overridden from Object)	Returns the string representation of the current value
Public Static Methods	Format	Converts a given value for a given enumeration type to a string, based on a provided format
	GetNames	Returns the array of string constants for a given enumeration type
	GetValues	Returns the array of values for the constants in a given enumeration type
	IsDefined	Returns whether a constant with a given value is defined in the given enumeration type
	Parse	Converts one or more string constants for a given enumeration type to the appropriate enumeration value

We use the `Enum.Parse` method to convert our `string` value to the appropriate `PictureBoxSizeMode` enumeration value. The `Parse` method used here takes an enumeration type and a string, and returns an `object` representing the enumeration value. It throws an `ArgumentException` object if an invalid string is provided.

The enumeration type is obtained using the `typeof` keyword. This keyword returns a `Type` object that represents the given type, in this case the `PictureBoxSizeMode` enumeration type.

Since the `Parse` method returns an `object` value, it must be converted to the appropriate enumeration value. This conversion is "down" the class hierarchy from the generic `object` type to the more specific `PictureBoxSizeMode` enumeration. In C++, such operations are dangerous since the language does not provide explicit support for such a downcast, as it is called. In C#, downcasting is explicitly permitted, and an illegal cast throws an exception of type `InvalidCastException`.

Using the `DropDownItemClicked` event ensures that our `PictureBox` is updated with the appropriate display behavior, regardless of which item was selected. Compile and run this code to see it in action.

TRY IT! The `PictureBoxSizeMode` enumeration contains more than just the three settings used here. Add a menu item to the Image menu called `menuImageCenter`, with the text "Center Image," to handle the `CenterImage` value. Set the `Tag` property appropriately to see how our existing code automatically handles the new menu.

4.2.2 Altering a submenu before it appears

Users appreciate feedback from an application. Our current interface does not yet do this. The user has to understand the possible display modes in order to know what is currently selected, and then choose a different setting. A more intuitive interface would highlight the current selection in the `menuImage` submenu. This would immediately indicate what mode is currently displayed, and help our user make a more informed selection.

The `ToolStripMenuItem` class provides a `Checked` property that, when `true`, displays a check mark next to the menu. We could set this property explicitly whenever the selection is modified, so our user would see the appropriate feedback. Of course, as our program changes, there might be other commands or user interactions that alter the display mode of the image, so this approach could get complicated. An alternate solution might ensure that the display modes are checked or unchecked as they are displayed to the user. This approach is more robust in the face of future changes, creating an application that users, documenters, and testers will appreciate for years to come.

The `DropDownOpening` event is designed for just this purpose. This event occurs just before the drop-down list associated with an item is displayed, allowing its appearance or contents to be modified and then immediately displayed to the user. Let's see how this works.

IMPLEMENT A DROPDOWNOPENING HANDLER FOR THE IMAGE MENU

	Action	Result

1	In the MainForm.cs [Design] window, add a `DropDownOpening` event handler for the Image menu.	`private void menuImage_DropDownOpening(`
		`    object sender, EventArgs e)`
		`{`

2	Within this handler, call a `ProcessImageOpening` method, with the given drop-down item as an argument.	`  ProcessImageOpening(`
		`      sender as ToolStripDropDownItem);`
		`}`

	IMPLEMENT A DROPDOWNOPENING HANDLER FOR THE IMAGE MENU *(CONTINUED)*	
	Action	**Result**

3	Implement the `ProcessImageOpening` method to assign the `Enabled` and `Checked` property for each menu item in the given drop-down list.	<pre>private void ProcessImageOpening(
		    ToolStripDropDownItem parent)
		{
		  if (parent != null)
		  {
		    string enumVal = pbxPhoto.SizeMode.ToString();
		    foreach (ToolStripMenuItem item
		                 in parent.DropDownItems)
		    {
		      item.Enabled = (pbxPhoto.Image != null);
		      item.Checked = item.Tag.Equals(enumVal);
		    }
		  }
		}</pre>

The handler for the `DropDownOpening` event is similar to what we have seen for the `Click` event, with an object as the first argument and an `EventArgs` object as the second parameter. Our implementation invokes a `ProcessImageOpening` method to perform the desired actions. We could avoid this method and implement the logic directly in the handler. Using a supporting method as we do here is useful if you ever want to invoke the same functionality in another part of the program.

The `ProcessImageOpening` method ensures the given item is not `null`, and uses the `ToString` method to obtain the string representation of the current `SizeMode` enumeration value. It also uses the C# `foreach` keyword, which provides an easy way to enumerate the items in a collection. A `foreach` loop is much like a `for` loop, except that each iteration of the loop processes the next item in the collection rather than the next integer-based value. We discuss this concept in more detail in chapter 5.

For each submenu item in the Image menu, our code sets the `Enabled` property based on whether the `PictureBox` control currently contains an image, and the `Checked` property based on a comparison of the `SizeMode` string with the subitem's `Tag` value. The `ToString` and `Equals` methods used here are inherited from the base `object` class, which we also discuss in chapter 5.

Figure 4.5 Our Actual Size display mode displays every pixel in the image within the window, starting with the upper-left corner.

Notice that there is nothing in the `ProcessImageOpening` method to indicate whether these menu items are part of a specific menu structure. The code works identically whether displayed from the View menu or as part of the context menu. Compile and run the application to verify that the menus work correctly. Figure 4.5 shows the application with an image displayed in Actual Size mode.

Unfortunately, this figure reveals a problem with our PictureBox control. In the figure, the image is larger than the display area, but there is no way to see the rest of the image without resizing the window. While this is possible when the image is small, a high-resolution image may contain more pixels than our screen. Ideally, the application would display scroll bars here. Since the PictureBox control does not support scroll bars, we are a bit stuck unless we display the picture in an alternate display mode.

You may be wondering about a book that teaches you how to build an application that doesn't quite work, and you should. We discuss how to solve this problem in chapter 13 using a scrollable panel or tab page to contain the picture box, and again in chapter 19 where we build a custom picture box that solves this problem directly.

TRY IT! Okay, I admit this has nothing to do with our application. Still, if you want to have fun with the DropDownOpening event, add a new menu, menuCounter, at the bottom of the ctxMenuPhoto context menu with the text "Counter" and insert a single menu with the text "DropDown" in its submenu. Define a DropDownOpening event for the menuCounter menu, which Visual Studio will name menuCounter_DropDownOpening. In this handler, dynamically create a new ToolStripMenuItem object and add it to the end of the menuCounter submenu. Set the Text property to your new menu to "Count #," where # is the number of drop-downs that have occurred on your new menu. Use a static integer dropdownCount in the MainForm class to track the number of drop-down occurrences. The lines to dynamically create the new menu in your DropDownOpening handler should look something like this:

```
ToolStripMenuItem mi = new ToolStripMenuItem();
mi.Text = "Count " + dropdownCount.ToString();
menuCounter.DropDownItems.Add(mi);
```

This example illustrates how easy it is to create menus on the fly with the .NET Framework, and how a parent menu can change the contents of its submenu as it is displayed. This might be used, for example, to display a list of files most recently opened by an application.

If all this makes no sense to you, download the code for this TRY IT! from the book's website. Have a look at the menuCounter_DropDownOpening handler to see the code required.

This concludes our discussion of menus for now. Before we leave this chapter, let's take a look at another type of tool strip: the status strip.

4.3 STATUS STRIPS

Most applications make a lot of information available to users. There is often a core subset that most users would appreciate having readily available. A status bar at the base of a window is a good place for this type of data, as it provides quick feedback related to the current task or cursor position. My word processor, for example, indicates the current page number, total number of pages, column and line position of the cursor, whether the Insert key has been pressed (which I seem to hit constantly while aiming for the Page Down key), and other information I may want to know at a glance. This helps me keep track of how this book is shaping up, when the Insert key has been pressed, and where these words you are reading appear on the page.

Status bars can also contain graphical information such as the status of a print request, whether the application is connected to the Internet, and pretty much anything else you can draw or animate.

In .NET, status bars are represented by the `StatusStrip` class, which is part of the `ToolStrip` class hierarchy we have been discussing. As a way to round out our discussion and examine another kind of tool strip, this section takes a quick look at this functionality. We discuss status strips and status panels, or labels, and add the status bar we saw in figure 4.1 to our MyPhotos application.

We should note that Win32 status bars are also supported by the `StatusBar` and `StatusBarPanel` classes. These classes are supported for existing and new applications, but are hidden in Visual Studio to encourage use of the new tool strip classes.

4.3.1 Creating a status strip

The `StatusStrip` control inherits directly from the base `ToolStrip` class. A summary of this control appears in .NET Table 4.5. We will not discuss the details of the

.NET Table 4.5 StatusStrip class

New in 2.0 The `StatusStrip` class is a tool strip used to show a status bar on a form. This class can display a collection of labels in the form of `ToolStripStatusLabel` objects. The `StatusStrip` class is part of the `System.Windows.Forms` namespace, and inherits from the `ToolStrip` class. See .NET Table 16.1 for a list of inherited members, and .NET Table 4.7 for information on the `ToolStripStatusLabel` class.

Public Properties	Dock (overridden from Control)	Gets or sets the docking style for the control. The default for status strips is `Bottom`.
	GripStyle (overridden from ToolStrip)	Gets or sets whether the move handle is hidden or visible. The default for status strips is `Hidden`.
	ShowItemToolTips (overridden from ToolStrip)	Gets or sets whether items display their tooltips. The default for status strips is `false`.
	SizingGrip	Gets or sets whether the sizing grip for resizing the form appears in the status bar.
	Stretch (overridden from ToolStrip)	Gets or sets whether the strip expands to fill the width of its parent's container. The default for status bars is `true`.

ToolStrip class until chapter 16, but one detail to take from our table here is that the StatusStrip class is basically a ToolStrip that overrides the base functionality to achieve the appearance of a Win32-style status bar. This includes docking the strip at the bottom of the form, hiding the move handle grip, not showing any tooltips, and stretching the strip across the entire width of the form.

A status strip can technically appear within any parent container and docked to any side of this container, so traditionally this control is placed only at the base of Form objects. The following step adds a status strip to our MyPhotos application.

ADD A STATUS STRIP TO OUR APPLICATION		
	Action	**Result**
1	In the MainForm.cs [Design] window, drag a StatusStrip control from the Toolbox window onto the form.	The new status strip appears at the base of the form in the designer window, and in the component tray below the form. menuStrip1 ctxMenuPhoto statusStrip1

Notice how the interface for populating a status strip is quite different than the one employed for menus. The small, mostly white icon on the left adds a ToolStripStatusLabel object, while the drop-down arrow next to this icon displays a context menu of various ToolStripItem objects that can be added to the strip.

The code generated in the MainForm.Designer.cs file is much like the code we have seen when adding other controls to our form. A statusStrip1 field is created at the top of the InitializeComponent method, its nondefault values assigned in the middle and added to the Form at the bottom of the method. The field is defined at the end of the generated file, as shown here:

```
private System.Windows.Forms.StatusStrip statusStrip1;
```

Most status strips contain one or more status panels, or labels. This is our next topic.

4.3.2 Adding status strip labels

In the Win32-based classes, status bars contain panels: the Windows Forms StatusBar class represents a status bar, and contains one or more StatusBarPanel components. In the tool strip world, the terminology is slightly different. The StatusStrip class represents a status bar, and contains one or more ToolStripStatusLabel objects. We will adopt the term *status labels* in this book to stay consistent with the new class name.

The ToolStripStatusLabel class for status labels is based on the ToolStripLabel class. A summary of this class appears in .NET Table 4.6. The ToolStripStatusLabel class adds some additional functionality specific to status bars, and is summarized in .NET Table 4.7.

.NET Table 4.6 ToolStripLabel class

New in 2.0 The `ToolStripLabel` class is a tool strip item that displays nonselectable text and image as well as hyperlink items. The `ToolStripLabel` class is part of the `System.Windows.Forms` namespace, and inherits from the `ToolStripItem` class. See .NET Table 3.4 for a list of inherited members.

Public Properties	*CanSelect* (overridden from ToolStripItem)	Gets whether the contents of the item are selectable. Always `false` for label items.
	IsLink	Gets or sets whether the label is a hyperlink.
	LinkBehavior	Gets or sets the `LinkBehavior` enumeration value representing the appearance of a link.
	LinkColor	Gets or sets the color to use for a normal link. The `ActiveLinkColor` and `VisitedLinkColor` properties represent the color to use for an active and visited link, respectively.
	LinkVisited	Gets or sets whether the link should display as though it were visited.

As you can see in .NET Table 4.6, the `ToolStripLabel` class overrides the `CanSelect` property from the `ToolStripItem` class to enforce that such labels cannot be selected. The other properties relate to treating the label as a hyperlink. In particular, the `IsLink` property identifies whether the label appears as a hyperlink. A `Click` event handler can be used to process the link when it is clicked.

In .NET Table 4.7, the `ToolStripLabel` class is extended to work within a status strip. As you can see, three new properties are added: two to define the borders for the label, and a `Spring` property that allows the label to grow or contract as the status strip is resized.

.NET Table 4.7 ToolStripStatusLabel class

New in 2.0 The `ToolStripStatusLabel` class is a label item for use within a `StatusStrip` control. The `ToolStripStatusLabel` class is part of the `System.Windows.Forms` namespace, and inherits from the `ToolStripLabel` class.

Public Properties	*BorderSides*	Gets or sets the sides of the status label that should display borders
	BorderStyle	Gets or sets the `Border3DStyle` enumeration value for how the label's borders should appear
	Spring	Gets or sets whether the panel should expand or shrink to fit the available space when the status strip is resized

Returning to our MyPhotos application, we already have a `StatusStrip` object on our form, so the next task is to define a reasonable set of labels. We start with the three labels mentioned at the start of the chapter.

When we added a status strip to our form, we mentioned the interface provided to add labels and other items to the strip. While we could use this interface here, we instead use the Items Collection Editor window as an alternate method for this task. This editor is available for other tool strips as well, including menu strips.

<table>
<tr><th colspan="3">ADD STATUS LABELS TO A STATUS STRIP</th></tr>
<tr><th></th><th>Action</th><th>Result</th></tr>
<tr><td>1</td><td>In the MainForm.cs [Design] window, display the items for the status strip.
How-to
Right-click the status strip and select the Edit Items entry.
Alternately
Click the smart tag associated with the status strip, and click Edit Items in the StatusStrip Tasks window.</td><td>The Items Collection Editor window appears. This editor allows a collection of items, in this case tool strip items on a status strip, to be configured for a parent control. A portion of this window is shown here.
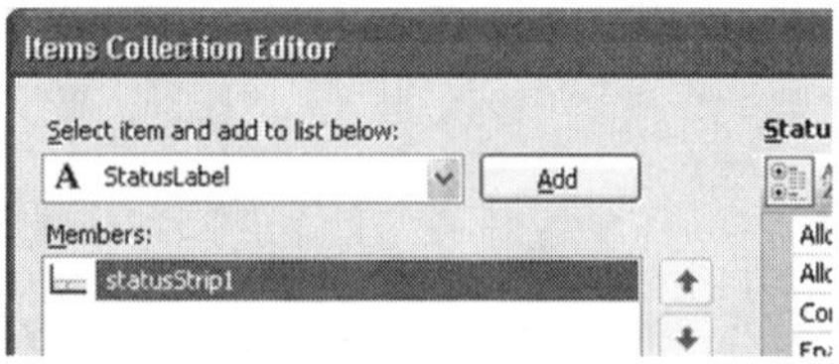
</td></tr>
<tr><td>2</td><td>Click the Add button twice to add two status labels to the control.</td><td>The new <code>ToolStripStatusLabel</code> objects are shown in the editor.</td></tr>
<tr><td>3</td><td>Modify the properties of the first label as follows.
Settings
<table><tr><th>Property</th><th>Value</th></tr><tr><td>(Name)</td><td>statusInfo</td></tr><tr><td>AutoSize</td><td>False</td></tr><tr><td>Spring</td><td>True</td></tr><tr><td>Text</td><td>Desc</td></tr><tr><td>TextAlign</td><td>MiddleLeft</td></tr></table></td><td>
</td></tr>
<tr><td>4</td><td>Close the Item Collections Editor window by clicking the OK button.</td><td>The two status labels are shown in the designer window.</td></tr>
</table>

ADD STATUS LABELS TO A STATUS STRIP *(CONTINUED)*		
	Action	**Result**

5	Click the second status label and modify its properties as follows.
	
	Settings
	
	Property — **Value**
	(Name) — statusImageSize
	BorderSides — All
	BorderStyle — SunkenInner
	Text — W x H
		The properties are assigned in the generated MainForm.Designer.cs file.
		
		`//`
		`// statusImageSize`
		`//`
		`this.statusImageSize.BorderSides`
		`  = ((System.Windows.Forms.`
		`      ToolStripStatusLabelBorderSides)`
		`    ((((System.Windows.Forms.ToolStrip-`
		`          StatusLabelBorderSides.Left`
		`      | System.Windows.Forms.ToolStrip-`
		`          StatusLabelBorderSides.Top)`
		`      | System.Windows.Forms.ToolStrip-`
		`          StatusLabelBorderSides.Right)`
		`      | System.Windows.Forms.ToolStrip-`
		`          StatusLabelBorderSides.Bottom)`
		`    ));`
		`this.statusImageSize.BorderStyle`
		`  = System.Windows.Forms.`
		`      Border3DStyle.SunkenInner;`
		`this.statusImageSize.Name`
		`  = "statusImageSize";`
		`this.statusImageSize.Size`
		`  = new System.Drawing.Size(40, 17);`
		`this.statusImageSize.Text = "W x H";`

6	Add a third status label to the status strip.
	
	How-to
	Click the small white icon at the right of the strip.
	
	W x H
	
	Settings
	
	Property — **Value**
	(Name) — statusAlbumPos
	BorderSides — All
	BorderStyle — SunkenInner
	Text — 1 / 1
		The third label appears in the designer window, and is initialized in the generated code. The three status labels are added to the `Items` property of the `StatusStrip` object using the `AddRange` method.
		
		`this.statusStrip1.Items.AddRange(new`
		`  System.Windows.Forms.ToolStripItem[] {`
		`    this.statusInfo,`
		`    this.statusImageSize,`
		`    this.statusAlbumPos});`

These three labels will show a description of the current image, the size of the image, and the current position of the image within an album. Of course, the album position label is not needed in this chapter. We add it here to save time and space in chapter 6, when our application displays an album rather than a single image.

In our property settings, note how the `BorderSides` and `BorderStyle` properties work together to define how the label appears within the status strip. In our example we set our size and position labels to have borders on all four sides using the `SunkenInner` value from the `Border3DStyle` enumeration.

As for the other two labels, the description and size, we should update them whenever we load an image to contain the filename as the description, and the width and height in pixels as the size. The `Text` property inherited from the `ToolStrip-Item` class defines the text to display on the label. You can also display an image by assigning the `Image` property, but we do not make use of this here.

One approach for updating these labels might be to assign each label's text in the `Click` event handler of our Load menu directly. This is another example where the most obvious approach may not be the best long-term solution. Since our status strip is likely to change, we encapsulate this logic in a private method. We continue our prior steps to make these changes.

ASSIGN TEXT TO STATUS LABELS

	Action	Result
7	In the MainForm.cs code window, define a new private method called `SetStatusStrip` that accepts a file path as the only argument.	`private void SetStatusStrip(string path)` `{`

8	If an image is assigned to the picture box, set the `statusInfo` label to the given path.	`  if (pbxPhoto.Image != null)`
		`  {`
		`    statusInfo.Text = path;`

9	Also set the `statusImageSize` label to the size of the image.
	
	How-to
	Use the `Width` and Height properties in the `Image` class.
		`    statusImageSize.Text`
		`      = String.Format("{0:#}x{1:#}",`
		`          pbxPhoto.Image.Width,`
		`          pbxPhoto.Image.Height);`
		`    // statusAlbumPos is set in ch. 6`
		`  }`

10	If no image is assigned to the picture box control, set the status labels to blank.
	
	How-to
	Set each `Text` property to `null`.
		`  else`
		`  {`
		`    statusInfo.Text = null;`
		`    statusImageSize.Text = null;`
		`    statusAlbumPos.Text = null;`
		`  }`
		`}`

11	Update the status bar at the end of the `menuFileLoad_Click` event handler.	`private void menuFileLoad_Click(`
		`    object sender, EventArgs e)`
		`{`
		`  . . .`
		`  if (dlg.ShowDialog() == DialogResult.OK)`
		`  {`
		`    . . .`
		`    `**`SetStatusStrip(dlg.FileName);`**
		`  }`
		`  dlg.Dispose();`
		`}`

	Action	**Result**

12	Also call `SetStatusStrip` in the form's constructor to initialize the status bar settings.	`public MainForm()`
		`{`
		`  InitializeComponent();`
		`  SetTitleBar();`
		`  **SetStatusStrip(null);**`
		
		`  menuView.DropDown = ctxMenuPhoto;`
		`}`

Table: ASSIGN TEXT TO STATUS LABELS *(CONTINUED)*

Compile and run the program to see the status strip update. Make sure you test loading a valid and an invalid file to see that the `SetStatusStrip` method handles both cases.

TRY IT! There are a number of changes you could make here to experiment with the various properties and settings supported by the `StatusStrip` and `ToolStripStatusLabel` classes. Here are a couple of suggestions:

- There is a slight problem with our first label, since if the file path is too long it cannot be read by the user. Assign the `ToolTipText` property for the `statusInfo` label so the user can see the full path in a tooltip. You will also need to modify the `ShowItemToolTips` property for the status strip, since this is set to `false` by default.
- For a more challenging task, create a new item in the status strip that modifies the `BorderStyle` property of the `statusImageSize` label. To do this, add a drop-down button to the strip by selecting the DropDownButton item from the drop-down menu, as shown in the graphic. Set the (Name) to "statusBorder" and `Text` to "Size Border." Look up the `Border3DStyle` enumeration in the .NET documentation to find the ten possible values for this enumeration.

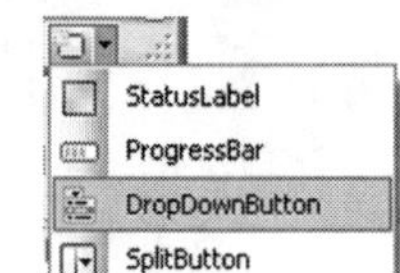

  Use these values to replicate the logic from our Image menu handlers earlier in the chapter. The new item is a `ToolStripDropDownButton object`, and you can add drop-down items for each enumeration value to the button, set the `Tag` property on each, and handle the `DropDownItemClick` event to modify the `statusImageSize.BorderStyle` property. Run the application to dynamically change the border style so you can view the effect of each option.

4.4 RECAP

This chapter discussed context menu strips and status strips. We began with the `ContextMenuStrip` class and its similarities to the `MenuStrip` control. An example in our MyPhotos application created an Image menu for altering how an image is displayed in our `PictureBox` control. A new View menu in our `MenuStrip` class cleverly linked to our context menu so both menus would exhibit the same contents and behavior. This logic for the Image menu required the use of the `Enum` structure to convert `PictureBoxSizeMode` enumeration values to and from `string` objects.

We concluded the chapter with a discussion of status strips. We showed how `StatusStrip` controls contain `ToolStripStatusLabel` items, and created a status strip with some labels within our application.

Some new C# keywords were examined along the way, namely the `foreach` and `as` keywords, and some common object methods such as `Equals` and `ToString` were employed. We looked at the Properties window in Visual Studio in more detail, and used this window to add various events to our program.

This chapter completes our early discussion of tool strips and tool strip items, done here in the context of menus and status strips. Future chapters rely on this knowledge to make additional menu or status strip changes as we progress through the book. We also discuss the `ToolStrip` and `ToolStripItem` classes in greater detail in chapter 16.

The next chapter takes us out of the Windows Forms namespace briefly in order to examine reusable libraries. This lays the foundation for our discussions on various Windows Forms controls in subsequent chapters.

CHAPTER 5

Reusable libraries

This chapter is our chance to lean back in our respective chairs, take stock of where we've been, and plan for the future. We are at the point where we need to build some infrastructure and introduce some programming concepts. Some of you may be familiar or comfortable with these concepts; others may not. My goal is to provide enough material to review what is needed without getting too bogged down in the details.

Looking at our MyPhotos application, it would be great if this application turned out to be somewhat useful. As such, it is worth laying the proper groundwork for the road ahead. So far, we have built an application with the following features:

- A title bar where the name and version number of the program is displayed
- A menu bar where the user can access commands such as loading an image
- A main window that displays a single image at a time in a variety of ways
- A status bar where information about the displayed image appears

So now what? In this book, we still need to cover a number of features: panels, combo boxes, splitters, and printing, to name a few. To do this, we need more than a single image in our application. If we can display one image, why not more than one? Let's display multiple photos. We call this, of course, a photo album.

To keep this chapter somewhat manageable, we do not mess with our main application window, focusing instead on suitable photograph and photo album abstractions as C# classes in a new library project. Chapter 6 integrates these changes into the MyPhotos application. Specifically, we perform the following tasks in this chapter:

- Create a `Photograph` class to represent a single photograph.
- Create a `PhotoAlbum` class to represent a collection of photographs.
- Compile the `Photograph` and `PhotoAlbum` classes into an external library.

Before we write any code for these classes, a short design discussion is in order.

5.1 CLASS LIBRARIES

A class library is a good way to encapsulate a common set of logic so it can be shared among multiple applications. This is useful both to promote reusability of the classes in the library and to keep the portions of an application down to a manageable size.

Let's begin with an example of this idea by creating a library to hold a `Photograph` class. For lack of a better term, we call this library MyPhotoAlbum. It is always a good idea to sketch out the structure of a class before you write code, so that is what we do here.

One simple approach might be to represent a photograph as a filename instance, or perhaps a `Bitmap` image. While both ideas would work just fine, neither is very flexible since it would be difficult to add settings and logic to such a photograph in the future. We would like to develop a more full-featured object that can hold additional changes later in the book.

Listing 5.1 shows the structure of the `Photograph` class we build, along with the properties and methods we expect to support. These members are used throughout the book, but are gathered here so we can define them in a single spot.

Listing 5.1 Photograph class overview

```
public class Photograph   <-- 1 Inherits from System.Object
{
  // Create a new instance from a filename.

  // Properties:
  //    - get the filename for the photograph
  //    - get the Bitmap for the photograph
  //    - get or set a caption (brief description) for the photograph
  //    - get or set the photographer who took the photograph
  //    - get or set the date the photograph was taken
  //    - get or set detailed comments on the photograph

  // Methods:
  //    - see if two Photographs are equal
  //    - obtain a string representing the Photograph
}  <-- 2 Ends the Photograph class
```

Some syntactic points here:

❶ Classes in C# are very similar to classes in the C++ and Java languages. Classes are created with the `class` keyword, with their contents enclosed in braces. All classes implicitly inherit from the `object` class even when it is not specified. So even though it is not shown, our `Photograph` class inherits from the base `System.Object` class implicitly, which is equivalent to the C# `object` class.

❷ If you haven't realized it by now, note that there are no header files in C#. Like Java, the entire class is specified in a single file. For C++ programmers, also note that a semicolon (;) is not required after the class definition.

We discuss the `PhotoAlbum` class later in the chapter. I don't know about you, but I'm ready to write some code.

5.1.1 Creating a class library

In Visual Studio, every assembly is typically a separate project within the solution. Practically, each library or executable is a separate directory in the file system. While our focus here is on Visual Studio, we give some hints for building such libraries from the command line later in the chapter.

It is certainly possible to define `Photograph` and `PhotoAlbum` classes in the MyPhotos application directly. This would work quite well but make it difficult to build other applications using our new classes. So, instead we place our new classes in a library that other programs can reuse. In Windows parlance, such a library is called a dynamic link library, or DLL.

In this section we create a new project for eventual use in our MyPhotos solution. This project builds a new MyPhotoAlbum library, as detailed in the following steps.

CREATE A REUSABLE LIBRARY IN VISUAL STUDIO		
	Action	**Result**
1	Open the Add New Project window for the MyPhotos solution. **How-to** a. In the Solutions window, right-click the MyPhotos solution. b. Select the New Project entry from the Add menu.	Add New Project Project types: Visual C#, Windows, Smart Device, Database, Starter Kits, Other Languages, Other Project Types Templates: Visual Studio installed tem… Windows Application, Class Library, Device

	Action	Result
	CREATE A REUSABLE LIBRARY IN VISUAL STUDIO *(CONTINUED)*	
2	Configure the new project as a class library named "MyPhotoAlbum." **How-to** a. Select Visual C# as the project type. b. Select Class Library as the template. c. Enter "MyPhotoAlbum" for the name.	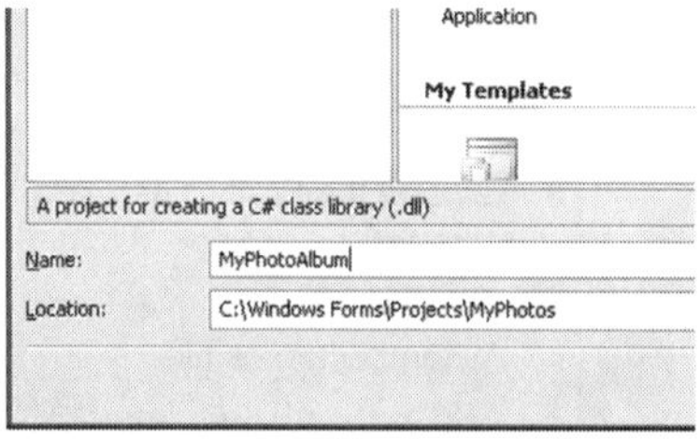 Application My Templates A project for creating a C# class library (.dll) Name: MyPhotoAlbum Location: C:\Windows Forms\Projects\MyPhotos
3	Click the OK button to create the new project.	In the Solution Explorer window, the new project appears with a single class named `Class1`. The main window displays the Class1.cs source file. 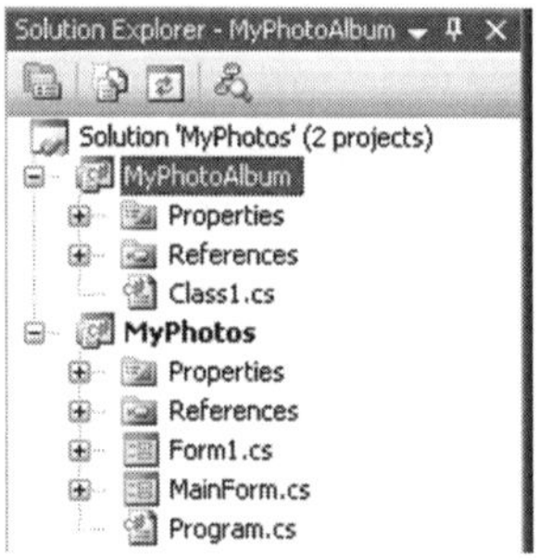 Solution Explorer - MyPhotoAlbum Solution 'MyPhotos' (2 projects) MyPhotoAlbum Properties References Class1.cs **MyPhotos** Properties References Form1.cs MainForm.cs Program.cs

That's all it takes. The solution MyPhotos now contains two projects: a MyPhotoAlbum project to create a DLL library, and a MyPhotos project to create a Windows Forms application. The new project has its own AssemblyInfo.cs file within its Properties entry and an initial class called `Class1`. The MyPhotos project is in bold to indicate that it is the default or *startup project* in Visual Studio terms.

Visual Studio automatically uses the project name as the namespace for all files in the project. While not shown here, the `Class1` class is in the `MyPhotoAlbum` namespace, to ensure it does not interfere with anyone else who may have a class called `Class1`. By convention, namespaces specify the company name, followed by the project name. Since our library might be used outside of this book (hey, you never know!), we should follow this convention as well. We use the publisher's name Manning as our top-level namespace.

The following table continues our prior steps creating our new MyPhotoAlbum project. We synchronize our version numbers, get rid of this unnecessary `Class1` class, add the `Photograph` class, and adjust our namespace name.

<table>
<tr><th colspan="3">CREATE THE PHOTOGRAPH CLASS</th></tr>
<tr><th></th><th>Action</th><th>Result</th></tr>
<tr><td>4</td><td>Set the MyPhotoAlbum version number to 5.1.
How-to
a. Expand the Properties item for the project.
b. Double-click the AssemblyInfo.cs file.
c. Assign the two version attributes the assembly and file, and other attributes as desired.</td><td>When you compile the MyPhotoAlbum library, the new version number is included, and will be visible when displaying the properties for the generated library assembly.
Note: Your main window may now display two AssemblyInfo.cs tabs for the corresponding files in each project. The displayed file is always selected in the Solution Explorer window, which identifies the project that contains the file. To display the Solution Explorer window while editing a file, use the keyboard shortcut Ctrl+Alt+L.</td></tr>
<tr><td>5</td><td>Delete the Class1.cs file.
How-to
Select the Class1.cs entry and press the Delete key.</td><td>The Class1.cs entry in the MyPhotoAlbum project is removed. The corresponding file in the MyPhotoAlbum project directory is deleted as well.</td></tr>
<tr><td>6</td><td>Display the Add New Item dialog box to add a new class to the project.
How-to
a. Right-click the MyPhotoAlbum project in Solution Explorer.
b. Select the Class item from the Add menu.</td><td>Add New Item - MyPhotoAlbum
Templates:
Visual Studio installed templates
Class Interface Code File Windows Fo</td></tr>
<tr><td>7</td><td>Add a new <code>Photograph</code> class to the project.
How-to
Enter "Photograph" as the name for the class and click the Add button (not shown).</td><td rowspan="2">A new PhotoAlbum.cs file is added to the project and appears in the main window.<pre>
using System;
using System.Collections.Generic;
using System.Text;

namespace Manning.MyPhotoAlbum
{
  public class Photograph
  {
  }
}
</pre></td></tr>
<tr><td>8</td><td>Make the class public, and modify the namespace to be <code>Manning.MyPhotoAlbum</code>.</td></tr>
</table>

Our library is now ready; all we need to do is add code. Notice how the Photograph.cs file contains using statements for the `System.Collections.Generic` and `System.Text` namespaces. These are not required right now, so we will not discuss them. Visual Studio adds these automatically, and we do make use of them eventually.

If you are not using Visual Studio to build your program, then you are missing out on a number of nice features. You must establish a directory for the library and set up your files manually. The command-line tools discussed in chapter 1 are used by Visual Studio to build the library. The next section provides a short discussion on this topic for completeness and to provide some insight into what Visual Studio does behind the scenes.

5.1.2 Using the command-line tools

As we saw in chapter 1, you can build Windows Forms applications without using Visual Studio. The interactive environment makes many tasks easier, but costs money and uses memory and other system resources on your computer. On a limited budget, or on a computer with limited resources, this can present some problems. If you have a favorite editor and are comfortable working with makefiles, you can create the examples in this book without using Visual Studio.

To create a class library such as MyPhotoAlbum.dll, create a MyPhotoAlbum directory for the library and place the required source files in it. In this case you would create a Photograph.cs file to hold the `Photograph` class source code and other files as required. You can create an AssemblyInfo.cs file if you wish, or simply include the version number and other assembly information at the top of your primary source file as we did in chapter 1.

The C# compiler (csc.exe) is used to produce both executables and libraries. The `/target` switch specifies the type of output file to produce, using the options shown in table 5.1. The `/out` switch specifies an output filename. Both `/out` and `/target` must appear before any source filenames.

Table 5.1 C# compiler output options (/target switch)

Switch	Output	Comments
/target:exe	Creates a console application (.exe)	This is the default.
/target:library	Creates a library file (.dll)	The library generated is an assembly that can be referenced by other .NET applications.
/target:module	Creates a library module (.dll)	The library generated is not an assembly that can be referenced by other .NET applications. It must be incorporated in an assembly manifest using the `/addmodule` switch. This permits collections of files to be built separately and merged into a single assembly.
/target:winexe	Creates a Windows application (.exe)	When a Windows application is run in a console window, the console does not wait for the application to exit. This is different than a console application, where the console does in fact wait.

For example, the following line creates a library assembly called MyPhotoAlbum.dll using a single source file PhotoAlbum.cs:

```
> csc /target:library /out:MyPhotoAlbum.dll PhotoAlbum.cs
```

To use this library with your MyPhotos application, you will need to include an `/r` reference when compiling the application. For example, if your MyPhotoAlbum.dll library was in a directory called `C:\MyProjects\MyPhotoAlbum`, then you would add the following switch when compiling the MyPhotos application:

```
/r:C:\MyProjects\MyPhotoAlbum\MyPhotoAlbum.dll
```

We discuss references in Visual Studio in the next section and again in chapter 6.

5.1.3 Creating the Photograph class

No matter how you compile your library, we are now ready to implement the `Photograph` class. This section takes us through the initial implementation of this class. If you find typing all this code rather tedious (or are a really bad typist!), the final code is available from the book's website. For the rest of us, let's forge ahead.

The `Photograph` class represents a photograph stored in a file. We define this class in three parts:

1. Create the constructor and properties for the filename and image.
2. Create the other properties in the class.
3. Create the methods for the class.

The following steps create the first part of this class.

DEFINE THE PHOTOGRAPH CONSTRUCTOR AND READ-ONLY PROPERTIES

	Action	Result

1	In the Photograph.cs window, create some documentation for the class.	`. . .`
		`namespace Manning.MyPhotoAlbum`
		`{`
		`  /// <summary>`
		`  /// The Photograph class represents a`
		`  /// photographic image stored in the`
		`  /// file system.`
		`  /// </summary>`
		`  class Photograph`
		`  {`

2	Create private member variables to track the filename and bitmap for the class.	`private string _fileName;`
		`private Bitmap _bitmap;`
		Note: As discussed in the introduction, we indicate these fields are `private` within the containing class by prefixing them with an underscore.

3	Create a constructor to initialize these members from a given filename.	`public Photograph(string fileName)`
		`{`
		`  _fileName = fileName;`
		`  _bitmap = null;`
		`}`
		Note: We allow a `Photograph` to be created with an invalid filename.

4	Create a `FileName` property to return the assigned filename.	`public string FileName`
		`{`
		`  get { return _fileName; }`
		`}`

	DEFINE THE PHOTOGRAPH CONSTRUCTOR AND READ-ONLY PROPERTIES *(CONTINUED)*	
	Action	**Result**

5	Create an `Image` property to return the corresponding `Bitmap` object.
	
	Note: An invalid filename will throw an `ArgumentException` exception. We allow this to occur here and expect the caller to handle the resulting error.
		<pre>public Bitmap Image
		{
		  get
		  {
		    if (_bitmap == null)
		    {
		      _bitmap = new Bitmap(_fileName);
		    }
		    return _bitmap;
		  }
		}</pre>

This is the first time we've created our own properties, so it is worth a short discussion. Don't compile this code yet, as it is not yet finished.

A property in C# is created much like a method. You define an access level, a type, and a name for the property. By Microsoft conventions, property names begin with a capital letter, and are a noun or noun phrase.[1] The lack of parentheses after the name informs the compiler that this is a property and not a method.

Inside the braces, the *access methods* for the property are defined. The access methods provide read access, via the `get` keyword, or write access, via the `set` keyword. The `get` access method must return the defined type, while the `set` access method uses the reserved word `value` to access the assigned value on the right side of the equals sign. For example, if we wanted users of our `Photograph` class to set the `FileName` property, we could code this as follows:

```
public string FileName
{
  get { return _fileName; }
  set { _fileName = value; }  // example only, not in our code
}
```

Of course, in an actual implementation it might be good to verify that the `value` provided to the `set` call is a real file and does indeed represent a photograph. For our purposes, the `Photograph` class is tied to a specific filename, so we do not provide a `set` implementation. In this case the `FileName` property is said to be *read-only*, since the value can be read but not written.

Also note that in production code it is a good idea to provide a three-slash (`///`) summary comment for all public class members, including properties. Visual Studio

[1] Microsoft has published a set of design guidelines for .NET, which includes naming conventions for properties and other constructs. We follow most of these conventions in this book. See the introduction for a brief discussion of these guidelines and a summary of the few conventions we do not follow exactly.

picks up these comments and presents them to other programmers who use your library, so this is a good way to communicate information about the interface.

Practically, properties permit safe access to a class without the need to expose internal variables or other features. To duplicate the `get` and `set` functionality for a filename member in C++, programmers typically provide methods such as `SetFileName` and `GetFileName`. Properties formalize this concept for C# so that all programs use a standard mechanism for this style of access.

Since properties are invoked similar to methods, additional calculations can be performed as part of their definition. In the code for the `Image` property, for example, the `Bitmap` is created as required before returning it to the user:

```
public Bitmap Image
{
  get
  {
    if (_bitmap == null)
    {
      _bitmap = new Bitmap(_fileName);
    }
    return _bitmap;
  }
}
```

Astute readers will note here that the given file may or may not exist as an actual image file. We expect this or any other exception to be handled by the caller, so that our code does not impose a particular behavior on the calling application.

If you happen to compile this code, the MyPhotoAlbum project does not compile. The error message is something like this:

```
Error       The type or namespace name 'Bitmap' could not be found (are
            you missing a using directive or an assembly reference?)
```

This occurs because `Bitmap` is part of the `System.Drawing` namespace, which is not referenced in our MyPhotoAlbum project. This namespace is provided in a separate library, namely the System.Drawing.dll library, so we need to reference this DLL directly in order to use it in our class.

	ADD THE SYSTEM.DRAWING REFERENCE	
	Action	**Result**
6	Display the Add Reference dialog for the MyPhotoAlbum project. **How-to** In the context menu for the MyPhoto-Album project in the Solution Explorer window, right-click the References item and select Add Reference.	A portion of this dialog box is shown here. 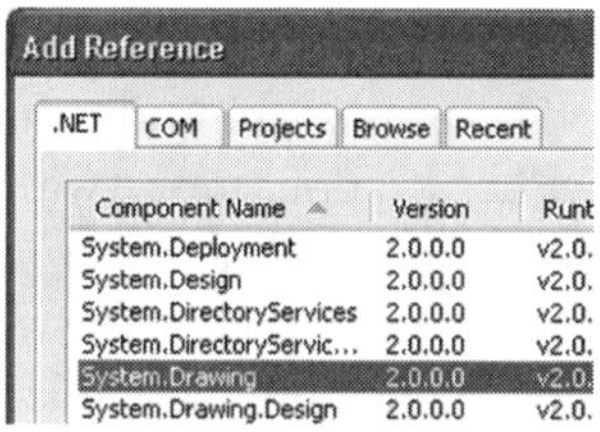
7	Add the System.Drawing.dll assembly as a reference. **How-to** a. Select the System.Drawing.dll entry in the .NET tab. b. Click the OK button.	The `System.Drawing` assembly appears as a reference for the MyPhotoAlbum project. 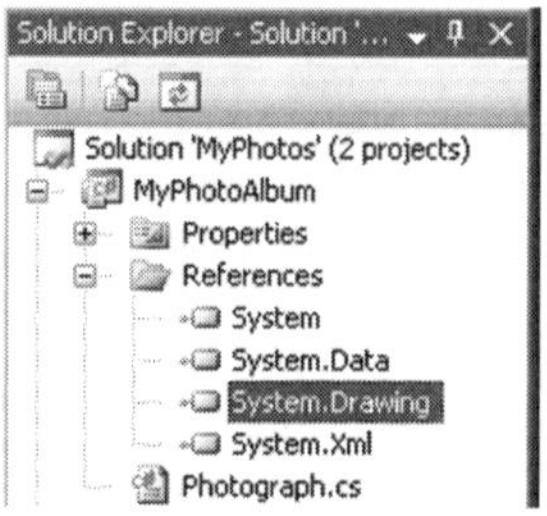

8	Add a `using` directive for the `System.Drawing` namespace at the top of the Photograph.cs file.	`using System;`
		`using System.Collections.Generic;`
		`using System.Drawing;`
		`. . .`

Now the project should compile with no errors. The next section defines the remaining properties for the class.

5.1.4 Defining class properties

Each of the remaining properties provides read and write access to a simple type of data. Some developers advocate defining a private member to hold the data, and a public property for external access. A `Caption` property, for example, might look like this:

```
private string _caption;

public string Caption
{
  get { return _caption; }
  set { _caption = value; }
}
```

This works well, provides the desired interface, and is a fine solution. Other developers argue that a public field provides equivalent functionality, is a little easier to type, and doesn't require properties that essentially do nothing. In this form, the Caption property is a single line:

```
public string Caption;
```

If required, this form can always be converted to a property later on. So is there anything wrong with this approach? As is often the case, that depends.

The purists point out that properties are invoked by external programs, like our MyPhotos application, with a method-like syntax. As you might guess, the get accessor is invoked via a get_*PropertyName* construct, while the set accessor is invoked via a set_*PropertyName* construct. So later on, if you convert a public Caption field into a public Caption property, then any code using the library must be recompiled in order to access these internal property methods. This could be a problem depending on where and how the application is built. As a result, the property construct is safer and better insulates external assemblies from future changes. In a large or highly distributed project, and perhaps even for most projects, I recommend the property approach since it is indeed the safer option.

In our case, we also want to track when a Photograph object has been modified, so the property approach is required as well as preferred.

ADD PUBLIC PHOTOGRAPH PROPERTIES		
	Action	**Result**

1	Add private fields to the Photograph class to hold a caption, photographer, date, notes for the picture, and an indication of whether this object has been modified.
	Also initialize these fields to an appropriate value.
		`private string _caption = "";`
		`private string _photographer = "";`
		`private DateTime _dateTaken = DateTime.Now;`
		`private string _notes = "";`
		`private bool _hasChanged = true;`
		Note: We can't really show it here, but it is good practice to group all private fields in a file in one location. The DateTime structure represents a specific day and time. We discuss this structure in more detail in chapter 14.

2	In the constructor, initialize the caption field to the base name of the file.	`public Photograph(string fileName)`
		`{`
		`  . . .`
		`  _caption = System.IO.Path.`
		`      GetFileNameWithoutExtension(fileName);`
		`}`

3	Define a HasChanged property so users can identify when a Photograph object has been modified.	`public bool HasChanged`
		`{`
		`  get { return _hasChanged; }`
		`  internal set { _hasChanged = value; }`
		`}`
		Note: Here we define a public get accessor available to all users, and an internal set accessor available only to members of the MyPhotoAlbum assembly. The ability to assign different access modifiers in C# is new as of .NET 2.0.

ADD PUBLIC PHOTOGRAPH PROPERTIES *(CONTINUED)*

<table>
<tr><th></th><th>Action</th><th>Result</th></tr>
<tr><td>4</td><td>Define a public <code>Caption</code> property.

How-to
In the get accessor, simply return the current value.

In the set accessor, indicate the class has been modified when a new value is assigned.</td><td>

```
public string Caption
{
  get { return _caption; }
  set
  {
    if (_caption != value)
    {
      _caption = value;
      HasChanged = true;
    }
  }
}
```

</td></tr>
<tr><td>5</td><td>Define similar public <code>Photographer</code>, <code>DateTaken</code>, and <code>Notes</code> properties.

Note: The code here is written in a compressed format to make this table a bit smaller. If you enter or cut and paste this text into Visual Studio, it will lay it out differently, which is fine.</td><td>

```
public string Photographer
{
  get { return _photographer; }
  set { if (_photographer != value) {
          _photographer = value;
          HasChanged = true; }
  }
}

public DateTime DateTaken
{
  get { return _dateTaken; }
  set { if (_dateTaken != value) {
          _dateTaken = value;
          HasChanged = true; }
  }
}

public string Notes
{
  get { return _notes; }
  set { if (_notes != value) {
          _notes = value;
          HasChanged = true; }
  }
}
```

</td></tr>
</table>

Our code defines a `_hasChanged` field to track when the object has changed. Note how a new photograph is always marked as changed so it will be stored if required (more on this later). Each property `set` accessor assigns `true` to the `HasChanged` property whenever the value has actually changed.

There are a few types used here that we have not seen before. The `DateTime` structure represents a date and time, with the `Now` property representing the current day and time.

The `Path` class, part of the `System.IO` namespace, provides methods for manipulating file paths. Here we use the `GetFileNameWithoutExtension` method, which returns the base filename without the dot and extension portions. So, for example, in a `Photograph` object constructed using the "C:\Images\castle.jpg" filename, the `Caption` property is set to "castle." Note how we use the fully qualified name of the method for this class so we can avoid adding a using directive for the `System.IO` namespace at the top of the file.

The last portion of our `Photograph` class is the method definitions. The methods proposed in listing 5.1 are based on methods provided by the `object` class, so we present them in a new section.

5.2 THE OBJECT CLASS

As we have repeatedly indicated, all classes in C# implicitly inherit from the `object` class, which is the same as `System.Object` class. In this section we look at the `Object` class in detail, and override some methods inherited from this class in our `Photograph` class.

5.2.1 Comparing object and Object

You may wonder why there is both an `object` and an `Object`, and the answer is both simple and confusing. The `object` class is part of the C# language definition, and all types, be they built-in or specific to your program, ultimately inherit from `object`.

Separate and somewhat independent of the C# language definition is the .NET Framework, containing classes and namespaces used to generate programs and services of all kinds. The `System` namespace in the framework defines various classes required by languages such as C#, including the `System.Object` class. In Microsoft's C# compiler, the `System.Object` class is equivalent to the C# `object` class. So `object` and `Object` are different but functionally equivalent. In this book, we use both classes interchangeably, with a preference toward the language-specific `object`. An overview of the `object` class is shown in .NET Table 5.2.

Note that a similar discussion applies to the classes `string` and `System.String` as well.

5.2.2 Overriding object methods

Look closely at the `Equals` method in .NET Table 5.2. In our `Photograph` class, we would like two photographs to be equal if they represent the same file. By default, this is not the case. Since `Photograph` is a reference type, two objects are currently equal only if they refer to the same physical storage in memory. It doesn't matter if both objects internally represent the same image file. If they are different references, they are not equal. This behavior should come as no surprise to any seasoned Java coders among us, but might seem a little strange to programmers accustomed to C++ or Visual Basic behavior.

To ensure that `Photograph` objects compare as expected, we must override the `Equals` method. Our override returns `true` if the two photos refer to the same file, and `false` in all other situations.

We should also override the `GetHashCode` method. The default `GetHashCode` implementation for the `object` class returns different hash values for different references, which works fine when two physically different objects are never equal. In our

.NET Table 5.2 object class

The `object` class is the base class for all objects in C#, including the built-in types such as `int` and `bool`. The `System.Object` class is equivalent to the C# language `object` class in the .NET Framework.

Public Static Methods	Equals	Determines if two objects are equal.
	ReferenceEquals	Determines if two objects both refer to the same object instance.
Public Methods	Equals	Determines whether a given object is the same as the current object. Performs bitwise equality for value types, and object equality for reference types.
	GetHashCode	Returns an integer suitable for use as a hash code for the object. Objects that are equal should return the same value, so you should override this method if you override `Equals`.
	GetType	Returns the `Type` object representing the C# language metadata associated with the object.
	ToString	Returns a `string` that represents the current object. By default, the fully qualified name of the object's type is returned.

case, since two different photographs are equal if they refer to the same file, this means that two `Photograph` objects that refer to the same filename would return different hash values.[2] This would make it rather difficult to look up `Photograph` objects in a hash table. As a rule, you should always (yes, always!) override `GetHashCode` if you are overriding the `Equals` method.

OVERRIDE THE EQUALS AND GETHASHCODE METHODS

	Action	Result

1	In the Photograph.cs file, provide an override of the `Equals` method that compares filenames.	`public override bool Equals(object obj)`
		`{`
		`  if (obj is Photograph)`
		`  {`
		`    Photograph p = (Photograph)obj;`
		
		`    return (FileName.Equals(p.FileName,`
		`      StringComparison.`
		`        InvariantCultureIgnoreCase));`
		`  }`
		
		`  return false;`
		`}`

[2] This discussion assumes you understand hashing and hash tables. A standard hash table uses a key, or hash code, as an index into a table. Each entry in the table is a linked list of objects that all hash to the same key. Look up these terms on the Internet for a detailed discussion of this topic.

	Override the Equals and GetHashCode methods *(continued)*	
	Action	**Result**

2	Override the `GetHashCode` method.
	How-to
	Use the `GetHashCode` method on the contained filename.
		`public override int GetHashCode()`
		`{`
		`  return FileName.`
		`      ToLowerInvariant().GetHashCode();`
		`}`

The `Equals` implementation here packs a number of new concepts into one method, so let's break this method down line by line:

1. In C#, the `override` keyword is required to override a virtual method. Using the `virtual` keyword here would cause a compile error, since the method name is already declared as virtual in the base class. The `override` keyword indicates that the `Equals` method here serves the same purpose as this base member. To define a new meaning for an inherited member and hide the original definition, the `new` modifier is used instead of the `override` keyword. The `Equals` method returns a boolean value, which is the `bool` type in C#. The possible values for a `bool` instance are `true` and `false`.
2. Since we must handle any given `object` here, we only perform our comparison if the given object is a `Photograph`. We use the `is` keyword for this purpose, which evaluates to `true` if the variable has the given type, and `false` otherwise. As a result this code may perform two cast operations—one for the `is` keyword, and one for the actual downcast to the `Photograph` type.
3. The default `String.Equals` method performs a case-sensitive comparison of strings. That is, "book" and "book" are equal, but "book" and "Book" are not. To ignore capitalization in our filename strings, we use an alternate form of the `String.Equals` method that accepts a `StringComparison` enumeration value to indicate how the strings should be compared. The `StringComparison.InvariantCultureIgnoreCase` setting causes a culture-insensitive comparison to be performed that ignores character case. Look up this enumeration in the documentation to see the other comparison values.
4. Note how `false` is always returned if the given object is not a `Photograph`.

It is also worth noting that the `String` class overrides the `Equals` method to perform a value-based case-sensitive comparison of its contents, even though it is a reference type. This ensures that two `String` objects are identical as long as they contain the same set of characters in the same order, based on the comparison method.

This code also introduces the invariant culture. A culture represents a specific language and region, such as U.S. English, or Canadian French. The *current culture* is the current system's culture. The *invariant culture* is associated with the English language but not with a country or region. We use it here to obtain a culture-independent result for our comparison. In the GetHashCode implementation, we use the invariant form of the ToLower method for a similar effect.

Let's override the ToString method here as well. The default implementation returns the string "Manning.MyPhotoAlbum.Photograph" every time, which is not very illuminating. A more useful implementation would return the filename associated with the photograph, as shown in the following step.

OVERRIDE THE TOSTRING METHOD		
	Action	**Result**

3	Override the ToString method to return the contained filename.	`public override string ToString()`
		`{`
		`  return FileName;`
		`}`

Compile the code to verify that we have not made any errors. These overrides of the base object methods will come in useful in future chapters. Since they are found in every object, Windows Forms controls make use of these methods whenever an object must be compared with another object or a corresponding string displayed in a window. In particular, in chapter 11 we show how list controls utilize the ToString method by default when displaying an object in a list. Because of this somewhat ubiquitous use, providing a reasonable ToString implementation for your classes is always a good idea.

This completes our implementation of the Photograph class for now. Our next topic discusses the implementation of the PhotoAlbum class.

5.3 INTERFACES

We need to represent an album in a way that facilitates the required actions, such as "add an image," "move to the next photo," and so forth. You may immediately think of some sort of array, and this is indeed our approach. This section presents a short design discussion as a way to introduce some terminology we require and lay the groundwork for writing our code.

We have already seen that C# and .NET provide some direct support for collections. In chapter 4 we used the foreach keyword to iterate through a menu item collection, and we have used the Add and AddRange methods to add objects to collections of one form or another. It would be nice if we could support such .NET collection methods in our PhotoAlbum class so that albums in our application could be handled in a similar manner.

This is, of course, possible, and is the subject of the next two sections. We begin with interfaces, and introduce generics as an alternate approach in the subsequent section.

5.3.1 Interfaces and collections

An *interface* is an abstraction of an abstraction, and should be familiar to programmers of COM or its UNIX ancestor, the distributed computing environment (DCE). While a class encapsulates a data structure and its operations, an interface encapsulates a type of data structure and its operations. This can be confusing. Said another way: a class defines a set of operations, while an interface defines a set of operations that classes can support.

This is similar to an abstract class, except that an interface does not provide implementations of any members; it just defines the properties, methods, and events that a class must implement in order to support the interface. An interface encapsulates a common idea for use by unrelated classes, while an abstract class encapsulates a common idea for use by related classes.

For example, the .NET `ICollection` interface defines a type that serves as a collection for other objects. A number of classes hold or behave as collections throughout the .NET Framework, including the `Array`, `ToolStrip`, `Form`, and `DataSet` classes. Languages such as C++ provide multiple inheritance for this kind of support. In C++, `ICollection` could be an abstract class and inherited where needed. In C# and Java, only single inheritance is supported, so this is not possible. Instead, both languages provide interfaces as a way to encapsulate common functionality that can be used by a wide range of classes.

For example, the `ArrayList` class holds an array of objects, and supports the `ICollection` interface. You can create an instance of `ArrayList`, since it is a class, but you cannot create an instance of `ICollection` except as a by-product of an existing class that happens to support this interface.

The .NET Framework provides interfaces for everything from enumerating members of a collection to transferring data between applications. Some interfaces related to our current discussion on albums are listed in table 5.3.

Table 5.3 Interfaces related to data collections

Interface	Description	Members
IEnumerable	Interface that supports the creation of an enumerator class for iterating over the elements in a collection. **Usage:** Supporting this interface allows the C# `foreach` statement to be used with instances of a class or structure.	`GetEnumerator` method, which returns a class that supports the `IEnumerator` interface

Table 5.3 Interfaces related to data collections *(continued)*

Interface	Description	Members
IEnumerator	Interface for stepping through the elements in a collection.	`Current` property, to retrieve the current element from the collection `MoveNext` method, which advances to the next element in the collection `Reset` method, which sets the enumerator just before the first element
ICollection	An `IEnumerable` interface that provides sizing and synchronization capabilities. This interface is the basis for all collections in the .NET Framework.	`Count` property, to retrieve the number of elements in the collection `SyncRoot` property, to retrieve an object for synchronizing multithreaded access to the collection `CopyTo` method, which copies the elements in the collection into an `Array` object
IList	An `ICollection` interface that provides indexing of its elements. **Usage:** Supporting this interface allows a class or structure to be treated as an array. This permits objects to be used as targets of data bound controls, as discussed in chapter 21.	`Item` property, to support array-style indexing of elements using [brackets], much like a `[]` override in C++ `Add` method, which adds a new element to the collection `Contains` method, which determines if the collection contains a specific object `Remove` method, to remove the element from the collection at a given index value

5.3.2 Appreciating collection classes

Suppose we wish to implement our `PhotoAlbum` class in terms of a collection interface. Looking over the interfaces in the table 5.3, the `IList` interface seems particularly appropriate for the task at hand. This allows elements to be added and removed from the collection, and supports array-style indexing. Some of the data collection classes in the .NET Framework are shown in table 5.4. Note, in particular, those classes in the table that support the `IList` interface.

Since we do not have a database here, the `DataView` class is not appropriate. The `StringCollection` class would be great for a collection of filenames. This leaves us with a simple array or the `ArrayList` or `CollectionBase` class. A simple fixed-size array is not appropriate since we would like our album to grow dynamically. So we are left to choose between the `ArrayList` and `CollectionBase` classes.

An overview of the `ArrayList` class is shown in .NET Table 5.5. We do not ultimately use this implementation, but it is worth a short discussion. Deriving our `PhotoAlbum` class from `ArrayList` would look like this:

```
// Deriving PhotoAlbum from ArrayList (not our approach)
public class PhotoAlbum : System.Collections.ArrayList
{
    // Inherits all properties and methods from ArrayList
}
```

An advantage of this approach is that we would not need to explicitly implement most methods, since they would be directly inherited from `ArrayList`. A disadvantage is that all methods would accept any `object`, and not just `Photograph` objects. If you look at the documentation, you will see that the methods in `ArrayList` operate on `object` instances. For example, the `PhotoAlbum.Add` method would have the following signature:

```
// PhotoAlbum.Add when derived from ArrayList
public int Add( object value );
```

Programmers using our class could add filename strings, bitmap images, or any other object directly to the album. So although this would be a very easy implementation, the methods in our `PhotoAlbum` class would not be type-safe, and therefore not be so robust.

Table 5.4 Some of the .NET collection classes

Class	Description	Interfaces supported
Array	A fixed-sized array. This abstract class is the base class for all simple arrays in .NET.	`ICloneable`, `IList`, `ICollection`, `IEnumerable`
ArrayList	A dynamically sized array.	`ICloneable`, `IList`, `ICollection`, `IEnumerable`
CollectionBase	An abstract class for creating a strongly typed collection.	`IList`, `ICollection`, `IEnumerable`
DataView	A customized view of a database table.	`IList`, `ICollection`, `IEnumerable`, and others
Hashtable	A collection that stores values based on a hash code, called a key.	`ICloneable`, `ICollection`, `IEnumerable`, `IDictionary`, and others
Queue	A FIFO queue; a first-in, first-out collection of objects.	`ICloneable`, `ICollection`, `IEnumerable`
SortedList	A sorted collection of keys and values accessible by both key and index.	`ICloneable`, `ICollection`, `IEnumerable`, `IDictionary`
StringCollection	A collection of `string` objects.	`IList`, `ICollection`, `IEnumerable`
Stack	A LIFO queue; a last-in, first-out collection of objects.	`ICloneable`, `ICollection`, `IEnumerable`

.NET Table 5.5 ArrayList class

The `ArrayList` class is a collection of indexed objects where the number of objects can change dynamically. This class is part of the `System.Collections` namespace, and is very similar to the `Array` class for fixed-length collections of objects. The `ArrayList` class supports the `ICloneable`, `IEnumerable`, `ICollection`, and `IList` interfaces.

Public Properties	Capacity	Gets or sets the maximum number of objects the list can contain.
	Count	Gets or sets the actual number of objects in the array.
Public Methods	Add	Adds an object to the end of the array.
	AddRange	Adds a given array or collection to the end of the array.
	Clear	Removes all objects from the array.
	Contains	Determines if an object is in the array. Comparison is done using the `Equals` method.
	CopyTo	Copies the `ArrayList`, or a portion of it, into a one-dimensional `Array` object.
	IndexOf	Returns the zero-based index of the first occurrence of the given object in the array, or `-1` if the object is not found. Comparison is done using the `Equals` method.
	Remove	Removes an object from the array.
	RemoveAt	Removes the object at a given index from the array.
	Sort	Sorts the array based on a given `IComparable` interface.
	TrimToSize	Sets the capacity to the actual number of objects in the array list.

Another alternative would use a private `ArrayList` object in a class derived directly from System.Object. This alternative is sketched out in listing 5.2. This implementation is now type-safe, since the programmer does not have access to the internal `ArrayList` used to store the photographs.

Listing 5.2 PhotoAlbum class with private ArrayList (not our approach)

```
public class PhotoAlbum : IList, IEnumerable
{
  // internal (not inherited) ArrayList
  private ArrayList _photoList;

  // Constructor and other wrappers
  . . .

  #region IList interface implementation
  // Custom Add wrapper
```

```
    public int Add(Photograph photo)
    {
      return _photoList.Add(photo);
    }

    // Custom Clear wrapper
    . . .
    #endregion // IList interface

    #region IEnumerable interface implementation
    // Custom GetEnumerator wrapper
    . . .
    #endregion // IEnumerable interface
  }
```

As it turns out, the CollectionBase class exists to support this type of implementation directly, avoiding some of the code outlined in listing 5.2. An overview of this class is shown in .NET Table 5.6. This class is abstract, and requires derived classes to implement the additional methods required to support the appropriate interfaces. This requires a little more work than inheriting from ArrayList, but less work than the type of implementation shown in listing 5.2. A ReadOnlyCollectionBase class also exists for building read-only collections.

.NET Table 5.6 CollectionBase class

The CollectionBase class is an abstract class for creating strongly typed collections. A class is *strongly typed* if it only allows a specific type or types in its methods, rather than a general type such as object. Strongly typed classes allow the compiler to ensure that the proper objects are passed to methods in the class, and can prevent errors that would otherwise occur only at runtime.

The CollectionBase class is part of the System.Collections namespace. It supports the IEnumerable, ICollection, and IList interfaces.

Public Properties	Capacity	Gets or sets the number of objects the collection can contain
	Count	Gets the actual number of objects in the collection
Public Methods	Clear	Removes all objects from the collection
	GetEnumerator	Returns an IEnumerator object that can iterate through the elements in the collection
	RemoveAt	Removes the object at a given index from the array
Protected Properties	InnerList	Gets an ArrayList instance representing the collection
	List	Gets an IList instance representing the collection

Deriving from the CollectionBase class used to be the recommended way to build strongly typed collections, such as the PhotoAlbum class as a collection of

Photograph objects. Prior to .NET 2.0, this was the best approach for building such collections. As of .NET 2.0, C# supports a concept called *generics*, with even better support. If you wish to build your own, however, CollectionBase is the way to go.

Since we plan to implement the PhotoAlbum class using generics, we do not show an entire CollectionBase solution. An implementation is outlined in listing 5.3. The numbered sections are discussed in the subsequent paragraphs.

Listing 5.3 PhotoAlbum class derived from CollectionBase (not our approach)

```
using System;
using System.Collections;

namespace Manning.MyPhotoAlbum
{
  public class PhotoAlbum : CollectionBase        <-- 1 Inherits from CollectionBase
  {
    // No constructor required     <-- 2 Lacks a constructor

    // IEnumerable interface is provided by the CollectionBase class
    // This allows use of the foreach construct with albums

#region ICollection members
    public virtual bool IsSynchronized
    {
      get { return false; }
    }

    public void CopyTo(Photograph[] array, int index)
    {
      List.CopyTo(array, index);
    }
    // not shown: SyncRoot
    . . .
#endregion ICollection members
                                   3 Implements ICollection members
#region IList members
    public int Add(Photograph p)
    {
      return List.Add(p);
    }
    public Photograph this[int index]
    {
      get { return (Photograph)(List[index]);
      set { List[index] = value; }
    }
                                   4 Implements array-style indexing
    // not shown: IsFixedSize, IsReadOnly
    // not shown: Contains(), IndexOf(), Insert(), Remove()
    . . .
#endregion IList members
  }
}
```

❶ As already mentioned, classes in C# support inheritance from a single class only, in this case from the `CollectionBase` class, although multiple interfaces can be specified. This is the same as Java, and a break from C++. Also unlike the C++ language, C# classes do not support private or protected inheritance.

❷ A constructor is not required, and in fact an empty constructor may hurt your performance. As in C++, classes without an explicit constructor automatically provide a default constructor with no arguments.

❸ The members of the `ICollection` and `IList` interfaces are implemented using the `Photograph` class in place of the `object` parameter. This ensures compile-time checks and helps prevent programming errors. Properties such as `IsSynchronized` can be implemented to return `false`. Methods like `CopyTo` or `Add` can use the corresponding method on the protected `List` property.

❹ The C# language allows an *indexer* to define array-style access into a collection or other class. Here we define integer-based indexing, so `myAlbum[0]` retrieves the first `Photograph` in the collection, `myAlbum[1]` the second, and so forth. The syntax employs accessor methods similar to the declaration of properties, with the `this` keyword referring to the class itself and a variable defining the index value within the definition. In this example, the indexer defines retrieval and assignment access to the array of `Photograph` objects in the collection. Any collection class can be treated as an indexed array through the use of a similar indexer definition.

Collection classes are used throughout the .NET Framework, so it is good to understand what they are and how to implement them explicitly. In practice, the best way to implement a collection class, including our `PhotoAlbum` class, is by leveraging the generics support in C#.

5.4 GENERICS

As already indicated, version 2.0 of the .NET Framework provides support for generics and more specifically generic collections. This section defines this concept and applies it to the `PhotoAlbum` class we have been discussing.

5.4.1 Generic classes

One of the great benefits of object-oriented programming is the ability to encapsulate an object and reuse it in different applications. Our `Photograph` class is one example of this idea. This is great for encapsulating a specific abstraction, such as a photograph or a database table. Where object encapsulation comes up short is when you need to encapsulate a concept rather than an object.

The idea of a collection is a good example. While interfaces such as `ICollection` and `IList` allow us to define what a collection might look like, they do not let us define an actual collection. It would be great if we could define some sort of reusable model for a collection class, and then plug in any arbitrary type to automatically define a collection for that type. Such a feature would allow us, for example, to easily create a PhotoAlbum class as a collection for the Photograph type.

Generics attempt to address this issue with a mechanism for defining generalized solutions and design patterns that are type-safe and efficient. Generic classes use angle brackets (<>) to define a generalized type that is referenced within the class. Listing 5.4 shows an example of this in a type-safe stack implementation using generics. A stack works like a stack of dishes. You *push* onto the top of the stack, and can only remove, or *pop*, off the top.

Listing 5.4 Stack implementation using generics

```
using System;
using System.Collections;

  public class MyStack<T>
  {
    private ArrayList _list;

    public Stack()
    {
      _list = new ArrayList();
    }

    public void Push(T item)
    {
      _list.Add(item);
    }

    public T Pop()
    {
      int len = _list.Count;
      object item = _list[len - 1];
      _list.RemoveAt(len - 1);

      return (T)item;
    }
  }
```

❶ Generic type definition
❷ Push implementation
❸ Pop implementation

Let's look at the salient points of listing 5.4:

❶ The angle brackets indicate to the compiler that this is a generic class definition. By convention, a T is typically used to indicate the *type parameter*, as it is called. Multiple type parameters can be specified, separated by commas. When MyStack<T> is instantiated with a concrete type, each occurrence of T is replaced with the given type. The T type parameter can be used throughout the class definition, in properties, methods, and even nested classes.

❷ The generic Push method accepts a parameter T and adds it to an internal list. When the class is instantiated, this ensures that only objects of type T can be placed on the stack. The .NET Stack class provides identical functionality for object types, but without any type safety. This implementation is type-safe, providing compile-time checking for the given type parameter.

❸ The generic `Pop` method returns an object of type `T`. In this code the last object in the list is removed and cast to the generic type `T`.

The generic `MyStack<T>` class allows a type-safe stack object of any type to be defined. For example, an integer, string, and photo stack are defined by the following lines:

```
MyStack<int> integerStack = new MyStack<int>();
MyStack<string> stringStack = new MyStack<string>();
MyStack<Photograph> photoStack = new MyStack<Photograph>();
```

With this brief introduction to generics in place, let's take a look at the generic collections provided by .NET.

5.4.2 Appreciating generic collections

The `System.Collections.Generic` namespace provides a rather extensive set of generic classes for supporting and manipulating type-safe collections in .NET. With the introduction of these classes in .NET 2.0, there is little reason to implement custom collections in .NET except for compatibility with prior versions of the .NET Framework or for applications that require strict compliance with the Common Language Specification (CLS). A summary of the types in this namespace appears in .NET Table 5.7.

As you can see from the table, an extensive set of collection-related types are provided. These allow us to create type-safe objects quickly and easily. You want a queue that contains only strings and a dictionary indexed on integers that stores `ToolStripMenuItem` objects. This is easily done:

```
Queue<string> stringQueue = new Queue<string>();
Dictionary<int, ToolStripMenuItem> menuDictionary
    = new Dictionary<int, ToolStripMenuItem>();
```

In a similar manner, we can create an album object as a list collection of `Photograph` objects with this code:

```
List<Photograph> album = new List<Photograph>();
```

While this certainly works, we would like to encapsulate the concept of an album in a class definition. Doing so defines this concept as a type, namely the `PhotoAlbum` class, and allows us to add functionality in future chapters.

We also need to support the more general `IList` interface that can be customized to fit our needs. The `System.Collections.ObjectModel` namespace provides additional generic classes that more directly support custom collections. This namespace includes the `Collection<T>` class for creating custom lists, the `KeyedCollection<T>` class for creating custom dictionaries, and the `ReadOnlyCollection<T>` class for creating custom read-only collections.

.NET Table 5.7 System.Collections.Generic namespace

New in 2.0 The System.Collections.Generic namespace provides generic classes and interfaces for strongly typed collections. The classes in this namespace provide type safety and robust performance, and are generally preferred over non-generic collections.

Classes	*Comparer<T>*	Defines a comparison class for equivalence and sorting of a generic type.
	Dictionary<K, V>	Defines a collection of key-value pairs organized by key.
	LinkedList<T>	Defines a generic doubly linked list.
	List<T>	Defines a generic list that supports the IList interface.
	Queue<T>	Defines a FIFO collection class. This is a type-safe version of the Queue class.
	Stack<T>	Defines a LIFO collection class. This is a type-safe version of the Stack class.
Interfaces	*ICollection<T>*	Specifies methods that define and manipulate generic collections. This mimics the ICollection interface for nongeneric collections.
	IEnumerable<T>	Specifies the GetEnumerator method to support simple iteration over a generic collection. This method returns an IEnumerator<T> interface instance. This mimics the IEnumerable interface for nongeneric collections.
Structures	*KeyValuePair<K, V>*	Defines a type-safe key-value pair for use in generic dictionary classes.
	List<T>.Enumerator	Enumerates the elements of a List<T> collection.

The difference between Collection<T> and List<T> is apparent when you try to customize the internal behavior of the list. The List<T> class is basically a straight implementation of the methods required by the IList interface. The Collection<T> class additionally defines protected methods that can affect how items are internally handled. These methods are shown in .NET Table 5.8.

As you can see, the Collection<T> class provides protected members that allow a class to alter the logic for clear, add, insert, and set operations. We need these methods to implement a HasChanged property for our album.

.NET Table 5.8 Collection<T> class

New in 2.0 The Collection<T> class is a base class for generic collections. This class provides an extensible IList implementation suitable for creating custom generic collections, and is part of the System.Collections.ObjectModel namespace. The Collection<T> class supports the IList, ICollection, and IEnumerable interfaces.

The public members of this class are the standard properties and methods required by the supported interfaces. Here, we only show the protected methods that enable customized behavior.

Protected Methods	*ClearItems*	Removes all elements from the collection
	InsertItem	Inserts an element into the collection at a given index
	RemoveItem	Removes an element from the collection at a given index
	SetItem	Replaces the element in the collection at a given index

The subsequent steps add the PhotoAlbum.cs class file to our project, in the proper Manning.MyPhotoAlbum namespace. Just to show it can be done, we also extend the generic collection to support an alternate form of the Add method.

DEFINE THE PHOTOALBUM CLASS

	Action	Result
1	Modify the project so that Manning.MyPhotoAlbum is the default root namespace. **How-to** a. Right-click the MyPhotoAlbum project in Solution Explorer and select the Properties option. b. In the Application section, set the Default namespace to "Manning.MyPhotoAlbum."	A portion of the properties tab for the MyPhotoAlbum project is shown here.
2	Add a new class file to the MyPhotoAlbum project called "PhotoAlbum.cs."	The new class is added to the project and displayed in the window.

3	Indicate that we are using the System.Collections.ObjectModel namespace in this file.	Note how the Generic namespace is included by default and how our new default namespace is assigned.
		`using System;`
		`using System.Collections.Generic;`
		`using System.Collections.ObjectModel;`
		`using System.Text;`
		
		`namespace Manning.MyPhotoAlbum`
		`{`

DEFINE THE PHOTOALBUM CLASS *(CONTINUED)*

	Action	Result

4	Modify the `PhotoAlbum` class to be public, and to derive from the generic `Collection<Photograph>` collection class.	`public class PhotoAlbum`
		`        :Collection<Photograph>`
		`{`
		
		Note: This alone defines a complete album class that implements the entire `IList` interface. The rest of these steps extend the behavior of this class.

5	Define a private field to record whether the album has been modified, and initialize it to `false`.	`private bool _hasChanged = false;`

6	Implement a `HasChanged` property that identifies whether the album has been modified.
	
	How-to
	a. For the `get`, return `true` if the local setting is `true`.
	b. Otherwise return `true` only if a contained photo has changed.
	c. Make the `set` internal.
	d. Assign the given value.
	e. If the new setting is `false`, also reset each photo's setting to `false`.
		`public bool HasChanged`
		`{`
		`  get {`
		`    if (_hasChanged) return true;`
		
		`    foreach (Photograph p in this)`
		`      if (p.HasChanged) return true;`
		
		`    return false;`
		`  }`
		
		`  internal set {`
		`    _hasChanged = value;`
		`    if (value == false)`
		`    {`
		`      foreach (Photograph p in this)`
		`        p.HasChanged = false;`
		`    }`
		`  }`
		`}`

7	Implement an alternate `Add` method that accepts the name of a file and adds it to the collection as a new `Photograph` object. Return the new photograph.	`public Photograph Add(string fileName)`
		`{`
		`  Photograph p = new Photograph(fileName);`
		`  base.Add(p);`
		`  return p;`
		`}`

8	Override the protected `ClearItems` method in the `Collection<Photograph>` class to indicate that the collection has changed.	`protected override void ClearItems()`
		`{`
		`  if (Count > 0)`
		`  {`
		`    base.ClearItems();`
		`    HasChanged = true;`
		`  }`
		`}`

	DEFINE THE PHOTOALBUM CLASS *(CONTINUED)*	
	Action	**Result**

9	Similarly, override the other protected methods in the `Collection<Photograph>` class.
	
	Note: We assign the `HasChanged` property after performing the base operation in each method here to ensure that the operation completes successfully before marking the object as changed.
		`protected override void InsertItem(`
		`    int index, Photograph item)`
		`{`
		`  base.InsertItem(index, item);`
		`  HasChanged = true;`
		`}`
		
		`protected override void RemoveItem(int index)`
		`{`
		`  base.RemoveItem(index);`
		`  HasChanged = true;`
		`}`
		
		`protected override void SetItem(`
		`    int index, Photograph item)`
		`{`
		`  base.SetItem(index, item);`
		`  HasChanged = true;`
		`}`

This code completely defines the `PhotoAlbum` class, more succinctly and efficiently than the implementations outlined in listings 5.2 and 5.3. We add, remove, enumerate, and otherwise manipulate `Photograph` objects using this class in the next chapter.

One new concept employed by this code is the use of the `base` keyword. There are two primary uses for this keyword. The first is as a placeholder in the constructor for invoking a constructor in the base class. This is not shown here.

The second use is to access a member of the base class from a derived class. In our specialized `Add` method, we call the `Add` method in the base `Collection<Photograph>` class to add the new `Photograph` to the collection. The `base` keyword facilitates this call.

5.4.3 Disposing of resources

Our `PhotoAlbum` and `Photograph` classes are now fairly well defined. We can create photographs from image files, add photos to—and remove them from—albums, and iterate through the contents of an album. A topic we haven't touched on is the issue of cleaning up a photo or album when we have finished. This is not part of generics per se, but we squeeze this concept into section 5.4 regardless.

You might wonder why we even care. Isn't this the purpose of garbage collection? When we have finished with an album, the garbage collector cleans it up eventually, so why worry about it?

This is true to a point. The problem is that we have no idea when the garbage collector runs. It could be immediately, it could be hours later, or it could even be when the program exits. This is fine for most application memory, but might present a problem for system resources. For example, the creation of a `Bitmap` object requires that a file be opened and loaded into memory. The `Bitmap` object retains a file handle to the disk file. Resources like file handles are limited, so it is a good idea to release them when you have finished.

The preferred method for doing this is through a `Dispose` method as part of the `IDisposable` interface. This interface is summarized in .NET Table 5.9. Since the `Component` class supports the `IDisposable` interface and is the basis for most classes in the `System.Windows.Forms` namespace, most objects in the Windows Forms namespace provide a `Dispose` method for just this purpose.

.NET Table 5.9 IDisposable interface

The `IDisposable` interface indicates that an object can be disposed of. Instances of objects that support this interface should call the `Dispose` method to free system resources before the last reference to the object is discarded. This interface is part of the `System` namespace.

Public Method	Dispose	Releases any system resources used by the object.

Since our `Photograph` class uses a `Bitmap` instance, we should support this interface to enable users of this class to clean up the associated `Bitmap` object. In many cases, it is an error to reference a disposed object. In our case, we allow a user to clear and reuse a `PhotoAlbum` instance, so we leave the album object in a usable state after the `Dispose` method has been called.

SUPPORT THE IDISPOSABLE INTERFACE

	Action	Result

1	In the Photograph.cs source file, indicate that this class supports the `IDisposable` interface.	`public class Photograph : IDisposable`
		`{`
		`. . .`

2	Implement the `Dispose` method.
	How-to
	Implement a `ReleaseImage` method to dispose of the contained bitmap if it exists, and invoke this method from `Dispose`.
		`public void ReleaseImage()`
		`{`
		`if (_bitmap != null)`
		`{`
		`_bitmap.Dispose();`
		`_bitmap = null;`
		`}`
		`}`
		
		`public void Dispose()`
		`{`
		`ReleaseImage();`
		`}`
		`. . .`
		`}`

3	Also support the `IDisposable` interface in the `PhotoAlbum` class.	`public class PhotoAlbum :`
		`Collection<Photograph>, IDisposable`
		`{`
		`. . .`
		Note: The base class must precede any implemented interfaces.

	Support the IDisposable interface *(continued)*	
	Action	**Result**

4	Implement the `Dispose` method for the `PhotoAlbum` class.
	How-to
	Dispose of each `Photograph` in the album.
		`public void Dispose()`
		`{`
		`  foreach (Photograph p in this)`
		`    p.Dispose();`
		`}`
		`. . .`

5	Also modify the `ClearItems` and `RemoveItem` overrides to dispose of the referenced items appropriately.	`protected override void ClearItems()`
		`{`
		`  if (Count > 0)`
		`  {`
		`    Dispose();`
		`    base.ClearItems();`
		`    HasChanged = true;`
		`  }`
		`}`
		`. . .`
		`protected override void RemoveItem(int index)`
		`{`
		`  Items[index].Dispose();`
		`  base.RemoveItem(index);`
		`  HasChanged = true;`
		`}`

Our objects now dispose of their contents properly. Be aware that it may not always be a good idea to dispose of contained objects as we do for the `PhotoAlbum` class here. There are times when an object in a list may be in use elsewhere in the program, and it is best to let the caller or even the garbage collector decide when and how to dispose of any contents. For example, if a single `Photograph` object could be stored in two `PhotoAlbum` objects at the same time, then our `PhotoAlbum.Dispose` implementation would not be appropriate. In our design a single `Photograph` can be a member of at most one album, so the implementation presented here works just fine.

This ends our discussion of the `Photograph` and `PhotoAlbum` classes for now. These classes will serve us throughout the rest of the book, although we make some additional modifications along the way. As usual, we end the chapter with a recap of where we've been.

5.5 Recap

In this chapter we created an external library that applications everywhere can use when a photograph or photo album is required. We implemented a `Photograph` class to encapsulate a photographic image, and a `PhotoAlbum` class to encapsulate a collection of `Photograph` objects. Along the way we examined properties, interfaces, .NET collections, the `object` class, generics, generic collections, and disposable objects.

The MyPhotoAlbum.dll library is ready for use. Integrating this library into our MyPhotos application is the topic of the next chapter. We also make use of this library in future chapters to develop alternate applications based on the photo and album abstractions.

You can find more on collections and generics in .NET on the Internet, of course. One source for additional classes is the Power Collections project. This is a community project aimed at building, in their words, "the best public license collection classes for .NET." This project defines an open source collection class library that extends the collection classes provided by the .NET Framework. The code and specification for this library are available at www.wintellect.com.

CHAPTER 6

Files and common dialog boxes

In chapter 5 we created the `Photograph` and `PhotoAlbum` classes as a way to encapsulate a photographic image and a collection of photographs. In this chapter we make use of these classes in our MyPhotos application to display a photo album to the user. We keep our model of one photo at a time, but allow a user to move forward and backward within the album. This permits us to focus on integrating the MyPhotoAlbum library without changing the user interface too much.

This chapter builds on our library to introduce some additional concepts. We expand our menu bar and introduce some additional Windows Forms features. Specifically, this chapter shows how to perform the following tasks:

- Use the `PhotoAlbum` and `Photograph` classes to display, navigate, and manage a set of photographs in the MyPhotos application.
- Insert a standard set of menus into a menu strip.
- Allow multiple files to be selected using the `OpenFileDialog` class.

- Save a file using the `SaveFileDialog` class.
- Utilize the `StreamReader` and `StreamWriter` classes to read and write text files to and from the file system.
- Create a custom exception class to encapsulate a specific type of error.

Our discussion begins with the standard menu bars provided by Visual Studio.

6.1 STANDARD MENUS

Figure 6.1 illustrates some of the changes we make in this chapter, with the new File menu displayed. The name for this album, Leeds Castle, is displayed on the title bar of the form as well. The status strip displays a short caption for the photograph, as well as the current position within the album.

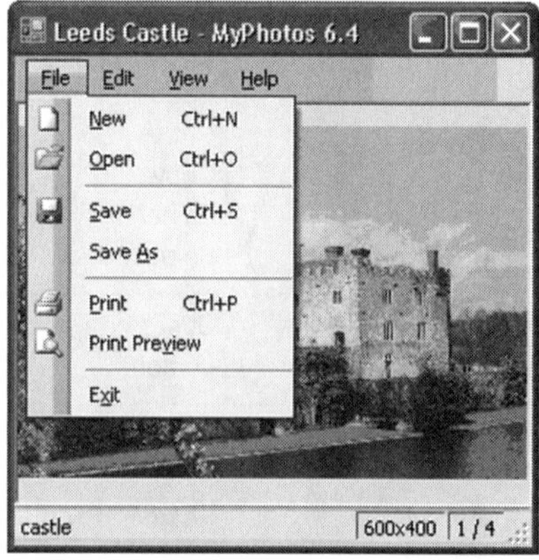

Figure 6.1 This chapter implements a more traditional File menu structure in our application.

The changes planned for this chapter require that we rewrite our menu bar. It is always a good idea to sketch your graphical elements and changes up front. You can even do this on paper. The point is to have in mind the graphical interface you wish to implement before you start writing code. While it is always possible to move menus and other objects around, it can also waste a lot of time. This is especially true if the application has to be approved by a manager, the customer, or anyone else. Doing a prototype or even a quick sketch on paper creates a basis for discussion and allows initial thoughts and ideas to be aired before a more formal design document or any code is written.

That said, the .NET Framework provides a standard set of menus that make sense in many applications. So here we simply incorporate the standard menus into our application and define a way to access an album manager within our form.

6.1.1 Changing the menu bar

The good folks at Microsoft realize how tedious it is to lay out a whole bunch of menus for an application. In an effort to simplify the task, and perhaps to standardize application menu layout, a standard set of menus and menu items is provided for use in Windows programs. These mimic what is seen in many Microsoft products, and therefore define a reasonable starting point for most applications. The standard menu items supported by Visual Studio are shown in table 6.1.

Table 6.1 The standard menu items provided by Visual Studio

Menu	Menu item	Shortcut	Usage in MyPhotos application
File	New	Ctrl+N	Creates a new album; see section 6.2.1.
	Open	Ctrl+O	Opens an existing photo album file; see section 6.2.2.
	Save	Ctrl+S	Saves the current album; see section 6.2.3.
	Save As	Ctrl+P	Saves the current album in a new file; see section 6.2.3.
	Print		Prints the current image; see section 23.1.
	Print Preview		Previews the current print selection; see section 23.1.
	Exit		Exits the application; see section 6.2.4.
Edit	Undo	Ctrl+Z	Undoes the latest change; not used in this book.
	Redo	Ctrl+Y	Redoes an undone change; not used in this book.
	Cut	Ctrl+X	Cuts an image from the album; see section 15.1.1.
	Copy	Ctrl+C	Copies an image from the album; see section 15.1.1.
	Paste	Ctrl+V	Pastes a copied image into the album; see section 15.1.1.
	Select All		Selects all items on the form; not used in this book.
Tools	Customize		Customizes application settings; not used in this book.
	Options		Modifies application options; not used in this book.
Help	Contents		Displays contents; not used in this book.
	Index		Displays index; not used in this book.
	Search		Searches help; not used in this book.
	About		Displays About Box for an application; see section 23.3.

It is tempting to use our own terminology and establish our own conventions here. For example, why not use an "Album" main menu instead of the File menu, or save Ctrl+N as the shortcut for a Next photo rather than the New album menu? The short answer: don't do it. Computer users appreciate familiarity and resist change (so do most consumers and small children, but I digress). The File menu is standard in most Windows applications, and Ctrl+N is used for creating a new object (be it a document in Microsoft Word, or an image in Adobe PhotoShop). Unless you intend your application to be somewhat contrary, use existing standards where possible.[1]

So even though Ctrl+N and Ctrl+P would make nice shortcuts for Next and Previous, we stick with Ctrl+N for New and Ctrl+P for printing. We replace our existing menu with the standard structure with the following steps.

[1] For detailed information on these and other guidelines recommended by Microsoft, see the "Official Guidelines for User Interface Developers and Designers" at http://msdn.microsoft.com/library/en-us/dnwue/html/welcome.asp. See appendix B of these guidelines for keyboard shortcuts.

Modify menu strip to use standard items		
	Action	**Results**
1	In the MainForm.cs [Designer] window, display the Tasks dialog box associated with the MenuStrip control. **How-to** With the menu strip highlighted, click the smart tag arrow at the top right of the strip.	MenuStrip Tasks Embed in ToolStripContainer Insert Standard Items RenderMode: ManagerRenderMode Dock: Top GripStyle: Hidden Edit Items...
2	Insert the standard menu items. **How-to** Click the Insert Standard Items link.	The standard menu items are added to the menu strip. MyPhotos File View File Edit Tools Help
3	Delete the prior File menu. **How-to** Select the menu and press the Delete key.	The first File menu and the contained Load and Exit menu items are deleted. **Note:** The existing event handlers for the Load and Exit menu items remain in the source file. We make use of this code later in the chapter.
4	Move the View menu between the new Edit and Tools menus. **How-to** Click and drag the View menu to the desired location.	MyPhotos File Edit View Tools Help
5	Delete the Undo, Redo, and Select All items from the Edit menu, the entire Tools menu, and all of the items from the Help menu except for the About menu item.	We do not make use of these menu items in this book.
6	Rename the new menus to our naming convention if desired. **How-to** Unfortunately there is no easy way to rename these items, so each one must be modified manually.	**Note:** Our convention from chapter 3 is *menu[item]*. So the File menu is `menuFile`, and contains items `menuFileNew`, `menuFileOpen`, `menuFileSave`, and so forth. The default name is fine for item separators, since these are not typically manipulated. Renaming these items is optional, of course, but we use the modified names in this book.

The standard items can be created manually, of course. Visual Studio simply provides a shortcut that is normally quicker than creating these menus by hand. Visual Studio includes separator items and assigns images and keyboard shortcuts to the menus as well.

We also add a few menu items specific to our application, for navigating between photographs and inserting or removing items in an album.

<table>
<tr><th colspan="3">CREATE OUR NEW MENU</th></tr>
<tr><th></th><th>Action</th><th>Result</th></tr>
<tr><td>7</td><td>Enter new Add and Remove menus at the end of the Edit submenu.
Settings
<table>
<tr><th>MenuItem</th><th>Property</th><th>Value</th></tr>
<tr><td>separator</td><td></td><td></td></tr>
<tr><td>Add</td><td>(Name)
Shortcut
Text</td><td>menuEditAdd
Ctrl+Shift+A
Ad&d</td></tr>
<tr><td>Remove</td><td>(Name)
Shortcut
Text</td><td>menuEditRemove
Ctrl+Shift+R
Remo&ve</td></tr>
</table></td><td>Edit View Help Type Here
Cut Ctrl+X
Copy Ctrl+C
Paste Ctrl+V
Add Ctrl+Shift+A
Remove Ctrl+Shift+R
Type Here</td></tr>
<tr><td>8</td><td>Add Next and Previous menu items to the <code>ctxMenuPhoto</code> strip.
Settings
<table>
<tr><th>MenuItem</th><th>Property</th><th>Value</th></tr>
<tr><td>separator</td><td></td><td></td></tr>
<tr><td>Next</td><td>(Name)
Shortcut
Text</td><td>menuNext
Ctrl+Shift+N
&Next</td></tr>
<tr><td>Previous</td><td>(Name)
Shortcut
Text</td><td>menuPrevious
Ctrl+Shift+P
&Previous</td></tr>
</table></td><td>ContextMenuStrip
Image
Next Ctrl+Shift+N
Previous Ctrl+Shift+P
Type Here

Note: If you recall, this menu is attached to the View menu as well.</td></tr>
</table>

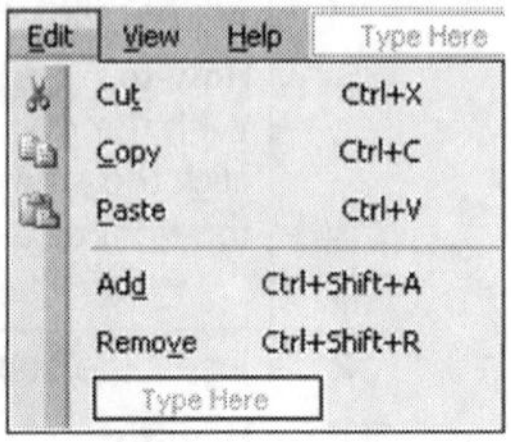

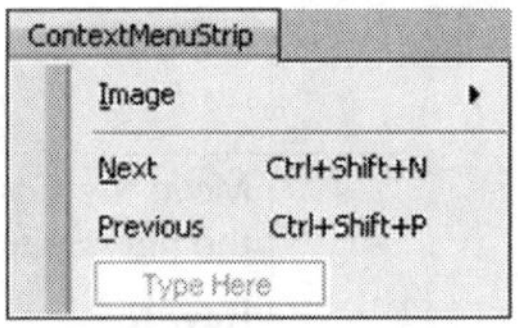

The generated code does not use anything we have not already discussed in prior chapters, so we do not explore these changes in any further detail. The rest of this chapter implements event handlers for many of these menus using the `Photograph` and `PhotoAlbum` classes.

6.1.2 Managing an album

Before we can implement any event handlers for our menus, and in particular before we can open and save album files, we must have a `PhotoAlbum` at our disposal in the `MainForm` class. We could certainly add an album explicitly to the class, and then manipulate this album as required in each event handler.

While such an approach would work, it places all of the code to manage an album in our `Form` class. In addition to complicating our user interface code, this would limit our ability to reuse such logic in other applications. So we will look for an alternate approach.

In thinking about the types of actions required, we need to track a current position in the album so we can move around the album, as well as add or remove a photo at a given position. In addition, we probably want to save and open albums to some sort of storage device. One possibility is to define this logic in the `PhotoAlbum` class directly. This would work, but is not necessarily the best approach. Along with complicating our album code, this makes the `PhotoAlbum` class do more than just represent an album.

Instead, we implement an `AlbumManager` class to handle such actions, and we interact with the album from our UI through this class. This approach clearly defines the tasks available to our UI in a single class, and preserves the "purity" of our `Photograph` and `PhotoAlbum` classes to simply represent the photo and album abstractions. Listing 6.1 sketches an interface for this class.

Listing 6.1 AlbumManager class overview

```
public class AlbumManager
{
  // Create a manager for a new album
  // Create a manager for an existing album

  // Properties:
  //    Album - gets the managed album.
  //    Current - gets the photo at the current position.
  //    Index - gets or sets the current position in the managed album.

  // Methods:
  //    AlbumExists - returns whether a given album already exists
  //    Save() - saves the album under the current name, or a new name
  //    MoveNext() - move the position to the next photo
  //    MovePrev() - move the position to the prior photo
}
```

In large enterprise systems, such classes are often called *boundary classes*, since they define how two layers in the system, in this case our UI and object abstraction layers, interact at the boundary where the layers meet. In such systems, boundary classes might be defined in an entirely new class library so they are kept distinct from other layers. In our case, we define this class as part of our existing MyPhotoAlbum.dll library for simplicity. This code introduces a few new features worth mentioning. Listing 6.2 shows an excerpt of this code.

The `AlbumManager` class implementation is provided in the following steps.

CREATE THE ALBUMMANAGER CLASS

	Action	Result

1	Add a new public class called `AlbumManager` to the MyPhotoAlbum library.
	Indicate we will use the `System.Drawing` and `System.IO` namespaces in this class.
		`. . .`
		`using System.Drawing;  // for Bitmap class`
		`using System.IO;       // for Path class`
		`. . .`
		`namespace Manning.MyPhotoAlbum`
		`{`
		`  public class AlbumManager`
		`  {`

2	Define a static private field and public property to hold a default storage location for photo albums.	`static private string _defaultPath;`
		`static public string DefaultPath`
		`{`
		`  get { return _defaultPath; }`
		`  set { _defaultPath = value; }`
		`}`

3	Define a static constructor to initialize the default location to an Albums directory in the user's My Documents folder.	`static AlbumManager()`
		`{`
		`  _defaultPath = Environment.GetFolderPath(`
		`     Environment.SpecialFolder.Personal)`
		`     + @"\Albums";`
		`}`

4	Define private fields to hold the album, position within the album, and album name.	`private int _pos = -1;`
		`private string _name = String.Empty;`
		`private PhotoAlbum _album;`

5	Define a default constructor that initializes the class for an empty album.	`public AlbumManager()`
		`{`
		`  _album = new PhotoAlbum();`
		`}`

6	Define a constructor that loads an existing album.
	How-to
	For now, throw an exception here to prevent accidental use before this is fully implemented.
		`public AlbumManager(string name) : this()`
		`{`
		`  _name = name;`
		`  // TODO: load the album`
		`  throw new NotImplementedException();`
		`}`

7	Define a read-only `Album` property, and a `FullName` property that can only be set internally.	`public PhotoAlbum Album`
		`{`
		`  get { return _album; }`
		`}`
		
		`public string FullName`
		`{`
		`  get { return _name; }`
		`  private set { _name = value; }`
		`}`

	Create the AlbumManager class *(continued)*	
	Action	**Result**

8	Define a read-only `ShortName` property that returns the base name for the album.	`public string ShortName`
		`{`
		`  get`
		`  {`
		`    if (String.IsNullOrEmpty(FullName))`
		`      return null;`
		`    else`
		`      return Path.`
		`        GetFileNameWithoutExtension(FullName);`
		`  }`
		`}`

9	Implement a `Current` property to get the `Photograph` at the current position.	`public Photograph Current`
		`{`
		`  get`
		`  {`
		`    if (Index < 0 || Index >= Album.Count)`
		`      return null;`
		
		`    return Album[_pos];`
		`  }`
		`}`

10	Implement a `CurrentImage` property to return the image for the current photograph.
	
	Note: For now, ignore any exception thrown by the `Image` property.
		`public Bitmap CurrentImage`
		`{`
		`  get`
		`  {`
		`    if (Current == null)`
		`      return null;`
		
		`    return Current.Image;`
		`  }`
		`}`

11	Implement an `Index` property to get or set the current position within the album.
	
	Note: Unfortunately, we need to ensure the position is valid in the `get` accessor here, to account for any photographs added to or removed from the album.
		`public int Index`
		`{`
		`  get`
		`  {`
		`    int count = Album.Count;`
		`    if (_pos >= count)`
		`      _pos = count - 1;`
		`    return _pos;`
		`  }`
		
		`  set`
		`  {`
		`    if (value < 0 || value >= Album.Count)`
		`      throw new IndexOutOfRangeException(`
		`        "The given index is out of bounds");`
		
		`    _pos = value;`
		`  }`
		`}`

12	Create a placeholder for a static `AlbumExists` method to check if an album already exists.	`static public bool AlbumExists(string name)`
		`{`
		`  // TODO: implement AlbumExists method`
		`  return false;`
		`}`

	CREATE THE ALBUMMANAGER CLASS *(CONTINUED)*	
	Action	**Result**

13	Create a placeholder for some eventual `Save` methods.	`public void Save()`
		`{`
		`  // TODO: Implement Save method`
		`  throw new NotImplementedException();`
		`}`
		
		`public void Save(string name, bool overwrite)`
		`{`
		`  // TODO: Implement Save(name) method`
		`  throw new NotImplementedException();`
		`}`

14	Implement a `MoveNext` method to safely move to the next position in the album.	`public bool MoveNext()`
		`{`
		`  if (Index >= Album.Count)`
		`    return false;`
		
		`  Index++;`
		`  return true;`
		`}`

15	Implement a `MovePrev` method to safely move to the previous position in the album.	`public bool MovePrev()`
		`{`
		`  if (Index <= 0)`
		`    return false;`
		
		`  Index--;`
		`  return true;`
		`}`
		`  }`
		`}`

Listing 6.2 Excerpt of the AlbumManager class

```
. . .
  public class AlbumManager
  {
    static private string _defaultPath;
    . . .
    static AlbumManager()
    {
      _defaultPath = Environment.GetFolderPath(
         Environment.SpecialFolder.Personal)
         + @"\Albums";
    }

    public AlbumManager()
    {
      _album = new PhotoAlbum();
    }

    public AlbumManager(string name) : this()
    {
      _name = name;
      // TODO: load the album
```

❶ **Defines static constructor**

❷ **Defines constructor dependency**

❸ **Specifies TODO task item**

```
        throw new NotImplementedException();
      }
      . . .
      public string FullName
      {
        get { return _name; }
        private set { _name = value; }
      }
      . . .
    }
  }
```

4 Defines private set accessor

Let's look at the details of listing 6.2:

1. As mentioned in chapter 1, C# classes can define a static constructor that is invoked exactly once for a class, typically just before the first reference to a member of that class. Here we initialize a default location for storing albums; namely an Albums folder in the user's My Documents folder. This is done using the `GetFolderPath` method and `SpecialFolder` enumeration as indicated in the code. The `Environment` class contains members that reference the operating system environment of the user, as summarized in .NET Table 6.2.

2. In chapter 5, we discuss how a class can use the `base` keyword to invoke a constructor in the base class as part of the derived class's constructor. Here, the `this` keyword is used to invoke a local constructor from another `AlbumManager` constructor. This ensures that the logic in the default constructor code is executed prior to the current constructor code.

3. The comment here begins with the token `TODO`. Visual Studio can display such comments in the Task List window so they are easily found and addressed at a later time. This window can be displayed via the Other Window item of the View menu, or with the keyboard shortcut Ctrl+Alt+K. The tokens HACK and UNDONE are also recognized, or you can add custom tokens in the Environment section of the Visual Studio Options dialog box.

4. `FullName` property defines a public `get` accessor to obtain the name assigned to the managed album. The `set` accessor is defined as private, so that only members of the `AlbumManager` class can assign a new name for the album.

The `AlbumManager` class defines how a user interface can interact with the `PhotoAlbum` class. This management functionality is now available to our MyPhotos application, and to other applications we write in this book.

You may have noticed that we use a generic `name` parameter to represent an album. This permits the `AlbumManager` class to interpret this value in a variety of ways. Our implementation treats this value as a file system path and stores albums in files. An alternate implementation might store an album in a database or by some other means.

.NET Table 6.2 Environment class

The `Environment` class represents the current user's operating system environment, providing the ability to retrieve and specify environmental information. This class is sealed and the members defined by this class are static. The `Environment` class is part of the `System` namespace.

Public Static Properties	CurrentDirectory	Gets or sets the fully qualified path of the current directory for this process.
	ExitCode	Gets or sets the exit code for the process.
	MachineName	Gets the NetBIOS name of this local computer.
	OSVersion	Gets an `OperatingSystem` instance under which this process is currently running.
	ProcessorCount	Gets the number of processors on the machine.
	TickCount	Gets the number of milliseconds elapsed since the system started.
	UserName	Gets the user name that started the current thread for this process.
	WorkingSet	Gets the amount of physical memory mapped to this process context.
Public Static Methods	Exit	Terminates the calling process and returns the given exit code to the operating system.
	FailFast	Writes a given message to the event log and terminates the process without invoking any `finally` blocks.
	GetCommandLineArgs	Returns an array of `string` objects containing the command-line arguments for the current process.
	GetEnvironmentVariable	Returns the value of a specified environment variable as a `string`. The `GetEnvironmentVariables` method returns the names and values of all environment variables.
	GetFolderPath	Returns the path of a folder identified by the `Environment.SpecialFolder` enumeration. For example, the `Personal` value returns the directory where the user's documents are typically stored, while `StartMenu` returns the directory containing the Start menu items.
	GetLogicalDrives	Returns an array of `string` objects containing the names of the logical drives on the computer under which this process is running.
	SetEnvironmentVariable	Create, modifies, or deletes a specified environment variable.

6.2 COMMON FILE DIALOG BOXES

With our management functionality defined, we can start implementing our various menus. We begin with the File menu, and implement `Click` handlers for the New, Open, Save, Save As, and Exit menu items. The two print menus we save for chapter 23.

Supporting the ability to save and open files is a common task in many applications. The Windows Forms namespace includes a set of common dialog boxes to support these types of activities. We already utilized one of these in the `OpenFileDialog` class in chapter 1. In this section we take a second look at `OpenFileDialog` and its companion, the `SaveFileDialog` class.

6.2.1 Creating a new album

The New menu seems fairly straightforward. We need to have an `AlbumManager` in our form, and the New menu handler should create a new instance of this manager. We should handle closing and saving any existing album, and refreshing the form to display the new, albeit empty, album.

The following steps handle this menu.

CREATE A CLICK EVENT HANDLER FOR THE NEW MENU

	Action	Result
1	In the MyPhotos project, add a reference to the MyPhotoAlbum project. **How-to** a. Right-click the MyPhotos project in the Solution Explorer window. b. Select Add Reference. c. Click the Projects tab in the Add Reference dialog box. d. Double-click the MyPhotoAlbum entry.	The MyPhotoAlbum assembly is added as a reference in the MyPhotos project.

2	In the MainForm.cs code window, indicate we are using the `Manning.MyPhotoAlbum` namespace.	`. . .`
		`using Manning.MyPhotoAlbum;`
		`. . .`

3	Add a private field called `_manager` to hold an `AlbumManager` instance.	`public partial class MainForm : Form`
		`{`
		`  private AlbumManager _manager;`

4	Add a private `Manager` property to retrieve or assign the current manager.	`  private AlbumManager Manager`
		`      { get { return _manager; }`
		`        set { _manager = value; } }`

CREATE A CLICK EVENT HANDLER FOR THE NEW MENU *(CONTINUED)*		
	Action	**Result**

5	In the `MainForm` constructor, initialize the form by calling a `NewAlbum` method. This call replaces the existing calls to `SetTitleBar` and `SetStatusStrip`.	`public MainForm()`
		`{`
		`  InitializeComponent();`
		
		`  `**`NewAlbum();`**
		`  menuView.DropDown = ctxMenuPhoto;`
		`}`

6	Modify the `SetStatusStrip` method to use the new manager class.
	How-to
	Create the handler by double-clicking the New item in the designer window.
	Note: Also change this method to have no arguments.
		`private void SetStatusStrip()`
		`{`
		`  if (pbxPhoto.Image != null)`
		`  {`
		`    statusInfo.Text`
		`      `**`= Manager.Current.FileName;`**
		`    statusImageSize.Text = . . .;`
		`  }`
		`  else`
		`    . . .`

7	Create a new `DisplayAlbum` method to update the form with the current photograph.	`private void DisplayAlbum()`
		`{`
		`  pbxPhoto.Image = Manager.CurrentImage;`
		`  SetStatusStrip();`
		`  SetTitleBar();`
		`}`

8	Add a `Click` event handler for the New menu that calls the `NewAlbum` method.	`private void menuFileNew_Click`
		`    (object sender, System.EventArgs e)`
		`{`
		`  NewAlbum();`
		`}`

9	Implement the `NewAlbum` method to clean up and save the current album, create a new empty album, and update the form.	`private void NewAlbum()`
		`{`
		`  // TODO: clean up, save existing album`
		`  Manager = new AlbumManager();`
		`  DisplayAlbum();`
		`}`

This code makes a number of changes, but carefully encapsulates the display functionality in a `DisplayAlbum` method so we can modify and reuse it in the future. Four other points worth noting here:

1. While we could use our private `_manager` field directly, creating the private `Manager` property in step 4 allows us to modify how the manager is accessed in the future without changing the rest of our code. As we discussed for the `Photograph` class in chapter 5, creating simple properties for your public fields is usually a good idea, and this discussion applies to private fields as well.
2. The `NewAlbum` method is somewhat optional. Another approach is to implement this code in the New menu's `Click` handler directly and invoke the `PerformClick` method to simulate a click of the New menu. Either approach

works, though Microsoft recommends our implementation since it separates the logic from the `Click` handler.

3 Note our use once again of a `TODO` comment in step 9. Since Visual Studio tracks such comments on our behalf, using `TODO` comments is a good way to make sure we come back to this work eventually.

4 Encapsulating the `DisplayAlbum` logic is a good idea, of course, and will simplify some of our future code. Another approach here would be to create an `AlbumModified` event in our `Album` class. The event approach would define a standard mechanism for this or any other application that manages albums, and require that we only hook up these events to handle changes to our albums now or in the future. Using events may well be a better approach, but we opted for the `DisplayAlbum` method here to simplify our discussion.

Some of these changes affect code from prior chapters, in particular the use of `SetStatusStrip` in the `menuFileLoad_Click` method. We address this in the next section, but you can adjust your application now to ensure it still compiles if you wish. Next up is the Open menu item.

6.2.2 Opening an album

We did not define an explicit Open or Load method in the `AlbumManager` class. Instead, we defined a constructor that accepts a name for a new album. Our implementation uses a filename to represent the album, so our Open menu item can use the `OpenFileDialog` class to locate an album file.

Since we must save and open album files on disk, we need a way to identify that a particular file is an album file. On Windows platforms, this is typically done with a three-letter extension. While we could use an existing file type such as text (.txt) or XML (.xml), such extensions would not be unique to our albums.

So the question becomes: what extension should we use? This is somewhat subjective, although extensions typically avoid numbers and represent an acronym or abbreviation of the file type. Well-known extensions such as .xml, for Extensible Markup Language, or .gif, for Graphics Interchange Format, should also be avoided. With this in mind, we choose the extension .abm for an album file.

We used the `OpenFileDialog` class in chapter 1 to load a bitmap file, where we briefly discussed the `FileDialog` class it derives from. The functionality specific to the `OpenFileDialog` class is shown in .NET Table 6.3. Here we use it to locate an album file and create a new manager for it. Of course, we do not have any album files yet, but we can still write the code.

.NET Table 6.3 OpenFileDialog class

The `OpenFileDialog` class represents a common file dialog for loading one or more files from disk, and is part of the `System.Windows.Forms` namespace. This class inherits from the `FileDialog` class, and is the standard class for opening existing files. See .NET Table 1.2 for a list of members in the base class.

Public Properties	CheckFileExists	Gets or sets whether to display a warning dialog box if the specified file does not exist.
	Multiselect	Gets or sets whether multiple files can be selected. The inherited `FileNames` property retrieves the selected files.
	ReadOnlyChecked	Gets or sets whether the read-only check box is selected.
	ShowReadOnly	Gets or sets whether the dialog box should contain an open-read-only check box.
Public Methods	OpenFile	Returns a `Stream` with read-only access to the file specified by the `FileName` property.

IMPLEMENT A CLICK HANDLER FOR THE OPEN MENU

	Action	Result

1	Delete the `menuFileLoad_Click` method and add a `Click` handler for the Open menu item in the `MainForm` class.	`protected void menuFileOpen_Click`
		`    (object sender, System.EventArgs e)`
		`{`
		Note: You can copy the code from the existing `menuFileLoad_Click` method to use as a basis for this handler, or simply delete this method and retype the code as shown here.

2	Allow the user to select an album file with the `OpenFileDialog` class.	`// Allow user to select a new album`
		`OpenFileDialog dlg = new OpenFileDialog();`
		
		`dlg.Title = "Open Album";`
		`dlg.Filter = "Album files (*.abm)|*.abm|"`
		`    + "All files (*.*)|*.*";`
		`dlg.InitialDirectory`
		`    = AlbumManager.DefaultPath;`
		`dlg.RestoreDirectory = true;`

3	Use the `AlbumManager` constructor to open the album.	`if (dlg.ShowDialog() == DialogResult.OK)`
		`{`
		`  // TODO: save any existing album.`
		
		`  // Open the new album`
		`  // TODO: handle invalid album file`
		`  Manager = new AlbumManager(dlg.FileName);`

4	Display the new album in the application.	`  DisplayAlbum();` `}`

IMPLEMENT A CLICK HANDLER FOR THE OPEN MENU *(CONTINUED)*		
	Action	**Result**

5	Dispose of any system resources used by the dialog box.	`dlg.Dispose();`
		`}`
		Note: This is the `IDisposable` interface discussed in chapter 5. We discuss this method for `Form` classes in detail in section 7.2.

This code uses the `OpenFileDialog` class in a way quite similar to how it was used in chapter 1. We use the `InitialDirectory` property to define the starting directory to display in the dialog box, and the `RestoreDirectory` property to ensure that the current operating system directory is restored to its prior value when the dialog box closes.

When we handle the Add menu item, we will use the `Multiselect` property to permit multiple files to be added at once. For now, let's move on to the Save menus.

6.2.3 Saving an album

The Save menu handler saves an existing album, while the Save As menu handler saves the album under a new name. In our `AlbumManager` class, we implemented placeholders for this functionality, which we can make use of here. The next section discusses the actual writing of an album to disk.

As you might expect, .NET provides a `SaveFileDialog` class to store information to a file. A summary of this class is shown in .NET Table 6.4.

.NET Table 6.4 SaveFileDialog class

The `SaveFileDialog` class represents a common file dialog box for saving a file to disk, and is part of the `System.Windows.Forms` namespace. This class inherits from the `FileDialog` class, described in .NET Table 1.2.

Public Properties	CreatePrompt	Gets or sets whether to display a dialog box requesting permission to create the specified file if it does not exist
	OverwritePrompt	Gets or sets whether to display a dialog box requesting permission to overwrite a specified file if it already exists
Public Methods	OpenFile	Returns a `Stream` object with read/write permission for the selected file

Before we use this class to handle the Save As menu, let's take a quick look at the Save menu. This item saves the album using the existing name and so does not require a file dialog box.

HANDLE THE SAVE MENU ITEM		
	Action	**Result**

1	Create a `SaveAlbum` method to save the album under a given name.	`private void SaveAlbum(string name)`
		`{`
		`  Manager.Save(name, true);`
		`}`

2	Create an alternate `SaveAlbum` method that handles the case where a name is not assigned.	`private void SaveAlbum()`
		`{`
		`  if (String.IsNullOrEmpty(Manager.FullName))`

3	If no name is assigned, invoke a `SaveAsAlbum` method so the user can select a name.	`    SaveAsAlbum();   // Force user to select name`

4	If the album has already been assigned a name, save the album under the existing name.	`  else`
		`  {`
		`    // Save the album under the existing name`
		`    SaveAlbum(Manager.FullName);`
		`  }`
		`}`

5	In the designer window, add a `Click` handler for the Save menu that employs these methods.	`private void menuFileSave_Click`
		`  (object sender, EventArgs e)`
		`{`
		`  SaveAlbum();`
		`}`

Note how the Save handler invokes the SaveAlbum method to save an album without a name. The `SaveAsAlbum` method employs the `SaveFileDialog` class. The following steps continue our changes and implement this logic.

HANDLE THE SAVE AS MENU ITEM		
	Action	**Result**

6	Add a `Click` handler for the Save As menu that calls a `SaveAsAlbum` method.	`protected void menuFileSaveAs_Click`
		`    (object sender, System.EventArgs e)`
		`{`
		`  SaveAsAlbum();`
		`}`

7	Create the `SaveAsAlbum` method to use a `SaveFileDialog` instance.	`private void SaveAsAlbum()`
		`{`
		`  SaveFileDialog dlg = new SaveFileDialog();`

<table>
<tr><th colspan="3">HANDLE THE SAVE AS MENU ITEM (CONTINUED)</th></tr>
<tr><th></th><th>Action</th><th>Result</th></tr>
<tr><td>8</td><td>Initialize the dialog box properties as shown.

Note: In the <code>Filter</code> property setting, allow all files to be shown, even though .abm is the only recognized extension. This is not necessary, but a nice convenience to allow the user to see all files in a directory.</td><td><pre> dlg.Title = "Save Album";
  dlg.DefaultExt = "abm";
  dlg.Filter = "Album files (*.abm)|*.abm|"
      + "All files|*.*";
  dlg.InitialDirectory
    = AlbumManager.DefaultPath;
  dlg.RestoreDirectory = true;</pre></td></tr>
<tr><td>9</td><td>If the user selects a file, save the album under this new name.</td><td><pre> if (dlg.ShowDialog() == DialogResult.OK)
  {
    SaveAlbum(dlg.FileName);

    // Update title bar to include new name
    SetTitleBar();
  }</pre></td></tr>
<tr><td>10</td><td>Dispose of any system resources used by the dialog box.</td><td><pre> dlg.Dispose();
}</pre></td></tr>
<tr><td>11</td><td>Modify the <code>SetTitleBar</code> method to include the album name in the title bar.</td><td><pre>private void SetTitleBar()
{
  Version ver = new Version(
    Application.ProductVersion);
  string name = Manager.FullName;
  this.Text = String.Format(
    "{2} - MyPhotos {0:0}.{1:0}",
      ver.Major, ver.Minor,
      String.IsNullOrEmpty(name)
          ? "Untitled" : name);
}</pre></td></tr>
</table>

Notice how our use of the `SaveFileDialog` class is reminiscent of our prior use of the `OpenFileDialog` class. The default extension .abm is added to the name automatically if the user does not specify an extension.

The `OpenFileDialog` and `SaveFileDialog` classes are dialog boxes provided by the .NET Framework that implement a standard interface for common functionality required by applications. They inherit from the `FileDialog` class, which in turn inherits from the `CommonDialog` class directly.

Two other such dialog boxes provided by .NET are the `ColorDialog` and `FontDialog` classes. The `ColorDialog` class permits a user to select a color and corresponding `Color` structure, while the `FontDialog` class permits a user to select a font name, family, size, and corresponding `Font` class instance. The use of these dialog boxes is similar to the use of the `FileDialog` objects in this chapter, although the actual windows are quite different.

We should also note that these dialog boxes, including the `OpenFileDialog` and `SaveFileDialog` classes, can be configured directly in the Windows Forms Designer window. They are available in the Toolbox, and can be dragged onto the form and configured in the Properties window much like any other component. We elected not to do this here since the dialogs would then exist for the life of the form, which is not really necessary for our purposes.

6.2.4 Printing and exiting

Two other `CommonDialog` classes are the `PageSetupDialog` and `PrintDialog` classes. These dialog boxes support printing from within Windows Forms applications, and are discussed in section 23.1. We leave discussion of the Print Preview and Print menus until this section as well.

Our final menu item, Exit, brings us back to familiar territory. Unless you deleted it, the `menuFileExit_Click` method is still in your code, so all we need to do is hook it up to the menu.

HANDLE THE EXIT MENU

	Action	Result
1	Display the events for the Exit command in the Properties window.	
2	Display the list of possible handlers for the `Click` event. **How-to** a. Find the Click entry in the window. b. Click the down arrow to the right of the Click entry.	
3	Select the `menuFileExit_Click` entry in this list as the `Click` event handler.	The selected method is assigned as the handler for this event.

This completes our implementation of the File menu for now. Before we move on to the other menus in our menu strip, we provide some support for actually writing and reading an album from the disk.

TRY IT! The Print and Print Preview menus are currently misleading, since the user can click on them and nothing happens. Try addressing this issue in the following ways to see the results:

- Set the `Visible` property of these menu items to `false`.
- Set the `Enabled` property of these menu items to `false`.
- Create an event handler called `menu_NotImplemented` in the code that displays a dialog box indicating that this menu is not yet implemented. Use the `MessageBox.Show` method to display this dialog box, and add this handler to each of these menus via the Properties window as we did for the Exit menu item.

Whichever mechanism you prefer, you can use it throughout this chapter for menu items that are not yet handled in the book.

6.3 STREAMS AND WRITERS

So far in this chapter we have implemented an `AlbumManager` class to manage an album on behalf of our application. We used this class to implement the File menu in the prior section. One loose end is the actual reading and writing of album data on the disk. This section addresses this problem by introducing the `Stream` classes.

6.3.1 Stream classes

The abstract `Stream` class in the `System.IO` namespace provides a generic view of a sequence of bytes, and is the key to managing bytes in .NET from all manner of sources. The `MemoryStream` class manages bytes in memory, the `FileStream` class manages bytes in a file, and the `BufferedStream` class provides buffered access to the bytes in a stream.

Other namespaces utilizes the `Stream` class as well. For example, the `System.IO.Compression` namespace provides classes for compressing and decompressing streams, and the `System.Net.Sockets` namespace manages network bytes via the `NetworkStream` class. See the .NET documentation for a complete list of classes derived from the `Stream` class.

One unique feature of streams is the ability to link, or chain, them together to achieve multiple effects on a single base stream. For example, you can chain the `GZipStream` and `FileStream` classes together to compress data as it is written to disk.

For reading and writing text, .NET provides the `TextReader` and `TextWriter` classes. These abstract classes encapsulate the notion of reading characters, rather than bytes, and are useful for managing textual data. A summary of these classes is shown in .NET Tables 6.5 and 6.6.

Returning to our application, the `StreamReader` and `StreamWriter` classes mentioned in the two .NET Tables are good choices for managing album files on disk. We have already noted places in our `AlbumManager` class where this logic is required, so all we have to do is decide how to fit this into the class.

.NET Table 6.5 TextReader class

The `TextReader` class represents a reader for a sequence of characters, and is part of the `System.IO` namespace. This class inherits from the `System.MarshalByRefObject` class. The `StreamReader` class for reading characters from a stream derives from this class.

Public Methods	Close	Releases any system resources associated with the reader and closes it
	Peek	Returns the next character without actually reading it from the input stream
	Read	Retrieves one or more characters from the input stream
	ReadLine	Retrieves a line of characters from the input stream as a string
	ReadToEnd	Retrieves all characters from the current position to the end of the reader as a string

.NET Table 6.6 TextWriter class

The `TextWriter` class represents a writer for a sequence of characters, and is part of the `System.IO` namespace. This class inherits from the `System.MarshalByRefObject` class. The `StreamWriter` class for writing characters to a stream derives from this class.

Public Properties	NewLine	Gets or sets the line terminator string for this writer
Public Methods	Close	Releases any system resources associated with the writer, flushes all buffered data to the underlying device, and closes the writer
	Flush	Writes any buffered data to the underlying device, and clears all internal buffers
	Write	Sends a given data type to the output stream
	WriteLine	Sends the given data to the output stream, followed by a line terminator

As usual, we have some choices here. Do we just add this code in our manager class, or do we create a separate class for it? If we create a separate class, does it go in our existing assembly or in a new one? As you might guess, we will separate this logic into a separate class, called `AlbumStorage`. It might make sense in a large project to isolate such storage logic in its own assembly, but for the purposes of our book the existing assembly works just fine. A sketch of the public methods in our `AlbumStorage` class appears in listing 6.3.

Listing 6.3 AlbumStorage class overview

```
public static class AlbumStorage
{
  static public void WriteAlbum(PhotoAlbum album, string path)
  static public PhotoAlbum ReadAlbum(string path)
}
```

It is often a good idea to make use of a class before you actually implement it. This may sound counterintuitive, but the idea is to write a test program or application that uses your class to verify that the methods make sense and accomplish the desired tasks. We can simulate this idea here by examining how our `AlbumManager` class would use the new storage methods.

<table>
<tr><th colspan="3">UTILIZE ALBUMSTORAGE METHODS IN THE ALBUMMANAGER CLASS</th></tr>
<tr><th></th><th>Action</th><th>Result</th></tr>
<tr><td>1</td><td>In the <code>AlbumManager</code> class, implement the second constructor to read in the album with the given name.

Note: You can double-click on the appropriate TODO item in the Task List window to jump directly to this code.</td><td><pre>public class AlbumManager
{
  . . .
  public AlbumManager(string name) : this()
  {
    _name = name;
    _album = AlbumStorage.ReadAlbum(name);
    if (Album.Count>0)
      Index=0
  }</pre></td></tr>
<tr><td>2</td><td>Locate and implement the two <code>Save</code> methods in this class to write the current album with the assigned name.

How-to
a. Throw an exception if an argument is bad.
b. Use <code>WriteAlbum</code> to save the file.
c. Set the <code>FullName</code> value last, in case an exception occurs.</td><td><pre> public void Save()
  {
    if (FullName == null)
      throw new InvalidOperationException(
          "Unable to save album with no name");

    AlbumStorage.WriteAlbum(Album, FullName);
  }

  public void Save(string name, bool overwrite)
  {
    if (name == null)
      throw new ArgumentNullException("name");
    if (name != FullName
        && AlbumExists(name) && !overwrite)
      throw new ArgumentException(
          "An album with this name exists");

    AlbumStorage.WriteAlbum(Album, name);
    FullName = name;
  }</pre></td></tr>
<tr><td>3</td><td>Implement the <code>AlbumExists</code> method to return whether the given filename already exists.

How-to
Use the <code>Exist</code> method in the <code>File</code> class.</td><td><pre> static public bool AlbumExists(string name)
  {
    return File.Exists(name);
  }
  . . .
}</pre></td></tr>
</table>

This certainly makes sense, so we can forge ahead and create these methods in a new `AlbumStorage` class. The `File` class used in step 3 is a static class that defines methods for creating and managing operating system files.

6.3.2 Writing an album to disk

Before we create an album with the `WriteAlbum` method, there is the issue of how best to handle errors. Handling errors is really a policy decision for an application or system, so we do not want to hard-code such decisions into our class unless absolutely necessary. Instead, we will raise an exception when something unexpected occurs so that the parent application can deal with it.

There are a number of defined exceptions in .NET, among them the `ApplicationException` class for general application errors, or the `IOException` class for I/O errors. While either would work, neither is appropriate for an error that occurs trying to store a photo album. A better strategy is to create a custom exception class for this purpose, as it allows an external application to isolate the specific exceptional condition that our class generates.

With this in mind, let's walk through the logic to write an album to disk.

CREATE THE ALBUMSTORAGE CLASS AND WRITEALBUM METHOD		
	Action	**Result**

1	Create a new AlbumStorage.cs class file in the MyPhotoAlbum project.	`using System;`
		`using System.IO;`
		
		`namespace Manning.MyPhotoAlbum`
		`{`

2	Create an exception class to represent a failed attempt to read or write an album.
	
	Note: This class exists for the name only, allowing us to distinguish album storage exceptions from other errors that might occur.
		`public class AlbumStorageException : Exception`
		`{`
		`  public AlbumStorageException() : base() { }`
		`  public AlbumStorageException(string msg)`
		`      : base(msg) { }`
		`  public AlbumStorageException(string msg,`
		`      Exception inner) : base(msg, inner) { }`
		`}`

3	Make the `AlbumStorage` class static to indicate that it only contains static members.	`public static class AlbumStorage` `{`
4	Define a private field to hold the current version number for new album files.	`static private int CurrentVersion = 63;` **Note:** We use version 63 since we are in section 6.3.

	Action	Result
CREATE THE ALBUMSTORAGE CLASS AND WRITEALBUM METHOD *(CONTINUED)*		

5	Implement the `WriteAlbum` method to write an album to disk.
	
	How-to
	a. Accept an album and album file.
	b. Use the `StreamWriter` class with a `try` block.
	c. Write the current version number on a line by itself.
	d. Loop through the photos in the album and write each one to disk.
	e. After all photos are written, reset the `HasChanged` property to `false`.
	f. If a recognized error occurs, rethrow it as an `AlbumStorageException` error.
	g. Use a `finally` block to ensure the `StreamWriter` is closed regardless of whether an error occurs in the code.
		`static public void WriteAlbum(`
		`    PhotoAlbum album, string path)`
		`{`
		`  StreamWriter sw = null;`
		
		`  try`
		`  {`
		`    sw = new StreamWriter(path, false);`
		`    sw.WriteLine(CurrentVersion.ToString());`
		
		`    // Store each photo separately`
		`    foreach (Photograph p in album)`
		`      WritePhoto(sw, p);`
		
		`    // Reset changed after all photos written`
		`    album.HasChanged = false;`
		`  }`
		`  catch (UnauthorizedAccessException uax)`
		`  {`
		`    throw new AlbumStorageException(`
		`      "Unable to access album " + path, uax);`
		`  }`
		`  finally`
		`  {`
		`    if (sw != null)`
		`      sw.Close();`
		`  }`
		`}`

6	Implement the `WritePhoto` method to write an individual photo to the open file.
	
	How-to
	a. Accept the open `StreamWriter` and a `Photograph`.
	b. Write each property on a separate line. Make sure you handle `null` string values appropriately.
		`static private void WritePhoto(`
		`    StreamWriter sw, Photograph p)`
		`{`
		`  sw.WriteLine(p.FileName);`
		
		`  sw.WriteLine(p.Caption != null`
		`      ? p.Caption : "");`
		`  sw.WriteLine(p.DateTaken.ToString());`
		`  sw.WriteLine(p.Photographer != null`
		`      ? p.Photographer : "");`
		`  sw.WriteLine(p.Notes != null`
		`      ? p.Notes : "");`
		`}`

The use of a `try-catch-finally` block is a key component of this logic. Listing 6.4 shows the key points of this concept in our `WriteAlbum` method. The numbered portions are discussed in more detail.

Listing 6.4 Using try-catch-finally in the WriteAlbum method

```
static public void WriteAlbum(
    PhotoAlbum album, string path)
{
  StreamWriter sw = null;

  try
  {
    sw = new StreamWriter(path, false);     <-- 1 Creates object in try block
    . . .
  }
  catch (UnauthorizedAccessException uax)    <-- 2 Catches possible exceptions
  {
    throw new AlbumStorageException(. . .);
  }
  finally
  {
    if (sw != null)     <-- 3 Cleans up resources in finally block
      sw.Close();
  }
}
```

❶ The `StreamWriter` object is created inside the `try` block. This ensures that any exceptions raised while creating the object can be caught and handled appropriately. While the writer can be created before entering the block, this is not a good idea for just this reason.

❷ Exceptions that might occur are caught in one or more `catch` blocks. Here we catch the `UnauthorizedAccessException` in case access to the given file is denied. The `StreamWriter` constructor might throw other exceptions such as `ArgumentNullException` or `SecurityException` that might also be worth catching here.

❸ The code in the `finally` block executes regardless of whether an exception is thrown in the `try` block. By placing our cleanup code here, we guarantee that our writer is closed no matter what happens. To be safe, we only close the writer if the variable is not `null` in case the `StreamWriter` constructor throws an exception so that the `sw` variable is never assigned.

In chapter 7 we see how the `using` statement can represent this concept more succinctly, but for now this code suffices. We can write an album to disk. The next step is to read a previously written album into memory.

TRY IT! As just mentioned, our `WriteAlbum` method only catches the `UnauthorizedAccessException` class. Look up the `StreamWriter` constructor that accepts a `string` and `bool` value in the .NET documentation, and add additional catch blocks to handle any exceptions you think can safely be turned into `AlbumStorageException` errors.

6.3.3 Reading an album from disk

The code to read an existing album is similar to writing an album. We use the version number to provide some verification that we are given a file in the proper format.

CREATE THE READALBUM METHOD

	Action	Result

1	Implement the `ReadAlbum` method to read an existing album into a `PhotoAlbum` object.
	
	How-to
	a. Accept an album file.
	b. Use the `StreamReader` class in a `try` block.
	c. Read the version number from the file.
	d. If a known version is found, read in the album.
	e. If the version is not recognized, throw an exception.
	f. After reading the album, set it as unchanged and return the new album.
		`static public PhotoAlbum ReadAlbum(`
		`    string path)`
		`{`
		`  StreamReader sr = null;`
		
		`  try`
		`  {`
		`    sr = new StreamReader(path);`
		`    string version = sr.ReadLine();`
		
		`    PhotoAlbum album = new PhotoAlbum();`
		`    switch (version)`
		`    {`
		`      case "63":`
		`        ReadAlbumV63(sr, album);`
		`        break;`
		`      default:`
		`        throw new AlbumStorageException(`
		`          "Unrecognized album version");`
		`    }`
		
		`    album.HasChanged = false;`
		`    return album;`
		`  }`

2	If a recognized error occurs, rethrow it as an `AlbumStorageException` error.	`  catch (FileNotFoundException fnx)`
		`  {`
		`    throw new AlbumStorageException(`
		`     "Unable to read album " + path, fnx);`
		`  }`

3	Use a `finally` block to clean up the `StreamReader`.	`  finally`
		`  {`
		`    if (sr != null)`
		`      sr.Close();`
		`  }`
		`}`

4	Implement a `ReadAlbumV63` method to read an album in version 63 format.
	
	How-to
	a. Create a new `PhotoAlbum`.
	b. Read a photo from the file until no more exist.
	c. Return the album.
		`static private void ReadAlbumV63(`
		`    StreamReader sr, PhotoAlbum album)`
		`{`
		`  // Read each photo into album.`
		`  Photograph p;`
		`  do`
		`  {`
		`    p = ReadPhotoV63(sr);`
		`    if (p != null)`
		`      album.Add(p);`
		`  } while (p != null);`
		`}`

CREATE THE READALBUM METHOD *(CONTINUED)*

	Action	Result

5	Implement a `ReadPhotoV63` method to read a photo in version 63 format.
	How-to
	a. Read the first line containing the filename.
	b. If at the end of the file, return `null`.
	c. Otherwise, create a new `Photograph` with the filename.
	d. Read each property in the correct order.
	e. Return the new `Photograph`.
		`static private Photograph ReadPhotoV63(`
		`    StreamReader sr)`
		`{`
		`  // Presume at the start of photo`
		`  string file = sr.ReadLine();`
		`  if (file == null || file.Length == 0)`
		`    return null;`
		
		`  // File not null, should find photo`
		`  Photograph p = new Photograph(file);`
		
		`  p.Caption = sr.ReadLine();`
		`  p.DateTaken`
		`      = DateTime.Parse(sr.ReadLine());`
		`  p.Photographer = sr.ReadLine();`
		`  p.Notes = sr.ReadLine();`
		
		`  return p;`
		`}`

We need to make two points here. First, note the use of the `DateTime.Parse` method. Most base types define a `Parse` method to convert a given string into that type. The `Convert` class provides another mechanism for such conversions, all of which throw a `FormatException` if the object cannot be converted.

Also note our use of the `PhotoAlbum.HasChanged` property. We defined this property with an internal set accessor. Since the `AlbumStorage` class is in the same `Manning.MyPhotoAlbum` assembly as the `Photograph` class, we can assign this property here to reset this property for the album and all containing photographs.

You can compile and test our application if you wish. Of course, since we cannot add images to an album yet, you cannot do much yet. The next section finishes up our menus for the purposes of this chapter.

6.4 ALBUM MANAGEMENT

So far we have an album, albeit an empty one, in our application that we can save and open from disk. In this final section, we allow a user to add and remove photos, and navigate to the next or previous photo in the album. We look at the Add and Remove items in the Edit menu, followed by the Next and Previous items in the View menu.

6.4.1 Adding and removing images

In previous chapters, we allowed a user to load a single image, first using a button and later with a menu item. In our new structure, this is replaced by the ability to add multiple photos to the album or remove the current photo from the album.

As you would expect, we provide `Click` handlers for both menu items. The Add menu item should allow one or more photos to be selected and added to the album, while the Remove item should delete the currently displayed photo from the album.

The Add menu item uses the `Multiselect` property of the `OpenFileDialog` class to enable selection of multiple files.

The steps required for this functionality are as follows.

	Implement Add and Remove Handlers	
	Action	**Result**

1	In the MainForm designer window, add a `Click` event handler for the Add menu item.	`protected void menuEditAdd_Click`
		`    (object sender, System.EventArgs e)`
		`{`

2	Initialize an `OpenFileDialog` instance to allow multiple selections of various image file types.
	
	Note: The `Filter` setting here includes most of the common formats users are likely to see. These formats are all supported by the `Bitmap` class.
		`OpenFileDialog dlg = new OpenFileDialog();`
		
		`dlg.Title = "Add Photos";`
		`dlg.Multiselect = true;`
		`dlg.Filter`
		`  = "Image Files (JPEG, GIF, BMP, etc.)|"`
		`    + "*.jpg;*.jpeg;*.gif;*.bmp;"`
		`    + "*.tif;*.tiff;*.png|"`
		`   + "JPEG files (*.jpg;*.jpeg)|*.jpg;*.jpeg|"`
		`    + "GIF files (*.gif)|*.gif|"`
		`    + "BMP files (*.bmp)|*.bmp|"`
		`   + "TIFF files (*.tif;*.tiff)|*.tif;*.tiff|"`
		`    + "PNG files (*.png)|*.png|"`
		`    + "All files (*.*)|*.*";`
		`dlg.InitialDirectory`
		`    = Environment.CurrentDirectory;`

3	Invoke the dialog box and process an OK response.	`if (dlg.ShowDialog() == DialogResult.OK)` `{`
4	Extract the array of files selected by the user.	`string[] files = dlg.FileNames;`

5	Iterate through the selected files.	`int index = 0;`
		`foreach (string s in files)`
		`{`

6	Add each image to the album if it is not already present.
	
	How-to
	Use the `IndexOf` method to see if the photo is already in the album.
		`Photograph photo = new Photograph(s);`
		
		`// Add the file (if not already present)`
		`index = Manager.Album.IndexOf(photo);`
		`if (index < 0)`
		`  Manager.Album.Add(photo);`
		`else`
		`  photo.Dispose();  // photo already there`
		`}`
		`Manager.Index=Manager.Album.Count-1`
		`}`
		
		Note: The `IndexOf` method used here relies on the `Equals` override we implemented in chapter 5.

7	Dispose of any system resources used by the dialog box, and display the updated album.	`dlg.Dispose();`
		`DisplayAlbum();`
		`}`

8	Add a `Click` handler for the Remove menu item.	`private void menuEditRemove_Click(`
		`    object sender, EventArgs e)`
		`{`

	IMPLEMENT ADD AND REMOVE HANDLERS *(CONTINUED)*	
	Action	**Result**

9	If the album is not empty, remove the current image and display the updated album.	`if (Manager.Album.Count > 0)`
		`{`
		`  Manager.Album.RemoveAt(Manager.Index);`
		`  DisplayAlbum();`
		`}`
		`}`

In the Add handler code, the `Multiselect` property permits multiple file selections. This is one of the few `OpenFileDialog` members not inherited from the `FileDialog` class. The `FileNames` property returns the set of files selected as an array of `string` objects.

The Remove handler employs the `RemoveAt` method from our `PhotoAlbum` class to remove the current photo. The issue of adjusting the current position in case we remove the last photo from the album is left to the `AlbumManager` class.

This permits us to add images to an album. The last task is to enable a user to view more than just the first image.

6.4.2 Navigating an album

This section implements the Next and Previous menu items in our application. These items are part of the context strip assigned to the `PictureBox` on our form. As you'll recall, this context menu is assigned to the View menu as well, so the two menus always behave identically. The new menu is shown in figure 6.2.

The handlers for Next and Previous use some familiar concepts, so let's get to it.

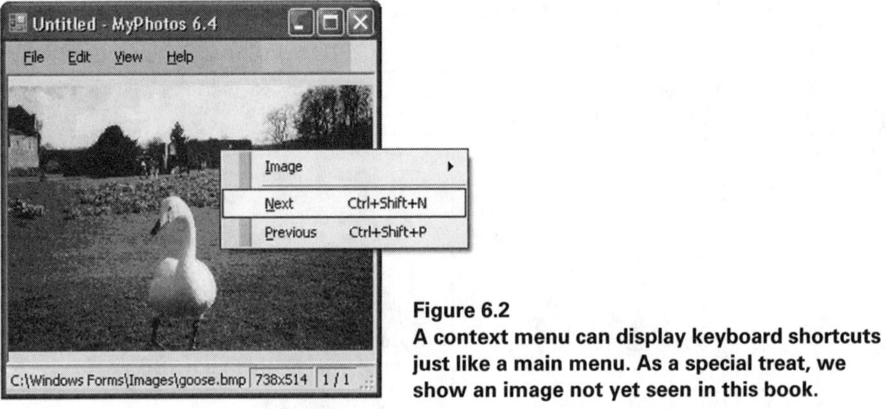

Figure 6.2
A context menu can display keyboard shortcuts just like a main menu. As a special treat, we show an image not yet seen in this book.

	IMPLEMENT NEXT AND PREVIOUS HANDLERS	
	Action	**Result**

1	In the `ctxMenuPhoto` strip, add a `Click` handler for the Next menu item.	`private void menuNext_Click(`
		`    object sender, EventArgs e)`
		`{`

2	Implement this handler to increment the current index and redisplay the album.	`  if (Manager.Index < Manager.Album.Count - 1)`
		`  {`
		`    Manager.Index++;`
		`    DisplayAlbum();`
		`  }`
		`}`

3	Add a `Click` handler for the Previous menu item.	`private void menuPrevious_Click(`
		`    object sender, EventArgs e)`
		`{`

4	Implement this handler to decrement the current index and redisplay the album.	`  if (Manager.Index > 0)`
		`  {`
		`    Manager.Index--;`
		`    DisplayAlbum();`
		`  }`
		`}`

Note how each handler only modifies the index if there are additional photos before or after the current photo. This prevents the user from navigating outside the bounds of the album. It would be even nicer if we could disable the Next menu item at the end of the album, and the Previous menu item at the start of the album.

	DISABLE NEXT AND PREVIOUS MENUS AS APPROPRIATE	
	Action	**Result**

5	Add an `Opening` event handler for the `ctxMenuPhoto` context strip.	`private void ctxMenuPhoto_Opening(`
		`    object sender, CancelEventArgs e)`
		`{`
		Note: We discuss the `CancelEventArgs` class shown in this code in the next chapter.

6	Enable the Next menu item if the current index is before the last photo in the album.	`  menuNext.Enabled` `    = (Manager.Index < Manager.Album.Count - 1);`
7	Enable the Previous menu item if the current index is after the first photo in the album.	`  menuPrevious.Enabled = (Manager.Index > 0);` `}`

Compile and run the application to verify that the application can navigate images in an album. This completes our integration of the `PhotoAlbum` class into the MyPhotos application. As discussed earlier in the chapter, the remaining menus do nothing right now. If you wish, you can disable or otherwise handle these inactive menus in a consistent fashion.

TRY IT! It would be useful to have First and Last menu items here as well. These would display the first or last photo in the album, respectively. Add these two items to the context menu and implement a `Click` event handler for each.

6.4.3 Displaying album status

As a final change for this chapter, let's improve our status bar a bit by displaying the position of the current photograph within the album. While we are here, let's also display the current photograph's caption, rather than the filename. The following steps update our status strip with these changes.

ADD A POSITION STATUS BAR PANEL		
	Action	**Result**

1	In the MainForm.cs source code window, modify the `SetStatusStrip` method to display the caption in the description panel, as well as the current position in the album position panel.	`private void SetStatusStrip()`
		`{`
		`  if (pbxPhoto.Image != null)`
		`  {`
		`    statusInfo.Text = **Manager.Current.Caption;**`
		`    statusImageSize.Text = . . .;`
		`    **statusAlbumPos.Text**`
		`      **= String.Format(" {0:0}/{1:0} ",**`
		`          **Manager.Index + 1,**`
		`          **Manager.Album.Count);**`
		`  }`
		`  else`
		`    . . .`
		`}`

Compile and run the application, and it should look something like figure 6.1 shown at the start of the chapter.

6.5 RECAP

In this chapter, we rewrote the menu bar and began using the MyPhotoAlbum project developed in chapter 5. We saw how Visual Studio can insert a standard set of menus on a menu strip, saving our poor fingers from doing so manually. We examined the `OpenFileDialg` and `SaveFileDialog` classes to open and save files from and to disk. To support these efforts, we implemented an `AlbumManager` class to manage an album on behalf of our application, and an `AlbumStorage` class to deal with storage issues for an album. The `StreamReader` and `StreamWriter` classes proved useful to store and load text data for an album file.

Other topics included creating a custom exception class, called `AlbumStorageException`, to represent recognizable album storage errors, using TODO tasks in Visual Studio, and ensuring that certain menu items, namely our Next and Previous items, are enabled only when appropriate

We seem to have a knack for introducing little problems into our application. In chapter 4 we were unable to scroll when the full-size image was displayed, and in this chapter we left ourselves a number of TODO tasks to address, plus we ignored the exceptions that might occur when opening, saving, and displaying albums.

The next chapter clears up these problems while introducing the `MessageBox` class, as part of a more general discussion on dialog boxes.

Before we move on to the next chapter, it is worth noting that Microsoft provides a number of Internet newsgroups for questions on C#, Windows Forms, and other aspects of .NET. These are available at Microsoft's News Server at news.microsoft.com, or through a number of websites such as http://groups.google.com. Among the groups provided are microsoft.public.dotnet.framework.windowsforms for questions regarding Windows Forms application development, and microsoft.public.dotnet.languages.csharp for questions regarding the C# programming language. Microsoft also provides online technical forums on Windows Forms and other topics at http://forums.microsoft.com.

CHAPTER 7

Dialog boxes

So far we have used a single window for our MyPhotos application. We have changed its appearance in each chapter, adding controls such as a picture box, menu strip, and status strip, but all controls, events, and other activities have occurred within our one `Form` window. In this chapter we branch out.

Aside from a main application window, another common use for `Form` classes is the creation of dialog boxes. In this chapter we look at both simple message boxes and more complex custom dialog boxes. By the end of the chapter we learn how to

- Create simple message boxes with the `MessageBox` class
- Close and dispose of `Form` objects
- Intercept when a form closes with the `OnFormClosing` method
- Create modal and modeless dialog boxes using the `Form` class

Before we get into generating custom dialog boxes, we first look at how simple messages are displayed using the `MessageBox` class.

7.1 MESSAGE BOXES

Developers, especially object-oriented developers, are always looking for shortcuts. Classes such as `OpenFileDialog` and `SaveFileDialog` not only provide a standard way to prompt a user for files; they also save programmers a lot of time and effort by encapsulating the required window display and interaction code. Another common task programmers face is the need to display a simple message to the user. Our photo album application, for example, should display an error message when an album cannot be saved successfully, or it could pose a question by asking the user if they would like to save the album to an alternate file location.

The .NET Framework provides a `MessageBox` class for this purpose. This class is very similar to the MFC function of the same name, if you happen to be familiar with it. This section shows how this class handles simple interactions with a user. While not actually a `Form` object, this class is the most basic of modal dialog boxes.

All dialog boxes are either modal or modeless. A *modal* dialog box requires the user to respond before the associated program continues. *Modeless* or *nonmodal* dialog boxes allow the application to continue while the dialog box is displayed.

All `MessageBox` windows are modal, while `Form` windows are modal if invoked via the `Form.ShowDialog` method and modeless if invoked via the `Form.Show` method.

Figure 7.1 shows some sample message boxes that we create in this section. The figure shows various button configurations. As you can see, No is defined as the default button in the Unable to Save dialog box. An overview of the `MessageBox` class is provided in .NET Table 7.1.

As indicated in the table, a `MessageBox` instance cannot be instantiated. Instead, the `Show` method creates the message box and returns the result. A number of overloads are available for this method, from a version that takes a single message string to one that accepts a parameter for everything from the title bar text to which button should be the default. We use a few of these variations in this chapter. See the .NET documentation for the complete list.

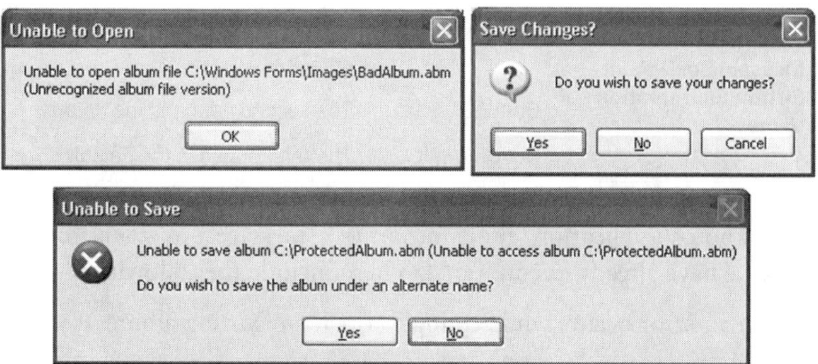

Figure 7.1 A message box consists of message text and a caption shown in the title bar, an optional icon on the left, and one or more buttons at the base of the window.

.NET Table 7.1 MessageBox class

The `MessageBox` class represents a modal dialog box that displays a message or question to the users and waits for their response. This class is part of the `System.Windows.Forms` namespace. A `MessageBox` cannot be instantiated as an object with the `new` keyword; instead the static `Show` method is used to display the dialog box.

By default, a message box displays with no icon and a single OK button. The `Show` method is overloaded to allow these and other settings to be customized. Four enumerations are used for this purpose: `MessageBoxButtons`, `MessageBoxIcon`, `MessageBoxDefaultButton`, and `MessageBoxOptions`. In the following table, the enumeration values for the first three of these four types are described as well.

Public Static Methods	Show	Displays a message box and returns the `DialogResult` enumeration value corresponding to the button selected by the user.
MessageBoxButtons Enumeration Values	OK	Displays an OK button only.
	OKCancel	Displays OK and Cancel buttons.
	YesNo	Displays Yes and No buttons.
	YesNoCancel	Displays Yes, No, and Cancel buttons.
MessageBoxIcon Enumeration Values	Error	Displays an error icon: a white X in a red circle. Use this for unexpected problems that prevent an operation from continuing.
	Information	Displays an information icon: a lowercase letter i in a circle. Use this for general messages about the application such as a status or notification.
	Question	Displays a question mark icon. Use this for Yes/No questions where a choice by the user is required.
	Warning	Displays a warning icon: an exclamation point in a yellow triangle. Use this for problems that may interfere with an operation's ability to continue.
MessageBoxDefault-Button Enumeration Values	Button1	The first button in the message box is the default.
	Button2	The second button is the default.
	Button3	The third button is the default.

In our MyPhotos application, the addition of a message box would be beneficial in situations we have already encountered. These include the following:

- When an error occurs while trying to open an existing album
- When an error occurs while trying to save the current album
- When the current album has changed and is about to be discarded

We create a MessageBox for each of these instances in the subsequent sections.

7.1.1 Creating an OK message box

We begin with the Unable to Open message box shown in figure 7.1. When a selected album cannot be opened, there is not much to do other than inform the user that something is wrong. An error message box is appropriate since a failure here is not typically expected.

HANDLE AN EXCEPTION IN THE MENUFILEOPEN_CLICK METHOD

	Action	Result

1	In the `menuFileOpen_Click` method of the `MainForm` class, enclose the code to open an album in a `try` block.
	
	How-to
	a. Delete to TODO line and select the two lines to enclose.
	b. Right-click and select the Surround With option.
	c. Double-click the `try` item in the pop-up list.
		`private void menuFileOpen_Click(. . .)`
		`{`
		`  . . .`
		`  if (dlg.ShowDialog() == DialogResult.OK)`
		`  {`
		`    **string path = dlg.FileName;**`
		`    // TODO: save any existing album.`
		
		`    **try**`
		`    **{**`
		`      // Open the new album`
		`      Manager = new AlbumManager(**path**);`
		`    **}**`
		
		Note: Of course, you can type this code manually. The how-to steps provide an alternative approach available within Visual Studio. We also altered this code to include a local path variable so we could use this in our `catch` block.

2	Catch the album storage exception that might occur.	`    catch (AlbumStorageException aex)` `    {`

3	In the `catch` block, display a message box and reset the album manager.	`      string msg = String.Format(`
		`        "Unable to open album file {0}\n({1})",`
		`        path, aex.Message);`
		`      MessageBox.Show(msg, "Unable to Open");`
		`      Manager = new AlbumManager();`
		`    }`

4	Either way, display any changes made in the main window and dispose of the `OpenFileDialog` instance.	`    DisplayAlbum();`
		`  }`
		
		`  dlg.Dispose();`
		`}`

We only catch the AlbumStorageException error in this code, since this is the one error we recognize and know how to deal with. A totally unexpected error such as OutOfMemoryException or IOException causes the application to crash. This is not necessary wrong; these are serious errors beyond the scope of our application, and we would not want our application to continue if such an error occurs.

You can, in fact, handle such unexpected errors in an application-wide manner using the AppDomain class. Although a bit beyond our current discussion, the

UnhandledException event in this class is available to process any uncaught exception in a common way for an entire application.

Looking back at the code we created in the previous steps, it is also worth noting that the result returned by the MessageBox.Show method in step 3 is ignored. This is appropriate since there is only a single OK button in the message box.

7.1.2 Creating a YesNo message box

As an alternate example, what happens when an error occurs while saving an album? We could simply display an OK message box as we did while opening an album. This would just duplicate the previous code, so instead we allow the user to save the album under an alternate filename. This is the Unable to Save message box in figure 7.1, and it permits a user to save the album to an alternate location that is less likely to fail.

HANDLE AN EXCEPTION IN THE SAVEALBUM METHOD

	Action	Result
1	Locate the SaveAlbum method that accepts a string.	`private void SaveAlbum(string name)` `{`

2	Enclose the code to save the album in a try block.	`  try`
		`  {`
		`    Manager.Save(name, true);`
		`  }`

3	Catch the storage exception that may occur.	`  catch (AlbumStorageException aex)` `  {`

4	Within the catch block, display a Yes-No error message box with No as the default. Also record the button selected by the user.	`    string msg = String.Format(`
		`      "Unable to save album {0} ({1})\n\n"`
		`      + "Do you wish to save the album "`
		`      + "under an alternate name?",`
		`      name, aex.Message);`
		`    DialogResult result = MessageBox.Show(`
		`      msg,`
		`      "Unable to Save",`
		`      MessageBoxButtons.YesNo,`
		`      MessageBoxIcon.Error,`
		`      MessageBoxDefaultButton.Button2);`

5	If the user wishes to save under an alternate name, prompt the user for a new filename.
	How-to
	Use the SaveAsAlbum method.
		`    if (result == DialogResult.Yes)`
		`      SaveAsAlbum();`
		`  }`
		`}`

Unlike our message for the Open handler, this code examines the value returned by the Show method. This value is a DialogResult enumeration that indicates the button clicked. The values in this enumeration are shown in .NET Table 7.2, and correspond to the kinds of buttons available in many Windows dialog boxes.

Compile and run this code if you wish to see these message boxes in action. You can generate an open error message box easily enough by selecting a file that is not, in

.NET Table 7.2 DialogResult enumeration

The `DialogResult` enumeration represents a value returned by a dialog box. This class is part of the `System.Windows.Forms` namespace, and is used with all dialog boxes in Windows Forms. In particular, a `DialogResult` is returned by the `MessageBox.Show` method, as well as the `ShowDialog` method in both the `Form` and `CommonDialog` classes. This enumeration is also used by the `Button` class to indicate the result that is automatically returned from a modal dialog box when the button is clicked.

Enumeration Values	Abort	The return value is Abort. Typically, this means the user clicked an Abort button in the dialog box.
	Cancel	The return value is Cancel, typically from a Cancel button.
	Ignore	The return value is Ignore, typically from an Ignore button.
	No	The return value is No, typically from a No button.
	None	The return value is not set. Normally this indicates that the dialog box is still running.
	OK	The return value is OK, typically from an OK button.
	Retry	The return value is Retry, typically from a Retry button.
	Yes	The return value is Yes, typically from a Yes button.

fact, an album file. A save error message box can be generated by attempting to save to a read-only CD, or by manually setting an album file to be read-only or protected, and then trying to save to it.

Our last example generates a message box for closing an existing album.

7.1.3 Creating a YesNoCancel message box

As a final example, consider the case where an album has changed but is about to be discarded. This could occur when the application is about to exit, when loading a new album with the Open menu item, and when creating a new album with the New menu item. This is the Save Changes? message box in figure 7.1.

To handle these situations in a consistent manner, let's create a method to gracefully close the current album for all three cases. We call this method `SaveAndCloseAlbum` and have it return a boolean value indicating whether the album was closed or the user clicked the Cancel button.

The three buttons in our message box correspond to the following behavior in our `SaveAndCloseAlbum` method:

- Yes saves the album, then closes the album and returns `true`.
- No does not save the album, but closes the album and returns `true`.
- Cancel does not save or close the album, but returns `false` to indicate that the calling operation should be canceled.

The following steps implement this method.

	Action	Result
	ADD A SAVEANDCLOSEALBUM METHOD	
1	Add a `SaveAndCloseAlbum` method to the `MainForm` class.	`private bool SaveAndCloseAlbum()` `{`

2	Only offer to save the album if it has been modified.	`if (Manager.Album.HasChanged)`
		`{`
		`// Offer to save the current album`

3	Define an appropriate message to display.
	
	Note: We vary the message text depending on whether or not the current album has a name.
		`string msg;`
		`if (String.IsNullOrEmpty(Manager.FullName))`
		`msg = "Do you wish to save your changes?";`
		`else`
		`msg = String.Format("Do you wish to "`
		`+ "save your changes to \n{0}?",`
		`Manager.FullName);`

4	Display the message box and record the result.	`DialogResult result`
		`= MessageBox.Show(this, msg,`
		`"Save Changes?",`
		`MessageBoxButtons.YesNoCancel,`
		`MessageBoxIcon.Question);`

5	Perform the action requested by the user.	`if (result == DialogResult.Yes)`
		`SaveAlbum();`
		`else if (result == DialogResult.Cancel)`
		`return false;  // do not close`
		`}`

6	If the Yes or No button was clicked, close the album and return `true`.	`// Close the album and return true`
		`if (Manager.Album != null)`
		`Manager.Album.Dispose();`
		
		`Manager = new AlbumManager();`
		`SetTitleBar();`
		`return true;`
		`}`

We use this new method in three different places to ensure that the user has the option of saving any changes they might make to the album:

- In `menuFileNew_Click` to save the existing album before a new album is created
- In `menuFileOpen_Click` to save the album before a new album is selected
- In `menuFileExit_Click` to save the album before the application exits

We modify the handlers for the New and Open menu items here. The Exit menu item presents some additional issues, which we take up in the next section. The following table continues our prior steps.

	Action	Result
UPDATE THE HANDLERS FOR THE NEW AND OPEN MENU ITEMS		

7	Modify the `NewAlbum` method to use the `SaveAndCloseAlbum` method.
	
	Note: Since this method is called during initial startup, we need to make sure our manager is not `null` before calling `SaveAndCloseAlbum`.
		`private void NewAlbum()`
		`{`
		`  if (Manager == null || SaveAndCloseAlbum())`
		`  {`
		`    // Album closed, create a new one`
		`    Manager = new AlbumManager();`
		`    DisplayAlbum();`
		`  }`
		`}`

8	Modify the `menuFileOpen_Click` method to use the `SaveAndCloseAlbum` method.	`private void menuFileOpen_Click(. . .)`
		`{`
		`  // Allow user to select a new album`
		`  OpenFileDialog dlg = new OpenFileDialog();`
		`  . . .`
		`  if (dlg.ShowDialog() == DialogResult.OK)`
		`  {`
		`    string path = dlg.FileName;`
		
		`    // Close any existing album`
		`    if (!SaveAndCloseAlbum())`
		`      return;  // Close canceled`
		
		`    try`
		`    {`
		`      // Open the new album`
		`      Manager = new AlbumManager(path);`
		`    }`
		`    . . .`
		`}`

These changes make our application much more user-friendly by interacting with users when they are about to discard a modified album. Our code for the New menu item uses a boolean or (||) expression:

```
if (Manager == null || SaveAndCloseAlbum())
  . . .
```

This is required since our `menuFileNew_Click` method is invoked during startup when the manager is `null`. The `SaveAndCloseAlbum` logic requires that `Manager` is a valid object. Like the C++ language, C# guarantees that an or expression evaluates left to right, so the second item is only evaluated if the first item is `false`. This ensures that the `SaveAndCloseAlbum` method is only called when the `Manager` is, in fact, assigned.

TRY IT! Before moving on, create a `MessageBox` instance in the `menuFile-Remove_Click` method, where the current photograph is removed without any confirmation by the user. Add a question box here to verify that the user does indeed want to remove the current photo.

For the Exit menu item, life is not so easy. We discuss this topic in the next section.

7.2 THE FORM.CLOSE METHOD

In this section we continue our prior discussion of the SaveAndCloseAlbum method from section 7.1.3, after a short interlude on the Close and Dispose methods. You may think this is a little off-topic from dialog boxes, but in fact it is quite relevant. One of the key issues for C# programming in .NET is when to call the Dispose method to clean up window handles and other system resources. This section discusses this topic as it relates to dialog boxes, and introduces the FormClosing event as a way to intercept a user's request to close a form.

7.2.1 Comparing Close and Dispose

Before we return to the topic of calling SaveAndCloseAlbum as our application exits, let's look at the relationship between Close and Dispose in .NET. It's actually quite simple: they are the same. For all classes in the .NET Framework, a call to Close is equivalent to calling the Dispose method, and a call to Dispose is equivalent to calling the Close method. The term *close* traditionally applies to objects like files and windows, and .NET has preserved this terminology. When you have finished with a form or a file, it seems silly to require a call to both Close and Dispose, so it makes sense to merge these two concepts together. The .NET design team could have chosen a common method name for all classes, but programmers naturally expect to close objects such as forms and files, and closing objects like arrays or drawing objects seems a bit odd. Instead, the designers chose to use both methods and define them as equivalent.

When a user closes a Form, the actual behavior varies depending on whether the object is displayed as a modal or modeless window. For a modeless window, displayed with the Form.Show method, the system resources are automatically cleaned up when the form is closed. This makes life much easier for us programmers, since we do not have to remember anything in this case. You cannot use a modeless Form after it is closed because all of its resources are gone. The Hide method can be used if you simply want to remove a Form from the desktop and display it later via the Show method. We see this in chapter 16 when we use a tool strip button to hide the modeless dialog box created in section 7.4 of this chapter.

For modal windows, displayed with the Form.ShowDialog method, there is a problem in that the class is typically accessed after the window disappears. As a result, classes that implement a modal dialog box must call Close or Dispose explicitly to release its system resources. Listing 7.1 illustrates the typical code used to create and destroy such a class.

In this listing, if the resources for the dlg variable disappeared after the ShowDialog method returned, you could not access any of its settings. For this reason, .NET only calls the Hide method after a user responds to a modal dialog box, so that any class settings may still be accessed. This can be a little confusing since we still say the user closes the dialog box, even though the class's `Close` method is not actually called.

Listing 7.1 Typical modal dialog code

```
MyModalDialog dlg = new MyModalDialog();

// Initialize any dlg settings

if (dlg.ShowDialog() == DialogResult.OK)
{
  // Use dlg settings to do something
}
dlg.Dispose()
```

Fortunately, modal dialog boxes tend to have *deterministic scope*, meaning that you can predict when the dialog box is created and destroyed. The application waits until the user responds to a modal dialog box, so it's clear where the `Dispose` method must be called. We have already seen this method used with `OpenFileDialog` and `SaveFileDialog` objects in chapter 6, both of which are modal windows.

The C# language provides a `using` statement to call `Dispose` on our behalf in deterministic situations such as this. We have seen how the `using` directive defines an alias or shortcut for an object or members of a namespace. The `using` statement defines the scope in which a given object should exist. The syntax is as follows:

```
using (object)
{
  // Do something with object
}
```

At the end of the block of code associated with the statement, the identified object is automatically disposed. For example, the code in listing 7.1 can be written to call `Dispose` automatically at the end of the block, as shown in listing 7.2. As another example, listing 7.3 illustrates how our `SaveAsAlbum` method can be rewritten with the `using` statement. The changes from our current implementation are shown in bold.

Listing 7.2 Modal dialog code with using statement

```
using (MyModalDialog dlg = new MyModalDialog)
{
  // Initialize any dlg settings

  if (dlg.ShowDialog() == DialogResult.OK)
  {
    // Use dlg settings to do something
  }
}
```

Listing 7.3 Implementation of menuFileSaveAs_Click with using statement

```
private void SaveAsAlbum()
{
  using (SaveFileDialog dlg = new SaveFileDialog())
  {
    // Display a dialog for saving the album
    dlg.Title = "Save Album";
    dlg.DefaultExt = "abm";
    dlg.Filter = "Album files (*.abm)|*.abm|"
      + "All files|*.*";
    dlg.InitialDirectory = AlbumManager.DefaultLocation;
    dlg.RestoreDirectory = true;
    if (dlg.ShowDialog() == DialogResult.OK)
    {
      // Save the album under the new name
      SaveAlbum(dlg.FileName);

      // Update title bar to include new name
      SetTitleBar();
    }
  } // end of using: dlg.Dispose() is called
}
```

In general, any object that supports the `IDisposable` interface is a candidate for a `using` statement. In particular, you may recall that we supported this interface in our `PhotoAlbum` and `Photograph` classes in chapter 6, so we can apply this statement to our album and photo objects.

For the remainder of the book, we generally employ the `using` statement in our examples to dispose of system resources rather than calling the `Dispose` method explicitly. The resulting code is typically shorter and easier to read and maintain.

7.2.2 Intercepting the Form.Close method

Let's get back to our application and the `SaveAndCloseAlbum` method. Since our application is a modeless dialog box, `Close` should be called when the application exits. In fact, we already call the `Close` method explicitly in the `Click` handler for our Exit menu item.

We could certainly use the `SaveAndCloseAlbum` method directly in our `menuFileExit_Click` handler. While this would work for the Exit menu item, it would not work when the application exits via the Alt+F4 keyboard shortcut or the Close option on the system menu.[1]

[1] The *system menu,* as you probably know, is the menu of operating system commands that appears when you click the control box icon in the upper-left corner of a window. You can also right-click an application's title bar or its entry in the Taskbar to display this menu.

To handle both situations, the Form class provides a FormClosing event that occurs whenever the form is about to close. The protected OnFormClosing method is invoked whenever the Close method is called, and it in turn raises the FormClosing event by invoking any registered event handlers. The signature for this method is as follows:

```
protected virtual void OnFormClosing(FormClosingEventArgs ce);
```

The FormClosingEventArgs object received by this method defines a CloseReason property that indicates why the form is closing, and inherits a Cancel property from the CancelEventArgs base class to help determine whether the application actually exits. If the Cancel property is set to true by an override of the OnFromClosing method or a FormClosing event handler, then the close operation is canceled and the application continues to run. The Cancel property defaults to false, so that the close operation is not canceled and the application exits.

We should also note that a Closing event and OnClosing method also exist in the Form class and provide similar behavior. These members use the CancelEventArgs class directly, so that only a Cancel property is available to a handler or override. I tend to prefer the FormClosing event, which is new in .NET 2.0, since it provides additional information over the Closing event defined as part of .NET 1.*x*. Both approaches work equally well and are fully supported.

We override the OnFormClosing method in our MainForm class to make sure the SaveAndCloseAlbum method is called regardless of how the application exits.

OVERRIDE THE ONFORMCLOSING METHOD

	Action	Result

1	Override the OnFormClosing method in the MainForm class.	`protected override void OnFormClosing`
		`    (FormClosingEventArgs e)`
		`{`

2	Within this method, call the SaveAndCloseAlbum method to see if the current album should be saved.	`  if (SaveAndCloseAlbum() == false)`
3	If the user canceled the operation, then cancel the close operation.	`    e.Cancel = true;` **Note:** This cancels the Close operation so that the application does not exit.

4	Otherwise, allow the application to close.	`  else`
		`    e.Cancel = false;`
		Note: Since false is the default value, these lines are not strictly required. They are here simply to illustrate the setting when the application is permitted to exit.

OVERRIDE THE ONFORMCLOSING METHOD *(CONTINUED)*		
	Action	**Result**

5	Remember to call `OnFormClosing` in the base class.	`base.OnFormClosing(e);`
		`}`
		Note: This call ensures that logic internal to the `Form` class is performed, and ensures that any `FormClosing` event handlers for the form are called before the application exits. Of course, any registered handler can prevent the application from exiting by setting `e.Cancel` to `true`.

Compile and run the application to see this method in action. Add a few photos and try to exit the application using the Exit menu item, the Alt+F4 key, and the Close option from the system menu. In all cases, you should be queried by the `SaveAndCloseAlbum` method—via the question dialog box—whether you want to save the current album. If you click the Cancel button the application does not, in fact, exit.

Before we go on, we should point out that our `OnFormClosing` override can be written more succinctly by taking advantage of the boolean value returned by our close album method:

```
protected override void OnFormClosing(FormClosingEventArgs e)
{
  e.Cancel = !SaveAndCloseAlbum();
  base.OnFormClosing(e);
}
```

Now that we know all about closing a dialog box, let's see how to create one of our own.

7.3 FORMS AND PANELS

In earlier chapters, we added controls such as a `Button`, a `PictureBox`, and a `StatusBar` to our main form, and displayed and managed these objects within the `Form` class on behalf of our application. Forms are one of a number of controls that are designed to contain other controls within their borders. This section introduces two of these controls: the `Form` and `Panel` classes.

Figure 7.2 shows the class hierarchy for these two controls. The `ToolStrip` class is also shown in this diagram to illustrate how it relates to these controls. Let's take a closer look:

❶ The hierarchy for the `Form` class was briefly discussed in chapter 3 along with figure 3.2. The `Form` class is the basis for all desktop windows, so, as you might guess, it contains quite a few members. Some of these are presented in .NET Table 7.3 later in this section.

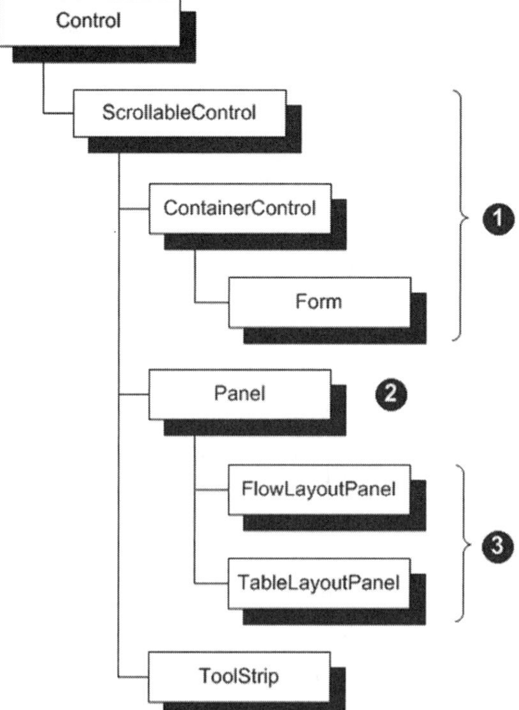

Figure 7.2
The ContainerControl, Panel, and ToolStrip classes are all based on the ScrollableControl class.

❷ The `Panel` class is a scrollable control that acts as a container for other controls. Panels are discussed in the next section.

❸ While the panel control is quite useful, it does not impose any organization on its contained controls. With the .NET 2.0 release, the `FlowLayoutPanel` and `TableLayoutPanel` classes are panels that also define how contained controls are organized for display. The `FlowLayoutPanel` organizes controls one after the other in the panel, while the `TableLayoutPanel` organizes controls in a grid. The `TableLayoutPanel` class is discussed in more detail in section 7.4. The `FlowLayoutPanel` class works in a somewhat similar manner and is not illustrated in this book.

7.3.1 The Form class

The `Form` class is a monster of a class that represents almost any type of window that can appear on the Windows desktop. As a result, it contains all kinds of members intended for various types of windows. A sampling of members specific to the `Form` class appears in .NET Table 7.3.

The `MainForm` class in our MyPhotos application is, of course, derived from the `Form` class. We have also seen modal dialog boxes created using the `SaveFileDialog` and `OpenFileDialog` classes that behave much like a form, using the `ShowDialog` method to display the form and wait for a response.

.NET Table 7.3 Form class

The `Form` class represents a window that can be displayed by an application, including standard windows as well as modal or modeless dialog boxes and multiple document interface (MDI) windows. This class is part of the `System.Windows.Forms` namespace and inherits from the `ContainerControl` class. The contents of a form can be drawn directly by a program, consist of a collection of controls, or some combination of the two. These contents can also be larger than the visible area, with scrolling supported by the `ScrollableControl` class (see .NET Table 13.3).

Public Static Properties	ActiveForm	Gets the `Form` currently active in the application, or `null` if no `Form` is active.
Public Properties	AcceptButton	Gets or sets the button to invoke when the Enter key is pressed. The `CancelButton` property gets or sets the button to invoke when the Esc key is pressed.
	ControlBox	Gets or sets whether a control box appears at the left of the title bar.
	DialogResult	Gets or sets the dialog box result to return when the form is a modal dialog box.
	FormBorderStyle	Gets or sets the border style for the form.
	Icon	Gets or sets the icon for the form.
	IsMdiChild	Gets whether this form is an MDI child form. MDI forms are discussed in chapter 20.
	MaximumSize	Gets or sets the maximum size for a form.
	MinimizeBox	Gets or sets whether a Minimize button appears in the title bar of the form.
	Modal	Gets whether this form is displayed modally.
	ShowInTaskBar	Gets or sets whether the form is displayed in the Windows Taskbar.
	StartPosition	Gets or sets the initial position of the form when it is displayed.
	WindowState	Gets or sets how the form is displayed on the desktop (normal, maximized, or minimized).
Public Methods	Activate	Activates the form and gives it focus.
	Close	Closes the form.
	ShowDialog	Displays this form as a modal dialog box.
Public Events	Deactivate	Occurs when the form has lost the focus.
	FormClosing	Occurs when the main form is about to close. The `FormClosed` event occurs after the form closes.
	Load	Occurs before a form is initially displayed.
	Shown	Occurs when a form is first displayed.

In section 7.4 we construct a modeless dialog box using the `Form` class. Before we do so, a discussion on dialog boxes is in order.

7.3.2 Creating a dialog box

In previous Windows development environments, an explicit class such as `CDialog` created a dialog box directly. In .NET, dialog boxes are created directly from the `Form` class. Table 7.4 summarizes the properties required to turn the default `Form` into a somewhat standard dialog box.

Table 7.4 Turning a Form into a dialog box

Property	Default	Value for Dialog Box	Comments
AcceptButton	(none)	OK button instance	For a modal dialog box, set to the OK or other `Button` the user clicks when finished.
CancelButton	(none)	Cancel button instance	For a modal dialog box, set to the Cancel or other `Button` the user clicks to abort the dialog box.
FormBorderStyle	Sizable	FixedDialog	This creates a fixed-sized window with a thick dialog-style border and no control box on the title bar. Assuming the `ControlBox` setting is `true`, the system menu is still available by right-clicking on the title bar. This value is based on the `FormBorderStyle` enumeration.
HelpButton	False	True or False	Set to `true` if you would like the question mark box to appear on the title bar. The `HelpRequested` event fires when this box is clicked. Note that the question box only appears if the `MaximizeBox` and `MinimumBox` properties are both `false`.
MaximizeBox	True	False	Removes the Maximize button from the title bar.
MinimizeBox	True	False	Removes the Minimize button from the title bar.
ShowInTaskBar	True	False	Does not display the dialog box on the Windows Taskbar.
StartPosition	WindowsDefault-Location	CenterParent	Establishes the initial position for the form. Typically, dialog boxes are centered over the parent window.
Size	300, 300	(varies)	For a fixed-size dialog box, set the window to an appropriate size.

Of course, you may need to modify other properties as well, but these settings establish the appropriate features for a standard dialog box. This table is a good reference when you're creating dialog boxes within an application.

As an example using many of these properties, listing 7.4 illustrates how a `FormDialog` class might be constructed. This class is just a `Form` class that assigns the dialog box properties appropriately so you don't have to. We do not actually use this class in our MyPhotos application, but it might be useful in an application that creates dialog boxes dynamically or that requires a large number of dialog boxes.

Listing 7.4 Sample FormDialog class

```
using System;
using System.Windows.Forms;

namespace MyFormNamespace
{
  public class FormDialog : Form
  {
    public FormDialog()
    {
      FormBorderStyle = FormBorderStyle.FixedDialog;
      MaximizeBox = false;
      MinimizeBox = false;
      ShowInTaskbar = false;
      StartPosition = FormStartPosition.CenterParent;
    }
  }
}
```

7.4 MODELESS DIALOG BOXES

Now that we have briefly discussed form and panel controls in .NET, let's see how to construct one as part of our MyPhotos application. The dialog boxes we have seen thus far are modal. Modal dialog boxes tend to be "in and out"—you open one, you do something, and you close it. Modeless dialog boxes tend to show some information relevant to the program. In a stock analysis program, for example, you might have a stock ticker window that runs independently of the program. This would be a modeless, or nonmodal, dialog box and would update continuously with stock information, perhaps related to a displayed portfolio or to what the user is viewing in the main application window.

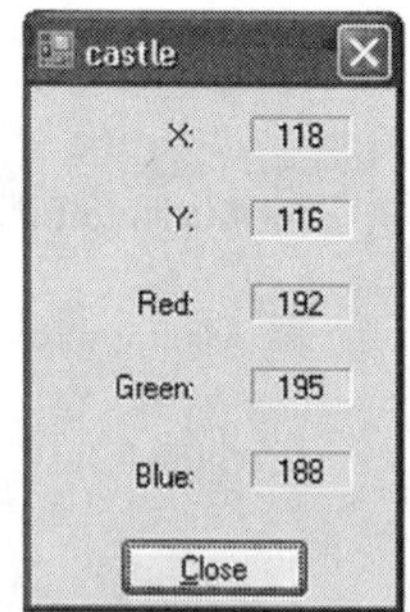

Figure 7.3 Our modeless dialog box shows the image coordinates and RGB color of the pixel indicated by the current location of the cursor.

In this section we create a modeless dialog box to display the pixel location of the mouse pointer within the image window, as well as the color of the image at this location. This information updates continuously as the location of the mouse pointer changes, using the dialog box in figure 7.3. As you can see, the pixel position of the mouse pointer within the image is shown as X and Y coordinates, along with the color in red, green, and blue (RGB) coordinates. This particular figure indicates that the mouse pointer is over the image at pixel (118, 116) of the image, and the current color at that pixel has an RGB value of (192, 195, 188).

We divide the creation of this dialog box into six separate discussions. First, we create the box, then lay out the controls, write some update code, display it from our main form, update the form when the image changes, and finally track when the mouse moves.

7.4.1 Creating a modeless dialog box

The creation of a dialog box is much the same whether it is modal or modeless. First you create a new `Form` class for the dialog box, update properties, add controls, and then process events.

So let's begin by creating the dialog class itself. One question to answer is exactly where to place this class. Creating the dialog class within the MyPhotos project would be fine, but that would restrict our ability to reuse the dialog class in other applications. On the other hand, placing the class in the MyPhotoAlbum project would mix our basic photo and album abstraction with the display medium, in this case Windows Forms. Right now there is nothing in our MyPhotoAlbum project that would prevent it from appearing as part of a web application, and it would be nice to keep it that way.

As you might guess, we solve this by adding a third project to our application, which we call the MyPhotoControls project. The following steps create the basic form within this new project.

CREATE THE PIXELDIALOG CLASS

	Action	Result
1	Add a new MyPhotoControls project to the MyPhotos solution. **How-to** Right-click the MyPhotos solution. Select Windows Control Library as the template in the Add New Project dialog box. **Note:** If you're using an Express edition, this template is not available. Use the Class Library template instead.	The project is added to the solution. Solution Explorer - Solution '... Solution 'MyPhotos' (3 projects) MyPhotoAlbum MyPhotoControls Properties References UserControl1.cs MyPhotos
2	Modify the project so that `Manning.MyPhotoControls` is the default root namespace. **Note:** This is set in the properties for the project, as explained in section 5.4.2.	

<table>
<tr><th colspan="3">CREATE THE PIXELDIALOG CLASS (CONTINUED)</th></tr>
<tr><th></th><th>Action</th><th>Result</th></tr>
<tr><td>3</td><td>Delete the UserControl1.cs file from the solution.

Note: We discuss user controls in chapter 14.</td><td rowspan="4"></td></tr>
<tr><td>4</td><td>Set the assembly version for the library to 7.4.</td></tr>
<tr><td>5</td><td>Add a new Windows Form to the project called PixelDialog.</td></tr>
<tr><td>6</td><td>Within the MyPhotoControls project, add a reference to the existing MyPhotoAlbum project.</td></tr>
<tr><td>7</td><td>Set the properties for the new form as indicated.

Settings<table><tr><th>Property</th><th>Value</th></tr><tr><td>FormBorderStyle</td><td>FixedSingle</td></tr><tr><td>MaximizeBox</td><td>False</td></tr><tr><td>MinimizeBox</td><td>False</td></tr><tr><td>Size</td><td>150,230</td></tr><tr><td>Text</td><td>Pixel Values</td></tr></table>
Note: The border style <code>FixedSingle</code> used here is similar to <code>FixedDialog</code>, except that the control box appears on the form. Since this will be a modeless dialog box, it seems appropriate to display the control box and allow the form to show on the Taskbar.</td><td></td></tr>
</table>

Listing 7.5 shows the code for the PixelDialog.cs file after these steps have been completed. As for the `MainForm` class in our application, all of the designer-generated code is in a separate file, PixelDialog.Designer.cs. The contents of this file are quite similar to the MainForm.Designer.cs file we first examined in chapter 2, so we do not discuss it here. Instead, let's move on to the contents of this new form.

Listing 7.5 Initial contents of PixelDialog.cs file

```
using System;
. . .

namespace Manning.MyPhotoControls
{
  public partial class PixelDialog : Form
  {
    public PixelDialog()
    {
      InitializeComponent();
```

```
        }
    }
}
```

7.4.2 Adding panels and labels to a form

With our form created, we can add the appropriate controls to create the form in figure 7.3. We use the `Label` control for both the headings and values displayed in the dialog box. The `Label` control is mainly used in situations where the user does not need to interact with the control. While labels can respond to events like any other control, they are mainly intended to display text or images. A summary of this class appears in .NET Table 7.5.

.NET Table 7.5 Label class

The `Label` class is a control that displays a text string or image. This class is part of the of the `System.Windows.Forms` namespace, and inherits from the `Control` class. A `Label` object can be assigned a tab index, but when activated the next control in the tab order always receives focus. See .NET Table 3.1 for a list of members inherited from the `Control` class.

Public Properties	AutoSize	Gets or sets whether the label should automatically resize to the size of its contents.
	AutoEllipse	Gets or sets whether the ellipse character is shown when the text extends beyond the width of the control.
	BorderStyle	Gets or sets the `BorderStyle` enumeration value representing the border for the label.
	FlatStyle	Gets or sets the `FlatStyle` enumeration value for the label.
	Image	Gets or sets the image to appear on the label.
	ImageList	Gets or sets an `ImageList` object to associate with the label. The `ImageIndex` property determines which image is displayed on the label.
	PreferredHeight	Gets the height of the control, in pixels, assuming a single line of text is displayed.
	TextAlign	Gets or sets how text is aligned in the label. The `ImageAlign` property gets or sets the image alignment.
	UseMnemonic	Gets or sets whether an ampersand (`&`) in the `Text` property is interpreted as an access key prefix character
Public Events	AutoSizeChanged	Occurs when the value of the `AutoSize` property changes.
	TextAlignChanged	Occurs when the value of the `TextAlign` property changes.

As you can see from the table, the properties and methods in this class are geared toward defining and laying out text and graphics in the control. We use text in this class here, but use this class with graphics later in the book, most notably in section 23.3.

One approach for creating our `PixelDialog` form is to simply drag ten `Label` objects onto the form, adjust their position and properties, add a `Button` control, and we are finished. This is certainly possible, and pretty much the only way to create this form prior to .NET 2.0. If you have some time, this is a good exercise to perform to understand the monotony of the task.

.NET Table 7.6 TableLayoutPanel

New in 2.0 The `TableLayoutPanel` class is a panel that displays contained controls in a grid. The caller determines the number and size of the rows and columns in the grid, and can place a single control within each cell of the grid. Control layout properties such as `Anchor` and `Dock` apply within each cell rather than within the panel. This class is part of the `System.Windows.Forms` namespace, and inherits from the `Panel` class.

The `Panel` class is a `ScrollableControl` that contains other controls, with an added `BorderStyle` property that gets or sets a border. We do not show a separate .NET Table for this class.

Public Properties	*CellBorderStyle*	Gets or sets the border style for the cells panel. Uses the `TableLayoutPanelCellBorderStyle` enumeration.
	ColumnCount	Gets or sets the number of columns to display in the table layout panel.
	ColumnStyles	Gets a collection of `ColumnStyle` objects representing the style of each column in the panel.
	GrowStyle	Gets or sets how the table panel expands when new controls are added, based on the `TableLayoutPanelGrowStyle` enumeration.
	RowCount	Gets or sets the number of rows to display in the table layout panel.
	RowStyles	Gets a collection of `RowStyle` objects representing the style of each column in the panel.
Public Methods	*SetColumnSpan*	Sets the number of columns spanned by a given control in the table panel. The `SetRowSpan` method sets the number of rows spanned by a contained control.
	GetColumnSpan	Gets the number of columns spanned by a given control. The `GetRowSpan` method sets the number of rows spanned by a contained control.
	GetControlFromPosition	Returns the `Control` at a given row and column.
Public Events	*CellPaint*	Occurs when a cell is about to be painted.

The `TableLayoutPanel` class gives us a way to create this form in a kinder, simpler fashion. This class inherits the containment and scrolling capabilities of the `Panel` class, and adds a table layout capability. An overview of this support appears in .NET Table 7.6.

Controls in a `TableLayoutPanel` control can span rows, columns, or both, and table panels can be nested within a cell of another table panel to achieve various layout configurations.[2]

When a control is placed within a cell of a table panel in Visual Studio, a Column, ColumnSpan, Row, and RowSpan "property" appears in the Properties window for the control. They are not real C# properties, but allow the location and span of the control within the table panel to be assigned. In the designer code the appropriate properties or methods are called to set the assigned values. Such properties are called *extender providers*, a topic we present in detail in chapter 9.

We use the `TableLayoutPanel` class to simplify the layout of the `PixelDialog` form, as defined by the following steps.

<table>
<tr><th colspan="3">ADD CONTROLS TO THE PIXELDIALOG CLASS</th></tr>
<tr><th></th><th>Action</th><th>Result</th></tr>
<tr><td>1</td><td>In the designer window for the <code>PixelDialog</code> class, add a <code>TableLayoutPanel</code> that fills all but the bottom portion of the form.

Settings
<table><tr><th>Property</th><th>Value</th></tr><tr><td>GrowStyle</td><td>FixedSize</td></tr><tr><td>RowCount</td><td>5</td></tr></table></td><td rowspan="2">Note: If your rows are not evenly spaced as in the graphic, click the small button for the <code>Rows</code> property item to display the <code>RowStyles</code> collection. Set each row to have size type <code>Percent</code> with value 20.</td></tr>
<tr><td>2</td><td>Add a Close button at the base of the form.

Settings
<table><tr><th>Property</th><th>Value</th></tr><tr><td>(Name)</td><td>btnClose</td></tr><tr><td>Text</td><td>&Close</td></tr></table></td></tr>
</table>

---

[2] In many ways the `TableLayoutPanel` control is similar to the table construct in HTML for building Web pages. This is outside the scope of the book, of course, but worth a mention.

ADD CONTROLS TO THE PIXELDIALOG CLASS		
	Action	**Result**
3	Lock the Toolbox window on the form by clicking the small thumbtack icon at the top of the form.	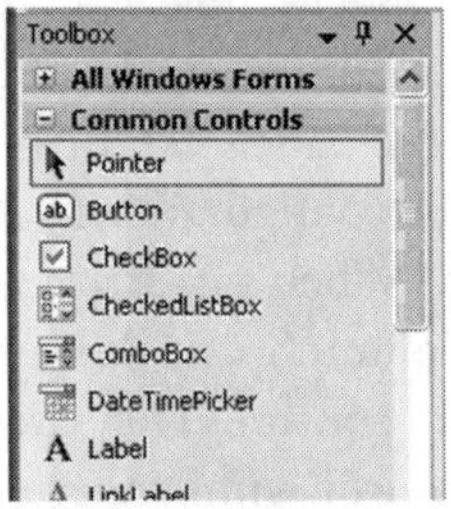
4	Add ten `Label` controls to the table layout panel. **How-to** a. Click the table layout panel so it is the active control. b. Double-click the Label entry in the Toolbox ten times to add the labels. **Note:** In this step you are placing these controls inside the `TableLayoutPanel`, rather than inside the `Form`. This is an important distinction.	The labels are placed in successive cells of the table across and down the panel. 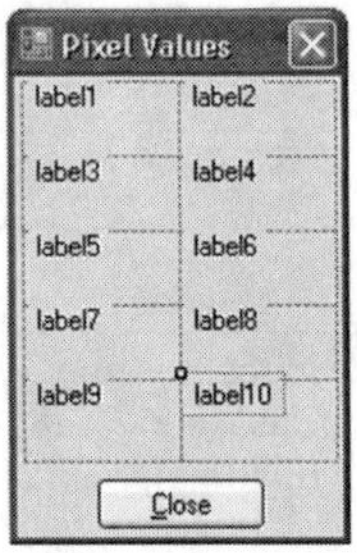
5	Set the `Text` property for the five left-hand labels to X:, Y:, Red:, Green:, and Blue:, respectively.	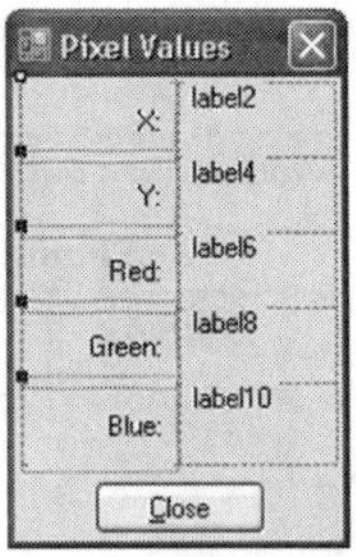
6	Set the properties for all left-hand labels simultaneously as follows. **How-to** a. Click the first label so it is selected. b. Hold down the Ctrl key and click each label in turn until all five are selected. c. Assign the property values as shown. **Settings** Property: Dock — Value: Fill Property: TextAlign — Value: MiddleRight	

ADD CONTROLS TO THE PIXELDIALOG CLASS

	Action	Result
7	Leave the default names for the left-hand controls, and assign the (Name) value for the five right-hand controls to lblX, lblY, lblRed, lblGreen, lblBlue, respectively.	Pixel Values dialog: X:, Y:, Red:, Green:, Blue:, Close
8	Simultaneously set the properties for the five right-hand labels to the indicated values. **Settings** Property / Value AutoSize: False BorderStyle: Fixed3D Margin: 15, 9, 3, 0 Size: 40, 15 Text: *space* TextAlign: MiddleCenter	

This completes the layout of the form. In the final step, the `Margin` property is used to somewhat center each label in the cell. The next task is to figure out how to assign these values for an external image.

TRY IT! Within the `TableLayoutPanel` class, the `Anchor` property of contained controls is interpreted rather differently than for other controls. Reset the `Margin` setting to 0, 0, 0, 0 for one of the labels, and try setting various `Anchor` property combinations to see this behavior.

7.4.3 Updating the PixelDialog controls

With our form established, we need to allow our main application to modify the display values, and make sure the dialog box exits when the Close button is clicked. As usual, we can cram all of this logic into the MyPhotos project, but we know by now that we want to enable reuse of our logic as much as possible.

So ideally we would like to have a method that updates the dialog box controls within the class itself. This allows our `Form` to be used in alternate applications, with the logic required to update the contained controls readily available.

Another feature we need is the ability to close the dialog box. As we see in the next chapter, a modal dialog box can be configured to exit automatically. Since this is a modeless dialog box, we have created the Close button for this purpose.

So our first steps here are to properly close the form and establish an internal way to assign values to the labels.

	Action	Result
ADD ABILITY TO CLOSE AND UPDATE PIXELDIALOG FORM		
1	In the PixelDialog.cs [Design] window, set both the `AcceptButton` property and the `CancelButton` property for the form to `btnClose`.	The properties are set in the `InitializeComponent` method of the PixelDialog.Designer.cs file, and ensure that the dialog box closes when the user presses the Enter or Esc key.

2	Add a `Click` handler for the Close button that closes the form.	`private void btnClose_Click`
		`    (object sender, EventArgs e)`
		`{`
		`  Close();`
		`}`

3	Define a private `SetPixelData` method to assign the labels on the form.	`private void SetPixelData(int x, int y,`
		`  int red, int green, int blue)`
		`{`
		`  lblX.Text = x.ToString();`
		`  lblY.Text = y.ToString();`
		`  lblRed.Text = red.ToString();`
		`  lblGreen.Text = green.ToString();`
		`  lblBlue.Text = blue.ToString();`
		`}`

This ensures our dialog box can be closed, and provides a way for other methods to update the label text. Note how the `Form.Close` method is used to close the form, just like in the Exit menu handler for our main form. The .NET Framework keeps track of which form is the top-level application window, so the `Close` method here closes just the `PixelDialog` window and not the entire application. As you may recall, this method disposes of any system resources allocated by the form as well.

The next task is to provide a way for an external form to update this dialog box. We do this in two ways. The first simply resets all values to zero. The second performs the various calculations necessary to update the values. There is a bunch of math here to translate values between the rectangle where the bitmap is displayed and the actual portion of the bitmap displayed within this rectangle. We won't discuss this math in detail—just trust me when I say it is correct. Of course, I said this in the first edition of the book and some astute readers broke my code, so feel free to scour my logic and prove me wrong again.

ADD THE ABILITY TO UPDATE THE PIXELDIALOG FORM EXTERNALLY

	Action	Result

4 In the MyPhotoAlbum project, define a new `ImageUtility` class that contains a public static method `ScaleToFit` to determine the best fit of a given bitmap within a target rectangle.

```
using System;
using System.Drawing;

namespace Manning.MyPhotoAlbum
{
 public class ImageUtility
 {
  public static Rectangle ScaleToFit(
      Bitmap bmp, Rectangle targetArea)
  {
    Rectangle result = new Rectangle(
        targetArea.Location, targetArea.Size);
```

5 Within this method, determine whether the bitmap fits best along the width or the height. If width, then adjust the result to fit to the width.

```
    // Determine best fit: width or height
    if (result.Height * bmp.Width
        > result.Width * bmp.Height)
    {
      // Final width should match target,
      // determine and center height
      result.Height = result.Width * bmp.Height
                      / bmp.Width;
      result.Y += (targetArea.Height
                   - result.Height) / 2;
    }
```

6 If the bitmap fits best along the height, adjust the result to fit to the height.

```
    else
    {
      // Final height should match target,
      // determine and center width
      result.Width = result.Height * bmp.Width
                     / bmp.Height;
      result.X += (targetArea.Width
                   - result.Width) / 2;
    }
```

7 Either way, return the resulting rectangle.

```
    return result;
  }
 }
}
```

8 Back in the `PixelDialog` class, indicate we are using the MyPhotoAlbum project.

```
. . .
using Manning.MyPhotoAlbum;
. . .
```

9 Implement a public `ClearPixelData` method to reset the values to all zeros.

```
  public void ClearPixelData()
  {
    SetPixelData(0, 0, 0, 0, 0);
  }
```

10 Define a public `UpdatePixelData` that accepts all the information necessary to update the pixel data values.

```
  public void UpdatePixelData(int xPos,
    int yPos,
    Bitmap bmp,            // displayed bitmap
    Rectangle displayRect, // area of display
    Rectangle bmpRect,     // area of bitmap
    PictureBoxSizeMode sizeMode)
  {
```

11 Implement this method to determine the position within the bitmap using the given size mode setting.

```
    // Determine (x,y) position within image
    int x = 0, y = 0;

    switch (sizeMode)
    {
```

	ADD THE ABILITY TO UPDATE THE PIXELDIALOG FORM EXTERNALLY *(CONTINUED)*	
	Action	**Result**

12	For now, do not implement the `AutoSize` and `CenterImage` values.	`case PictureBoxSizeMode.AutoSize:`
		`case PictureBoxSizeMode.CenterImage:`
		`  throw new NotSupportedException(`
		`  "The AutoSize and CenterImage size modes"`
		`    + " are not supported at this time.");`

13	For the `Normal` mode, this image is displayed at actual size. Display the portion of the image shown in the display.	`case PictureBoxSizeMode.Normal:`
		`  // Rectangle coords are image coords`
		`  if (xPos >= bmp.Width`
		`      || yPos >= bmp.Height)`
		`    return; // position outside image`
		
		`  x = xPos - bmpRect.X;`
		`  y = yPos - bmpRect.Y;`
		`  break;`

14	For the `StretchImage` mode, the image fills the entire display area. Translate the given coordinates into image coordinates.	`case PictureBoxSizeMode.StretchImage:`
		`  // Translate rect coords to image`
		`  x = xPos * bmp.Width / displayRect.Width;`
		`  y = yPos * bmp.Height`
		`          / displayRect.Height;`
		`  break;`

15	For the `Zoom` mode, the image is scaled to fit the display area. Translate the position within the display area into the position within the scaled image.	`case PictureBoxSizeMode.Zoom:`
		`  // Determine image rectangle`
		`  Rectangle r2`
		`    = ImageUtility.ScaleToFit(`
		`        bmp, displayRect);`
		
		`  if (!r2.Contains(xPos, yPos))`
		`    return; // position outside image`
		
		`  x = (xPos - r2.Left)`
		`          * bmp.Width / r2.Width;`
		`  y = (yPos - r2.Top)`
		`          * bmp.Height / r2.Height;`
		`  break;`
		`}`

16	Once the image coordinates are calculated, determine the color at this position and display it within the dialog box.	`// Extract color at calculated position`
		`Color c = bmp.GetPixel(x,y);`
		
		`// Update dialog values`
		`SetPixelData(x, y, c.R, c.G, c.B);`
		`}`

And there you have it. These methods update the displayed values each time they are called. An application such as our MyPhotos application can use this to update the values as the mouse moves about the form.

7.4.4 Displaying a modeless dialog box

For modal dialog boxes such as those you create using `OpenFileDialog`, the `Form.ShowDialog` method displays the dialog box and waits for a response, preventing the parent form from accepting any external input until this occurs. For a modeless dialog box, a different method is required to allow the parent form to continue processing user input.

The `Form.Show` method is used for this purpose. The `Show` method is inherited from the `Control` class and sets a control's `Visible` property to `true`. For a `Form`, this means it displays in a modeless fashion. The `Show` method is a `void` method since no immediate result is returned.

As you would expect, we display the form from a menu item.

ADD PIXEL DATA MENU TO THE MYPHOTOS APPLICATION

	Action	Result
1	In the MainForm.cs [Design] window of the MyPhotos project, add a separator at the end of the context menu.	
2	Add a Pixel Data item to the end of this menu. **Settings** **Property** / **Value** (Name): menuPixelData Text: Pi&xel Data...	MyPhotos File Edit View Tools Help ContextMenuStrip Image Next Ctrl+Shift+N Previous Ctrl+Shift+P Pixel Data... Type Here

Before we use this to display the dialog box, let's ponder what support we need for our new class. Since this is a modeless dialog box, it displays while the main form is displayed. So the user may change which photo is displayed, or modify the display mode used. Such changes require that we modify what appears in the dialog.

Since our class does the bulk of the work, all we need to do is keep a reference to a class instance, and update it as required. A handler for the menu item added in step 2 can create the class.

HANDLE THE PIXEL DATA MENU ITEM

	Action	Result
3	In the MyPhotos project, add a reference to the MyPhotoControls project.	The project appears in the list of references for the project in Solution Explorer.
4	In the `MainForm` class, indicate we use this new library.	`. . .` `using Manning.MyPhotoControls;`

5	Add a private field to hold the `PixelDialog` form object, and a corresponding property.	`private PixelDialog _dlgPixel = null;`
		`private PixelDialog PixelForm {`
		`  get { return _dlgPixel; }`
		`  set { _dlgPixel = value; }`
		`}`

6	Add a `Click` handler for the Pixel Data menu.	`protected void menuPixelData_Click(`
		`    object sender, EventArgs e)`
		`{`

	HANDLE THE PIXEL DATA MENU ITEM *(CONTINUED)*	
	Action	**Result**

7	If the `PixelForm` class has not been created or the existing dialog box has been disposed of, create a new dialog box.	`if (PixelForm == null || PixelForm.IsDisposed)`
		`{`
		`  PixelForm = new PixelDialog();`
		`  PixelForm.Owner = this;`
		`}`
		Note: The `Owner` property used here ensures that the `PixelDialog` form is minimized and maximized along with the parent form.

8	Display the dialog box.	`PixelForm.Show();`

9	Assign the initial data to display in the dialog box.	`Point p = pbxPhoto.PointToClient(`
		`  Form.MousePosition);`
		`UpdatePixelDialog(p.X, p.Y);`
		`}`

The code to create and display the dialog box should seem familiar, but what about that code in step 9 of our task? Let's talk about it.

The first line in step 9 converts the current screen coordinates of the mouse pointer to the corresponding coordinates in the `PictureBox` object. This uses the static `Form.MousePosition` property to retrieve the screen coordinates of the mouse pointer as a `Point` instance. The point contains the current X and Y positions of the pointer on the screen in pixels.

The location on the screen is not what we need. We need to know the location of the mouse pointer within the `PictureBox` object—that is, in the `pbxPhoto` control. We can then use this information to calculate what part of the image is at that location.

The `PointToClient` method does this conversion. It accepts a point in screen coordinates and returns the same point in client coordinates. If the given point happens to be outside the control, the returned `Point` contains values outside the display area of the control.

The final line calls an as-yet-undefined `UpdatePixelDialog` method. We write this method in the next section to accept the current position of the mouse pointer in `PictureBox` coordinates and call the `PixelDialog.UpdatePixelData` method with the appropriate settings.

7.4.5 Updating the PixelDialog form

So far we have created and displayed our form as a modeless dialog box. In this section we implement the code to update this dialog box based on the current location of the mouse pointer in the `pbxPhoto` control. We account for the fact that a photo might not be displayed, and that the mouse pointer may be located outside of the control.

The code for UpdatePixelData utilizes the support we already defined in our PixelDialog class.

IMPLEMENT THE UPDATEPIXELDIALOG METHOD		
	Action	**Result**
1	In the MainForm class, add an UpdatePixelDialog method.	`private void UpdatePixelDialog(int x, int y)` `{`
2	Only update the pixel data if the dialog box exists and is visible.	`if (PixelForm != null && PixelForm.Visible)` `{`
3	Get the currently displayed image.	`Bitmap bmp = Manager.CurrentImage;`

4	Display the caption as the title of the pixel dialog box.	`PixelForm.Text = (Manager.Current == null`
		`? "Pixel Data"`
		`: Manager.Current.Caption);`
		
		Note: The question mark (?) works the same as in C++. If the expression evaluates to true, the value before the colon (:) is used; otherwise the value after the colon is used.

5	If no image is displayed or the point is outside the picture box, clear the pixel data values.	`if (bmp == null || !pbxPhoto.`
		`DisplayRectangle.Contains(x, y))`
		`PixelForm.ClearPixelData();`

6	Otherwise, update the data based on the current position, the displayed bitmap, the display area of the picture box, the bitmap area, and the current PictureBoxSizeMode setting.	`else`
		`PixelForm.UpdatePixelData(x, y, bmp,`
		`pbxPhoto.DisplayRectangle,`
		`new Rectangle(0, 0,`
		`bmp.Width, bmp.Height),`
		`pbxPhoto.SizeMode);`
		`}`
		`}`

And once again, there you have it. This method updates the PixelDialog form each time it is called. Most of the work is performed by the class itself. This code simply makes sure the appropriate values are sent to the UpdatePixelData method.

Our final task is to make sure this method is called each time the mouse pointer moves or the displayed information changes.

7.4.6 Tracking mouse movement

In the previous section we created a method to update the dialog box for a given position within the PictureBox control. Now we need to ensure that UpdatePixelDialog is called whenever appropriate.

The most obvious time is whenever the location of the mouse pointer changes. We can use the MouseMove event inherited from the Control class for this purpose. The protected OnMouseMove method raises this event for the form, so we could override OnMouseMove in our Form class. In this case, we would have to convert from Form coordinates to PictureBox coordinates, so handling the event for the

PictureBox class directly is probably a better choice. More importantly, by handling mouse pointer movements in the PictureBox control directly, our code is only called when the movement occurs inside the picture box.

CALL THE UPDATEPIXELDIALOG METHOD WHEN THE MOUSE MOVES		
	ACTION	**RESULT**

1	In the MainForm.cs [Design] window, add a `MouseMove` event handler for the `pbxPhoto` object.	`private void pbxPhoto_MouseMove(`
		`    object sender, MouseEventArgs e)`
		`{`

2	Call the `UpdatePixelData` method with the current mouse pointer coordinates.	`  UpdatePixelDialog(e.X, e.Y);` `}`

The MouseMove event handler receives a MouseEventArgs parameter containing, among other event data, an X and Y property defining the current coordinates of the mouse pointer in the control's coordinates. We discuss this and other mouse events in chapter 10, so we do not go into more detail on this handler here.

The one other instance when the pixel values must be updated is when the displayed image changes. The easiest place to track this is when the DisplayAlbum method is called. Continuing the previous steps:

CALL UPDATEPIXELDATA WHEN CURRENT PHOTO CHANGES		
	Action	**Result**

3	Locate the `DisplayAlbum` method in the MainForm.cs source file.	`private void DisplayAlbum()`
		`{`
		`  pbxPhoto.Image = Manager.CurrentImage;`
		`  SetStatusStrip();`
		`  SetTitleBar();`

4	Call `UpdatePixelDialog` to update the dialog box.	**`  Point p = pbxPhoto.PointToClient(`** **`      Form.MousePosition);`** **`  UpdatePixelDialog(p.X, p.Y);`** `}`

This code uses the same Form.MousePosition property and PointToClient method we saw earlier in this section.

Our modeless dialog box is finished. Compile your code, show your friends, and otherwise verify that the dialog box works properly. Both the main and pixel dialog form can be manipulated at the same time, and the dialog box updates automatically when you display the next or previous image in an album or when the mouse cursor moves inside the control. Also notice that the TableLayoutPanel control cannot be seen since it has no borders, even though it was so critical in positioning the labels on the form.

TRY IT! One change you might make here is to modify the cursor used for the `PictureBox` control to use a small cross-hair rather than the normal arrow. Do this by changing the `Cursor` property for the `PictureBox` object to use the `Cross` cursor.

Another interesting change is to allow the user to hide the `PixelDialog` window from the main application. You can implement this by modifying the `Text` displayed for the `menuPixelData` menu to "Hide Pi&xel Data" whenever the dialog box is displayed and back to "Pi&xel Data..." whenever the box is hidden or closed. Set the appropriate menu text in the `ctxMenuPhoto_Opened` handler, and use the `Hide` or `Visible` property to hide or show the dialog box.

Before we move on to the next topic, let's give a quick summary of what we covered in this chapter.

7.5 RECAP

In this chapter we looked at dialog boxes. We began with simple dialog boxes using the `MessageBox` class, and by the end of the chapter we built a custom modeless dialog box. Along the way we discussed the difference between modal and modeless dialog boxes, caught potential exceptions when opening and saving our album files, examined the relationship between the `Close` and `Dispose` methods, saw how to intercept a closing window using the `OnFormClosing` method, and learned how to track mouse movement within a control.

We also discussed some new controls. The panel classes were presented, and we used the `TableLayoutPanel` control while constructing our `PixelDialog` form. The `Label` class was used, as well, to display information within the `PixelDialog` form.

We are not done with dialog boxes. Since our main form is getting rather full, future topics require additional dialog boxes to expand the capabilities of our program. In particular, the next chapter creates a dialog box for editing the properties of a photograph as a way to introduce specific Windows Forms controls in more detail.

CHAPTER 8

Text boxes

The .NET Framework provides a number of controls for use in Windows Forms applications. The original version of Windows supported `Label`, `TextBox`, `Button`, `RadioButton`, `CheckBox`, `ListBox`, and `ComboBox` controls, inheriting these concepts from other graphical environments and other operating systems. Over the next few chapters we examine these core controls in more detail. As we saw the `Label` control in the previous chapter, this chapter focuses on text box controls.

As usual, we discuss these controls both generally and in the context of our MyPhotos application. Our `PhotoAlbum` and `Photograph` classes already define a number of properties eager to be displayed and edited, so we can focus on the controls themselves and how they are utilized in an application. Specific Windows Forms concepts we cover including the following:

- Inheriting from a Form
- Displaying data in TextBox controls
- Masking data in the MaskedTextBox control
- Processing keyboard input in a text box
- Converting strings into types with the `Parse` method
- Validating masked text box data against a specific type

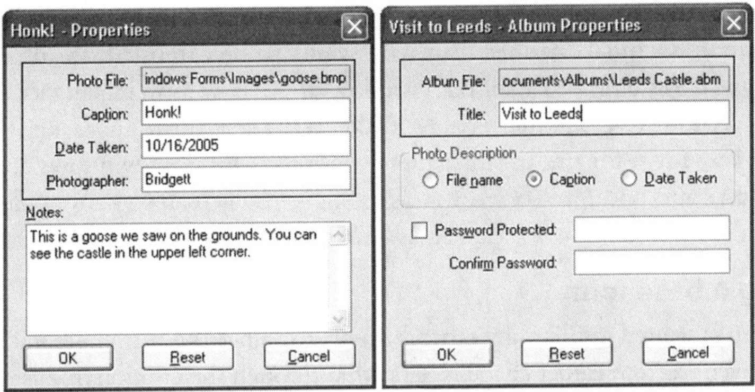

Figure 8.1 These dialog boxes are created using the controls discussed in this and the next chapter.

To enable our discussion of all this and more, we create two modal dialog boxes for our form, shown in figure 8.1. These represent various settings the user can modify on an individual photograph or entire album. While we discuss each control generally, these two dialog boxes serve to demonstrate the creation and usage of each control as we move through this and the next chapter. This chapter builds the dialog box for `Photograph` objects, and chapter 9 builds the `PhotoAlbum` dialog box.

We begin our discussion with form inheritance.

8.1 Form inheritance

The concept of class inheritance is often explained with the canonical `Employee` class derived from a `Person` class. The derived class, in this case `Employee`, inherits the properties and functionality found in the parent class, in this case `Person`. For example, the `Person` class might provide properties and methods for tracking the address of a person. The `Employee` class inherits these members and supports this functionality without the addition of any new code.

Since all Windows Forms controls are classes, a similar behavior is available for forms and other controls. You can create a form, and then reuse that form in the creation of additional forms. The parent form defines various members and controls that child forms inherit. Controls on the form define their access level, such as `private`, `protected`, or `public`, just like members of any other class. A child form can modify these controls to the extent of their assigned access level.

We illustrate this in our application with the two dialog boxes shown in figure 8.1. The first is for editing the properties of a photograph, the second for editing the properties of an album. While the contents of these two windows are entirely different, they are both modal dialog boxes and share a common set of buttons at the base of the form and a panel at the top.

We could just be very careful here, and ensure that the two dialog boxes appear and behave in a similar manner. But who wants to be careful? Instead, this is a great chance to use a common `Form` for both windows to see how form inheritance works.

In this section we create the base `BaseEditDialog` form and a derived `PhotoEditDialog` form for use in subsequent sections. Our new windows are specific to the `PhotoAlbum` and `Photograph` classes but generally usable by any application, so we place them in the `MyPhotoControls` assembly created in the previous chapter.

8.1.1 Creating a base form

A base form is created just like any other form object. Since this form does not use any controls we haven't seen in earlier chapters, let's whip through the creation of this new window, starting with the form and its controls.

CREATE THE BASEEDITDIALOG FORM

	Action	Result
1	Add a new `Form` called `BaseEditDialog` to the MyPhotoControls project.	The new class appears in the Solution Explorer window and the BaseEditDialog.cs [Design] window is shown.
2	Add three buttons to the bottom of the form, with properties and positioning as shown. **Settings** **Button** / **Property** / **Value** OK: (Name) = btnOk; DialogResult = OK; Text = &OK Reset: (Name) = btnReset; Text = &Reset Cancel: (Name) = btnCancel; DialogResult = Cancel; Text = &Cancel	BaseEditDialog window with buttons OK, Reset, Cancel
3	Set the properties for the `BaseEditDialog` form to make it a dialog box. **Settings** **Property** / **Value** AcceptButton = btnOk CancelButton = btnCancel FormBorderStyle = FixedDialog MaximizeBox = False MinimizeBox = False ShowInTaskBar = False	BaseEditDialog window with buttons OK, Reset, Cancel

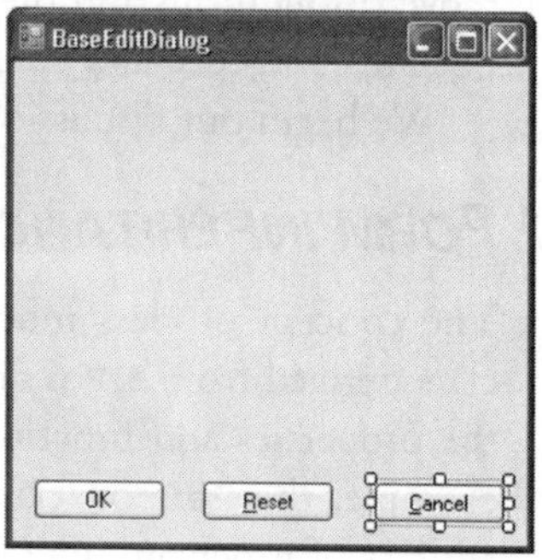

	CREATE THE BASEEDITDIALOG FORM *(CONTINUED)*	
	Action	**Result**
4	Finally, add a `Panel` control to the top of the form. **Settings** **Property** / **Value** BorderStyle / FixedSingle Modifiers / Protected	BaseEditDialog

The generated code for this form is similar to what we have seen for other forms in our application. The one exception is our `Panel` control. Display the BaseEditDialog.Designer.cs file, an extract of which is shown in listing 8.1. As you can see, the three buttons are defined as `private` controls just like controls we created in earlier chapters. The `Panel` is a `protected` control. This small change was accomplished by assigning a Modifiers setting for the panel, and allows our child forms to alter the settings for this control.

Listing 8.1 Initial BaseEditDialog.Designer.cs file contents

```
namespace Manning.MyPhotoControls
{
  partial class BaseEditDialog
  {
    . . .
    #region Windows Form Designer generated code
    . . .
    #endregion

    private System.Windows.Forms.Button btnOK;
    private System.Windows.Forms.Button btnReset;
    private System.Windows.Forms.Button btnCancel;
    protected System.Windows.Forms.Panel panel1;
  }
}
```

While the Modifiers setting appears in the Properties window for all controls, it is not a property in the C# sense, nor does it appear in the .NET documentation for the `Panel` or any other class. This setting exists to allow the access level for a control to be assigned within Visual Studio. There are five possible values for this setting, as shown in table 8.1.

Since our intent was to allow a subclass to modify this panel, we could have used either the Protected or Protected Internal setting here. There is no reason to prevent

Table 8.1 Values for the Modifiers setting for controls in Visual Studio

Value	C# equivalent	Form inheritance notes
Public	public	Any class, regardless of where and how it is defined, can modify the control. This is not typically recommended, since you do not want any object to modify the location, size, or other internal settings for the control.
Protected	Protected	Any subclass of the form, regardless of where it is defined, can modify the control.
Protected Internal	protected internal	Any subclass defined in the same assembly as the base form can modify the control.
Internal	internal	Any class in the same assembly, regardless of how it is defined, can modify the control. This is safer than public access, since you normally have control over the classes that appear in an assembly.
Private	private	No subclass of the form can modify the control. This is the default setting.

derived forms in external assemblies from modifying the panel, so we used the Protected value.

Before we move on, notice that, since our OK, Reset, and Cancel buttons are private, subclasses of `BaseEditDialog` cannot add `Click` event handlers for these buttons. The OK and Cancel buttons have assigned actions due to their `DialogResult` property setting. The `DialogResult` property causes the parent form to hide[1] the dialog box and receive the assigned value as the result from the `ShowDialog` method. So the OK and Cancel buttons work as expected. We need a way to perform an action when the Reset button is clicked, in a way that can be modified in our child forms. In light of this, the following steps establish a standard mechanism for resetting the dialog box.

DEFINE A METHOD TO RESET THE DIALOG BOX

	Action	Result

5	Create a virtual `ResetDialog` method that can be overridden in child classes.	`protected virtual void ResetDialog()`
		`{`
		`  // Does nothing in base class`
		`}`

6	Handle the `Click` event for the Reset button to invoke this method.	`private void btnReset_Click(`
		`    object sender, EventArgs e)`
		`{`
		`  ResetDialog();`
		`}`

[1] The term "hide" here is intentional. Pursuant to our discussion on `Close` and `Dispose` in chapter 7, modal dialog boxes must be disposed of manually. As a result, the framework only hides our dialog box by calling the `Hide` method when the OK or Cancel button is clicked.

Next, let's create a derived form for editing a photograph's settings. The `BaseEditDialog` form is the parent for this new form.

8.1.2 Creating a derived form

A new form is derived from an existing form the same way that any new class is derived from an existing class. The base form is defined as the parent class of the new form (the `partial` keyword here is optional, of course):

```
public partial class PhotoEditDialog :
      Manning.MyPhotoControls.BaseEditDialog
{
  // class definition goes here
}
```

In our case, we create a derived form and leave the addition of new members for subsequent sections. Visual Studio supports the creation of inherited forms graphically via an Add Inherited Form item in the Project menu, or from the context menu of the project itself. This is detailed in the following steps.

DERIVE A PHOTOEDITDIALOG FORM FROM THE BASEEDITDIALOG FORM		
	Action	**Result**
1	Add a new form called `PhotoEditDialog` to the MyPhotoControls project. **How-to** a. Use the keyboard shortcut Ctrl+Shift+A. b. Click the Inherited Form template. c. Enter the name "PhotoEditDialog." d. Click the Add button. **Note:** In the Express Edition, this template does not exist. In this case, create a new `Form` and modify it manually to match the code preceding this table.	The Inheritance Picker window appears. Inheritance Picker Specify the component to inherit from: Component Name / Namespace / Location BaseEditDialog / Manning.MyPhotoControls / C:\Windows Forms\Projects\MyPhotos\MyPhotoContr PixelDialog / Manning.MyPhotoControls / C:\Windows Forms\Projects\MyPhotos\MyPhotoContr New component name: PhotoEditDialog Browse... OK Cancel

	DERIVE A PHOTOEDITDIALOG FORM FROM THE BASEEDITDIALOG FORM *(CONTINUED)*	
	Action	**Result**
2	Select `BaseEditDialog` as the base form, and click OK. **Note:** Only compiled forms are shown in the Inheritance Picker window, so the MyPhotoControls project must be built for the `BaseEditDialog` form to appear.	The new form is added to the project and inherits from the `BaseEditDialog` class. The PhotoEditDialog.cs [Design] window is shown. Photo Properties OK Reset Cancel **Note:** Each control displays a small graphic to indicate that it is inherited by the form.
3	Set the `Text` property for the new form to "Photo Properties."	

That's all it takes. There are a couple interesting features to point out here. The code in the PhotoEditDialog.cs file is similar to the code shown at the start of this section. The `InitializeComponent` method in the generated PhotoEditDialog.Designer.cs file is shown in listing 8.2. The generated `InitializeComponent` method is interesting not for what it contains, but for what it is missing.

Listing 8.2 Excerpt of initial PhotoEditDialog.Designer.cs file

```
namespace Manning.MyPhotoControls
{
  partial class PhotoEditDialog
  {
    . . .
    #region Windows Form Designer generated code
    . . .
    private void InitializeComponent()
    {
      this.SuspendLayout();
      //
      // PhotoEditDialog
      //
      this.AutoScaleDimensions = new System.Drawing.SizeF(6F, 13F);
      this.ClientSize = new System.Drawing.Size(292, 266);
      this.Name = "PhotoEditDialog";
      this.Text = "Photo Properties";
      this.ResumeLayout(false);
```

```
    }
    #endregion
  }
}
```

In the code, notice how the panel and button controls are not listed, as they are inherited from the base form. As a result, only the `Form` properties are assigned here. If you click the OK button in the designer window, a small lock appears to indicate that the button cannot be moved or modified. The properties for this button are grayed out and read-only to indicate this fact as well.

We are ready to discuss the specific controls for our `PhotoEditDialog` form now. Before we do, realize how powerful this inheritance feature really is. Consider, for example, a standard form showing the contents of a database table. Applications that use this table can customize the form for their specific needs, or libraries that extend the existing database can build a new form based on the original. In many cases, changes to the original database can be encoded in the base class in such a way that no changes are required in the inherited forms.

When you need a set of forms in your application based on a common concept or theme, consider creating a base form from which other forms can be derived.

8.2 STANDARD TEXT BOXES

We took a brief look at labels in chapter 7, so here we expand our repertoire to include text boxes as well. Both controls are required to build the `PhotoEditDialog` as it appears in figure 8.1. This dialog box displays the following settings, corresponding to the properties we created in our `Photograph` class:

- `Caption`—A brief string describing the photo.
- `DateTaken`—The date the photograph was taken. In this chapter we present the date as a string. In chapter 14 we replace this with a `DateTimePicker` control.
- `Photographer`—The person who took the photograph. This setting is a string. In chapter 12 we utilize a `ComboBox` control for this setting so the user can see a drop-down list of photographers for the album.
- `Notes`—Random notes or other comments about the photograph. This is a potentially long string, so we employ text box with multiple lines for this property.

This section creates `TextBox` controls on the form for these settings: first the panel area and then the Notes section. We finish by hooking the new dialog box into our MyPhotos application.

8.2.1 Adding text boxes

In chapter 7 we used the `TableLayoutPanel` control to align a set of labels on the `PixelDialog` form. Here we align a set of labels and text boxes, but the concept is much the same. Let's add the required controls to the table panel, and then discuss some features of the `TextBox` control.

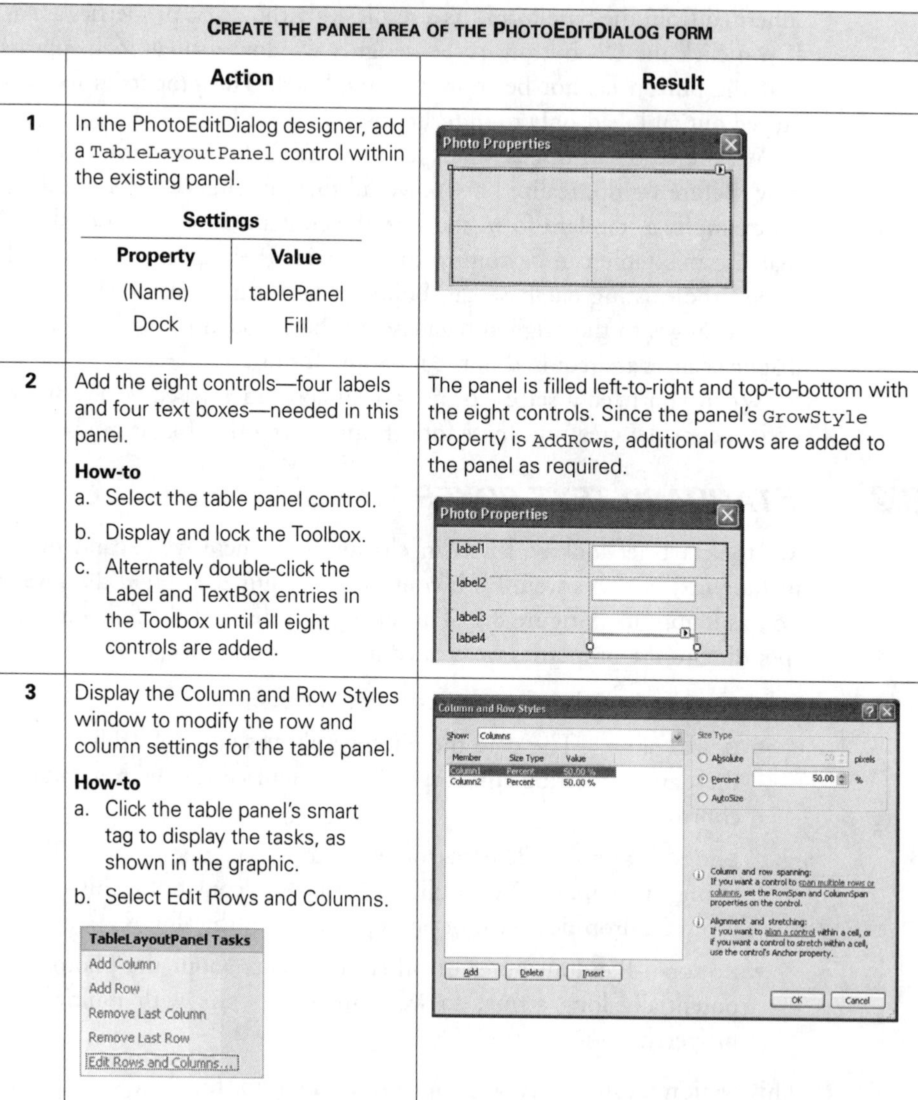

CREATE THE PANEL AREA OF THE PHOTOEDITDIALOG FORM

	Action	Result
1	In the PhotoEditDialog designer, add a `TableLayoutPanel` control within the existing panel. **Settings** **Property** — **Value** (Name) — tablePanel Dock — Fill	
2	Add the eight controls—four labels and four text boxes—needed in this panel. **How-to** a. Select the table panel control. b. Display and lock the Toolbox. c. Alternately double-click the Label and TextBox entries in the Toolbox until all eight controls are added.	The panel is filled left-to-right and top-to-bottom with the eight controls. Since the panel's `GrowStyle` property is `AddRows`, additional rows are added to the panel as required.
3	Display the Column and Row Styles window to modify the row and column settings for the table panel. **How-to** a. Click the table panel's smart tag to display the tasks, as shown in the graphic. b. Select Edit Rows and Columns.	

CREATE THE PANEL AREA OF THE PHOTOEDITDIALOG FORM *(CONTINUED)*		
	Action	**Result**
4	Use this window to modify the panel's columns to use 35% and 65% of the space, respectively, and set each row to use 25% of the available space. **How-to** a. Click Column1 and set its Size Type to Percent with a 35% value. b. Click Column2 and set its Size Type to Percent with a 65% value. c. In the Show drop-down, select the Rows option. d. Hold down the mouse and select all four rows. e. Set the Size Type for all rows to Percent with a 25% value. f. Click the OK button.	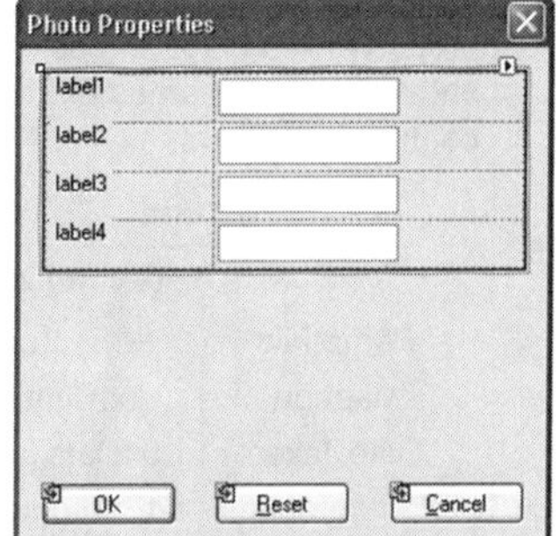
5	For all label controls, set the `Dock` property to `Fill` and the `TextAlign` property to `MiddleRight`. Set the `Text` property for each label as follows. **Settings** **Label** / **Text Property** label1 — Photo &File: label2 — Cap&tion: label3 — &Date Taken: label4 — &Photographer:	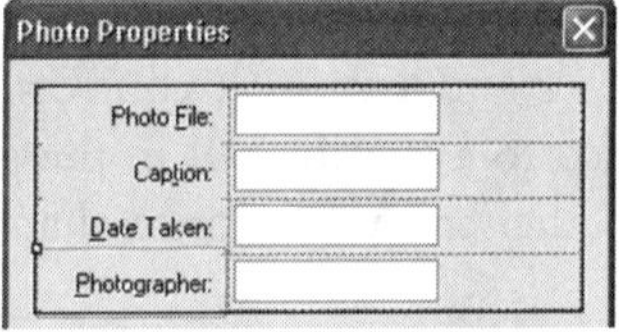

	CREATE THE PANEL AREA OF THE PHOTOEDITDIALOG FORM *(CONTINUED)*	
	Action	**Result**
6	For the text boxes, set the `ReadOnly` property of the first text box to True, and the variable names for the four controls as follows. **Settings** **TextBox** — **(Name) value** Photo File — txtPhotoFile Caption — txtCaption Date Taken — txtDateTaken Photographer — txtPhotographer	Photo Properties Photo File: Caption: Date Taken: Photographer: OK Reset Cancel
7	Expand the four `TextBox` controls simultaneously to fill their cells, so they appear as in the graphic.	

Note how the `txtPhotoFile` text box displays a gray background to indicate that it is read only. The label and text box controls are defined within the table layout panel control, which in turn is defined within the panel. Listing 8.3 shows the generated code in the generated `InitializeComponent` method for the panels and the first `Label` and `TextBox` controls. In the listing, note how each control in the table is added to a specific cell in the grid, with control properties assigned as we have seen for other controls in prior chapters.

Listing 8.3 TableLayoutPanel settings for the PhotoEditDialog form

```
//
// panel1
//
this.panel1.Controls.Add(this.tablePanel);
//
// tablePanel
//
this.tablePanel.ColumnCount = 2;
this.tablePanel.ColumnStyles.Add(
    new System.Windows.Forms.ColumnStyle(
      System.Windows.Forms.SizeType.Percent, 35F));
this.tablePanel.ColumnStyles.Add(
    new System.Windows.Forms.ColumnStyle(
      System.Windows.Forms.SizeType.Percent, 65F));
this.tablePanel.Controls.Add(this.label1, 0, 0);
this.tablePanel.Controls.Add(this.txtPhotoFile, 1, 0);
this.tablePanel.Controls.Add(this.label2, 0, 1);
this.tablePanel.Controls.Add(this.txtCaption, 1, 1);
this.tablePanel.Controls.Add(this.label3, 0, 2);
this.tablePanel.Controls.Add(this.txtDateTaken, 1, 2);
```

```
this.tablePanel.Controls.Add(this.label4, 0, 3);
this.tablePanel.Controls.Add(this.txtPhotographer, 1, 3);
this.tablePanel.Dock = System.Windows.Forms.DockStyle.Fill;
this.tablePanel.Location = new System.Drawing.Point(0, 0);
this.tablePanel.Name = "tablePanel";
this.tablePanel.RowCount = 4;
this.tablePanel.RowStyles.Add(
    new System.Windows.Forms.RowStyle(
      System.Windows.Forms.SizeType.Percent, 25F));
this.tablePanel.RowStyles.Add(
    new System.Windows.Forms.RowStyle(
      System.Windows.Forms.SizeType.Percent, 25F));
. . .
//
// label1
//
this.label1.AutoSize = true;
this.label1.Dock = System.Windows.Forms.DockStyle.Fill;
this.label1.Location = new System.Drawing.Point(3, 0);
this.label1.Name = "label1";
this.label1.Size = new System.Drawing.Size(87, 26);
this.label1.TabIndex = 0;
this.label1.Text = "Photo &File:";
this.label1.TextAlign = System.Drawing.ContentAlignment.MiddleRight;
//
// txtPhotoFile
//
this.txtPhotoFile.Location = new System.Drawing.Point(96, 3);
this.txtPhotoFile.Name = "txtPhotoFile";
this.txtPhotoFile.ReadOnly = true;
this.txtPhotoFile.Size = new System.Drawing.Size(167, 20);
this.txtPhotoFile.TabIndex = 1;
```

The control for the photograph's filename is set to read only, since we do not want our user modifying this value. We could have used a label with a 3D border here, much like we did for the values shown in the `PixelDialog` form in chapter 7. The difference is that a read-only `TextBox` permits the user to select and copy text out of the control, while a `Label` does not. I generally prefer the `TextBox` control in most situations for this reason, just in case a user wants to copy the displayed information.

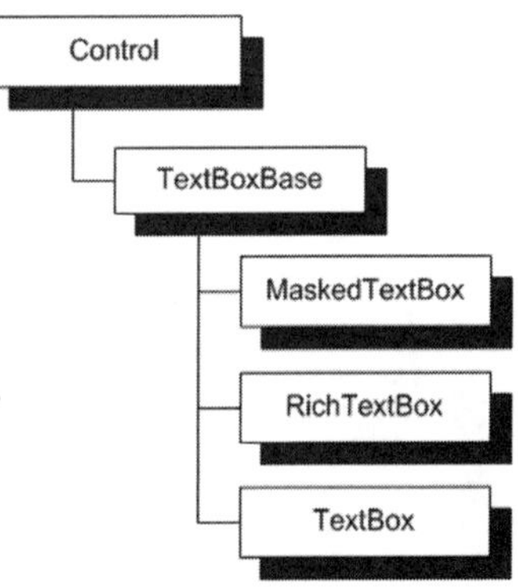

Figure 8.2 The various text box classes display and manipulate text within the bounds of a control.

As shown in figure 8.2, the `TextBox` class is based on the `TextBoxBase` class. The base class provides much of the core functionally for all text boxes, and is summarized in .NET Table 8.2. We discuss the MaskedTextBox control later in this chapter. The RichTextBox class supports more advanced formatting features than a standard text box, displaying both plain text and Rich Text Format (RTF) information. Various character and paragraph formatting can be

.NET Table 8.2 TextBoxBase class

The TextBoxBase class is a control that displays editable text and can interact with the Clipboard class to permit cut and paste operations. This class is part of the of the System.Windows.Forms namespace, and inherits from the Control class. The Control class is summarized in .NET Table 3.1.

Public Properties	AcceptsTab	Gets or sets whether a multiline text box displays a Tab character or moves focus to the next control when the Tab key is pressed.
	CanUndo	Gets or sets whether the user can undo the previous edit performed in the text box.
	Lines	Gets or sets the lines of text in the text box as an array of strings.
	MaxLength	Gets or sets the maximum number of characters the control will accept.
	Multiline	Gets or sets whether this is a multiline text box.
	ReadOnly	Gets or sets whether the text is read only.
	SelectedText	Gets or sets the currently selected text in the control. The SelectedStart property indicates the location of the first selected character.
	TextLength	Gets the length of text in the text box. The Text property is overridden to contain the text for the control.
	WordWrap	Gets or sets whether long lines in a multiline text box wrap to the next line as required.
Public Methods	AppendText	Adds a string to the end of the existing text.
	Copy	Moves the current text into the Windows clipboard.
	Paste	Replaces the current selection with the contents of the clipboard.
	SelectAll	Selects all text in the control. The Select method selects a substring.
	Undo	Undoes the last edit operation in the text box.
Public Events	MultilineChanged	Occurs when the Multiline property changes.
	ReadOnlyChanged	Occurs when the ReadOnly property changes.

assigned to a portion or all of the text in the control. For more on this class, see the .NET Framework Reference documentation for `RichTextBox`, which contains an example that loads an RTF file into a `RichTextBox` control and then changes the font style for a portion of the text.

The `TextBox` and `RichTextBox` classes manage a single line of text by default, and only support multiple lines when the `Multiline` property is set to `true`. This is our next topic.

8.2.2 Adding a multiline text box

In this section we create the Notes section of our dialog box to illustrate a multiline text box. A number of properties affect the behavior of text boxes generally and multiline text boxes in particular. Many of these are inherited from the `TextBoxBase` control, such as the `WordWrap` property, which specifies whether long lines of text automatically wrap to the next line. Additional properties specific to the `TextBox` control are summarized in .NET Table 8.3.

.NET Table 8.3 TextBox class

The `TextBox` class is a text box that displays a single font. This control is part of the `System.Windows.Forms` namespace, and inherits from the `TextBoxBase` control. Through its parent class, text boxes can support single or multiple lines, and interact with the clipboard to cut, copy, and paste text.

Public Properties	AcceptsReturn	Gets or sets whether the Enter key in a multiline text box adds a new line or activates the default accept button for the form.
	AutoCompleteMode	Gets or sets the style of automatic completion applied to the control.
	AutoCompleteSource	Gets or sets the source for automatic completion strings applied to the control.
	CharacterCasing	Gets or sets a `CharacterCasing` enumeration value that defines the capitalization of characters in the box.
	PasswordChar	Gets or sets the character used to mask the text in the control. When assigned, cutting and copying from the control is disabled.
	ScrollBars	Gets or sets which scroll bars, if any, appear in a multiline text box.
	TextAlign	Gets or sets how text is aligned in the control.
	UseSystemPasswordChar	Gets or sets whether the OS-supplied password character should be used.
Public Events	TextAlignChanged	Occurs when the `TextAlign` property changes.

Some of the properties shown in .NET Table 8.3 are required for the Notes section of our `PhotoEditDialog` form. We get to these in a minute. First, a brief mention of the automatic completion properties is in order, since these are new in .NET 2.0. These enable suggested completions of the initial text entered by a user, much like most Internet browsers do these days, where possible completions of an entered URL string are displayed below the text. We use this feature while discussing the `ComboBox` class, so we see an example of this feature in chapter 12.

In our MyPhotos application, we make use of the properties to accept return characters, create a text box with multiple lines, and enable scrolling within the control. The following steps are required to make these changes. We use the password feature while building a dialog box for `PhotoAlbum` objects in chapter 9.

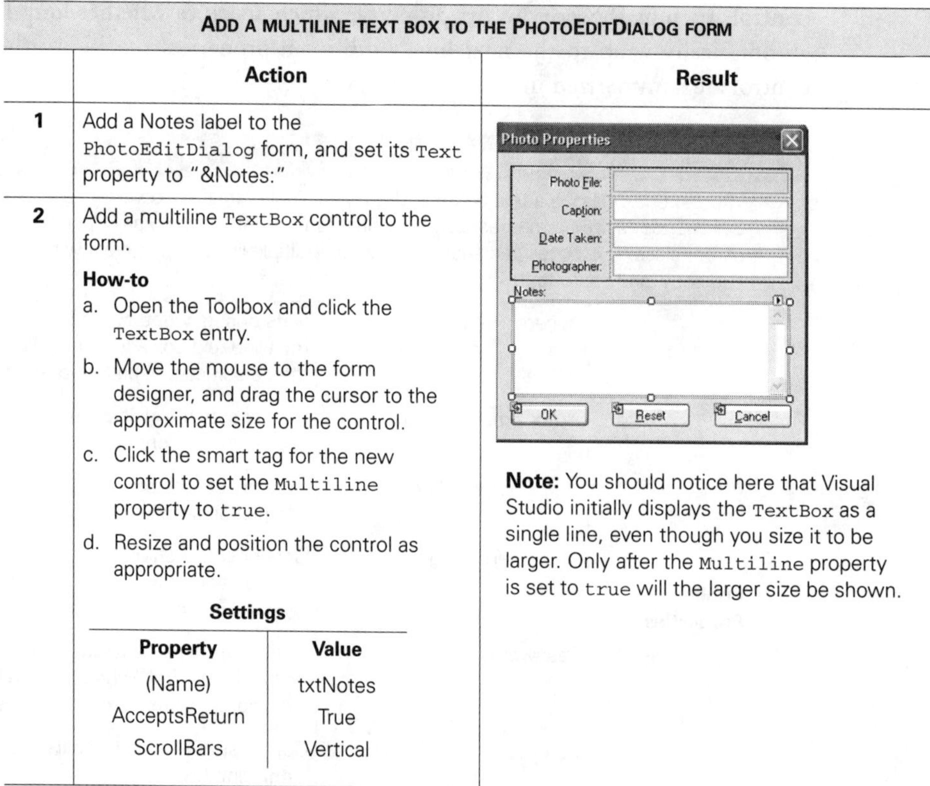

ADD A MULTILINE TEXT BOX TO THE PHOTOEDITDIALOG FORM

	Action	Result
1	Add a Notes label to the `PhotoEditDialog` form, and set its `Text` property to "&Notes:"	Photo Properties Photo File: Caption: Date Taken: Photographer: Notes: OK Reset Cancel **Note:** You should notice here that Visual Studio initially displays the `TextBox` as a single line, even though you size it to be larger. Only after the `Multiline` property is set to `true` will the larger size be shown.
2	Add a multiline `TextBox` control to the form. **How-to** a. Open the Toolbox and click the `TextBox` entry. b. Move the mouse to the form designer, and drag the cursor to the approximate size for the control. c. Click the smart tag for the new control to set the `Multiline` property to `true`. d. Resize and position the control as appropriate. **Settings** **Property** / **Value** (Name) / txtNotes AcceptsReturn / True ScrollBars / Vertical	

Let's clarify a couple points about these changes. In Visual Studio, the `AutoSize` property in the `Label` control is set to `true` by default. This causes the control to resize automatically based on the assigned text. If you change the text to "Notes on this photograph:" the size will automatically expand to fit the new text.

For the `TextBox`, step 2 illustrates one method of creating a multiline control. No matter how the control is added, the `Multiline` property must be set to `true` before Visual Studio allows the TextBox to be resized vertically and displayed with more than a single line.

By default, the text within a text box is aligned on the left side of the control. The TextBox class is one of a number of controls that provide alignment properties to define how information within the control is displayed. Typically, these properties define either a ContentAlignment enumeration value or a HorizontalAlignment enumeration value. The ContentAlignment enumeration is part of the System.Drawing namespace, and defines how text or objects align both vertically and horizontally on the drawing surface of the control. The values for this enumeration define a vertical alignment of Bottom, Middle, or Top and a horizontal alignment of Left, Center, or Right. This results in the nine possible values from BottomLeft, BottomCenter, and so forth on to TopRight. The Label class presented in chapter 7 uses this enumeration for both the TextAlign and ImageAlign properties, as does the ButtonBase class we examine in chapter 9.

The HorizontalAlignment enumeration is part of the System.Windows.Forms namespace, and defines how text or objects aligns horizontally within the control. Three values are possible: Center, Left, and Right. This enumeration is used by numerous Windows Forms classes, including the ComboBox, Label, ListBox, and TextBox classes.

Returning to our MyPhotos application, the PhotoEditDialog form is now fully defined, so all that remains is to link up a Photograph object within the form. If this is not your first introduction to Windows Forms, you might think about using data binding to bind values in the Photograph class to controls on our form. We save our discussion on data binding for chapters 21 and 22, so here we link our class values to controls by hand. It is important to understand the various options the framework provides, and to keep our chapters and discussions to a manageable length.

The following table extends our prior steps and completes our dialog box.

ASSIGNING PHOTOGRAPH VALUES TO PHOTOEDITDIALOG CONTROLS

	Action	Result

3	In the PhotoEditDialog.cs file, indicate that the Manning.MyPhotoAlbum namespace will be used.	`. . .`
		`using Manning.MyPhotoAlbum;`
		`. . .`
		` public partial class PhotoEditDialog : . . .`
		` {`

4	Add a private field and property for a Photograph and AlbumManager instance.	`private Photograph _photo;`
		`private Photograph Photo`
		`    { get { return _photo; } }`
		
		`private AlbumManager _manager = null;`
		`private AlbumManager Manager`
		`    { get { return _manager; } }`

ASSIGNING PHOTOGRAPH VALUES TO PHOTOEDITDIALOG CONTROLS *(CONTINUED)*		
	Action	**Result**

5	Make the default constructor protected.	`protected PhotoEditDialog()`
		`{`
		`  // Call required by Windows Form Designer.`
		`  InitializeComponent();`
		`}`

6	Create an `InitializeDialog` method that sets the `_photo` field and calls the `ResetDialog` method to initialize the controls.	`private void InitializeDialog(`
		`    Photograph photo)`
		`{`
		`  _photo = photo;`
		`  ResetDialog();`
		`}`

7	Create a public constructor that accepts a valid `Photograph` instance and initializes the class.	`public PhotoEditDialog(Photograph photo)`
		`    : this()`
		`{`
		`  if (photo == null)`
		`    throw new ArgumentNullException(`
		`        "The photo parameter cannot be null");`
		
		`  InitializeDialog(photo);`
		`}`

8	Create a second constructor that accepts a valid `AlbumManager` instance and initializes the class.
	Note: Our two constructors allow reuse of this form in a variety of applications.
		`public PhotoEditDialog(AlbumManager mgr)`
		`    : this()`
		`{`
		`  if (mgr == null)`
		`    throw new ArgumentNullException(`
		`        "The mgr parameter cannot be null");`
		
		`  _manager = mgr;`
		`  InitializeDialog(mgr.Current);`
		`}`

9	Override the `ResetDialog` method to set the `Text` property for each control on the form to the value of the corresponding property the associated `Photograph`.	`protected override void ResetDialog()`
		`{`
		`  Photograph photo = Photo;`
		`  if (photo != null)`
		`  {`
		`    txtPhotoFile.Text = photo.FileName;`
		`    txtCaption.Text = photo.Caption;`
		`    txtDateTaken.Text`
		`      = photo.DateTaken.ToString();`
		`    txtPhotographer.Text`
		`      = photo.Photographer;`
		`    txtNotes.Text = photo.Notes;`
		`  }`
		`}`

10	Override the `OnClosing` method to save the settings when the OK button is clicked.	`protected override void OnClosing(`
		`    CancelEventArgs e)`
		`{`
		`  if (DialogResult == DialogResult.OK)`
		`    SaveSettings();`
		`}`

<table>
<tr><th colspan="3">ASSIGNING PHOTOGRAPH VALUES TO PHOTOEDITDIALOG CONTROLS (CONTINUED)</th></tr>
<tr><th></th><th>Action</th><th>Result</th></tr>
<tr><td>11</td><td>Implement the <code>SaveSettings</code> method to store any changes in the form to the current photograph.</td><td><pre>
private void SaveSettings()
{
  Photograph photo = Photo;
  if (photo != null)
  {
    photo.Caption = txtCaption.Text;
    photo.Photographer = txtPhotographer.Text;
    photo.Notes = txtNotes.Text;

    // On parse error, do not set date
    try
    {
      photo.DateTaken
        = DateTime.Parse(txtDateTaken.Text);
    }
    catch (FormatException) { }
  }
}
</pre></td></tr>
</table>

We do not need to discuss this code in detail, except for the `DateTime.Parse` method. Most of the base types in .NET define a `Parse` method to convert a `string` into the base type. If the string cannot be converted into that type, then a `FormatException` is thrown. In our code, right now users can enter any text they wish into the Date Taken control, which could quite easily throw an exception in this code. We fix this in section 8.3 by replacing this text box with a masked text box, so for now we simply ignore the user's input if it cannot be converted to a date.

Before we discuss the `MaskedTextBox` control, we have one more task to perform so we can interact with our new dialog box.

8.2.3 Hooking up a dialog box

Our new form is ready; we just need to display it from our MyPhotos application. This section integrates the dialog box into our application, much as we integrated the `PixelDialog` form in chapter 7. The following table details this integration.

<table>
<tr><th colspan="3">DISPLAY THE PHOTOEDITDIALOG FORM FROM THE MAIN WINDOW</th></tr>
<tr><th></th><th>Action</th><th>Result</th></tr>
<tr><td>1</td><td>In the MainForm.cs [Design] window of the MyPhotos project, add a new menu item to the <code>ctxMenuPhoto</code> menu.
Settings
<table><tr><th>Property</th><th>Value</th></tr><tr><td>(Name)</td><td>menuPhotoProps</td></tr><tr><td>Text</td><td>Phot&o Properties...</td></tr></table></td><td>ContextMenuStrip
Image
Next
Previous
Pixel Dialog...
Photo Properties...
Type Here</td></tr>
</table>

	Action	Result
DISPLAY THE PHOTOEDITDIALOG FORM FROM THE MAIN WINDOW *(CONTINUED)*		

2	Update the `Opening` event handler for the context menu to set the `Enabled` property appropriately for the new menu item.	`private void ctxMenuPhoto_Opening(. . .)`
		`{`
		`  menuNext.Enabled = (. . .);`
		`  menuPrevious.Enabled = (. . .);`
		`  menuPhotoProps.Enabled`
		`      = (Manager.Current != null);`
		`}`

3	Add a `Click` event handler for the newly added item.	`private void menuPhotoProps_Click(`
		`    object sender, EventArgs e)`
		`{`

4	Implement this handler to display the new dialog box. If the user makes any changes, display them on the main form.	`  if (Manager.Current == null)`
		`    return;`
		
		`  using (PhotoEditDialog dlg`
		`          = new PhotoEditDialog(Manager))`
		`  {`
		`    if (dlg.ShowDialog()`
		`          == DialogResult.OK)`
		`      DisplayAlbum();`
		`  }`
		`}`

Since the dialog box itself handles the initialization and storage of any changes made by the user, and the `using` statement disposes of the dialog box when finished, there is not much work required by our handler. The `Photograph` class tracks whether it has changed as well, so the `Click` handlers for our Save menu items do not require any changes.

So let's see if your code actually works. Compile and run the application and open a previously saved album file. Display the Photo Properties dialog box. Note in particular the following features:

- Observe the differences between the read-only and editable text boxes.
- Labels cannot be highlighted, while text boxes can, even when read-only.
- The access key for a label automatically sets the focus to the subsequent text box, based on the assigned tab order.
- Pressing the Enter key within the single-line text boxes is the same as if you clicked the OK button, while pressing the Enter key within the Notes text box adds a new line. This is because we set the `AcceptsReturn` property to `true` in the Notes box.

Figure 8.3 The standard context menu for the TextBox control disables commands that are not currently available.

- A right-click within any text box displays a default context menu. This menu contains various commands for editing text, as shown in figure 8.3. The items in this menu correspond to methods in the `TextBoxBase` class shown in .NET Table 8.2.

8.3 MASKED TEXT BOXES

As pointed out in the prior section, the text box we created for the `DateTaken` property of the `Photograph` class is of questionable use. The text box accepts any input from the user, so the user may or may not enter a valid date. The `MaskedTextBox` class provides one approach for ensuring that the user can only enter date values.

This section examines various ways of manipulating the data entered by a user into a text box. The masked text box is perhaps the most important of these, but we utilize some keyboard-related events for the standard `TextBox` control as well.

8.3.1 Handling key presses

Before we get all fancy with masks and data type validation, we should point out that the `MaskedTextBox` is only useful for well-described data. The standard text box also supports some events that can alter or otherwise place restrictions on the entered text.

One such event is the `KeyPress` event. We look at keyboard events more generally in chapter 19, but let's do a quick example here. Suppose we wanted the caption for a photo to contain only letters, numbers, and spaces—that is, no punctuation characters and no symbols. The `KeyPress` event is invoked as characters are entered, and allows processing of these characters before they are sent to the control. Event handlers for this event receive a `KeyPressEventArgs` object, as shown in .NET Table 8.4.

The following steps illustrate the use of this event to filter characters that appear in a text box.

HANDLE KEYPRESS EVENT TO DISCARD PUNCTUATION

	Action	Result

1	In the PhotoEditDialog.cs [Design] window, add a `KeyPress` event handler for the `txtCaption` text box control.	`private void txtCaption_KeyPress(`
		`    object sender, KeyPressEventArgs e)`
		`{`

2	Implement this handler to permit only letters, numbers, white space, or control characters to appear within the control.	`char c = e.KeyChar;`
		
		`e.Handled = !(Char.IsLetterOrDigit(c)`
		`  || Char.IsWhiteSpace(c)`
		`  || Char.IsControl(c));`

3	If the character is consumed by the handler, emit a system beep to alert the user.	`if (e.Handled)`
		`  Console.Beep();`
		`}`

.NET Table 8.4 KeyPressEventArgs class

The `KeyPressEventArgs` class represents the event data for the `KeyPress` event. This class is part of the `System.Windows.Forms` namespace, and inherits from the `System.EventArgs` class.

Public Properties	Handled	Gets or sets whether the keyboard character was handled. If set to `true`, the control does not receive the character.
	KeyChar	Gets the `char` value corresponding to the keyboard character entered by the user.

This handler restricts the characters that can appear in the control, while still allowing spaces and control characters, such as the backspace key, to appear. When our handler sets the `Handled` property to `true`, the control does not receive the character. When this occurs, we emit a system beep sound using the `Beep` method provided by the `Console` class.

This handler may not be a good idea, by the way, since a caption such as "one-way street" is now not permitted, since the hyphen character (-) is punctuation. Feel free to remove this handler if you do not want this behavior in your program.

The `TextChanged` event is another useful event for text boxes, as it occurs just after new characters have been added to the control. This is quite useful when you need to process the text as it is typed.

We can use this event in the `PhotoEditDialog` form to display the caption for the photograph in the title bar. Of course, as the caption can be edited, we would not want the text box and the title bar to display different values. We could, of course, use the `KeyPress` event to do this. Aside from the existing handler we just created, the `KeyPress` event receives control characters that we really do not care about, so this is not the best approach here.

Let's continue our previous steps and use the `TextChanged` event for this purpose.

HANDLE TEXTCHANGED EVENT TO UPDATE TITLE BAR

	Action	Result

4	Add a `TextChanged` event handler for the `txtCaption` text box control.	`private void txtCaption_TextChanged(`
		`    object sender, EventArgs e)`
		`{`

5	Implement this handler to update the title bar for the dialog box with the modified text.	`  Text`
		`    = txtCaption.Text + " - Properties";`
		`}`

Compile and run the application to view these new changes. Verify that the caption entry beeps whenever you type a punctuation character, and that the title bar updates automatically as the caption is modified.

Hopefully these examples illustrate some of the processing you can perform on behalf of a text box control. Before we move on to the `MaskedTextBox` control, try the following exercise to further test your text box skills.

TRY IT! As an exercise in using some of the `TextBox` methods, create the standard context menu for text boxes manually and assign it to the Notes control. To do this, you will need a `ContextStrip` object on the form that is assigned to the `txtNotes.ContextStrip` property. Assigning this property disables the default context menu. Add the eight menu items to the menu: Undo, a separator, Copy, Cut, Paste, Delete, another separator, and Select All.

To process this menu, use the `Opened` event handler for the context menu to enable or disable the appropriate items. The `CanUndo`, `SelectedText`, `SelectionLength`, and `SelectionStart` properties, as well as the `Copy`, `Cut`, `Paste`, `SelectAll`, and `Undo` methods, should prove useful in completing this implementation.

8.3.2 Masking text

At last we come to the `MaskedTextBox` class. This class is based on the similar control in Visual Basic 6, and ensures that a specific type of input is received by the control. We use this to ensure that a valid date is entered into the Date Taken portion of the `PhotoEditDialog` form we just completed, but let's begin with a more general discussion of the control.

A summary of this class is shown in .NET Table 8.5. As you can see, there are a lot of confusing properties defined by this control. In addition, a number of properties are inherited from the `TextBoxBase` class that are not supported by the `MaskedTextBox` control. These include the `CanUndo`, `MaxLength`, `Multiline`, and `WordWrap` properties, as well as `GetFirstCharIndexFromLine` and other line-based methods.

At the heart of the `MaskedTextBox` control is the `Mask` property. This property defines the length and contents of user input that can be accepted by the user. The mask causes the control to prohibit any input that does not conform to the defined format. For example, a zip code mask accepts exactly five digits.

A number of characters, or *character elements*, as they are called, are available when defining a mask. The set of possible characters is shown in table 8.6. The following sample mask strings illustrate some of these characters:

- `00000` represents five required digits, such as a five-digit U.S. zip code.
- `(999) 000-0000` represents a U.S. phone number with an optional area code.
- `$00,000.99` represents a currency value. The currency, thousandths, and decimal characters are replaced at runtime with the appropriate culture-specific characters.

- `>LLLL` represents a four-letter string that is output as all capital letters.
- `&&&&CCCC` represents a four- to eight-character string.

.NET Table 8.5 MaskedTextBox class

New in 2.0 The `MaskedTextBox` class is a text box that supports a mask string to define acceptable input for the control. This control is part of the `System.Windows.Forms` namespace, and inherits from the `TextBoxBase` control. See .NET Table 8.2 for members inherited from the base class.

Public Properties	*AllowPromptAsInput*	Gets or sets whether the `PromptChar` character can be entered as valid data by the user.
	AsciiOnly	Gets or sets whether the control allows characters outside the ASCII character set.
	BeepOnError	Gets or sets whether the control causes a system beep for each key stroke that it rejects.
	HidePromptOnLeave	Gets or sets whether the `PromptChar` characters are visible when the control does not have focus.
	Mask	Gets or sets the character used to mask text in the control. When assigned, cutting and copying from the control is disabled.
	MaskCompleted	Gets or sets whether all required inputs have been entered.
	MaskFull	Gets or sets whether all required and optional inputs have been entered.
	MaskedTextProvider	Gets a clone of the mask-parsing engine associated with the masked text box.
	PromptChar	Gets or sets the character to display to represent the absence of user input in the control.
	Text (overridden from Control)	Gets or sets the text as it is currently displayed to the user.
	TextMaskFormat	Gets or sets a `MaskFormat` enumeration value that determines how to format text returned by members such as the `Text` property.
	ValidatingType	Gets or sets a `Type` object that supports a static `Parse` method used to verify the user's input.
Public Methods	*ValidateText*	Attempts to convert the formatted string into an instance of the validating type.
Public Events	*MaskChanged*	Occurs when the `Mask` property changes.
	MaskInputRejected	Occurs when the input or assigned text does not match the current mask position.
	TypeValidationCompleted	Occurs when the `ValidatingType` property is assigned just after the output text has been validated against the assigned `Type`.

Table 8.6 Character meanings for the MaskedTextBox.Mask property

Char	Meaning	Description
0	Required digit	Accepts any digit from 0 to 9.
9	Optional digit or space	Accepts any digit from 0 to 9 or a space. Nothing is rendered if not specified.
#	Option digit or space	Accepts any digit from 0 to 9, a space, plus (+), or minus (-). Rendered as a space if not specified.
L	Required letter	Accepts any ASCII letter from a to z or A to Z.
?	Optional letter	Accepts any ASCII letter from a to z or A to Z. Nothing is rendered if not specified.
&	Required character	Accepts any non-control character.
C	Optional character	Accepts any character. Nothing is rendered if not specified.
A	Required alphanumeric	Accepts any letter or digit.
a	Optional alphanumeric	Accepts any letter or digit. Nothing is rendered if not specified.
.	Decimal character	Displays and renders the specified type of character. The actual character used is appropriate for the current culture assigned to the control, based on the control's `Culture` property. This `Culture` property defaults to the application's current culture.
,	Thousands character	
:	Time separator	
/	Date separator	
$	Currency symbol	
<	Shift down	Converts all characters that follow to lowercase.
>	Shift up	Converts all characters that follow to uppercase.
|	Disable prior shift	Disable a previous shift up or shift down for all characters that follow.
\	Escape	Escapes a mask character, turning it into a literal. For example, `\C` displays and renders a capital C, while `\\` renders a backslash.
All others	Literal	Displays and renders any non-mask character as itself. Literals always occupy a fixed position in the mask at runtime, and cannot be moved or deleted by the user.

Internally, the actual processing of a mask is handled by a `MaskedTextProvider` object. This class is defined by the `System.ComponentModel` namespace, and defines a generic engine for processing masked text. One of the constructors for the `MaskedTextBox` control accepts a custom `MaskedTextProvider` instance for customized processing.

So let's create an example. The `PhotoEditDialog` form created in the previous section uses a `TextBox` to hold the `Photograph.DateTaken` property. We can improve this using a `MaskedTextBox` control instead to ensure that the user enters a date in the proper format. This requires the following steps.

CONVERT THE DATE TAKEN TEXT BOX INTO A MASKEDTEXTBOX CONTROL		
	Action	**Result**
1	In the PhotoEditDialog.cs [Design] window, delete the existing `txtDateTaken` control.	The text box is removed from the form.
2	Insert a `MaskedTextBox` control in the open spot on the table. **Settings** **Property** / **Value** (Name): mskDateTaken Mask: 00/00/0000 **How-to** You can enter this mask manually, or click the small button next to the Mask property value to display the Input Mask dialog box. This dialog box displays predefined masks, and has a Preview section where you can experiment with an assigned setting.	Photo Properties Photo File: Caption: Date Taken: __/__/____ Photographer: Notes: OK Reset Cancel
3	Modify the `ResetDialog` and `SaveSettings` methods to use the new `mskDateTaken` control instead of `txtDateTaken`, which is no longer valid.	These changes are required so the code compiles correctly.
4	Reset the tab order for the form so the new control is in the proper tab sequence. **How-to** a. In the PhotoEditDialog.cs [Design] window, select the Tab Order item from the View menu. b. Click the controls in the preferred tab order: begin with buttons at the bottom, then click the label and text box pairs in the panel, then the Notes label and text box.	Photo Properties 3.0.0 Photo File: 3.0.1 3.0.2 Caption: 3.0.3 3.0.4 Date Taken: 3.0.5 3.0.6 Photographer: 3.0.7 4 Notes: 5 0 - Read Only 1 - Read Only 2 - Read Only

In these steps, replacing the control and modifying the code is nothing new. The final step to reset the tab order we have not seen before (at least in this book). We were careful with our original form to create the controls in the proper tab order. Here, since we replace a control, the new control is added to the end of the tab order within our panel. Rather than requiring us to modify the properties by hand, Visual Studio supports the tab order display shown in step 4, where the desired order is imposed graphically. Note how the controls within our table panel display the order of the panel (3), the order of the table panel within this panel (3.0), and finally the order of each control within the table panel (3.0.0, 3.0.1, 3.0.2, and so forth).

If you compile and run this change, you are now forced to enter numeric values in the format of a date, and you can still use the keyboard shortcut Alt+D to edit the Date Taken value. The new control is an improvement, but not quite right. The user can enter the value "12/99/2077," which fits the mask but is not actually a date.

To address such issues, masked text boxes provide the `ValidatingType` property. This property defines a `Type` for further validation of the input. Any type can be specified as long as it defines a static `Parse` method that accepts a string and returns an object. The .NET base types provide such a method, so types such as `Int16` and `DateTime` can be assigned to this property.

Whenever the input focus leaves a `MaskedTextBox` control with a validating type assigned, type validation is performed. The `TypeValidationComplete` event is raised after this validation completes, and can be used to interpret the results. Handlers for this event receive a `TypeValidationEventArgs` parameter that contains validation information, as shown in .NET Table 8.7.

.NET Table 8.7 TypeValidationEventArgs class

New in 2.0 The `TypeValidationEventArgs` class defines event data for the `TypeValidationComplete` event in the `MaskedTextBox` control. This class is part of the `System.Windows.Forms` namespace, and inherits from the `System.EventArgs` class.

Public Properties	*Cancel*	Gets or sets whether to cancel the event
	IsValidInput	Gets whether the current input text is complete and valid
	Message	Gets a string that records the results of the validation
	ReturnValue	Gets the object returned by the `Parse` method when the input is valid
	ValidatingType	Gets the `Type` defined by the sender's `ValidatingType` property

Taken together, the `ValidatingType` property and `TypeValidationComplete` event allow an application to enforce specific constraints on the control, both with the base .NET types and with custom objects that apply specific parsing logic.

In our application, we could simply use the `DateTime` type as the validating type. This would work great, but does not really convey the power of custom parsing. Instead, let's define a `CurrentDate` class to perform validation of the `MaskedTextBox` control instead. This new class ensures that the given input is a valid date that is not in the future. The following steps continue our changes for this section.

VALIDATE THE INPUT FOR THE DATE TAKEN MASKED TEXT BOX

	Action	Result

5	Within the `PhotoEditDialog` class, define a nested `CurrentDate` class.	`public partial class PhotoEditDialog : . . .`
		`{`
		`  . . .`
		`  private static class CurrentDate`
		`  {`

	Action	Result
VALIDATE THE INPUT FOR THE DATE TAKEN MASKED TEXT BOX *(CONTINUED)*		

6	Implement a static `Parse` method for this class that verifies a given string is a valid date that is not in the future.	`public static DateTime Parse(string input)`
		`{`
		`  DateTime result = DateTime.Parse(input);`
		`  if (result > DateTime.Now)`
		`    throw new FormatException(`
		`      "The given date is in the future.");`
		
		`  return result;`
		`}`
		`}`

7	Modify the `InitializeDialog` method to define this new class as the validating type for the `mskDateTaken` control.	`private void InitializeDialog(`
		`    Photograph photo)`
		`{`
		`  . . .`
		`  mskDateTaken.ValidatingType`
		`    = typeof(CurrentDate);`
		`}`

8	In the designer window, add a `TypeValidationCompleted` event handler for the `MaskedTextBox` control.	`private void`
		`  mskDateTaken_TypeValidationCompleted(`
		`    object sender, TypeValidationEventArgs e)`
		`{`

9	Implement this handler to query the user if the current input is invalid.	`  if (!e.IsValidInput)`
		`  {`
		`    DialogResult result = MessageBox.Show(`
		`      "The Date Taken entry is invalid or "`
		`      + "in the future and may be ignored."`
		`      + " Do you wish to correct this?",`
		`      "Photo Properties",`
		`      MessageBoxButtons.YesNo,`
		`      MessageBoxIcon.Question);`

10	If the user wished to correct the input, cancel the validation so focus remains with the masked text box.	`    e.Cancel = (result == DialogResult.Yes);`
		`  }`
		`}`

This change relies on the existing `SaveSettings` method we previously defined that ignores the input if it is not a valid date. Here, we warn users this is about to occur, and give them the option of correcting the problem if they wish.

The `CurrentDate` class is defined as private within the `PhotoEditDialog` class since it is only required within the context of this dialog box. If we had other classes that needed to use the `CurrentDate` class, it would make sense to define it in a separate assembly.

This completes our discussion of text box controls. Compile, run, test, tell your friends, and otherwise enjoy our application.

TRY IT! The MaskedTextBox control defines a number of properties that tweak the behavior of the control. As an exercise, build the application shown in figure 8.4 so you can modify and otherwise experiment with this control. This application accepts a mask string in a text box, and applies it to a masked text box. Use the Leave event to determine when a new mask string is defined, and the TextChanged event to display various property values for the MaskedTextBox as the user enters input text. Feel free to display other information in the panel if you wish.

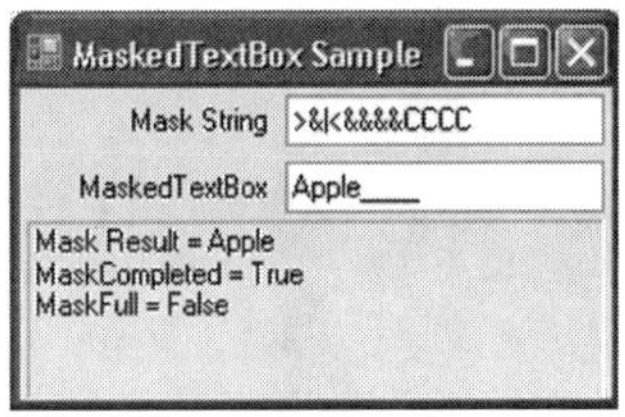

Figure 8.4 Sample MaskedTextBox application

The mask shown in the figure accepts a five- to nine-character string, and capitalizes the first letter. Here, the user has entered the string "apple," which completes the required portion of the mask.

8.4 RECAP

In this chapter we looked at text boxes. We began with form inheritance as a way to encapsulate common properties and controls for multiple forms. We built a base form to serve as a shared dialog box for some forms to edit Photograph and PhotoAlbum properties.

This base form allowed us to build the PhotoEditDialog form, which conveniently contains various text boxes to hold the properties on a photograph. We looked at various features of the base TextBoxBase class, read-only text boxes, and multiline text boxes. We also examined a couple of different ways of processing keyboard input within the TextBox control.

The final part of the chapter presented the MaskedTextBox control. This control includes a mask string to define acceptable user input, and supports various members to manipulate and modify how this input is interpreted. As an example, we defined a MaskedTextBox to manage the DateTime property value in a Photograph object, and configured the control to ensure that the input is a valid date on or before the current date.

The next chapter presents Button controls in the Windows Forms namespace. As part of this discussion, we build the dialog box in figure 8.1 for editing PhotoAlbum objects.

CHAPTER 9

Buttons

Buttons come in all shapes and sizes, on clothes as well as computer applications. On a computer, a button is a control that establishes a specific state, typically some form of "on" or "off." Buttons are used to perform immediate actions in an interface, define the behavior for a specific feature, or enable or disable a specific setting. The various styles of buttons in Windows Forms are as follows:

- A *push button* is a button that performs some immediate action, such as displaying or deactivating a dialog box, or modifying the values in the window. In Windows Forms, the `Button` class represents a push button.
- A *radio button*, sometimes called an *option button*, is used to select from a set of mutually exclusive options. When one of a group of radio buttons is selected, the other radio buttons in the group are typically deselected. Windows Forms provides the `RadioButton` class for the creation of these objects. All radio buttons in the same container are automatically part of the same group. Use container classes such as `GroupBox` and `Panel` to support multiple groups of radio buttons on your forms.
- A *check box button* allows a user to turn a specific option on or off, such as whether a file should be saved as read-only or not. In .NET, the `CheckBox` class

can represent either a check box button or a *toggle button.* A toggle button appears as a normal button, but preserves an up or down state to represent a checked or unchecked mode, respectively.

While we have used a push button or two on most of our forms, this chapter presents a more formal discussion of the concept. We examine the following aspects of buttons:

- Exploring the .NET classes for Windows Forms buttons
- Creating and using radio buttons
- Creating and using check boxes
- Using buttons to enable and disable controls
- Aligning images and text within buttons

In presenting these topics, we continue our use of the MyPhotos application to demonstrate each feature. In chapter 8 we built a dialog box for the properties of a photograph, so in this chapter we build one for the properties of an album. Of course, our `PhotoAlbum` class does not have much in the way of properties right now, which enables us to discuss the following aspects of the .NET Framework:

- Adding properties to classes
- Using version numbers to manage different file formats
- Applying simple encryption to a file
- Displaying tooltips for the controls in a dialog box

We begin, of course, with the basic button.

9.1 PUSH BUTTONS

All Windows Forms buttons in .NET inherit from the `ButtonBase` class. In this section we review the basic button classes and build some supporting code for our album class to aid our examples in this chapter. As you may know, a `Button` class also exists for web applications, but this is not of interest to us here. When we talk about or mention buttons, we always mean the Windows Forms variety unless otherwise indicated.

9.1.1 The Button class

The `Button` class, as we have indicated, inherits from the `ButtonBase` class. These classes appear in .NET Table 9.1 and .NET Table 9.2, respectively. As you can see, the base class provides basic alignment and appearance properties, with the `Button` class adding functionality to support dialog boxes and click-related behavior.

In contrast to text boxes, text within a button can be aligned both vertically and horizontally. The `TextAlign` property for text boxes is a `HorizontalAlignment` enumeration value. For buttons, as for labels, the `TextAlign` and `ImageAlign` properties are `ContentAlignment` enumeration values, allowing them to be aligned both vertically and horizontally. There is a Try It! exercise later in the chapter where this feature can be explored.

.NET Table 9.1 ButtonBase class

The `ButtonBase` class is the base control for simple buttons. This abstract class is part of the `System.Windows.Forms` namespace, and inherits from the `Control` class. The `Button`, `CheckBox`, and `RadioButton` classes all inherit from this class. See .NET Table 3.1 for members inherited from the `Control` class.

Public Properties	*AutoEllipse*	Gets or sets whether the ellipse character is shown when the text extends beyond the width of the control
	FlatAppearance	Gets the appearance of the border and colors used to indicate various button states
	FlatStyle	Gets or sets the button's flat style appearance
	Image	Gets or sets the image to display on the button
	ImageAlign	Gets or sets the alignment of the button image
	ImageIndex	Gets or sets the image as an index into the `ImageList` property value
	ImageList	Gets or sets an `ImageList` object to associate with this button
	Text (overridden from Control)	Gets or sets the text assigned to the button
	TextAlign	Gets or sets the alignment of the button text
	TextImageRelation	Gets or sets the relative position of the text and image as a `TextImageRelation` enumeration value

Looking at the `Button` class, the `DialogResult` property, `NotifyDefault` method, and `PerformClick` method are all defined by the `IButtonControl` interface. This interface represents a generic button on a `Form`, and is of course implemented by the `Button` class. The `AcceptButton` and `CancelButton` properties in the `Form` class are both of type `IButtonControl` so that custom controls can act as the OK and Cancel buttons for a dialog box or other form.

Since we have been using standard buttons since chapter 1, the rest of this section does not spend much time on them. The work here is aimed at preparing to build an `AlbumEditDialog` form in the rest of the chapter. This requires that we expand the `PhotoAlbum` class and update the storage and retrieval of the modified class.

Of course, there are a number of ways to modify and otherwise use buttons in an application. In chapter 15 we illustrate placing an image on a button, and in chapter 17 we build a custom `RoundButton` class as an example of a custom control.

.NET Table 9.2 Button class

The `Button` class represents a standard push button. A button may display text, an image, or both text and an image. This class is part of the `System.Windows.Forms` namespace, inherits from the `ButtonBase` class, and implements the `IButtonControl` interface.

Public Properties	*AutoSizeMode*	Gets or sets how the control resizes when `AutoSize` is enabled
	DialogResult	Gets or sets a value that is returned to the parent form when the button is clicked
Public Methods	NotifyDefault	Informs the button whether or not it is the default button, so the control can adjust its appearance accordingly
	PerformClick	Generates a `Click` event on the button

9.1.2 Expanding the PhotoAlbum class

In order to demonstrate the various styles of buttons and provide some interesting code, this section expands the `PhotoAlbum` class to include the following properties:

- `Title`: A title or name for the album as a string. Shown as a `TextBox` control.
- `PhotoDescriptor`: The `Photograph` setting to use as the short display name for all photos in the album. This supports display of the base filename, the caption, or the date assigned to the photo. This property has three possible values, making it a good candidate for a `RadioButton` example.
- `Password`: If present, the password required for the album. We use a `CheckBox` to indicate whether a password is desired, and basic encryption via the `System.Security.Cryptography` namespace to encrypt and decrypt the album on disk. This is a bit beyond our "Buttons" chapter title, so we save the cryptography for chapter 10. Here, we simply store the password for the current album in the `AlbumManager` class.

The first step is to add properties for these values to our `PhotoAlbum` class.

ADD NEW SETTINGS TO THE PHOTOALBUM CLASS

	Action	Result

1	In the PhotoAlbum.cs file, add a `DescriptorOption` enumeration to define different ways to represent a photograph.	`public class PhotoAlbum`
		`    : Collection<Photograph>, IDisposable`
		`{`
		`  public enum DescriptorOption`
		`      { FileName, Caption, DateTaken }`

2	Define two private fields to hold the album title and display option setting.	`  private string _title;` `  private DescriptorOption _descriptor;`

<table>
<tr><th colspan="3">ADD NEW SETTINGS TO THE PHOTOALBUM CLASS (CONTINUED)</th></tr>
<tr><th></th><th>Action</th><th>Result</th></tr>
<tr><td>3</td><td>Define a <code>ClearSettings</code> method to initialize these fields.</td><td><pre>private void ClearSettings()
{
  _title = null;
  _descriptor = DescriptorOption.Caption;
}</pre></td></tr>
<tr><td>4</td><td>Call this new method in a constructor and when the album is disposed.</td><td><pre>public PhotoAlbum()
{
  ClearSettings();
}

public void Dispose()
{
  ClearSettings();
  foreach (Photograph p in this)
    p.Dispose();
}</pre></td></tr>
<tr><td>5</td><td>Also define properties for these new fields.</td><td><pre>public string Title
{
  get { return _title; }
  set { _title = value;
        HasChanged = true; }
}

public DescriptorOption PhotoDescriptor
{
  get { return _descriptor; }
  set { _descriptor = value;
        HasChanged = true; }
}</pre></td></tr>
<tr><td>6</td><td>Add some methods to retrieve the description for a photo.
How-to
Use the new <code>Photo-Descriptor</code> property and create one method to retrieve by <code>Photograph</code> object and another by index.</td><td><pre>public string GetDescription(Photograph photo)
{
  switch (PhotoDescriptor)
  {
    case DescriptorOption.Caption:
      return photo.Caption;

    case DescriptorOption.DateTaken:
     return photo.DateTaken.ToShortDateString();

    case DescriptorOption.FileName:
      return photo.FileName;
  }

  throw new ArgumentException(
      "Unrecognized photo descriptor option.");
}

public string GetDescription(int index)
{
  return GetDescription(this[index]);
}</pre></td></tr>
<tr><td>7</td><td>In the AlbumManager.cs file, add a new field and property to hold a password for the album.</td><td><pre>private string _pwd;

public string Password
{
  get { return _pwd; }
  set { _pwd = value; }
}</pre></td></tr>
</table>

This modifies our PhotoAlbum class to include some additional properties, and prepares the AlbumManager class for managing a password for an album. It is, of course, a bit of a security risk to expose the password setting in this manner, since the password is stored as clear text in memory. The System.Security namespace defines a SecureString class in order to store in-memory strings in a secure fashion. If you wish, you can use this class here.

Since the definition of an album has changed, we also need to modify the routines that store and retrieve our album files.

9.1.3 Storing album data

We created the AlbumStorage class to manage the interaction, or boundary, between the album and photo classes and the actual disk. As a result, we can focus our attention on the AlbumStorage class now in order to alter how album data is stored and retrieved. As long as we preserve the existing interface, any classes using our AlbumStorage class do not have to change.

Modifying our storage logic may present a slight problem. A user may have created a lot of albums using the existing format defined in chapter 6, so if we change this all of their album data would be useless. We do not want this to happen, of course, so we need a way to understand both the existing format and a new format.

As you may recall, we defined a version number in our album file. To create an alternate format, we simply need to create a new version number. We are in section 9.1, so let's create version 91 here. The following table enumerates the steps required for this change.

STORE AND RETRIEVE THE NEW ALBUM FORMAT		
	Action	**Result**
1	In the AlbumStorage.cs file, change the default version number to 91.	`static private int CurrentVersion = 91;`
2	Modify the `WriteAlbum` method to store the album properties prior to writing photos into the file. **How-to** Insert code to write the album properties into the file.	See code below

```
static public void WriteAlbum(
    PhotoAlbum album, string path)
{
  StreamWriter sw = null;

  try
  {
    sw = new StreamWriter(path, false);
    sw.WriteLine(CurrentVersion.ToString());

    // Save album properties
    sw.WriteLine(album.Title);
    sw.WriteLine(
        album.PhotoDescriptor.ToString());

    // Store each photo separately
    . . .
}
```

STORE AND RETRIEVE THE NEW ALBUM FORMAT *(CONTINUED)*		
	Action	**Result**

3	Modify the `ReadAlbum` method to distinguish between version 63 and version 91.
	
	How-to
	Modify the `switch` statement to distinguish between the two version numbers.
		<pre>static public PhotoAlbum ReadAlbum(string path)
		{
		  StreamReader sr = null;
		
		  try
		  {
		    sr = new StreamReader(path);
		    string version = sr.ReadLine();
		
		    PhotoAlbum album = new PhotoAlbum();
		    switch (version)
		    {
		      case "63":
		        ReadAlbumV63(sr, album);
		        break;
		      case "91":
		        ReadAlbumV91(sr, album);
		        break;
		      default:
		        throw new AlbumStorageException(. . .);
		    }
		    . . .
		  }
		  . . .
		}</pre>

4	Implement a `ReadAlbumV91` method to read the version 91 format for an album.
	
	How-to
	a. Read the album properties from the start of the file.
	b. Use the `ReadAlbumV63` method to read the remainder of the file.
		<pre>static private void ReadAlbumV91(
		    StreamReader sr, PhotoAlbum album)
		{
		  // Read album properties
		  album.Title = sr.ReadLine();
		  string enumVal = sr.ReadLine();
		  album.PhotoDescriptor
		    = (PhotoAlbum.DescriptorOption)Enum.Parse(
		        typeof(PhotoAlbum.DescriptorOption),
		        enumVal);
		
		  // Version 91 finishes with Version 63
		  ReadAlbumV63(sr, album);
		}</pre>

The `AlbumStorage` class now stores and retrieves the new `PhotoAlbum` settings in album files, while still preserving the ability to read our older format from section 6.3. Note that no changes were required to our `AlbumManager` class or the application itself to support this new functionality.

Of course, while these changes work fine, the goal here is to allow a user to modify these new properties. We take up this topic in the next section on radio buttons.

9.2 RADIO BUTTONS

Radio buttons display a set of mutually exclusive options. The users select their choice, and the application acts accordingly. User interface studies have shown that users work best with no more than seven "choices" at a time, and I generally apply this to radio buttons as well. When there are lots of options for a setting, a list control such as the ComboBox class usually provides a better interface. An advantage of radio buttons is that the user sees all possible options at once, but this gets confusing when the set of options is large.

9.2.1 The RadioButton class

A summary of the RadioButton control appears in .NET Table 9.3. A radio button typically appears as a small circle followed by a text description, although the Appearance property can alter the control to display as a toggle button and the CheckAlign property can alter the alignment of the radio button in relation to its text.

As mentioned in the table, radio buttons are always grouped within a parent container. Any control that acts as a container for other controls serves to define the group. Controls like the Panel or TabPage class are often used to define distinct regions of a form where radio buttons and other controls are displayed. For a more lightweight grouping of radio buttons, the GroupBox class may suffice.

.NET Table 9.3 RadioButton class

The RadioButton class represents a button that displays a selectable option within a group. By default, only one radio button in the group may be selected at a time. When a radio button is clicked, it is selected and all others in the same group are deselected. The AutoCheck property disables this behavior.

The parent container for this control defines its group. If four radio buttons are contained within a form, then by default only one of the four buttons may be checked at any one time. Use container classes such as GroupBox and Panel to provide multiple independent groups of radio buttons on a single form.

This control is part of the System.Windows.Forms namespace, and inherits from the ButtonBase class. See .NET Table 9.1 for members inherited from this class.

Public Properties	Appearance	Gets or sets whether the button appears as a standard radio button or toggle button.
	AutoCheck	Gets or sets the behavior of related radio buttons when this button is clicked. If true, radio buttons in the same group are deselected; if false, radio buttons in the same group must be deselected manually.
	CheckAlign	Gets or sets the alignment of the radio button within the control. This determines the location of the text for the button as well.
	Checked	Gets or sets whether the radio button is currently checked.
Public Methods	PerformClick	Sends a Click event to the control.
Public Events	CheckedChanged	Occurs when the Checked property changes.

The `GroupBox` control is shown in .NET Table 9.4. As you can see, there is not much to a group box. Although group boxes do not support scrolling, they are quite useful visually to define a region within a form or other container for a specific feature or setting. Group boxes behave a bit like labels when it comes to receiving focus. A group box cannot receive focus, so when focus is set to this control or a user tabs to it, the group box assigns the focus to the first control in the group. Our `PhotoAlbum` dialog box illustrates this feature.

.NET Table 9.4 GroupBox class

The `GroupBox` class lets you create a control that displays a frame around a group of contained controls. The `GroupBox` control is part of the `System.Windows.Forms` namespace, and inherits from the `Control` class. See .NET Table 3.1 for members inherited from this base class.

Public Properties	Text (overridden from Control)	Gets or sets an optional caption displayed on the frame for the control.
	TabStop (overridden from Control)	Gets or sets whether this control is a tab stop. A group box can never receive focus, so this property is ignored.

With this brief explanation of radio buttons and group boxes, let's work on creating an `AlbumEditDialog` form to illustrate these and other types of buttons.

9.2.2 Creating an album dialog box

In section 9.1 we expanded the `PhotoAlbum` class in preparation for a property dialog box for `PhotoAlbum` objects. This form was shown in figure 8.1 of the prior chapter, but is reproduced here in figure 9.1.

Figure 9.1 The album dialog box reduces the height of the panel inherited from the BaseEditDialog class. This is possible since the panel is a protected member of the base form.

As you may recall, we built a `BaseEditDialog` form to encapsulate a shared structure for our dialog boxes, with a panel at the top and the three buttons at the bottom. In chapter 8 we embedded a `TableLayoutPanel` control within the panel to provide some structure for the labels and text boxes. While we could certainly take the same approach here, let's examine the option of arranging these controls by hand within Visual Studio.

The following steps lay out the panel and radio button portion of this form.

CREATE THE PHOTO DESCRIPTION PORTION OF THE ALBUMEDITDIALOG FORM		
	Action	**Result**

1	Add a new Inherited Form called `AlbumEditDialog` to the MyAlbumControls project. Inherit from the `BaseEditDialog` class, and set its Text property to "Album Properties."	`using System;`
		`. . .`
		`namespace Manning.MyPhotoControls`
		`{`
		`  public partial class AlbumEditDialog`
		`      : BaseEditDialog`
		`  {`

2	In the panel, add and position the labels and text boxes as shown in the graphic, and set their properties as follows. **Settings** **Control** / **Property** / **Value** First Label: Text = Album &File; TextAlign = Middle Right File TextBox: (Name) = txtAlbumFile; ReadOnly = True Second Label: Text = &Title; TextAlign = Middle Right Title TextBox: (Name) = txtTitle	Album Properties Album File: Title: **Note:** You need to resize the panel to reproduce the controls as shown. Use the colored guide lines when aligning the controls, and the Layout toolbar or Align submenu of the Format menu to select two controls and align them with each other. Also note that we do not give a (Name) for our `Label` controls. You may do so, if you wish.
3	Place a `GroupBox` control on the form below the existing panel.	Photo Description
4	Set the `Text` property for the group box to "Phot&o Description."	
5	Place three RadioButton controls in the group box, positioned as in the graphic. **Settings** **Button** / **Property** / **Value** File name: (Name) = rbtnFileName; Text = File &name Caption: (Name) = rbtnCaption; Text = Ca&ption Date Taken: (Name) = rbtnDateTaken; Text = &Date Taken	Album Properties Album File: Title: Photo Description File name Caption Date Taken

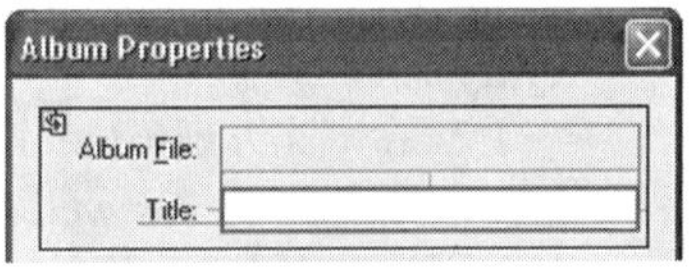

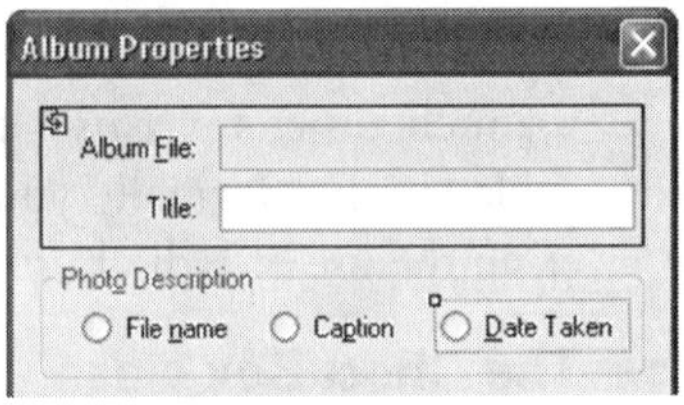

The behavior of our radio buttons are automated by .NET, so no code is required to manage these controls at this point. As we will see when we hook this dialog box up to our main form, radio buttons in a group are treated as a single tab index. When a user tabs to a group of radio buttons, the selected button receives the focus, and the arrow keys alter the selected button.

Experienced users often prefer the assigned access keys to set a desired radio button. In our form, the Alt+N key selects the File name radio button, Alt+P the Caption button, and Alt+D the Date Taken button. The Alt+O access key selects the Photo Descriptor group box, which in turn assigns focus to the radio button currently selected.

If you wish, examine the generated `InitializeComponent` code. In the interest of time and space, as well as the fact that there is nothing really new to see, we do not show the code here. Instead, we finish our new form by discussing check box buttons.

9.3 CHECK BOX BUTTONS

The `CheckBox` control is similar to a radio button in that both have a clickable graphic associated with some text. While a radio button is used for a set of mutually exclusive options, a check box is used for a single option that can be turned on or off. This section discusses check box buttons, and completes the layout of the `AlbumEditDialog` begun in the prior section.

Try not to use radio buttons where a `CheckBox` control belongs. I have seen interfaces where two-value options are displayed as radio buttons. For example, a form might display the question "Does this person wear glasses?" with Yes and No radio buttons as possible choices. This is generally poor design. The form contains three controls to implement this, and the user must read a question and then decide which of two options to select. A check box with the text "This person wears glasses." is much easier for a user to understand, since there is a single control with a brief explanation. Normally you should have at least three possible options before considering the use of radio buttons.

9.3.1 The CheckBox class

A summary of this class appears in .NET Table 9.5. A check box button normally appears as a small square followed by a textual description, although once again the `Appearance` property causes the control to display as a toggle button and the `CheckAlign` property can alter the alignment of the check box in relation to the textual description.

Check boxes are not grouped like radio buttons, as they represent a single setting on the form. A check box can, of course, be placed within a container the same as other controls.

.NET Table 9.5 CheckBox class

The `CheckBox` class represents a button that displays a boolean option to the user. Typically, a check box represents one of two states, either *checked* or *unchecked*. A three-state check box can also be established, with an additional *intermediate* state. This third state is useful to represent an unset value, such as a database null value, or for a set of objects that individually would have both checked and unchecked states.

This control is part of the `System.Windows.Forms` namespace, and inherits from the `ButtonBase` class. See .NET Table 9.1 for members inherited from this class.

Public Properties	Appearance	Gets or sets whether the button appears as a standard check box or toggle button.
	AutoCheck	Gets or sets whether the button is checked automatically or manually when clicked.
	CheckAlign	Gets or sets the alignment of the check box within the control. This determines the location of the text for the button as well.
	Checked	Gets or sets whether the check box is currently checked.
	CheckState	Gets or sets the state of a three-state check box as a `CheckState` enumeration value. This is `Checked`, `Unchecked` (the default), or `Intermediate`.
	ThreeState	Gets or sets whether the check box supports three states rather than two.
Public Events	CheckedChanged	Occurs when the `Checked` property changes.
	CheckStateChanged	Occurs when `CheckState` changes.

9.3.2 Using check box buttons

Check boxes are typically used in one of two ways. The first is a simple on or off state, often as a yes or no answer to some implicit question. For example, display the properties dialog box for a file in the Windows file system, and a check box displays whether the file is read-only or not.

Another common usage for check boxes is to enable or disable a set of controls on a form, typically related to some specific option. When checked, the related controls are enabled so the user can assign values for each control. When unchecked, the related controls are disabled and not accessible by the user.

In our dialog box, we implement the second kind of check box to indicate whether an album should be password-protected. If so, the user enters a password, which is used to encrypt the album data in the file. The implementation of this encryption appears in the next chapter, so here we simply set up the controls to work as expected.

CREATE THE PASSWORDPORTION OF THE ALBUMEDITDIALOG FORM		
	Action	**Result**
1	Drag a `CheckBox` control from the Toolbox window onto the form, just below the existing group box. **Settings** Property / Value (Name) / cbxPassword Text / Pass&word Protected:	Photo Description File name / Caption / Date Taken Password Protected:
2	To the right of this check box, add a text box to receive the password from the user. **Settings** Property / Value (Name) / txtPassword Enabled / False UseSystem-PasswordChar / True	The text box appears on the form. **Note:** The `PasswordChar` property replaces any entered text with the assigned character. The `UseSystem-PasswordChar` property supersedes this setting, and uses the system-defined password character.
3	Below the check box, add a label and text box for password confirmation. **Settings** Control / Property / Value Label / (Name) / lblConfirm Label / Enabled / False Label / Text / Confir&m Password: Label / TextAlign / MiddleRight TextBox / (Name) / txtConfirm TextBox / Enabled / False TextBox / UseSystem-Password-Char / True	Album Properties Album File: Title: Photo Description File name / Caption / Date Taken Password Protected: Confirm Password: OK / Reset / Cancel

4	Add a `CheckedChanged` event handler for the check box control.
	How-to
	This is the default event, so simply double-click the check box.
		`private void`
		`  cbxPassword_CheckedChanged(`
		`      object sender, EventArgs e)`
		`{`

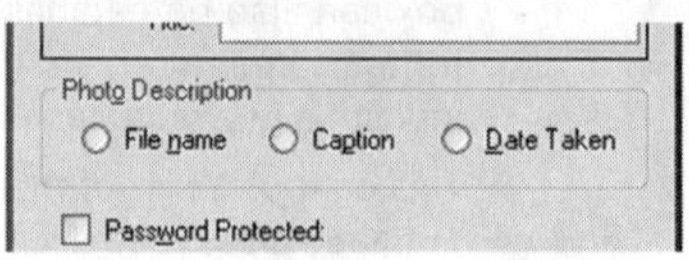

CREATE THE PASSWORDPORTION OF THE ALBUMEDITDIALOG FORM *(CONTINUED)*		
	Action	**Result**

5	Implement this handler to enable or disable the password controls depending on the state of the check box.	`bool enabled = cbxPassword.Checked;`
		`txtPassword.Enabled = enabled;`
		`lblConfirm.Enabled = enabled;`
		`txtConfirm.Enabled = enabled;`
		
		`// If enabled, assign focus`
		`if (enabled)`
		`  txtPassword.Focus();`
		`}`

Each time the user selects or deselects the check box, the `cbxPassword_Checked-Changed` method is called to handle the event. When checked, this method enables the three password-related controls and assigns focus to the initial password text box. When unchecked, this method disables the three controls.

Right now we rely on the user to ensure that the password and confirmation text boxes contain the same string. This is not quite fair, since the user cannot actually read these passwords due to our use of the system password character in each text box. We write the code to enforce this requirement in section 9.4.

9.3.3 Completing the AlbumEditDialog form

With our form layout completed, the final tasks to see our new dialog box in action are to handle the reset and save logic and use the new class in our MyPhotos application. The following steps perform the first of these tasks.

FINISH THE ALBUMEDITDIALOG FORM		
	Action	**Result**

1	In the AlbumEditDialog.cs file, indicate that we use the `Manning.MyPhotoAlbum` namespace.	`. . .`
		`using Manning.MyPhotoAlbum;`
		`. . .`

2	In the `AlbumEditDialog` class, add a private `AlbumManager` field and property to hold the album to edit.	`private AlbumManager _manager;`
		`private AlbumManager Manager`
		`    { get { return _manager; } }`

3	Modify the constructor to require a manager parameter and assign the initial values for the dialog box.	`public AlbumEditDialog(AlbumManager mgr)`
		`{`
		`  if (mgr == null)`
		`    throw new ArgumentException(`
		`        "AlbumManager cannot be null");`
		
		`  InitializeComponent();`
		
		`  _manager = mgr;`
		`  ResetDialog();`
		`}`

FINISH THE ALBUMEDITDIALOG FORM *(CONTINUED)*

<table>
<tr><th></th><th>Action</th><th>Result</th></tr>
<tr><td>4</td><td>Override the <code>ResetDialog</code> method.</td><td><pre>protected override void ResetDialog()
{
  PhotoAlbum album = Manager.Album;</pre></td></tr>
<tr><td>5</td><td>Implement this method to reset the dialog box controls to the initial album settings.

How-to
a. Assign the album file name and text boxes.
b. Check the radio button corresponding to the current descriptor setting.
c. Select the check box if the manager contains a password.
d. Set the password and confirm text to the current password.</td><td><pre> // Assign text boxes
  txtAlbumFile.Text = Manager.FullName;
  txtTitle.Text = album.Title;

  // Assign radio button
  switch (album.PhotoDescriptor)
  {
   case PhotoAlbum.DescriptorOption.Caption:
      rbtnCaption.Checked = true;
      break;
   case PhotoAlbum.DescriptorOption.DateTaken:
      rbtnDateTaken.Checked = true;
      break;
   case PhotoAlbum.DescriptorOption.FileName:
      rbtnFileName.Checked = true;
      break;
  }

  // Assign check box
  string pwd = Manager.Password;
  cbxPassword.Checked
      = (pwd != null && pwd.Length > 0);
  txtPassword.Text = pwd;
  txtConfirm.Text = pwd;
}</pre></td></tr>
<tr><td>6</td><td>Implement a <code>ValidPassword</code> method to validate an assigned password. A valid password has matching password strings and is non-empty.</td><td><pre>private bool ValidPassword()
{
  if (cbxPassword.Checked)
    return (txtPassword.TextLength > 0
      && txtConfirm.Text == txtPassword.Text);
  else
    return true;
}</pre></td></tr>
<tr><td>7</td><td>Override the <code>OnClosing</code> method to save the settings when the OK button is clicked.</td><td><pre>protected override void OnClosing(
    CancelEventArgs e)
{
  if (DialogResult == DialogResult.OK)
  {</pre></td></tr>
<tr><td>8</td><td>In this override, if the password is invalid, cancel the close operation to force the user to fix the problem.</td><td><pre>   if (!ValidPassword())
    {
      DialogResult result = MessageBox.Show(
        "The current password is blank "
         + " or the two password entries "
         + "do not match.",
        "Invalid Password",
        MessageBoxButtons.OK,
        MessageBoxIcon.Information);

      e.Cancel = true;
    }</pre></td></tr>
<tr><td>9</td><td>If the operation is not canceled, save the dialog box settings.</td><td><pre>   if (!e.Cancel)
      SaveSettings();
  }
}</pre></td></tr>
</table>

	FINISH THE ALBUMEDITDIALOG FORM *(CONTINUED)*	
	Action	**Result**

10	Implement a `SaveSettings` method to store the results
	How-to
	a. Assign the album title.
	b. Assign the descriptor based on which radio button is checked.
	c. Assign the password if the check box is selected and the password is valid.
		`private void SaveSettings()`
		`{`
		`  PhotoAlbum album = Manager.Album;`
		`  if (album != null)`
		`  {`
		`    album.Title = txtTitle.Text;`
		
		`    if (rbtnCaption.Checked)`
		`      album.PhotoDescriptor = PhotoAlbum.`
		`          DescriptorOption.Caption;`
		`    else if (rbtnDateTaken.Checked)`
		`      album.PhotoDescriptor = PhotoAlbum.`
		`          DescriptorOption.DateTaken;`
		`    else if (rbtnFileName.Checked)`
		`      album.PhotoDescriptor = PhotoAlbum.`
		`          DescriptorOption.FileName;`
		
		`    if (cbxPassword.Checked && ValidPassword())`
		`      Manager.Password = txtPassword.Text;`
		`    else`
		`      Manager.Password = null;`
		`  }`
		`}`

11	Finally, add a `TextChanged` event handler to the Title text box to update the title bar as the title text is modified.	`private void txtTitle_TextChanged(`
		`    object sender, EventArgs e)`
		`{`
		`  Text = txtTitle.Text + " - Album Properties";`
		`}`

The `AlbumEditDialog` is now ready for use. The next section puts it all together.

9.3.4 Hooking up a dialog box (again)

The final task required before we can view our new form is almost identical to section 8.2.3 where we hooked up the `PhotoEditDialog` form. These steps are as follows.

	DISPLAY THE ALBUMEDITDIALOG FORM FROM THE MAIN WINDOW	
	Action	**Result**
1	In the designer window for the `MainForm` class of the MyPhotos project, add a new menu item to the `ctxMenuPhoto` menu. **Settings** **Property** / **Value** (Name) / menuAlbumProps Text / Albu&m Properties...	

	Display the AlbumEditDialog form from the main window *(continued)*	
	Action	**Result**

2	Update the `ctxtMenuPhoto_Opening` event handler to set the `Enabled` property appropriately for the new menu.	`private void ctxMenuPhoto_Opening(`
		`    object sender, CancelEventArgs e)`
		`{`
		`  menuNext.Enabled = (. . .);`
		`  menuPrevious.Enabled = (. . .);`
		`  menuPhotoProps.Enabled = (. . .);`
		`  menuAlbumProps.Enabled`
		`      = (Manager.Album != null);`
		`}`

3	Add a `Click` event handler for the newly added menu.	`private void menuAlbumProps_Click(`
		`    object sender, EventArgs e)`
		`{`

4	Implement this handler to display the new dialog box. If the user makes any changes, display them on the form.	`  if (Manager.Album == null)`
		`    return;`
		
		`  using (AlbumEditDialog dlg`
		`         = new AlbumEditDialog(Manager))`
		`  {`
		`    if (dlg.ShowDialog()`
		`          == DialogResult.OK)`
		`      DisplayAlbum();`
		`  }`
		`}`

Compile, run, display an album, and use the new dialog box. The password setting should work fine, although it does not actually do anything to the album yet. We discuss encryption and decryption, using this setting for an example, in chapter 10.

While our new dialog box works well, some fine-tuning is still possible. It would be nice if we could provide more information on the meaning of each setting, and we need to tell users when the two password entries do not match before they try to save their changes. These two improvements are part of the final topic in this chapter.

9.4 Tooltips and error providers

The .NET Framework provides a mechanism for extending the behavior of objects using an external class called an *extender provider*. Extender providers implement additional behavior or effects across one or more components.

Two examples of extender providers are the `ToolTip` and `ErrorProvider` classes. The `ToolTip` class implements small pop-up windows for controls on a form, while the `ErrorProvider` class implements a mechanism for indicating an error associated with a control on a form.

We discuss each class separately, as well as extender providers in general.

9.4.1 The ToolTip class

You never know when a good tip might come in handy. In Windows applications, tooltips provide short and quick explanations of the purpose of a control or other object. A number of classes provide their own tooltip mechanism through a `ToolTipText` property, in particular the ToolStripItem classes. For classes derived from the Control object, the ToolTip class supports this feature in a general fashion. An overview of this class appears in .NET Table 9.6.

A ToolTip object is not a control at all. Instead it is a component that is typically associated with a Form object. A single ToolTip can create the tips for all controls on a single form.

.NET Table 9.6 ToolTip class

The ToolTip class is a component that provides a small pop-up window for a control. This window displays a short phrase describing the purpose of the control, and appears whenever the mouse hovers over the control for a configurable amount of time. This class is part of the System.Windows.Forms namespace, implements the IExtenderProvider interface, and derives from the System.ComponentModel.Component class.

Public Properties	Active	Gets or sets whether the ToolTip is currently active.
	AutomaticDelay	Gets or sets the default delay time in milliseconds. When this property is set, the AutoPopDelay, InitialDelay, and ReshowDelay properties are initialized. The default is 500.
	AutoPopDelay	Gets or sets the time before a displayed tooltip disappears. The default is ten times the AutomaticDelay setting.
	InitialDelay	Gets or sets the time before a tooltip appears when the mouse is stationary. This defaults to the AutomaticDelay.
	IsBalloon	Gets or sets whether the tooltip displays in a balloon or a rectangular graphic.
	OwnerDraw	Gets or sets whether the tooltip is custom drawn using the Draw event or drawn by the framework.
	ReshowDelay	Gets or sets the time in milliseconds after the first tooltip displays before subsequent tooltips appear as the mouse moves from one assigned control to another. The default is one-fifth the AutomaticDelay setting.
	ShowAlways	Gets or sets whether to display the tooltip for an inactive control.
	UseFading	Gets or sets whether or not the tooltip fades in and out.
Public Methods	GetToolTip	Retrieves the tooltip string associated with a control.
	RemoveAll	Removes all tooltip strings defined in this component.
	SetToolTip	Associates a tooltip string with a control.
Public Events	*Draw*	Occurs when the OwnerDrawn property is true and the tooltip should be displayed.
	Popup	Occurs just before the tooltip is drawn.

9.4.2 Displaying tooltips

While it is certainly possible to assign tooltips for our `MainForm` controls in the `MyPhotos` project, doing so would not make a very exciting example. The `ToolStripItem` classes that build the menu and status bar components provide their own tooltip mechanism, which leaves us with the `PictureBox` control as the sole target for a potential tip.

Figure 9.2 The framework displays tooltip text just below the mouse cursor, which in most cases does not obscure the control's contents from view.

Instead, we look to our now-famous MyPhotoControls library for a rich source of tooltip-hungry controls. Figure 9.2 shows the `AlbumEditDialog` form with a tooltip displayed for the Title text box.

Let's crank up an Action-Result table and create a `ToolTip` object for this dialog box. Once the tooltip exists, we can discuss how to associate specific messages with individual controls.

ADD A TOOLTIP OBJECT TO THE ALBUMEDITDIALOG FORM

	Action	Result
1	In the AlbumEditDialog.cs [Design] window, add a `ToolTip` object to the form.	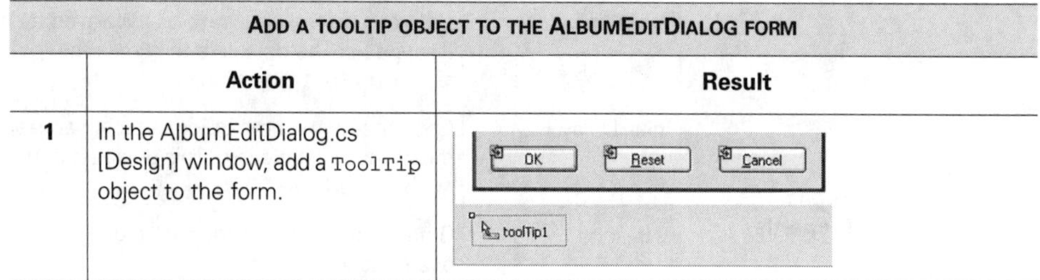 OK Reset Cancel toolTip1

As usual, the new object is defined in the class and initialized in the `InitializeComponent` method. Listing 9.1 shows an excerpt of generated code related to the tooltip component. Let's examine the numbered portions of the code in greater detail.

Listing 9.1 Generated code excerpt showing tooltip creation

```
namespace Manning.MyPhotoControls
{
  partial class AlbumEditDialog
  {
    /// <summary>
    /// Required designer variable.
    /// </summary>
    private System.ComponentModel.IContainer components = null;
    . . .
    protected override void Dispose(bool disposing)
   {
```

Holds components for form ❶

```
      if (disposing && (components != null))      ❷ Disposes of
      {                                              components
        components.Dispose();
      }
      base.Dispose(disposing);

    }

    #region Windows Form Designer generated code
    . . .
    private void InitializeComponent()
    {
      this.components = new System.ComponentModel.Container();
      . . .
      this.toolTip1 = new System.Windows.Forms.ToolTip(this.components); <-
      . . .                                          Creates tooltip object ❸

    }
    #endregion

    . . .
    private System.Windows.Forms.ToolTip toolTip1;
  }
}
```

❶ We first saw the `components` field in chapter 2, where we indicated that this field was required to properly manage the form's components. This field is a `Container` object, and holds any components added to the form.

❷ When a form is disposed of, the components field allows any components associated with the form to be properly disposed of as well. The `Container` object implicitly disposes of all contained objects when its `Dispose` method is called.

❸ The `ToolTip` class is defined and managed much like any other object on the form. The one difference is that, since it is a `Component` object, it is created within the components container, so that the tooltip is disposed of when the `Form` is closed.

We can add a series of tooltip strings for our controls using Visual Studio directly. This table continues our prior steps.

	ADD TOOLTIP STRINGS TO THE FORM'S CONTROLS	
	Action	**Result**
2	Add the tooltip "Album file name" for the Album File text box control on the form. **How-to** a. Display the properties for the `txtAlbumFile` control. b. Locate the entry "ToolTip on toolTip1." c. Enter the setting "Album file name."	Properties window: txtAlbumFile System.Windows.Forms.TextBox — Text; TextAlign: Left; ToolTip on toolTip1: **Album file name**; UseSystemPassword: False; UseWaitCursor: False; Visible: True; WordWrap: True **ToolTip on toolTip1** Determines the ToolTip shown when the mouse hovers over the control.

3	Define tooltip strings for the other controls on the form.
	
	Settings
	Control — **ToolTip String**
	txtTitle — Title for the album
	rbtnFileName — When set, describes each photo using its filename
	rbtnCaption — When set, describes each photo using its caption
	rbtnDateTaken — When set, describes each photo using its date taken
	cbxPassword — Whether to encrypt the album file on disk
	txtPassword — Password for album
	txtConfirm — Confirms password for album
		Visual Studio generates the code required for each tooltip in the `InitializeComponent` method.
		`private void InitializeComponent()`
		`{`
		`  . . .`
		`  //`
		`  // txtTitle`
		`  //`
		`  this.txtTitle.Location = . . .;`
		`  this.txtTitle.Name = . . .;`
		`  . . .`
		`  this.toolTip1.SetToolTip(`
		`      this.txtTitle,`
		`      "Title for the album");`
		`  . . .`
		`}`
		Note: You can assign tooltips to labels and group boxes as well. Since the user does not normally interact with such controls, tooltips are not typically assigned.

That's all it takes. Visual Studio generates a call to `SetToolTip` for each control, as is shown in the table for the `txtTitle` control. Of course, you can define tooltips explicitly in your code using the `SetToolTip` method without using Visual Studio. The steps used here simply demonstrate the support provided by the development environment.

The `ToolTip` class is a specific kind of Windows Forms class called an *extender provider*. We discuss such classes in more detail in a moment. Before we do, compile and run the program to make sure our tooltips work. Open an album and display the `AlbumEditDialog` form for the album. Place the mouse over a control and watch the tooltip appear. As you look at the tooltips we just defined, note the following features:

- There is a short pause, about half a second, before the tooltip text appears, and then it disappears after about 5 seconds. These intervals are controlled by the `InitialDelay` and `AutoPopDelay` properties.
- Display a tooltip, then move the mouse to another control and note how the tooltip for the second control appears almost immediately. This secondary delay defaults to 100 milliseconds, and is specified by the `ReshowDelay` property.
- The tooltips for the password text boxes do not appear when these buttons are disabled. The behavior for inactive or disabled controls is determined by the `ShowAlways` property.

TRY IT! Create a `ToolTip` object for the `PhotoEditDialog` form and set tooltip text for the interactive controls in this form. Try setting the `IsBalloon` property to `true` to see how this style of tooltip appears. Instead of setting the tips in Visual Studio, use the `SetToolTip` method in the `PhotoEditDialog` constructor to create a tooltip for each control on the form.

That's a quick introduction to tooltips. You can also create custom-drawn tooltips by setting the `OwnerDrawn` property to `true`. The procedure for drawing custom tooltips is somewhat similar to how custom list items are drawn, which is discussed in chapter 12. Check out the `Draw` event and the `DrawToolTipEventArgs` class in the .NET documentation for more information on this topic.

9.4.3 Building extender providers

Tooltips are one of the *extender providers* built into Windows Forms. Extender providers are classes that implement the `IExtenderProvider` interface. An overview of this interface appears in .NET Table 9.7.

.NET Table 9.7 IExtenderProvider interface

The `IExtenderProvider` interface defines the interface for providing additional properties to other components. Extender providers are typically components, and must be assigned a `ProvideProperty` attribute. Examples of extender providers include the `ToolTip` and the `HelpProvider` classes in the Windows Forms namespace. This class is part of the `System.ComponentModel` namespace.

Public Methods	CanExtend	Returns whether the given object can receive the extended properties
Required Attributes	ProvideProperty	Specifies the name of the property that the provider offers to other components

Extender providers follow a somewhat standard format for their implementation. In chapter 10 we implement a class called `FlybyTextProvider` to support fly-by text on menu strip items. This class only supports `ToolStripMenuItem` objects, and displays temporary text describing a menu item in a status bar label. Listing 9.2 illustrates the key parts of this implementation.

Listing 9.2 Sample class that implements IExtenderProvider

```
[ProvideProperty("FlybyText", typeof(ToolStripMenuItem))]
public class FlybyTextProvider : Component, IExtenderProider
{
  public FlybyTextProvider(IContainer container)
  {
    container.Add(this);
  }

  private Hashtable _flybyTable = new Hashtable();

  #region IExtenderProvider members
  public bool CanExtend(object extendee)
  {
    return (extendee is ToolStripMenuItem);
  }
  #endregion

  #region FlybyText property code
  public void SetFlybyText(ToolStripMenuItem item, string text)
  {
    // Assign or clear text for given item
  }

  public string GetFlybyText(ToolStripMenuItem item)
  {
    // Return text for given item
  }
  #endregion

  /*
   * Implementation logic goes here
   */
}
```

Annotations: ❶ Defines properties and class; ❷ Uses hash table to hold settings; ❸ Implements IExtenderProvider interface; ❹ Implements Get property method

❶ The `FlybyTextProvider` class is defined to implement the `IExtenderProvider` interface. Each extended property is defined by a `ProvideProperty` attribute. An attribute appears before a class, method, or other definition and defines some feature or behavior that is applied to or supported by the class. In this case, the `ProvideProperty` attribute indicates that the `FlybyTextProvider` class extends `ToolStripMenuItem` objects to include a new `FlybyText` property.

❷ Since extender providers support a property on multiple objects, some sort of collection is required to define the value of the property for each object. A `Hashtable` class is often used since it provides a relatively efficient mechanism for associating values with objects.

❸ The `CanExtend` method is the only member required by the `IExtenderProvider` interface. It returns `true` if a given object can be extended by this class and `false` otherwise. In our case, `true` is returned if the given object is a menu item object.

❹ Properties defined by `ProvideProperty` attributes are not actual C# properties. As we saw for the `ToolTip` class, they only appear as properties in Visual Studio, as in "ToolTip on toolTip1." The implementation of the property is an explicit Set and Get method, as in the `ToolTip.SetToolTip` and `ToolTip.GetToolTip` methods. In our case, since our property is "FlybyText," we implement the `SetFlybyText` method to assign the fly-by text value for a menu item, and the `GetFlybyText` method to retrieve the fly-by text assigned to a menu item.

The implementation of this extender provider requires use of the mouse events, so we save the complete implementation for the next chapter. We finish this chapter with a discussion of another extender provider object, the `ErrorProvider` class.

9.4.4 The ErrorProvider class

Good user interfaces provide feedback to their users. One useful mechanism is the ability to indicate portions of a form that do not meet the requirements for the associated data. The `ErrorProvider` class, summarized in .NET Table 9.8, provides one way to implement such functionality.

Much like the `ToolTip` class, when an `ErrorProvider` is assigned to a form, each control can assign error text through the `GetError` and `SetError` methods. Controls with an assigned error display the icon assigned to the class, subject to the icon alignment setting for the control. The `Get` and `SetIconAlignment` methods support a second `ProvideProperty` attribute defined for the `ErrorProvider` class. There is also a third property to control the padding between the control and the icon, set via `GetIconPadding` and `SetIconPadding` methods, that is not shown in .NET Table 9.8.

We demonstrate an error provider in our application on the `AlbumEditDialog` form, as illustrated in figure 9.3. If you recall, we did not verify that the given password and confirmation strings were valid until the user attempted to close the dialog box. The following steps define an error provider and illustrate its use for this purpose.

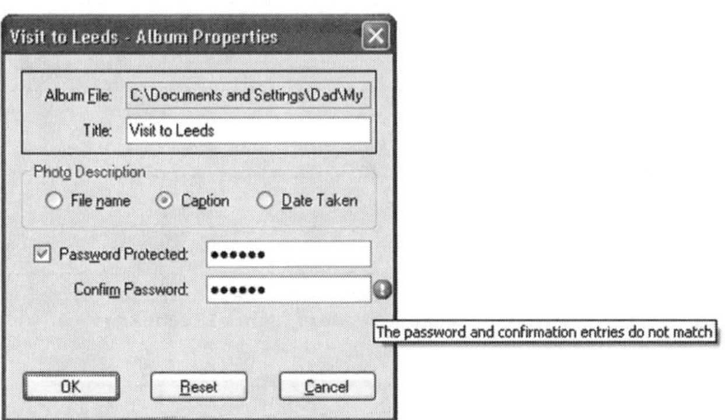

Figure 9.3 An error provider notifies a user that an error exists, without preventing additional actions from occurring within the form.

.NET Table 9.8 ErrorProvider class

The `ErrorProvider` class is a component that provides a mechanism for indicating when a control on a form has an error associated with it. This consists of a small icon that appears next to the control. This class is part of the `System.Windows.Forms` namespace, implements the `IExtenderProvider` interface, and derives from the `System.ComponentModel.Component` class.

Public Properties	BlinkRate	Gets or sets the rate in milliseconds used to flash the error icon when blinking is enabled.
	BlinkStyle	Gets or sets an `ErrorBlinkStyle` enumeration value that indicates whether and how the error icon should blink.
	DataSource	Gets or sets a data source that this class should monitor. The `DataMember` property indicates the list within the data source to monitor.
	Icon	Gets or sets the `Icon` object to display when an error is assigned to a control. By default, a red circle containing an exclamation point is used.
	Tag	Gets or sets an object associated with this error provider.
Public Methods	CanExtend	Indicates whether a given object supports the `ErrorProvider` extended property.
	Clear	Removes all errors currently assigned to controls.
	GetError	Gets the error description, if any, associated with a given control. The `SetError` method assigns the error description for a control.
	GetIconAlignment	Gets the alignment for the error icon to use with a specific control, using the `ErrorIconAlignment` enumeration. The `SetIconAlignment` method assigns this alignment.

DEFINE AN ERRORPROVIDER FOR THE ALBUMEDITDIALOG CLASS

	Action	Result
1	In the AlbumEditDialog.cs designer window, drag an `ErrorProvider` object into the component tray for the form.	OK Reset Cancel toolTip1 errorProvider1

2	Add a `Validating` event handler for the `txtPassword` text box.	`private void txtPassword_Validating(`
		`  object sender, CancelEventArgs e)`
		`{`

DEFINE AN ERRORPROVIDER FOR THE ALBUMEDITDIALOG CLASS *(CONTINUED)*		
	Action	**Result**

3	Implement this handler to assign an error message if the password is blank.	`if (txtPassword.TextLength > 0)`
		`errorProvider1.SetError(txtPassword, "");`
		`else`
		`errorProvider1.SetError(txtPassword,`
		`"The assigned password cannot be blank");`
		`}`

4	Add a `Validating` event handler for the `txtConfirm` text box.	`private void txtConfirm_Validating(`
		`object sender, CancelEventArgs e)`
		`{`

5	Implement this handler to assign an error message if the two passwords do not match.	`if (txtConfirm.Text == txtPassword.Text)`
		`errorProvider1.SetError(txtConfirm, "");`
		`else`
		`errorProvider1.SetError(txtConfirm,`
		`"The password and confirmation entries "`
		`+ "do not match");`
		`}`

As you may recall, the `ValidPassword` method created in section 9.3.3 returns `true` if the password is blank or the two text boxes contain different strings. We implement this requirement here with error notifications for the different conditions. Note the use of the `Validating` event for the `TextBox` controls, and the assignment of the error string within the event handlers.

The `Validating` event is one of a series of events related to entering and leaving a control. Collectively, these events are sometimes referred to as the *focus events*. The focus events, in the order in which they occur, are as follows: `Enter`, `GotFocus`, `Leave`, `Validating`, `Validated`, and `LostFocus`. These events can be used to fine-tune the behavior of a control as the user moves from one control to the next.

The validation events, namely `Validating` and `Validated`, occur during and after validation whenever the `CausesValidation` property is set to `true`. This property defaults to `true`, so validation events normally occur in all controls. The `Validating` event receives a `CancelEventArgs` parameter much like the `OnClosing` event discussed for the `Form` class in chapter 7. We could alternately implement the `Confirm` event handler to cancel the operation with code similar to this:

```
private void txtConfirm_Validating(
    object sender, CancelEventArgs e)
{
  if (txtPassword.Text != txtConfirm.Text)
  {
    MessageBox.Show(this,
        "The password and confirm values do not match");
    e.Cancel = true;
  }
}
```

The problem with this code is that when a Validating operation is canceled, the focus is not permitted to leave the associated control. The user is thus forced to enter a valid matching password before they can leave the confirmation text box. This is a problem if the user entered the incorrect value in the password text box, or if they simply wish to cancel the dialog box.

As an alternative to the Cancel property, the ErrorProvider object presents feedback to users without preventing them from leaving the text box or canceling the form. The SetError method is used to assign an error string:

```
public void SetError(Control control, string value);
```

The first parameter is the control to receive the error. The second parameter contains the error string. If the given error string is blank or empty, the error is cleared for the given control.

If you recall, our implementation of the OnClosing override prevents users from saving their changes if the password is invalid. So our new ErrorProvider object informs the user when the dialog box contains an error, and if the user clicks the OK button, the OnClosing override prevents the Form from closing with an error present. When the user clicks the Cancel button, the dialog box can safely close since any new values are discarded.

TRY IT! Add a Validating event for the Album Title text box whenever the title is blank. If you wish, modify the BlinkRate and BlinkStyle for the error provider to see the different effects available with these settings.

9.5 RECAP

This chapter discussed buttons in Windows Forms. We looked at the three basic types of buttons: push buttons, radio buttons, and check box buttons, and presented a dialog box for editing the properties of a PhotoAlbum object using these button classes. We saw how radio buttons are grouped within a container control, either the Form itself or a Panel, GroupBox, or other container, and illustrated how a check box control can be used to enable and disable a collection of controls.

The chapter finished with a discussion of tooltips and error providers. The ToolTip and ErrorProvider components are both examples of extender providers, which implement the IExtenderProvider interface to define optional properties for controls on a form.

Another extender provider implemented in the Windows Forms namespace is the HelpProvider class, which provides support for adding pop-up or online help to an application. This class works much like other extender providers in that a set of properties defines the behavior for a specific control.

A good source for examples, both for extender providers and the button classes, is the Code Project website at www.codeproject.com. This site provides free access to samples and articles provided by its user community on .NET and other programming topics.

This chapter left two tasks unfinished to complete in our next chapter. The first is to implement encryption using the password captured by the `AlbumEditDialog` form; the second is to provide the complete code for the `FlybyTextProvider` class as an example of an extender provider implementation.

Both topics are included in the next chapter, which presents an assortment of .NET features related to Windows Forms application development, most notably the handling of keyboard and mouse events. Our discussion of Windows Forms controls resumes in chapter 11 and 12, where we discuss list and combo boxes.

CHAPTER 10

Handling user input and encryption

This chapter provides a brief interlude between the text box and button controls in chapters 8 and 9, and the list box and combo box controls in chapters 11 and 12. Here we turn our attention to interacting with the keyboard and mouse. We also look at the cryptographic support built into .NET, and take a peek at the `LinkLabel` control.

User input refers to any type of input made by a user. This includes touch pads, joysticks, audio hook-ups, and just about anything else you might imagine. The most common interaction is with the mouse and keyboard, of course, and this is our focus here. Be careful in your applications not to overly favor one over the other. Supporting mouse interaction is important in any modern interface since mouse users are comfortable with menus and other click-based interaction. Do not discount those of us who prefer the keyboard, though, since expert users generally prefer the quicker access provided by keyboard shortcuts and other keyboard-based navigation.

10.1 KEYBOARD EVENTS

We looked briefly at keyboard events in chapter 8 while discussing the `TextBox` class. There we used the `KeyPress` event to limit what characters could appear in a text box control. In this section we look more generically at keyboard events, and use them in our application to provide some quick shortcuts for the user.

10.1.1 The three events

Three distinct events occur whenever a key is pressed and released. Note that we did not say whenever a *character* is pressed and released. A character may involve multiple key presses. For example, the letter "A" requires the use of the Shift key and the A key, typically abbreviated as Shift+A (of course, this is not true if the Caps Lock key is pressed, but you understand).

The three keyboard events are summarized in table 10.1. These events occur for a control in the order shown in the table whenever the control has the focus.

Table 10.1 The keyboard events

Event	Description	Event Argument
KeyDown	Occurs when a key on the keyboard is pressed down	`KeyEventArgs` class
KeyPress	Occurs when a character is pressed on the keyboard, and again each time the character is repeated while it continues to be pressed	`KeyPressEventArgs` class
KeyUp	Occurs when a key on the keyboard is released	`KeyEventArgs` class

10.1.2 Handling the KeyPress event

The `KeyPress` event is used for generic handling of keyboard characters. Event handlers of this type receive an instance of the `KeyPressEventArgs` class as its event parameter. We saw this class in .NET Table 8.4 in chapter 8. As you may recall, a `Handled` property defines whether the event handler consumes the key, and a `Key-Char` property contains the character pressed.

It is important to realize that the `KeyPress` event, as well as the `KeyDown` and `KeyUp` events, is received by the control that currently has the focus. In particular, keyboard events are not normally received by parent controls such as `Panel` and `Form` objects that contain the control. Normally this is a good thing. The per-character behavior is defined by each control, with no need for parental involvement. For example, if a `TextBox` control handles the `KeyPress` event to ensure that only integer values are entered, there is no need to spend precious operating system cycles percolating this event up through the set of `Panel` or other controls that contain the text box. A parent control such as a `Panel` or `GroupBox` only receives a keyboard event if it specifically has the focus.

This presents a slight problem for subclasses of the `ContainerControl` object, and in particular the `Form` object. As you may recall, container control objects manage the focus for the contained controls, and do not receive the focus directly. There are plenty of situations where you would like to initiate an action from the keyboard regardless of the current control.

The good folks at Microsoft created the `KeyPreview` property in the `Form` class for just this purpose. When this property is set to `true`, the `Form` object receives all keyboard events before they are passed to the current control. If the event handler sets the `Handled` property to `true`, the active control does not receive the keyboard key or corresponding character.

Let's create an example of this in our MyPhotos program by handling the plus (+) and minus (–) characters. It would make sense for the plus character to display the next photograph, and the minus the previous photograph. These should occur at the `Form` level and not just in our `PictureBox` instance where the image is displayed. The following steps detail this change.

MAP THE PLUS AND MINUS KEYS TO THE NEXT AND PREVIOUS MENU ITEMS

	Action	Result
1	In the MainForm.cs [Design] window of the MyPhotos project, modify the `KeyPreview` property for the `MainForm` object to be `true`.	Properties MainForm System.Windows.Forms.Form HelpButton False Icon (Icon) ImeMode NoControl IsMdiContainer False KeyPreview True Language (Default) Localizable False

2	Override the protected `OnKeyPress` method in the `MainForm` class.	`protected override void OnKeyPress(`
		`    KeyPressEventArgs e)`
		`{`

3	When a plus sign is pressed, invoke the Next menu handler.
	
	Note: Invoking a menu directly like this is generally discouraged. We do it anyway to keep our code shorter.
		`  switch (e.KeyChar)`
		`  {`
		`    case '+':`
		`      menuNext.PerformClick();`
		`      e.Handled = true;`
		`      break;`

4	When a minus sign is pressed, invoke the Previous menu handler.	`    case '-':`
		`      menuPrevious.PerformClick();`
		`      e.Handled = true;`
		`      break;`

5	For all other characters, do nothing to allow child controls to receive the character.	`  }`
		
		`  // Invoke the base method`
		`  base.OnKeyPress(e);`
		`}`

We could have used an `if` statement in this code, especially with only two items to check. Since we may wish to add behavior for additional characters in the future, a `switch` statement seems like a better approach here. We simulate a user click of the appropriate menu item with the PerformClick method. A more robust approach might be to encapsulate the required logic in a supporting method that both this code and the menu handlers could employ. This is typically preferred, but we take the shortcut of invoking the menu directly.

Let's move on to the KeyDown and KeyUp events.

10.1.3 Handling the KeyDown and KeyUp events

The key up and down events are useful to fine-tune an application's behavior as keyboard keys are pressed and released, and for handling noncharacter keys such as the function or arrow keys. Handlers for these events receive a KeyEventArgs class instance as their event parameter, which is summarized in .NET Table 10.2

.NET Table 10.2 KeyEventArgs class

The KeyEventArgs class represents the event data for the KeyDown and KeyUp events. This class represents the keyboard key pressed down or released by the user. It is part of the System.Windows.Forms namespace, and inherits from the System.EventArgs class.

Public Properties	Alt	Gets whether the Alt key was pressed.
	Control	Gets whether the Ctrl key was pressed.
	Handled	Gets or sets whether the key event was handled.
	KeyCode	Gets the specific keyboard key pressed as a value in the Keys enumeration.
	KeyData	Gets the combination of keyboard keys pressed at the same time using the values from the Keys enumeration.
	KeyValue	Gets the int character value corresponding to the keyboard combination.
	Modifiers	Gets the combination of modifier keys pressed or released using the Keys enumeration values. This is a combination of the Control, Shift, and Alt values, or None if no keys were pressed.
	Shift	Gets whether the Shift key was pressed.
	SuppressKeyPress	Gets or sets whether the key should be passed to the current control. Setting this to true also sets Handled to true.

As you can see, while the KeyPress event works at the character level, the KeyUp and KeyDown events work at the keyboard key level. The KeyEventArgs members allow you to determine exactly which combination of keys are pressed or released when the event occurs.

We can demonstrate this class by setting the Page Up and Page Down keys to invoke the Previous and Next menu items, respectively. We use the KeyDown event

	Map the Page Down and Page Up keys to the Next and Previous menu items	
	Action	**Result**

1	In the `MainForm` class, override the `OnKeyDown` method.	`protected override void OnKeyDown(`
		`    KeyEventArgs e)`
		`{`

2	Invoke the Previous menu item when the Page Up key is pressed down.	`  switch (e.KeyCode)`
		`  {`
		`    case Keys.PageUp:`
		`      menuPrevious.PerformClick();`
		`      e.Handled = true;`
		`      break;`

3	Invoke the Next menu item when the Page Down key is pressed down.	`    case Keys.PageDown:`
		`      menuNext.PerformClick ();`
		`      e.Handled = true;`
		`      break;`

4	Invoke the base method at the end of the method.	`  }`
		
		`  base.OnKeyDown(e);`
		`}`

for this purpose. We have already set the `KeyPreview` property to receive keyboard events in our `Form`, so we can override the `OnKeyDown` method to process this event.

Run the program to verify that all four keys we handled work as expected. It should be noted here that not all characters are received by the keyboard events. Depending on the control, some characters may be preprocessed or otherwise handled before this event is raised. To process these characters, yet another approach is required.

TRY IT! Modify the `OnKeyDown` method to recognize the Home and End keys as well. Have the Home key display the first photograph in the album, and the End key display the last.

As an alternate approach, modify this method so that Shift+Page Down will display the last photograph and Shift+Page Up the first photograph in the album. To implement this change, you need to check the `Shift` property within the `PageUp` and `PageDown` case blocks, or modify the `switch` statement to use the `e.KeyData` property instead.

10.1.4 Preprocessing command keys

This topic is a little esoteric, but quite useful if you ever need to intercept a key that is preprocessed by the control you are using. Take, for example, the Tab key. This key is used to navigate between controls on a `Form`, and so is not available to the keyboard events. A similar situation applies if you wish to process a Down or Up arrow key within a list. Typically, you do not need to do this unless you are creating a new control or looking to fine-tune the use of an existing control.

There are three protected methods in the `Control` class that are called during message preprocessing and can be overridden to modify or augment the behavior of a control. These methods are summarized in table 10.3, in the order they are invoked within a control.

Table 10.3 Protected methods for preprocessing keyboard keys in controls

Method	Description
ProcessCmdKey	Process a command key for a control, such as an accelerator or menu shortcut.
ProcessDialogKey	Process a dialog box key for a control, such as a Tab, Return, or arrow key. This method is called if the protected `IsInputKey` method indicates that the control does not process the key.
ProcessDialogChar	Process a dialog box character for a control, such as a control mnemonic. This method is called if the protected `IsInputChar` method indicates that the control does not process the character.

We can show a quick example using the `ProcessCmdKey` method to handle the Tab and Shift+Tab keys for yet another way to move forward and backward within the album. If you try processing the `Keys.Tab` value in the `KeyDown` event handler, you will discover that this value is never received by the handler.

The `ProcessCmdKey` method receives two parameters: the operating system message and the key data. The operating system message arrives as a `Message` structure, which contains a `Msg` property with the message value.

OVERRIDE THE PROCESSCMDKEY METHOD

	Action	Result
1	In the MainForm.cs source window, define a private constant for the keyboard down message.	`private const int WM_KEYDOWN = 0x100;` **Note:** This and other message values are defined by the operating system. The `WM_KEYDOWN` message is the keystroke down message. You can also test for `WM_SYSKEYDOWN`, with value 104, to catch keystroke messages that include control keys such as Alt or Ctrl.

2	Override the `ProcessCmdKey` method.	`protected override bool ProcessCmdKey(`
		`  ref Message msg, Keys keyData)`
		`{`
		
		Note: The `ref` parameter modifier causes a reference to be passed into a method, so that any changes made to the parameter are visible outside the method. This requires the caller to provide an initialized non-`null` value.

OVERRIDE THE PROCESSCMDKEY METHOD *(CONTINUED)*		
	Action	**Result**

3	Invoke the Next or Previous menu item when the Tab or Shift+Tab key is pressed, respectively.
	How-to
	Invoke the appropriate menu, and return `true` to indicate that the keystroke was processed by the form.
		<pre>if (msg.Msg == WM_KEYDOWN)
		{
		  switch (keyData)
		  {
		    case Keys.Tab:
		      menuNext.PerformClick();
		      return true;
		
		    case Keys.Shift
			Keys.Tab:
			      menuPrevious.PerformClick();
			      return true;
			  }
			}</pre>

4	If the keystroke was not processed, call the method in the base class to determine the appropriate return value.	<pre> return base.ProcessCmdKey(ref msg, keyData); }</pre>

The set of Windows message values is rather large. If you search the Microsoft Developer Network (MSDN) at http://msdn.microsoft.com for the phrase "keyboard message notification," you will find more information on possible message values.

Note that this code could be problematic if the form changes in the future to include additional controls. Since the Tab key is consumed by our class, the user can never use this key to navigate between controls on the form. This example is simply intended to illustrate how to handle command keys, so feel free to remove it from your application if you wish.

Our next topic is the events related to mouse interactions.

10.2 MOUSE EVENTS

The mouse device has gone through its own little evolution since it was invented by Xerox Corporation over 30 years ago. The number of buttons has varied from one to three, and the shape has evolved from a rather uncomfortable rectangle to the hand-fitting contours found in most modern versions. The mouse wheel is a rather recent addition, permitting automated scrolling from the comfort of your mouse. An even newer addition is a five-button mouse, with the extra buttons intended for backward/forward navigation in applications such as web browsers.

Regardless of the type of mouse you own, the possible events in .NET are the same. In chapter 7 we used the `MouseMove` event to update the `PixelDialog` form as the mouse pointer changed its position. Here we discuss the mouse events in a bit more detail.

10.2.1 The MouseEventArgs class

Mouse events are somewhat similar to keyboard events. Mouse buttons go down and up just like keyboard keys, and the events `MouseDown` and `MouseUp` occur

Table 10.4 The mouse events in Windows Forms controls

Event	Description	Event Argument
MouseDown	Occurs when a mouse button is pressed down while the pointer is over the control.	`MouseEventArgs` class
MouseEnter	Occurs when the mouse pointer enters the control.	`EventArgs` class
MouseHover	Occurs when the mouse pointer remains, or hovers, over a control for a configurable amount of time.	`EventArgs` class
MouseLeave	Occurs when the mouse pointer leaves the control.	`EventArgs` class
MouseMove	Occurs when the mouse pointer moves over the control.	`MouseEventArgs` class
MouseUp	Occurs when a mouse button is released while the pointer is over the control.	`MouseEventArgs` class
MouseWheel	Occurs when the mouse wheel moves while the control has focus. The read-only `MouseWheelPresent` property in the `SystemInformation` class indicates whether the operating system believes a mouse wheel is present.	`MouseEventArgs` class

accordingly. Since the mouse also controls the mouse pointer, there are events related to pointer movement as well. The complete list of mouse events is shown in table 10.4. These events occur with respect to a specific control.

As you can see from the table, many of the mouse event handlers received an instance of the `MouseEventArgs` class as their event parameters. The `MouseEventArgs` class, summarized in .NET Table 10.5, provides properties to identify which button was pressed, how it was pressed, and exactly where the cursor was located when this occurred.

.NET Table 10.5 MouseEventArgs class

The `MouseEventArgs` class is the event argument class associated with mouse events. This class represents information about the mouse device and the mouse pointer position when the event occurs. It is part of the `System.Windows.Forms` namespace, and inherits from the `System.EventArgs` class.

Public Properties	Button	Gets the `MouseButtons` enumeration value corresponding to the mouse button pressed by the user.
	Clicks	Gets the number of times the mouse button was pressed and released. Note that the `DoubleClick` event is normally used to process double-clicks of the mouse.
	Delta	Gets a signed integer representing the number of detents the mouse wheel has rotated. A *detent* is a rotation of the mouse wheel by one notch.
	Location	Gets the current location of the mouse.
	X	Gets the x-coordinate of the current mouse pointer position.
	Y	Gets the y-coordinate of the current mouse pointer position.

A simple application using mouse events is shown in listing 10.1. This application displays a form, and modifies the background color of the form whenever the left or right mouse button is pressed.

Listing 10.1 Sample application using mouse events

```
using System.Drawing;
using System.Windows.Forms;

public class MouseSample : Form
{
  public MouseSample()
  {
    Text = "Mouse Sample";
    MouseDown += HandleMouseDown;
    MouseUp += HandleMouseUp;
  }

  public void HandleMouseDown(object sender, MouseEventArgs e)
  {
    if (e.Button == MouseButtons.Left)
      BackColor = Color.Purple;
    else if (e.Button == MouseButtons.Right)
      BackColor = Color.Yellow;
  }

  public void HandleMouseUp(object sender, MouseEventArgs e)
  {
    BackColor = SystemColors.Control;
  }

  public static void Main()
  {
    Application.Run(new MouseSample());
  }
}
```

❶ **Defines event handlers**

❷ **Processes MouseDown event**

❸ **Processes MouseUp event**

Let's highlight some aspects of this code:

❶ In the constructor, event handlers for the `MouseDown` and `MouseUp` events are established. The syntax here uses the abbreviated syntax supported as of .NET 2.0. The compiler determines the event type automatically and creates a new `MouseEventHandler` class internally to define the handler. These handlers could be created explicitly as follows:

```
MouseDown += new MouseEventHandler(HandleMouseDown);
MouseUp += new MouseEventHandler(HandleMouseUp);
```

❷ When a mouse button is pressed, the `MouseDown` handler assigns the background color using the `BackColor` property for the `Form` class. The color assigned depends on which mouse button is clicked. The `Color` structure defines numerous static properties for various colors.

❸ When a mouse button is released, the MouseUp handler assigns the background color to the default background color for controls, regardless of the button. The SystemColors class defines static properties that reference the colors assigned in the operating system. These are available from the Display Properties dialog box available on the Windows desktop. Click the Advanced button on the Appearance tab page to display the Advanced Appearance dialog box. The Control property used in this code references the 3D Objects color.

This simple application shows how an application can distinguish between different mouse buttons. You may also recall our use of the MouseMove event in chapter 7 while creating the PixelDialog form. For another example, let's turn once again to our MyPhotos application.

10.2.2 Implementing FlybyTextProvider using mouse events

In chapter 9 we showed an outline of an extender provider class called FlybyTextProvider. This class requires some mouse events, so we delayed the completed implementation until this section. The purpose of this class is to display temporary, or flyby, text for menu item objects.

The goal here is to display the flyby text on a status bar panel when the mouse is over a configured menu. The MouseHover event occurs in this situation, and the MouseLeave event occurs when the mouse pointer exits the control and the text should disappear. It might also be nice to stop displaying the text when the user clicks on a menu to display the submenu, so we handle the MouseDown event as well.

The steps to implement the FlybyTextProvider class are as follows.

START IMPLEMENTATION OF THE FLYBYTEXTPROVIDER CLASS		
	Action	**Result**

1	In the MyPhotoControls project, add a new class called FlybyTextProvider.	`using System;`
		`using System.Collections;`
		`using System.ComponentModel;`
		`using System.Windows.Forms;`
		
		`namespace Manning.MyPhotoControls`
		`{`

2	Define the class as an extender provider component with an extender property called FlybyText.	`[ProvideProperty("FlybyText",`
		`    typeof(ToolStripMenuItem))]`
		`public class FlybyTextProvider`
		`    : Component, IExtenderProvider`
		`{`
		
		Note: A ProvideProperty attribute can also be defined using the string form of the type as the second parameter, as in "ToolStripMenuItem" for this example. However, this form may not work properly in Visual Studio, so use the Type form with the typeof keyword as shown here if possible.

<table>
<tr><th colspan="3">START IMPLEMENTATION OF THE FLYBYTEXTPROVIDER CLASS (CONTINUED)</th></tr>
<tr><th></th><th>Action</th><th>Result</th></tr>
<tr><td>3</td><td>Define a constructor that adds the provider to a given container.</td><td><pre>public FlybyTextProvider(IContainer container)
{
 container.Add(this);
}</pre></td></tr>
<tr><td>4</td><td>Define some private fields:
a. A hash table to hold assigned flyby text
b. A status label to hold the location for flyby text
c. A string to hold the currently displayed text</td><td><pre>private Hashtable _flybyTable = new Hashtable();
private ToolStripStatusLabel _statusLabel = null;
private string _currentText = null;</pre></td></tr>
<tr><td>5</td><td>Define properties for these fields as well.</td><td><pre>private Hashtable FlybyTable
 { get { return _flybyTable; } }

private string CurrentStatusText
{ get { return _currentText; }
   set { _currentText = value; } }

public ToolStripStatusLabel StatusLabel
{ get { return _statusLabel; }
   set { _statusLabel = value; } }</pre></td></tr>
<tr><td>6</td><td>Implement the single method in the <code>IExtender-Provider</code> interface to return <code>true</code> if a given item is a <code>ToolStripMenuItem</code> object.</td><td><pre>public bool CanExtend(object extendee)
{
 return (extendee is ToolStripMenuItem);
}</pre></td></tr>
<tr><td>7</td><td>Implement the <code>SetFlyby-Text</code> method to assign or clear text for an item.
How-to
a. If the text is <code>null</code> or blank, clear any settings for the item.
b. Otherwise, assign the given text for the item.
c. Also assign event handlers for the hover, leave, and down mouse events.</td><td><pre>public void SetFlybyText(
  ToolStripMenuItem item, string text)
{
 if (text == null || text.Length == 0)
 {
  // Clear the item's text, if necessary
  if (FlybyTable.Contains(item))
  {
   FlybyTable.Remove(item);
   item.MouseHover -= OnMouseHover;
   item.MouseLeave -= OnMouseLeave;
   item.MouseDown -= OnMouseDown;
  }
 }
 else
 {
  // Write or overwrite the item's text
  FlybyTable[item] = text;
  item.MouseHover += OnMouseHover;
  item.MouseLeave += OnMouseLeave;
  item.MouseDown += OnMouseDown;
 }
}</pre></td></tr>
</table>

START IMPLEMENTATION OF THE FLYBYTEXTPROVIDER CLASS *(CONTINUED)*		
	Action	**Result**

8	Implement the `GetFlybyText` method to return any text assigned for the given item.	`public string GetFlybyText(`
		`    ToolStripMenuItem item)`
		`{`
		` return FlybyTable[item] as string;`
		`}`

These steps define the internal settings required for the class, and implement the extended FlybyText "property" in the `SetFlybyText` and `GetFlybyText` methods. As mentioned briefly in chapter 5, the `Hashtable` class here represents a collection of key-value pairs. In our case, the key is the menu item, with the value the assigned text. The `Hashtable` class uses the `Object.GetHashCode` method to retrieve the hash code for each key, which is used internally to organize the collection for more efficient access.[1]

Note in this code how the mouse event handlers are registered with the += operator when the flyby text is assigned, and deregistered with the -= operator when the flyby text is cleared. All we have to do now is define these event handlers as part of our class.

FINISH IMPLEMENTATION OF THE FLYBYTEXTPROVIDER CLASS		
	Action	**Result**

9	Define a `ShowFlyby` method to display the assigned flyby text for a given item on the assigned status label.	`private void ShowFlyby(object item)`
		`{`
		` string flybyText = FlybyTable[item] as string;`
		` if (flybyText != null && StatusLabel != null)`
		` {`
		`  CurrentStatusText = StatusLabel.Text;`
		`  StatusLabel.Text = flybyText;`
		` }`
		`}`

10	Define a `RevertFlyby` method to restore the original status bar text to the assigned label.	`private void RevertFlyby(object item)`
		`{`
		` if (StatusLabel != null)`
		` {`
		`  StatusLabel.Text = CurrentStatusText;`
		`  CurrentStatusText = null;`
		` }`
		`}`

11	Implement the `OnMouseHover` event handler to display the flyby text assigned to the given `sender` object.	`private void OnMouseHover(`
		`    object sender, EventArgs e)`
		`{`
		` // Display flyby text on hover if assigned`
		` ShowFlyby(sender);`
		`}`

[1] It is not my intent here to explain and define hash tables. I just wanted to point out some of the terminology and methods used to implement hash tables in .NET. For a general discussion of hash tables, see the .NET documentation.

FINISH IMPLEMENTATION OF THE FLYBYTEXTPROVIDER CLASS *(CONTINUED)*		
	Action	**Result**

12	Implement the `OnMouseLeave` event handler to revert to the original text displayed on the label.	<pre>private void OnMouseLeave(
		    object sender, EventArgs e)
		{
		 // Revert to status text when mouse leaves
		 RevertFlyby(sender);
		}</pre>

13	Implement the `OnMouseDown` event handler to revert to the original text displayed on the label.	<pre>private void OnMouseDown(
		    object sender, MouseEventArgs e)
		{
		 // Revert to status text when mouse pressed
		 RevertFlyby(sender);
		}
		}
		}</pre>

This completes the `FlybyTextProvider` implementation. Compile the code to see that it builds. When you do, you may notice an interesting change in the Toolbox window when a designer window is displayed. As shown in figure 10.1, the Toolbox now displays the new `FlybyTextProvider` class. This makes it easy to drag our new component onto a form, which is our final topic in this section.

Figure 10.1 The Toolbox window automatically displays controls and components that are defined in the current solution.

10.2.3 Using the FlybyTextProvider class

This is not related to mouse events, but while we are here let's make use of our new extender provider class. The class compiles and appears in our Toolbox, so all we must do is make use of this new component in our MyPhotos application.

ADD FLYBY TEXT TO THE MYPHOTOS MENU ITEMS		
	Action	**Result**
1	In the MainForm.cs [Design] window for the MyPhotos project, drag a `FlybyTextProvider` component.	The new component appears in the component tray of the form, with a default name supplied by Visual Studio. oto statusStrip1 flybyTextProvider1

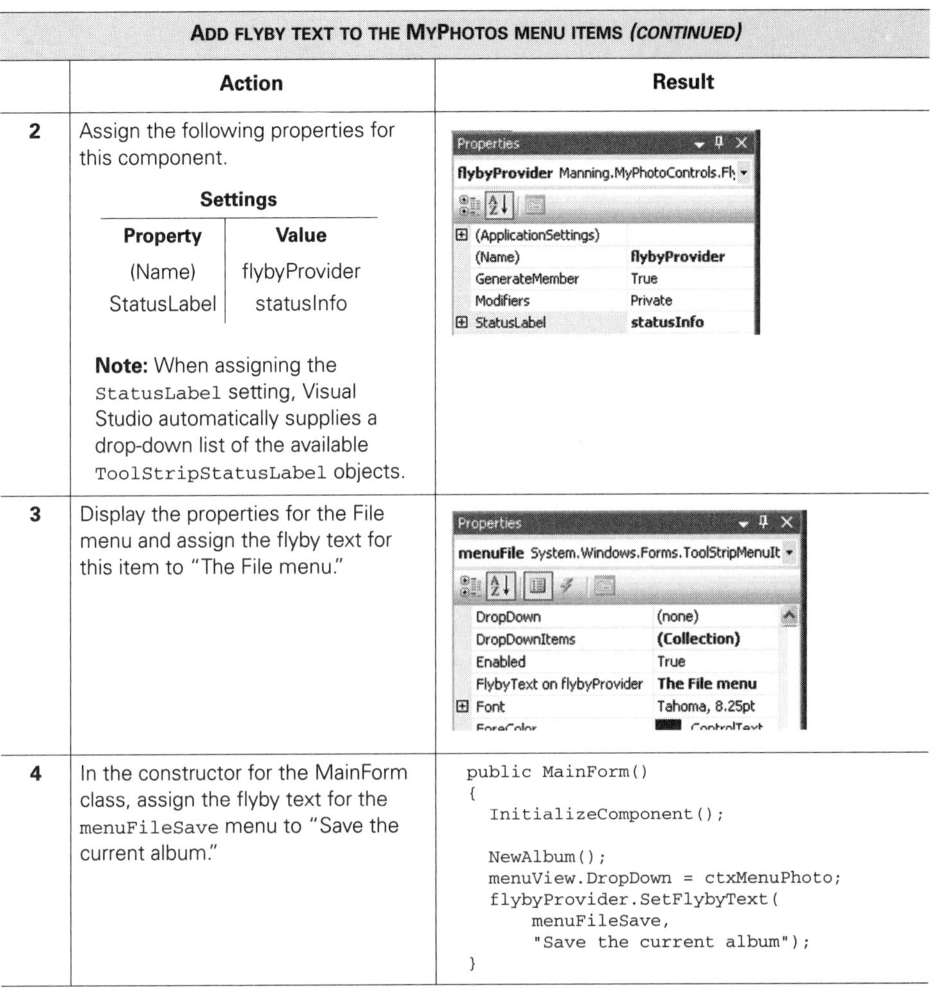

ADD FLYBY TEXT TO THE MYPHOTOS MENU ITEMS *(CONTINUED)*

	Action	Result
2	Assign the following properties for this component. **Settings** **Property** / **Value** (Name) / flybyProvider StatusLabel / statusInfo **Note:** When assigning the `StatusLabel` setting, Visual Studio automatically supplies a drop-down list of the available `ToolStripStatusLabel` objects.	Properties flybyProvider Manning.MyPhotoControls.Fl (ApplicationSettings) (Name) / **flybyProvider** GenerateMember / True Modifiers / Private StatusLabel / **statusInfo**
3	Display the properties for the File menu and assign the flyby text for this item to "The File menu."	Properties menuFile System.Windows.Forms.ToolStripMenuIt DropDown / (none) DropDownItems / **(Collection)** Enabled / True FlybyText on flybyProvider / **The File menu** Font / Tahoma, 8.25pt

4	In the constructor for the MainForm class, assign the flyby text for the `menuFileSave` menu to "Save the current album."	`public MainForm()`
		`{`
		`  InitializeComponent();`
		
		`  NewAlbum();`
		`  menuView.DropDown = ctxMenuPhoto;`
		`  flybyProvider.SetFlybyText(`
		`      menuFileSave,`
		`      "Save the current album");`
		`}`

These steps assign flyby text to two of our many menus, first through the Visual Studio designer window, and then explicitly in the constructor. In Visual Studio, the "FlybyText on flybyProvider" entry only appears when a `ToolStripMenuItem` is selected. This is because our `CanExtend` implementation only returns `true` for this type of object. If you select the `MenuStrip`, `PictureBox`, or any other control, you do not see this property. Visual Studio does all the work of displaying the appropriate properties and settings for our new component.

Assign flyby text for additional menu items as well if you wish. When you are finished, compile and run the application to see our new feature. Position the mouse pointer over the Save menu, and you should see something similar to figure 10.2. We could, of course, add other features to the `FlybyTextProvider` class. For example, a `Font` property could be added so the font used for flyby text differs from the normal font used in the status panel. You can probably think of additional features as well.

This brings us to the end of our keyboard and mouse events discussion. Our next topic is data encryption.

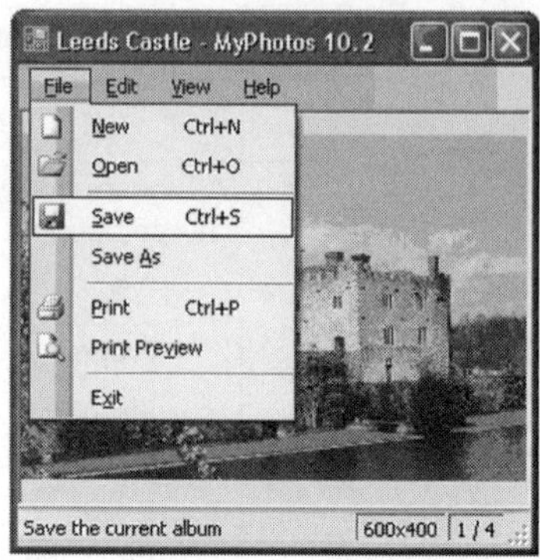

Figure 10.2 The flyby text for the Save menu item displays when the mouse hovers over this item.

10.3 ENCRYPTION

While this is definitely not a book on security or encryption, we divert our attention to a small example of encrypting data in a file. This example introduces some of the key terms and classes required to perform encryption, and illustrates some interesting points that hopefully makes this worth our time.

There is, or course, more than one way to encrypt files programmatically. The `File` class in the `System.IO` namespace provides `Encrypt` and `Decrypt` methods that secure a file based on the current user account. This works well if the data only applies to a specific user. Be careful with this, however, since if the user account goes away there is no way to decrypt the data.

For our example, we perform encryption manually using a given password. Encryption depends on a secret, normally some sort of key. Symmetric encryption uses a single key, or password, for both encryption and decryption. Learn the password and you can compromise the entire system. Asymmetric encryption, or public-key encryption as it is often called, relies on two independent but related keys. These keys, a public key and a private key, provide a more secure system at the expense of added complexity and slower performance.

10.3.1 The Cryptography namespace

The .NET Framework provides the `System.Security.Cryptography` namespace to define various cryptographic features, including both symmetric and asymmetric algorithms. A brief summary of this namespace appears in .NET Table 10.6.

For our purposes, symmetric encryption with a password will work just fine. The default symmetric algorithm in .NET is the Rijndael algorithm, which is a block cipher algorithm designed by Joan Daemen and Vincent Rijmen. This algorithm was selected as the Advanced Encryption Standard (AES) by the United States in 2001, so it should serve our purposes just fine.

.NET Table 10.6 System.Security.Cryptography namespace

The `System.Security.Cryptography` namespace provides cryptographic services such as the encoding and decoding of data, random number generation, message authentication, and other operations.

Classes	AsymmetricAlgorithm	The abstract base class for all asymmetric algorithm implementations
	CryptographicException	The exception class that is thrown when an error occurs during cryptographic operations
	CryptoStream	A stream class that links data streams to cryptographic transformations
	PasswordDeriveBytes	A class for deriving byte sequences from password strings
	ProtectedMemory	A class that supports protecting sensitive data in memory
	Rijndael	The base class for all implementations of the Rijndael symmetric encryption algorithm
	SignatureDescription	A class that defines properties of digital signatures
	SymmetricAlgorithm	The abstract base class for all symmetric algorithm implementations
Interfaces	ICryptoTransform	Defines basic operations for cryptographic transformations
Enumerations	CipherMode	Specifies the block cipher mode to use for encryption
	CryptoStreamMode	Specifies the access mode for a cryptographic stream, either `Read` or `Write`
	PaddingMode	Specifies how a message data block is padded when the block is shorter than the number of bytes required for an operation

All symmetric algorithms depend on a key and an initialization vector. Both are an array of bytes of predetermined length. The key is used to encrypt the data. The initialization vector (IV) is required to support cipher block chaining (CBC). CBC is the default cipher mode for the Rijndael algorithm, and encrypts each block of data using both the key and information from the prior block. This chaining prevents recurring patterns when similar blocks of text are encrypted. Such similarities might otherwise be used to break the code. The first block does not have a prior block, so the IV is used to initialize the first block in the chain.

In our case, we have a textual password, so we need a way to convert a password into a fixed-length array of bytes. The `PasswordDeriveBytes` class supports this requirement, as we see momentarily. We begin with a short discussion of our requirements.

10.3.2 Encrypting data

We already have two album formats, the 63 and 91 versions created in sections 6.3 and 9.1. It would be nice to support encryption while preserving our existing versions. We also have some code written in our `AlbumStorage` class that uses the `StreamWriter` and `StreamReader` classes. So the question is: can we preserve our existing formats and not have to rewrite all the code involved?

If you recall, our album format is based on storing each piece of information on a separate line in the file. If we encrypt each line separately, then we continue to operate on a line at a time. So what we need are some stream writer and reader classes that support encryption at the line level. With this in mind, we can create a `CryptoReader` and a `CryptoWriter` class for this purpose.

Before we do, we need a base class to support the actual encryption and decryption of data. This class should accept a password and provide a method for encrypting a string of data or decrypting a previously encrypted string. Of course, the decryption only works if we are given the same password used during encryption.

The `CryptoTextBase` class serves as our base class, and is shown in listing 10.2. This class employs the `SymmetricAlgorithm`, `PasswordDerivedBytes`, and `CryptoStream` classes mentioned in .NET Table 10.6, as well as a few other classes and interfaces to manipulate the data.

Listing 10.2 The CryptoTextBase class

```
using System;
using System.IO;
using System.Security.Cryptography;
using System.Text;

namespace Manning.MyPhotoAlbum
{
  class CryptoTextBase
  {
    // A larger salt would provide more secure encryption here
    public readonly byte[] SaltBytes
        = { 0x39, 0x38, 0x14, 0x05, 0x68 };

    private byte[] _pwd;
    private MemoryStream _ms;
    private CryptoStream _cs;

    protected Byte[] Password { get { return _pwd; } }
    protected MemoryStream MStream
        { get { return _ms; } set { _ms = value; } }
    protected CryptoStream CStream
        { get { return _cs; } set { _cs = value; } }

    public CryptoTextBase(string password)
    {
      if (password == null || password.Length == 0)
        throw new ArgumentNullException("password");
```

```
        _pwd = Encoding.UTF8.GetBytes(password);      <-- ❶ Encodes password as bytes
      }

      /// <summary>
      /// Encrypt or decrypt a given string
      /// </summary>
      public string ProcessText(string text, bool encrypt)
      {
        // Encode text as byte array
        byte[] bytes = encrypt
          ? Encoding.UTF8.GetBytes(text)                   ❷ Converts text to bytes
              : Convert.FromBase64String(text);

        MStream = new MemoryStream();

        // Create default symmetric algorithm for cryption
        SymmetricAlgorithm alg = SymmetricAlgorithm.Create();
        PasswordDeriveBytes pdb                                ❸ Creates symmetric algorithm
            = new PasswordDeriveBytes(Password, SaltBytes);
        alg.Key = pdb.GetBytes(alg.KeySize / 8);
        alg.IV = pdb.GetBytes(alg.BlockSize / 8);
        ICryptoTransform transform
          = encrypt ? alg.CreateEncryptor()
                    : alg.CreateDecryptor();

        // Create cryptographic stream
        CStream = new CryptoStream(MStream,
                                   transform,
                                   CryptoStreamMode.Write);

        // Encrypt data and flush result to buffer
        CStream.Write(bytes, 0, bytes.Length);
        CStream.FlushFinalBlock();                        ❹ Encrypts or decrypts to memory stream

        // Retrieve the resulting bytes
        byte[] result = MStream.ToArray();

        // Convert result to a string
        return encrypt
          ? Convert.ToBase64String(result)
              : Encoding.UTF8.GetString(result);
      }
    }
  }
```

Once you understand the basic approach outlined here, you should be able to construct your own cryptographic classes for various purposes. The following paragraphs discuss details of the annotated portions of our `CyptoTextBase` implementation.

❶ The `System.Text` namespace provides an `Encoder` class to convert characters into bytes. The `Encoding` class in this namespace provides access to various encoders, including the `ASCII` encoder and various Unicode encoders. The `UTF8` encoder used here converts characters into UTF-8 Unicode format.

❷ We define a single method to perform both encryption and decryption of a given `string`. During encryption, the string is converted into a byte array in UTF-8 format. For decryption, the string should be a prior encryption encoded with base-64 digits, so we convert the string back into a byte array using the `FromBase64String` method in the `Convert` class. The `Convert` class defines a rather large set of static methods that convert data from one type into another.

❸ We create a default symmetric algorithm with an appropriate key and initialization vector. As we mentioned, .NET uses the Rijndael algorithm by default. We could create a specific algorithm here by invoking the `Create` method on the desired algorithm. For example, the `Rijndael.Create` method creates the default Rijndael algorithm explicitly.

Note also the use of the `PasswordDeriveBytes` class in this code. The constructor for this class accepts the password and an array of bytes called the salt value to convert the password string into a byte array. As long as we pass the same salt value every time, we produce the same byte arrays to initialize the symmetric algorithm. The `GetBytes` method of the `PasswordDeriveBytes` class obtains a byte array of a given length. The `KeySize` and `BlockSize` properties of the `SymmetricAlgorithm` class return the number of bits expected for the key and initialization vector, so we divide by 8 to obtain the required number of bytes.

The final line of this code creates the cryptographic transformation to perform the actual encryption or decryption based on the assigned settings.

❹ Our transformation code takes advantage of the `Stream` class's ability to chain two or more streams together. Here we chain a `MemoryStream`, which manages a stream in a block of memory, to a `CryptoStream` object, which applies a cryptographic transformation to a stream. The result is that we write our converted string through the cryptographic transformation and into the memory buffer. This produces an encrypted or decrypted array of bytes, which is then converted to a string and returned to the caller.

This code is the foundation of our encrypted album, as it does all the hard work of encrypting and decrypting data. To use this code in our `AlbumStorage` class, we use the `CryptTextBase` class to build cryptographic versions of the `StreamReader` and `StreamWriter` classes. We build these classes in the next two sections.

10.3.3 Writing encrypted data

This section creates a `CryptoWriter` class to write encrypted data into a file. This requires the following steps.

	Define cryptographic classes for writing text	
	Action	**Result**
1	In the MyPhotoAlbum project, add the `CryptoTextBase` class as shown in listing 10.2.	This code may be useful in other contexts as well, but for our purposes placing this class in the MyPhotoAlbum project will suffice. **Note:** Of course, ideally we would build this class in a stand-alone exercise. I'm cheating here to save space in the chapter by including listing 10.2 by reference.

2	Also in this project, add a new `CryptoWriter` class that extends the `StreamWriter` class.	`using System;`
		`using System.IO;`
		`using System.Text;`
		
		`namespace Manning.MyPhotoAlbum`
		`{`
		` class CryptoWriter : StreamWriter`
		` {`

3	Create a private `CryptoTextBase` field.	`  private CryptoTextBase _base;`
		`  private CryptoTextBase CryptoBase`
		`      { get { return _base; } }`

4	In the constructor, accept a file path and password.	`  public CryptoWriter(`
		`    string path, string password) : base(path)`
		`  {`
		`    if (path == null || path.Length == 0)`
		`      throw new ArgumentNullException("path");`
		`    if (password == null || password.Length == 0)`
		`      throw new ArgumentNullException("password");`
		
		`    _base = new CryptoTextBase(password);`
		`  }`

5	Use the path to initialize the `StreamWriter`, and the password to initialize the `CryptoTextBase` field.	

6	Override the `WriteLine` method to encrypt and write a line to the stream.	`  public override void WriteLine(string value)`
		`  {`
		`    string encrypted`
		`      = CryptoBase.ProcessText(value, true);`
		`    base.WriteLine(encrypted);`
		`  }`

7	Also provide a `Write-UnencryptedLine` method to write a line without any encryption.	`  public void WriteUnencryptedLine(string value)`
		`  {`
		`    base.WriteLine(value);`
		`  }`
		` }`
		`}`

As you can see, our code only overrides the `WriteLine(string)` method, since that is all we expect to use in our `AlbumStorage` class. The other write methods in the `StreamWriter` class could be overridden in a similar manner.

10.3.4 Reading encrypted data

This section creates a `CryptoReader` class to read encrypted data from a file. This class is implemented in a similar manner to the `CryptoWriter` class.

	Action	Result
	DEFINE CRYPTOGRAPHIC CLASSES FOR READING TEXT	

1	Define a new `CryptoReader` class that extends the `StreamReader` class.	`using System;`
		`using System.IO;`
		`using System.Text;`
		
		`namespace Manning.MyPhotoAlbum`
		`{`
		` class CryptoReader : StreamReader`
		` {`

2	Create a private `CryptoTextBase` field.	`private CryptoTextBase _base;`
		`private CryptoTextBase CryptoBase`
		`    { get { return _base; } }`

3	In the constructor, accept a file path and password.	`public CryptoReader(`
		`  string path, string password) : base(path)`
		`{`
		`  if (path == null || path.Length == 0)`
		`    throw new ArgumentNullException("path");`
		`  if (password == null || password.Length == 0)`
		`    throw new ArgumentNullException("password");`
		
		`  _base = new CryptoTextBase(password);`
		`}`

4	Use the path to initialize the `StreamReader`, and the password to initialize the `CryptoTextBase` field.	

5	Override the `ReadLine` method to read and decrypt a line from the stream.	`public override string ReadLine()`
		`{`
		`  string encrypted = base.ReadLine();`
		`  if (encrypted == null || encrypted.Length == 0)`
		`    return encrypted;`
		`  else`
		`    return CryptoBase.ProcessText(encrypted, false);`
		`}`

6	Also provide a `ReadUnencryptedLine` method to read a line without any decryption.	`public string ReadUnencryptedLine()`
		`{`
		`  return base.ReadLine();`
		`}`
		` }`
		`}`

In the `ReadLine` method, note how we handle the case where we are at the end of the file or retrieve a blank line. Otherwise, this class is quite similar to the `CryptoWriter` class.

10.3.5 Storing encrypted albums

So far we've created classes to write and read encrypted text; our final task is to utilize these objects in our `AlbumStorage` class. With the ability to encrypt and decrypt data a line at a time, we can hook these classes into our code without too much impact on our existing implementation.

When performing encryption, it is important to provide a mechanism to verify that the user has provided the correct password. One way to do this is to encrypt a well-known string during encryption that you can then verify during decryption. Ideally this is not a fixed string, since an attacker might gain insight into the encryption algorithm by analyzing different encryptions of the same string. In our case, we use both a fixed string and the password itself for this purpose, to provide some obscurity of the password and still have a varying string.

The following steps make these changes.

<table>
<tr><th colspan="3">SUPPORT AN ENCRYPTED ALBUM FORMAT</th></tr>
<tr><th></th><th>Action</th><th>Result</th></tr>
<tr><td>1</td><td>In the <code>AlbumStorage</code> class, modify the <code>WriteAlbum</code> method to accept a password parameter.</td><td><pre><code>static public void WriteAlbum(
  PhotoAlbum album, string path, string password)
{
  StreamWriter sw = null;</code></pre></td></tr>
<tr><td>2</td><td>If no password is provided, create a <code>StreamWriter</code> object.</td><td><pre><code> try
  {
    if (password == null || password.Length == 0)
    {
      sw = new StreamWriter(path);
      sw.WriteLine(CurrentVersion.ToString());
    }</code></pre></td></tr>
<tr><td>3</td><td>If a password is given, create a <code>CryptoWriter</code>, add the character 'e' to the end of the version string, and write a check string into the encrypted file.

Also assign the stream writer to the new cryptographic writer.</td><td><pre><code>   else
    {
      // Create CryptoWriter to use as StreamWriter
      CryptoWriter cw
        = new CryptoWriter(path, password);
      cw.WriteUnencryptedLine(
              CurrentVersion.ToString() + 'e');
      cw.WriteLine(password);
      sw = cw;
    }

    // Save album properties
    sw.WriteLine(album.Title);
    sw.WriteLine(album.PhotoDescriptor.ToString());
    . . .
  }
  catch (UnauthorizedAccessException uax)
  . . .
}</code></pre></td></tr>
<tr><td>4</td><td>Also implement a <code>WriteAlbum</code> method with the old signature for backward compatibility.</td><td><pre><code>static public void WriteAlbum(
    PhotoAlbum album, string path)
{
  WriteAlbum(album, path, null);
}</code></pre></td></tr>
<tr><td>5</td><td>Similarly, modify the <code>ReadAlbum</code> method to take a password parameter.</td><td><pre><code>static public PhotoAlbum ReadAlbum(
    string path, string password)
{
  StreamReader sr = null;</code></pre></td></tr>
</table>

SUPPORT AN ENCRYPTED ALBUM FORMAT *(CONTINUED)*		
	Action	**Result**

6	If no password is given, create a `StreamReader` and ensure the file does not contain encrypted data.	<pre>try
		{
		  string version;
		  if (password == null || password.Length == 0)
		  {
		    sr = new StreamReader(path);
		    version = sr.ReadLine();
		    if (version.EndsWith("e"))
		      throw new AlbumStorageException(
		        "A password is required to open the album");
		  }</pre>

7	Otherwise, create a `CryptoReader` object. If the file does not in fact contain encrypted data, revert to a `StreamReader` instance.	<pre> else
		  {
		    // Create CryptoReader to use as StreamReader
		    CryptoReader cr
		      = new CryptoReader(path, password);
		    version = cr.ReadUnencryptedLine();
		    if (!version.EndsWish("e"))
		    {
		      // Decryption not required
		      cr.Close();
		      sr = new StreamReader(path);
		      version = sr.ReadLine();
		    }</pre>

8	If the file is encrypted, read the path line to verify that the given password properly decrypts the file, and assign the stream reader to the new cryptographic reader.	<pre> else
		    {
		      string checkLine = cr.ReadLine();
		      if (checkLine != password)
		        throw new AlbumStorageException(
		          "The given password is not valid");
		      sr = cr;
		    }
		  }</pre>

9	Also account for the new 91e version string that is now possible.	<pre> PhotoAlbum album = new PhotoAlbum();
		  switch (version)
		  {
		    . . .
		    case "91":
		    case "91e":
		      ReadAlbumV91(sr, album);
		      break;
		    default:
		      . . .</pre>

10	Catch cryptographic exceptions in case an incorrect password causes a decryption exception.	<pre>catch (System.Security.Cryptography.
		           CryptographicException cex)
		{
		  throw new AlbumStorageException(
		    "Unable to decrypt album "+ path, cex);
		}
		. . .
		}</pre>**Note:** Place this new `catch` block before the existing block for the `FileNotFoundException` class.

	Action	Result
SUPPORT AN ENCRYPTED ALBUM FORMAT *(CONTINUED)*		

11	Also implement `ReadAlbum` with the old signature for backward compatibility.	<pre>static public PhotoAlbum ReadAlbum(string path)
		{
		  return ReadAlbum(path, null);
		}</pre>

12	Finally, create an `IsEncrypted` method to identify whether a given album file is encrypted.	<pre>static public bool IsEncrypted(string path)
		{
		  StreamReader sr = null;
		
		  try
		  {
		    using (sr = new StreamReader(path))
		    {
		      string version = sr.ReadLine();
		      return version.EndsWith ("e");
		    }
		  }
		  catch (FileNotFoundException fnx)
		  {
		    throw new AlbumStorageException(
		       "Unable to find album " + path, fnx);
		  }
		}</pre>

Our code is now ready for encryption. Note how this code verifies the given password. When an encrypted file is written, we write a check string into the file that includes the password in an encrypted form. When reading the file, we read this line and verify that it matches the provided password. If it does not, then we know the password was invalid.

If you want to test this code for yourself, you can modify the `MainForm` in the MyPhotos application to always pass in a fixed password when reading or writing albums. This allows you to see this code in action and view the encryption version of the album file.

For the rest of us, we apply our new code to the MyPhotos application using the `LinkLabel` class.

10.4 LINK LABELS

The `LinkLabel` class is to Windows Forms what a hyperlink is to a web page. This class extends the `Label` class to support hyperlink-style behavior. The application can do pretty much anything it wants when the user clicks the label, much like when a user clicks a button. In fact, you may recall the `IButtonControl` interface mentioned in the previous chapter. If you think about it, a hyperlink on a web page works much like a button, which is what the `LinkLabel` control is fashioned after. The `LinkLabel` class supports the `IButtonControl` interface and can therefore act as a button on a form.

10.4.1 The LinkLabel class

So how exactly does the LinkLabel class fit into our grand schemes? The goal here is to enable our MyPhotos application to save and open encrypted album files. To save an encrypted album, the AlbumEditDialog created in chapter 9 allows the user to assign a password for the album. When assigned, we can use this password to write the album in an encrypted form.

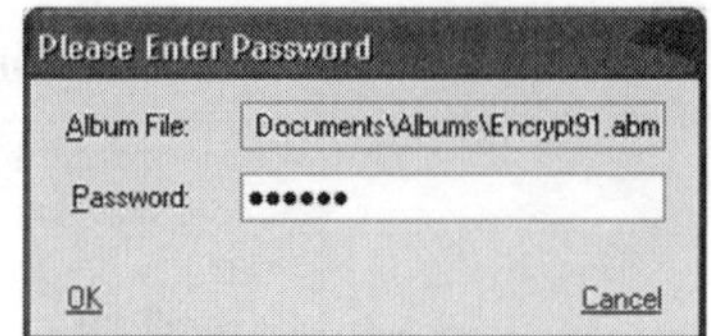

Figure 10.3 This dialog box permits a user to enter the password for an album.

To open an encrypted album, we can use the AlbumStorage.IsEncrypted method to identify an encrypted album and prompt the user for a password. The password dialog box we use is shown in figure 10.3. As you can see, two LinkLabel controls replace the standard OK and Cancel buttons. A summary of the LinkLabel control appears in .NET Table 10.7.

.NET Table 10.7 LinkLabel class

The LinkLabel class is a label that can appear as a hyperlink. This class is part of the System.Windows.Forms namespace, inherits from the Label class, and implements the IButtonControl interface. See .NET Table 7.5 for members of the base class.

Public Properties	ActiveLinkColor	Gets or sets the color for an active link.
	DisabledLinkColor	Gets or set the color for a disabled link.
	LinkArea	Gets or sets the portion of text to treat as a link.
	LinkBehavior	Gets or sets how the link appears within the control. Uses the LinkBehavior enumeration.
	LinkColor	Gets or sets the color for a normal link.
	LinkVisited	Gets or sets whether the link has been visited.
	VisitedLinkColor	Gets or sets the color for a link previously visited.
Public Events	LinkClicked	Occurs when the link is clicked.

In .NET Table 10.7, note that the members of the IButtonControl interface, for instance the DialogResult property, do not appear in the table. These members are implemented, but hidden because they are not public within the class. To access these members, a link label must first be cast to the interface, as illustrated here:

```
LinkLabel link1;
. . .
// Use link label as button
IButtonControl btn = (IButtonControl) link1;
btn.PerformClick();
. . .
```

We revisit link labels in chapter 23 to discuss the hyperlink aspects of the control. For now, let's talk about how to open and save our album in an encrypted form.

10.4.2 Saving encrypted albums

Our `MainForm` window is well prepared to deal with this change. One slight problem is that our application works through the `AlbumManager` class, and all we have done so far is make it work through the `AlbumStorage` class. So we need to update our manager class to understand passwords, and then utilize this within our application.

The following steps update `AlbumManager` to support passwords.

SUPPORT AN ENCRYPTED ALBUM FORMAT

	Action	Result

1	In the MyPhotoAlbum project, add a new constructor for the `AlbumManager` class that accepts a name and password for a potentially encrypted album.	`public class AlbumManager`
		`{`
		`  . . .`
		`  public AlbumManager(string name, string pwd) : this()`
		`  {`
		`    _name = name;`
		`    _album = AlbumStorage.ReadAlbum(name, pwd);`
		`    Password = pwd;`
		`  }`

2	Modify the existing `Save` methods to include the password setting when writing the album.	`public void Save()`
		`{`
		`  if (FullName == null)`
		`    throw new InvalidOperationException(. . .);`
		
		`  AlbumStorage.WriteAlbum(Album, FullName, `**`Password`**`);`
		`}`
		
		`public void Save(string name, bool overwrite)`
		`{`
		`  if (name == null)`
		`    throw new ArgumentNullException("name");`
		`  if (name != FullName && AlbumExists(name)`
		`                                  && !overwrite)`
		`    throw new ArgumentException(. . .);`
		
		`  AlbumStorage.WriteAlbum(Album, name, `**`Password`**`);`
		`  FullName = name;`
		`}`

This is, in fact, the only change required to save an album in an encrypted form. In chapter 9 we assigned the `AlbumManager.Password` property as part of our `AlbumEditDialog` class, so we can now save encrypted albums. Compile and run the program, open an existing album, assign a password for this album in the Album Properties dialog box, and then save the album under a new name. If you look at the resulting .abm file, you should see something similar to listing 10.3. The first line of the file is the readable version number, in this case 91e, with the remainder of the file unintelligible.

Listing 10.3 Excerpt of an encrypted album file


```
91e
6NTNxsEOjdZ1Prc3bX946w==
b5oqjg0CoSbtBHNe99yYeQ==
XTK3PEEMvrZvHAPxSWevxg==
nyAKVI+buPgwz/IcprY2HN+KF7ynEpMaFwGNsYQDfBcw91YhB9/feaxaeoOMsHUH
c5KS54iq1fxImHG4nxLhTw==
. . .
```


Of course, an encrypted album is not all that useful unless we can also open it. The next section adds this rather important feature.

10.4.3 Opening encrypted albums

To open an encrypted album, we need the password. Figure 10.3 displayed a form for accepting the password for an album. In this section we create this form and then use it in our MyPhotos application.

CREATE AN ALBUMPASSWORDDIALOG CLASS

	Action	Result
1	In the MyPhotoControls project, create a new `AlbumPasswordDialog` form with the following settings. **Settings** Property: Value ControlBox: False FormBorderStyle: FixedDialog Size: 285, 136 StartPosition: CenterParent Text: Please Enter Password	Please Enter Password
2	Add the controls indicated in the graphic. **Settings** Album label — Text: &Album File: Album text box — (Name): txtAlbum; ReadOnly: True Password label — Text: &Password: Password text box — (Name): txtPassword; UseSystem-PasswordChar: True	Please Enter Password Album File: Password:

CREATE AN ALBUMPASSWORDDIALOG CLASS *(CONTINUED)*

<table>
<tr><th></th><th>Action</th><th>Result</th></tr>
<tr><td>3</td><td>Drag two <code>LinkLabel</code> controls from the Toolbox and position them as shown.

Settings
<table>
<tr><th>Control</th><th>Property</th><th>Value</th></tr>
<tr><td rowspan="2">OK label</td><td>(Name)</td><td>lnkOK</td></tr>
<tr><td>Text</td><td>OK</td></tr>
<tr><td rowspan="2">Cancel label</td><td>(Name)</td><td>lnkCancel</td></tr>
<tr><td>Text</td><td>Cancel</td></tr>
</table></td><td></td></tr>
</table>

This creates the form. We need to establish our button-oriented settings to the links, which are not visible in Visual Studio. As a result, we assign these properties in code.

COMPLETE THE ALBUMPASSWORDDIALOG CLASS

<table>
<tr><th></th><th>Action</th><th>Result</th></tr>
<tr><td>4</td><td>In the constructor for the new dialog box, define the button result settings for the link label controls.</td><td><pre>
public AlbumPasswordDialog()
{
  InitializeComponent();

  // Define dialog results for link labels
  IButtonControl btn = (IButtonControl)lnkOK;
  btn.DialogResult = DialogResult.OK;
  btn = (IButtonControl)lnkCancel;
  btn.DialogResult = DialogResult.Cancel;
}
</pre></td></tr>
<tr><td>5</td><td>Also define properties for the two text box entries.</td><td><pre>
public string Album
{
  get { return txtAlbum.Text; }
  set { txtAlbum.Text = value; }
}

public string Password
{
  get { return txtPassword.Text; }
  set { txtPassword.Text = value; }
}
</pre></td></tr>
</table>

COMPLETE THE ALBUMPASSWORDDIALOG CLASS *(CONTINUED)*

<table>
<tr><th></th><th>Action</th><th>Result</th></tr>
<tr><td>6</td><td>In the AlbumPasswordDialog.cs [Design] window, assign the accept and cancel buttons for the form to our two link labels.

Settings
<table><tr><th>Property</th><th>Value</th></tr><tr><td>AcceptButton</td><td>lnkOK</td></tr><tr><td>CancelButton</td><td>lnkCancel</td></tr></table></td><td>When assigning these values, Visual Studio automatically displays any controls that support the <code>IButtonControl</code> interface in the dropdown for these settings.
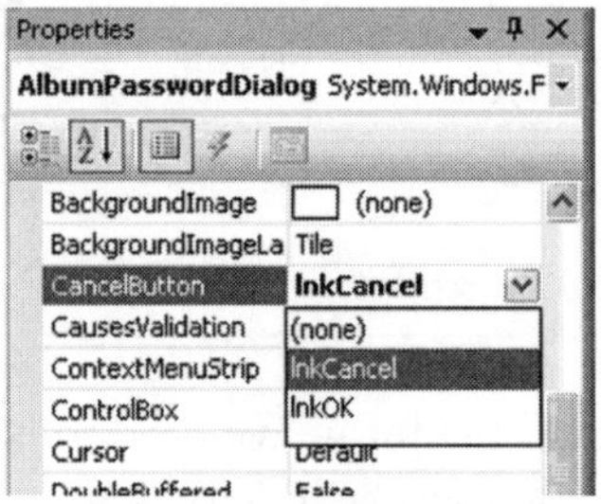
</td></tr>
<tr><td>7</td><td>Create a new <code>lnk_LinkClicked</code> method to handle a click on either link label.

How-to
Use the <code>IButtonControl</code> interface to assign the link's dialog box result to the form.</td><td><pre>
private void lnk_LinkClicked(object sender,
    LinkLabelLinkClickedEventArgs e)
{
  IButtonControl btn
      = sender as IButtonControl;
  if (btn != null)
  {
    DialogResult = btn.DialogResult;
    Close();
  }
}
</pre></td></tr>
<tr><td>8</td><td>Assign this method as the handler for the <code>LinkClicked</code> event on both link labels.</td><td>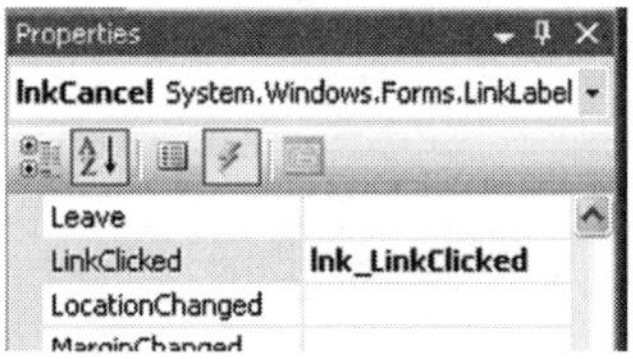
</td></tr>
</table>

This completes our form. Notice how we use the `IButtonControl` interface to define a shared event handler for both link labels. Unfortunately, link labels do not support the automatic click handling provided by `Button` objects, so we have to handle the `LinkClicked` event here.

Our final task here is to update the application to utilize this new dialog box.

OPEN AN ENCRYPTED ALBUM		
	Action	**Result**

9	In the `MainForm` class of the MyPhotos project, locate the `Click` event handler for the Open menu item.	`private void menuFileOpen_Click(`
		`    object sender, EventArgs e)`
		`{`
		` // Allow user to select a new album`
		` OpenFileDialog dlg = new OpenFileDialog();`
		` . . .`

10	When the user selects an album, define a local variable to hold any password for the album.	` if (dlg.ShowDialog() == DialogResult.OK)`
		` {`
		`  string path = dlg.FileName;`
		`  string pwd = null;`

11	If the album is encrypted, use the `AlbumPasswordDialog` form to receive the password.	`  // Get password if encrypted`
		`  if (AlbumStorage.IsEncrypted(path))`
		`  {`
		`   using (AlbumPasswordDialog pwdDlg`
		`           = new AlbumPasswordDialog())`
		`   {`
		`    pwdDlg.Album = path;`
		`    if (pwdDlg.ShowDialog() != DialogResult.OK)`
		`      return; // Open cancelled`
		
		`    pwd = pwdDlg.Password;`
		`   }`
		`  }`

12	Open the album using the provided path and password.	`  // Close existing album`
		`  if (!SaveAndCloseAlbum())`
		`    return; // Close cancelled`
		
		`  // Open the new album`
		`  try`
		`  {`
		`    Manager = new AlbumManager(path, **pwd**);`
		`  }`
		`  . . .`
		`}`

This code ensures that the user can enter a password for an album if it is required. The existing album is not closed with a call to `SaveAndCloseAlbum` until the user has committed to opening the new album by providing the filename and password, if required.

This completes the changes required to support encrypted albums. Compile, run, test, and otherwise enjoy your new code. Although an encrypted album is protected from other users viewing the album, there is nothing to protect a malicious user from destroying the album by modifying the content such that the program can no longer read and decrypt each line. Fixing this would require appropriate security for files in the file system, since this problem also exists for unencrypted files.

10.5 RECAP

This chapter discussed user input and encryption. We began with keyboard and mouse events, and utilized these events in our MyPhotos application. Keyboard event handlers receive a KeyPressEventArgs parameter for KeyPress events, and a KeyEventArgs parameter for KeyDown and KeyUp events. Mouse event handlers receive either the standard EventArgs parameter or a MouseEventArgs parameter.

We completed the implementation of the extender provider class outlined in chapter 9. The new FlybyTextProvider class displays temporary text on a status label that describes a menu item. Visual Studio does most of the work required to enable our extender provider to work within the Windows Forms Designer.

Also included in this chapter was a discussion of encryption. We presented one approach to encrypting data sent to a file. This required a number of classes from the System.Security.Cryptographic namespace, and the ability to encode and decode characters using the encoding classes of the System.Text namespace.

The final topic was the LinkLabel class. This class is basically a hyperlink, and can behave like a button on a form. We saw this directly in the password entry dialog created to assist with opening an encrypted album file.

We now return to our discussion of various Windows Forms controls. The ListBox control is discussed in chapter 11, and the ComboBox control in chapter 12.

CHAPTER 11

List boxes

The previous chapter was a bit of an aside to the Windows Forms controls discussed in chapters 8 and 9. Here we continue our control discussion with the `ListBox` control, and then move on to the related `ComboBox` control in chapter 12. The `TextBox` and `Button` controls present a single item to the user: a string of text or a button with associated text. The `ListBox` and `ComboBox` classes present a collection of items to a user.

While it is certainly possible to use a multiline text box to present a scrollable list of strings, a text box does not allow the user to select and manipulate individual items. The list controls present a scrollable list of objects that can be individually selected, highlighted, moved, and otherwise manipulated by your program. In this chapter we cover the following topics:

- Understanding the `ListControl` class hierarchy
- Presenting a collection of objects in a `ListBox` class
- Supporting single and multiple selections in a list box
- Manipulating items in a multiselection list box

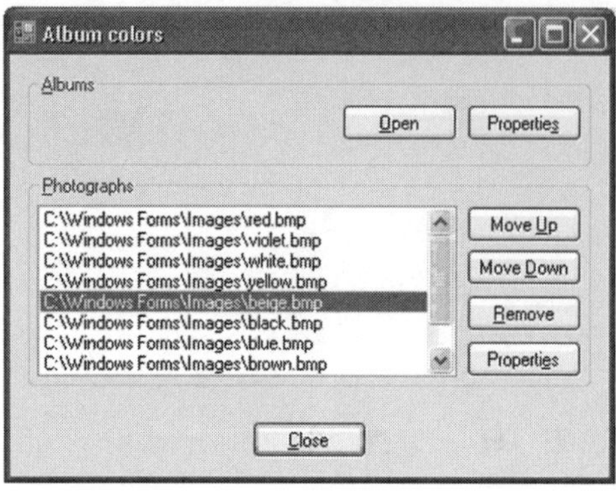

Figure 11.1
The MyAlbumEditor application does not include a menu or status bar.

We take a slightly different approach in this chapter. Rather than using the MyPhotos application we have come to know and love, we build a new application for displaying the contents of an album, using the existing MyPhotoAlbum.dll and MyPhotoControls.dll libraries. This demonstrates the reuse of our libraries to build a different view of the same data. Our new application is called MyAlbumEditor, as shown in figure 11.1.

11.1 List controls

List controls present a collection of objects as a scrollable list of items. In this section we look at the `ListControl` class and discuss controls that depend on this base class. We also create a new project called MyAlbumEditor to use throughout the rest of this chapter, and discuss ways to share code between this new project and our existing MyPhotos application.

Like text boxes and buttons, the list control classes date back to the original version of Windows. Since then more complex list classes such as the `ListView` and `TreeView` classes have appeared, but these basic classes still prove useful when a simple list of items is required. The `ListView` and `TreeView` classes are discussed in chapters 18 and 19.

One big advantage of the list control classes is that they hold a list of items directly, and do not require secondary classes to define and manipulate the list. As we see in part 3, classes such as `ListView`, `TreeView`, and `DataGridView` are not as easy to use. When a single piece of information for an object is required in a list, the classes derived from `ListControl` are normally the simplest approach.

11.1.1 The ListControl classes

All list control classes derive from the base `ListControl` class, which in turn derives from the `Control` class. This class hierarchy is shown in figure 11.2. The base `ListControl` class defines common behavior for all list controls, and is summarized in .NET Table 11.1.

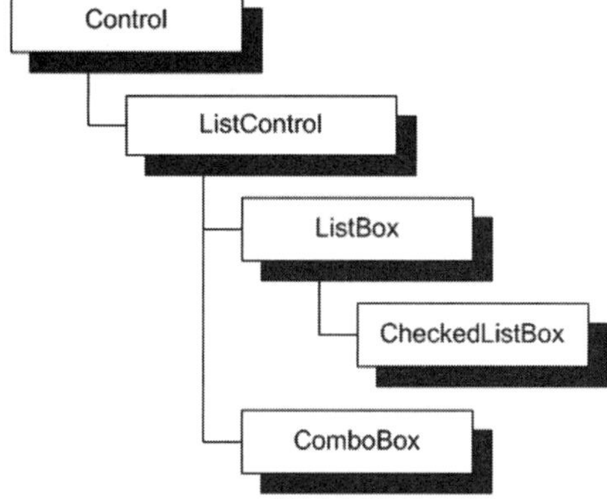

Figure 11.2
The various list control classes display and manipulate a collection of items within the control.

.NET Table 11.1 ListControl class

The `ListControl` class presents a collection of objects to the user as a scrollable list, and is the basis for the `ListBox` and `ComboBox` classes. This abstract class is part of the `System.Windows.Forms` namespace, and inherits from the `Control` class. See .NET Table 3.1 for members inherited from this base class.

Public Properties	DataSource	Gets or sets the data source for this control. When assigned, items can only be added or removed from the list through the data source.
	DisplayMember	Gets or sets the name of the property to display. If not set, the `ToString` method is used.
	FormatInfo	Gets or sets an `IFormatProvider` interface to use when formatting is enabled.
	FormatString	Gets or sets a string to use when formatting each list item.
	FormattingEnabled	Gets or sets whether formatting is enabled. The individual objects must support the `IFormattable` interface to enable formatting.
	SelectedIndex	Gets or sets the zero-based index of the `object` selected in the control.
	SelectedValue	Gets or sets the value for the `object` selected in the control.
	ValueMember	Gets or sets the name of the property to use when retrieving the value for an item in the list. If not set, the object itself is returned.
Public Methods	GetItemText	Retrieves the display text associated with a specified item.
Public Events	DataSourceChanged	Occurs when the `DataSource` property changes.
	Format	Occurs when the format for an item in the list is required.

The ListBox class presents a selectable list of items within the bounds of the control, while the ComboBox class displays a selected item in an editing control similar to a text box, with a drop-down arrow that displays an associated list box. The ComboBox class is the subject of chapter 12.

The CheckListBox class is a list box that displays a check box in front of each item in the list. This permits a set of options to display as a scrollable list with a check box to enable or display each option.

We illustrate and discuss most of the members shown in .NET Table 11.1 throughout the course of this chapter, with additional discussion in the next chapter. The DataSource and DisplayMember properties support the display of data directly from an assigned collection, called the data source. These properties are presented in section 11.2 on simple list boxes. As of .NET 2.0, list controls also support automatic formatting of list items with members such as the FormatString property and Format event. This formatting support is examined in chapter 12.

The SelectedIndex and SelectedValue properties enable the selection of an item within the list. The ListBox class extends this concept to support selection of multiple items. Selection of a single item is discussed as part of section 11.2, while multiple selections are the subject of section 11.3.

11.1.2 Creating a new solution

We return to creating and manipulating list boxes in a moment. First, let's create the new MyAlbumEditor solution we mentioned at the start of this chapter.

CREATE THE MYALBUMEDITOR SOLUTION		
	Action	**Result**
1	Create a new project and solution for a Windows Application called "MyAlbumEditor." **How-to** Select New from the File menu, or use the keyboard shortcut Ctrl+Shift+N.	Solution Explorer - Solution '... Solution 'MyAlbumEditor' (1 project) MyAlbumEditor Configuration References Form1.cs Program.cs
2	Rename the Form1.cs file to EditorForm.cs. Click Yes in the dialog box to rename the Form1 class as well.	The file is renamed, and any use of the Form1 class is renamed to EditorForm.

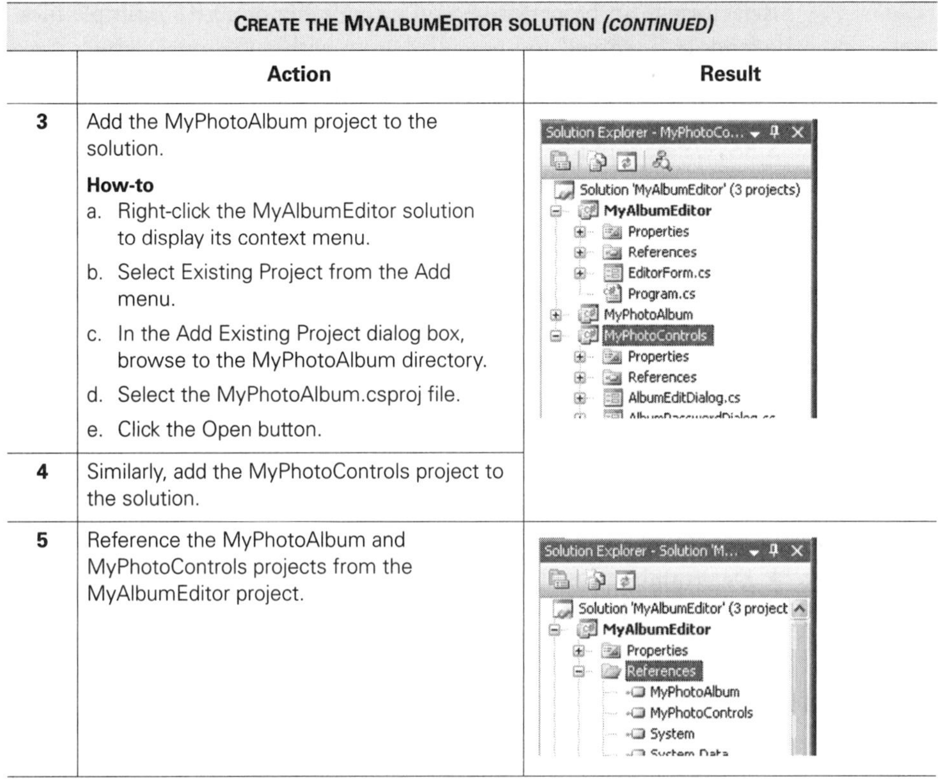

CREATE THE MYALBUMEDITOR SOLUTION *(CONTINUED)*		
	Action	**Result**
3	Add the MyPhotoAlbum project to the solution. **How-to** a. Right-click the MyAlbumEditor solution to display its context menu. b. Select Existing Project from the Add menu. c. In the Add Existing Project dialog box, browse to the MyPhotoAlbum directory. d. Select the MyPhotoAlbum.csproj file. e. Click the Open button.	
4	Similarly, add the MyPhotoControls project to the solution.	
5	Reference the MyPhotoAlbum and MyPhotoControls projects from the MyAlbumEditor project.	

These steps should be familiar if you have been following along from the beginning of the book. Since we encapsulated the `Photograph` and `PhotoAlbum` classes in chapter 5, as well as various other classes in chapters 6 through 10, these objects are now available for use in our new application. This is an important point, so I will say it again. The proper encapsulation of our objects in the MyPhotoAlbum and MyPhotoControls libraries makes the development of our new application much easier, and permits us to focus our attention on the list controls.

Generally speaking, there are two ways to reuse code. The first is what we have done so far: create object and form classes in separate libraries so they can be reused. A second approach is to look at some existing code and pull out functionality that you would like to reuse in another context.

This second approach is called *refactoring*, and is worth a brief discussion.

11.1.3 Refactoring application code

Refactoring is aimed at improving the design of existing code without changing the observable behavior of the code. As of .NET 2.0, Visual Studio provides direct support for some common refactoring tasks, such as renaming an item or extracting a region of code into a new method.

Refactoring can be performed on a single file or across multiple files. Over time, code tends to be copied and reapplied, even within the same class. It is worth taking a step back every so often to see if code can be refactored to simplify or consolidate the logic. Refactoring normally makes code easier to read, understand, and maintain.

Since we are building a new MyAlbumEditor application, it is worth considering what aspects of our existing MyPhotos application might be extracted into reusable methods. By refactoring some of the common tasks in the MyPhotos application, we can end up with code that is also reusable in the MyAlbumEditor application and perhaps by future applications as well.

One area worth our consideration is the file dialog boxes. We most likely need to open and save albums in our new application, so perhaps there is some code we previously wrote that might be encapsulated in a way that could be reused.

Refactoring is often a bit of an art. The trick is to find a section that is generally useful without embedding too much logic in the refactored code such that it is only usable in very narrow circumstances. In our existing MyPhotos code, the following aspects are good candidates for refactoring:

- Determining the file path and, if required, password when opening an album. This would encapsulate the `OpenFileDialog` logic in the `menuFileOpen_Click` method of the `MainForm` class.
- Determining the file path when saving an album under a new name. This encapsulates the `SaveAsAlbum` logic used in the `Click` handler for the Save As menu item.
- Asking users if they wish to save the changes made to an album. This should simplify the `SaveAndCloseAlbum` method in the `MainForm` class.

The following steps illustrate the newly created code based on these considerations. We could easily create new methods within the EditorForm.cs file of the MyPhotos application here. Since our goal is to eventually reuse this code elsewhere, we make the leap of refactoring this code into a reusable class in the MyPhotoControls library.

EXTRACT THE OPEN DIALOG CODE FROM THE MYPHOTOS APPLICATION

	Action	Result

1	In the MyPhotos solution, create a public and static class called `AlbumController` in the MyPhotoControls project.	`using System;`
		`using System.Windows.Forms;`
		`using Manning.MyPhotoAlbum;`
		
		`namespace Manning.MyPhotoControls`
		`{`
		` public static class AlbumController`
		` {`

	Extract the open dialog code from the MyPhotos application *(continued)*	
	Action	**Result**

2	Create a static `OpenAlbumDialog` method to determine the file path and password for a new album.	`public static bool OpenAlbumDialog(`
		`  ref string path, ref string password)`
		`{`

3	Implement this method to display an `OpenFileDialog` window to the user.
	How-to
	Copy the code from the `Click` handler for the Open menu, or type it in as shown.
		`  // Allow user to select a new album`
		`  using (OpenFileDialog dlg = new OpenFileDialog())`
		`  {`
		`    dlg.Title = "Open Album";`
		`    dlg.Filter = "Album files (*.abm)|*.abm|"`
		`      + "All files (*.*)|*.*";`
		`    dlg.InitialDirectory`
		`        = AlbumManager.DefaultPath;`
		`    dlg.RestoreDirectory = true;`
		`    if (dlg.ShowDialog() == DialogResult.OK)`
		`    {`
		`      path = dlg.FileName;`

4	Check to see if the file is encrypted, and obtain the password if required.	`      return CheckAlbumPassword(path, ref password);`
		`    }`
		`  }`

5	Return `false` if the user cancels the request.	`  return false;` `}`

6	Implement a public `CheckAlbumPassword` method to retrieve the password for an album, if required.	`public static bool CheckAlbumPassword(`
		`    string path, ref string password)`
		`{`
		`  // Get password if encrypted`
		`  if (AlbumStorage.IsEncrypted(path))`
		`  {`
		`    using (AlbumPasswordDialog pwdDlg`
		`             = new AlbumPasswordDialog ())`
		`    {`

7	Return `false` from this method if the user cancels the request. Otherwise, return `true`.	`      pwdDlg.Album = path;`
		`      if (pwdDlg.ShowDialog() != DialogResult.OK)`
		`        return false; // Open cancelled`
		
		`      password = pwdDlg.Password;`
		`    }`
		`  }`
		`  return true;`
		`}`
		`}`
		`}`

It is worth experimenting with the Visual Studio Refactor menu to understand its capabilities as well. For example, right-click the `PhotoAlbum` class name in the PhotoAlbum.cs file, and use the Refactor submenu to rename it to `PhotoCollection`. You will find that the class is renamed correctly in all three projects in the solution. Build the solution to verify this fact, and then rename it back to `PhotoAlbum`.

You can also create new methods with the Refactor menu. Highlight a section of code within a large method, and select the Extract Method item in this menu. You are prompted for a new method name, and Visual Studio does the work of encapsulating the new code within the new method and calling this method from the existing code.

In our code so far, the `OpenAlbumDialog` method uses `ref` parameters to return a selected album file and associated password to a caller. Using `ref` parameters ensures that caller can see any new values we assign to these parameters.

Let's continue with our changes. As in the prior steps, you can copy and paste code from the existing methods in the `MainForm` class, or enter this new code by hand.

EXTRACT THE SAVE DIALOG BOX CODE FROM THE MYPHOTOS APPLICATION

	Action	Result

8	In the `AlbumController` class, create a static `SaveAlbumDialog` method to determine a file path in which to save an album.	`public static bool SaveAlbumDialog(ref string path)`
		`{`
		`  using (SaveFileDialog dlg = new SaveFileDialog())`
		`  {`
		`    // Display a dialog for saving the album`
		`    dlg.Title = "Save Album";`
		`    dlg.DefaultExt = "abm";`
		`    dlg.Filter = "Album files (*.abm)`|`*.abm`|`"`
		`      + "All files`|`*.*";`
		`    dlg.InitialDirectory`
		`      = AlbumManager.DefaultPath;`
		`    dlg.RestoreDirectory = true;`

9	Return `true` if an album was selected, and `false` if the user cancels the request.	`    if (dlg.ShowDialog() == DialogResult.OK)`
		`    {`
		`      // Save the album under the new name`
		`      path = dlg.FileName;`
		`      return true;`
		`    }`
		
		`    return false;`
		`  }`
		`}`

10	Also create an `AskForSave` method to accept an `AlbumManager` and query the user on whether they wish to save any changes made to the contained album.	`public static DialogResult AskForSave(`
		`    AlbumManager manager)`
		`{`
		`  if (manager.Album.HasChanged)`
		`  {`

	Action	Result
EXTRACT THE SAVE DIALOG BOX CODE FROM THE MYPHOTOS APPLICATION *(CONTINUED)*		

11	Query the user with the `YesNoCancel` message box used in the MainForm.cs file, and return the selected result to the caller.	<pre> string msg;
		    if (manager.FullName == null)
		      msg = "Do you wish to save your changes?";
		    else
		      msg = "Do you wish to save your changes to "
		        + manager.ShortName + "?";
		
		    // Ask user if they wish to save file
		    DialogResult result = MessageBox.Show(
		      msg, "Save Changes?",
		      MessageBoxButtons.YesNoCancel,
		      MessageBoxIcon.Question);
		
		    return result;
		  }
		
		  return DialogResult.No;
		}</pre>

This completes the three methods that should prove useful in future applications. Note how we made the `AlbumController` class static to simplify the use of these methods. Our final step in our little refactoring exercise is to hook these methods into our MyPhotos application.

	Action	Result
USE THE ALBUMCONTROLLER METHODS IN THE MAINFORM CLASS		

12	In the MyPhotos project, modify the `menuFileOpen_Click` method of the `MainForm` class to use of the new `OpenAlbumDialog` method.	<pre>private void menuFileOpen_Click(
		  object sender, EventArgs e)
		{
		  string path = null;
		  string password = null;
		  if (AlbumController.OpenAlbumDialog(
		          ref path, ref password))
		  {
		    // Close existing album
		    if (!SaveAndCloseAlbum())
		      return; // Close cancelled
		
		    try
		    {
		      // Open the new album
		      Manager = new AlbumManager(path, password);
		    }
		    catch (AlbumStorageException aex)
		    . . .
		    DisplayAlbum();
		  }
		}</pre>

	Action	Result
USE THE ALBUMCONTROLLER METHODS IN THE MAINFORM CLASS *(CONTINUED)*		

13	Modify the `SaveAsAlbum` method to use the new `SaveAlbumDialog` method.	`private void menuFileSaveAs_Click(`
		`  object sender, EventArgs e)`
		`{`
		`  string path = null;`
		`  if (AlbumController.SaveAlbumDialog(ref path))`
		`  {`
		`    // Save the album under the new name`
		`    SaveAlbum(path);`
		
		`    // Update title bar to include new name`
		`    SetTitleBar();`
		`  }`
		`}`

14	Modify the `SaveAndCloseAlbum` method to use the new `AskForSave` method.	`private bool SaveAndCloseAlbum()`
		`{`
		`  DialogResult result`
		`    = AlbumController.AskForSave(Manager);`
		
		`  if (result == DialogResult.Yes)`
		`    SaveAlbum();`
		`  else if (result == DialogResult.Cancel)`
		`    return false;  // do not close`
		
		`  // Close album and return true`
		`  . . .`
		`  return true;`
		`}`

As you can see, our new methods have simplified the `MainForm` class code, without modifying the behavior of the application. As a rule, you should never refactor and modify functionality at the same time. Do one task first, then thoroughly test the change, then perform the other task. The reason for this is that the more you change, the harder it becomes to find any resulting errors. By changing only one aspect at a time, you know where to look if (when?) things go wrong.

Whole books have been written on refactoring, some of which are shown in the bibliography at the back of the book. This is enough of an introduction for our purposes, and prepares us for creating our list control application.

11.2 SIMPLE LIST BOXES

The `ListBox` class is the simplest form of list control. It can display a collection of objects directly, or be customized to contain a variety of items from various sources. Use this class to show more than one item on a form, especially to allow the selection of one or more of these items.

Typically, the objects in a list box are all the same type. In our example, the list holds a `PhotoAlbum` object, so all items are `Photograph` objects. There are times, however, when you may wish to show different types in the list. This can be done using the base `object` class, or by creating either an encapsulating class or a shared base class to define the members shared by the various types.

.NET Table 11.2 ListBox class

The `ListBox` class is a list control that displays a scrollable list of items. The control allows single or multiple items to be selected from the list, and displays each item as a simple text string or a custom-drawn graphic. This class is part of the `System.Windows.Forms` namespace, and inherits from the `ListControl` class. See .NET Table 11.1 for members inherited from the base class.

Public Static Fields	DefaultItemHeight	Holds the constant value representing the default height of an owner-drawn list box item.
	NoMatches	Holds the constant value returned by `ListBox` methods when no matches are found during a search.
Public Properties	DrawMode	Gets or sets how this list box should be drawn.
	ItemHeight	Gets or sets the height of an item when the list is drawn with a fixed item height.
	Items	Gets the collection of items to display.
	MultiColumn	Gets or sets whether multiple columns are supported.
	ScrollAlwaysVisible	Gets or sets whether the vertical scroll bar is shown at all times. The `HorizontalScrollBar` property gets or sets whether a horizontal scroll bar is shown.
	SelectedIndices	Gets the collection of zero-based indices for the items selected in the list.
	SelectedItem	Gets or sets the currently selected item.
	SelectedItems	Gets the collection of items selected in the list.
	SelectionMode	Gets or sets how items are selected in the list.
	Sorted	Gets or sets whether the contained items are automatically sorted.
	TopIndex	Gets the index of the first visible item in the list.
Public Methods	BeginUpdate	Prevents the control from repainting its contents until the `EndUpdate` method is called.
	ClearSelected	Deselects all items currently selected in the list.
	FindString	Returns the index of the first item with a display value beginning with a given string.
	GetSelected	Indicates whether a specified item is selected. The `SetSelected` method selects or deselects a given item.
	IndexFromPoint	Returns the index of the item at the given coordinates.
Public Events	DrawItem	Occurs when an item in an owner-drawn list box requires painting.
	MeasureItem	Occurs when the size of an owner-drawn item is required.
	SelectedIndex-Changed	Occurs when a new item in the list is selected, in both single- and multiple-selection modes.

This section discusses the `ListBox` class in general, and its support for the display and selection of items in the list. The discussion illustrates the use of this class using the MyAlbumEditor application we created in the prior section.

11.2.1 The ListBox class

A summary of the `ListBox` class appears in .NET Table 11.2 (on page 309). While the core functionality is defined by the base `ListControl` class, the `ListBox` class adds support for scrolling, multiple selection, custom drawing, and other functionality as indicated in the table. The ability to scroll the list and control item selection is discussed in this chapter. Custom drawing of list items is examined in section 13.4.

The `CheckedListBox` class is a list box that supports a check box next to each item. The `CheckedItems` property retrieves the collection of items checked in the control.

Let's look at an example of some of the selection and display properties inherited from the base `ListControl` class. The following steps implement some code for our MyAlbumEditor project as a basis for this discussion.

<table>
<tr><th colspan="3">CREATE CONTROLS FOR THE MYALBUMEDITOR APPLICATION</th></tr>
<tr><th></th><th>Action</th><th>Result</th></tr>
<tr><td>1</td><td>Open the MyAlbumEditor solution, and drag two <code>GroupBox</code> controls onto the EditorForm.cs [Design] window.
Settings
<table>
<tr><th>GroupBox</th><th>Property</th><th>Value</th></tr>
<tr><td rowspan="3">First</td><td>(Name)</td><td>grpAlbums</td></tr>
<tr><td>Anchor</td><td>Top, Left, Right</td></tr>
<tr><td>Text</td><td>&Albums</td></tr>
<tr><td rowspan="4">Second</td><td>(Name)</td><td>grpPhotos</td></tr>
<tr><td>Anchor</td><td>Top, Bottom, Left, Right</td></tr>
<tr><td>Enabled</td><td>False</td></tr>
<tr><td>Text</td><td>&Photographs</td></tr>
</table></td><td></td></tr>
</table>

<table>
<tr><th colspan="3">CREATE CONTROLS FOR THE MYALBUMEDITOR APPLICATION (CONTINUED)</th></tr>
<tr><th></th><th>Action</th><th>Result</th></tr>
<tr><td>2</td><td>Drag a <code>Button</code> control into the Album group box, a <code>ListBox</code> control into the Photos group box, and a <code>Button</code> control at the base of the form.
Settings
<table>
<tr><th>Control</th><th>Property</th><th>Value</th></tr>
<tr><td rowspan="3">Open Button</td><td>(Name)</td><td>btnOpen</td></tr>
<tr><td>Anchor</td><td>Top, Right</td></tr>
<tr><td>Text</td><td>&Open</td></tr>
<tr><td rowspan="3">ListBox</td><td>(Name)</td><td>lstPhotos</td></tr>
<tr><td>Anchor</td><td>Top, Bottom, Left, Right</td></tr>
<tr><td>HorizontalScrollbar</td><td>True</td></tr>
<tr><td rowspan="4">Close Button</td><td>(Name)</td><td>btnClose</td></tr>
<tr><td>Anchor</td><td>Bottom</td></tr>
<tr><td>DialogResult</td><td>OK</td></tr>
<tr><td>Text</td><td>&Close</td></tr>
</table>
</td><td>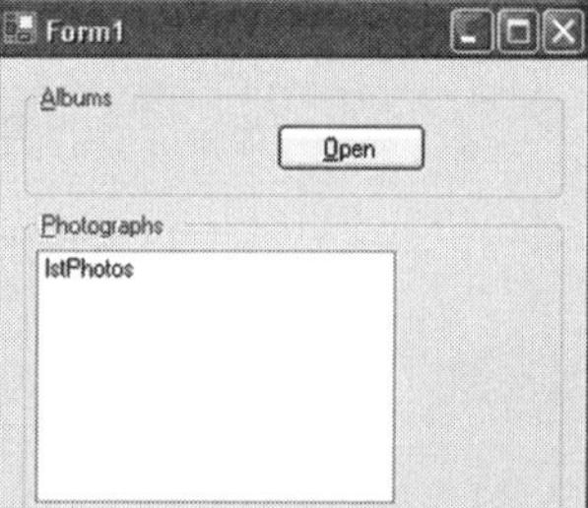

Note: Since our application does not have a menu bar, we use the standard Close button as the mechanism for exiting the application.</td></tr>
<tr><td>3</td><td>Set the properties for the <code>EditorForm</code> form as follows.
Settings
<table>
<tr><th>Property</th><th>Value</th></tr>
<tr><td>AcceptButton</td><td>btnClose</td></tr>
<tr><td>Size</td><td>400, 300</td></tr>
<tr><td>Text</td><td>MyAlbumEditor</td></tr>
</table>
Note: When you enter the <code>Size</code> setting, notice how the controls automatically resize within their containers based on the assigned <code>Anchor</code> settings.</td><td>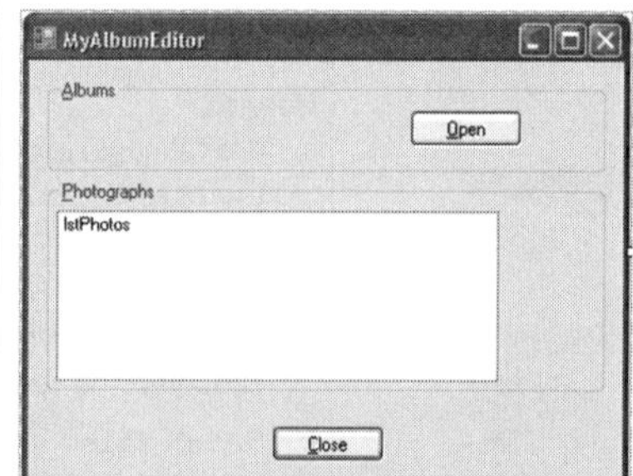
</td></tr>
</table>

We use the `Anchor` property from the `Control` class here to establish the positioning of each control within its parent container. So the group boxes and Close button are anchored within the form, while the Open button and list box are anchored within their respective group boxes.

So far all we've done is toss some controls on a form with some assigned properties. Next we link these controls to our photograph and album classes.

11.2.2 Displaying a data source

Windows Forms controls can interact directly with collection classes in various ways, including custom classes such as our `PhotoAlbum` class. The process is called *data binding*, a topic we cover in detail in chapters 21 and 22. List controls such as `ListBox` support this notion through the `DataSource` and `DataMember` properties.

The following steps introduce some basic functionality into our application and display an album using the `DataSource` property.

<table>
<tr><th colspan="3">DISPLAY THE CONTENTS OF AN ALBUM IN A LIST BOX</th></tr>
<tr><th></th><th>Action</th><th>Result</th></tr>
<tr><td>1</td><td>In the EditorForm.cs file, indicate we are using the <code>Manning.MyPhotoAlbum</code> namespace.</td><td><pre>. . .
using Manning.MyPhotoAlbum;
using Manning.MyPhotoControls;</pre></td></tr>
<tr><td>2</td><td>Add a private field and property to hold an <code>AlbumManager</code> object.</td><td><pre>private AlbumManager _manager;
private AlbumManager Manager
{ get { return _manager; }
  set { _manager = value; } }</pre></td></tr>
<tr><td>3</td><td>Modify the constructor to initialize this field with a new manager.</td><td><pre>public EditorForm()
{
  InitializeComponent();
  Manager = new AlbumManager();
}</pre></td></tr>
<tr><td>4</td><td>Create a <code>CloseAlbum</code> method to save any changes to the existing album and close it.
How-to
a. If a manager exists, use the <code>AskForSave</code> method in the <code>AlbumController</code> class to query the user.
b. Return <code>true</code> if the user canceled the request.
c. Return <code>false</code> if the user selected whether to save the album.</td><td><pre>private bool CloseAlbum()
{
  if (Manager != null)
  {
    DialogResult result
      = AlbumController.AskForSave(Manager);
    switch (result)
    {
      case DialogResult.Yes:
        Manager.Save();
        break;
      case DialogResult.Cancel:
        return true;
    }

    Manager.Album.Dispose();
    Manager = null;
  }

  return false;
}</pre></td></tr>
<tr><td>5</td><td>Override the <code>OnClosing</code> method to make sure any changes are saved before exiting.</td><td><pre>protected override void OnClosing(
    CancelEventArgs e)
{
  e.Cancel = CloseAlbum();
}</pre></td></tr>
<tr><td>6</td><td>Exit the application by closing the form when the Close button is clicked.</td><td><pre>private void btnClose_Click(
    object sender, EventArgs e)
{
  Close();
}</pre></td></tr>
<tr><td>7</td><td>Add a <code>Click</code> event handler for the Open button.</td><td><pre>private void btnOpen_Click(
    object sender, EventArgs e)
{</pre></td></tr>
</table>

	Action	Result
DISPLAY THE CONTENTS OF AN ALBUM IN A LIST BOX *(CONTINUED)*		

8	Implement this handler to allow the user to open a new album file.
	How-to
	a. Use the `OpenAlbumDialog` method in the `AlbumController` class.
	b. If the use selects a new album, close the existing album.
	c. Open the selected album.
	d. If an album error occurs, set the manager to `null`.
	e. Display the updated album.
		`string path = null;`
		`string password = null;`
		`if (AlbumController.OpenAlbumDialog(`
		`ref path, ref password))`
		`{`
		`if (CloseAlbum())`
		`return; // cancel open`
		
		`try`
		`{`
		`Manager = new AlbumManager(`
		`path, password);`
		`}`
		`catch (AlbumStorageException)`
		`{`
		`Manager = null;`
		`}`
		`}`
		
		`DisplayAlbum();`
		`}`

9	Implement a `DisplayAlbum` method to display an album within the form.
	How-to
	a. If a manager does not exist, disable the photo portion of the control.
	b. If a manager does exist, display the contents of the album in the list box.
		`private void DisplayAlbum()`
		`{`
		`if (Manager == null)`
		`{`
		`grpPhotos.Enabled = false;`
		`Text = "The selected album "`
		`+ "could not be opened";`
		`lstPhotos.BackColor = SystemColors.Control;`
		`lstPhotos.Items.Clear();`
		`}`
		`else`
		`{`
		`grpPhotos.Enabled = true;`
		`Text = "Album " + Manager.ShortName;`
		`lstPhotos.BackColor = SystemColors.Window;`
		`lstPhotos.DataSource = Manager.Album;`
		`}`
		`}`

The assignment of the `DataSource` property here may be less glamorous than you expected, but that really is all it takes to display the list of photograph filenames within the list box. The `DisplayAlbum` code is repeated in listing 11.1 so we can add commentary in the subsequent paragraphs.

Listing 11.1 Initial code to display an album in a list box

```
private void DisplayAlbum()
{
  if (Manager == null)
  {
    Text = "The selected album could not be opened";
    grpPhotos.Enabled = false;                          ❶ Disables the Photographs group box
    lstPhotos.BackColor = SystemColors.Control;         ❷ Modifies the list box background color
    lstPhotos.Items.Clear();
```

```
    }
    else
    {
      Text = "Album " + Manager.ShortName;
      grpPhotos.Enabled = true;
      lstPhotos.BackColor = SystemColors.Window;
      lstPhotos.DataSource = Manager.Album;
    }
}
```

❷ **Modifies the list box background color**

❸ **Assigns the Album as the data source**

❶ When no album is present, we need to indicate this to the user. This line disables the Photographs group box control. Since this control is a collection, all contained controls are disabled as well.

❷ When a `ListBox` control is disabled, it still displays the standard window color as the background. To make it more apparent when an album is not present, our code modifies the background color of the control to the standard control color, and resets it to the default window color when an album is assigned. The `SystemColors` class used here allows the colors assigned to the desktop to be accessed in code.

❸ This line assigns the current `PhotoAlbum` collection as the source of data for the `ListBox` control. The `DataSource` property accepts any collection that supports the `IList` interface.[1] In our case, the album collection contains photographs, so each `Photograph` object in the album is displayed in the list. By default, the `ToString` method is called for each contained item to obtain the text to display. As you may recall, we overrode the `ToString` method for the `Photograph` class to return the filename associated with the object.

An example of our application so far is shown in figure 11.3, where an album named "colors" is displayed. Each photograph in this album is named after a well-known

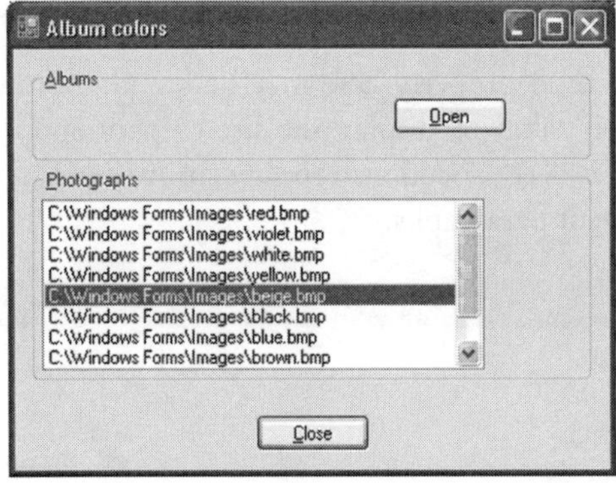

Figure 11.3
By default, a list box displays a vertical scroll bar when the number of items exceeds the size of the box.

[1] For a more detailed discussion of data sources, see chapters 21 and 22, and in particular table 21.2, for a list of interfaces related to data binding.

color. Notice how the group box controls display their keyboard access keys, namely Alt+A and Alt+P. When activated, the focus is set to the first control in the group box, based on the assigned tab order.

You may also notice that there is a lot of blank space in our application. These spaces fill up as we progress through the chapter.

TRY IT! The `DisplayMember` property for the `ListControl` classes indicates the name of the property to use for display purposes, rather than the default `ToString` method. Modify this property in the `DisplayAlbum` method to a property specific to the `Photograph` class, such as "FileName" or "Caption." Run the program again to see how this affects the displayed items.

The related property `ValueMember` specifies the value returned by members such as the `SelectedValue` property. By default, this property returns the `object` instance itself.

11.2.3 Selecting list items

The `ListBox` class includes the ability to select one or more items in the displayed list. By default, a single item can be selected at a time. We discuss single selection here, and save the selection of multiple items for the next section.

Two key properties for this feature are the `SelectedItem` and `SelectedIndex` properties—which obtain the object or index of the selected item, respectively—and the `SelectedIndexChanged` event—which occurs when a new item is selected.

We can illustrate the use of the index property using the property dialog boxes created in chapters 8 and 9. The following steps add the ability to display these dialog boxes from our application. The album dialog box can be displayed using a normal button. The photo dialog box shows the properties for the selected photograph.

<table>
<tr><th colspan="3">DISPLAY THE ALBUM AND PHOTO PROPERTY DIALOG BOXES</th></tr>
<tr><th></th><th>Action</th><th>Result</th></tr>
<tr><td>1</td><td>In the EditorForm.cs [Design] window, add two new buttons to the form as shown.

Settings
<table>
<tr><th>Button</th><th>Property</th><th>Value</th></tr>
<tr><td rowspan="4">Album</td><td>(Name)</td><td>btnAlbumProps</td></tr>
<tr><td>Anchor</td><td>Top, Right</td></tr>
<tr><td>Enabled</td><td>False</td></tr>
<tr><td>Text</td><td>Propertie&s</td></tr>
<tr><td rowspan="3">Photo</td><td>(Name)</td><td>btnPhotoProps</td></tr>
<tr><td>Anchor</td><td>Top, Right</td></tr>
<tr><td>Text</td><td>Properti&es</td></tr>
</table></td><td>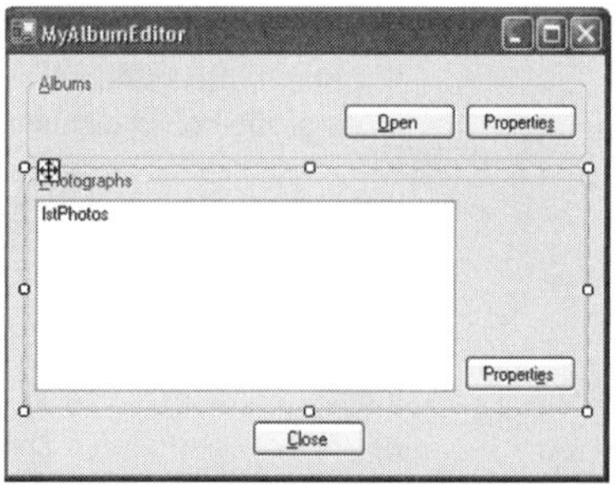
</td></tr>
</table>

<table>
<tr><th colspan="3">DISPLAY THE ALBUM AND PHOTO PROPERTY DIALOG BOXES (CONTINUED)</th></tr>
<tr><th></th><th>Action</th><th>Result</th></tr>
<tr><td>2</td><td>Add a <code>Click</code> event handler for the album Properties button that displays an <code>AlbumEditDialog</code> for the current album.</td><td><code>private void btnAlbumProp_Click(
    object sender, EventArgs e)
{
  if (Manager == null)
    return;

  using (AlbumEditDialog dlg
     = new AlbumEditDialog(Manager))
  {
    if (dlg.ShowDialog()
          == DialogResult.OK)
      DisplayAlbum();
  }
}</code></td></tr>
<tr><td>3</td><td>Add a <code>Click</code> event handler for the photo Properties button. Do nothing if no manager exists or nothing is selected.</td><td><code>private void btnPhotoProps_Click(
    object sender, EventArgs e)
{
  if (Manager == null
      || lstPhotos.SelectedIndex < 0)
    return; // nothing selected</code></td></tr>
<tr><td>4</td><td>Otherwise, display a <code>PhotoEditDialog</code> form for the selected photograph.</td><td><code> Manager.Index
      = lstPhotos.SelectedIndex;
  using (PhotoEditDialog dlg
      = new PhotoEditDialog(Manager))
  {
    if (dlg.ShowDialog()
          == DialogResult.OK)
      DisplayAlbum();
  }
}</code></td></tr>
<tr><td>5</td><td>Also display a <code>PhotoEditDialog</code> when the user double-clicks on a list item.

How-to
Handle the <code>DoubleClick</code> event for the list box control.</td><td><code>private void lstPhotos_DoubleClick(
    object sender, EventArgs e)
{
  btnPhotoProps.PerformClick();
}</code></td></tr>
<tr><td>6</td><td>Finally, update the <code>DisplayAlbum</code> method to disable the album Properties button when a manager is not assigned.

Note: We do not need to disable the photo button since it is disabled when its group box is disabled.</td><td><code>private void DisplayAlbum()
{
  if (Manager == null)
  {
    grpPhotos.Enabled = false;
    btnAlbumProps.Enabled = false;
    Text = . . .;
    . . .
  }
  else
  {
    grpPhotos.Enabled = true;
    btnAlbumProps.Enabled = true;
    Text = . . .;
    . . .
  }
}</code></td></tr>
</table>

In the code to display the `Photograph` properties dialog box in step 4, the `Selected-Index` property retrieves the index into the album of the selected photograph:

```
Manager.Index = SelectedIndex;
```

This works because the order of items in the list box matches the order of photographs in the album. It is possible, of course, to construct a list where the order of items in the list differs from that within the collection. In this case, the code must search for the item in the list or each item must define a way to determine its actual positioning within the collection. One way to do this is with the `SelectedItem` property. This property retrieves the item as an `object`, so in our code we would have to convert this to a `Photograph` using the `as` keyword. This approach would use the following line of code:

```
Manager.Index = Manager.Album.IndexOf(
                    lstPhotos.SelectedItem as Photograph);
```

Our code also updates the `DisplayAlbum` method to ensure that the album Properties button is only enabled when an album is successfully opened. Figure 11.4 illustrates the use of this button to display the properties for an album called "colors."

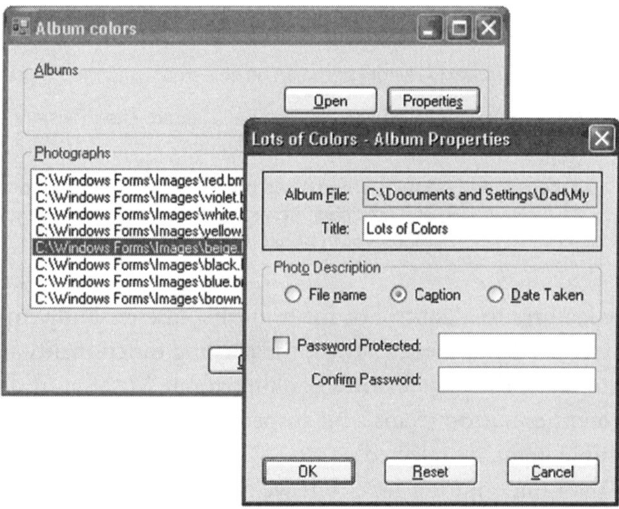

Figure 11.4 Since our properties dialog boxes were encapsulated in the MyAlbumControls library, we can easily reuse them in our new application as shown here.

This example relies on the fact that only a single item is selected at a time. List boxes also permit multiple item selection, which is our next topic.

11.3 MULTISELECTION LIST BOXES

In this section we discuss various aspects of selecting multiple items in a list box. We examine the different kinds of selection supported by the `ListBox` control, and illustrate these features in our MyAlbumEditor application.

A list box can allow no selection, single selection, or one of two kinds of multiple selection. Unless a list box is read only, you typically want to allow some sort of selection from the list. If a user needs to manipulate multiple list items at the same time, then one of the multiple selection options should be used. Otherwise, stick with single selection as it is the easiest to use and understand.

11.3.1 Enabling multiple selection

Enabling a list box to allow multiple selections simply requires setting the right property value: `SelectionMode`. This property is based on the `SelectionMode` enumeration, as shown in .NET Table 11.3. Most Windows applications these days use the `MultiExtended` mode to select multiple items, so the `MultiSimple` mode should be avoided except when an application truly requires this behavior.

.NET Table 11.3 SelectionMode enumeration

The `SelectionMode` enumeration specifies the selection behavior of a list box control. This enumeration is part of the `System.Windows.Forms` namespace.

Enumeration values	None	Items cannot be selected.
	One	A single item can be selected using the mouse or spacebar.
	MultiSimple	Multiple items can be selected. The mouse or spacebar selects or deselects an item.
	MultiExtended	Multiple items can be selected. In addition to the mouse and spacebar, items can be selected using a drag of the mouse or the Shift, Ctrl, and arrow keys.

When adding new features to a control or form, in this case enabling multiple selection in our list box, it is a good idea to review the existing functionality to determine how best to accommodate the new feature. Looking at our MyAlbumEditor application, the photo Properties button seems a bit suspect, since it is not clear what should happen when multiple items are selected.

There is more than one solution here, but we adopt the behavior that the photo Properties button only applies when a single item is selected. We add three new buttons that are appropriate when multiple items are selected. The first two rearrange the selected items within the album while the third button removes selected items from the album.

The following code adds these buttons and enables or disables them depending on how many items are selected. These changes are discussed in the subsequent paragraphs.

<table>
<tr><th colspan="3">ENABLE MULTIPLE SELECTION IN THE LIST BOX</th></tr>
<tr><th></th><th>Action</th><th>Result</th></tr>
<tr><td>1</td><td>In the EditorForm.cs [Design] window, modify the <code>SelectionMode</code> property for the list box to be <code>MultiExtended</code>.</td><td>The list box now allows multiple items to be selected, in the same manner files can be selected in Windows Explorer.</td></tr>
<tr><td>2</td><td>Add three new buttons to the form, as shown in the graphic.

Settings
<table>
<tr><th>Button</th><th>Property</th><th>Value</th></tr>
<tr><td rowspan="3">Move Up</td><td>(Name)</td><td>btnMoveUp</td></tr>
<tr><td>Anchor</td><td>Top, Right</td></tr>
<tr><td>Text</td><td>Move &Up</td></tr>
<tr><td rowspan="3">Move Down</td><td>(Name)</td><td>btnMoveDown</td></tr>
<tr><td>Anchor</td><td>Top, Right</td></tr>
<tr><td>Text</td><td>Move &Down</td></tr>
<tr><td rowspan="3">Remove</td><td>(Name)</td><td>btnRemove</td></tr>
<tr><td>Anchor</td><td>Top, Right</td></tr>
<tr><td>Text</td><td>&Remove</td></tr>
</table></td><td>Note: Controls can be copied and pasted in the designer window much like text in a document editor. One way to add these three buttons is to copy and paste the Properties button.</td></tr>
<tr><td>3</td><td>Rewrite the <code>DisplayAlbum</code> method to add each item to the list manually.

Note: This allows us to manipulate the individual items in the list, which is prohibited when filling the list with the <code>DataSource</code> property.</td><td><pre>
private void DisplayAlbum()
{
  if (Manager == null)
    . . .
  else
  {
    . . .
    lstPhotos.BackColor = . . .;

    lstPhotos.BeginUpdate();
    lstPhotos.Items.Clear();
    foreach (Photograph p
               in Manager.Album)
    {
      lstPhotos.Items.Add(p);
    }
    lstPhotos.EndUpdate();
  }
}
</pre></td></tr>
</table>

In step 3, we assign the items in the list explicitly rather than using the `DataSource` property. The `Items` property gets or sets a `ListBox.ObjectCollection` value that holds the collection of objects in the list. This collection supports the normal collection interfaces such as `IList` and `IEnumerable`, so we can invoke standard collection operations such as the `Clear` and `Add` method.

This code also uses the `BeginUpdate` and `EndUpdate` methods. These methods are supported by list controls to prevent the list from redrawing its contents while the items in the list are manipulated. These are especially useful when making multiple changes to a list, as they improve performance and prevent the screen from flickering by ensuring that the list is drawn only once.

The last task for this section is to enable or disable our new buttons depending on how many items are selected in the list.

HANDLE THE SELECTEDINDEXCHANGED EVENT

	Action	Result

4	Handle the `SelectedIndexChanged` event in the `ListBox` control to enable the photo buttons appropriately.	`private void lstPhotos_SelectedIndexChanged(`
		`    object sender, EventArgs e)`
		`{`
		`  EnablePhotoButtons();`
		`}`

5	Implement the `EnablePhotoButtons` method to determine whether any list items are selected.	`private void EnablePhotoButtons()`
		`{`
		`  int selCount`
		`      = lstPhotos.SelectedIndices.Count;`
		`  bool someSelected = (selCount > 0);`

6	If so, then enable the Move Up and Move Down buttons based on whether the selected items can be moved up and/or down.	`  if (someSelected)`
		`  {`
		`    bool firstSelected = lstPhotos.GetSelected(0);`
		`    bool lastSelected = lstPhotos.GetSelected(`
		`            lstPhotos.Items.Count - 1);`
		
		`    btnMoveUp.Enabled = !firstSelected;`
		`    btnMoveDown.Enabled = !lastSelected;`
		`  }`

7	If not, disable the Move Up and Move Down buttons.	`  else`
		`  {`
		`    btnMoveUp.Enabled = false;`
		`    btnMoveDown.Enabled = false;`
		`  }`

8	In either case, enable the Remove button if any items are selected, and the photo Properties button if a single item is selected.	`  btnRemove.Enabled = someSelected;`
		`  btnPhotoProps.Enabled = (selCount == 1);`
		`}`

9	Also use this method when opening an album to set the initial state of the photo-related buttons.	`private void btnOpen_Click(. . .)`
		`{`
		`  string path = null;`
		`  string password = null;`
		`  if (AlbumController.OpenAlbumDialog(. . .))`
		`    . . .`
		`  DisplayAlbum();`
		`  EnablePhotoButtons();`
		`}`

We already mentioned the `Items` property that holds the object collection for the list. Two other collections are defined within the `ListBox` class. The `ListBox.SelectedObjectCollection` class represents a collection of objects selected in a list box, and the `ListBox.SelectedIndexCollection` class represents a collection of indices selected in a list box. The `SelectedItems` and `Selected-Indices` properties get or set these collections for the list. Our code uses the `SelectedIndices` property to determine the number of items selected.

The `lstPhotos_SelectedIndexChanged` code also utilizes the `GetSelected` method to determine whether a specific index is selected. This is required to ensure that our Move Up button is not enabled when the first item is selected and that the Move Down button is not enabled when the last item is selected. A `SetSelected` method also exists to select or deselect a specific list item.

TRY IT! Our code uses the `MultiExtended` selection mode to enable selecting a range of items using the mouse or keyboard. Run the application to observe this behavior, then change the list box to use the `MultiSimple` selection mode to see how these two modes differ.

11.3.2 Reordering list items

Now that our list box allows multiple selections, we need to process these selections in some button `Click` event handlers. We look at the Move Up and Move Down buttons first, which should move the selected set of photographs up or down within both the album and the list, while still preserving the selection state.

There are two problems we need to solve in order to do this. The first is that our album does not explicitly support this notion. We could move each item directly in our `Form` class, but it might be easier if we create a utility method in our `AlbumMan-ager` class to facilitate these operations.

The second problem is that we need to preserve the order of our selections. Whenever we move an item up or down, we affect the index of other items in the album. As illustrated in figure 11.5, when we move an item down, then the subsequent item has a new index. In the figure, if we move item 3 down, and then move item 4 down, we would effectively move the original item 3 into the fifth position. The trick here, as you may realize, is to work backward. When moving items down, we start at the bottom and work our way up to ensure that each item is only moved once. Conversely, when moving items up, we start at the top and work our way down.

Let's begin with some new methods in the `AlbumManager` class.

1	Photo A
2	Photo B
3	**Photo C**
4	Photo D
5	Photo E
6	Photo F

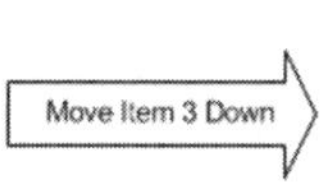

1	Photo A
2	Photo B
3	Photo D
4	**Photo C**
5	Photo E
6	Photo F

Figure 11.5
When the third item in the list is moved down, the original fourth item moves into position 3.

<table>
<tr><th colspan="3">IMPLEMENT MOVE METHODS IN THE ALBUMMANAGER CLASS</th></tr>
<tr><th></th><th>Action</th><th>Result</th></tr>
<tr><td>1</td><td>In the <code>AlbumManager</code> class of the MyPhotoAlbum project, define a <code>MoveItemBackward</code> method to move the photo at a given index to the prior position.</td><td><pre><code>public void MoveItemBackward(int index)
{
  if (index <= 0 || index >= Album.Count)
    throw new IndexOutOfRangeException();

  // Remove photo and reinsert at prior position
  Photograph photo = Album[index];
  Album.RemoveAt(index);
  Album.Insert(index - 1, photo);
}</code></pre></td></tr>
<tr><td>2</td><td>Also define a <code>MoveItemForward</code> method to move the photo at a given index to the subsequent position.</td><td><pre><code>public void MoveItemForward(int index)
{
  if (index < 0 || index > Album.Count - 1)
    throw new IndexOutOfRangeException();

  // Remove photo and reinsert at subsequent pos
  Photograph photo = Album[index];
  Album.RemoveAt(index);
  Album.Insert(index + 1, photo);
}</code></pre></td></tr>
</table>

These methods move the `Photograph` at a given index forward or backward within the collection represented by the album. If an invalid index is provided, we throw an exception.

With these methods in place, we can write the code for the Move Up and Move Down buttons in our MyAlbumEditor application.

<table>
<tr><th colspan="3">IMPLEMENT MOVE HANDLERS IN THE EDITFORM CLASS</th></tr>
<tr><th></th><th>Action</th><th>Result</th></tr>
<tr><td>3</td><td>In the EditorForm.cs [Design] window, add a <code>Click</code> event handler for the Move Up button.</td><td><pre><code>private void btnMoveUp_Click(
    object sender, EventArgs e)
{</code></pre></td></tr>
<tr><td>4</td><td>Implement this handler to move the selected photographs to the prior positions in the album.</td><td><pre><code> ListBox.SelectedIndexCollection indices
    = lstPhotos.SelectedIndices;
  int count = indices.Count;
  int[] newIndices = new int[count];

  // Move each selection up
  for (int i = 0; i < count; i++)
  {
    int x = indices[i];
    Manager.MoveItemBackward(x);
    newIndices[i] = x - 1;
  }

  ReselectMovedItems(newIndices);
}</code></pre></td></tr>
</table>

	Action	Result
IMPLEMENT MOVE HANDLERS IN THE EDITFORM CLASS *(CONTINUED)*		

5	Implement a `ReselectMoved-Items` method to display the modified album and reselect a given set of indices.	`private void ReselectMovedItems(`
		`    int[] newIndices)`
		`{`
		`  DisplayAlbum();`
		
		`  // Reselect moved items`
		`  foreach (int x in newIndices)`
		`    lstPhotos.SetSelected(x, true);`
		`}`

6	Add a `Click` event handler for the Move Down button.	`private void btnMoveDown_Click(`
		`    object sender, EventArgs e)`
		`{`

7	Implement this handler similar to the Move Up handler.	`  ListBox.SelectedIndexCollection indices`
		`    = lstPhotos.SelectedIndices;`
		`  int count = indices.Count;`
		`  int[] newIndices = new int[count];`
		
		`  // Move each selection down`
		`  for (int i = count - 1; i >= 0; i--)`
		`  {`
		`    int x = indices[i];`
		`    Manager.MoveItemForward(x);`
		`    newIndices[i] = x + 1;`
		`  }`
		
		`  ReselectMovedItems(newIndices);`
		`}`

Both of these event handlers employ a number of members of the `ListBox` class. Let's walk through the Move Down event handler in detail as a way to discuss our changes as well as these members.

```
private void btnMoveDown_Click(object sender, EventArgs e)
{
```

The method employs a local indices variable to hold the index values of the selected items. As we mentioned earlier, the `SelectedIndices` property is used to retrieve this collection. Also note here how an array of integers is created to hold the resulting index for each photograph after it has been moved:

```
  ListBox.SelectedIndexCollection indices
      = lstPhotos.SelectedIndices;
  int count = indices.Count;
  int[] newIndices = new int[count];
```

A `for` loop is used to iterate through the selected indices, starting from the back of the list. Each photograph is moved to the subsequent position in the collection, using the `MoveItemForward` method we created in the `AlbumManager` class. If you recall, the Move Down button is disabled if the last item is selected, so we know for certain that `x + 1` is a valid index within the collection.

```
        // Move each selection down
        for (int i = count - 1; i >= 0; i--)
        {
          int x = indices[i];
          Manager.MoveItemForward(x);
          newIndices[i] = x + 1;
        }
```

After moving the selected items, we need to redisplay the album within the list and reselect the items we moved. This is common to both methods, so we create a `ReselectMovedItems` method to encapsulate this logic:

```
        ReselectMovedItems(newIndices);
      }
```

This new method appears in step 5. The `SetSelected` method in this method accepts an index into the collection and a flag that indicates whether the item should be selected or deselected.

You can run the application here if you wish. The next section implements the Remove button to complete our application for this chapter.

11.3.3 Removing list items

The Remove button is a bit like the Move Down button. We need to be careful when removing an item that we do not alter the index of additional entries that should also be removed. This is handled in a similar fashion, by iterating through the items starting from the end of the selection list.

Also note that by removing selected photographs, we make an irreversible change to an album. As a result, we should warn users that they are about to make such a change, and give them a chance to cancel the request. A user might be annoyed if they click a button in our application just to see what happens, and cause a change that cannot be undone.

HANDLE THE CLICK EVENT FOR THE REMOVE BUTTON

	Action	Result

1	Add a `Click` event handler for the Remove button.	`private void btnRemove_Click(`
		`    object sender, EventArgs e)`
		`{`
		`  ListBox.SelectedIndexCollection indices`
		`    = lstPhotos.SelectedIndices;`
		`  int count = indices.Count;`

	Action	Result
	HANDLE THE CLICK EVENT FOR THE REMOVE BUTTON *(CONTINUED)*	

2	Implement this handler to confirm that the user really wants to remove the selected photographs.	`string msg;`
		`if (count == 1)`
		`  msg = "Do you really want to remove the "`
		`    + "selected photograph?";`
		`else`
		`  msg = String.Format("Do you really want to "`
		`    + "remove the {0} selected photographs?",`
		`    count);`
		
		`DialogResult result = MessageBox.Show(msg,`
		`  "Remove Photos?",`
		`  MessageBoxButtons.YesNo,`
		`  MessageBoxIcon.Question,`
		`  MessageBoxDefaultButton.Button2);`

3	If the user clicks `Yes`, then remove the selected items, and redisplay the album	`if (result == DialogResult.Yes)`
		`{`
		`  for (int i = count - 1; i >= 0; i--)`
		`    Manager.Album.RemoveAt(indices[i]);`
		
		`  DisplayAlbum();`
		`}`
		`}`

This code is similar in spirit to the code discussed for the Move Down button, so we won't discuss it in detail here. Compile and run the application to see our new buttons in action.

TRY IT! It is typically considered bad form to allow a user to perform an action without supporting the inverse action as well, in this case removing a photo without the ability to add new photos. Insert a new Add button into the Photographs group box that allows the user to add new photographs to the album. You may need to adjust the size of the form to make room for this button.

11.4 RECAP

This chapter discussed list box classes in the .NET Framework, and illustrated the creation and manipulation of items in a new sample application, which we called MyAlbumEditor.

We began with a discussion of the various types of list controls, which we learned are all based on the `ListControl` class. One such class, the `ListBox` class, was the focus of the remainder of our discussion.

We explored functionality supported by list controls generally and additional features specific to list boxes. In our sample application, we illustrated creating a list box first with single selection, and then with multiple selection supported. We enabled and disabled controls based on the number of items selected, and handled the `DoubleClick` event for quick access to a standard operation.

The next chapter continues the discussion on list controls by focusing on the `ComboBox` control. The `ComboBox` control reduces the space required for a list by only displaying the associated list when the user clicks on a small down arrow associated with the control.

There are some additional topics related to `ListBox` controls that warrant further discussion as well. These were left out of this chapter due to space constraints, but fit nicely into the next two chapters on combo boxes and tab controls. The custom formatting of list items is discussed in the next chapter, and the custom drawing of items, which applies to a number of Windows Forms controls, is examined in chapter 13. Both topics apply equally well to `ListBox` and `ComboBox` controls, even though our examples focus on the `ListBox` control we created in this chapter.

CHAPTER 12

Combo boxes

A list box is useful for presenting a list of strings, such as the photographs in an album. There are times when only one item should be selected, or when the extra space necessary to display a list box is problematic or unnecessary. The `ComboBox` class is a type of `ListControl` that displays a single item in a text box and permits selection from an associated list box. Since a user can enter new values into the text box control directly, a `ComboBox` allows additional items to be added much more simply than a `ListBox` control.

This chapter presents various aspects of combo boxes in the .NET Framework, including the following areas:

- Creating `ComboBox` controls
- Handling selection in a combo box list
- Editing the contents of a combo box
- Supporting automatic completion of text in a combo box
- Formatting the display text for items in a list

In addition, we cover a number of other .NET and Windows Forms topics over the course of this chapter, including:

- The `FolderBrowserDialog` class
- Automatic completion in the `TextBox` control
- The .NET formatting interfaces: `IFormattable`, `IFormatProvider`, and `ICustomFormatter`
- Formatting of strings for numeric values
- The `NumberFormatInfo` class

The examples in this chapter continue using the MyAlbumEditor application built in chapter 11. As shown in figure 12.1, over the course of our discussion we add a `ComboBox` control to this application and support alternate formatting for the text displayed for each `Photograph` in the list box.

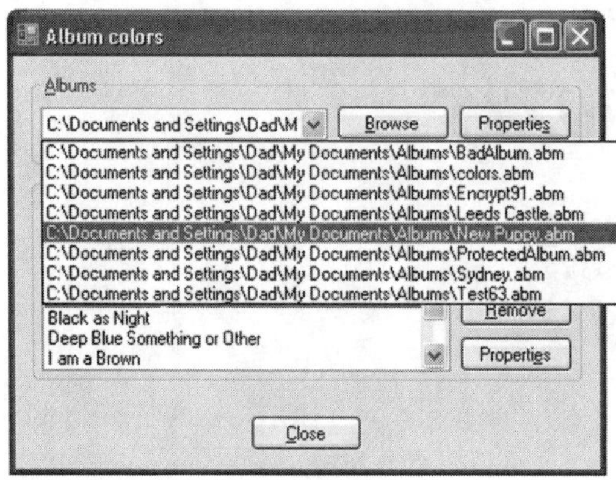

Figure 12.1
The drop-down list for a combo box is hidden until the user clicks the down arrow associated with the control.

12.1 STANDARD COMBO BOXES

A combo box consists of a text box portion and a list portion, and can display its contents in a couple of different ways. The text box can be read only or editable, and the list box control can be visible or hidden. When offering a fixed set of entries, the text box should be read only to prevent the user from modifying the selected entry. Most of the time the list box portion of a combo box is kept hidden to conserve space on the form.

This chapter introduces the `ComboBox` class and discusses some key features of this control class.

12.1.1 The ComboBox class

An overview of the `ComboBox` class is shown in .NET Table 12.1. As you can see, a number of members are reminiscent of members from both the `ListBox` and `TextBox` classes. The `TextBox` area is sometimes called the editable portion of the control, even though it is not always editable, and the `ListBox` area is also referred to as the drop-down portion, since the list drops down below the text box portion for some display styles.

.NET Table 12.1 ComboBox class

The `ComboBox` class is a list control that presents a `TextBox`-like control, also called an edit control, with an associated `ListBox` control. Typically, a user selects a value from the list box for display within the text area. The text area can be editable or not, and the list box can be shown or hidden. When the list box is hidden, the text area displays a down arrow that, when clicked, displays the list of available items.

This class is part of the `System.Windows.Forms` namespace, and inherits from the `ListControl` class. See .NET Table 11.1 for members inherited from this base class.

Public Properties	*AutoCompleteCustomSource*	Gets or sets a custom collection to use when `AutoCompleteSource` is set to `CustomSource`.
	AutoCompleteMode	Gets or sets the automatic completion style for the control.
	AutoCompleteSource	Gets or sets the source for automatic completion strings applied to the control.
	DrawMode	Gets or sets how elements in the list are drawn.
	DropDownStyle	Gets or sets how the edit and list controls appear.
	DropDownWidth	Gets or sets the width of the list portion of the control. The `DropDownHeight` property gets or sets the height of the list.
	DroppedDown	Gets or sets whether the list portion is currently shown.
	Items	Gets or sets the collection of items in the list.
	MaxDropDownItems	Gets or sets the maximum number of items to display in the list portion of the control at any time.
	MaxLength	Gets or sets the maximum number of characters permitted in the text box portion of the control.
	SelectedItem	Gets or sets the currently selected item in the list.
	SelectedText	Gets or sets any text selected in the text box.
	Sorted	Gets or sets whether the items in the list portion are automatically sorted.
Public Methods	FindString	Finds the first item in the list that begins with a given string. A `FindStringExact` method also exists.
	SelectAll	Selects all text in the text box portion of the control.
Public Events	DrawItem	Occurs when an item in an owner-drawn combo box requires painting.
	DropDown	Occurs just before the drop-down portion is displayed.
	DropDownClosed	Occurs when the drop-down portion is no longer visible.
	SelectionChangeCommitted	Occurs when new item has been chosen from the list and the drop-down list is closed.

The various members of the `ComboBox` class are discussed throughout this chapter. This section, along with section 12.2, covers members that access and manipulate the text and list areas of the control. Section 12.2 also covers automatic completion, a feature added for the .NET 2.0 release of the framework.

Members that support automatic formatting of list items are inherited from the base `ListControl` class, and apply equally well to `ComboBox` and `ListBox` controls. This is discussed in section 12.3. The `DrawMode` property, `DrawItem` event, and other aspects of owner drawn lists are discussed in section 13.4.

12.1.2 Creating a combo box

As you might expect, a `ComboBox` control is added to a form much like any other control. The following steps replace the Open button used in chapter 11 with a combo box that displays the album files in the default album directory.

<table>
<tr><th colspan="3">REPLACE THE OPEN BUTTON WITH A COMBOBOX CONTROL</th></tr>
<tr><th></th><th>Action</th><th>Result</th></tr>
<tr><td>1</td><td>In the EditorForm.cs [Design] window, delete the Open button from the form.</td><td>The button and related code are removed from the application. The <code>btnOpen_Click</code> event handler remains in the code.</td></tr>
<tr><td>2</td><td>Drag a <code>ComboBox</code> control into the Albums group box as shown in the graphic.
Settings
<table>
<tr><th>Property</th><th>Value</th></tr>
<tr><td>(Name)</td><td>comboAlbums</td></tr>
<tr><td>Anchor</td><td>Top, Left, Right</td></tr>
<tr><td>DropDownStyle</td><td>DropDownList</td></tr>
<tr><td>DropDownWidth</td><td>400</td></tr>
</table></td><td>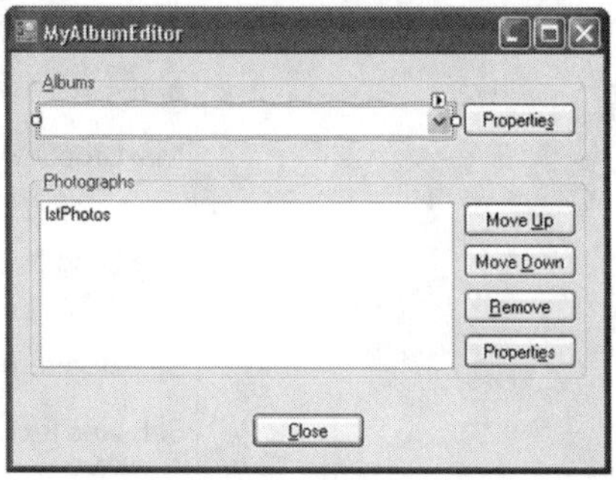
</td></tr>
<tr><td>3</td><td>In the EditorForm.cs file, indicate that we plan to use members of the <code>System.IO</code> namespace.</td><td><pre>. . .
using System.IO;
. . .</pre></td></tr>
<tr><td>4</td><td>In the <code>EditorForm</code> class, override the <code>OnLoad</code> method.</td><td><pre>protected override void OnLoad(
    EventArgs e)
{</pre></td></tr>
</table>

	Action	Result
	REPLACE THE OPEN BUTTON WITH A COMBOBOX CONTROL *(CONTINUED)*	

5	In this method, assign the collection of album files in the default location as the data source for the items in the `ComboBox` control.	`comboAlbums.DataSource`
		`  = Directory.GetFiles(`
		`      AlbumManager.DefaultPath,`
		`      "*.abm");`
		`base.OnLoad(e);`
		`}`
		
		Note: The `GetFiles` method requires the directory to exist, so you may receive a `DirectoryNotFoundException` on this line if you have not created an Albums directory in your MyDocuments folder.

As we saw in our `ListBox` control, the `DataSource` property provides a quick way to assign a collection of objects to the `comboAlbums` control. The static `GetFiles` method in the `Directory` class returns an array of strings containing the filenames in the given directory that match a given search string. In our case, the `DataSource` property is set to the array of album filenames in the default album directory defined by the `AlbumManager` class.

These items are assigned within the `OnLoad` method override. This method raises the `Load` event, which occurs before a form is displayed for the first time. As a result, the items in the combo box are initialized exactly once when the form is about to be displayed.

Our `ComboBox` control is created in the Albums group box at the top of the form. Since we expect to display filenames in this control, we set the default width of the drop-down via the `DropDownWidth` property to be a bit wider than the control itself.

The `DropDownStyle` property is set to `DropDownList`, which is one of three values defined by the `ComboBoxStyle` enumeration. This enumeration is shown in .NET Table 12.2.

.NET Table 12.2 ComboBoxStyle enumeration

The `ComboBoxStyle` enumeration specifies the display behavior of a combo box control. This enumeration is part of the `System.Windows.Forms` namespace.

Enumeration values	DropDown	The text portion of the control is editable. The list portion is only displayed when the user clicks the down arrow button on the control.
	DropDownList	The text portion of the control is not editable. The list portion is only displayed when the user clicks the down arrow button on the control.
	Simple	The text portion of the control is editable. The list portion of the control is always visible.

You can run this program to see the combo box display the available album files, without the ability to actually open an album. This task is part of our next topic.

12.1.3 Selecting combo box items

Selection of items in a combo box is a bit different than in a list box. The `ListBox` class permits multiple selection, and supports various members to manipulate the collections of selected indices or items. In a `ComboBox` control, selection can only occur when the list box portion is displayed, so the members are slightly different.

Both classes support the `SelectedIndexChanged` event, which occurs when the value of the `SelectedIndex` property changes. In the `ComboBox` class, this occurs when the list portion is displayed as the user selects an item in the list. The `SelectionChangeCommitted` event occurs after the user has selected an item and closed the list box.

We should also note here that text displayed in a `ComboBox` control can also be selected, much like text within a `TextBox` control. A number of members relate to the text selected in the control, which is quite different from the selected item in the list. These include the `SelectAll` method and the `SelectedText`, `SelectionLength`, and `SelectionStart` properties. These members behave just like the equivalent methods in the `TextBox` class.

In our MyAlbumEditor application, we need to open the selected album whenever a new item is selected. We can do this by handling the `SelectionChangeCommitted` event for our `ComboBox` control, as illustrated in these steps.

OPEN THE ALBUM SELECTED IN THE COMBO BOX		
	Action	**Result**

1	Add a `SelectionChange-Committed` event handler for the `comboAlbums` control.	`private void`
		`  comboAlbums_SelectionChangeCommitted(`
		`    object sender, EventArgs e)`
		`{`

2	In this handler, retrieve the selected album file using the `Text` property.	`  string path = comboAlbums.Text;`

3	If a new album file is selected, open it.	`  // Don't reopen the existing album`
		`  if (Manager != null && path == Manager.FullName)`
		`    return;`
		
		`  // Open the new album`
		`  OpenAlbum(path);`
		`}`

4	For the `OpenAlbum` method, replace the name of the `btnOpen_Click` method with `OpenAlbum`, and modify the parameters to accept the album file to open.	`private void OpenAlbum(`**`string path`**`)`
		`{`
		
		Note: Also remove the declaration of the `path` variable here (`string path = null;`), since this is now a parameter.

OPEN THE ALBUM SELECTED IN THE COMBO BOX *(CONTINUED)*

	Action	Result

5	Modify this method to use the `CheckAlbumPassword` method in the `Album-Controller` class rather than the `OpenAlbumDialog` method. The remainder of this method remains the same.	`string password = null;`
		`if (path != null && path.Length > 0`
		`&& AlbumController.CheckAlbumPassword(path, ref password))`
		`{`
		`if (CloseAlbum())`
		`return; // cancel open`
		`. . .`
		`}`
		
		`DisplayAlbum();`
		`EnablePhotoButtons();`
		`}`

6	Modify the `OnLoad` method to open the first album in the list, if any.	`protected override void OnLoad(EventArgs e)`
		`{`
		`comboAlbums.DataSource`
		`= Directory.GetFiles(. . .);`
		`OpenAlbum(comboAlbums.Text);`
		
		`base.OnLoad(e);`
		`}`

This code relies on much of the existing code written in chapter 11 to display the album. As you may recall, the `DisplayAlbum` method disables the controls if an `AlbumManager` does not exist, and displays the contents of the open album when a manager is defined. An example of the application with an invalid album selected appears in figure 12.2.

Our final topic in this section is the use of the `FolderBrowserDialog` class to specify an alternate album directory.

12.1.4 Modifying the data source

So far we have assigned items in the combo box using the default album directory. This works fine, but what if the user wants to view albums in an alternate directory? This section addresses this problem by allowing the user to select an alternate album location.

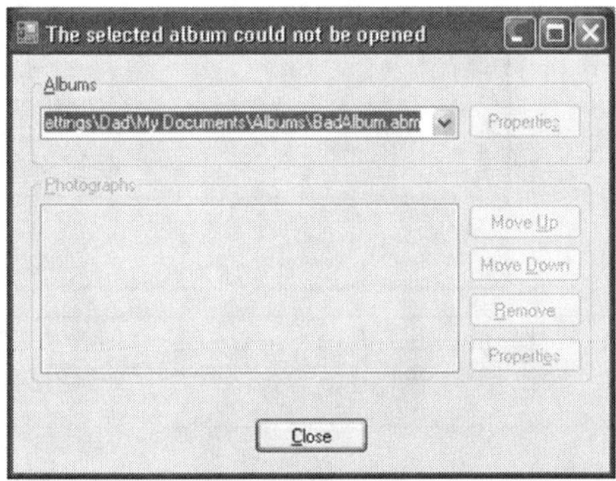

Figure 12.2
When a selected album cannot be opened, only the Close button remains active.

To do this, we insert a new Browse button and display a dialog box that allows the user to locate a new directory. Fortunately for us, Windows Forms provides the `FolderBrowserDialog` class for just this purpose. A summary of this class appears in .NET Table 12.3.

.NET Table 12.3 FolderBrowserDialog class

The `FolderBrowserDialog` class is a common dialog class that allows a user to view and select directory folders. This class is part of the `System.Windows.Forms` namespace, and inherits from the `CommonDialog` class.

Public Properties	Description	Gets or sets the text displayed at the top of the dialog box.
	RootFolder	Gets or sets the base folder. This is the topmost folder the user is able to view in the dialog box.
	SelectedPath	Gets or sets the directory folder currently selected.
	ShowNewFolderButton	Gets or sets whether the New Folder button appears.
Public Methods	Reset (overridden from CommonDialog)	Reset the controls in the dialog box to their default values.

The `FolderBrowserDialog` is a common dialog class in the same class hierarchy as the `OpenFileDialog` and `SaveFileDialog` we used in chapter 6. The following steps add a Browse button to our application and implement a handler that permits the user to request a new album.

<table>
<tr><th colspan="3">ADD A BROWSE BUTTON TO THE MYALBUMEDITOR APPLICATION</th></tr>
<tr><th></th><th>Action</th><th>Result</th></tr>
<tr><td>1</td><td>In the EditorForm.cs [Design] window, resize the <code>ComboBox</code> control and add a Browse button as in the graphic.

Button Settings
<table><tr><th>Property</th><th>Value</th></tr><tr><td>(Name)</td><td>btnBrowse</td></tr><tr><td>Anchor</td><td>Top, Right</td></tr><tr><td>Text</td><td>&Browse</td></tr></table></td><td>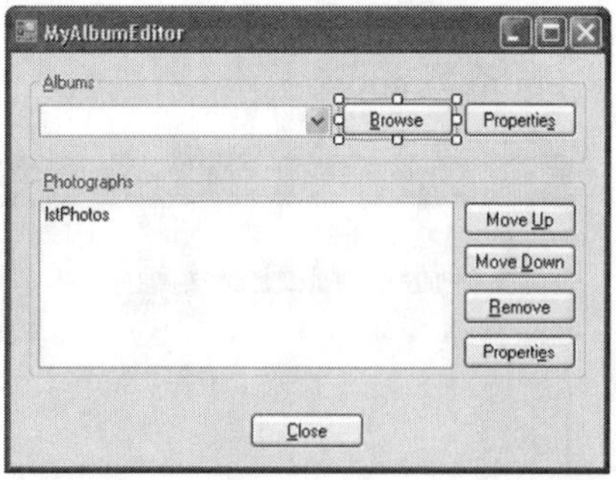
</td></tr>
<tr><td>2</td><td>Handle the <code>Click</code> event for the Browse button.</td><td><pre>private void btnBrowse_Click(
    object sender, EventArgs e)
{</pre></td></tr>
</table>

	Add a Browse button to the MyAlbumEditor application *(continued)*	
	Action	**Result**

3	Implement this handler to display a `FolderBrowserDialog` to prompt the user for the album directory path.	`using (FolderBrowserDialog dlg`
		`        = new FolderBrowserDialog())`
		`{`
		` dlg.Description = "Select an album file "`
		`   + "directory to add to the dialog.";`
		`  dlg.SelectedPath`
		`   = AlbumManager.DefaultPath;`

4	If the user selects a new directory, close the existing album and set the new directory as the source for album files.	`  if (dlg.ShowDialog() == DialogResult.OK)`
		`  {`
		`    if (CloseAlbum())`
		`      return;  // cancel browse`
		
		`    comboAlbums.Text = null;`
		`    comboAlbums.DataSource`
		`      = Directory.GetFiles(`
		`          dlg.SelectedPath, "*.abm");`

5	Open the first album in the list, if any.	`    OpenAlbum(comboAlbums.Text);`
		`  }`
		` }`
		`}`

Compile and run the application to make use of this new dialog class. An example of the resulting `FolderBrowserDialog` is shown in figure 12.3.

12.2 Editable combo boxes

The `ComboBox` control created in our MyAlbumEditor application uses a fixed set of list entries taken from a directory. The `DataSource` property assigns the list of items, and the `DropDownList` combo box style prevents users from editing the displayed text.

In this section we create another `ComboBox` that permits manual updates to its contents by the user. Such a control is useful when you do not wish to display all

Figure 12.3
The Make New Folder button shown here can be hidden by setting the ShowNewFolderButton property to false.

possible entries or you want the user to create additional entries as necessary. It so happens that we have just this situation for the Photographer property of our Photograph class.

Within a given album, there are likely to be only a handful of photographers for the images in that album. A combo box control is a good choice to permit the user to select the appropriate entry from the drop-down list. When a new photographer is required, the user should also be able to enter the name of the new photographer.

Figure 12.4 The drop-down list for the ComboBox control here extends outside the Panel control. This is permitted even though the control is contained within the panel.

We can implement this functionality in the PhotoEditDialog form, as shown in figure 12.4. This list only displays four photographers in the scrollable list, whereas our prior combo box displayed eight album files before scrolling. A ComboBox control displays eight items by default, but provides the MaxDropDown property to assign an alternate maximum.

This change allows us to illustrate and discuss dynamic update of a ComboBox control using the Items property, accepting manual input in the text area of the control and using automatic completion to present users with matching items as they enter text.

12.2.1 Creating a combo box (again)

If you recall, our PhotoEditDialog form includes a Reset button to restore the current settings and an OK button to accept the modified properties. To change the Photographer text box into a combo box, we need to update the methods for these buttons as well. Our first task is to simply replace the existing text box.

REPLACE THE PHOTOGRAPHER TEXT BOX WITH A COMBO BOX		
	Action	**Result**
1	In the PhotoEditDialog designer window, delete the TextBox control associated with the Photographer label.	The generated code for this control is removed from the form.

REPLACE THE PHOTOGRAPHER TEXT BOX WITH A COMBO BOX *(CONTINUED)*		
	Action	**Result**
2	Place a `ComboBox` control on the form where the text box used to be. **Settings** **Property** / **Value** (Name): comboPhotographer MaxDropDown: 4 Sorted: True	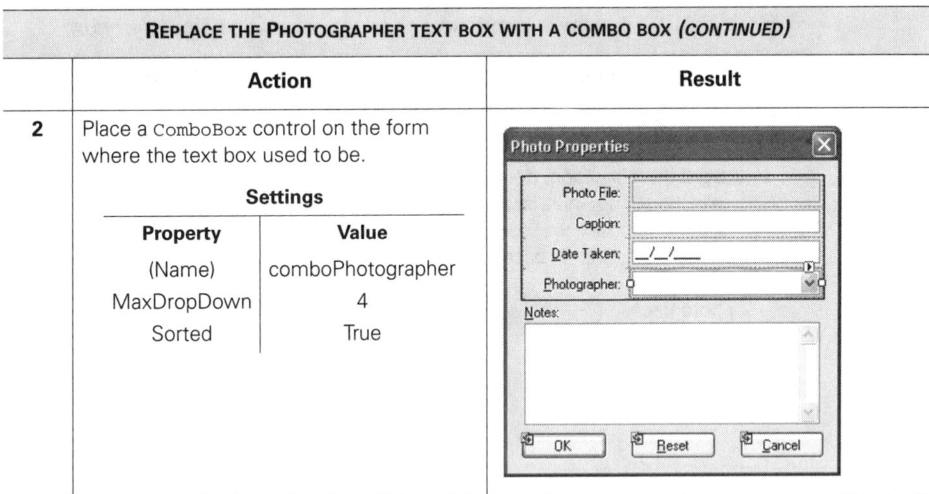

The `Sorted` property sorts the items in the list alphabetically. This property can only be used when assigning items explicitly—that is, it cannot be used when a data source for the list is assigned.

To fill in the items for the combo box, we need to determine the set of photographers defined by the current album. There are a number of ways to do this. One approach is to iterate through the photographs in the album explicitly when initializing the form and fill in the combo box items as required. A more robust approach might be to define a `Photographers` method in the `AlbumManager` class that would retrieve the collection of photographs in the album. This method would preserve the list so it could be reused, and only reconstruct the list when the album changes. As you would expect, we opt for the second approach.

DISPLAY THE CONTENTS OF AN ALBUM IN A LIST BOX		
	Action	**Result**

3	In both the `AlbumManager` class of the MyPhotoAlbum project and the `PhotoEditDialog` class of the MyPhotoControls project, indicate that we use the specialized collections namespace.	`. . .`
		`using System.Collections.Specialized;`
		`. . .`

4	In the `AlbumManager` class, add a private field to hold the collection of photographers in the album.	`private StringCollection _photographers = null;`

<table>
<tr><th colspan="3">DISPLAY THE CONTENTS OF AN ALBUM IN A LIST BOX (CONTINUED)</th></tr>
<tr><th></th><th>Action</th><th>Result</th></tr>
<tr><td>5</td><td>Implement a <code>Photographers</code> property to get this collection. If the collection is not initialized or the album has changed, create the collection based on the current set of photographs.</td><td><pre>public StringCollection Photographers
{
  get
  {
    if (Album.HasChanged || _photographers == null)
    {
      _photographers = new StringCollection();
      foreach (Photograph p in Album)
      {
        // Make sure we add each person only once
        string person = p.Photographer;
        if (person != null && person.Length > 0
            && !_photographers.Contains(person))
        {
          _photographers.Add(person);
        }
      }
    }

    return _photographers;
  }
}</pre></td></tr>
<tr><td>6</td><td>In the <code>PhotoEditDialog</code> class, rewrite the <code>ResetDialog</code> method to initialize the combo box prior to initializing the controls.</td><td><pre>protected override void ResetDialog()
{
  // Fill combo box with photographers in album
  comboPhotographer.BeginUpdate();
  comboPhotographer.Items.Clear();</pre></td></tr>
<tr><td>7</td><td>If an album manager is present, add each photographer in the album to the combo box list.</td><td><pre> if (Manager != null)
  {
    StringCollection coll = Manager.Photographers;
    foreach (string s in coll)
      comboPhotographer.Items.Add(s);
  }
  else
    comboPhotographer.Items.Add(Photo.Photographer);

  comboPhotographer.EndUpdate();</pre></td></tr>
<tr><td>8</td><td>Initialize the <code>Text</code> property of each control to the appropriate setting in the current <code>Photograph</code> object.</td><td><pre> // Initialize form contents
  Photograph photo = Photo;
  if (photo != null)
  {
    txtPhotoFile.Text = photo.FileName;
    txtCaption.Text = photo.Caption;
    mskDateTaken.Text
      = photo.DateTaken.ToString();
    comboPhotographer.Text = photo.Photographer;
    txtNotes.Text = photo.Notes;
  }
}</pre></td></tr>
</table>

	DISPLAY THE CONTENTS OF AN ALBUM IN A LIST BOX *(CONTINUED)*	
	Action	**Result**

9	Modify the `SaveSettings` method to save the photographer entered into the combo box control.	`private void SaveSettings()`
		`{`
		`  Photograph photo = Photo;`
		`  if (photo != null)`
		`  {`
		`    photo.Caption = txtCaption.Text;`
		`    photo.Photographer = `**`comboPhotographer`**`.Text;`
		`    . . .`
		`  }`
		`}`

The `Text` property for the `ComboBox` control retrieves the string entered in the text area of the control. Typically, this corresponds to the string associated with the `SelectedItem` object. This is not always true when the user can manipulate the text value directly, as we see in a moment.

This code also uses the `StringCollection` class from the `System.Collections.Specialized` namespace. This class is a standard collection of `string` values, making it a good choice for situations where a dynamically sized array of strings is required.

12.2.2 Updating a combo box dynamically

As you would expect, the collection defined by the `Items` property can be used to add or remove entries to or from the combo box list. In our case, we want to add an entry whenever the user updates the photographer in the dialog box. The `Leave` event occurs whenever focus leaves a control, and can be used for this purpose.

We make this change with the following steps.

	UPDATE THE COMBO BOX LIST WHEN THE PHOTOGRAPHER CHANGES	
	Action	**Result**

1	Add a `Leave` event handler for the `comboPhotographer` control.	`private void comboPhotographer_Leave(`
		`  object sender, EventArgs e)`
		`{`

2	If the current text is not already in the list, add it to the `Items` collection.	`  string person = comboPhotographer.Text;`
		`  if (!comboPhotographer.Items.Contains(person))`
		`    comboPhotographer.Items.Add(person);`
		`}`

This code only updates the items in the combo box list. The value is assigned to the `Photograph` object when the user clicks the OK button.

The `Leave` event is one many members inherited from the `Control` class. The keyboard and mouse events, the `ContextMenuStrip` property, and other members used throughout this book also apply to `ComboBox` controls in a similar manner.

Members specific to the ComboBox class are often similar to members of the TextBox and ListBox classes. We already discussed the various selection properties and events related both to selection of items in the list and selection of text in the text area. Other members related to these classes are available as well.

For an example that combines these two kinds of members, consider the code in listing 12.1. This code illustrates a TextChanged event handler for the Photographer combo box control. The purpose of this handler is to match the text a user enters with the entries in the list box, in order to automatically complete a user's entry. Windows Forms provides full support for this feature, which we examine in a moment. Listing 12.1 is a good exercise to illustrate how a portion of this feature can be implemented directly.

Listing 12.1 TextChanged event handler for ComboBox control

```
private void comboPhotographer_TextChanged(object sender, EventArgs e)
{
  // See if a matching string exists in the list
  string text = comboPhotographer.Text;
  int index = -1;
  if (text.Length > 0)
    index = comboPhotographer.FindString(text);      // 1 Locates matching list entry

  // Show list box only if a match was found
  if (index < 0)
    comboPhotographer.DroppedDown = false;           // 2 Shows drop-down list
  else
  {
    comboPhotographer.DroppedDown = true;            // 3 Displays first matching entry

    // Display and select remaining portion of matched entry
    string newText = comboPhotographer.Items[index].ToString();
    comboPhotographer.Text = newText;
    comboPhotographer.SelectionStart = text.Length;
    comboPhotographer.SelectionLength = newText.Length - text.Length;
  }
}
```

Let's look at the annotated portions of this listing:

1. The FindString method is available in both the ListBox and ComboBox controls to locate the first entry in the list that matches a given string. Here, we use it to find any list entries that begin with the text entered by the user. The comparison ignores case, so it matches an entry regardless of whether the user enters lower- or uppercase letters.

2. When a match is found, we display the list area of the control so the user can see the matching entries. The DroppedDown property gets or sets whether the list is shown.

❸ The final code in this listing displays the matched entry in the text area, and selects the portion of text the user has not yet entered. This is shown in the graphic here, where the user has entered "Ed" and the remaining text of the first match is selected. If the user enters the letter "w" next as part of the name "Edward," then the selection and drop-down list disappear.

The code in listing 12.1 is only the beginning of automatic completion support for the control. If you add this event handler to your code, you will find that the backspace key does not work correctly, and ideally only the matching items would appear below the text area, rather than the entire list. The purpose of this code is to illustrate additional features of the `ComboBox` control rather than provide a complete implementation.

For a full-featured implementation of this feature, we make use of the automatic completion support built into Windows Forms as part of the .NET 2.0 release.

12.3 AUTOMATIC COMPLETION

Automatic completion of text is supported in text box and combo box controls, including the standard `TextBox` and `ComboBox` classes as well as the more specialized `ToolStripTextBox` and `ToolStripComboBox` classes. This section discusses this feature generally and provides some examples of how to use this feature in code.

12.3.1 Understanding automatic completion

Support for automatic completion, also referred to as auto-completion, essentially boils down to three properties, regardless of the control. The `AutoCompleteMode` property defines the style of completion performed and the `AutoCompleteSource` property defines the source of completion strings. When a custom source is specified, the `AutoCompleteCustomSource` property specifies the custom collection of completion strings.

The `AutoCompleteMode` property represents an `AutoCompleteMode` enumeration value, a summary of which appears in .NET Table 12.4. The mode is set to `None` by default to indicate that automatic completion is not used by the control. When assigned, completion strings may be appended to the user's text, presented as suggestions that the user can select, or both appended and presented for the user. The possible modes are shown in the table.

An example of the `SuggestAppend` completion mode is shown in figure 12.5, where a Web Sites text box is configured to complete a URL string entered by a user. In the figure, the user has entered "www.man" and the system has appended "ning.com" to complete the first matching string, namely "www.manning.com." This is the `Append` mode of completion.

.NET Table 12.4 AutoCompleteMode enumeration

New in 2.0 The `AutoCompleteMode` enumeration specifies if and how automatic completion of text is enabled within a control. This enumeration is part of the `System.Windows.Forms` namespace.		
Enumeration values	*Append*	Appends and selects the remaining characters of the most likely match for the existing string.
	None	Disables automatic completion within the control.
	Suggest	Displays the most likely matches for the existing string in an auxiliary drop-down list associated with the control. The user can select a desired string from this list.
	SuggestAppend	The behavior for both the `Append` and `Suggest` options is applied to the control.

Also in the figure, the list of possible matches is displayed in a drop-down list below the control. As you can see, five sites are listed. The user can click an entry to have it display in the text box. This is the `Suggest` mode of completion.

The code to build the sample shown in figure 12.5 appears in listing 12.2. This code creates two text box controls with automatic completion enabled and lays out these controls in a `TableLayoutPanel`. We discuss the annotated sections in the following paragraphs.

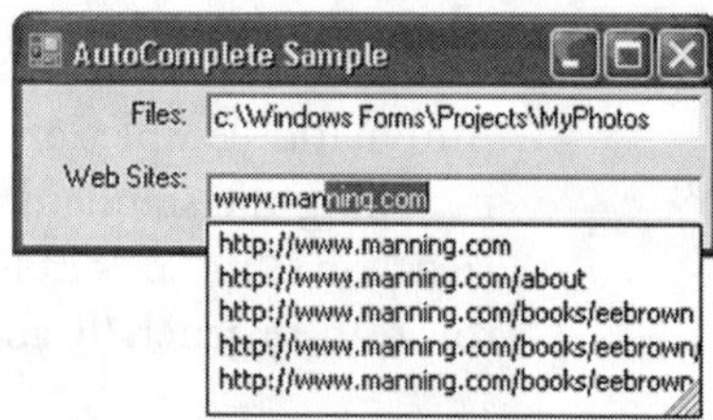

Figure 12.5 Note the corner grip at the bottom right of the drop-down list. This grip is used to resize the drop-down if desired.

Listing 12.2 AutoComplete sample program using TextBox controls

```
using System;
using System.Drawing;
using System.Windows.Forms;

namespace AutoCompleteSample
{
  static class Program
  {
    [STAThread]
    static void Main()
    {
      Form f = new Form();
      f.Text = "AutoComplete Sample";
      f.Size = new Size(300, 100);

      TableLayoutPanel panel = new TableLayoutPanel();
      panel.Dock = DockStyle.Fill;
      panel.ColumnCount = 2;
      panel.ColumnStyles.Add(new ColumnStyle(SizeType.Absolute, 75));
```

Creates TableLayoutPanel ❶

```
            panel.ColumnStyles.Add(new ColumnStyle(SizeType.Absolute, 200));

            Label l1 = new Label();
            l1.Text = "Files:";
            l1.TextAlign = ContentAlignment.MiddleRight;

            Label l2 = new Label();
            l2.Text = "Web Sites:";
            l2.TextAlign = ContentAlignment.MiddleRight;

            TextBox txtFiles = new TextBox();
            txtFiles.Width = 120;
            txtFiles.Anchor = AnchorStyles.Left | AnchorStyles.Right;
            txtFiles.AutoCompleteMode = AutoCompleteMode.Suggest;
            txtFiles.AutoCompleteSource = AutoCompleteSource.FileSystem;

            TextBox txtSites = new TextBox();
            txtSites.Width = 120;
            txtSites.Anchor = AnchorStyles.Left | AnchorStyles.Right;
            txtSites.AutoCompleteMode = AutoCompleteMode.SuggestAppend;
            txtSites.AutoCompleteSource = AutoCompleteSource.AllUrl;

            panel.Controls.Add(l1);
            panel.Controls.Add(txtFiles);
            panel.Controls.Add(l2);
            panel.Controls.Add(txtSites);

            f.Controls.Add(panel);
            Application.Run(f);
        }
    }
}
```

Auto-completes based on file paths ❷

Auto-completes based on URL strings ❸

❶ A `TableLayoutPanel` control is created to handle the layout of the controls on the form. This panel has two columns, with the styles defined so the first column is 75 pixels wide and the second 200 pixels wide. Two labels and two text boxes are placed within this panel.

❷ The first text box uses the `Suggest` completion mode, and is defined to use file system paths as the source for completion strings. The `AutoCompleteSource` enumeration defines the possible sources of completion strings for a control. The complete list of values for this enumeration is shown in .NET Table 12.5.

❸ The second text box uses the `SuggestAppend` completion mode, and is defined to use Uniform Resource Locator (URL) strings from the history and recently used lists as the source for completion strings.

As indicated in .NET Table 12.5, the `Custom` value indicates that a custom collection is used as the source for auto-completion strings. In this case, an `AutoCompleteStringCollection` class must be created to hold the set of completion strings. This class is a standard collection, and supports the various collection methods such as Add and AddRange.

Listing 12.2 illustrates the use of auto-completion in a TextBox control. We can use our PhotoEditDialog form to demonstrate auto-completion in a ComboBox control.

.NET Table 12.5 AutoCompleteSource enumeration

New in 2.0 The AutoCompleteSource enumeration specifies the source for the collection of completion strings when the AutoCompleteMode property is set to a value other than None. This enumeration is part of the System.Windows.Forms namespace.

Enumeration values	*AllSystemSources*	Completion strings consist of all strings indicated by the AllUrl and FileSystem values.
	AllUrl	Completion strings consist of all URLs indicated by the HistoryList and RecentlyUsedList values.
	CustomSource	Completion strings are taken from a custom source, as specified by an associated AutoCompleteStringCollection object.
	FileSystem	Completion strings consist of valid file paths in the file system.
	FileSystemDirectories	Completion strings consist of valid directory names in the file system.
	HistoryList	Completion strings are taken from the URLs in the history list.
	ListItems	Completion strings are taken from the items in the combo box list. Only valid for combo boxes.
	None	No completion source is available, effectively disabling auto-completion.
	RecentlyUsedList	Completion strings are taken from the URLs in the recently used list.

12.3.2 Using auto-completion in a combo box

When you're designing a text box or combo box control, Visual Studio presents the three auto-completion properties in the Properties window. When the AutoCompleteSource is set to Custom, a dialog box is even provided where you can specify a fixed set of custom completion strings.

In the MyAlbumEditor application, the completion strings consist of the photographers shown in the list portion of the ComboBox control. We can enable auto-completion of these values by performing the following step.

ENABLE AUTO-COMPLETION IN THE PHOTOGRAPHER COMBO BOX		
	Action	**Result**
1	In the PhotoEditDialog.cs [Design] window, modify the properties in the `comboPhotographer` control as indicated. **Settings** **Property** / **Value** AutoCompleteMode / SuggestAppend AutoCompleteSource / ListItems	The values are assigned to the control properties in the generated PhotoEditDialog.Designer.cs file.

That's all it takes. The result is similar to what happened with the `TextChanged` event handler code from listing 12.1. Since the combo box already contains a list box, setting the source to the `ListItems` value causes the drop-down list to display when a match is found for the text entered by a user. The result looks much like the `TextBox` example shown in figure 12.5.

Another feature added for the .NET 2.0 release is the ability to format each item in the list according to a specified format. This is our final topic.

12.4 *ITEM FORMATTING*

In chapter 11, we discussed how the `DataSource` and `DisplayMember` properties of the `ListControl` class indicate a source of list items and the property of these items to display in the list. This is useful to display a custom string in the list based on a given property member name.

There are cases, of course, where a property does not exist for the desired display string. The formatting interfaces in .NET allow a common syntax to be defined that can apply to any instance of a class. This section discusses formatting in general and implements this feature for the `Photograph` object in our MyAlbumEditor application.

12.4.1 The formatting interfaces

Three interfaces are related to the formatting of objects in .NET: `IFormattable`, `IFormatProvider`, and `ICustomFormatter`. Each interface requires a single method, as described in .NET Table 12.6.

This section discusses each interface in the table, and provides a sample implementation of the `IFormattable` interface for `Photograph` objects. By the end of this section, the list box in our application will be able to show custom strings as illustrated in figure 12.1 at the start of this chapter.

Note that a custom format can also be defined by overriding the `ToString` method in a newly derived class. For example, we could create a custom `NewPhotograph` class

.NET Table 12.6 Format interfaces

The .NET Framework provides three formatting interfaces. The `IFormattable` interface defines the ability to format an object into a corresponding string representation, the `IFormatProvider` interface defines a mechanism for obtaining an object to control formatting, and the `ICustomFormatter` interface defines the ability to support custom user-defined formatting of an object.

These interfaces are all part of the `System` namespace, and each requires a single method to implement the interface.

IFormattable interface	ToString method	Formats the current object using the specified format and provider
IFormatProvider interface	GetFormat method	Returns an object that provides formatting services for the specified type
ICustomFormatter interface	Format method	Returns a string representation of the given object using the specified format and provider

that defines a new display string as follows. The formatting performed in this code is discussed within this section, so we don't explain it here.

```
public class NewPhotograph : Photograph
{
  public NewPhotograph(string file) : base(file) { }

          public override string ToString()
  {
    return String.Format("Photo: {0} (Taken {1})",
      this.Caption, this.DateTaken.ToString("MMMM dd, yyyy"));
  }
}
```

Of course, our `PhotoAlbum` class employs `Photograph` objects, not `NewPhotograph` objects, so replacing our existing class would take some work. What we need is a way to specify formatting for a class without having to change its definition. This is exactly what the formatting interfaces enable.

12.4.2 Implementing an IFormattable interface

As indicated in .NET Table 2.6, the `IFormattable` interface specifies an alternate form of the `ToString` method. This method has the following signature:

```
string ToString(string format, IFormatProvider fp)
```

The first parameter is a format string; the second is an object that provides formatting information for the type. The syntax supported by the format string is dependent on the class that implements the interface. An `IFormatProvider` interface is used to interpret this string. Typically, an `IFormatProvider` interface is associated with a specific culture.

A *culture*, as you may know, represents a specific language and region. The unique name for each culture is typically a two-letter abbreviation for the language, followed by a dash, followed by a two-letter abbreviation for the country or region. So the string "en-US" represents U.S. English, while the string "en-GB" represents U.K. English. Similarly, "fr-FR" represents French in France, while "fr-CA" specifies French in Canada.

So an `IFormatProvider` interface defines formatting for a specific type, often in the context of an assigned culture. For example, when you're formatting numbers, the currency symbol character changes depending on the type of currency, as do the decimal point and thousands separator characters. For numeric values, the `NumberFormatInfo` class implements the `IFormatProvider` interface in order to define a mechanism for retrieving this information. More on this class in a moment.

First, however, let's implement the `IFormattable` interface for our `Photograph` class. The following steps implement this interface.

<table>
<tr><th colspan="3">IMPLEMENT THE IFORMATTABLE INTERFACE IN THE PHOTOGRAPH CLASS</th></tr>
<tr><th></th><th>Action</th><th>Result</th></tr>
<tr><td>1</td><td>In the Photograph.cs file, modify the class definition to indicate that the <code>IFormattable</code> interface is supported.</td><td><pre>public class Photograph
    : IDisposable, IFormattable
{</pre></td></tr>
<tr><td>2</td><td>Provide an implicit implementation of this interface.
How-to
a. Right-click the newly added "IFormattable" string in the class definition.
b. Under Implement Interface, select the Implement Interface option, as in the graphic.</td><td>A region containing an implementation of this interface is inserted at the end of the file.<pre>#region IFormattable Members
public string ToString(string format,
    IFormatProvider formatProvider)
{
  throw new Exception("The method or "
    + "operation is not implemented.");
}
#endregion</pre></td></tr>
<tr><td></td><td colspan="2">IFormattable
Implement Interface ▸ | Implement Interface
Refactor ▸ | Implement Interface Explicitly</td></tr>
<tr><td>3</td><td>Implement the new <code>ToString</code> method to format the letters c, d, and f as the <code>Caption</code>, <code>DateTaken</code>, and <code>FileName</code> properties, respectively.
Note: We treat lower- and uppercase letters the same. This not required, as some formattable classes interpret upper- and lowercase letters differently.</td><td><pre>public string ToString(string format,
    IFormatProvider fp)
{
  if (String.IsNullOrEmpty(format))
    format = "f";

  char first = format.ToLower()[0];
  if (format.Length == 1)
  {
    switch (first)
    {
      case 'c': return Caption;
      case 'd': return DateTaken.
                  ToShortDateString();
      case 'f': return FileName;
    }
  }</pre></td></tr>
</table>

IMPLEMENT THE IFORMATTABLE INTERFACE IN THE PHOTOGRAPH CLASS *(CONTINUED)*		
	Action	**Result**

4	If the letter d is followed by one or more characters, format the `DateTaken` property using this as the date format string.	`else if (first == 'd')`
		`  return DateTaken.ToString(`
		`      format.Substring(1), fp);`

5	Otherwise, throw a `FormatException` to indicate that the format string is not recognized.	`  throw new FormatException();` `}`

As you can see, this code interprets the given format string to support three characters: c, d, and f. The c character is formatted as the `Caption` property, the d character as the `DateTaken` property, and the f character as the `FileName` property. The `DateTaken` property is additionally formatted according to the `DateTime` formatting syntax using any characters following the d character. We discuss `DateTime` formatting while discussing the `DateTimePicker` control in chapter 14, so we do not go into detail on this subject here.

Some important implementation notes from this code are as follows.

- The .NET Framework requires that all `IFormattable` implementations define a default format when a `null` or empty string is given. The static `IsNullOrEmpty` method in the `String` class checks for this condition.
- For the d character, the `DateTime.ToString` method is called when a date format is specified. The given `IFormatProvider` is passed through to this call. The `SubString` method used in this line returns the portion of the string beginning at the given index.
- When a format string is not recognized, a `FormatException` instance should be thrown to indicate the error. This permits a caller to handle this specific condition in a `catch` block.

By convention, a `ToString` method with either of the two formats and provider parameters is also implemented whenever the `IFormattable` interface is supported. Not wanting to buck convention, we do this as well.

IMPLEMENT STANDARD TOSTRING METHODS IN THE PHOTOGRAPH CLASS		
	Action	**Result**

6	Implement a `ToString` method for the `Photograph` class that accepts a format string.	`public string ToString(string format)`
		`{`
		`  return ToString(format, null);`
		`}`

	Action	Result
IMPLEMENT STANDARD TOSTRING METHODS IN THE PHOTOGRAPH CLASS *(CONTINUED)*		

7	Implement a `ToString` method for the `Photograph` class that accepts an `IFormatProvider`.	`public string ToString(IFormatProvider fp)`
		`{`
		`  return ToString(null, fp);`
		`}`

In our implementation, we ignore the `IFormatProvider` parameter, except when we pass it on to the `DateTime.ToString` method. This parameter becomes important when the current culture or other context information is required to properly format an object.

As previously mentioned, the proper format of a number differs depending on the culture. The .NET Framework defines the `NumberFormatInfo` class to encapsulate this information for a specific culture. Table 12.7 shows some of the formatting codes supported for numeric values, along with related properties from the `NumberFormatInfo` class.

Table 12.7 Standard numeric format codes and associated NumberFormatInfo properties

Code	Description	Default U.S. English Examples	NumberFormatInfo Properties
c, C	Currency format	($49) $49.95	CurrencyGroupSizes CurrencyPositivePattern CurrencySymbol
d, D	Decimal format	-49	NegativeSign PositiveSign
e, E	Scientific or exponential notation	-4.999999e+001 4.995000e+001	NumberDecimalSeparator
g, G	General format	-49 49.95 4,995	NumberGroupSeparator
x, X	Hexidecimal format	ffffffcf	

In addition to the codes shown in table 12.7, a set of numeric format pattern characters is supported. When a numeric format string is longer than a single character, it is treated as a pattern and processed accordingly. A few of the pattern characters are shown in table 12.8. As always, consult the .NET documentation for the complete set of pattern characters. Look for the topic "Custom Numeric Format Strings" in the .NET Framework Developer's Guide.

Table 12.8 Standard numeric formatting characters

Char	Description	Example Pattern	Result for 7649.95
0	A digit is copied to this position. A zero (0) is inserted if no digit is available.	0000 00000.00	7650 07649.95
#	A digit is copied to this position. Nothing is inserted if no digit is available.	#### ######.##	7650 7649.95
.	A decimal character is inserted.	##.##	7649.95
,	A thousands separator is inserted	0,000	7,650

As a quick example that puts much of this discussion together, consider the following lines of code:

```
Type numType = typeof(NumberFormatInfo);
CultureInfo us = CultureInfo.CreateSpecificCulture("en-US");
CultureInfo gb = CultureInfo.CreateSpecificCulture("en-GB");

NumberFormatInfo usInfo = (NumberFormatInfo)us.GetFormat(numType);
NumberFormatInfo gbInfo = (NumberFormatInfo)gb.GetFormat(numType);
Console.WriteLine("USA value is " + (49.95).ToString("c", usInfo));
Console.WriteLine("GB value is " + (49.95).ToString("c", gbInfo));
```

This prints the number 49.95 in currency format for both the US and British cultures. The result of this code is:

```
USA value is $49.95
GB value is £49.95
```

Of course, this code only works if these two cultures are present on the local machine, which may not be true if your machine was installed with a non-English version of the operating system. We discuss cultures in slightly more detail in chapter 15, so we leave this topic for now.

Returning to our MyAlbumEditor application, we certainly want to make use of our `IFormattable` implementation to alter the appearance of items in the list. This is our next topic.

12.4.3 Using formatting in list controls

Formatting is used by a number of classes in the .NET Framework. The list controls, of course, are one such instance, and we look at these in a moment. Another place is in the `String.Format` method.

The `String.Format` method replaces format items in a given string with formatted object strings. The most commonly used override of this method is likely the following:

```
public string Format(string, object[]);
```

In all versions of this method, the `string` parameter can contain zero or more format items, each with this syntax:

```
{index[,alignment][:formatString]}
```

The index is required as are the braces, while the alignment and format string are optional. The index indicates the index into the `object` array of the item for format at this location. By default, the `Object.ToString` method is invoked to retrieve the value of each item. So, for example, the following line would return the string "We have 14 apples and 5 oranges":

```
String.Format("We have {0} {2} and {1} {3}",
              14, 5, "apples", "oranges");
```

The optional alignment indicates the minimum width for the item. The value is padded with spaces if necessary, and justified to the right for a positive alignment and to the left for a negative alignment. The comma is required if an alignment is specified.

The format string is applied when a given object supports the `IFormattable` interface. In this case, the formattable `ToString` method is called to format the string, with the given format string, or `null` if no format string is provided. This is why all classes that implement `IFormattable` should support a `null` format string.

The following code illustrates some examples of using the `String.Format` method. This code assumes a `PhotoAlbum` with three photographs is defined by an `album` variable, with the first `Photograph` defined to have caption "My House" and date taken 1/1/2000 at 5:54 PM.

```
// Set s1 to string "Album has    3 photos"
string s1 = String.Format("Album has {0,4} photos",
                          album.Count);

// Set s2 to string "First photo caption is My House"
string s2 = String.Format("First photo caption is {0:c}",
                          album[0]);

// Set s3 to string "First photo taken on 01/01/2000"
string s3 = String.Format("First photo taken on {0:d}",
                          album[0]);
```

The `ListControl` class defines three formatting properties that can be used to indicate how list items should be formatted within a list. The `FormattingEnabled` property indicates whether formatting can be performed, and defaults to `true`; the `FormatString` property defines the format string; and the `FormatProvider` property defines an `IFormatProvider` to pass to the `ToString` method.

As you may recall, we defined the `PhotoDescriptor` property in the `PhotoAlbum` class to indicate the preferred description method for photographs in the album. We use this property in our MyAlbumEditor application to assign the format of the photographs in the list box.

FORMAT PHOTOGRAPHS IN MYALBUMEDITOR APPLICATION		
	Action	**Result**

1	In the MyPhotoAlbum project, define a `GetDescriptorFormat` method in the `PhotoAlbum` class that returns the format string for the current descriptor setting.	`public string GetDescriptorFormat()`
		`{`
		`  switch (PhotoDescriptor)`
		`  {`
		`    case DescriptorOption.Caption: return "c";`
		`    case DescriptorOption.DateTaken: return "d";`
		
		`    case DescriptorOption.FileName:`
		`    default:`
		`      return "f";`
		`  }`
		`}`

2	In the MyAlbumEditor project, modify the `DisplayAlbum` method in the `EditorForm` class to assign the Photograph's list box format based on the current descriptor setting.
	
	Note: The `Album-EditDialog` form, as you may recall, allows users to modify the descriptor setting.
		`private void DisplayAlbum()`
		`{`
		`  if (Manager == null)`
		`    . . .`
		`  else`
		`  {`
		`    . . .`
		`    lstPhotos.BackColor = SystemColors.Window;`
		
		`    lstPhotos.FormatString`
		`      = Manager.Album.GetDescriptorFormat();`
		`    if (Manager.Album.PhotoDescriptor`
		`          == PhotoAlbum.DescriptorOption.DateTaken)`
		`      lstPhotos.FormatString = "dMMMM dd, yyyy";`
		
		`    lstPhotos.BeginUpdate();`
		`    . . .`
		`  }`
		`}`

As you can see, when the descriptor setting is assigned to `DateTaken`, the default format is replaced with a custom date format. The string used here specifies the full name of the month, two-digit day, and four-digit year, as in "November 12, 2004." The date and time format characters are shown in table 14.4 in chapter 14.

TRY IT! Modify the formatting syntax for the `Photograph` class to support the strings "fb" and "fB." The "fb" format should indicate the base filename of the photo's FileName property, while the "fB" format should indicate the base filename without the extension. To implement these, use the corresponding `GetFileName` methods in the `Path` class. Modify the application code to use these strings so you can see the result.

12.4.4 Implementing custom formatters

The final formatting interface, `ICustomFormatter`, provides an alternate or extended implementation of an existing format. For example, you can override string formatting to output strings in Morse code rather than normal text.[1] The interface

[1] There is an article by Heath Stewart on just this topic at the Code Project site (www.codeproject.com). Search for the article "custom string formatting" and you should find it.

requires a single method that accepts a format string, an object to format, and an `IFormatProvider` to use during formatting:

```
string Format(string, object, IFormatProvider);
```

Typically, this interface is implemented along with the `IFormatProvider` interface and provided to a method like the `String.Format` method to format a custom string. An alternate version of the `String.Format` method accepts an explicit format provider argument:

```
public string Format(IFormatProvider, string, object[]);
```

If a custom formatter is given as the format provider, this version of the `Format` method invokes the `ICustomFormatter.Format` method to construct each item. For this to work, the custom formatter must not interfere with the formatting of unrecognized objects.

It's not clear exactly what a custom formatting interface for our `Photograph` class might perform. Nonetheless, for the sake of an example, listing 12.3 shows an implementation of a `CustomPhotoFormatter` class that allows the color of a photograph at a given pixel to be included in a string. The class recognizes the syntax "pX,Y" where (X,Y) represents the coordinates of a pixel within an image, and outputs the RGB color values for the color at that pixel. It isn't the greatest of custom formatters, but we hope it demonstrates a custom formatter within the context of our application.

Listing 12.3 Sample ICustomFormatter implementation

```
using System;
using System.Drawing;

namespace Manning.MyPhotoAlbum
{
  public class CustomPhotoFormatter
          : IFormatProvider, ICustomFormatter
  {
    // IFormatProvider implementation
    public object GetFormat(Type formatType)
    {
      // Need to check for ICustomFormatter type, not current type
      if (formatType == typeof(ICustomFormatter))
        return this;
      else
        return null;
    }

    // ICustomFormatProvider Implementation
    public string Format(string format,
                         object arg, IFormatProvider provider)
    {
      if (arg == null)
```

```
        throw new ArgumentException("arg cannot be null");

      // Format a Photograph object
      if (!String.IsNullOrEmpty(format) && arg is Photograph)
      {
        Photograph photo = (Photograph)arg;
        if (Char.ToLower(format[0]) == 'p')
        {
          if (format.Length == 1)
            throw new FormatException("X,Y coordinate required");

          // Find coordinates for pixel by splitting on the comma
          string[] points = format.Substring(1).Split(
                                 new char[] { ',' });
          if (points.Length != 2)
            throw new FormatException(
                "Unable to determine X,Y coordinate");

          // Presume X and Y are valid integers
          int x = Int32.Parse(points[0]);
          if (x < 0 || x >= photo.Image.Width)
            throw new FormatException("Width is out of range");

          int y = Int32.Parse(points[1]);
          if (y < 0 || y >= photo.Image.Height)
            throw new FormatException("Height is out of range");
          // Return pixel color as RGB string
          Color c = photo.Image.GetPixel(x, y);
          return String.Format("R{0}G{1}B{2}", c.R, c.G, c.B);
        }
        else    // use default Photograph formatting
          return photo.ToString(format);
      }

      // Handle non-Photograph arguments appropriately
      if (arg is IFormattable)
        return ((IFormattable)arg).ToString(format, provider);
      else
        return arg.ToString();
    }
  }
}
```

This code should be somewhat self-explanatory, so we do not discuss it in detail. We complete this chapter with a suggested exercise and our standard recap.

TRY IT! Create a Console application project and use the `CustomColorFormatter` class in listing 12.3 to experiment with the `String.Format` method that accepts an `IFormatProvider` parameter. Create a pure red image file using Microsoft Paint (mspaint.exe) to test this formatter. The following code should produce the string "The pixel at (100,100) is R255G0B0":

```
photoFormatter = new CustomPhotoFormatter();
Photograph photo = new Photograph("c:\temp\MyRedImage.bmp");
Console.Writeline(String.Format(photoFormatter,
                    "The pixel at (100,100) is {0:p100,100}",
                    photo);
```

12.5 RECAP

This chapter extended our discussion of list controls from chapter 11 by presenting the `ComboBox` class. We saw how combo boxes combine a text control with a list control, and provided examples with both a fixed list of items and an editable list that allowed the user to enter a string manually. We added a combo box to our MyAlbumEditor application as well as the `PhotoEditDialog` form created in chapter 8.

Automatic completion of text is supported in both text box and combo box controls. We looked at a text box example, and modified our `PhotoEditDialog` form to support automatic completion in the newly added `ComboBox` control for the photographer assigned to a photograph.

For our final section, we explored features available in all list controls: item formatting. We looked at the formatting interfaces, namely `IFormattable`, `IFormatProvider`, and `ICustomFormatter`. This diverged into a discussion of formatting in general, the `Format` method in the `String` class, and the `NumberFormatInfo` class, before settling down into an example for our MyAlbumEditor application that altered the formatting of text displayed in the `ListBox` control.

One other topic applies to both `ListBox` and `ComboBox` classes: creating owner-drawn lists. Custom drawing applies to other controls as well, including the `TabControl` class that is the subject of the next chapter. Since we introduce owner-drawn tabs in section 13.3, we save the subject of owner-drawn list items for section 13.4.

CHAPTER 13

Tab controls and pages

Tab controls are used to compact a large amount of data into a single form by segmenting the data into different screens, or *tab pages.* One of the more well-known examples of this construct is the Properties window associated with files and directories in the Windows file system. Right-click a directory in Windows Explorer and select Properties, and a window with a tab control appears. Typically, a directory's Properties dialog box shows a General and a Sharing tab, as well as additional tabs depending on which applications, services, and features are installed on the machine.

This chapter discusses tab controls and tab pages. The following topics are covered:

- Members of the `TabControl` and `TabPage` classes
- Automated scrolling using the `ScrollableControl` class
- Owner-drawn tabs in a `TabControl` object
- Owner-drawn lists in a `ListBox` object
- Copy and paste of controls in Visual Studio

The MyAlbumEditor application continues to serve our needs at this point of the book, so we continue to use it in our examples. Before we modify this application, we create a sample viewer to illustrate the use of tab controls in code. Figure 13.1

Figure 13.1
The tabs for a collection of tab pages can appear above, below, or on either side of the containing tab control.

illustrates this application, which displays the image for each `Photograph` in an album as a separate tab on a form.

Our first topic, as you might guess, is the `TabControl` class.

13.1 TAB CONTROL FUNDAMENTALS

The `TabControl` class is a container for one or more `TabPage` objects, with each `TabPage` instance holding the collection of controls to display on that page. This section presents the classes used to construct tab controls and pages, and creates the form shown in figure 13.1.

13.1.1 The TabControl class

As is our practice, we begin by examining where these controls fit into the Windows Forms class hierarchy, shown in figure 13.2. It is also worth mentioning once again that the complete class hierarchy of all Windows Forms controls appears in appendix C.

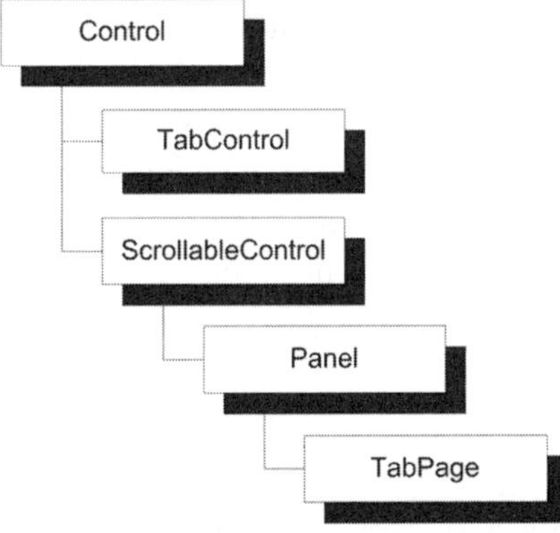

Figure 13.2
The TabPage class is a Panel control that exists within a TabControl object.

As indicated in figure 13.2, the `TabControl` class inherits directly from the `Control` class we first discussed in chapter 3. This class is a container that manages a collection of `TabPage` objects, and provides members to control the location, appearance, and behavior of the pages contained by the control. An overview of this class appears in .NET Table 13.1.

The `TabPage` class inherits from the `Panel` class. This makes sense, as each page in a tab control contains a collection of controls, exactly like a `Panel` object. This also permits tab pages to automatically scroll if the display area exceeds the size of the window by using members inherited from the `ScrollableControl` class. We return to this feature in a moment.

Many of the members in the `TabControl` class are similar to concepts and members we have seen for other Windows Forms controls, so we do not discuss every member shown in .NET Table 13.1. Our first example illustrates the simple creation of tab controls and pages, and demonstrates the scrolling provided by both `TabPage` and `Panel` controls. We then look at tabs within our MyAlbumEditor application, and show how the contents of a page can be copied in Visual Studio from one control to another.

13.1.2 Creating tab controls

Tab controls are often forgotten or perhaps forsaken by programmers. It is not uncommon to see a user interface packed full of buttons, labels, text boxes, and other controls. Often these are organized into group boxes to separate the information into somewhat logical groups. Although such interfaces are functional, they may not be effective since users must process so much information at once. Visual Studio supports multiple tab pages in an interface quite easily, so perhaps programmers will think to use these constructs more often in the future. As a rule of thumb, make sure the controls in each tab page are all related, and try to keep screens and dialog boxes to no more than seven concepts at a time. The number seven here is not completely arbitrary, as user interface research has shown that this is a reasonable maximum number of concepts to present to a user at once.[1]

Let's create a small application to illustrate the creation of a tab control. This is the application shown in figure 13.1, which we fashionably call the TabControlSample application. This application provides a context menu for selecting an album, and displays the image for each `Photograph` in the album on a separate tab page. There are two parts to this code. The first part is shown in listing 13.1, where the context menu and tab control are created and initialized. The second part creates the actual tab pages, and is shown in section 13.2.2.

---

[1] See "The Magical Number Seven, Plus or Minus Two: Some Limits on Our Capacity for Processing Information," by George A. Miller, at www.well.com/user/smalin/miller.html.

.NET Table 13.1 TabControl class

The `TabControl` class is a control that presents a collection of tab pages to the user. Each tab page is represented by a `TabPage` instance. This class is part of the `System.Windows.Forms` namespace, and inherits from the `Control` class. See .NET Table 3.1 for a list of members inherited from the `Control` class, and .NET Table 13.2 for details on the `TabPage` class.

Public Properties	Alignment	Gets or sets the area where tabs are displayed, called the *tab strip*.
	Appearance	Gets or sets how the tabs are displayed, such as a normal tab or 3D button.
	DrawMode	Gets or sets how tabs are drawn in the control.
	HotTrack	Gets or sets whether tabs change their appearance when the mouse passes over them.
	ImageList	Gets or sets the images to use on the control's tabs.
	ItemSize	Gets or sets the default size of each tab.
	Multiline	Gets or sets whether more than one line of tabs can be displayed. The `RowCount` property gets the number of rows currently displayed.
	SelectedIndex	Gets or sets the index of the selected page. The `SelectedTab` property gets or sets the currently selected `TabPage` instance.
	ShowToolTips	Gets or sets whether the tooltip for each tab page should be displayed.
	SizeMode	Gets or sets how tabs for the control are sized.
	TabCount	Gets the number of tab pages in the control.
	TagPages	Gets the control's collection of `TabPage` objects.
Public Methods	GetTabRect	Returns the bounding `Rectangle` for a given tab.
Public Events	DrawItem	Occurs when a tab must be drawn.
	Selecting	Occurs when a tab page is about to be selected. The `Selected` event occurs after page selection. Similar `Deselected` and `Deselecting` events also exist.
	SelectedIndexChanged	Occurs when a new tab page is selected.

Listing 13.1 Sample TabControl application (part 1)

```
using System;
using System.IO;
using System.Windows.Forms;
using Manning.MyPhotoAlbum;
using Manning.MyPhotoControls;

namespace TabControlSample
{
  static class TabControlSampleMain
  {
    [STAThread]
    static void Main()
    {
      // Create tab control
      TabControl tab = new TabControl();          ❶ Creates TabControl
      tab.Dock = DockStyle.Fill;
      tab.ShowToolTips = true;

      // Create anonymous Click handler for Open menu
      EventHandler openHandler = delegate(object s, EventArgs e)
        {
          string path = null;                      Defines inline ❷
          string pwd = null;                       event handler
          if (AlbumController.OpenAlbumDialog(ref path, ref pwd))
          {
            PopulateTabControl(tab, path, pwd);
          }
        };

      // Create context menu
      ContextMenuStrip menu = new ContextMenuStrip();
      menu.Items.Add("&Open Album", null, openHandler);   <-- Defines
                                                              context menu
      // Create and kick off form                             item and
      Form f = new Form();                                 ❸ Click handler
      f.Text = "Right click to open a new album";
      f.ContextMenuStrip = menu;
      f.Controls.Add(tab);
      Application.EnableVisualStyles();
      Application.Run(f);
    }

    static void PopulateTabControl(TabControl tab,
                        string path, string password)
    {
      PhotoAlbum album = tab.Tag as PhotoAlbum;
      try
      {
        if (album != null)        ❹ Disposes of prior album
          album.Dispose();

        album = AlbumStorage.ReadAlbum(path, password);
```

```
          tab.Tag = album;
        }
        catch (AlbumStorageException aex)
        {
          MessageBox.Show("Unable to open album: " + aex.Message);
        }

        // Fill tab control with contents of album
        // ... See section 13.2.2 ...
      }
    }
  }
```

We could, of course, use Visual Studio to create this application. But it is always nice to get your hands dirty every once in a while and create an application by hand, which is what we do here:

1. The `TabControl` class is created much like any other control, so there is not much to discuss here.

2. These lines illustrate a new feature in C# as of .NET 2.0.called *anonymous methods*. Anonymous methods are defined directly in code and not as explicit members of the class. The `delegate` keyword is required to create an anonymous method, and the code for the method follows the keyword in braces. Such methods are especially useful to create one-line event handlers. For example, a `Click` handler for a `button1` button control can be defined inline as follows:

```
button1.Click += delegate(object s, EventArgs e)
    { MessageBox.Show("Received button1 Click event"); };
```

The `delegate` keyword defines the parameters for the delegate as if it were a method definition. The compiler infers the delegate type, in this case `EventHandler`, and wraps the code in an internal method that can be invoked and processed during program execution.

In our code, we define the handler for the Open Album context menu item as an anonymous method. This code calls the `OpenAlbumDialog` method of the `AlbumController` class to select an album, and then invokes the `PopulateTabControl` method to process this album. This code also illustrates how objects defined outside of an anonymous method can be used within it, as it incorporates the local `tab` variable into the call to the `PopulateTabControl` method

3. The `Items` property of the `ContextStripMenu` class includes an `Add` method that accepts the text for the menu item, an image to display for the item, and the `Click` event handler to assign for the item. This is a convenient way to create a menu item dynamically, which we do in our code.

4. The `PopulateTabControl` method is where the tab pages are created, so we defer most of this implementation to the next section. Here we simply create the

`PhotoAlbum` required for the method, disposing of any prior album if necessary. `Bitmap` objects are, by their very nature, somewhat large, and reference file system resources when created from a filename as we do in our `Photograph` class. So it is important to clean up these objects as quickly as possible. If you run this application without this disposal logic and open a few albums, you will see that your memory utilization increases rather dramatically.

Overall, the code in listing 13.1 creates a single `TabControl` object docked to fill the entire window area of a standard resizable form. The title bar of the form tells users to right-click so they can view the context menu—perhaps not the greatest of interfaces, but it works for our purposes.

You can run this application if you wish, although you will find that a very empty `TabControl` object does not do very much. If you do build this application, make sure you reference the two `Manning` libraries required by this code.

We complete this code with `TabPage` controls in the next section.

13.2 TAB PAGE FUNDAMENTALS

Tab pages are the heart and soul of a tab control. They define the tabs displayed to the user and the layout of controls that appear when each page is displayed. This section presents the `TabPage` class and extends the application began in the prior section to include the required tab pages.

13.2.1 The TabPage class

An overview of the `TabPage` class appears in .NET Table 13.2. As you can see, the `TabPage` class adds very little functionality to the base `Panel` class. If the parent `TabControl` enables tooltips, the `ToolTipText` property defines the text for this tip. Similarly, if the parent control defines an `ImageList` setting, then the `ImageIndex` property identifies the image to display on each tab. We discuss image lists in chapter 16.

.NET Table 13.2 TabPage class

The `TabPage` class represents a `Panel` object with an associated tab that exists within a `TabControl` object. It contains the set of controls for a single *sheet*, or *page*, of the tab control. The appearance and location of the tab is controlled by the `TabControl` class, as discussed in .NET Table 13.1.

This class is part of the `System.Windows.Forms` namespace, and inherits from the `Panel` class. The `Panel` class is discussed in .NET Table 7.6.

Public Properties	ImageIndex	Gets or sets an index of the image in the parent tab control's `ImageList` to display on the tab for this page
	Text (overridden from Control)	Gets or sets the text to display on the tab for this page
	ToolTipText	Gets or sets the tooltip to display for this page's tab

Normally, the .NET Framework displays any assigned text and image on each tab automatically. If the `DrawMode` property for the containing `TabControl` object is set to `OwnerDrawFixed`, then the tab must be custom drawn by an application. In this case, the `DrawItem` event for the `TabControl` occurs each time a tab must be drawn. Owner-drawn tabs are discussed in section 13.3.

13.2.2 Creating tab pages

With this in mind, we can finish the application begun in listing 13.1 by providing a complete implementation for the `PopulateTabControl` method. This code appears in listing 13.2.

Listing 13.2 Sample TabControl application (part 2)

```
static void PopulateTabControl(TabControl tab,
                    string path, string password)
{
  PhotoAlbum album = tab.Tag as PhotoAlbum;
  try
  {
    if (album != null)
      album.Dispose();

    album = AlbumStorage.ReadAlbum(path, password);
    tab.Tag = album;
  }
  catch (AlbumStorageException aex)
  {
    MessageBox.Show("Unable to open album: " + aex.Message);
  }

  // Fill tab control with contents of album
  try
  {
    tab.SuspendLayout();
    tab.TabPages.Clear();
    // Creates a tab page for each photograph
    foreach (Photograph p in album)
    {
      PictureBox pbx = new PictureBox();
      pbx.Dock = DockStyle.Fill;
      pbx.Image = p.Image;
      pbx.SizeMode = PictureBoxSizeMode.AutoSize;

      string file
          = Path.GetFileNameWithoutExtension(p.FileName);
      TabPage page = new TabPage(file);
      page.BorderStyle = BorderStyle.FixedSingle;
      page.ToolTipText = p.FileName;
      page.AutoScroll = true;
      page.AutoScrollMinSize = pbx.Image.Size;
      page.Controls.Add(pbx);
```

5 Creates auto-sized PictureBox

6 Creates scrollable TabPage

```
          tab.TabPages.Add(page);
        }
      }
      finally
      {
        tab.ResumeLayout();
      }
    }
```

❺ The PictureBox object created here uses the AutoSize value for the SizeMode property setting. This causes the control to resize automatically to fit the actual size of the contained image. As a result, our PictureBox may well be much larger than the size of the containing TabPage object.

❻ The TabPage for the photograph uses the base filename for the name of the tab, and the complete filename as the tooltip. Scrolling is enabled in the control by setting AutoScroll to true, and the minimum size of the scrolling area is set to the actual size of the photographic image. See the subsequent discussion on scrolling for more detail on this feature.

The code in listing 13.2 creates the required tab pages for each image, resulting in the dialog box previously shown in figure 13.1. One interesting feature of these tab pages is their ability to scroll.

Scrolling in Panel and Form controls is enabled by the ScrollableControl class. This class, described in .NET Table 13.3, defines four main properties to manage scrolling within the control.

The AutoScroll property defines whether the control allows scrolling at all. In listing 13.2, this property is set to true to allow our tab page to scroll the contained picture box. If this property is set to false, the other scrolling properties are ignored.

The AutoScrollMinSize property defines the scrollable area. This must be at least as large as the area occupied by the page's contents to ensure that the user can view everything inside. In listing 13.2, to view the entire image, we set this value to the size of the contained image. We cannot use the size of the PictureBox control here because the updated size for this control is not set until the new layout for the form is determined, which is likely after our code has completed. Strictly speaking, the image size is slightly smaller than the size of the PictureBox, but it is close enough for our purposes.

To get a more exact minimum size, we could define the AutoScrollMargin property to account for the edges of the control. This property can ensure that the scrollable area goes slightly beyond the edge of any contained controls. In listing 13.2, we would add a couple of pixels on each side for the border plus the values defined by the PictureBox control's Padding property. The Padding property is inherited from the Control class, and gets or sets the Padding structure

.NET Table 13.3 ScrollableControl class

The `ScrollableControl` class represents a control that supports automated scrolling. This class is part of the `System.Windows.Forms` namespace and inherits from the `System.Windows.Forms.Control` class. This class is not typically used directly. Instead, derived classes such as `Form` and `Panel` are used. See .NET Table 3.1 for members inherited from the `Control` class.

Public Properties	AutoScroll	Gets or sets whether the user can scroll the container to any contents placed outside of its visible boundaries.
	AutoScrollMargin	Gets or sets the extra margin to add to the container's contents for scrolling purposes.
	AutoScrollMinSize	Gets or sets the `Size` object representing the minimum height and width of the scroll bars in pixels.
	AutoScrollPosition	Gets or sets the `Point` within the virtual display area to appear in the upper-left corner of the visible portion of the control.
	DockPadding	Gets or sets any extra padding for the inside border of this control when it is docked.
	HorizontalScroll	Gets the `HScrollProperties` object that defines how horizontal scrolling occurs.
	VerticalScroll	Gets the `VScrollProperties` object that defines how vertical scrolling occurs.
Public Methods	ScrollControlIntoView	When scrolling is enabled, adjusts the scrollable area so the given `Control` is visible in the viewable area. The `Control.AutoScrollOffset` property defines where the control is scrolled to when passed to this method.
Public Events	*Scroll*	Occurs when the client area is scrolled, whether by code or the user.

representing the internal margin settings for the control. This would require the `System.Drawing` namespace, but would result in something like this:

```
page.AutoScrollMargin = new Size(4 + pbx.Padding.Horizontal,
                                 4 + pbx.Padding.Vertical);
```

The final scrolling property is perhaps the most complex. The `AutoScrollPosition` property defines what coordinate of the scrollable area is placed at the upper-left corner of the viewable area. This property can be used in code to adjust exactly what information is shown within the viewable area of the control.

TRY IT! The TabControl in listing 13.1 is created with the default behavior. You can change the location and style for the tabs by altering the Alignment and Appearance properties. Try setting these properties to alternate values to see how the control then appears. Also set the Multiline property to true and resize the form to see how multiple rows of tabs are displayed. Feel free to experiment with other properties as well.

For a more interesting change, note that each image in listing 13.2 is created and displayed in a PictureBox control even if the user never clicks on the associated tab. This, of course, takes some time and may allocate a lot of memory for a large album. Fix this by handling the Selecting event in the TabControl to create the PictureBox control only if the user clicks on the tab. This may still allocate a lot of memory, but only if the user actually clicks on every tab. Of course, you still need to create the image for the first page that always appears to the user.

To address the memory issue, handle the Deselected event on the tab control to release the image associated with the Photograph when the user clicks away from the tab. This has to properly interact with the Selecting event to re-create the image as required, but ensures the images not currently in view do not lock up any system resources.

This example is a good reminder that a Windows Forms designer window is not needed to lay out a Windows Forms application. You can create tabs and pages directly in code, including altering the contents of a form in response to various events.

Of course, managing numerous controls on multiple tab pages gets rather confusing without a tool such as Visual Studio. In fact, it gets confusing even with Visual Studio, as the code for the tabs, pages, and controls all appears in the same source file.

We look at how to use Visual Studio to create tab controls and pages next, and talk about some approaches that reduce some of the inherent complexity of a multipage control in chapter 14.

13.2.3 Enclosing existing controls in a tab page

In this section we return our attention to the MyAlbumEditor application, and replace the existing Photographs group box with a tab control. The controls previously placed in the Photographs group box still exist, but within a TabPage rather than a GroupBox control. In this section we simply make the change illustrated in figure 13.3. We add more tab pages in future chapters.

As you can see, the ListBox and four Button controls have been moved inside a Photos tab page. To make this change, we need to delete the GroupBox control in Visual Studio. If we delete the group box directly, the contained controls are also deleted. While we could re-create the ListBox and Button controls inside a new TabPage control, it would be much nicer if we could somehow move the controls into a tab page directly.

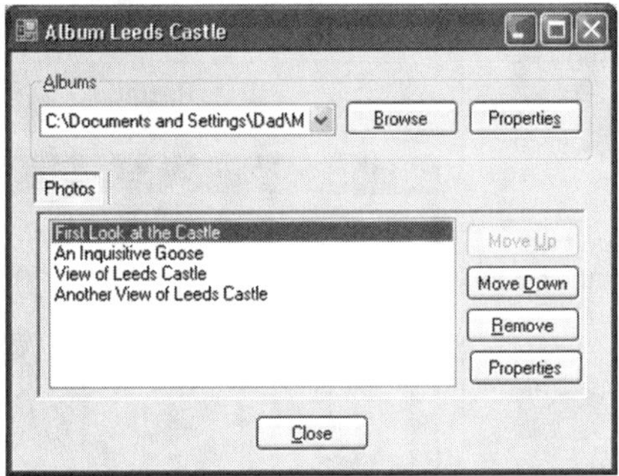

Figure 13.3
A tab control can display tabs or buttons for each tab page. Here a flat button is shown.

The solution is to use cut and paste just like you might when moving text around in a document. We cut the controls from the group box and then paste them inside a tab page. The steps required are as follows.

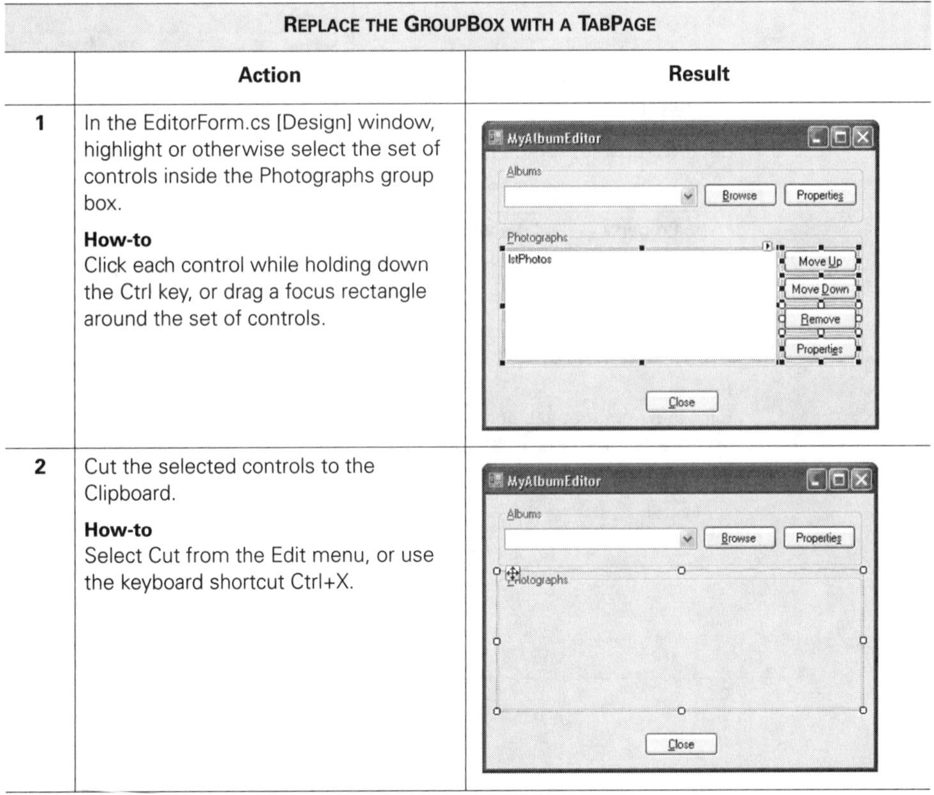

REPLACE THE GROUPBOX WITH A TABPAGE

	Action	Result
1	In the EditorForm.cs [Design] window, highlight or otherwise select the set of controls inside the Photographs group box. **How-to** Click each control while holding down the Ctrl key, or drag a focus rectangle around the set of controls.	
2	Cut the selected controls to the Clipboard. **How-to** Select Cut from the Edit menu, or use the keyboard shortcut Ctrl+X.	

REPLACE THE GROUPBOX WITH A TABPAGE *(CONTINUED)*		
	Action	**Result**
3	Delete the Photographs group box control from the form.	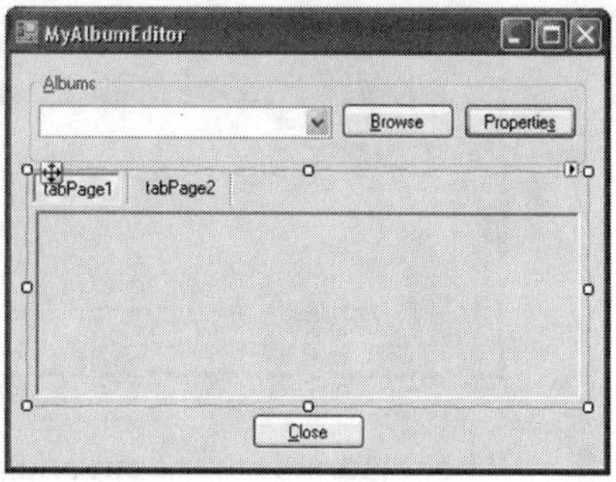
4	Drag a `TabControl` object onto the form, and resize it to be about the same size as the deleted group box. **Settings** **Property** / **Value** (Name) / tcPhotos Appearance / FlatButtons Anchor / Top, Bottom, Left, Right	
5	Paste the cut controls inside the first `TabPage` control, and resize them to fit the page. **How-to** Right-click within the `tabPage1` control and select Paste.	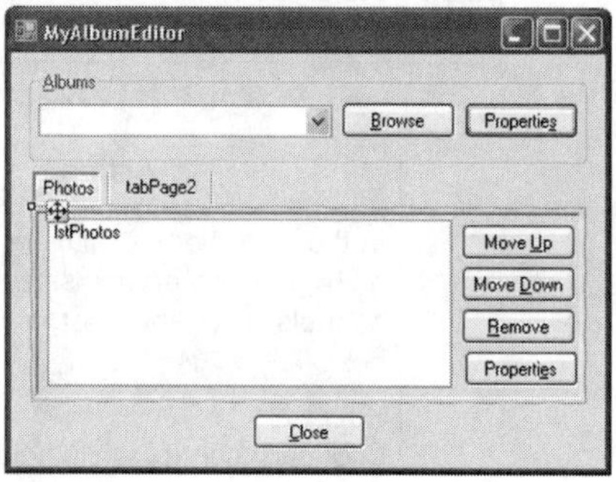
6	Set the properties for the tab page. **Settings** **Property** / **Value** (Name) / pagePhotos Text / Photos	
7	Remove the `tabPage2` control. **How-to** Click the `tabPage2` tab and select Remove Tab from the `TabControl`'s smart tag menu. TabControl Tasks Add Tab Remove Tab	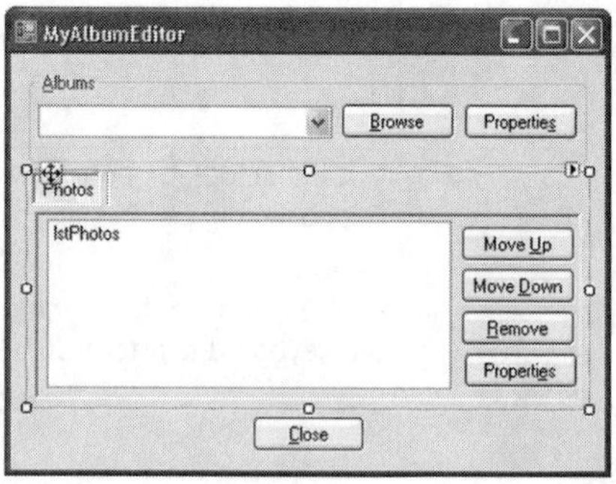

	Replace the GroupBox with a TabPage *(continued)*	
	Action	**Result**
8	Manually reestablish the `DoubleClick` and `SelectedIndexChanged` event handlers for the list box, and the `Click` handlers for each of the four button controls. **How-to** Use the list of Events for each control, and select the existing methods from the appropriate drop-down lists.	The event handlers for the controls are reassigned to the appropriate events. **Note:** This step is required whenever a control is cut from one location and pasted into another. The event handlers are not preserved, since they may not be valid in their new context. This does not apply to properties, which are preserved when cutting and pasting controls.
9	In the EditorForm.cs code file, replace all occurrences of the string "`grpPhotos`" with the string "`pagePhotos`".	This replaces our prior use of the `grpPhotos` `GroupBox` control with the new `pagePhotos` `TabPage` control.

The Photographs group box is now replaced with a Photos tab page. The `Appearance` property causes the tab control to display buttons rather than tabs, as shown in the table. I was hoping to set the `Alignment` property to `Left` so the tab would appear on the left side of the control, but this is broken when visual styles are enabled[2] so this was not possible.

Compile and run the application to make sure the controls still behave as expected, including the selection of multiple list items. We add a second `TabPage` control in chapter 14 as part of our discussion on the `MonthCalendar` class.

In this chapter, our next topic is one we have studiously avoided thus far: the custom drawing of controls. The `DrawMode` property of the `TabControl` class allows a tab to be custom drawn, and presents a reasonable opportunity to discuss this concept.

13.3 Owner-drawn tabs

There are times when changes to a standard control are desired. There may be functionality that requires such a change, or simply a desire to improve the usability or appearance of a form. Whatever the reason, some changes require the ability to modify how a control displays its contents. For the `TabControl` object, this often involves customizing the tabs for each page in the control.

This section discusses the members supported by the `TabControl` class to enable custom-drawn tabs. We begin with a discussion of the relevant members, as well as the classes provided by the `System.Drawing` namespace to support such an effort.

---

[2] According to a post on the Microsoft Forums, this is an OS limitation in the `WC_TABCONTROL` window class that the `TabControl` class wraps. I'm not sure how a "limitation" is different from a defect, but you can disable visual styles in the `Program` class if you would like to see a left-aligned tab actually work.

We show how to create a class that encapsulates a custom tab, and put this class to use in the AlbumViewer application created at the start of this chapter.

13.3.1 The DrawItem event

The DrawItem event is used by a number of classes to draw an item contained within some sort of larger collection. Classes that define this event include the ComboBox, ListBox, ListView, and TabControl classes. In the TabControl class, this event occurs whenever a tab should be drawn and the DrawMode property is set to the OwnerDrawFixed value.

The DrawMode property in the TabControl class gets or sets a TabDrawMode enumeration value. By default, this property is Normal to indicate that Windows Forms should handle the drawing of each tab automatically. When set to Owner-DrawFixed, each tab must be drawn manually.

All classes that support the DrawItem event employ the DrawItemEventArgs class to define the data associated with the event. An overview of this class appears in .NET Table 13.4.

When a DrawItem event occurs for a TabControl object, the properties of the corresponding DrawItemEventArgs object are assigned as you might expect. The Bounds property gets the rectangle for the tab to draw, while the Font and

.NET Table 13.4 DrawItemEventArgs class

The DrawItemEventArgs class defines the event data necessary to manually draw an element of a control. Controls with a DrawItem event that use this class include the ComboBox, ListBox, ListView, and TabControl classes. This class is part of the System.Windows.Forms namespace, and inherits from the System.EventArgs class.

Public Properties	Bounds	Gets the Rectangle of the area to be drawn with respect to the entire area for the object.
	Font	Gets a suggested Font to use for any text. Typically, this is the parent's Font property.
	ForeColor	Gets a suggested Color object to use for foreground elements, such as text.
	Graphics	Gets the Graphics object to use for painting the item.
	Index	Gets the index of the item to be painted. The exact meaning depends on the type of object.
	State	Gets additional state information on the object, using the DrawItemState enumeration. Examples include whether the item is selected, enabled, has the focus, or is disabled.
Public Methods	DrawBackground	Draws the Bounds rectangle with the default background color.
	DrawFocusRectangle	Draws a focus rectangle in the Bounds area.

FontColor properties provide the font information for the parent TabControl object. The Graphics property gets an appropriate drawing object, and the Index property gets the zero-based index of the TabPage associated with the tab to be drawn.

The State property defines various state information for the tab, using or'd values from the DrawItemState enumeration. For example, the DrawItemState.Focus value is set if the tab currently has the focus.

Within a DrawItem event handler, members of the System.Drawing namespace are normally used to draw the custom tab. This namespace provides various graphics functionality based on the GDI+ functionality built into the Windows operating system. A summary of the types in this namespace is shown in .NET Table 13.5. The namespace is too large to capture in this one-page table, but the types shown give you an idea of the functionality provided by this namespace.

We have already seen the Bitmap class defined by this namespace, and have utilized the Point structure when examining mouse coordinates in chapter 7. This chapter examines a number of drawing types related to custom-drawn controls, including the Graphics class and Color structure. Other types in this namespace are presented later in the book, most notably in chapter 17 on creating custom controls.

13.3.2 Drawing page tabs

So let's draw a custom tab within a TabControl object. We could create a TabControl object directly in a program and manipulate the members to perform drawing as required. This would employ code something like this:

```
TabControl tab = new TabControl();
tab.DrawMode = TabDrawMode.OwnerDrawFixed;
tab.DrawItem += new DrawItemEventHandler(HandleDrawItem);
```

The program would then need to assign this tab control to a form, and implement a HandlerDrawItem method that accepts the sender as an object parameter and the event data as a DrawItemEventArgs parameter. While this would work just fine, another alternative is to create a custom tab control that encapsulates the required functionality so it could be used in more than our sample program. We pursue this latter approach, since it is normally good to encapsulate functionality where possible.

Rather than artificially shove a solution into our carefully crafted MyPhotoAlbum application, we modify the sample AlbumViewer application shown in listings 13.1 and 13.2. Our new control is a standard tab control that also supports a custom color for the text on the tab. This control adds two properties to the TabControl class. A TabColor property gets or sets the color for a normal tab, and a SelectedTabColor property gets or sets the color of the currently selected tab.

The code for this control, which we call the ColorTabControl class, is shown in listing 13.3. For simplicity, this control is part of the AlbumViewer namespace. In a production application, such controls are normally encapsulated in a separate control library so they can be reused as required.

.NET Table 13.5 System.Drawing namespace

The `System.Drawing` namespace provides access to basic graphics functionality provided by the graphical device interface (GDI+). The classes in this namespace are used when drawing to any display device such as a screen or printer, and to represent drawing primitives such as rectangles and points.

Classes	Brush	An abstract class representing an object used to fill the interior of a graphical shape. For example, the `Graphics.FillRectangle` method uses a brush to fill a rectangular area on a drawing surface. Classes derived from this class include the `SolidBrush` and `TextureBrush` classes.
	Brushes	A sealed class that provides `Brush` objects for all standard colors. For example, the `Brushes.Red` property can be used to fill shapes with a solid red color.
	Font	Defines a style for drawing text. This includes the font style and size as well as the font face.
	Graphics	Represents a GDI+ drawing surface. Members of this class draw shapes, lines, images, and other objects on a drawing surface.
	Image	An abstract class for image objects such as `Bitmap`.
	Pen	Represents an object used to draw lines and curves. A pen can draw a line in any color and specify styles such as line widths, dashes, and ending shapes (such as arrows). For example, the `Graphics.DrawRectangle` method uses a pen to draw the outline of a rectangular area on a drawing surface.
	Region	Represents the interior of a graphical shape composed of rectangles and paths.
	SystemColors	A sealed class that provides `Color` objects for the colors configured in the local Windows operating system. For example, the `SystemColors.Control` property returns the color configured for filling the surface of controls. Similar `System` classes also exist for predefined `Brush`, `Pen`, and `Icon` objects based on the local system configuration.
Structures	Color	Defines a specific color. A number of static colors are defined, such as `Color.Red`, or custom colors can be created.
	Point	A two-dimensional point as an integral x and y coordinate. The `PointF` structure defines a point with floating point values.
	Rectangle	Stores the location and size of a rectangular region as integral coordinates within a two-dimensional area. The `RectangleF` structure defines coordinates as floating point values.
	Size	Represents a rectangular region as an integral width and height. The `SizeF` structure uses floating point values.

Listing 13.3 A custom tab control class

```
using System;
using System.Drawing;
using System.Windows.Forms;

namespace AlbumViewer
{
  public partial class ColorTabControl : TabControl
  {
    public ColorTabControl()
    {
      base.DrawMode = TabDrawMode.OwnerDrawFixed;
    }

    private Color _tabColor;
    private Color _selTabColor;

    public new TabDrawMode DrawMode
    {
      get { return TabDrawMode.OwnerDrawFixed; }
    }

    public Color TabColor
    {
      get { return _tabColor; }
      set { _tabColor = value; }
    }

    public Color SelectedTabColor
    {
      get { return _selTabColor; }
      set { _selTabColor = value; }
    }

    protected override void OnDrawItem(DrawItemEventArgs e)
    {
      base.OnDrawItem(e);
      TabPage page = TabPages[e.Index];

      Brush b;
      if (e.Index == SelectedIndex)
        b = new SolidBrush(SelectedTabColor);
      else
        b = new SolidBrush(TabColor);

      StringFormat sf = new StringFormat();
      sf.LineAlignment = StringAlignment.Center;
      sf.Alignment = StringAlignment.Center;

      if (Alignment == TabAlignment.Right)
      {
        sf.FormatFlags = StringFormatFlags.DirectionVertical;
        e.Graphics.DrawString(page.Text, e.Font, b, e.Bounds, sf);
      }
```

❶ **Assigns DrawMode property**

❷ **Gets page associated with tab**

❸ **Creates solid brush object**

❹ **Uses vertical text for right-hand tabs**

```
        else if (Alignment == TabAlignment.Left)
        {
          sf.FormatFlags = StringFormatFlags.DirectionVertical;

          Bitmap bmp = new Bitmap(e.Bounds.Width, e.Bounds.Height);
          Graphics g = Graphics.FromImage(bmp);
          g.DrawString(page.Text, e.Font, b,
                  bmp.Width/2 - 1, bmp.Height/2 - 1, sf);
          g.Dispose();

          bmp.RotateFlip(RotateFlipType.
              Rotate180FlipNone);
          e.Graphics.DrawImage(bmp, e.Bounds);
        }
        else
        {
          e.Graphics.DrawString(page.Text, e.Font, b, e.Bounds, sf);
        }
      }
    }
  }
```

5 Rotates bitmap text for left-hand tabs

As you can see, the ColorTabControl class in listing 13.3 is based on the TabControl class. We override the OnDrawItem method to customize the drawing of each tab. Note how we invoke OnDrawItem in the base class to invoke any registered event handlers for the event, and then use the Graphics.DrawString method to draw the text for the associated page into the tab area. Let's take a closer look at this listing:

1. The constructor for the class assigns the DrawMode property for the base class to OwnerDrawFixed to indicate that the control draws its own tabs. To prevent a programmer from resetting the DrawMode property to Normal, we also define a new DrawMode property that only permits a get accessor.[3]
2. The DrawItemEventArgs class provides an Index property that identifies the index for the current tab. The TabPages property retrieves the TabPage at this index.
3. The System.Drawing namespace provides two classes to specify the color when drawing objects. The Pen class is used to draw lines, and the Brush class is used to draw regions. Drawing text requires a Brush object since characters have thickness and shape. The SolidBrush class uses a single color for the entire region. In our code, the TabColor property provides the color to draw for normal tabs, and the SelectedTabColor property defines the color to draw for the displayed tab.
4. Ultimately, the DrawString method is used to draw the text for the tab. When tabs are aligned at the top or bottom, this is straightforward. For tabs aligned at the left

[3] As we learn in chapter 17, to use this class in Visual Studio we would also want to set the new DrawMode property's Browsable attribute to false so the property does not appear in the Properties window.

or right, we need to draw the text vertically. The `StringFormat` class defines formatting information for drawing text, such as how to align the text within the region. A number of formatting flags are set via the `StringFormatFlags` enumeration in the `FormatFlags` property. In particular, the `DirectionVertical` value indicates that text should be drawn vertically.

5 One problem with vertical text is that it is always drawn from top to bottom. This is fine for a right-hand tab, but a left-hand tab should draw its text from the bottom up. To accomplish this, we create a `Bitmap` object the size of the bounding rectangle, and use the `Graphics.FromImage` method to create a `Graphics` object for drawing into this `Bitmap`. We can then draw the text into this `Bitmap`, and flip it 180 degrees to achieve the proper effect. The `DrawImage` method draws the resulting image onto the tab.

This code defines a custom tab control for drawing the text on the tab in an alternate color than the default font. Using this control in our AlbumViewer code is the subject of the next section.

TRY IT! You may have noticed that the code in listing 13.3 for the `ColorTabControl` class only draws the text for the page on the control. Modify this class to also draw any image associated with the page on the tab. The `ImageList` property in the `TabControl` class defines the collection of images for the tabs. Each `TabPage` instance specifies the index into this collection using the `ImageIndex` property.

13.3.3 Using a custom tab control

In our AlbumViewer application, using our new custom tab control is quite simple. We replace our use of the `TabControl` object with the `ColorTabControl` class instead. This is a key advantage of encapsulating drawing logic in a custom control. The work creating the control is finished, allowing the use of this control to be quite straightforward.

Listing 13.4 illustrates the modified code for the `Main` entry point for the AlbumViewer application, based on the original AlbumViewer code from listing 13.1. As you can see, the tab control is now a `ColorTabControl` instance, and the color properties are assigned to blue for the selected tab and gray for normal tabs. Figure 13.4 illustrates the resulting application with these changes.

Figure 13.4 The AlbumViewer application uses the ColorTabControl class, with the tab alignment set to TabAlignment.Left.

Listing 13.4 Using the ColorTabControl class

```
[STAThread]
static void Main()
{
  // Create tab control
  ColorTabControl tab = new ColorTabControl();

  // Assign tab properties
  tab.Dock = DockStyle.Fill;
  tab.ShowToolTips = true;
  tab.SelectedTabColor = Color.Blue;
  tab.TabColor = Color.Gray;
  tab.Alignment = TabAlignment.Left;
  . . .
}
```

This completes our discussion of custom-drawn tab controls. As we indicated at the start of this section, the `ListBox` control supports custom drawing as well. This support uses a `DrawItem` event much like the `TabControl` class, so let's revisit this class in order to discuss this functionality.

13.4 OWNER-DRAWN LIST BOXES

As you probably recall from chapter 11, `ListControl` classes display a list of strings. You assign objects to the list, and the `ToString` method retrieves the string to display. An alternate string can be displayed by assigning the `DisplayMember` property to the name of a desired property, or a specific format for each object's display string can be defined using the formatting properties discussed in chapter 12. The .NET Framework retrieves, formats, and draws these strings within the control, and life is good.

There are times when you do not want to display a string, or when you wish to customize exactly how the string appears. For these situations you must draw the list manually. This section discusses exactly how to do this, and modifies the `ListBox` control in the MyAlbumEditor application to include a small representation of the image associated with each photograph. Such an image is sometimes called a *thumbnail*, since it is a "thumbnail-sized" image. The result of this work appears in figure 13.5.

This section presents custom list items in three parts. First, we discuss the topic generally, and contrast it with drawing tabs in a `TabControl` object. Next, we discuss how list items can vary in height. Our final topic covers the actual drawing of the custom list item in our MyAlbumEditor application.

Figure 13.5
The ListBox here shows both the image and text for each photograph. Note how the first item in the list is selected.

13.4.1 Custom list items

Owner-drawn lists are surprisingly similar to owner-drawn tab controls. The `DrawMode` property indicates whether the list is custom drawn, and the `DrawItem` event occurs when custom drawing is enabled and a list item should be drawn.

There are two main differences. First, the `DrawMode` property for both the `ListBox` and `ComboBox` classes is based on the `DrawMode` enumeration, rather than the `TabDrawMode` enumeration used with tab controls. This enumeration provides the three values shown in .NET Table 13.6.

.NET Table 13.6 DrawMode enumeration

The `DrawMode` enumeration specifies the drawing behavior for the elements in a control. Controls that use this enumeration include the `ListBox`, `CheckedListBox`, and `ComboBox` controls. This enumeration is part of the `System.Windows.Forms` namespace.

Enumeration Values	Normal	Elements in the control are drawn by the .NET Framework and are the same size.
	OwnerDrawFixed	Elements in the control are drawn manually and are the same size.
	OwnerDrawVariable	Elements in the control are drawn manually and may vary in size.

The second change is the item size. In a tab control, the size is set based on the `SizeMode` and `ItemSize` properties. By default, tabs vary in length based on the icon and label to display. List items are normally the same size, but are permitted to vary in size if the drawing mode is set to `OwnerDrawVariable`.

Taken together, custom drawing of list items is quite similar to custom drawing a tab. The next two sections discuss the differences in more detail, beginning with item size.

13.4.2 Assigning item size

Since most list boxes display list items with text in a specific font, the default height of each item is just large enough to accommodate the height of the assigned font, and the width of the longest string. When you're drawing custom list items, the height and even width can vary.

When the drawing mode is set to `DrawMode.Normal`, the size of each item is determined automatically. When the drawing mode is set to `DrawMode.OwnerDrawFixed`, the item size is fixed, but can be adjusted for all items by assigning the `ItemHeight` property to the desired height, in pixels, for all items. This height must be an integer between 0 and 255.

When the drawing mode is set to `DrawMode.OwnerDrawVariable`, the size of each item can vary. In this case, the `ItemHeight` property returns the height of the first item in the list. The size of each item is assigned using the `MeasureItem` event. Handlers for this event receive a `MeasureItemEventArgs` instance, summarized in .NET Table 13.7. The list box assigns the size of each item through the `ItemHeight` and `ItemWidth` properties in this event argument class.

.NET Table 13.7 MeasureItemEventArgs class

The `MeasureItemEventArgs` class defines the event data necessary to determine the size of an owner-drawn item. This class is part of the `System.Windows.Forms` namespace, and inherits from the `System.EventArgs` class.

Public Properties	Graphics	Gets the graphics object for this item
	Index	Gets the index of the item to measure
	ItemHeight	Gets or sets the height of the indicated item
	ItemWidth	Gets or sets the width of the indicated item

In our MyAlbumEditor application, our change is to draw the image and text for each item. This means the height of the default font may be a bit on the small side. Figure 13.6 illustrates the various measurements required to determine the width and height for each item.

The following steps convert our list box to be custom drawn, and implement a `MeasureItem` event handler to assign the size for each item.

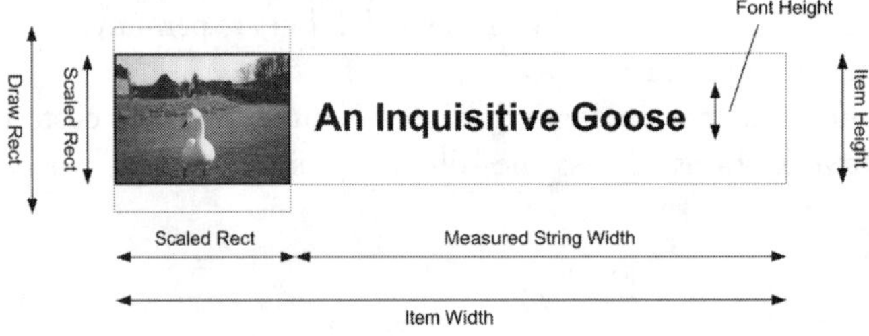

Figure 13.6 This figure shows the various measurements used to calculate a list item's width and height.

	Assign the list item size dynamically	
	Action	**Result**
1	In the EditorForm.cs [Design] window, set the `DrawMode` property for the `ListBox` control to `OwnerDrawVariable`.	Visual Studio assigns this property in the generated `InitializeComponent` code in the EditorForm.Designer.cs file.
2	In the EditorForm.cs source file, define a static `DrawRect` field to hold the maximum drawing size for thumbnail images.	`static private readonly Rectangle DrawRect` `  = new Rectangle(0, 0, 45, 45);`

3	Back in the designer window, handle the `MeasureItem` event in the `lstPhotos` control.	`private void lstPhotos_MeasureItem(`
		`    object sender, MeasureItemEventArgs e)`
		`{`

4	Implement this handler to determine the proper size for the image when scaled into the drawing rectangle.	`  Photograph p = Manager.Album[e.Index];`
		`  Rectangle scaledRect`
		`    = ImageUtility.ScaleToFit(`
		`        p.Image, DrawRect);`

5	Determine the text and width for the text portion of the item.
	How-to
	a. Use the `Font` assigned to the list control.
	b. Use the `GetItemText` method to retrieve the display text for the indicated item.
	c. Use the `Graphics` object to measure the display string against the assigned `Font`.
		`  Font f = lstPhotos.Font;`
		`  string text = lstPhotos.GetItemText(p);`
		`  int textWidth = (int)`
		`    e.Graphics.MeasureString(text, f).Width;`

6	Calculate the item width as the sum of the image and text width.	`  e.ItemWidth` `      = scaledRect.Width + textWidth + 2;`

7	Calculate the item height as the larger of the image and font height.	`  e.ItemHeight = Math.Max(scaledRect.Height,`
		`                          f.Height) + 2;`
		`}`

This code presumes that the image is drawn into a region 45 pixels square, and calculates the required width and height to accommodate both the image and text. The calculations in this code are based on figure 13.6 and explained within the code, so we do not discuss them further here.

It might be worth noting that we add 2 pixels of padding to both the width and height, to ensure that there is some spacing between the edges of the control as well as adjacent items. Our final task is to draw the actual items using the `DrawItem` event.

13.4.3 Drawing list items

Custom drawing of list items works much like drawing tabs for tab controls. The `DrawItem` event occurs each time an item should be drawn, with the properties for the item to draw defined by a `DrawItemEventArgs` instance.

In our MyPhotoAlbum application, we create items as illustrated in figure 13.6. The following steps accomplish this task.

CUSTOM DRAW THE LIST BOX ITEM

	Action	Result

1	Add a `DrawItem` event handler for the `lstPhotos` list box control.	`private void lstPhotos_DrawItem(`
		`    object sender, DrawItemEventArgs e)`
		`{`

2	Define local variables to hold the `Graphics` object and `Photograph` to draw.	`Graphics g = e.Graphics;`
		`if (e.Index < 0`
		`    || e.Index > Manager.Album.Count - 1)`
		`  return;`
		`Photograph p = Manager.Album[e.Index];`

3	Determine the region where the image should be drawn using the `Bounds` property.	`// Determine image rectangle`
		`Rectangle imageRect = ImageUtility.ScaleToFit(`
		`    p.Image, DrawRect );`
		`imageRect.X = e.Bounds.X + 2;`
		`imageRect.Y = e.Bounds.Y + 1;`

4	Draw the photographic image into this region, and add a black border.	`// Draw text image`
		`g.DrawImage(p.Image, imageRect);`
		`g.DrawRectangle(Pens.Black, imageRect);`
		`p.ReleaseImage();`

5	Determine the region where the text should be drawn, to the right of the image rectangle.	`// Determine text rectangle`
		`Rectangle textRect = new Rectangle();`
		`textRect.X = imageRect.Right + 2;`
		`textRect.Y = imageRect.Y + ((imageRect.Height`
		`              - e.Font.Height) / 2);`
		`textRect.Width`
		`  = e.Bounds.Width - imageRect.Width - 4;`
		`textRect.Height = e.Font.Height;`

6	Determine if this item is selected using the `State` property.	`// Determine text brush (handle selection)`
		`Brush textBrush;`
		`if ((e.State & DrawItemState.Selected)`
		`        == DrawItemState.Selected)`
		`{`
		
		Note: The `State` property defines additional settings for the current item. It contains an or'd set of `DrawItemState` enumeration values. Using this property is preferred over using a method such as `ListBox.GetSelected` since these and other methods may not reflect recent user changes until after the `DrawItem` event is processed.

7	If selected, use the system highlight colors to draw the text.	`  g.FillRectangle(`
		`        SystemBrushes.Highlight, textRect);`
		`  textBrush = SystemBrushes.HighlightText;`

CUSTOM DRAW THE LIST BOX ITEM *(CONTINUED)*		
	Action	**Result**

8	If not selected, use the normal window colors to draw the text.	`}`
		`else`
		`{`
		`  g.FillRectangle(`
		`        SystemBrushes.Window, textRect);`
		`  textBrush = SystemBrushes.WindowText;`
		`}`

9	Draw the text for the item in the appropriate font.	`// Draw the text`
		`g.DrawString(lstPhotos.GetItemText(p),`
		`          e.Font, textBrush, textRect);`
		`}`

Well done! You've just created your first owner-drawn list box. This code includes a number of features that should be useful in your own applications. It demonstrates how to draw an image as well as a string, and how to handle selected and deselected text. Compile and run the application to see this code in action.

Also note that our formatting code developed in chapter 12 assigns the item text appropriately. Step 9 uses the `GetItemText` method, which returns the displayed text based on formatting code assigned using the descriptor setting for the album.

TRY IT! Take a look at step 4 in the prior table. We use the photo's `Image` property to retrieve and draw the image, and then release this image so as not to consume too much memory and file resources in a large album. This is okay, except that every time a row must be redrawn the image is reloaded from disk. A cleaner and better-performing approach would be to define a `Thumbnail` property in the `Photograph` class that loaded the image, created a small version of the image, and then released the image. This would only load the `Image` value the first time, and then reuse the created thumbnail on subsequent calls.

Define a `Thumbnail` property in the `Photograph` class for this purpose, and use it in our `DrawItem` event handler to draw the list item.

13.5 RECAP

In this chapter we created tab controls and tab pages dynamically and using Visual Studio. We created a sample `AlbumViewer` application to demonstrate creating these controls in code without using Visual Studio. We also showed how to configure a `TabPage` control to accommodate a `PictureBox` object that is larger than the visible area by using the `ScrollableControl` class.

As an example within Visual Studio, we modified our MyAlbumEditor application to use a tab control in place of the Photographs group box created in chapter 10. This involved copying and pasting the existing controls out of the `GroupBox` and into a `TabPage` control.

Our discussion then turned to owner-drawn controls. We created a custom `ColorTabControl` class to utilize color within a tab, and then employed this new control in our AlbumViewer class.

We finished our discussion with owner-drawn list boxes, which turned out to be much like owner-drawn tabs. The key differences between owner-drawn tabs and lists are the enumerations used for the `DrawMode` properties and the ability to dynamically size each item in the list.

Of course, a `TabControl` object with only a single tab page is not all that useful. In the next chapter we examine date and time controls, and extend our `MyAlbumEditor` application to include not just one but two additional tab pages.

CHAPTER 14

Dates, calendars, and progress bars

Dealing with dates and times is one of those issues that prevent some programmers from getting a good night's sleep. With 3,600 seconds in an hour, 24 hours in a day, different days per month, and leap years almost but not quite every four years, it's no wonder. Fortunately, most languages and environments these days provide direct support for date-time values to simplify handling these constructs. In the .NET Framework, this support extends to Windows Forms controls as well.

In chapter 5 we saw how the `DateTime` structure is used to represent a date-time value within a program, and in chapter 8 we used the `MaskedTextBox` control to display and receive the `DateTaken` property in our `Photograph` class. In this chapter we look more closely at how to display and manipulate date-time values within a Windows Forms application. In particular, we look at these topics:

- Displaying dates and times with the `DateTimePicker` class
- Formatting `DateTime` objects with the `DateTimeFormatInfo` class
- Displaying weeks and months with the `MonthCalendar` class

- Processing mouse clicks within a `MonthCalendar` class
- Creating user controls with the `UserControl` class
- Managing tab pages within a `TabControl` by creating user control classes

Another topic we take up here is how to perform long-running operations while still allowing the user to interact with an application. One approach is to use the `ProgressBar` control with a `BackgroundWorker` instance to perform the operation. We present both classes and this approach in section 14.4.

14.1 DATE AND TIME DISPLAY

Since dates and times are an important part of any application, it seems appropriate that a specific control exists to display these values. This section discusses this control in detail and uses it in our `PhotoEditDialog` form.

14.1.1 The DateTimePicker class

The `DateTimePicker` class, described in .NET Table 14.1, displays a date and/or time to the user, and allows the user to alter the setting using the keyboard or a drop-down calendar control. The drop-down calendar is based on the `MonthCalendar` class, which we examine in section 14.3.

As you can see, the control supports properties to manipulate the appearance and contents of the control. We utilize many of these properties in this chapter, but let's take a quick look at the color-related properties defined by this control. Figure 14.1 shows a small sample program that includes a `DateTimePicker` control showing February 24, 2005, and a `ComboBox` control showing the text `CalendarTitleBackColor`.

This program is designed to dynamically modify the color settings for the `DateTimePicker` control. We won't go through the entire code for this program, but you can create this form in Visual Studio if you wish, with the `ComboBox.Items` property defined to hold the property names shown in the figure.

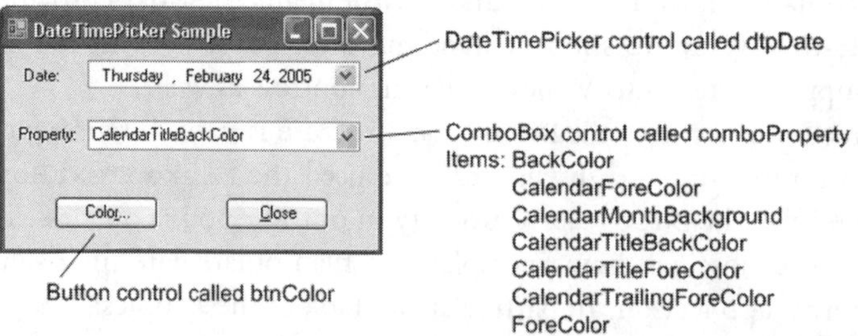

Figure 14.1 The DateTimePicker control looks a bit like a ComboBox control, except that it displays a calendar when the drop-down arrow is clicked, rather than a list of items.

.NET Table 14.1 DateTimePicker class

The `DateTimePicker` class represents a date and/or time value on a form. It allows the user to select a specific date and/or time, and presents this selection in a specified format. The `DateTime` value is presented in a text box control, with a down arrow providing access to a calendar from which an alternate date can be selected. The various parts of the `DateTime` value can alternately be modified using an up-down control or the arrow keys on the keyboard.

This class is part of the `System.Windows.Forms` namespace, and inherits from the `Control` class. See .NET Table 3.1 for members inherited from this base class.

Public Properties	CalendarFont	Gets or sets the font to apply to the calendar portion of the control.
	CalendarForeColor	Gets or sets the foreground color for the calendar.
	CalendarMonthBackground	Gets or sets the background color of the calendar month.
	CalendarTitleBackColor	Gets or sets the background color of the calendar title.
	Checked	When the `ShowCheckBox` property is `true`, gets or sets whether the check box is checked.
	CustomFormat	Gets or sets the custom date-time format.
	DropDownAlign	Gets or sets the alignment of the drop-down calendar on the control, using the `LeftRightAlignment` enumeration.
	Format	Gets or sets how the date-time value is formatted in the control.
	MaxDate	Gets or sets the maximum date-time value for the control. The `MinDate` property gets or sets the minimum value.
	ShowCheckBox	Gets or sets whether to show a check box to the left of the selected date.
	ShowUpDown	Gets or sets whether an up-down control is available to adjust the date-time value.
	Value	Gets or sets the `DateTime` value assigned to the control.
Public Events	CloseUp	Occurs when the drop-down calendar is dismissed and disappears.
	DropDown	Occurs when the drop-down calendar is shown.
	FormatChanged	Occurs when the `Format` property changes.
	ValueChanged	Occurs when the `Value` property changes.

The critical portion of this program is the event handler for the `Click` event of the Color button. The code for this handler is shown in listing 14.1, with the annotated portions discussed in the subsequent paragraphs.

Listing 14.1 Click handler for sample DateTimePicker application

```
using System;
using System.Drawing;
using System.Reflection;
using System.Windows.Forms;
. . .

    private void btnColor_Click(object sender, EventArgs e)
    {
      Type t = typeof(DateTimePicker);
      string prop = comboProperty.Text;

      PropertyInfo info = t.GetProperty(prop);
      if (info != null && info.PropertyType == typeof(Color))
      {
        using (ColorDialog dlg = new ColorDialog())
        {
          dlg.Color = (Color)info.GetValue(dtpDate, null);
          if (dlg.ShowDialog() == DialogResult.OK)
            info.SetValue(dtpDate, dlg.Color, null);
        }
      }
      else
        MessageBox.Show("Property not found, or property not a color.");
    }
```

❶ Obtains Type for DateTimePicker control

❷ Retrieves PropertyInfo for selected property

❸ Assigns property value to selected Color

❶ This code relies on the `Type` and `PropertyInfo` classes, both part of the `System.Reflection` namespace. This namespace provides classes and interfaces to examine, invoke, and create members of a defined type. A complete discussion of reflection would take more space than I care to devote to it, but this example is somewhat illustrative. This code retrieves the `Type` object for the `DateTimePicker` control. This could also be accomplished using the `GetType` method inherited from the `Object` type, using the method `dtpDate.GetType()`. Using the `typeof` keyword is preferred, since the `Type` is resolved by the compiler rather than at runtime by calling the `GetType` method.

❷ The members of the `Type` class allow access to the members of the corresponding type, even private and protected members. The `GetProperties` method returns the set of all properties for the type. Here we use the `GetProperty` method to retrieve information about the specific property name selected in the `ComboBox` control.

❸ The `PropertyInfo` class provides access to data associated with a corresponding property, usually referred to as the *metadata* for the property. A `PropertyInfo` object can be used to get or set the property value dynamically. In our code, we use the

PropertyType property in this class to ensure the Type of the property is a Color structure. If so, then we use the GetValue and SetValue methods to retrieve the current setting and then assign a new value to the property within our DateTimePicker control. The ColorDialog class, a common dialog class mentioned briefly in chapter 6, allows the user to define a new color for the selected property.

The result of this code is that a user can dynamically change the Color properties in the date-time control. The use of reflection permits a user to see how the various Color settings alter the appearance of the DateTimePicker control, and more specifically the colors in the drop-down calendar. An example of this application with the calendar showing an alternate set of colors appears in figure 14.2.

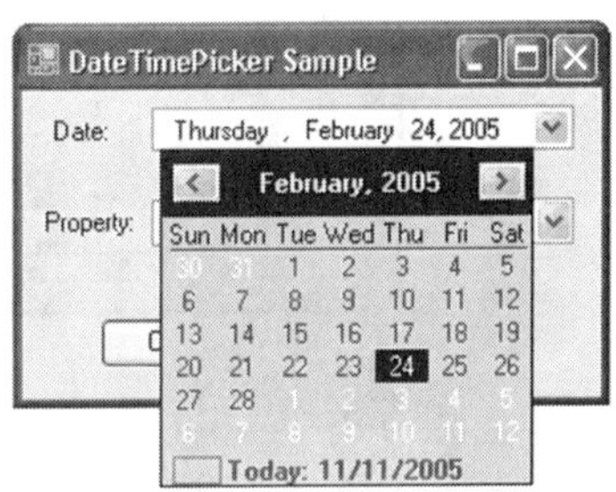

Figure 14.2 A modified drop-down calendar control

More generally, reflection allows a program to dynamically create, invoke, and alter objects within the program, making it a powerful tool that can generate forms on the fly or alter class instances based on user-defined configuration settings. Of course, this power and flexibility comes at the expense of performance. Using reflection is much slower than performing similar tasks using the actual member and class names.

While this is an interesting example, the user is not selecting an actual date or time here. For this, let's turn to the DateTaken property of our Photograph class.

14.1.2 Creating a DateTimePicker control

We can use the DateTimePicker control in our PhotoEditDialog form to display the photograph's DateTaken property. You may wonder why we switch to a DateTimePicker control for this property when the MaskedTextBox control worked just fine in chapter 8. The simple answer is that I need an example for the book, and this is it.

A better answer would be that the DateTimePicker control is probably more appropriate for a real DateTime value. The MaskedTextBox manipulates text, not dates and times, but is useful for formatting textual strings into and out of a specific form. The DateTimePicker control translates the data to and from DateTime values directly, whereas a MaskedTextBox must perform or configure such conversions by hand.

As a result, the DateTimePicker control works extremely well as long as the corresponding setting, in our case the DateTaken property, is indeed a DateTime structure. In situations where the corresponding value is a string or database value that might contain an invalid or null setting in addition to a date, you may find it easier to use a MaskedTextBox control to permit invalid dates to be shown and more easily manipulated.

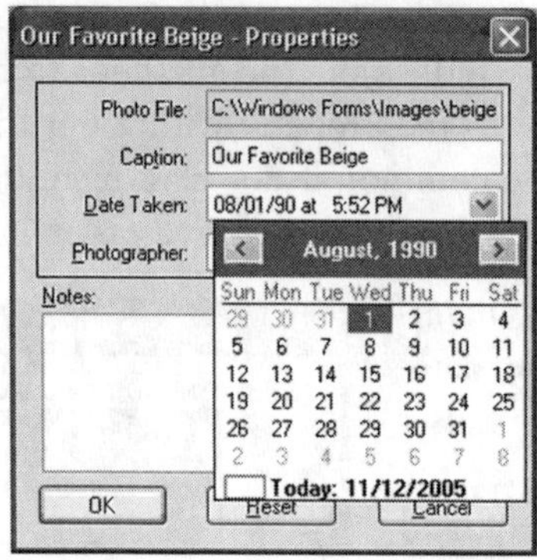

Figure 14.3
The DateTimePicker here displays a DateTime value with a custom format.

Since we do, in fact, have a `DateTime` value to display, the `DateTimePicker` control is probably the better choice here. The Photo Properties dialog box with a `DateTimePicker` control in place is shown in figure 14.3. The following steps add this control to our dialog box.

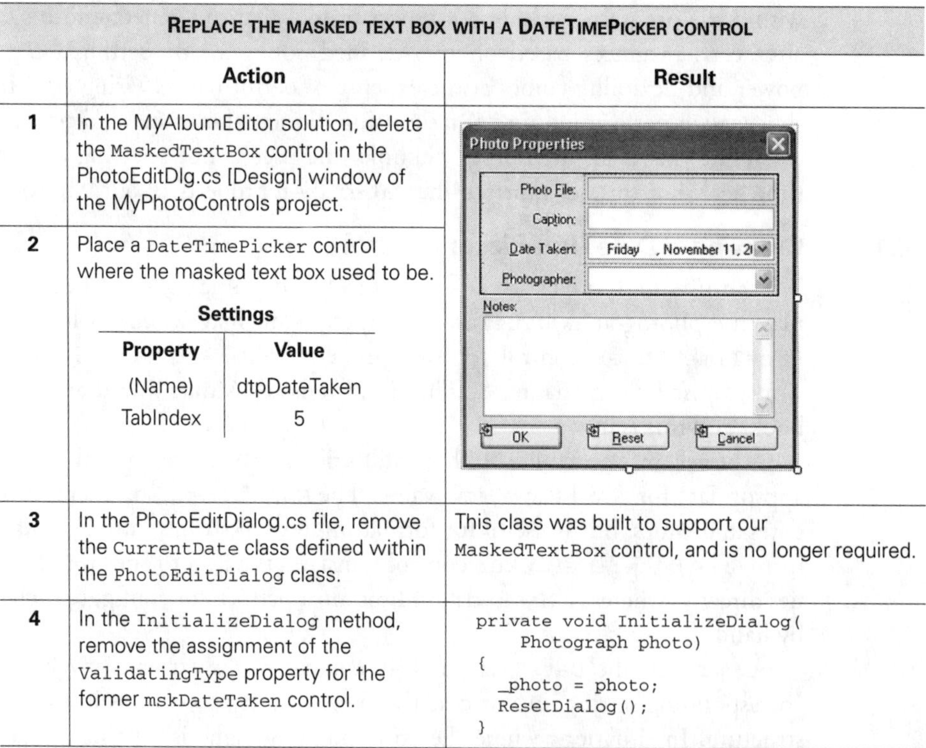

REPLACE THE MASKED TEXT BOX WITH A DATETIMEPICKER CONTROL

	Action	Result
1	In the MyAlbumEditor solution, delete the `MaskedTextBox` control in the PhotoEditDlg.cs [Design] window of the MyPhotoControls project.	*(screenshot: Photo Properties dialog — Photo File:, Caption:, Date Taken: Friday , November 11, 20…, Photographer:, Notes:, OK, Reset, Cancel)*
2	Place a `DateTimePicker` control where the masked text box used to be. **Settings** **Property** / **Value** (Name) / dtpDateTaken TabIndex / 5	
3	In the PhotoEditDialog.cs file, remove the `CurrentDate` class defined within the `PhotoEditDialog` class.	This class was built to support our `MaskedTextBox` control, and is no longer required.

4	In the `InitializeDialog` method, remove the assignment of the `ValidatingType` property for the former `mskDateTaken` control.	`private void InitializeDialog(`
		`    Photograph photo)`
		`{`
		`  _photo = photo;`
		`  ResetDialog();`
		`}`

	Action	Result
	REPLACE THE MASKED TEXT BOX WITH A DATETIMEPICKER CONTROL *(CONTINUED)*	

5	In the `ResetDialog` method, set the `Value` property for the date and time control to the `Photograph.DateTaken` property.	`protected override void ResetDialog()`
		`{`
		`  // Fill combo box with photos in album`
		`  comboPhotographer.BeginUpdate();`
		`  . . .`
		`  if (photo != null)`
		`  {`
		`    txtPhotoFile.Text = photo.FileName;`
		`    txtCaption.Text = photo.Caption;`
		`    dtpDateTaken.Value = photo.DateTaken;`
		`    comboPhotographer.Text`
		`        = photo.Photographer;`
		`    txtNotes.Text = photo.Notes;`
		`  }`
		`}`

6	In the `SaveSettings` method, set the `DateTaken` property to the date-time value specified by the user.
	
	Note: Since the `Value` property is a `DateTime` value, checking for a `FormatException` is no longer required.
		`private void SaveSettings()`
		`{`
		`  Photograph photo = Manager.Current;`
		`  if (photo != null)`
		`  {`
		`    photo.Caption = txtCaption.Text;`
		`    photo.Photographer`
		`        = comboPhotographer.Text;`
		`    photo.Notes = txtNotes.Text;`
		`    photo.DateTaken = dtpDateTaken.Value;`
		`  }`
		`}`

And there you have it. One `DateTimePicker` control ready to work. Since the `DateTimePicker` control works directly with `DateTime` values, the parsing and validating required with the `MaskedTextBox` control are no longer required. Compile and run the application, and notice the differences between our former use of a `MaskedTextBox` and our new control. Make sure your albums preserve the selected date after exiting and restarting the program.

You may have noticed that our control does not display the time. By default, the date and time control displays what .NET calls the *long date*. This includes the day of the week and month written out in the current language as well as the two-digit day and four-digit year. Modifying the format of the displayed `DateTime` value is our next topic.

14.2 DATE AND TIME FORMATS

We introduced formatting in .NET in chapter 12, where we discussed formatting interfaces in general, and numeric formatting more specifically. We also showed how to implement custom formatting for a class, using our `Photograph` class as an example. This section discusses the formatting of dates and times, and shows how the `DateTimePicker` control provides support for these formats.

14.2.1 Formatting date and time values

We looked at the formatting classes for numeric values back in chapter 12 (see section 12.4), so we should probably discuss the formatting of date-time values here. The `DateTimeFormatInfo` class encapsulates formatting information for date-time values for a specific culture. Similar to what we saw for numeric values, the formatting codes for dates and times fall into two types: single-digit format codes that express a specific format, and format characters that are used to define a custom formatting string.

Table 14.2 illustrates the most commonly used format codes for `DateTime` values. Unlike the numeric codes, there is often a difference in the meaning of the lower- and uppercase codes. An example using some of these codes is shown in listing 14.2.

Table 14.2 Standard date-time format codes and associated DateTimeFormatInfo properties

Code	Description	Default U.S. English Example	DateTimeFormatInfo Properties
d	Short date format	2/24/2005	ShortDatePattern
D	Long date format	Thursday, February 24, 2005	LongDatePattern
F	Full date and time format, using a long date and long time	Thursday, February 24, 2005 1:38:24 AM	FullDateTimePattern
g	General date and time format, using a short date and short time	2/24/2005 1:38 AM	
m, M	Month and day format.	February 24	YearMonthPattern
s	Sortable date and time format, using local time and the ISO 8601 standard.	2005-02-24T01:38:24	SortableDateTimePattern
t	Short time format	1:38 AM	ShortTimePattern
T	Long time format	1:38:24 AM	LongTimePattern
y, Y	Year and month format	February, 2005	YearMonthPattern

The most common format pattern characters for date-time values are shown in table 14.3. When a date-time format string is longer than a single character, it is treated as a pattern and processed accordingly.

A sample application that illustrates the formatting of both numeric and `DateTime` values is shown in listing 14.2. This example incorporates the sample code shown in chapter 12 in a console application, and includes additional code to demonstrate the format values for short dates and times, as well as a sample date-time formatting pattern

Table 14.3 Standard date-time formatting characters and associated DateTimeFormatInfo properties

Pattern	Description	Default U.S. English Values	DateTimeFormatInfo Property
d	Day of the month.	1 to 31	
dd	Two-digit day of the month.	01 to 31	
ddd	Abbreviated day of the week.	Sun to Sat	AbbreviatedDayNames
dddd	Full day of the week.	Sunday to Saturday	DayNames
M	Numeric month.	1 to 12	
MM	Two-digit numeric month.	01 to 12	
MMM	Abbreviated month name.	Jan to Dec	AbbreviatedMonthNames
MMMM	Full month name.	January to December	MonthNames
y	Year without century.	1 to 99	
yy	Two-digit year without century.	01 to 99	
yyyy	Four-digit century.	0001 to 9999	
gg	Period or era, if any.	B.C. or A.D.	
h	Hour on a 12-hour clock.	1 to 12	
hh	Two-digit hour on a 12-hour clock.	01 to 12	
H	Hour on a 24-hour clock.	1 to 24	
HH	Two-digit hour on a 24-hour clock.	01 to 24	
m	Minute.	0 to 59	
mm	Two-digit minute.	00 to 59	
s	Second.	0 to 59	
ss	Two-digit second.	00 to 59	
tt	AM/PM designator.	AM or PM	AMDesignator and PMDesignator
:	Default time separator	: (a colon)	TimeSeparator
/	Default date separator.	/ (a slash)	DateSeparator
"c"	Displays the specified character. For example, "s" will display the character s rather than the number of seconds.		

Listing 14.2 Sample formatting application

```
using System;
using System.Globalization;

namespace FormattingSample
{
  class Program
  {
```

```
        static void Main(string[] args)
        {
          // Get the culture information for USA and Great Britain
          CultureInfo us = CultureInfo.CreateSpecificCulture("en-US");
          CultureInfo gb = CultureInfo.CreateSpecificCulture("en-GB");

          // Numeric example
          Type numType = typeof(NumberFormatInfo);
          NumberFormatInfo usNumInfo = (NumberFormatInfo)us.GetFormat(numType);
          NumberFormatInfo gbNumInfo = (NumberFormatInfo)gb.GetFormat(numType);

          Console.WriteLine("USA value is " + (49.95).ToString("c", usNumInfo));
          Console.WriteLine("GB value is " + (49.95).ToString("c", gbNumInfo));

          // DateTime example
          Type dtType = typeof(DateTimeFormatInfo);
          DateTimeFormatInfo usDateInfo, gbDateInfo;
          usDateInfo = (DateTimeFormatInfo)us.GetFormat (dtType);
          gbDateInfo = (DateTimeFormatInfo)gb.GetFormat (dtType);

          DateTime date = new DateTime(2005, 2, 24, 1, 38, 24);
          string pattern = "dd MMM yyy 'at' HH:mm tt";
          Console.WriteLine("Short date: USA {0}, GB {1}",
            date.ToString("d", usDateInfo), date.ToString("d", gbDateInfo));
          Console.WriteLine("Short time: USA {0}, GB {1}",
            date.ToString("t", usDateInfo), date.ToString("t", gbDateInfo));
          Console.WriteLine("USA pattern: "
                            + date.ToString(pattern, usDateInfo));
          Console.WriteLine("GB pattern: "
                            + date.ToString(pattern, gbDateInfo));

          Console.Write("Press Enter to exit.");
          Console.ReadLine();
        }
      }
    }
```

If you compile and run this code on a machine that includes the cultural information for the United States and Great Britain, the following output is produced. Note the differences in the two format codes here, and how the format pattern produces the same result in either culture. Feel free to modify this code to view the output from alternate cultures or alternate format codes and patterns.

```
USA value is $49.95
GB value is £49.95
Short date: USA 2/24/2005, GB 24/02/2005
Short time: USA 1:38 AM, GB 01:38
USA pattern: 24 Feb 2005 at 01:38 AM
GB pattern: 24 Feb 2005 at 01:38 AM
```

As you might guess, the `DateTimePicker` control includes properties to define how the `DateTime` value should be formatted. This is our next topic.

14.2.2 Customizing a DateTimePicker control

As we have seen, the `DateTimePicker` control uses the long date format by default. The `Format` property defines the specific format to use in the control, using the `DateTimePickerFormat` enumeration described in .NET Table 14.4. As you can see, the enumeration exposes the short and long date formats, the long time format, and a custom format. For a custom format, the `CustomFormat` property defines the custom format string passed to the `DateTime.ToString` method to format the current date-time value.

.NET Table 14.4 DateTimePickerFormat enumeration

The `DateTimePickerFormat` enumeration specifies how to display a date-time value in a `DateTimePicker` control. This enumeration is part of the `System.Windows.Forms` namespace. For each value, the default setting for the U.S. English culture is provided. The format codes used here correspond to the codes supported by the `DateTimeFormatInfo` class.

Enumeration Values	Custom	A custom format is used, as specified by the `CustomFormat` property.
	Long	The long date format is used. This is the pattern defined by the `DateTimeFormatInfo.LongDatePattern` property for the current culture, or "dddd, MMMM dd, yyyy" for U.S. English environments.
	Short	The short date format is used. This is the pattern defined by the `DateTimeFormatInfo.ShortDatePattern` property for the current culture, or "M/d/yyyy" for U.S. English environments.
	Time	The time format is used. This is the pattern defined by the `DateTimeFormatInfo.LongTimePattern` property for the current culture, or "h:mm:ss tt" for U.S. English environments.

Let's modify our date and time control to display a customized value. We include both the date and time in the display.

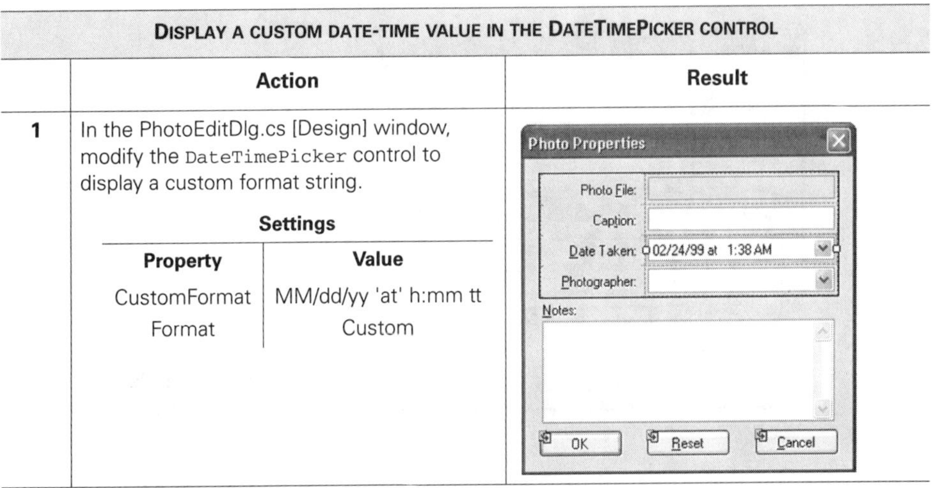

DISPLAY A CUSTOM DATE-TIME VALUE IN THE DATETIMEPICKER CONTROL

	Action	Result
1	In the PhotoEditDlg.cs [Design] window, modify the `DateTimePicker` control to display a custom format string. **Settings** **Property** / **Value** CustomFormat / MM/dd/yy 'at' h:mm tt Format / Custom	(dialog screenshot)

Compile and run these changes; notice that the drop-down calendar still appears to alter the date. The time values can be modified by hand or with the arrow keys. Try some alternate format strings, and set the `ShowUpDown` property to `true` so you can see the effect on the control.

The `DateTimePicker` class is great for displaying a single date-time value. When multiple dates or a range of dates are required, the `MonthCalendar` class can be used.

14.3 CALENDARS

Sometimes a single date does not do. A scheduling program, for example, might need to show a calendar with meeting days highlighted, or indicate a meeting that covers a range of dates. The `MonthCalendar` class allows one or more months to be displayed on a `Form`, with individual days highlighted or a range of days selected.

Since our `PhotoAlbum` class permits each photograph to specify its own date, it seems appropriate to demonstrate the calendar control by highlighting the days in a calendar on which a photograph was taken. We do this by adding a second `TabPage` object to our MyAlbumEditor main window. The result of our changes is shown in figure 14.4. Note how some dates are in bold to indicate one or more photographs were taken that day. If the user clicks on a date, a context menu pops up containing the corresponding photographs. When a photograph is selected from this context menu, the properties for that photograph are displayed.

The interface in figure 14.4 provides a very different view of our album. While the order of photographs in the album is not apparent, the specific days that a collection of pictures was taken are immediately available.

This section discusses the month calendar control in general and adds the control to a new tab page in our application. Our example includes how to bold the dates in the `MonthCalendar` control, and how to process and respond to mouse clicks within the control.

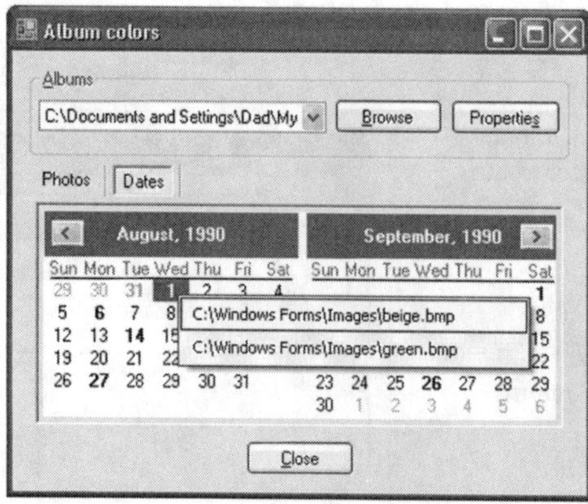

Figure 14.4
The MonthCalendar control displays multiple months when it is resized.

14.3.1 The MonthCalendar class

.NET Table 14.5 MonthCalendar class

The `MonthCalendar` class is a control that displays one or more months to the user. Days in each month can be displayed in bold, and the user can select single or multiple dates. This class is part of the `System.Windows.Forms` namespace, and inherits from the `Control` class. See .NET Table 3.1 for members inherited from this class.

Public Properties	AnnuallyBoldedDates	Gets or sets an array of `DateTime` objects that indicate which days to bold on an annual basis.
	BoldedDates	Gets or sets an array of `DateTime` objects of specific dates to show in bold.
	MaxDate	Gets or sets the maximum date. Months occurring after this date cannot be displayed.
	MaxSelectionCount	Gets or sets the maximum number of dates that can be selected in the control.
	ScrollChange	Gets or sets the number of months to scroll per click of a scroll button.
	SelectionRange	Gets or sets the range of dates selected in the control as a `SelectedRange` class instance. The `SelectionStart` and `SelectionEnd` properties get or set the initial and final date in the selected range.
	ShowToday	Gets or sets whether to display the `TodayDate` value at the bottom of the control.
	ShowTodayCircle	Gets or sets whether the `TodayDate` value is circled.
	TodayDate	Gets or sets the `DateTime` value used as today's date.
Public Methods	AddAnnuallyBoldedDate	Adds a day to display in bold on an annual basis.
	GetDisplayRange	Retrieves the range of dates displayed by the control, as a `SelectedRange` class instance.
	HitTest	Determines which aspect of the month calendar control is located at a specified point.
	RemoveBoldedDate	Removes a specific date from the list of nonrecurring bolded dates. The `RemoveAllBoldedDates` method clears the entire list of nonrecurring bolded dates.
	SetDate	Selects the given date in the control.
Public Events	DateChanged	Occurs when the current date in the control is modified, such as when a new month is displayed.
	DateSelected	Occurs when the dates selected in the control are modified.

An overview of the `MonthCalendar` class is provided in .NET Table 14.5. This class handles the entire range of dates possible in `DateTime` objects, which is basically any date until the year 9999. This class is a good way to display a series of dates related to an object or collection of objects.

As indicated in the table, the `MonthCalendar` control supports display of a single month, or months over multiple years. Dates can be bolded individually using the `BoldedDates` property, or on a monthly or yearly basis using the `MonthlyBoldedDates` and `AnnuallyBoldedDates` properties. A number of methods, some of which are shown in .NET Table 14.5, exist to add or remove some or all dates bolded in the calendar.

Other features of the calendar control include the minimum and maximum dates to display with the `MinDate` and `MaxDate` properties; the ability to show week numbers from 1 to 52 in the calendar with the `ShowWeekNumbers` property; and properties to control the colors used to draw various portions of each month for the control.

In our sample MyAlbumEditor application, we demonstrate many of these features of the `MonthCalendar` control. We use the ability to bold specific dates to indicate the dates when photographs in an album were taken, and the `HitTest` method to identify when a user clicks a specific date within the control.

Before we actually do this, let's take a short aside to discuss the `UserControl` class and its usefulness within `TabControl` objects.

14.3.2 The UserControl class

As we saw in chapter 13, the `TabControl` class enables multiple tab pages to display a complex set of information in an organized fashion. The user can click on the tab page of interest, and see only the information related to that page.

This feature is both a blessing and a curse. The blessing is that it can greatly improve the usability and organization of an interface. The curse is that you may end up with a huge `Form` object containing more controls and event processing code than you would otherwise wish for. For a small application or small number of pages, this is fairly manageable and does not normally cause headaches and other programmer frustrations. For larger applications, this can be quite a problem.

One way to deal with this issue is to use the `UserControl` class to create the contents of each tab page separately. This class is a container control, much like the `Form` class, except that it can be placed within a `Form`, much like a `Panel` object. The public members specific to this control are shown in .NET Table 14.6.

Since the `UserControl` class inherits from the `ContainerControl` class, which in turn inherits from the `ScrollableControl` class, our discussions in prior chapters on placing and managing controls within a form or panel apply to user controls as well. Similarly, our discussion on scrolling tab pages in section 13.2.2 also applies.

User controls are often used in two situations. The first is where an arrangement of controls is required in multiple locations throughout an application. A custom

.NET Table 14.6 UserControl class

The `UserControl` class is a container control that can serve as a basis for more complex control objects. User controls inherit the positioning and mnemonic-handling of the base `ContainerControl` class, while retaining the ability to be placed within the boundaries of other controls. This class is part of the `System.Windows.Forms` namespace, and inherits from the `ContainerControl` class.

Public Properties	*AutoSizeMode*	Gets or sets whether the control automatically resizes to fit its contents
	BorderStyle	Gets or sets the border to display around the edges of the control
Public Events	Load	Occurs just before the control is displayed for the first time

panel can sometimes serve this purpose as well, but in either case a predefined control is created that inherits from the `UserControl` or `Panel` class, and the controls positioned and managed within the new control.

The second situation we demonstrate in the next section, when a logical set of controls can be managed as a user-defined control to simplify or customize how the controls for an application are managed. The purpose in this second case is to simplify and organize an application rather than create a reusable control.

14.3.3 Creating a calendar control

Now that we have reviewed the `MonthCalendar` and `UserControl` classes, we are ready to create these controls in our MyAlbumEditor application. The goal here is to create a `UserControl` object that we can place within a tab page in the application, and have this control contain a `MonthCalendar` instance that references the currently selected album.

Let's begin by creating our new control and placing it within a new tab page in the MyAlbumEditor application.

CREATE THE DATES USER CONTROL

	Action	Result
1	In the MyAlbumEditor project, add a new `UserControl` called AlbumCalendar. **How-to** a. Click the project. b. Select Add User Control from the Project menu. c. Enter the name "AlbumCalendar" in the Add New Item dialog box. d. Click Add to add the new control.	AlbumCalendar.cs [Design] EditorForm.cs [Design] **Note:** Custom controls are named like any other class, beginning with a capital letter.

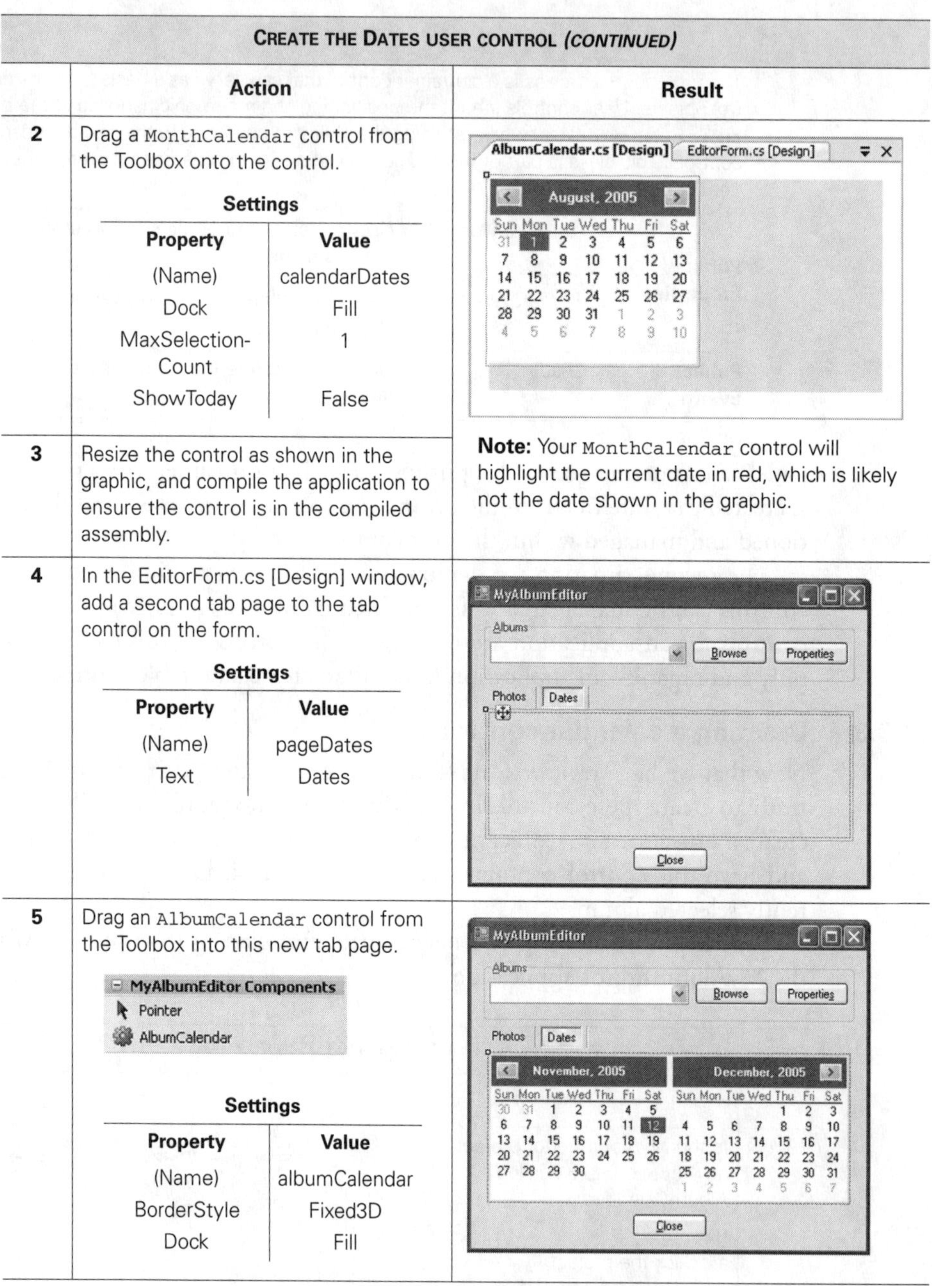

	CREATE THE DATES USER CONTROL ***(CONTINUED)***	
	Action	**Result**
2	Drag a `MonthCalendar` control from the Toolbox onto the control. **Settings** **Property** – **Value** (Name) – calendarDates Dock – Fill MaxSelection-Count – 1 ShowToday – False	
3	Resize the control as shown in the graphic, and compile the application to ensure the control is in the compiled assembly.	**Note:** Your `MonthCalendar` control will highlight the current date in red, which is likely not the date shown in the graphic.
4	In the EditorForm.cs [Design] window, add a second tab page to the tab control on the form. **Settings** **Property** – **Value** (Name) – pageDates Text – Dates	
5	Drag an `AlbumCalendar` control from the Toolbox into this new tab page. **Settings** **Property** – **Value** (Name) – albumCalendar BorderStyle – Fixed3D Dock – Fill	

These steps create a new `UserControl`-derived class called `AlbumCalendar` that we can use to manage a `MonthCalendar` control on behalf of an `AlbumManager` object. This will encapsulate all of our logic for managing this calendar within the new class, rather than cluttering the existing `EditorForm` class file with all of this code.

Note how Visual Studio automatically adds new user controls to the Toolbox. After we create the `AlbumCalendar` control and compile the code in step 3, the control is immediately available in the Toolbox under the "MyAlbumEditor Components" heading. In step 5, this feature is used to add the control to the form.

14.3.4 Initializing a calendar

Now that our `MonthCalendar` control is on the form, we can hook it up to our `AlbumManager` class. We do not want to initialize our calendar control needlessly, so we only do so when the Dates tab is displayed. By the same token, we do not want to initialize the `lstPhotos` list box needlessly, so we must ensure that this only occurs when the Photos tab is displayed.

The following steps are required for this change.

INITIALIZE THE MONTH CALENDAR CONTROL

	Action	Result

1	In the AlbumCalendar.cs source file, indicate that we use the two `Manning` namespaces.	`using Manning.MyPhotoAlbum;`
		`using Manning.MyPhotoControls;`
		Note: Within the MyAlbumEditor project, the default namespace of `MyAlbumEditor` is fine for this class.

2	Add a private `AlbumManager` field and public `Manager` method to the `AlbumCalendar` class.	`private AlbumManager _manager = null;`
		`public AlbumManager Manager`
		`{`
		`  get { return _manager; }`
		`  set`
		`  {`
		`    _manager = value;`
		`    UpdateCalendar();`
		`  }`
		`}`

3	Implement an `UpdateCalendar` method to update the `MonthCalendar` control within this user control.	`private void UpdateCalendar()`
		`{`
		`  DateTime minDate = DateTime.MaxValue;`
		`  DateTime maxDate = DateTime.MinValue;`
		`  calendarDates.RemoveAllBoldedDates();`

4	If an `AlbumManager` is not assigned, then display the current date in the calendar control.	`  if (Manager == null)`
		`  {`
		`    minDate = DateTime.Now;`
		`    maxDate = DateTime.Now.AddMonths(2);`
		`  }`

5	Otherwise, bold the `DateTaken` property for each photograph, and determine the smallest and largest dates when photographs were taken.	`  else`
		`  {`
		`    foreach (Photograph p in Manager.Album)`
		`    {`
		`      DateTime date = p.DateTaken;`
		`      calendarDates.AddBoldedDate(date);`
		
		`      if (date < minDate) minDate = date;`
		`      if (date > maxDate) maxDate = date;`
		`    }`
		`  }`

	INITIALIZE THE MONTH CALENDAR CONTROL *(CONTINUED)*	
	Action	**Result**

6	Update the `MonthCalendar` control with the calculated information.	`calendarDates.MinDate = minDate;`
		`calendarDates.MaxDate = maxDate;`
		`calendarDates.TodayDate = minDate;`
		`calendarDates.SelectionStart = minDate;`
		`calendarDates.UpdateBoldedDates();`
		`}`
		Note: Modified bolded dates are not automatically reflected in the control. The `UpdateBoldedDates` method must be called to force the control to update this information.

7	In the EditorForm.cs [Design] window, handle the `SelectedIndexChanged` event for the tab control.	`private void tcPhotos_SelectedIndexChanged`
		`    (object sender, System.EventArgs e)`
		`{`
		`  UpdateTabs();`
		`}`
		Note: This event occurs when a new tab is selected by the user.

8	Implement a private `UpdateTabs` method that handles the common logic for all tabs.	`private void UpdateTabs()`
		`{`
		`  bool nullManager = (Manager == null);`
		`  if (nullManager)`
		`    Text = "Selected album could not be opened";`
		`  else`
		`    Text = "Album " + Manager.ShortName;`

9	This includes disabling the Album Properties button and tab pages whenever a valid album is not selected.	`  btnAlbumProps.Enabled = !nullManager;` `  tcPhotos.Enabled = !nullManager;`

10	Also in this method, apply the appropriate logic to update the current tab.	`  if (tcPhotos.SelectedTab == pagePhotos)`
		`    DisplayAlbum();`
		`  else if (tcPhotos.SelectedTab == pageDates)`
		`    albumCalendar.Manager = Manager;`
		`}`

11	In the `OpenAlbum` method, replace the call to the `DisplayAlbum` method with a call to update the tabs.	`private void OpenAlbum(string path)`
		`{`
		`  . . .`
		`  UpdateTabs();`
		`  EnablePhotoButtons();`
		`}`

12	In the `DisplayAlbum` method, remove the common logic that is now part of the `UpdateTabs` method.	`private void DisplayAlbum()`
		`{`
		`  if (Manager == null)`
		`  {`
		`    lstPhotos.BackColor = SystemColors.Control;`
		`    lstPhotos.Items.Clear();`
		`  }`
		`  else`
		`  {`
		`    lstPhotos.BackColor = SystemColors.Window;`
		`    . . .`

Our calendar, as well as our list box, is updated whenever an album is opened and whenever the user displays an alternate tab page. The logic for manipulating our `MonthCalendar` control is entirely contained within the `AlbumCalendar` control, which greatly simplifies the code required in the `EditorForm` class.

Compile and run the application if you would like to see this in action. Load an album with photographs taken over the course of a few months, and note how multiple months are displayed in the `MonthCalendar` control as the MyAlbumEditor application window is resized.

The next section processes the user's mouse clicks on the calendar to provide access to the `PhotoEditDialog` form associated with a selected date.

14.3.5 Handling mouse clicks in a calendar control

Our `MonthCalendar` control is encapsulated in a user control, so we can add new functionality to this control and have it appear in our application. Right now we display the dates assigned to an album's photographs in bold. The next task is to handle mouse clicks by the user and link them with the associated photographs.

The `MouseDown` event for the `Control` class was discussed in chapter 10, and occurs when the user presses down a mouse button while the mouse pointer is within a control. We handle this event to create a `ContextMenuStrip` object on the fly that shows any photos associated with the selected date.

The key to our solution is the `HitTest` method in the `MonthCalendar` class. This method returns a `HitTestInfo` object for a given location within the control. The `MonthCalendar.HitTestInfo` class provides information about a location within the control, and is summarized in .NET Table 14.7.

.NET Table 14.7 MonthCalendar.HitTestInfo class

The `HitTestInfo` class contains information for a specific point within a `MonthCalendar` control, and is returned by the `MonthCalendar.HitTest` method. This class is defined within the `MonthCalendar` class, and is part of the `System.Windows.Forms` namespace.

Public Properties	HitArea	Gets the area of the calendar evaluated by the `HitTest` method as a `MonthCalendar.HitArea` enumeration value
	Point	Gets the point provided to the `HitTest` method
	Time	Gets date-time information specific to the area that was hit-tested

As you can see, the `HitTestInfo` class returns the specific area of the calendar that was hit-tested, along with the location of the test and date-time value associated with the hit area. The hit area is a `MonthCalendar.HitArea` enumeration value. The possible values are shown in .NET Table 14.8. For most values, the `HitTestInfo.Time` property is undefined. Values that define a specific meaning to the `Time` property are indicated in the table.

.NET Table 14.8 MonthCalendar.HitArea enumeration

The `HitArea` enumeration specifies the possible display areas in a `MonthCalendar` control. This enumeration is used when analyzing a specific point in a calendar control using the `HitTest` method, and is defined within the `MonthCalendar` class. The `MonthCalendar.HitArea` enumeration is part of the `System.Windows.Forms` namespace.

Enumeration Values	CalendarBackground	The specified point is part of the calendar's background.
	Date	The specified point is part of a specific date of the current month in the calendar. The `HitTestInfo.Time` property is set to the corresponding `DateTime` value.
	DayOfWeek	The point is part of a day abbreviation, such as "Mon." The `Time` property is set to the date on the top row of the calendar.
	NextMonthButton	The point is part of the next month button at the top right of the control.
	NextMonthDate	The point is part of the next month's dates shown at the end of a visible month in the control. The `Time` property is not set.
	Nowhere	The point is not in the `MonthCalendar` control, or is not in an active portion of the control.
	PrevMonthButton	The point is part of the previous month button at the top left of the control.
	PrevMonthDate	The point is part of the previous month's dates shown at the beginning of a visible month in the control. The `Time` property is not set.
	TitleBackground	The point is over the background of a month's title.
	TitleMonth	The point is over a month name in the title of the control.
	TitleYear	The point is over a year value in the title of the control.
	TodayLink	The point is over the "today" link at the bottom of the control.
	WeekNumbers	The point is over a week number when these values are displayed. The `Time` property should contain the first date of that week.

As you can tell, these two types allow an application to identify exactly where a user clicks within a `MonthCalendar` control. Our example only uses the `Date` value when a user clicks on an actual date, but illustrates the basic techniques required.

The following steps detail the code required to process the bolded dates in our application. We discuss the logic in more detail following the table.

HANDLE A MOUSE CLICK IN THE CALENDAR CONTROL		
	Action	**Result**

1	In the AlbumCalendar.cs [Design] window, add a `MouseDown` event handler for the `MonthCalendar` control.	`private void calendarDates_MouseDown(`
		`    object sender, MouseEventArgs e)`
		`{`
		`  // Ignore click if no album selected`
		`  if (Manager == null) return;`

2	Determine if the user clicked on a date.	`  MonthCalendar.HitTestInfo info`
		`    = calendarDates.HitTest(e.X, e.Y);`
		
		`  if (info.HitArea`
		`        == MonthCalendar.HitArea.Date)`
		`  {`

3	If so, create a new context menu strip to hold any photographs associated with this date.	`    ContextMenuStrip cms = new ContextMenuStrip();` `    cms.ShowImageMargin = false;`

4	Iterate through the photos in the album to locate any photographs taken on the date clicked by the user.
	
	How-to
	Use the `DateTime.Date` property to compare only the date portion of the `DateTime` objects.
		`    // See if any photos at date`
		`    for (int i = 0; i < Manager.Album.Count; i++)`
		`    {`
		`      Photograph p = Manager.Album[i];`
		`      if (p.DateTaken.Date == info.Time.Date)`
		`      {`

5	When a photo is found, add it to the context menu strip, with a method `cmsItem_Click` as the `Click` event handler.	`        ToolStripItem menuItem`
		`            = cms.Items.Add(p.FileName);`
		`        menuItem.Tag = i;`
		`        menuItem.Click += cmsItem_Click;`
		`      }`
		`    }`

6	If one or more matching photographs were found, display the context menu.
	
	How-to
	Use the `Show` method at the current mouse location.
		`    if (cms.Items.Count > 0)`
		`      cms.Show(calendarDates, e.Location);`
		`  }`
		`}`

7	Create the private `cmsItem_Click` method to display the associated Photo Properties dialog box.	`private void cmsItem_Click(object sender,`
		`                           EventArgs e)`
		`{`
		`  ToolStripItem item = sender as ToolStripItem;`

8	Implement this handler to display a `PhotoEditDialog` form when a photograph is selected.	`  if (item != null && item.Tag is int)`
		`  {`
		`    Manager.Index = (int)item.Tag;`
		`    using (PhotoEditDialog dlg`
		`            = new PhotoEditDialog(Manager))`
		`    {`

	Action	Result
	HANDLE A MOUSE CLICK IN THE CALENDAR CONTROL *(CONTINUED)*	

9	If the user modifies the `DateTaken` property, update the calendar control to display the modified date.	`DateTime oldDate`
		`    = Manager.Current.DateTaken;`
		`if (dlg.ShowDialog() == DialogResult.OK`
		`    && oldDate != Manager.Current.DateTaken)`
		`{`
		`  // DateTaken was modified`
		`  UpdateCalendar();`
		`}`
		`}`
		`}`
		`}`

When the user clicks on the `MonthCalendar` control, this code finds and displays any photographs associated with a selected date. The `HitTest` method in step 2 retrieves information about the selected point. The returned `HitTestInfo` object identifies exactly what was clicked within the control.

The `MonthCalendar` class also provides a `DateChanged` event that occurs whenever a date or range of dates is selected in the control. We could use this instead of the `MouseDown` event, although it would not work for the right mouse button and the current mouse position would still be required to display the context menu. Based on our requirements, the `MouseDown` event seems a more logical choice.

Another important part of this code is the dynamic creation of a `ContextMenu-Strip` instance to hold the photographs taken on the selected date. A `ToolStrip-Item` for this menu is created dynamically in step 5 to hold the information associated with the photo.

If any photographs are added to the menu, then the `ContextMenuStrip` object is displayed at the same location where the user clicked the mouse. We don't distinguish between which mouse button was clicked, so the user can click any button on the mouse and we happily display our context menu.

Each item within the context menu establishes a shared `Click` event handler. When a user clicks an item in our dynamic context menu, the `cmsItem_Click` method is invoked to process this click. We don't walk through this code, but you can see from the prior steps that we ensure the selected object represents one of our `ToolStripItem` objects, and display a `PhotoEditDialog` form for the associated photograph.

Compile and run the application to see this code in action. Click on a date where one or more photographs were taken and be amazed as a context menu pops up with the corresponding photos. Also try clicking on other aspects of the control to see what happens. In particular, see what happens when you click on the month and year in the title of the control. Note that your ability to alter the month and year displayed is restricted by the range of dates represented in the photo album.

14.4 PROGRESS BARS

To finish this chapter, let's build another tab page in our control to display the full-size images in the album. We add the somewhat artificial option of displaying each image as a black and white photograph. This allows us to discuss two other .NET classes: the `ProgressBar` control and the `BackgroundWorker` class.

There are times in a Windows application when some long-running task is required. This may be communication with an external server such as a database, a complex calculation that requires some time, or some other task. In such situations, the user should not be left wondering what is happening. The `BackgroundWorker` class allows such processing to occur behind the scenes from ongoing UI processing, and the `ProgressBar` control provides a mechanism for reporting on the progress of such activities.

We begin this discussion by building our new tab page, after which we examine the use of a progress bar on a form and the creation of a background worker.

14.4.1 Creating an images user control

Before we can discuss background processing, we need to build up an example where we can demonstrate this. Our approach is shown in figure 14.5, where a new tab page has been added that displays the images in the album in a picture box control.

There is not much new in this tab page, so we create it with the following steps.

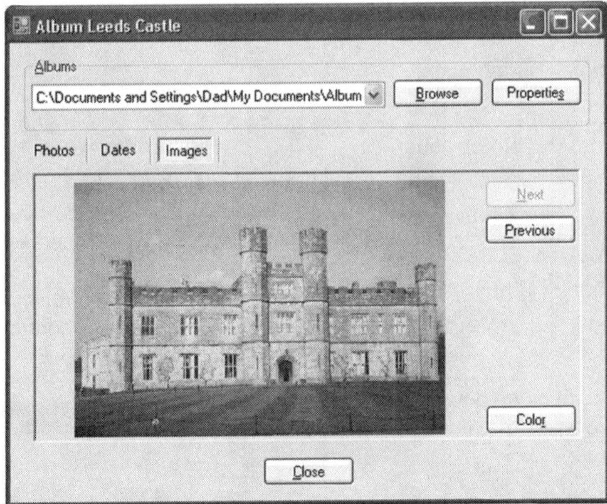

Figure 14.5
The tab page shown here allows the user to toggle between a color and black-and-white display of an image using the indicated button.

CREATE A NEW USER CONTROL TO DISPLAY AN IMAGE

	Action	Result
1	In the MyAlbumEditor project, add a new user control called `AlbumImage`. **Settings** Property / Value (Name): AlbumImage Padding: 5, 5, 5, 5 Size: 350, 200	
2	Drag a picture box onto the control as shown. **Settings** Property / Value (Name): pbxPhoto Anchor: Top, Button, Left, Right SizeMode: Zoom	
3	Add three buttons to the control. **Settings** Button / Property / Value Next: (Name) btnNext; Anchor Top, Right; Text &Next Previous: (Name) btnPrevious; Anchor Top, Right; Text &Previous B & W: (Name) btnColor; Anchor Bottom, Right; Text B && &W	Next Previous B & W **Note:** The last button here illustrates how to place an ampersand (&) character on a button, by using two ampersands in the `Text` setting. You need to build the project after this step, to ensure the new control is available for step 4.
4	In the EditorForm designer window, add a new tab page that contains the new user control. **Settings** Control / Property / Value Tab Page: (Name) pageImages; Border-Style Fixed3D; Text Images Album-Images: (Name) albumImages; Dock Fill	MyAlbumEditor Albums Browse Properties Photos Dates Images Next Previous B & W Close

This completes the visual aspects of our change. The rest is simply a small matter of programming.

<table>
<tr><th colspan="3">HANDLE A MOUSE CLICK IN THE CALENDAR CONTROL</th></tr>
<tr><th></th><th>Action</th><th>Result</th></tr>
<tr><td>5</td><td>In the AlbumImage.cs file, indicate we use the Manning namespaces.</td><td>. . .
using Manning.MyPhotoAlbum;
using Manning.MyPhotoControls;</td></tr>
<tr><td>6</td><td>Add a private AlbumManager field and public Manager property.</td><td>private AlbumManager _manager = null;
public AlbumManager Manager
{
  get { return _manager; }
  set
  {
    _manager = value;
    if (Manager != null) Manager.Index = 0;
    UpdateImage();
  }
}</td></tr>
<tr><td>7</td><td>Implement the UpdateImage method to assign an image for the picture box and enable the buttons appropriately.</td><td>private void UpdateImage()
{
  if (Manager == null || Manager.Current == null)
    pbxPhoto.Image = null;
  else
    AssignImage();

  EnableButtons();
}</td></tr>
<tr><td>8</td><td>Implement the Enable-Buttons method to enable or disable each button based on the current settings.</td><td>private void EnableButtons()
{
  bool haveImage = (pbxPhoto.Image != null);
  btnNext.Enabled = (haveImage
    && Manager.Index < Manager.Album.Count - 1);
  btnPrevious.Enabled = (haveImage
    && Manager.Index > 0);
  btnColor.Enabled = haveImage;
}</td></tr>
<tr><td>9</td><td>Implement Click handlers for the Next and Previous buttons.</td><td>private void btnNext_Click(
    object sender, EventArgs e)
{
  Manager.MoveNext();
  UpdateImage();
}

private void btnPrevious_Click(
    object sender, EventArgs e)
{
  Manager.MovePrev();
  UpdateImage();
}</td></tr>
<tr><td>10</td><td>Implement a private useColor field and UseColor method.</td><td>private bool _useColor = true;
private bool UseColor
{ get { return _useColor; }
  set { _useColor = value; } }</td></tr>
</table>

HANDLE A MOUSE CLICK IN THE CALENDAR CONTROL *(CONTINUED)*		
	Action	**Result**

11	Implement a `Click` handler for the `btnColor` button that toggles the `UseColor` setting and assigns its text accordingly.	<pre>private void btnColor_Click(
		    object sender, EventArgs e)
		{
		  Button btn = sender as Button;
		  UseColor = (btn.Text == "Colo&r");
		  if (UseColor)
		    btn.Text = "B && &W";
		  else
		    btn.Text = "Colo&r";
		
		  UpdateImage();
		}</pre>

12	Create a temporary `AssignImage` method that displays the current image.	<pre>private void AssignImage()
		{
		  pbxPhoto.Image = Manager.Current.Image;
		}</pre>

13	In the `EditorForm` class, add the logic to assign the album manager when the Images tab is selected.	<pre>private void UpdateTabs()
		{
		  . . .
		  if (tcPhotos.SelectedTab == pagePhotos)
		    DisplayAlbum();
		  else if (tcPhotos.SelectedTab == pageDates)
		    albumCalendar.Manager = Manager;
		  else if (tcPhotos.SelectedTab == pageImages)
		    albumImages.Manager = Manager;
		}</pre>

The new tab page is ready to go, and you can compile and run this to see it in action. With this in place, we are ready to discuss the `ProgressBar` control.

14.4.2 The ProgressBar class

A progress bar provides a way to track the completion of a task. As you can see in .NET Table 14.9, the members of the `ProgressBar` class are oriented around tracking a value between a minimum and maximum value.

The `Style` property in this class is new as of the .NET 2.0 release, and takes its values from the `ProgressBarStyle` enumeration. The values for this enumeration are `Blocks`, `Continuous`, and `Marquee`, corresponding to a line made of small blocks, a continuous line, or the Windows XP style where a small block repeatedly scrolls across the bounds of the control. The `Continuous` and `Marquee` styles are only available when visual styles are disable and enabled, respectively.

Figure 14.6 The progress bar here uses the Blocks style.

We demonstrate this control with the form shown in figure 14.6. This links up with our `AlbumImage` user control in the next section when we convert an image into black and white.

.NET Table 14.9 ProgressBar class

The `ProgressBar` class visually indicates the progress of a long operation or other activity. This class is part of the `System.Windows.Forms` namespace, and inherits from the `Control` class. See .NET Table 3.1 for members inherited from this base class.

Public Properties	Maximum	Gets or sets the largest value to display in the progress bar control
	Minimum	Gets or sets the smallest value to display
	Step	Gets or sets the incremental amount to add to the value when `PerformStep` is called
	Style	Gets or sets how progress should be indicated
	Value	Gets or sets the current progress value
Public Methods	Increment	Increases the value for the progress bar by the indicated amount

The following steps construct this form.

CREATE A FORM FOR TRACKING THE CONVERSION OF AN IMAGE

	Action	Result
1	In the MyAlbumEditor project, add a new form called `WorkerProgressDialog`, with a label, progress bar, and button on the form. **Settings** Control / Property / Value Label / Text / Converting image, please wait... Progress Bar / (Name) / pbarProgress Button / (Name) / btnCancel Button / DialogResult / Cancel Button / Text / &Cancel	WorkerProgressDi... Converting image, please wait... Cancel
2	Assign the properties for the form as follows. **Settings** Property / Value CancelButton / btnCancel ControlBox / False FormBorderStyle / FixedDialog MaximizeBox / False MinimizeBox / False StartPosition / CenterParent Text / Black & White	Black & White Converting image, please wait... Cancel

CREATE A FORM FOR TRACKING THE CONVERSION OF AN IMAGE *(CONTINUED)*		
	Action	**Result**

3	In the WorkerProgressDialog.cs file, define a `Progress` property to set or get the current value in the progress bar.	`public int Progress`
		`{`
		`  get { return pbarProgress.Value; }`
		`  set { pbarProgress.Value = value; }`
		`}`

This form displays a progress bar that tracks the conversion of a color image into a black and white image. The final section here performs this conversion.

14.4.3 Performing a background task

At last we are ready to pull this all together. The `AlbumImage` user control is ready to display photographs in either color or black and white, and the `WorkerProgressDialog` is ready to track the progress of a black-and-white conversion. The last piece we need is the `BackgroundWorker` class.

A background task is something that takes a lower priority than other tasks. In Windows Forms applications, responding to the user should always be the first priority. When a task is required that interferes with this ability, it is best to do this on a separate thread in the background. A thread is a sequence of execution—a train of thought if you will. Each thread in a program performs a separate, although sometimes interrelated, task. In our case, while our main thread responds to the user, a background thread performs the conversion into black and white. The `BackgroundWorker` class, summarized in .NET Table 14.10, simplifies this task.

.NET Table 14.10 BackgroundWorker class

New in 2.0 The `BackgroundWorker` class is a component that performs a task in a separate, dedicated thread. This class is part of the `System.ComponentModel` namespace, and inherits from the `Component` class.

Public Properties	*CancellationPending*	Gets whether the operation has been canceled
	IsBusy	Gets whether the worker is running an asynchronous operation
	WorkerReportsProgress	Gets or sets whether the worker can report progress updates
	WorkerSupportsCancellation	Gets or sets whether the worker allows asynchronous cancellation of an operation.
Public Methods	*CancelAsync*	Requests that an operation be canceled
	ReportProgress	Raises the `ProgressChanged` event to report on the progress of the background worker
	RunWorkerAsync	Starts execution of a background operation
Public Events	*DoWork*	Occurs to begin a background operation
	RunWorkerCompleted	Occurs when a background operation ends

The RunWorkerAsync method kicks off the operation. The DoWork event is invoked in a separate thread to perform the task, while the ProgressChanged and RunWorkerCompleted events occur in the main thread where the worker was created. Interaction with Windows Forms controls should only occur in the main thread where the Form containing the controls is managed. As a result, controls should not be manipulated in the DoWork event handler, and may be manipulated in the other events.

For our example, we create a background worker to convert a color image into black and white. This is done in the following steps.

CONVERT AN IMAGE TO BLACK AND WHITE IN THE BACKGROUND

	Action	Result

1	In the AlbumImage class, add a private field and property for a WorkerProgress-Dialog instance.	`private WorkerProgressDialog _worker;`
		`private WorkerProgressDialog WorkerDialog`
		`    { get { return _worker; } }`

2	Rewrite the Assign-Image method to create a black-and-white image when requested.	`private void AssignImage()`
		`{`
		`  Bitmap bmp = Manager.Current.Image;`
		`  if (UseColor)`
		`    pbxPhoto.Image = bmp;`
		`  else`
		`    CreateBlackWhiteImage(bmp);`
		`}`

3	Define the Create-BlackWhiteImage method to create a background worker to convert the image.	`private void CreateBlackWhiteImage(Bitmap bmp)`
		`{`
		`  BackgroundWorker bw = new BackgroundWorker();`
		`  bw.DoWork += worker_DoWork;`
		`  bw.ProgressChanged += worker_ProgressChanged;`
		`  bw.RunWorkerCompleted += worker_RunWorkerCompleted;`
		`  bw.WorkerSupportsCancellation = true;`
		`  bw.WorkerReportsProgress = true;`

4	Create the progress dialog box to display progress to the user, and pass the color bitmap image as an argument to the background process.	`  _worker = new WorkerProgressDialog();`
		`  WorkerDialog.Progress = 0;`
		
		`  pbxPhoto.Image = null;`
		`  bw.RunWorkerAsync(bmp);`

5	If the dialog box is canceled, cancel the background operation.	`  if (WorkerDialog.ShowDialog()`
		`          == DialogResult.Cancel)`
		`    bw.CancelAsync();`
		`}`

This code creates the background worker and assigns event handlers to track its progress. An instance of the WorkerProgressDialog is created to display the progress to the user. If the task completes, the dialog box exits normally. If the dialog box is canceled, the `CancelAsync` method is called to cancel the background operation.

All that is left is to implement the events for the background task.

	IMPLEMENT EVENT HANDLERS FOR THE BACKGROUND OPERATION	
	Action	**Result**

6	Implement the `worker_DoWork` method to process the `DoWork` event for the background worker.	`private void worker_DoWork(`
		`  object sender, DoWorkEventArgs e)`
		`{`
		`  BackgroundWorker bw`
		`      = sender as BackgroundWorker;`

7	Create a new `Bitmap` image to hold the black-and-white version of the image.	`  e.Result = null;`
		`  Bitmap bmp = e.Argument as Bitmap;`
		`  int width = bmp.Width;`
		`  int height = bmp.Height;`
		`  Bitmap bwImage = new Bitmap(width, height);`

8	Iterate through every pixel in the image to convert each color. If the operation is canceled, abort the task.	`  for (int i = 0; i < width; i++)`
		`  {`
		`    for (int j = 0; j < height; j++)`
		`    {`
		`      if (bw.CancellationPending) return;`
		
		`      Color c = bmp.GetPixel(i, j);`

9	Convert the color at each pixel to a grayscale value.
	
	Note: This uses a luminance algorithm for each pixel, which is based on typical monitor behavior and the color properties of the human eye.
		`      double redFactor = 0.30 * (double)c.R;`
		`      double greenFactor = 0.59 * (double)c.G;`
		`      double blueFactor = 0.11 * (double)c.B;`
		
		`      int x = (int)`
		`        (redFactor + greenFactor + blueFactor);`
		`      Color bwColor = Color.FromArgb(x, x, x);`
		`      bwImage.SetPixel(i, j, bwColor);`
		`    }`

10	After completing each row of pixels, report on progress. When complete, return the new image as the result of the operation.	`    bw.ReportProgress(i * 100 / width);`
		`  }`
		
		`  e.Result = bwImage;`
		`}`

11	Implement the `worker_ProgressChanged` method to update the progress bar in the worker dialog box.	`void worker_ProgressChanged(object sender,`
		`    ProgressChangedEventArgs e)`
		`{`
		`  if (WorkerDialog != null)`
		`    WorkerDialog.Progress = e.ProgressPercentage;`
		`}`

12	Implement the `worker_RunWorker-Completed` method to report any error in a message box.	`void worker_RunWorkerCompleted(object sender,`
		`    RunWorkerCompletedEventArgs e)`
		`{`
		`  if (e.Error != null)`
		`  {`
		`    MessageBox.Show("Unable to convert image "`
		`      + "to black and white ("`
		`      + e.Error.Message + ")");`
		`  }`

	Action	Result
IMPLEMENT EVENT HANDLERS FOR THE BACKGROUND OPERATION *(CONTINUED)*		

13	Otherwise, set the image in the picture box to `null` if the operation was canceled or returned no result, or to the returned bitmap if available.	`else`
		`{`
		`  Bitmap bmp = e.Result as Bitmap;`
		
		`  if (e.Cancelled || bmp == null)`
		`    pbxPhoto.Image = Manager.Current.Image;`
		`  else`
		`    pbxPhoto.Image = bmp;`
		`}`

14	Finish the method by closing the worker dialog box and updating the status of the control's buttons.	`  WorkerDialog.Close();`
		`  EnableButtons();`
		`}`

This completes our background operation. I should mention that this approach performs horribly when converting a large color image into black and white, even though it serves as an excellent example of background processing. If you need to manipulate an image at the pixel level, I don't recommend using the `SetPixel` and `GetPixel` methods. A better approach is described in the article "Unsafe Image Processing," by Eric Gunnerson, available through a search at msdn.microsoft.com. This article uses a rather poor conversion algorithm into black and white, but provides an excellent description of how to manipulate bitmap pixels in unsafe code to improve performance.

14.5 RECAP

In this chapter we examined date and time controls, most notably the `DateTimePicker` and `MonthCalendar` classes. We utilized both of these controls in our MyAlbumEditor application. A `DateTimePicker` control replaced the `MaskedTextBox` control in our `PhotoEditDialog` class, while a `MonthCalendar` control was utilized in a new `TabPage` within the existing tab control on the form.

We also discussed date and time formatting, continuing our discussion from chapter 12. We introduced the formatting codes and characters for the `DateTime` structure, and presented an example using the `DateTimeFormatInfo` class to hold culture-specific information such as how a date is formatted for a specific language and country.

We also discussed user controls. The `UserControl` class presents and manages a custom collection of controls, which can then be utilized within one or more applications. Our example created a new user control to hold the `MonthCalendar` control and logic for the new tab page in the MyAlbumEditor application.

We finished our discussion with the `ProgressBar` control and `BackgroundWorker` class. These classes are often used together to perform a long-running operation in a background thread and still allow the user to cancel the operation if necessary. Our example created yet another tab page to hold a new `AlbumImage` user control that displayed images from an album as either color or black-and-white images.

The next chapter provides another diversion from our ongoing discussion of Windows Forms controls by presenting various classes often used to improve the usability and appearance of applications. Chapter 16 finishes part 2 with a discussion on tool strips.

CHAPTER 15

Bells and whistles

It's the little things that make life, and computer programs, interesting. Colors, icons, sounds, and other such details make an application more useful and appealing than a similar application without such features. Much of our prior discussion has focused on the nuts and bolts of placing and interacting with controls and forms on the Windows desktop. In this chapter we look at a few Windows Forms classes that can help "dress up" a Windows program.

The topics covered here include the following. Our discussion presents each concept separately, in roughly the same order.

- Creating image files in Visual Studio
- Assigning a custom icon to a form or application
- Modifying the mouse cursor for a form or control
- Embedding resources within a project
- Playing sound within an application
- Using the `TrackBar` control
- Performing background tasks using the `Timer` component

Figure 15.1
This dialog box illustrates many of the features discussed in the chapter, including custom images, project resources, and track bars.

To demonstrate these features, we return to our MyPhotos application began in chapter 2. Over the course of our discussion, we extend this application to support the dialog box shown in figure 15.1.

15.1 IMAGES AND CURSORS

While we have discussed images a few different times, we have yet to present image classes in any formal manner. We introduced the `Bitmap` class in chapter 1, and this class still holds the images in our MyPhotos application.

In this chapter we discuss image types used in many applications: the `Bitmap` and `Icon` classes, and the Windows Forms `Cursor` class.

15.1.1 Bitmaps

We have already seen the `Bitmap` class in this book, both to represent image files loaded from disk and to display these files within a `PictureBox` control. The `Bitmap` class is quite interesting, and we could probably spend a few pages discussing the properties and methods provided by this class. Since this is a book on Windows Forms programming rather than on imaging, we do not do this. We continue to use new features of this class where appropriate, but keep our focus on creating and using bitmaps within Windows applications.

As we have seen, a number of Windows Forms classes provide an `Image` property to define the image to appear on or within a control. In some classes this is the only item shown in the control, as for the `PictureBox` class. Other classes can display text, an image, or both, as in the `Label` and `ButtonBase` classes.

The source for images to appear on controls is often a `Bitmap` instance. In our `Photograph` class, for example, an image file is loaded into a `Bitmap` object, and our MyPhotos application assigns the picture box `Image` property to this image.

You can also create bitmaps programmatically or within Visual Studio directly. We saw this in chapter 14 while converting a color image into black and white. As another example, the following lines of code create a red bitmap image 100 by 100 pixels:

```
Bitmap bmp = new Bitmap(100, 100);
Graphics g = Graphics.FromImage(bmp);
g.FillRectangle(Brushes.Red, 0, 0, bmp.Width, bmp.Height);
g.Dispose();
```

This code fills a `Graphics` object created from a new `Bitmap` instance using a red brush. For simple bitmap drawings, this technique is quite useful.

Bitmaps can also be created in an external file using a graphics program such as Microsoft Paint, the GIMP application (www.gimp.org), or a professional application such as Adobe Photoshop.

Visual Studio provides a Paint-like application for the creation of bitmap images. To see this, let's create some simple left and right arrows in our MyPhotos application.

CREATE ARROW BITMAP IMAGES

	Action	Result
1	Add a new Resources folder within the MyPhotos project of the MyPhotos solution. **How-to** a. Click the MyPhotos project. b. Select the New Folder item from the Project menu. c. Rename the folder to "Resources."	
2	Add a bitmap file called "NextBitmap" to the new Resources folder. **How-to** a. Right-click the new folder. b. Open the Add submenu. c. Select Add New Item. d. In the Add New Item dialog box, select the Bitmap File template. e. Enter "NextBitmap" as the Name. f. Click Add to add the new file. **Alternately** The Add New Item dialog box can be displayed using the keyboard shortcut Ctrl+Shift+A.	The new file appears in Solution Explorer. The Bitmap Editor displays the new bitmap in the main window, as shown in figure 15.2. 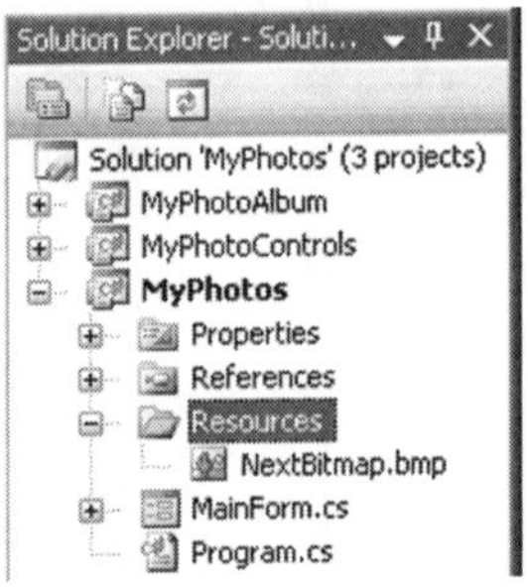 **Note:** If you are using the Visual C# Express Edition, a bitmap template and editor is not provided. Instead, create the bitmap file directly in Paint, and then drag the file into the Resources folder by hand.

CREATE ARROW BITMAP IMAGES *(CONTINUED)*

	Action	Result
3	Modify the properties of this bitmap to create an 18-pixel square bitmap. **Settings** **Property** / **Value** Height / 18 Width / 18	Properties Bitmap Editor IBmpEd (Name) Bitmap Editor Colors 16 Color Compressed False Filename C:\Windows Forms\ Height 18 Width 18 **Note:** The `Colors` property here defines the color depth of the bitmap: Monochrome, 16 Color, 256 Color, or True Color. For our purposes, the default of 16 Color is fine.
4	Edit the pixels for the bitmap to create a right-direction arrow. **How-to** Copy the graphic shown here, or create your own version of this arrow.	

This defines the first image, a right-pointing arrow. Figure 15.2 shows Visual Studio with this button displayed. If you are feeling creative, the editor supports a number of

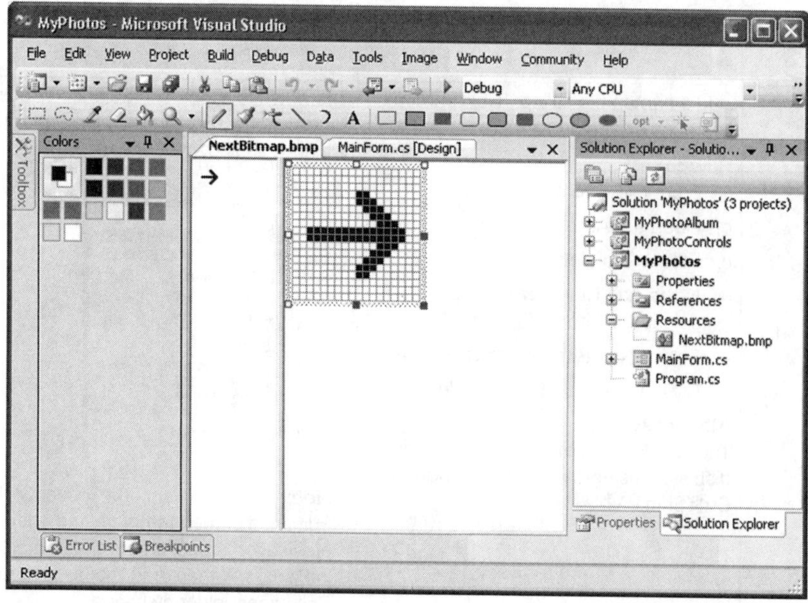

Figure 15.2 The Bitmap Editor displays an actual size and a per-pixel view of the bitmap.

drawing controls, quite similar to the Microsoft Paint application installed with Windows. In the figure, the drawing controls are available in the bottom row of toolbar buttons, and the Colors window is shown on the left side. If it's not shown, you can display the Colors window by right-clicking within the Bitmap Editor window and selecting Show Colors Window.

A bitmap for a left-pointing arrow can be created in a similar manner. An alternate method of creating this image is used in the following steps.

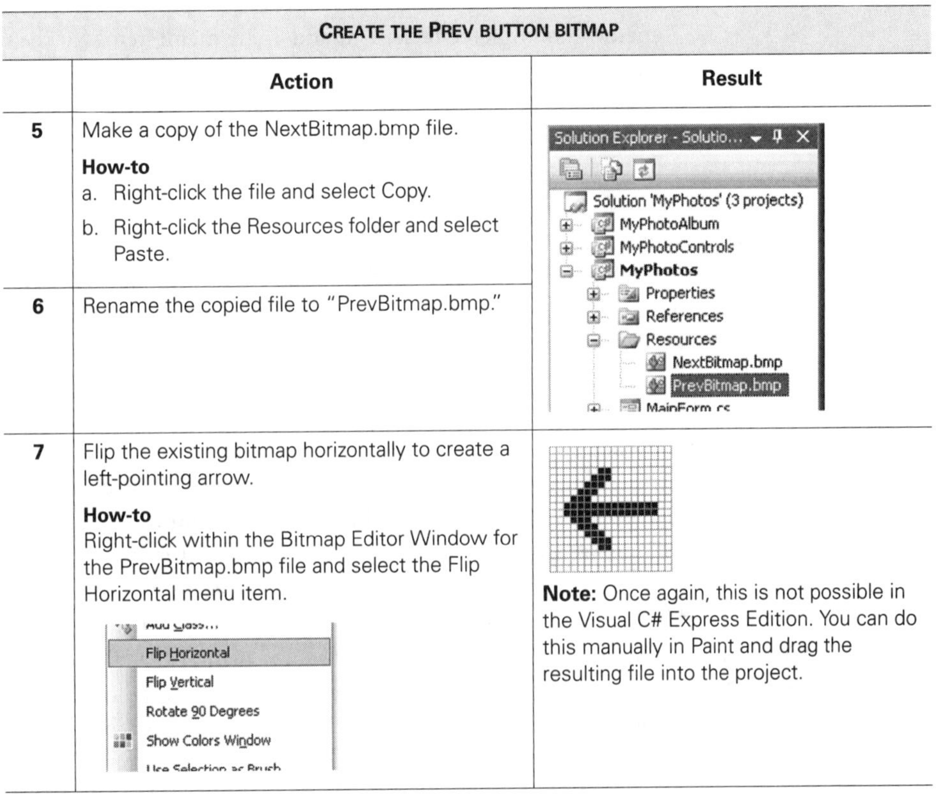

CREATE THE PREV BUTTON BITMAP

	Action	Result
5	Make a copy of the NextBitmap.bmp file. **How-to** a. Right-click the file and select Copy. b. Right-click the Resources folder and select Paste.	
6	Rename the copied file to "PrevBitmap.bmp."	
7	Flip the existing bitmap horizontally to create a left-pointing arrow. **How-to** Right-click within the Bitmap Editor Window for the PrevBitmap.bmp file and select the Flip Horizontal menu item.	**Note:** Once again, this is not possible in the Visual C# Express Edition. You can do this manually in Paint and drag the resulting file into the project.

These two bitmaps are now complete. As you might guess, we use these bitmaps later in the chapter on Next and Previous buttons for a new dialog window.

Personally, I am the kind of programmer who keeps good graphic artists employed, so we shy away from hand-drawing images or other graphics in the remainder of the book. Fortunately for us, Microsoft provides a fairly large collection of images that can be imported into your programs. These are installed by default along with Visual Studio in the Common7 directory underneath the main Visual Studio installation directory. For .NET 2.0, this is the directory C:\Program Files\Microsoft Visual Studio 8\ Common7. There you will find a folder or file called VS2005ImageLibrary or something similar. Locate the zip file with the same name, and unzip its contents into an appropriate folder. This collection contains animations, bitmaps, and icons that you can use in your applications.[1]

For the purposes of our discussions, we use the term *common image library* to refer to this directory rather than using the full directory name every time. In particular, we use this directory for our next topic: icons.

TRY IT! As an aside to our discussion, we still have the Cut, Copy, and Paste menu items in our Edit menu. Implement these menus to interact with the current album using the `Clipboard` class. Use the `SetFileDropList` method to implement the Cut and Copy menu items for the current photographic image; and the `Clipboard.ContainsFileDropList` method for the Paste menu item to identify if one or more files are available. If so, insert the available files into the album as required.

15.1.2 Icons

An *icon* is an image used to represent an object in a program or operating system. Icons are much like bitmaps, except they provide *transparency*, meaning that a certain color in the icon automatically blends in with the background when it is displayed. If the icon is displayed on a red background, the transparent areas appear red as well. If the icon is displayed on a purple background, the transparent areas appear purple. This behavior permits Windows icons to appear on the desktop and in file system windows as if they do not have a border. In fact, all icons are rectangular in shape.

It is worth mentioning that icons can be defined in a project just like any other object. You can create new icons from the Add New Item dialog box and edit them in Visual Studio as we did for our bitmap files. Unlike bitmaps, icons store multiple image types, or image sizes, in a single file. The most typical sizes are 16×16 and 32×32 pixels, so you should generally stick with these formats. New icons in Visual Studio are created with these two sizes by default, using 16 available colors, and the Icon Editor permits sizes to be deleted and custom sizes and colors to be assigned.

The `System.Drawing` namespace provides an `Icon` class to create and manipulate icons in your programs. It's a fine class, but we are not going to discuss it. Instead, we focus on how to assign icons to a project and to specific forms. The `Icon` property of the `Form` class defines the icon to display on the form.

By default, Visual Studio uses the graphic at the right as the icon on all forms. This icon is fine, but it would be nice to have a custom icon that represents a photo album in some manner. One such image is shown as the icon in figure 15.1. Microsoft provides this icon in the common image library discussed at the end of the prior section.

---

[1] Of course, if you customized your Visual Studio installation settings, or modified the installation directory, then these files may not exist on your machine or might be in an alternate location. You may need to reinstall Visual Studio to make sure these graphics are available, or use alternate graphics in place of the ones we use in the remainder of the book.

The following steps assign this icon to our form.

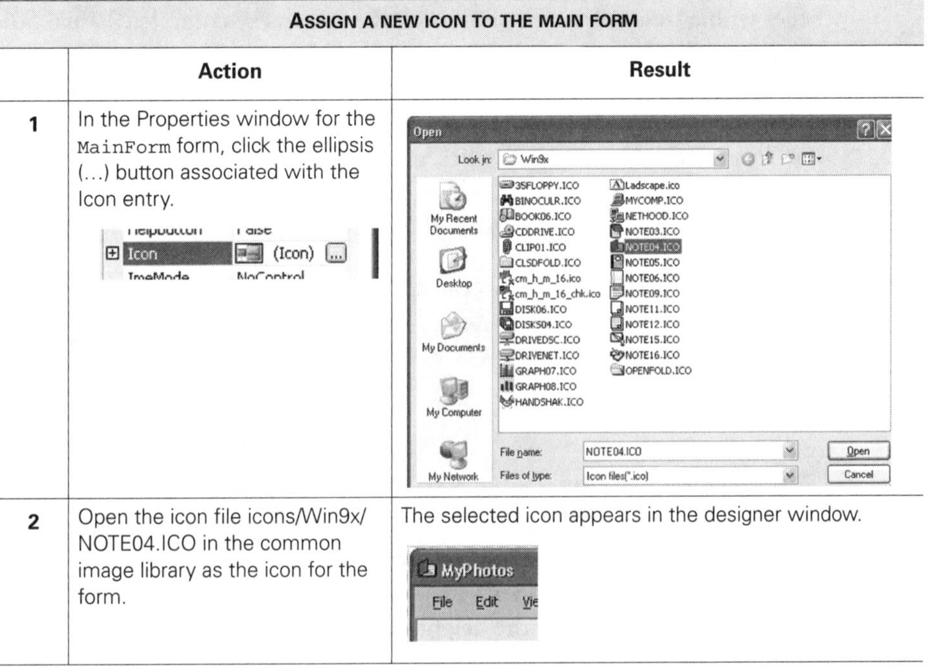

ASSIGN A NEW ICON TO THE MAIN FORM		
	Action	**Result**
1	In the Properties window for the `MainForm` form, click the ellipsis (…) button associated with the Icon entry.	
2	Open the icon file icons/Win9x/NOTE04.ICO in the common image library as the icon for the form.	The selected icon appears in the designer window.

These actions select an icon to display whenever the form is displayed. The generated code is quite interesting. The relevant excerpt of the `InitializeComponent` method in the MainFom.Designer.cs file is shown here:

```
private void InitializeComponent()
{
  this.components = new System.ComponentModel.Container();
  System.ComponentModel.ComponentResourceManager resources
      = new System.ComponentModel.ComponentResourceManager(
              typeof(MainForm));
  . . .
  this.Icon = ((System.Drawing.Icon)
                (resources.GetObject("$this.Icon")));
  . . .
}
```

This code employs the `ComponentResourceManager` class to load the icon into the application and assign it to the `Icon` property of the `MainForm` object. A short discussion of this functionality is in order.

A *culture-specific resource*, often referred to simply as a *resource*, is a file that encapsulates a set of data utilized by a component or assembly for a specific culture. A culture, as you may recall from chapter 12, represents a specific language and region.

Visual Studio creates a resource file for each project and component in an assembly automatically. Resource files use the .resx extension, and are compiled into binary files with a .resources extension using the resgen.exe compiler. Visual Studio invokes this compiler automatically, so we do not discuss it in detail here.

In our project, the file MainForm.resx represents the resources for the `MainForm` class. You can double-click on this file to view and manage the contained resources, as illustrated in figure 15.3. Click the down arrow associated with the first item and select the Icons option to view the icon we just added. You can view other resources as well, such as the images assigned to the form's menu items.

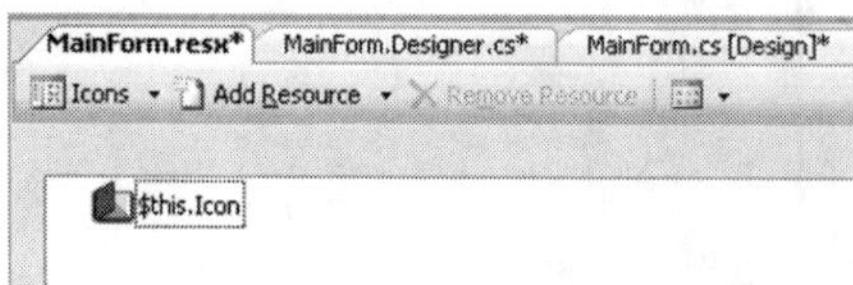

Figure 15.3
The Resource Editor displays the strings, images, icons, and other objects contained in the file.

Resource, or .resx, files use an XML format to represent each resource in the file. A short excerpt of this file is shown in listing 15.1 to give you an idea of its contents. As you can see, this resource file contains data for the application, such as the image associated with the New menu item or the icon associated with the form (`$this`), as well as metadata, such as the height of the component tray Visual Studio displays for the form.

Listing 15.1 Excerpt of MainForm.resx, the resource file for the MainForm class

```
<?xml version="1.0" encoding="utf-8"?>
<root>
. . .
  <xsd:schema id="root" . . .>
  . . .
  </xsd:schema>
  <resheader name="resmimetype">
    <value>text/microsoft-resx</value>
  </resheader>
  <resheader name="version">
    <value>2.0</value>
  </resheader>
  . . .
  <data name="menuFileNew.Image" type="System.Drawing.Bitmap,
      System.Drawing" mimetype="application/x
          -microsoft.net.object.bytearray.base64">
    <value>
      iVBORw0KGgoAAAANSUhEUgAAABAAAAAQCAYAAAAf8/9hAAAAAXNSR . . .
      YQUAAAAgY0hSTQAAeiYAAICEAAD6AAAAgOgAAHUwAADqYAAAOpgAA . . .
        . . .
    </value>
  </data>
```

```
  . . .
  <metadata name="$this.TrayHeight" type="System.Int32, mscorlib,
      Version=2.0.0.0, . . .>
    <value>43</value>
  </metadata>
  <data name="$this.Icon" type="System.Drawing.Icon, . . .>
    <value>
      AAABAAIAICAQAAAAAADoAgAAJgAAABAQEAAAAAAAKAEAAA4DAAAoA . . .
      AAAAAAAAAAAAAAAAAAAAAAAAAAAAAAAgAAAgAAAAICAAIAAAACAA . . .
    </value>
  </data>
</root>
```

When a solution is compiled, the resulting .resource files appear in the appropriate obj directory, using the fully qualified name of the associated class. Our MainForm.resx file is compiled into the MyPhotos.MainForm.resources file. This file is then linked into the resulting assembly, in this case the MyPhotos.exe file.

The `ResourceManager` class is part of the `System.Resources` namespace and provides access to culture-specific resources at runtime. The `ComponentResourceManager` class is part of the `System.ComponentModel` namespace and defines a resource manager for enumerating the resources associated with a component or object. A constructor for this class looks up the resource information associated with a given `Type`, in our case the `MainForm` type.

```
System.ComponentModel.ComponentResourceManager resources
    = new System.ComponentModel.ComponentResourceManager(
              typeof(MainForm));
```

The `ResourceManager` class provides a number of methods for retrieving objects from a resource file. The `GetString` method retrieves a specific `string` resource, while the `GetObject` method returns any `object` in the file. For the `GetObject` method, the `Type` of the object is stored in the resource file directory, so the returned `object` is of the proper type. This allows the generated code to cast the `object` directly into an `Icon` instance.

```
this.Icon = ((System.Drawing.Icon)(resources.GetObject("$this.Icon")));
```

Other resources are loaded in a similar manner. As an example, take a look at how images for the menu items are loaded in the `InitializeComponent` method.

Keep in mind that all of this resource management is performed automatically by Visual Studio. Unless you need to create and manage custom resources, or convert an application to work in an alternate culture or language, you should not need to deal with resources directly. For example, we can assign an icon for the `PixelDialog` form without referencing resources at all.

	Assign a new icon for the pixel dialog form	
	Action	**Result**
3	Modify the `PixelDialog` form in the MyPhotoControls project to use the icons/WinXP/search.ico icon from the common image library.	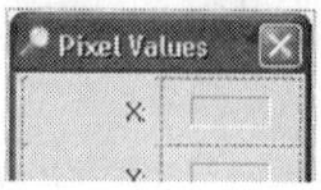 Pixel Values X: Y:

Compile and run the application to verify that these icons now appear on their respective forms. This method can be used to assign an existing icon to any form. Of course, the `Icon` property can be assigned to in code as well.

At times you may prefer that an icon not appear on a form. When set to `false`, the `Form.ControlBox` property removes the icon from the title bar.

You might think the icon for the application executable is based on the icon assigned to the main form, namely the form containing the `Main` entry point for the assembly. This is a fine notion—but it's not true. In fact, the application icon is totally separate from the icons assigned to any forms within the application. One simple reason for this is that applications do not always contain a main form, and console applications and libraries may not contain any forms at all.

For our purposes, we simply select an icon from the set of images provided by Microsoft in the common image library directory. The default application icon, visible by looking at the MyPhotos.exe file in the MyPhotos project's bin directory, is shown at the right.

We would prefer to use the same icon we assigned to the `MainForm` window as the application icon, so let's see exactly how to do this.

	Assign a new application icon to the MyPhotos project	
	Action	**Result**
4	Double-click the Properties entry in the MyPhotos project.	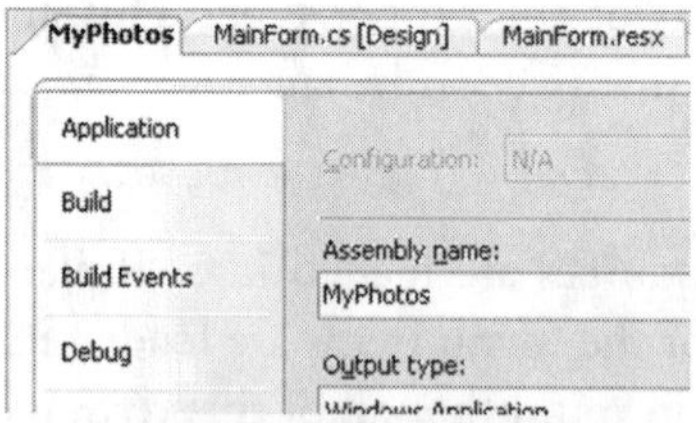 MyPhotos / MainForm.cs [Design] / MainForm.resx Application, Build, Build Events, Debug Configuration: N/A Assembly name: MyPhotos Output type: Windows Application
5	Click the ... button to the right of the Icon entry on the Application tab.	 Add existing file to project Look in: Win9x 35FLOPPY.ICO, BINOCULR.ICO, BOOK06.ICO, CDDRIVE.ICO, CLIP01.ICO, CLSDFOLD.ICO, cm_h_m_16.ico, Ladscape.ico, MYCOMP.ICO, NETHOOD.ICO, NOTE03.ICO, NOTE04.ICO, NOTE05.ICO, NOTE06.ICO Desktop, My Projects
6	Select the icons/Win9x/NOTE04.ICO file.	

ASSIGN A NEW APPLICATION ICON TO THE MYPHOTOS PROJECT *(CONTINUED)*		
	Action	**Result**
7	Click the Open button to assign the icon to the project.	

The only visual indication of this change in Visual Studio is the display of the icon to the right of the ... button, as shown in the result for step 7. When you rebuild the application, the MyPhotos.exe executable file on the bin directory is now displayed with this icon.

15.1.3 Cursors

As long as we are talking images in Windows Forms applications, a brief mention of cursors is in order. The `Cursor` class is part of the `System.Windows.Forms` namespace, and represents an image used to paint the mouse pointer. You can create and manipulate cursors using this class, but more typical is to use members of the `Cursors` class.

The `Cursors` class is also part of the `System.Windows.Forms` namespace, but provides access to the mouse pointer settings in the operating system through a set of static properties in the class. The list of properties in the `Cursors` class would not be very helpful without the graphics to go with it, so instead figure 15.4 is provided. This figure shows a sampling of the default cursor graphics in Windows XP Professional as seen in the Properties window of Visual Studio.

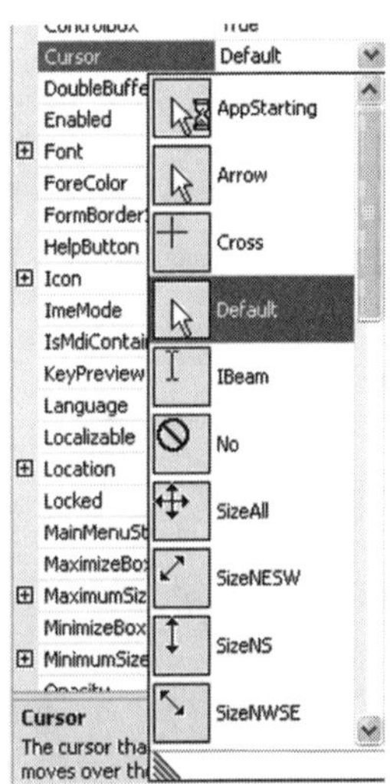

Figure 15.4 The mouse properties available from the Windows Control Panel allows the graphics associated with the cursor values to be modified.

The cursor for each control on a form can be assigned visually or programmatically. If unassigned, a control inherits its cursor from its parent control. Some controls, such as the `TextBox` control, define their own cursor for use within the control.

One common use of cursors is to assign a wait cursor while a potentially long operation is occurring. Assigning the `Cursor` property for the associated `Form` object does this. You can also assign the static `Current` property to a new cursor. When the `Cursor.Current` property is set, the assigned cursor is displayed and the application stops listening for mouse events until the `Current` property is set to `Cursors.Default`.[2]

[2] Calling the `Application.DoEvents` method prior to resetting the `Current` property to `Cursors.Default` will also cause the application to resume listening for mouse events and display the assigned cursor for each control.

As an example, listing 15.2 modifies our `Click` event handler for the Open menu item to display a wait cursor while opening the selected album. The changes are shown in bold type. Note how a finally block is used to ensure that the current cursor is reset regardless of whether an exception occurs. Using a finally block in such situations is important to prevent the application from entering an errant state.

Listing 15.2 Using a wait cursor while opening an album

```
private void menuFileOpen_Click(object sender, EventArgs e)
{
  string path = null;
  string password = null;
  if (AlbumController.OpenAlbumDialog(ref path, ref password))
  {
    // Close existing album
    if (!SaveAndCloseAlbum())
      return;  // Close canceled

    // Open the new album
    try
    {
      Cursor.Current = Cursors.WaitCursor;
      Manager = new AlbumManager(path, password);
    }
    catch (AlbumStorageException aex)
    {
      . . .
    }
    finally
    {
      Cursor.Current = Cursors.Default;
    }

    DisplayAlbum();
  }
}
```

15.2 Embedded resources and sounds

The previous section examined the use of images in Windows applications, and included a short discussion of resource files for an application or form. In this section, we expand on this discussion to cover embedded resources in an application, and the automatic support provided by Visual Studio for such resources.

One of the resources we embed in our MyPhotos application is a .wav sound file, so this section also discusses the `SoundPlayer` class for playing such files within an application.

15.2.1 Embedding a resource

As we have seen, Visual Studio creates resource files automatically for components that required them, such as our `MainForm` and `PixelDialog` classes. They are created with the same name as the component, with an .resx extension.

There are also times when an application requires a specific file as part of its execution. This might be an image or video clip used by the application, or perhaps test or seed data that is required for proper execution of the program. In this case two different approaches can be used to include, or embed, the data into the application.

The first approach is to embed the resource directly into the assembly. Every file in a project has a defined Build Action associated with it, accessible by selecting the Properties entry from the context menu for a file. The possible Build Action settings are shown in table 15.1. As you can see, the Embedded Resource action causes a file to be included in the assembly created for the project.

Table 15.1 Build action settings for Visual Studio project files

Build Action	Description
None	The file is not included in any output generated by the project. An example might be a project readme file.
Compile	The file is compiled and included in the build output. A source code file is the prime example.
Content	The file is not compiled, but is included as content for the project for deployment purposes. An example might be a documentation or HTML file required by the project.
Embedded Resource	The file is embedded in the build output and available in the resulting assembly. This is typically used for project resource or data files.

Examine any resource file in a project and you will find that its Build Action is set to Embedded Resource. You may also note that the Custom Tool property on project resource files may be set to "ResXFileCodeGenerator" to ensure that the appropriate .resources file is generated prior to embedding the file in the project assembly. The `ResourceManager` classes know how to extract this data and make it available to the application in the appropriate format.

It is also possible to embed data or other files in a project. In this case, the `Assembly` class in the `System.Reflection` namespace provides a few methods that can be used to retrieve embedded resources. The `GetManifestResourceNames` method returns an array populated with the names of all resources in the assembly, while the `GetManifestResourceStream` method loads a resource by name and returns a `Stream` object representing the resource. There is also a `GetManifestResourceInfo` method that returns a `ManifestResourceInfo` object containing information about the given resource name.

As a quick example, suppose two resources are embedded in a project called ResourceSample that uses the namespace `Samples.ResourceSample`. The first is an image file within an Images directory called MyImage.jpg. The second is an XML file called MyData.xml at the top level of the project directory.

Each resource is named using the project namespace, the directory structure within the project, and the name of the resource file. The directory structure is referred to as the *extended namespace*, so that the name is constructed as follows:

```
project namespace.extended namespace.filename
```

With this in mind, the following code excerpt retrieves these two resources from the current assembly:

```
// Determine the assembly for this class
Assembly asm = GetType().Assembly;

// Load the embedded image
Stream imageStream = asm.GetManifestResourceStream(
  "Samples.ResourceSample.Images.MyImage.jpg");
Image img = Image.FromStream(imageStream);

// Load the embedded XML file
Stream xmlStream = asm.GetManifestResourceStream(
  "Samples.ResourceSample.MyData.xml");
XmlReader reader = XmlReader.Create(xmlStream);
```

This code assumes that the resources are being loaded by a class within the `Assembly` that contains the resource, and that the `System.Reflection` and `System.Xml` namespaces are available within the class. We also use the `Image.FromStream` and `XmlReader.Create` methods to convert the retrieved `Stream` object into the desired data type. We do not discuss these methods or classes in detail here.

We should also note that the `Bitmap` class provides a constructor designed to load embedded images directly. This constructor allows the image in our prior example to be loaded with a single line:

```
Bitmap bmp = new Bitmap(GetType(), "Images.MyImage.jpg");
```

15.2.2 Using the project resource file

As an alternative to embedding a file directly into the project, a file can be included through the project's resource file. The Properties section of each project contains a Resources.resx file, and Visual Studio provides some fairly nice support for inserting and retrieving resources from this file.

The best way to see this is through an example, so let's include the two bitmap files we created in section 15.1.1 in the resource file for the MyPhotos project.

ASSIGN A NEW ICON FOR THE PIXEL DIALOG FORM		
	Action	**Result**
1	Set the Build Action for the NextBitmap.bmp file to None. **How-to** a. Right-click the file to display the context menu. b. Select the Properties item. c. Set the Build Action property to None.	
2	Similarly, set the Build Action for the PrevBitmap.bmp file to None.	
3	Display the resources for the MyPhotos project. **How-to** Double-click the Resources.resx file underneath the Properties entry in the Solution Explorer window.	
4	Add the NextBitmap.bmp file as a resource for the project. **How-to** Drag the NextBitmap.bmp file into the Resource Editor window.	
5	Similarly, add the PrevBitmap.bmp file as a resource for the project.	

So what exactly happened here? The short answer is that we turned these two bitmap files into project resources. To do this, we set the Build Action for both files to None to ensure that the files are not included in any output for the project. Then we added these bitmaps to the project resource file, Resources.resx, so they are available as resources in the project. The Resource Editor used here has some buttons to control what information is shown in the window—you can experiment with these settings to determine their meaning.

There is more happening here than you might guess. You may have realized that the Resources.resx file is updated with the bitmap data for these two images. This is quite similar to listing 15.1, so we won't repeat the bulk of this file here. Since the resources are based on a file within the project, the resource value is set to the file rather than the actual data. For example, the NextBitmap resource is defined like this:

```
<data name="NextBitmap" type="System.Resources.ResXFileRef,
                               System.Windows.Forms">
  <value>..\resources\nextbitmap.bmp;System.Drawing.Bitmap,
      System.Drawing, Version=2.0.0.0, Culture=neutral,
```

```
        PublicKeyToken=b03f5f7f11d50a3a</value>
  </data>
```

A less obvious change is that Visual Studio automatically regenerated the Resources.Designer.cs file. This file is generated using the `StronglyTypedResourceBuilder` class, but can be generated manually with the Resource File Generator (resgen.exe) tool using the /str option. An excerpt of the generated file is shown in listing 15.3.

Listing 15.3 Excerpt of Resources.Designer.cs file

```
namespace MyPhotos.Properties {
. . .
 internal class Resources {
  private static global::
      System.Resources.ResourceManager resourceMan;
  private static global::
      System.Globalization.CultureInfo resourceCulture;
  . . .
  /// <summary>
  ///   Returns the cached ResourceManager instance...
  /// </summary>
  [global::System.ComponentModel.EditorBrowsableAttribute(
     global::System.ComponentModel.EditorBrowsableState.Advanced)]
  internal static global::
     System.Resources.ResourceManager ResourceManager {
    get {
      if (object.ReferenceEquals(resourceMan, null)) {
        global::System.Resources.ResourceManager temp = new
          global::System.Resources.ResourceManager(
            "MyPhotos.Properties.Resources",
            typeof(Resources).Assembly);
        resourceMan = temp;
      }
      return resourceMan;
    }
  }

  /// <summary>
  ///   Overrides the current thread's CurrentUICulture
  ///   property for all resource lookups...
  /// </summary>
  internal static global::System.Globalization.CultureInfo Culture {
    get {
        return resourceCulture;
      }
      set {
        resourceCulture = value;
      }
    }

  internal static System.Drawing.Bitmap NextBitmap {
```

1 Defines static resource manager and culture

2 Defines internal properties

```
      get {
        return ((System.Drawing.Bitmap) (ResourceManager.GetObject(
            "NextBitmap", resourceCulture)));
      }
    }

      internal static System.Drawing.Bitmap PrevBitmap {
        get {
          return ((System.Drawing.Bitmap) (ResourceManager.GetObject(
              "PrevBitmap", resourceCulture)));          Retrieves typed  ❸
        }                                                       resource
      }
    }
  }
```

As you can see, the generated file defines a `Properties` namespace for the project with an internal `Resources` class. This code is available only to files within the MyPhotos.exe assembly using the fully qualified name `MyPhotos.Properties.Resources`. Other notable aspects of this code are as follows:

❶ The `Resources` class defines two static fields and corresponding properties to hold a `ResourceManager` and `CultureInfo` class. The `ResourceManager` instance creates the object the first time it is accessed. The `CultureInfo` defaults to `null` so that the default application culture is used, or an application can override the default by setting an explicit culture.

❷ The generator creates a static property for each resource defined in the source file, in this case the Resources.resx file. This property provides read-only access to the associated resource.

❸ The `get` accessor for each resource property loads the resource using the cached `ResourceManager` by calling the `GetObject` method. The retrieved object is cast to the appropriate type and returned.

We utilize these resources shortly in a slide show dialog box built in section 15.3. Our final topic in this section is sound.

15.2.3 Playing a sound

Curiously, the first release of the .NET Framework did not include any direct support for playing sound files. This is addressed in version 2.0 with the `SoundPlayer` class, shown in .NET Table 15.2. The `SoundPlayer` class loads and plays .wav files either synchronously or asynchronously. Typically, asynchronous playback is preferred so that the sound plays in the background, allowing the user to interact with the application at the same time.

The use of this class is rather straightforward. Listing 15.4 shows a short sample that plays a ringing sound from the Media directory on a Windows XP machine. This sample illustrates the difference between the `Play` and `PlaySync` methods.

.NET Table 15.2 SoundPlayer class

New in 2.0 The `SoundPlayer` class controls the playback of sound from a .wav sound file. This class is part of the `System.Media` namespace, and inherits from the `Component` class.

Public Properties	*IsLoadCompleted*	Gets whether the .wav file has finished loading.
	LoadTimeout	Gets or sets the maximum time, in milliseconds, to wait for the .wav file to load.
	SoundLocation	Gets or sets the file path or URL to the .wav file to load.
	Stream	Gets or sets the `Stream` object from which to load the .wav file.
	Tag	Gets or sets an `object` to associate with the player.
Public Methods	*Load*	Loads the .wav file in a synchronous manner. The `LoadAsync` method loads the file from a new thread (asynchronously).
	Play	Plays the .wav file from a new thread. The `PlaySync` method plays the .wav file synchronously.
	PlayLooping	Plays the .wav file from a new thread, and repeats the file until the application exits or `Stop` is called.
	Stop	Stops playback of the .wav file.
Public Events	*LoadCompleted*	Occurs when a load of the .wav file is complete, whether the load was successful or not.
	SoundLocationChanged	Occurs when the value of the `SoundLocation` property changes.
	StreamChanged	Occurs when the value of `Stream` changes.

Listing 15.4 Sample program using the SoundPlayer class

```
using System;
using System.Media;

namespace SoundSample
{
  class Program
  {
    static void Main(string[] args)
    {
      SoundPlayer player = new SoundPlayer(@"C:\WINDOWS\Media\ringin.wav");

      Console.WriteLine("Execution waits while sound plays with PlaySync");
      player.PlaySync();
      Console.WriteLine("Execution continues while sound plays with Play");
      player.Play();
```

```
            Console.WriteLine("This displays while sound is playing.");
            Console.Write("Press Enter to exit.");
            Console.ReadLine();
        }
    }
}
```

We can add a sound file to our project resources much as we added the bitmap files in the prior section.

ADD AN AUDIO RESOURCE TO THE PROJECT		
	Action	**Result**
1	Add the file "ding.wav" in the Windows Media directory as a new resource for the MyPhotos project. **How-to** a. Display the Resources.resx file for the project. b. Click the down arrow next to the Add Resource button in the Resource Editor Window. c. Select Add Existing File. d. Browse to the file "ding.wav" (in Windows XP, this is at the location C:\Windows\Media\ding.wav"). e. Click Open to add the file.	Resources.resx* MainForm.cs [Design] Audio Add Resource Remove ding
2	Rename the resource to "DingSound." **How-to** Right-click on the resource and select Rename.	The property for this resource in the Resources.Designer.cs file has the corresponding name.

The result of these changes is a new `DingSound` property in the internal `Resources` class, as shown in listing 15.5. The next section discusses the `Timer` and `TrackBar` classes, and makes use of the resources created in this section.

Listing 15.5 Resulting DingSound property

```
internal static System.IO.UnmanagedMemoryStream DingSound {
  get {
    return ResourceManager.GetStream("DingSound", resourceCulture);
  }
}
```

15.3 TRACK BARS

The `TrackBar` class is not a bell or whistle, per se, but it is often overlooked by developers when building Windows Forms applications, so it seems appropriate to include it here. The `TrackBar` control is sometimes compared to the progress bar control presented in the prior chapter. Both essentially display a graphical representation of a numeric value, so this is not surprising. The intent of each control is very different, so you should try to use them appropriately in your applications.

A track bar presents a numeric value, and provides the user with a way to modify it by dragging the bar to a new location. A progress bar is intended to display the completion progress of some operation or activity. Both are numeric values, but each has its own specialized purpose.

In this section we discuss the `TrackBar` class and begin building the dialog box shown in figure 15.1 to illustrate many of the concepts discussed in this chapter.

15.3.1 The TrackBar class

The `TrackBar` class provides a visual mechanism for tracking an integer value on a form. A summary of this class appears in .NET Table 15.3.

.NET Table 15.3 TrackBar class

The `TrackBar` class is a control that presents an integer value with a scrolling interface. The control may appear horizontally or vertically. This class is part of the `System.Windows.Forms` namespace, and inherits from the `Control` class.

Public Properties	LargeChange	Gets or sets the amount added or subtracted from the `Value` property for a large scroll in the control
	Maximum	Gets or sets the maximum value for this track bar
	Minimum	Gets or sets the minimum value for this track bar
	Orientation	Gets or sets the orientation of the track bar
	SmallChange	Gets or sets the amount added or subtracted from the `Value` property for a small scroll in the control
	TickFrequency	Gets or sets the delta between tick marks on the control
	TickStyle	Gets or sets how the tick marks are displayed.
	Value	Gets or sets the numeric setting for the track bar
Public Methods	SetRange	Sets the minimum and maximum values for the control
Public Events	Scroll	Occurs when the slider moves as a result of a mouse or keyboard action
	ValueChanged	Occurs when the `Value` property of the control is modified, whether by the user or from code

As you can see, the `TrackBar` class supports a numeric value between an assigned minimum and maximum setting. The `SmallChange` and `LargeChange` properties control how the slider in the control alters the assigned `Value` for the control in response to user interaction. By default, the small change is 1 and the large change is

5. A series of small lines, or *ticks*, are displayed, with the `TickFrequency` property defining the numeric spacing between each tick mark.

The next section illustrates the use of this control in our MyPhotos application.

15.3.2 Using track bars

Now that we've taken a quick look at the members of the `TrackBar` control, let's use one in our MyPhotos application. The following steps lay out a new `SlideShowDialog` form that includes a track bar.

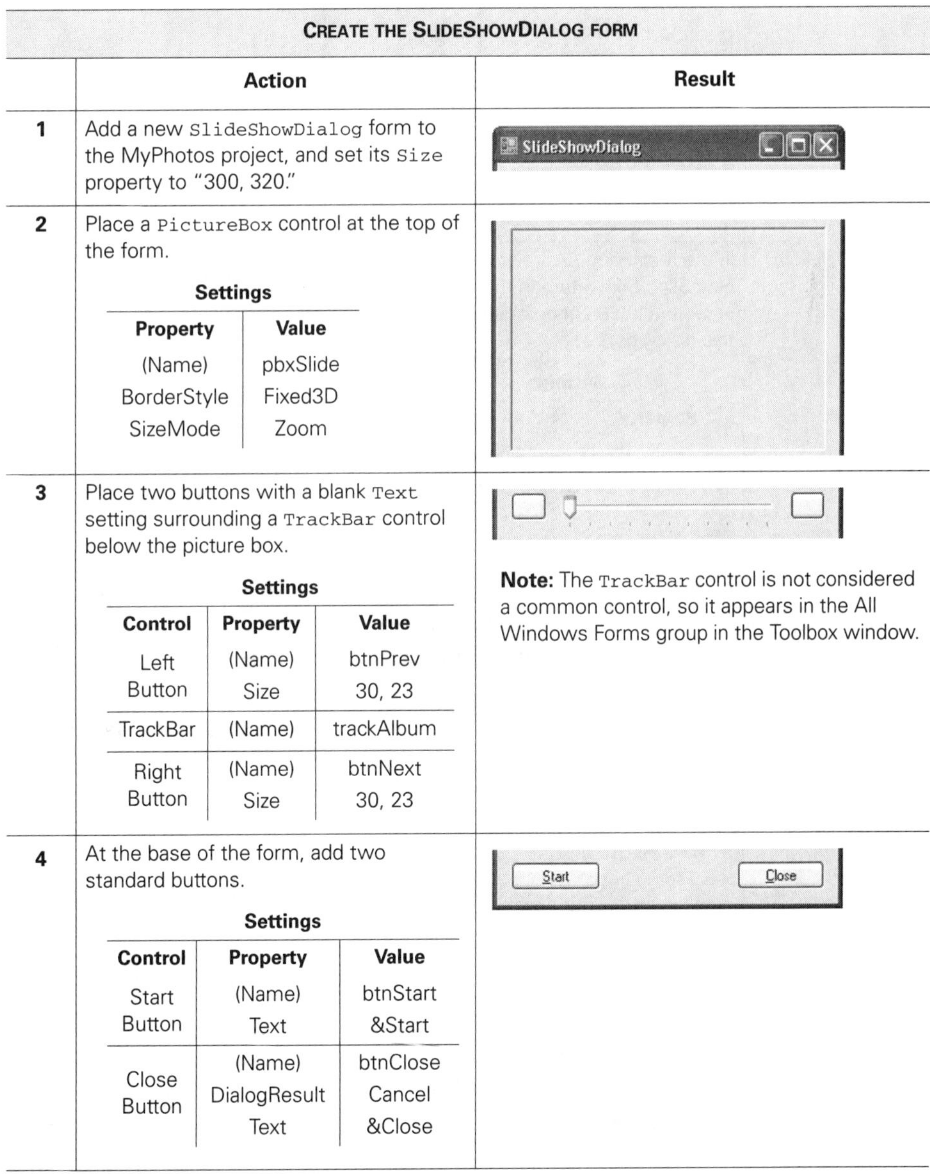

<table>
<tr><th colspan="3">CREATE THE SLIDESHOWDIALOG FORM</th></tr>
<tr><th></th><th>Action</th><th>Result</th></tr>
<tr><td>1</td><td>Add a new <code>SlideShowDialog</code> form to the MyPhotos project, and set its <code>Size</code> property to "300, 320."</td><td>SlideShowDialog</td></tr>
<tr><td>2</td><td>Place a <code>PictureBox</code> control at the top of the form.
Settings
<table>
<tr><th>Property</th><th>Value</th></tr>
<tr><td>(Name)</td><td>pbxSlide</td></tr>
<tr><td>BorderStyle</td><td>Fixed3D</td></tr>
<tr><td>SizeMode</td><td>Zoom</td></tr>
</table></td><td></td></tr>
<tr><td>3</td><td>Place two buttons with a blank <code>Text</code> setting surrounding a <code>TrackBar</code> control below the picture box.
Settings
<table>
<tr><th>Control</th><th>Property</th><th>Value</th></tr>
<tr><td>Left Button</td><td>(Name)
Size</td><td>btnPrev
30, 23</td></tr>
<tr><td>TrackBar</td><td>(Name)</td><td>trackAlbum</td></tr>
<tr><td>Right Button</td><td>(Name)
Size</td><td>btnNext
30, 23</td></tr>
</table></td><td>Note: The <code>TrackBar</code> control is not considered a common control, so it appears in the All Windows Forms group in the Toolbox window.</td></tr>
<tr><td>4</td><td>At the base of the form, add two standard buttons.
Settings
<table>
<tr><th>Control</th><th>Property</th><th>Value</th></tr>
<tr><td>Start Button</td><td>(Name)
Text</td><td>btnStart
&Start</td></tr>
<tr><td>Close Button</td><td>(Name)
DialogResult
Text</td><td>btnClose
Cancel
&Close</td></tr>
</table></td><td>Start   Close</td></tr>
</table>

CREATE THE SLIDESHOWDIALOG FORM *(CONTINUED)*		
	Action	**Result**
5	Set the tab order for these controls as shown in the graphic, and set the `Form` properties as follows. **Settings** **Property** / **Value** AcceptButton / btnClose ControlBox / False FormBorderStyle / FixedDialog MaximizeBox / False MinimizeBox / False ShowInTaskbar / False StartPosition / CenterScreen	SlideShowDialog 2 3 4 0 Start 1 Close
6	In the MainForm designer window, add new Slide Show item in the `ctxMenuPhoto` context menu to display this dialog box. **Settings** **Property** / **Value** (Name) / menuSlideShow Text / &Slide Show...	ContextMenuStrip Image Next Ctrl+Shift+N Previous Ctrl+Shift+P Pixel Dialog... Photo Properties... Album Properties... Slide Show... Type Here

This completes our dialog class. Within this class we want to track a location in an album, and display the photograph at this location in the `PictureBox` control. The `TrackBar.Value` property defines a numeric value we can use for this purpose.

TRACK AN ALBUM LOCATION USING THE VALUE PROPERTY		
	Action	**Result**

7	Indicate we are using the `System.Media` and `Manning.PhotoAlbum` namespaces in our new `SlideShowDialog` class.	`. . .`
		`using System.Media;`
		
		`using Manning.MyPhotoAlbum;`
		`. . .`

8	Within the class, define private `AlbumManager` and `SoundPlayer` fields with associated read-only properties.	`private AlbumManager _manager;`
		`private SoundPlayer _soundPlayer;`
		
		`private AlbumManager Manager`
		`    { get { return _manager; } }`
		`private SoundPlayer Player`
		`    { get { return _soundPlayer; } }`

TRACK AN ALBUM LOCATION USING THE VALUE PROPERTY *(CONTINUED)*		
	Action	**Result**

9	Modify the constructor to receive an `AlbumManager` instance and initialize the form.	<pre>public SlideShowDialog(AlbumManager manager)
		{
		  if (manager == null || manager.Album == null
		      || manager.Album.Count == 0)
		    throw new ArgumentException("manager");
		
		  InitializeComponent();
		
		  // Other initialization
		  _manager = manager;
		  InitializeForm();
		}</pre>

10	Implement an `InitializeForm` method to perform custom initialization of the form.
	How-to
	a. Place the custom bitmap images on the button controls.
	b. Initialize the controls appropriately.
	c. Create a `SoundPlayer` object to play the ding sound.
		<pre>private void InitializeForm()
		{
		  // Set button images, with White transparent
		  Bitmap bmp
		     = MyPhotos.Properties.Resources.NextBitmap;
		  bmp.MakeTransparent(Color.White);
		  btnNext.Image = bmp;
		
		  bmp
		    = MyPhotos.Properties.Resources.PrevBitmap;
		  bmp.MakeTransparent(Color.White);
		  btnPrev.Image = bmp;
		
		  trackAlbum.Maximum = Manager.Album.Count - 1;
		  UpdateDialog();
		
		  // Assign sound for slide show
		  _soundPlayer = new SoundPlayer(
		      MyPhotos.Properties.Resources.DingSound);
		}</pre>

11	Implement an `UpdateDialog` method to display the photo at the current track bar value.	<pre>private void UpdateDialog()
		{
		  int index = trackAlbum.Value;
		  if (index < Manager.Album.Count)
		  {
		    Photograph p = Manager.Album[index];
		    pbxSlide.Image = p.Image;
		    Text = p.Caption;
		  }
		}</pre>

12	Handle the `ValueChanged` event for the `TrackBar` control to call the update method.	<pre>private void trackAlbum_ValueChanged(
		    object sender, EventArgs e)
		{
		  UpdateDialog();
		}</pre>

TRACK AN ALBUM LOCATION USING THE VALUE PROPERTY *(CONTINUED)*		
	Action	**Result**

13	Handle the `Click` events for the previous and next buttons to modify the current value for the track bar.
	
	Note: These in turn invoke the `ValueChanged` event to update the picture box.
		private void btnPrev_Click(
		    object sender, EventArgs e)
		{
		  if (trackAlbum.Value > 0)
		    trackAlbum.Value--;
		}
		
		private void btnNext_Click(
		    object sender, EventArgs e)
		{
		  if (trackAlbum.Value < trackAlbum.Maximum)
		    trackAlbum.Value++;
		}

14	In the `MainForm` class, update the `Opening` event handler for the `ctxMenuPhoto` strip to properly enable the slide show menu item.	private void ctxMenuPhoto_Opening(
		    object sender, CancelEventArgs e)
		{
		  . . .
		  menuAlbumProps.Enabled
		    = (Manager.Album != null);
		  menuSlideShow.Enabled = (Manager.Album != null
		    && Manager.Album.Count > 0);
		}

15	Handle the `Click` event for the Slide Show menu to display the new dialog box.	private void menuSlideShow_Click(
		    object sender, EventArgs e)
		{
		  using (SlideShowDialog dlg
		        = new SlideShowDialog(Manager))
		  {
		    dlg.ShowDialog();
		  }
		}

This code maintains a location in the album using the value set in the `TrackBar` control. Each time the `Value` property is modified, the image in the `PictureBox` control is updated.

Note how our custom bitmaps stored in the project resources are used in the code for step 9. The `Bitmap` properties generated by Visual Studio in the `Resources` class are displayed on the corresponding buttons, and our `Ding` sound is used to create a `SoundPlayer` instance. For each bitmap, we use the `MakeTransparent` method in the `Bitmap` class to ensure the white background in our images does not appear on the form.

One advantage of our approach is that the `Index` property in the `AlbumManager` class is not modified. This ensures that the photo displayed in the MainForm window is not altered.

The `SoundPlayer` instance here is used in the next section, where we discuss the Windows Forms `Timer` class.

15.4 TIMERS

A *timer* in .NET is an object that raises an event after a configurable period of time has elapsed. There are, in fact, multiple `Timer` classes in the .NET Framework. There is one in the `System.Threading` namespace for use among multiple threads, one in the `System.Timers` namespace for server-based recurring tasks, and one in the `System.Windows.Forms` namespace that is optimized for the single-threaded processing environment used to handle events in a `Form` object. Unless you are doing some specialized processing among multiple threads, you should stick with the Windows Forms version for any timers required in your applications.

Timer classes provide a way to perform recurring tasks in the background. The `BackgroundWorker` class presented in chapter 14 performs a similar function, except that background workers are intended for single event-driven operations. In the example in chapter 14, whenever the user selects a new image while in black and white mode, a background worker is started to perform the conversion. The task is not required until the user initiates the action.

Timers, on the other hand, handle operations that are performed on a regular basis, regardless of what the user happens to do. Examples include updating the hands of a clock, or retrieving new email messages, or other possible time-based activities. This section presents the `Timer` class and incorporates a timer into our slide show dialog box.

15.4.1 The Timer class

The Windows Forms timer object is normally associated with and configured in a form, and raises a `Tick` event whenever the timer is enabled and an established period has elapsed. A summary of this class is given in .NET Table 15.4.

As you can see, the Windows Forms `Timer` class is started and stopped through the corresponding methods or by assigning the `Enabled` property. When the timer is enabled and the assigned `Interval` setting has elapsed, the `Tick` event occurs with the `Timer` object as the `sender` property. Custom data can be associated with the object and retrieved in a `Tick` event handler using the `Tag` property.

Timers are often used to perform ongoing processing in the background, with minimal impact on a user's ability to interact with the form directly. Since the `Tick` event occurs in the form's processing thread, you should keep any processing as short as possible.

15.4.2 Using timers

We demonstrate the `Timer` class in our `SlideShowDialog` form, of course. When the user clicks the Start button, we enable a timer to display the next picture in the album every 1.5 seconds. The timer runs in the background, allowing the user to pause and resume the timer, or even close the form, at the same time.

.NET Table 15.4 Timer class

The Windows Forms `Timer` class is a component that raises events at a defined interval. This timer is optimized for use in Windows Forms applications and its events occur within the processing thread for the associated `Form` object. This class is part of the `System.Windows.Forms` namespace, and inherits from the `System.ComponentModel.Component` class.

Public Properties	Enabled	Gets or sets whether the timer is currently active.
	Interval	Gets or sets the time in milliseconds between timer ticks.
	Tag	Gets or sets an `object` to associate with this timer.
Public Methods	Start	Starts the timer. This is equivalent to setting the `Enabled` property to `true`.
	Stop	Stops the timer. Equivalent to setting `Enabled` to `false`.
Public Events	Tick	Occurs when the timer is enabled and the specified interval has elapsed.

The steps required are as follows.

ADD A TIMER TO THE SLIDESHOWDIALOG FORM

	Action	Result
1	In the SlideShowDialog.cs [Design] window, drag a `Timer` object from the Toolbox to the form. **Settings** Property / Value (Name): timerSlide Interval: 1500	The timer appears in the component tray below the form. Start Close timerSlide
2	Handle the `Click` event for the Start button to start the timer, or stop the timer if it is already running. **Note:** We allow this button to display Start, Pause, or Restart, depending on the state of the timer. In all cases we preserve "s" as the keyboard shortcut for the button.	`private void btnStart_Click(object sender, EventArgs e) { if (btnStart.Text == "Pau&se") { timerSlide.Stop(); btnStart.Text = "Re&sume"; } else // "&Start" or "Re&sume" { timerSlide.Start(); btnStart.Text = "Pau&se"; } }`

```
private void btnStart_Click(
    object sender, EventArgs e)
{
  if (btnStart.Text == "Pau&se")
  {
    timerSlide.Stop();
    btnStart.Text = "Re&sume";
  }
  else // "&Start" or "Re&sume"
  {
    timerSlide.Start();
    btnStart.Text = "Pau&se";
  }
}
```

	Add a Timer to the SlideShowDialog form *(continued)*	
	Action	**Result**

3	Handle the `Tick` event for the timer to increment the `Value` setting of the track bar control. If the current setting is at the end of the album, then stop the timer and reset `Value` to zero.
	
	Note: Modifying the `Value` setting invokes the `ValueChanged` event, which updates the displayed image.
		`private void timerSlide_Tick(`
		`    object sender, EventArgs e)`
		`{`
		`  int n = trackAlbum.Value + 1;`
		`  if (n >= Manager.Album.Count)`
		`  {`
		`    // We are finished`
		`    timerSlide.Stop();`
		`    Text = "Finished";`
		`    btnStart.Text = "&Start";`
		`    n = 0;`
		`  }`
		
		`  trackAlbum.Value = n;`

4	Play the loaded sound each time the `Value` setting changes as a result of the timer.	`  Player.Play();` `}`

The Start button is used to start, pause, and resume the timer on behalf of the album. When the timer is active, clicking this button pauses the timer; clicking it again resumes the timer. When the end of the album is reached, the button reverts to the original "Start" text to indicate that the entire album has been shown.

Also in this code we illustrate the use of the `SoundPlayer.Play` method to play back our audio resource in the project. The sound is played asynchronously, so it does not interfere with the user's ability to interact with the form.

This completes our various bells and whistles. Compile and run the application to see the new dialog box, with its image buttons, track bar, and timer, in action.

TRY IT! Programmers often ask how to represent numeric values in a `TextBox` control. Although this can certainly be done, it is often easier to use the `NumericUpDown` class instead. This class derives from the `UpDownBase` class and represents a numeric value within a specified range of numbers. A spin box, also known as an up-down control, allows the user to graphically increase or decrease the displayed value. The related `DomainUpDown` class displays text values from a defined collection of strings.

To see the `NumericUpDown` class in action, try adding this control to our `SlideShowDialog` form to represent the timer interval. Allow users to alter this interval from 1 to 5 seconds so they can assign the amount of time to pause between photographs.

15.5 RECAP

This chapter explored various features of Windows Forms that can help make an application more user-friendly. We began with images, including bitmaps and icons, and the `Cursor` class, which encapsulates an image that can appear as the mouse pointer.

We then discussed how resources such as images are stored on behalf of a form in an .resx file. During compilation, the resource generator resgen.exe is used to build a corresponding .resources file for inclusion in the project assembly. A project can also embed project resources in a Resources.resx file. We embedded bitmap images and audio files, and saw how other resources such as strings or objects can also be included.

Our next topic was the `SoundPlayer` class, which is used to play back .wav files within an application. We demonstrated this class in our MyPhotos application in the dialog box built over the final two sections.

The main example in this chapter was the addition of a `SlideShowDialog` form to our MyPhotos project. This included a discussion of the `TrackBar` class for tracking a numeric value graphically, and the `Timer` class for performing background tasks at regular intervals.

The next chapter returns to where we started: tool strips. Way back in chapters 3 and 4 we presented various aspects of menu and status strips. As we discussed briefly in these chapters, both classes derive from the `ToolStrip` class, and contain items derived from the `ToolStripItem` class. Chapter 16 presents tool strips more generally.

CHAPTER 16

Tool strips

In this final chapter of part 2 of the book, we round out our discussion of Windows Forms programming back where we began: with the `ToolStrip` classes. You may wonder why these concepts were not presented earlier in our discussion, and they certainly could have been. The reason is either poor planning or clever organization—you decide which. Tool strips can get rather involved, so it makes sense to devote an entire chapter to this topic, even though we already discussed some aspects of these classes in chapters 3 and 4.

Prior to version 2.0 of the framework, toolbars in Windows Forms applications created were created using the Win32-based `ToolBar` and `ToolBarButton` classes. These classes still exist in .NET 2.0 for backward compatibility and future use, but are hidden in Visual Studio to encourage use of the newer constructs.

We also look at the `ImageList` class in this chapter. While we recommend using the project resources introduced in chapter 15, image lists provide another option for tool strips and other controls when a set of images is required. As a result, it is worth a quick look at this class to contrast the two approaches.

Specific topics we examine here include the following:

- Adding a tool strip to a window
- Creating tool strip buttons to duplicate menu item functionality
- Creating other tool strip items: toggle, drop-down, and split buttons
- Creating and managing image lists
- Using tool strip containers to define tool strip location within a form
- Supporting special features such as item overflow and reordering
- Hosting Windows Forms controls within a tool strip

We begin our discussion with the tool strip class.

16.1 TOOL STRIP FUNDAMENTALS

Toolbars were added to windowing environments as an alternate shortcut method for common tasks, especially menu bar items. While keyboard shortcuts are fine for more experienced users, they do not have a graphical presence in the window. Toolbars, implemented in .NET 2.0 as tool strips, provide a graphic for each shortcut button, so users should be able to quickly perform common tasks without having to hunt through the menus or documentation all the time.

At least that was the theory. Personally, I prefer keyboard shortcuts, and find the plethora of toolbars a distraction in many interfaces. Although common tasks such as opening and closing a file or selection of a bold or italic font style have developed somewhat standard graphical buttons, I have trouble deciphering the tiny graphics shown on many toolbars and prefer to learn the keyboard shortcuts instead. When creating toolbars in your programs, make sure their meaning is clear, and do not use a toolbar as an excuse to avoid keyboard shortcuts and access keys. Some users prefer the keyboard over the mouse, so it is a good idea to provide keyboard as well as mouse access to program functions.

But I digress. Let's get back to toolbars in .NET. Whether or not you employ them yourself, your users expect them. The `ToolStrip` classes are much more flexible than prior toolbar implementations, so perhaps they will prove useful even to skeptical users like me.

In this section we look at the `ToolStrip` class in detail and create a blank toolbar in our MyPhotos project. Later sections look at image lists and the creation of the various kinds of tool strip items. By the end of this chapter, our efforts produce the interface shown in figure 16.1.

Figure 16.1 Two of our three tool strips contain various button styles, while the third contains a drop-down and split button item.

16.1.1 The ToolStrip classes

As we have already seen, there is a `ToolStrip` class in the Windows Forms namespace, so this is a good spot for the corresponding .NET Table with some details about this class. As you can see from .NET Table 16.1, the `ToolStrip` class defines properties and events that define the behavior of the strip itself and of items within the strip.

All tool strips serve as containers for one or more `ToolStripItem` objects. The Win32 `ToolBar` class presents a fairly static collection of buttons, so the Windows Forms team at Microsoft sought to create a more flexible class that could support various features found in more advanced applications such as the Microsoft Office suite of products. The resulting `ToolStrip` class supports dynamic reordering of items, runtime merging of multiple strips, automatic overflow of items during form resize, and built-in classes to provide custom render and layout logic.

The tool strip classes are intended to provide a single base class for menus, status bars, and toolbars. The ability to combine items from multiple strips in the `AllowMerge` property comes from the Win32 menu classes that allow multiple-document interfaces (MDI) to merge menus for a parent and child window into a single menu. Similarly, the requirement to hide tooltips and stretch across the length of the form was taken from the Win32 status bar class, and defined by the `ShowItemToolTips` and `Stretch` properties.

We have already seen the `MenuStrip`, `ContextMenuStrip`, and `StatusStrip` classes during our discussions in chapters 3 and 4. The complete `ToolStrip` class hierarchy was shown in figure 3.5. Table 16.2 summarizes these and a few other classes related to tool strips, and indicates where in the book the class is discussed in more detail.

.NET Table 16.1 ToolStrip class

New in 2.0 The `ToolStrip` class is a scrollable control for displaying one or more `ToolStrip-Item` objects on a form. This provides a base class for menus, status bars, and toolbar objects. Tool strips typically provide shortcuts to menu commands and other commonly used tasks, or display important information about the current state of the form. This class is part of the `System.Windows.Forms` namespace, and inherits from the `ScrollableControl` class. See .NET Table 13.3 for a list of members inherited from the base class.

Public Properties	*AllowItemReorder*	Gets or sets whether drag-and-drop and item reordering are handled automatically by the tool strip.
	AllowMerge	Gets or sets whether multiple strips can be combined.
	CanOverflow	Gets or sets whether items in the tool strip can be sent to an overflow menu.
	DefaultDrop-DownDirection	Gets or sets the default direction a `ToolStripDropDown` object is displayed relative to the tool strip.
	GripStyle	Gets or sets whether the move handle is visible. Additional properties define the orientation, margin, and graphical boundary for the move handle.
	LayoutStyle	Gets or sets a `ToolStripLayoutStyle` value that defines an alignment for items displayed within the tool strip.
	OverflowButton	Gets the item that is the overflow button for the tool strip.
	Renderer	Gets or sets the `ToolStripRenderer` object used to customize the look of feel of a tool strip.
	Stretch	Gets or sets whether the tool strip fills the entire width or height of its container, depending on its orientation.
	TextDirection	Gets or sets a `ToolStripTextDirection` value that defines how text should be oriented within the strip.
Public Events	*ItemAdded*	Occurs when a new item is added to the tool strip.
	ItemClicked	Occurs when an item in the tool strip is clicked.
	ItemRemoved	Occurs when an item is removed from the tool strip.
	LayoutCompleted	Occurs when the layout of the tool strip is finished.
	LayoutStyleChanged	Occurs when the `LayoutStyle` property changes.
	PaintGrip	Occurs when the move handle should be painted.
	RendererChanged	Occurs when the `Renderer` property changes.

Table 16.2 Summary of tool strip classes

Class	Description	See Section
ToolStrip	The base class of all tool strips	16.1.1
MenuStrip	A tool strip that acts as a menu bar	3.3
StatusStrip	A tool strip that acts as a status bar	4.3
ContextMenuStrip	A drop-down strip that acts as a context menu	4.1
ToolStripOverflow	A tool strip that supports the overflow behavior for another tool strip	16.2.3
ToolStripContainer	A container control that supports one or more tool strips in side panels and other controls in a central panel	16.4
ToolStripManager	A sealed class that supports the arrangement and merging of tool strips	20.3.1
ToolStripRenderer	An abstract class that supports custom painting of tool strips	16.6

16.1.2 Creating a tool strip

While a menu bar is typically at the top of a form, and a status bar is typically at the base of a form, a toolbar can appear pretty much anywhere. In most applications a standard set of toolbars appear by default at the top of the form, so we do the same within our MyPhotos application.

The following adds a `ToolStrip` object to the top of our `MainForm` window.

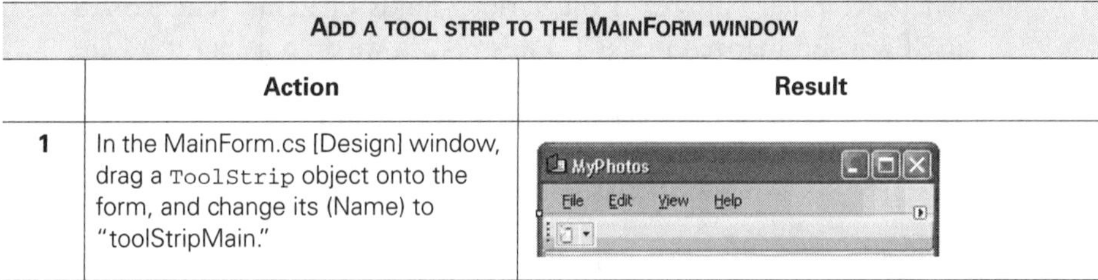

ADD A TOOL STRIP TO THE MAINFORM WINDOW		
	Action	**Result**
1	In the MainForm.cs [Design] window, drag a `ToolStrip` object onto the form, and change its (Name) to "toolStripMain."	

So far, so good. Note that you need to be careful with tool strips at times. Since menus and status bars are also tool strips, the positioning of these strips within the form can be altered depending on the settings. To see this, right-click the new `ToolStrip` control and select Send To Back. Hit Ctrl+Z to undo this change.

Also, if your form holds a container such as a panel, the strip can be placed within the panel or within the form. When a `Panel` or other container control is docked to fill the entire form, it is easy to accidentally place a tool strip within the panel. Just keep this in mind as you design and implement your forms.

If you look at the properties for the new `ToolStrip`, you may notice that the `Dock` property is set to `Top` by default. This causes the strip to appear at the top of the form, as shown in the table.

The code generated here is nothing unusual, so we move on to tool strip items.

16.2 TOOL STRIP ITEM FUNDAMENTALS

By themselves, tool strips do not present much information to the user. These objects take on meaning and purpose once they have one or more tool strip items placed on them. In this section we begin our look at the `ToolStripItem` classes.

Before we do this, a short speech. While it is certainly possible to create all sorts of cool toolbars with the `ToolStrip` and `ToolStripItem` classes, make sure the tool strips in your application are presented in a usable fashion. Group tool strip items logically into one or more strips, and try not to place too many items in each tool strip. There is a trade-off between the number of items on each strip and the number of strips in an application. It is quite easy to create a single tool strip with lots of items, or lots of tool strips with a few items each. Somewhere between these two extremes is a logical balance between the number of tool strips and the number of items per strip. Work with your potential users to select a reasonable solution for your specific application.

In our MyPhotos application, we create a few different tool strips. This section presents a summary of `ToolStripItem` classes and adds the standard set of items to the strip created in the prior section. We take a quick look at the various features related to tool strip items, including item alignment, overflow, and reordering.

16.2.1 The ToolStripItem classes

As you may recall, we examined the `ToolStripItem` class hierarchy in chapter 3, where we briefly discussed the various kinds of items. The `ToolStripItem` class itself was summarized in .NET Table 3.4, so we do not repeat it here.

Table 16.3 Summary of tool strip item classes

Class	Description	See Section
ToolStripItem	Base class for all tool strip items.	3.3.3 and 16.2.1
ToolStripButton	A tool strip item that presents a button to the user.	16.2.2
ToolStripControlHost	An item that can host other controls within a tool strip. The Windows Forms namespace provides hosting classes for the combo box, progress bar, and text box controls.	16.5.3
ToolStripDropDownButton	A drop-down item that presents a button with an associated drop-down tool strip.	16.5.2
ToolStripLabel	A nonselectable item that displays text and images.	4.3.2
ToolStripMenuItem	A drop-down item in a menu or context menu strip.	3.3.2
ToolStripOverflowButton	A drop-down button in a `ToolStripOverflow` control.	16.2.3
ToolStripSeparator	An item that separates other items in a tool strip.	3.3
ToolStripSplitButton	A drop-down item that presents a button and an arrow. Clicking the button selects a default action; clicking the arrow displays an associated drop-down tool strip.	16.5.3
ToolStripStatusLabel	A label item that can appear on a status strip.	4.3.2

It is worth reviewing the various kinds of items, as shown in table 16.3. This table provides a short description of each class along with the section of the book where this class is discussed. As you can see in the table, items related to menus and status strips were covered in chapters 3 and 4. Other items are discussed over the course of this chapter.

16.2.2 Adding standard tool strip items

As we saw with our menu and status strips, tool strip items can be added to tool strips programmatically or directly in Visual Studio. There is also a standard set of items supported by Visual Studio that can be added directly to a strip. We begin with this standard set of items, and look at alternate ways of placing items in subsequent sections.

In chapter 6, and specifically in table 6.1, we used the `MenuStrip` smart tag to add the standard menu items to our menu. Table 16.4 shows the standard items supported by Visual Studio for `ToolStrip` objects, along with the equivalent menu item within our MyPhotos application and the default image used for each item.

Table 16.4 The standard tool strip items provided by Visual Studio

Item	Equivalent Menu Item	Image	Usage in MyPhotos application
New	File > New		Create a new album as in section 6.2.1
Open	File > Open		Open an existing photo album file as in section 6.2.2.
Save	File > Save		Save the current album as in section 6.2.3.
Print	File > Print		Print the current image as in section 23.1.
Cut	Edit > Cut		Cut the selected item from the album. See the exercise in section 15.1.1 for a discussion of Cut, Copy, and Paste.
Copy	Edit > Copy		Copy the selected item from the album.
Paste	Edit > Paste		Paste a cut or copied object into the album.
Help	Help > About		Display help, in our case the about box as in section 23.3.

Each item in table 16.4 becomes a `ToolStripButton` object within the application. The button item is probably the most common of the tool strip items, as it represents a standard clickable button. Typically, such buttons are linked to a menu item and provide a visual shortcut for invoking the associated menu.

Most of the behavior for button items is inherited from the `ToolStripItem` class. Additional features supported by tool strip buttons are summarized in .NET Table 16.5; the main addition is the ability to appear in a pressed or unpressed state. By default, the `CheckOnClick` property is `true` to enable this feature, so that the

.NET Table 16.5 ToolStripButton class

New in 2.0 The `ToolStripButton` class is a selectable tool strip item that can present text and images to a user. This class is part of the `System.Windows.Forms` namespace, and inherits from the `ToolStripItem` class. See .NET Table 3.4 for a list of members inherited from the base class.

Public Properties	*Checked*	Gets or sets whether the button is pressed
	CheckOnClick	Gets or sets whether the button should be pressed and unpressed when clicked
	CheckState	Gets or sets whether the button is in a pressed, unpressed, or indeterminate state
Public Events	*CheckedChanged*	Occurs when the `Checked` property changes
	CheckStateChanged	Occurs when the `CheckState` property changes

button appears pressed when the user clicks the button and unpressed when the user releases the mouse click.

So let's see how this all fits together. The following steps create the standard items in our `toolStripMain` object and handle the `Click` events on these items so they mimic their corresponding menu items.

ADD THE STANDARD TOOL STRIP ITEMS TO THE TOOL STRIP

	Action	Result
1	Add the standard tool strip items to the `toolStripMain` object. **How-to** a. Click the smart tag associated with the tool strip control. b. Click Insert Standard Items.	 MyPhotos File Edit View Help
2	Modify the variable name for each button to use a more succinct naming convention. **Note:** This is not strictly required, but I prefer the shorter name with a common prefix. I use the "tsb" prefix followed by the button name, as in tsbNew, tsbOpen, tsbSave, etc.	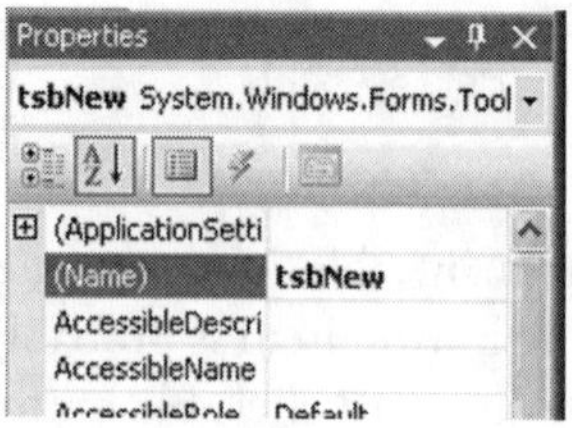 Properties tsbNew System.Windows.Forms.Tool (ApplicationSetti (Name) tsbNew AccessibleDescri AccessibleName

ADD THE STANDARD TOOL STRIP ITEMS TO THE TOOL STRIP *(CONTINUED)*

	Action	Result

3	In the `MainForm.cs` file, overload the `OnLoad` method to assign the `Tag` property for each button item to the corresponding `ToolStripMenuItem` object that represents the identical feature.
	
	Note: The `OnLoad` method raises the `Load` event, which occurs before a form is initially displayed. This makes it a good place to perform any final initialization of controls.
		`protected override void OnLoad(EventArgs e)`
		`{`
		`  this.tsbNew.Tag = menuFileNew;`
		`  this.tsbOpen.Tag = menuFileOpen;`
		`  this.tsbSave.Tag = menuFileSave;`
		`  this.tsbPrint.Tag = menuFilePrint;`
		`  this.tsbCut.Tag = menuEditCut;`
		`  this.tsbCopy.Tag = menuEditCopy;`
		`  this.tsbPaste.Tag = menuEditPaste;`
		`  this.tsbHelp.Tag = menuHelpAbout;`
		
		`  base.OnLoad(e);`
		`}`

4	Define a `tbs_Click` method that performs a click on the menu item associated with the assigned tool strip button.
	
	Note: We define this code to avoid an error even if the calling object does not have an associated menu item.
		`private void tbs_Click(`
		`    object sender, EventArgs e)`
		`{`
		`  // Ensure sender is a menu item`
		`  ToolStripItem item`
		`      = sender as ToolStripItem;`
		`  if (item != null)`
		`  {`
		`    ToolStripMenuItem mi`
		`        = item.Tag as ToolStripMenuItem;`
		`    if (mi != null)`
		`      mi.PerformClick();`
		`  }`
		`}`

5	In the MainForm.cs [Design] window, define this new method as the `Click` event handler for each tool strip item. **How-to** a. Click the New button item. b. Hold down the Shift key and click the other button items so that all items are selected. c. In the Properties window, assign the `Click` handler for the selected items to `tbs_Click`.	The top combo box is blank here to indicate that multiple items are selected.

This code handles all button items using a single event handler. The `Tag` property for each item is set to the corresponding menu item. Our shared `Click` handler uses this setting to call the `PerformClick` method on the associated menu.

An alternate way to provide this functionality is to implement a custom event handler for each button item. For example, the New item might have the following handler:

```
private void tbsNew_Click(object sender, EventArgs e)
{
    menuFileNew.PerformClick();
}
```

While this handler may be simpler in that it is a single line, the code reuse employed by the shared `tbs_Click` handler is lost. The shared handler also allows us to modify or augment the behavior of all buttons in the future without having to alter individual handlers. As a result, I prefer the shared handler approach.

16.2.3 Item alignment, overflow, and other features

As long as we are discussing tool strip items, there are some built-in features that are worth mentioning. Table 16.6 lists a number of key features supported by the `ToolStripItem` classes. The table also includes properties of the `ToolStripItem` and `ToolStrip` classes related to each feature. The description and example are probably sufficient for all except the item overflow feature, which is worth some additional discussion.

Table 16.6 Some features of the tool strip item classes

Feature	Description	ToolStripItem Properties	ToolStrip Properties
Alignment	The ability to align an item at one end of the tool strip. Create the example here by setting the strip's `Stretch` property to `true` and the `tsbHelp.Alignment` property to `Right`.	Alignment	
Display Style	The ability to display text, images, or a combination of the two. In the example here, the Open button displays only text, while the Cut button displays both image and text.	DisplayStyle, Image, Text, TextImageRelation	ImageScalingSize, TextDirection
Merge	The ability to merge items from two separate tool strips and display them as a single strip. This is discussed in chapter 20.	MergeAction, MergeIndex	AllowMerge
Overflow	The ability to move items into an overflow menu when the containing tool strip shrinks. In this example the width of the MainForm window is reduced. The tool strip here supports overflow, but the menu strip does not.	IsOnOverflow, Overflow	CanOverflow, OverflowButton

Table 16.6 **Some features of the tool strip item classes** *(continued)*

Feature	Description	ToolStripItem Properties	ToolStrip Properties
Reordering	The ability for a user to reorder the tool strip items in a running application, as shown here.		AllowItemReorder
Tool Tips	The ability to display a tooltip on an item in a tool strip. This example shows a Save tooltip.	AutoToolTip, ToolTipText	ShowItemToolTips

The table illustrates item overflow in our MyPhotos application when the form is resized. Tool strips can overflow their items into an *overflow menu* whenever an item no longer fits in the display area of the strip. The `ToolStripOverflow` class derives from the `ToolStripDropDown` class and implements the overflow menu. You can access the overflow button used for this menu programmatically using the `ToolStrip.OverflowButton` property, which retrieves the `ToolStripOverflowButton` object that holds the overflow menu.

You can turn off overflow by setting the `ToolStrip.CanOverflow` property to `false`. In this case items simply disappear and reappear as the form is resized, which is the standard behavior for menu strips.

Within the `ToolStripItem` class, two properties are related to overflow. The `IsOnOverflow` property returns `true` if overflow is enabled and the current item is on the overflow menu, and `false` otherwise. The `Overflow` property defines how the item will overflow. This second property gets or sets a `ToolStripItemOverflow` enumeration value that defines the conditions for placing an item on the overflow menu. The default is `AsNeeded`, which allows the item to move to the overflow menu as soon as it is no longer visible. The other values are `Never`, so that the item only appears in the containing tool strip, and `Always`, so that the item never appears directly within the containing strip.

You can experiment with the various tool strip item features presented here. When you are finished, join us for a diversion into the `ImageList` class.

16.3 IMAGE LISTS

The `ToolStrip` class is one of a number of controls that allow an image as part of their contents. In some cases, the requirement is for a set of images, rather than a single image. While Microsoft recommends using resource files to manage the images required on a tool strip, the `ImageList` class provides another way to do this.

The `ImageList` class is part of .NET 1.0, and is still available for use in 2.0 on buttons, lists, and tree views, as well as the `ToolStrip` classes. We go with the recommended resource file approach in the remainder of the book, but it is worth a quick look at image lists to understand how they work in the .NET Framework.

16.3.1 The ImageList class

The `ImageList` class represents a collection of `Image` objects, and provides a convenient way to store and access images required by various Windows Forms classes. The class inherits from the `System.ComponentModel.Component` class, and works much like an array of `Image` objects.

We do not present a .NET Table of the `ImageList` class members but instead provide a quick summary. The contained images are accessed using the `Images` property, a standard `IList` collection of images encapsulated by the `ImageList.ImageCollection` class. The `ColorDepth` and `ImageSize` properties define aspects of each image, while the `TransparentColor` property defines a color that is not rendered whenever an image is drawn. As in most Windows Forms components, a `Tag` property is provided to associate an arbitrary object with the class.

Classes that utilize an `ImageList` construct specify an index into the list, designating which image they wish to display. Typically, a containing class provides an `ImageList` property to specify a list to use, and classes that display an image from such lists provide an `ImageIndex` property to indicate which image to display. We see this feature for the `ToolStrip` and `ToolStripItem` classes in a moment.

In Visual Studio, since the `ImageList` class is not a preferred mechanism, some of the properties related to image lists are not available in the Properties window. This is a bit unfortunate since it means associated images do not appear in the designer. Let's look at an example where we can see this.

16.3.2 Creating an image list

For the `ToolStrip` object already created in our `MainForm` class, the standard items created on the strip were added without the use of an image list. In fact, if you examine the resources in the MainForm.resx file, you will see that many of the images occur twice: once for the standard menu strip items and once for the standard tool strip buttons.

In this chapter we add two items to our tool strip. We use icons from the common image library provided with Visual Studio. If you skipped chapter 15, or were simply not paying attention, this directory is typically C:\Program Files\Microsoft Visual Studio 8\Common7\VS2005ImageLibrary.

The following steps create an `ImageList` with an associated set of image files.

CREATE AN IMAGE LIST FOR OUR TOOLBAR		
	Action	**Result**
1	Associate an `ImageList` component with the `MainForm` form in the MainForm.cs [Design] window. **Settings** **Property** / **Value** (Name): imageListArrows TransparentColor: Magenta	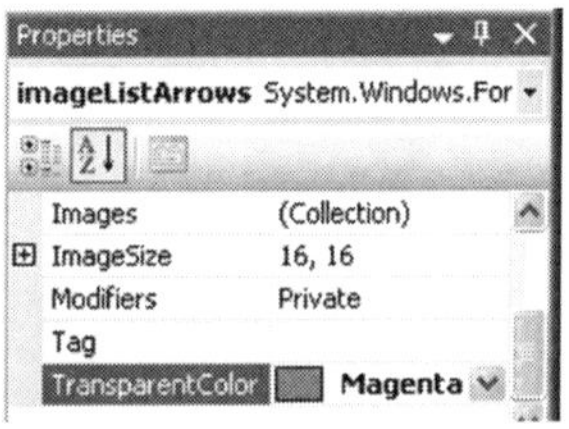
2	In Windows Explorer, create a left arrow bitmap that we can use. **How-to** a. Browse to the file RightArrow.bmp in the common image library folder bitmaps\commands\16color. b. Flip this image horizontally in Microsoft Paint to create a left-facing arrow. c. Save the image as a 16-color bitmap called LeftArrow.bmp	I'm not sure why Microsoft offered a right-facing arrow bitmap without a corresponding left one, but the steps here create a left-facing arrow for use in our application.
3	Back in Visual Studio, display the Image Collection Editor window. **How-to** Click the ... button next to the Images property.	A blank Image Collection Editor dialog box appears.
4	Add an image for moving to the next photograph in the collection. **How-to** a. Click the Add button. b. In the Open dialog box, select the RightArrow.bmp file mentioned in step 2. c. Click the Open button to add the image.	The right arrow image appears as item 0 within the Image Collection Editor dialog box. The left arrow becomes item 1 in the collection. 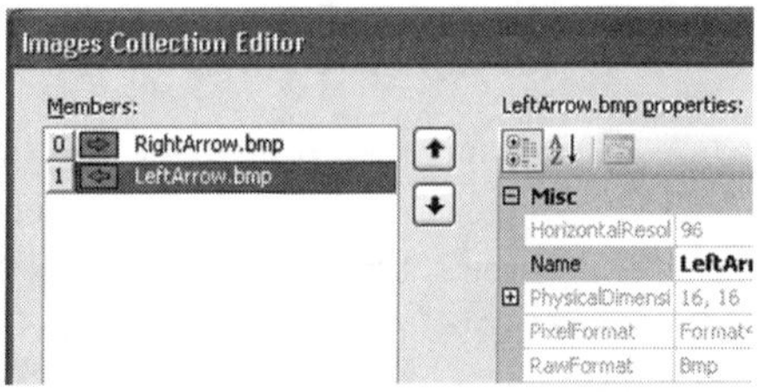
5	Similarly, add the LeftArrow.bmp image file created in step 2.	
6	Store the images in the list by clicking the OK button.	The assigned images are stored in the image list.

This creates a collection of the two images we wish to add to our toolbar. An excerpt of the code generated by these changes is shown in listing 16.1. Notice how the `ImageList` object is created within the `components` container so that the list is properly disposed of in the `Dispose` method. We discussed this behavior in chapter 9 for the `ToolTip` class.

Listing 16.1 Excerpt of InitializeComponent method after creating ImageList

```
private void InitializeComponent()
{
  . . .
  this.imageListArrows
    = new System.Windows.Forms.ImageList(this.components);
  . . .
  //
  // tsbHelp
  //
  this.tsbHelp.DisplayStyle
    = System.Windows.Forms.ToolStripItemDisplayStyle.Image;
  this.tsbHelp.Image = ((System.Drawing.Image)
      (resources.GetObject("tsbHelp.Image")));
  this.tsbHelp.ImageTransparentColor
    = System.Drawing.Color.Magenta;
  . . .
  //
  // imageListArrows
  //
  this.imageListArrows.ImageStream
    = ((System.Windows.Forms.ImageListStreamer)
        (resources.GetObject("imageListArrows.ImageStream")));
  this.imageListArrows.TransparentColor
    = System.Drawing.Color.Magenta;
  this.imageListArrows.Images.SetKeyName(0, "RightArrow.bmp");
  this.imageListArrows.Images.SetKeyName(1, "LeftArrow.bmp");
  . . .
}
```

❶ Gets Help image from resource file

❷ Gets image list stream from resource file

❸ Assigns key for each image

The annotated lines merit some additional discussion.

❶ Notice how the image for the Help button is loaded using a `ResourceManager` object as discussed in chapter 15. The resource file stores the image directly with the name `tbsHelp.Image`. This image is retrieved and assigned to the `tbsHelp.Image` property.

❷ For the `ImageList` object, the collection of images is stored within an `ImageListStreamer` object. This class encapsulates the image data required for the list so it can be stored and loaded as a single unit. In this case, the data is stored under the name `imageListArrows.ImageStream`. You can view this entry in the MainForm.resx resources file within Visual Studio by displaying the Other entries from the drop-down list. You can view the raw data for the `ImageListStreamer` object by viewing the raw MainForm.resx file in Visual Studio or a text editor.

❸ One special feature provided by the `ImageList.ImageCollection` class is the ability to associate a string key with each image. The `SetKeyName` method assigns this name, and the class provides members to retrieve and remove items based on the key. Visual Studio assigns and displays the key name of each image in the Image Collection Editor dialog box.

This completes our brief discussion of image lists. Let's use this new list in our application to create two additional items on our existing `ToolStrip` object.

16.3.3 Adding custom tool strip buttons

To illustrate the use of an `ImageList` object, we add next and previous buttons to our existing toolbar, and associate them with the Next and Previous menu items in the context menu associated with the form. This illustrates adding a `ToolStripButton` item within Visual Studio as well as the use of an `ImageList` object in a tool strip.

ADD PREVIOUS AND NEXT BUTTONS TO THE TOOL STRIP

	Action	Result
1	In the MainForm.cs [Design] window, add two `ToolStripButton` items and a `ToolStripSeparator` item to the tool strip. Rearrange the items as shown in the graphic. **How-to** Click the white Add Button item to add the buttons, and select the Separator entry from the drop-down list to add the separator. **Settings** Item: Previous — (Name): tsbPrevious; Text: Previous Item: Next — (Name): tsbNext; Text: Next	The two buttons display a default image since an actual image has not been assigned. MyPhotos File Edit View Help Desc WxH 1/1
2	Assign the `tbs_Click` method as `Click` event handler for both buttons.	The method is assigned as the handler for both buttons in the generated code.

3	In the MainForm.cs file, modify the `OnLoad` method to assign the appropriate menu item to each button's `Tag` property.	`protected override void OnLoad(. . .)`
		`{`
		`. . .`
		`tsbPrevious.Tag = menuPrevious;`
		`tsbNext.Tag = menuNext;`

4	Assign the tool strip's `ImageList` property to the new image list.	`toolStripMain.ImageList` `= imageListArrows;`

ADD PREVIOUS AND NEXT BUTTONS TO THE TOOL STRIP *(CONTINUED)*		
	Action	Result

5	Assign the two buttons' `ImageIndex` property to the appropriate index value within the list.	`tsbPrevious.ImageIndex = 1;`
		`tsbNext.ImageIndex = 0;`
		
		`base.OnLoad(e);`
		`}`

Since Visual Studio does not expose the `ImageList` properties in Windows Forms Designer, we assign these properties directly in the `OnLoad` method. Compile and run the application to see these new buttons in action. Another change we could make here is to disable the buttons when there is no next or previous image, much like we disabled our Next and Previous menu items in chapter 6. In the interest of keeping this section brief, we did not do this. Feel free to add this feature to your application if you wish.

As we already mentioned, Microsoft recommends the use of application resource files over image lists. In the remainder of this book we favor the recommended resource file approach, but it is good to understand image lists as well. Let's turn our attention to some other aspects of tool strips.

16.4 TOOL STRIP CONTAINERS

Now that we have some understanding of tool strips and tool strip items, we can take a look at some other features of these classes. This section discusses tool strip containers.

The `ToolStripContainer` class solves the problem of managing multiple tool strips within a single form. This class provides side panels that hold one or more `ToolStrip` objects and a central panel for other controls. This container also allows a user to move tool strips among the side panels at runtime.

16.4.1 The ToolStripContainer class

In applications such as Microsoft Word or Visual Studio, movable toolbars have become common practice. A user can place multiple toolbars in the same horizontal area, move them to the side or base of the application window, or stack them next to each other on any edge of the application. With the addition of the `ToolStrip` class, the Windows Forms team wished to add these features as well.

Their first attempt was a `RaftingContainer` control. A rafting container could be docked to each side of a form and hold one or more tool strips. Multiple tool strips could *raft* within each such container, and at runtime a user could move tool strips between the rafting containers on the form. While this worked just fine, it proved to be a bit cumbersome, so the design team sought an alternate solution.

The result is the `ToolStripContainer` class, summarized in .NET Table 16.6. This class provides a central panel much like a standard `Panel` class, surrounded by side panels for holding tool strips. The layout of these panels is illustrated in figure 16.2.

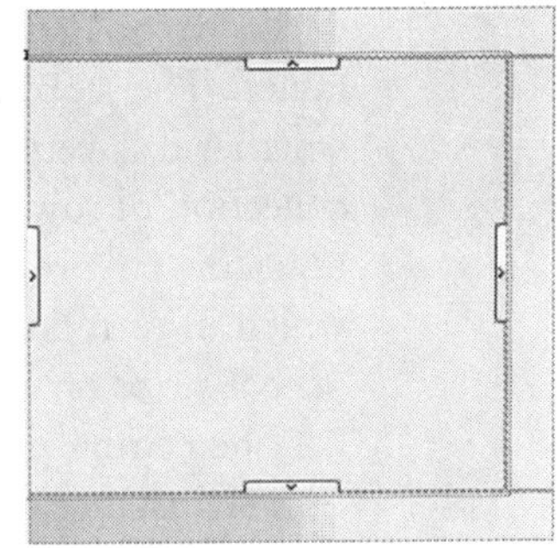

Figure 16.2 The ToolStripContainer class as it appears in Visual Studio. The arrow tabs here allow you to expose or hide the side panels. In the figure, the left panel is hidden.

The `ToolStripContainer` class provides members for accessing each panel and controlling the overall behavior of the container. It overrides a number of properties from the `Control` class, such as the `BackColor`, `Controls`, `Cursor`, and other properties, to define their behavior within the `ToolStripContainer` class. The four side panels are instances of the `ToolStripPanel` class, with associated properties to access each panel and define whether or not it is accessible, or visible, within the container. These properties are listed in .NET Table 16.7.

.NET Table 16.7 ToolStripContainer class

New in 2.0 The `ToolStripContainer` class is a container control for managing a set of `ToolStrip` objects on the sides of a form surrounding a central panel area. This Windows Forms control manages the docking and reordering of tool strips on a form, and inherits from the `ContainerControl` class.

The central panel in a tool strip container is a `ToolStripContentPanel` object, which represents a panel that fits inside a tool strip container and supports tool strip rendering. It is part of the `System.Windows.Forms` namespace, and inherits from the `Panel` class.

Each side panel in this container is a `ToolStripPanel` object, which is a container for holding `ToolStrip` objects in one or more rows within a tool strip container. It is part of the `System.Windows.Forms` namespace, and inherits from the `ContainerControl` class.

Public Properties	*BottomToolStripPanel*	Gets the bottom `ToolStripPanel` of the tool strip container
	BottomToolStripPanelVisible	Gets or sets whether the bottom panel is visible
	ContentPanel	Gets the central panel of the tool strip container
	LeftToolStripPanel	Gets the left panel of the tool strip container
	LeftToolStripPanelVisible	Gets or sets whether the left panel is visible
	RightToolStripPanel	Gets the right panel of the tool strip container
	RightToolStripPanelVisible	Gets or sets whether the right panel is visible
	TopToolStripPanel	Gets the top panel of the tool strip container
	TopToolStripPanelVisible	Gets or sets whether the top panel is visible

Each `ToolStripPanel` instance manages the tool strips on one side of the container. The `ToolStripPanel` class defines an `Orientation` property to define whether it is vertically or horizontally oriented, with a `Rows` property that holds the collection of rows within the panel. The spacing between each row is defined by the `RowMargin` property. Each row is defined as a `ToolStripPanelRow` instance, which in turn defines properties and methods that enable placement and movement of tool strips on and between `ToolStripPanelRow` objects.

The central panel in a `ToolStripContainer` class is a `ToolStripContentPanel` instance, accessible via the `ContentPanel` property. For the most part this class behaves exactly like a `Panel` instance. One additional feature is the ability to define a `ToolStripRenderer` via the `Renderer` property.

As you can see, there is a lot to absorb when it comes to tool strip containers. There is nothing like a little code to clarify what a control can do, so let's turn our attention to an example.

16.4.2 Embedding a tool strip in a container

We already have a tool strip in our MyPhotos application, but right now this tool strip is fixed and cannot be moved by the user. Embedding this strip in a `ToolStripContainer` would allow users to move this toolbar around the form, and prepare our form for additional tool strips in sections to come.

The following steps move our existing tool strip into a tool strip container.

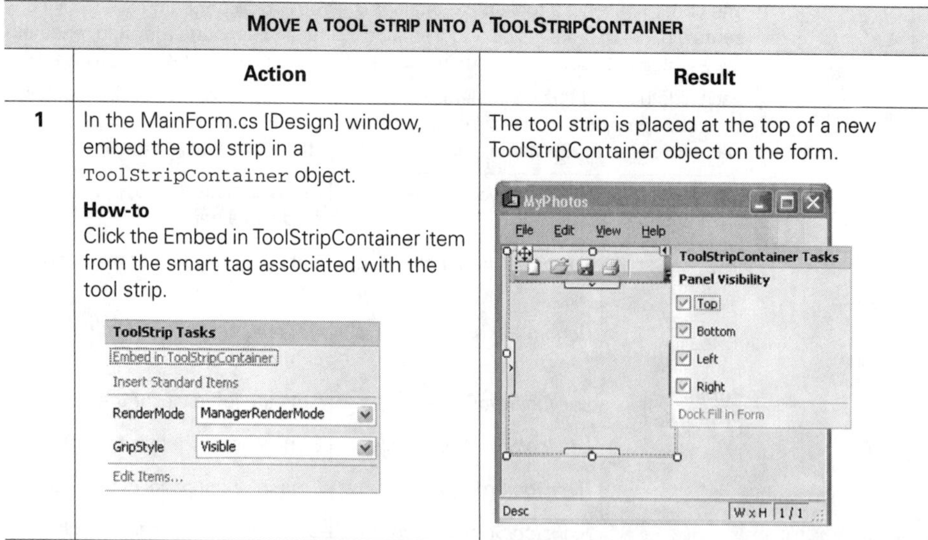

MOVE A TOOL STRIP INTO A TOOLSTRIPCONTAINER

	Action	Result
1	In the MainForm.cs [Design] window, embed the tool strip in a `ToolStripContainer` object. **How-to** Click the Embed in ToolStripContainer item from the smart tag associated with the tool strip.	The tool strip is placed at the top of a new ToolStripContainer object on the form.

Move a tool strip into a ToolStripContainer *(continued)*		
	Action	**Result**
2	Modify the `PictureBox` control so it is docked within the `ToolStripContainer` rather than the form. **How-to** a. Undock the `PictureBox` by clicking the "Undock in parent container" item from the box's smart tag tasks. b. Resize the picture box to a manageable size and drag it into the `ToolStripContainer` control's central panel. c. Dock the picture box in this panel by clicking the "Dock in parent container" item from the box's smart tag tasks.	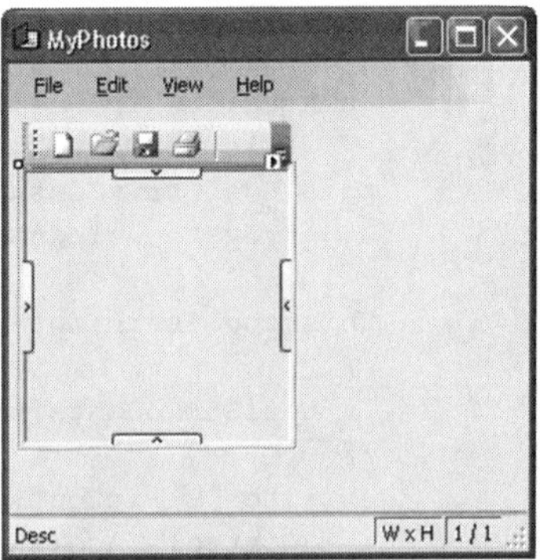
3	Modify the `ToolStripContainer` control to fill the entire form by setting its `Dock` property to `Fill`.	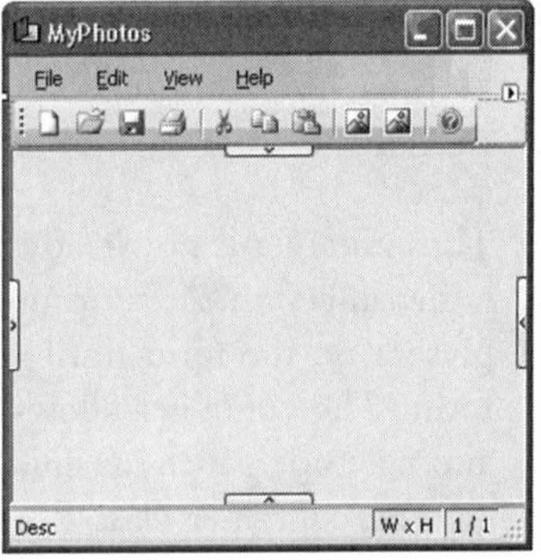

There seems to be a number of things going on here, but in fact the resulting code is rather straightforward. Listing 16.2 shows an excerpt of the generated code for our `MainForm` class after the prior steps have been completed. As you can see, the `ToolStripContainer` is created at notation 1; the picture box is placed within the central `ToolStripContentPanel` of the container at notation 2; and our existing tool strip is placed within the top `ToolStripPanel` of the container at notation 3.

Listing 16.2 MainForm.Designer.cs file after creating ToolStripContainer

```
. . .
private void InitializeComponent()
{
  . . .                                        Creates ToolStripContainer
  this.toolStripContainer1
      = new System.Windows.Forms.ToolStripContainer();
  . . .
```

```
    //
    // toolStripContainer1
    //
    //
    // toolStripContainer1.ContentPanel
    //
    this.toolStripContainer1.ContentPanel.Controls.Add(
        this.pbxPhoto);
    this.toolStripContainer1.Dock
        = System.Windows.Forms.DockStyle.Fill;
    . . .
    this.toolStripContainer1.Text = "toolStripContainer1";
    //
    // toolStripContainer1.TopToolStripPanel
    //
    this.toolStripContainer1.TopToolStripPanel.
        Controls.Add(this.toolStripMain);
    . . .
    this.Controls.Add(this.toolStripContainer1);
    this.Controls.Add(this.statusStrip1);
    this.Controls.Add(this.menuStrip1);
    . . .
}
```

Adds PictureBox to central panel

Adds tool strip to top panel

The container is now ready for use. Compile and run the application to see the container in action. At runtime, you cannot really tell that a `ToolStripContainer` is present on the form until you try to drag the `ToolStrip` to alternate sides of the form. The container allows the user to move the strip within any side panel or to alternate side panels, as illustrated in figure 16.3.

The container class is especially useful for managing multiple tool strips on a form, as we see in the next section. In this and prior sections, we focused on tool strip

Figure 16.3 The tool strip container allows our tool strip to appear on any side of the control. Note how the example on the right employs the overflow menu to hold some of the items.

buttons and various tool strip features. Next we look at some various tool strip items other than the button type we have seen thus far.

TRY IT! Try the following changes to see how the runtime behavior of the sample application changes.

Disable the right panel in the `ToolStripContainer` by setting the `RightToolStripPanelVisible` property to `false`. Run the application to verify that you cannot drag the strip to the right side of the application.

Set the `GripStyle` property of the `ToolStrip` control to `Hidden` so the moving grip is not shown. Run the application to verify that you can no longer move the strip within the container.

16.5 SPECIALIZED BUTTON ITEMS

We have already seen how the standard `ToolStripButton` class works, and created a `toolStripMain` tool strip full of such buttons in our MyPhotos application. There are some alternate kinds of tool strip buttons, and this section is a good place to discuss them.

In this section we look at toggle buttons, drop-down buttons, and split buttons. A *toggle button* is nothing more than a standard button that can display two states: pressed and unpressed. Toggle buttons are useful to indicate the state of a specific feature or window. For example, in Microsoft Word and other Windows-based document editors, the font style buttons for bold, italic, and underline are typically toggle buttons to indicate when the associated style is enabled or disabled.

Drop-down buttons work much like an item on a traditional menu bar. When a user clicks a drop-down button, an associated menu or other pop-up is displayed. The overflow button discussed in section 16.2.3 is an example of a drop-down button.

Split buttons work much like drop-down buttons, except that they differentiate between the standard button and drop-down button portion of the item. Among other features, split buttons permit a specific drop-down menu item to be associated with the standard button portion of the control.

16.5.1 Toggle buttons

A toggle button is just a `ToolStripButton` object that employs the `Checked` property to display a button with two possible states. As you may recall from section 16.2, the `Checked` property gets or sets the pressed state of the button. Since we have already discussed this class, let's move straight to an example.

Let's create a new tool strip that displays the dialog boxes associated with the MyPhotos application. This includes the album properties, photograph properties, and pixel dialog windows. As you may recall, the album and photograph dialog windows are modal so a standard tool strip button that simply displays the appropriate dialog box when clicked is appropriate.

For the pixel dialog form, this is a modeless dialog window. As a result, the user can interact with the main window when the `PixelDialog` form is displayed. A toggle button is a good option here, since the button can indicate whether the dialog box is shown by displaying a pressed state. To emphasize this point, we also display an alternate image when the button is pressed.

Figure 16.4 This figure illustrates how two tool strips can display side by side in a ToolStripContainer object.

Figure 16.4 shows the results of our endeavors. In the figure, a new `ToolStrip` with an album, photograph, and pixel graphic are shown. Since the pixel dialog window is visible, the pixel toggle button is in a pressed state.

The steps required to implement this new tool strip are shown in the following table.

<table>
<tr><th colspan="3">ADD NEW TOOL STRIP</th></tr>
<tr><th></th><th>Action</th><th>Result</th></tr>
<tr><td>1</td><td>In the MainForm.cs [Design] window, drag a new <code>ToolStrip</code> object onto the top panel of the <code>ToolStripContainer</code> control, and set its (Name) to "toolStripDialogs."</td><td>A second tool strip appears in the component tray and on the form.
toolStripDialogs</td></tr>
<tr><td>2</td><td>Add four (yes, four) tool strip buttons to this new strip.
Settings
<table>
<tr><th>Button</th><th>Property</th><th>Value</th></tr>
<tr><td>First</td><td>(Name)
ToolTipText</td><td>tsbAlbumProps
Album Properties</td></tr>
<tr><td>Second</td><td>(Name)
ToolTipText</td><td>tsbPhotoProps
Photo Properties</td></tr>
<tr><td>Third</td><td>(Name)
ToolTipText</td><td>tsbPixelData
Pixel Data</td></tr>
<tr><td>Fourth</td><td>(Name)
Visible</td><td>tsbPixelData2
False</td></tr>
</table></td><td>MyPhotos
File Edit View Help
Note: Although our buttons only display an image, we could also assign the <code>Text</code> for each button to keep our settings consistent. This is not required so we do not include this change here.</td></tr>
</table>

	ADD NEW TOOL STRIP *(CONTINUED)*	
	Action	**Result**
3	Assign the icons/Win9x/NOTE03.ICO image from the common image library as the image for the `tsbAlbumProps` tool strip button. **How-to** a. Locate the Image entry on Properties window for the first button. b. Click the ... button for this entry to display the Select Resource dialog box. c. Click the Import button to assign a local resource. d. Locate and select the desired image file. e. Click Open to select the image. f. Click OK to assign the image.	MyPhotos File Edit View Help
4	Similarly, assign the following images to the other buttons in the tool strip. **Settings** **Button** — **Image Value** tsbPhotoProps — icons/Win9x/NOTE12.ICO tsbPixelData — icons/WinXP/search4doc.ico tsbPixelData2 — icons/WinXP/search.ico	MyPhotos File Edit View Help

Our new tool strip holds four new buttons in the top panel of the tool strip container. The code here is much like the code generated for the standard buttons earlier in the chapter, so we do not discuss it in detail.

You may wonder why we create four buttons when our plan was to present three new buttons to the user. The reason we do this is to capture an alternate image in our fourth button. Although it is possible to store the icon as a resource in the project, it is a bit cumbersome to import an `Icon` and turn it into the `Image` required for our button. By using a fourth button and setting its `Visible` property to `false`, this task becomes much easier to accomplish.

Our buttons are ready; we just need to add the required implementation code.

	IMPLEMENT BUTTON EVENTS FOR NEW TOOL STRIP	
	Action	**Result**
5	Assign the `tsb_Click` method as the `Click` event handler for the Album and Photo buttons.	The handler is assigned in the generated MainForm.Designer.cs code.

IMPLEMENT BUTTON EVENTS FOR NEW TOOL STRIP *(CONTINUED)*		
	Action	**Result**

6	In the MainForm.cs file, modify the `OnLoad` method to assign the corresponding menus to the `Tag` property for the Album and Photo buttons.	`protected override void OnLoad(EventArgs e)`
		`{`
		`  . . .`
		`  // Set up toolStripDialogs`
		`  tsbAlbumProps.Tag = menuAlbumProps;`
		`  tsbPhotoProps.Tag = menuPhotoProps;`

7	Also assign the `Tag` setting for the `tsbPixelData` button to its own `Image` property setting.	`  tsbPixelData.Tag = tsbPixelData.Image;`
		
		`  base.OnLoad(e);`
		`}`

8	Add a new `Click` event handler for the `tsbPixelData` toolbar button.	`private void tsbPixelData_Click(`
		`    object sender, EventArgs e)`
		`{`

9	Implement this handler to display the `PixelDialog` form if it is not visible, and hide the dialog box if it is visible.	`  Form f = PixelForm;`
		`  if (f == null || f.IsDisposed || !f.Visible)`
		`    menuPixelData.PerformClick();`
		`  else`
		`    f.Hide();`

10	Also call an `UpdatePixel-Button` method with the visibility state of the dialog box.	`  UpdatePixelButton(PixelForm.Visible);` `}`

11	Implement the `UpdatePixel-Button` method to assign the checked state of the button to the given `visible` state.
	
	Note: This puts the button in a pressed state when the pixel dialog box is visible.
		`private void UpdatePixelButton(bool visible)`
		`{`
		`  tsbPixelData.Checked = visible;`

12	Also in this method, display the image on the hidden button when the pixel dialog box is visible, and display the default image when the pixel dialog box is not visible.	`  if (visible)`
		`    tsbPixelData.Image = tsbPixelData2.Image;`
		`  else`
		`    tsbPixelData.Image`
		`        = (Image)tsbPixelData.Tag;`
		`}`

13	In the menu handler for the pixel dialog, call the `UpdatePixelButton` method to press the button when the dialog box is displayed.	`private void menuPixelData_Click(. . .)`
		`{`
		`  . . .`
		`  Point p = pbxPhoto.PointToClient(. . .);`
		`  UpdatePixelDialog(p.X, p.Y);`
		`  UpdatePixelButton(true);`
		`}`

We are not quite done, but a short discussion is in order here. The toolbar buttons to display the Properties dialog box for the current album and photograph simply duplicate the behavior of an existing menu. So these buttons are handled through our existing `tsb_Click` method.

For our `tsbPixelData` button, we create a custom `Click` handler that displays or hides the `PixelDialog` form as required. We also create an `UpdatePixelButton` method that adjusts the button based on the visible state of the dialog box, including the use of our alternate image when the `PixelDialog` form is displayed.

Our dialog box can also display the `PixelDialog` form from the menu bar, so we modify the menu handler to invoke the `UpdatePixelButton` method as well. This handles all cases except one: the user can close the `PixelDialog` form directly, and right now we have no way to update our button.

We can fix this by activating the main form whenever the user closes the pixel dialog box, as per the following steps. The `Activated` event occurs when a form is made active from code or by the user.

HANDLE CASE WHERE PIXELDIALOG FORM IS MANUALLY CLOSED

	Action	Result

14	In the MainForm.cs file, handle the `Activated` event by overriding the `OnActivated` method.	`protected override void OnActivated(`
		`    EventArgs e)`
		`{`

15	Implement this method to update the pixel button whenever the `PixelDialog` form exists.	`  if (_dlgPixel != null)`
		`    UpdatePixelButton(_dlgPixel.Visible);`
		
		`  base.OnActivated(e);`
		`}`

16	In the `PixelDialog` class in the MyPhotoControls project, override the `OnFormClosed` event.	`protected override void OnFormClosed(`
		`    FormClosedEventArgs e)`
		`{`

17	Within this method, activate the owning form, if one exists.	`  Visible = false;`
		`  if (Owner != null)`
		`    Owner.Activate();`
		
		`  base.OnFormClosed(e);`
		`}`

This code ensures that the main form is activated whenever the `PixelDialog` form is closed. This in turn executes the `MainForm.OnActivated` method, which updates the pixel toolbar button with the appropriate image.

16.5.2 Drop-down buttons

Another type of button item is the drop-down button. Unlike toggle buttons, drop-down buttons are defined by a separate class: `ToolStripDropDownButton`. This class inherits from the `ToolStripDropDownItem` class, presented in .NET Table 4.2 in chapter 4 during our discussion of context menu strips.

The one additional public property defined by the `ToolStripDropDown-Button` class is `ShowDropDownArrow`. This property gets or sets whether a small arrow appears on the button to indicate that additional options are available.

As an example, let's add an Image drop-down button that mimics the behavior of the Image menu already present in the context menu of our form. As you may recall, the context menu drop-down is also used as the View menu for the application, so ideally we would like to reuse the existing drop-down associated with the Image menu.

The result of this change completes the application shown in figure 16.1 at the start of this chapter. The steps required are as follows.

ADD A TOOL STRIP DROP-DOWN BUTTON

	ACTION	RESULT
1	In the MainForm.cs [Design] window, add a new tool strip called `toolStripImages`.	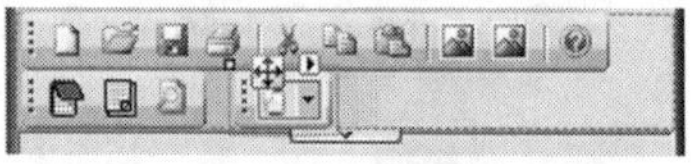
2	Add a DropDownButton item to this strip. **Settings** **Property** / **Value** (Name) / tsdImage AutoToolTip / False DisplayStyle / Text Text / &Image	MyPhotos File Edit View Help Image Type Here

3	In the `OnLoad` method in the `MainForm` class, set the `DropDown` for the new item to the drop-down associated with the existing Image menu.	`protected override void OnLoad(EventArgs e)`
		`{`
		`  . . .`
		`  // Set up toolStripDialogs`
		`  . . .`
		`  // Set up toolStripImages`
		`  tsdImage.DropDown = menuImage.DropDown;`
		
		`  base.OnLoad(e);`
		`}`

4	Assign the `DropDownItem-Clicked` event handler for the new button to use the matching handler from the `menuImage` menu item.	Properties **tsdImage** System.Windows.Forms.ToolStripDropDownButton DropDownClosed DropDownItemClick **menuImage_DropDownItemClicke** DropDownOpened DropDownOpening **menuImage_DropDownOpening**
5	Similarly, assign the `DropDown-Opening` event handler to match the one for the `menuImage` menu item.	

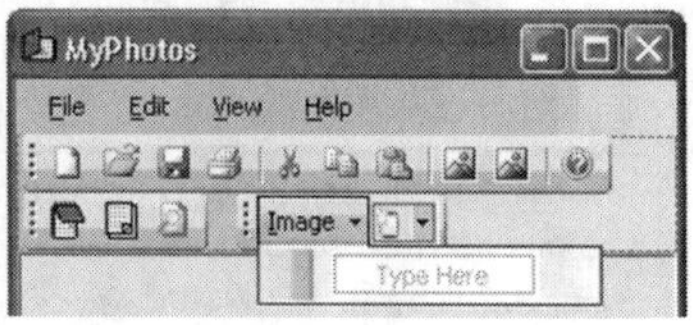

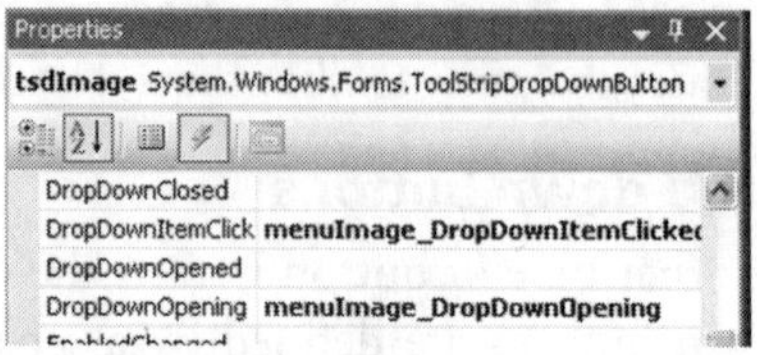

Ah, the power of reuse. At first glance you might think the implementation of a drop-down button might take a more than a few lines of code. In fact, we carefully constructed everything we needed way back in chapter 4, so here we simply reuse the existing menus and event handlers.

16.5.3 Split buttons

There is one more drop-down item to discuss: the `ToolStripSplitButton` class. This class is similar to the `ToolStripDropDownButton` class, except that it distinguishes between the various portions of the item. In `ToolStripDropDownButton`, the class internally defines the location, layout, and behavior of the image or text and drop-down arrow portions. The `ToolStripSplitButton` class provides properties for the three portions of the item: the image or text area, the drop-down arrow, and the space between them. More importantly, it allows an application to define alternate behavior for the standard button and dropdown button portions of the control. An overview of this class appears in .NET Table 16.8.

To demonstrate this control, we could replace our existing `ToolStripDropDownButton` with a split button. One change we might make is to assign the Scale to Fit menu as the default item for the split button, so that when a user clicks the button the image is automatically scaled to fit the window.

This would be a fine example, but we have bigger goals in mind. Our example adds a split button that allows the user to select an image from the album. This requires the use of the `ToolStripControlHost` class to display the images available in the album. Figure 16.5 illustrates our new change: a new Select button with a drop-down that shows the images in the album.

The various tool strip items allow for all sorts of interfaces, but there are times when what you really want is to place some other control within the bounds of a tool strip. The `ToolStripControlHost` class makes this possible by defining a generic mechanism for hosting Windows Forms controls on a strip. In particular, the `ToolStripComboBox`, `ToolStripProgressBar`, and `ToolStripTextBox` classes allow a combo box, progress bar, or text box to appear within a tool strip, and are based on the control host item. We do not present these specialize tool strip items in additional detail, but a summary of the `ToolStripControlHost` class appears in .NET Table 16.9.

Figure 16.5 The Select drop-down menu here is constructed dynamically whenever a new album is assigned to the album manager.

.NET Table 16.8 ToolStripSplitButton class

New in 2.0 The `ToolStripSplitButton` class is a drop-down tool strip item consisting of a standard button and a drop-down button. This class is part of the `System.Windows.Forms` namespace, and inherits from the `ToolStripDropDownItem` class. See .NET Table 4.2 for a list of members inherited from this base class.

Public Properties	*ButtonBounds*	Gets the size and location of the standard button portion of the split button item.
	ButtonPressed	Gets whether the button portion of the split button is in a pressed state.
	ButtonSelected	Gets whether the button portion is selected or the `DropDownButtonPressed` property is `true`.
	DefaultItem	Gets or sets the portion of the split button that is activated when the control is initially selected.
	DropDownButtonBounds	Gets the size and location of the drop-down button portion of the split button item.
	DropDownButtonPressed	Gets whether the drop-down button portion is in a pressed state. The `DropDownButtonSelected` property gets whether this portion is selected.
	DropDownButtonWidth	Gets or sets the width in pixels of the drop-down button portion of the split button.
	SplitterBounds	Gets the bounds for the separator between the standard and drop-down button portions of the split button.
	SplitterWidth	Gets or sets the width in pixels of the separator between the button portions of the split button.
Public Events	*ButtonClick*	Occurs when the standard button portion of the split button is clicked.
	ButtonDoubleClick	Occurs when the standard button portion of the split button is double-clicked.
	DefaultItemChanged	Occurs when the `DefaultItem` property changes.

While not listed in the table, the `ToolStripControlHost` class overrides a number of members inherited from `ToolStripItem` class. Properties like `DisplayStyle`, `Image`, and `Text` are not relevant for hosted items, and are essentially disabled. Other properties like `Font` and `ForeColor` are overridden to reflect the state of the hosted control. In addition, new members are defined to mimic commonly used members of the `Control` class and are passed through to the hosted control. This includes properties such as `CausesValidation` and `Focused`, and events such as `Enter`, `Leave`, `KeyDown`, `KeyUp`, `Validated`, and `Validating`.

.NET Table 16.9 ToolStripControlHost class

New in 2.0 The `ToolStripControlHost` class is a tool strip item that can host other Windows Forms controls on a tool strip. This class is part of the `System.Windows.Forms` namespace, and inherits from the `ToolStripItem` class. See .NET Table 3.4 for a list of members inherited from this base class.

Public Properties	*Control*	Gets the `Control` hosted by this item
	ControlAlign	Gets or sets the alignment of the hosted control
	Focused	Gets whether the hosted control has input focus
Public Events	*Enter*	Occurs when the hosted control is entered
	KeyDown	Occurs when a key is pressed while the hosted control has focus
	Validating	Occurs when the hosted control is about to be validated

The .NET documentation contains a number of examples using the `DateTimePicker` or `MonthCalendar` control hosted within a tool strip. In our application, we host a PictureBox control within a tool strip in order to offer a quick way for the user to select a specific image in an album.

The following steps add the new item to our form.

<table>
<tr><th colspan="3">ADD A TOOL STRIP SPLIT BUTTON</th></tr>
<tr><th></th><th>ACTION</th><th>RESULT</th></tr>
<tr><td>1</td><td>In the MainForm.cs [Design] window, add a split button item to the <code>toolStripImages</code> tool strip.

Settings
<table><tr><th>Property</th><th>Value</th></tr><tr><td>(Name)</td><td>tssSelect</td></tr><tr><td>AutoToolTip</td><td>False</td></tr><tr><td>DisplayStyle</td><td>Text</td></tr><tr><td>Text</td><td>&Select</td></tr></table></td><td></td></tr>
<tr><td>2</td><td>In the <code>MainForm</code> class, define a new <code>AssignSelectDropDown</code> method that defines the drop-down for this item.</td><td><pre>private void AssignSelectDropDown()
{
  ToolStripDropDown drop
      = new ToolStripDropDown();</pre></td></tr>
<tr><td>3</td><td>Within this method, loop through the photos in the current album.</td><td><pre> PhotoAlbum a = Manager.Album;
  for (int i = 0; i < a.Count; i++)
  {</pre></td></tr>
</table>

	ADD A TOOL STRIP SPLIT BUTTON *(CONTINUED)*	
	ACTION	**RESULT**

4	Define a `PictureBox` control that holds the image for each photo.	<pre>PictureBox box = new PictureBox();
		box.SizeMode = PictureBoxSizeMode.Zoom;
		box.Image = a[i].Image;
		box.Dock = DockStyle.Fill;</pre>

5	Host this picture box in a `ToolStripControlHost` tool strip item.	<pre>ToolStripControlHost host
		  = new ToolStripControlHost(box);
		host.AutoSize = false;
		host.Size = new Size(tssSelect.Width,
		                     tssSelect.Width);
		host.Tag = i;</pre>

6	Define an anonymous method as the `Click` handler for this control to select the associated image in the album.	<pre>host.Click += delegate(object o,
		                       EventArgs e)
		{
		  int x = (int)(o as ToolStripItem).Tag;
		  Manager.Index = x;
		  drop.Close();
		  DisplayAlbum();
		};</pre>

7	Add the control host item to the split button's drop-down list.	<pre> drop.Items.Add(host); }</pre>

8	If the resulting drop-down has any members, assign the drop-down to the split button, and set the first image as the default item.	<pre> if (drop.Items.Count > 0)
		  {
		    tssSelect.DropDown = drop;
		    tssSelect.DefaultItem = drop.Items[0];
		  }
		}</pre>

9	Modify the `Manager` property to call this new method whenever a new album manager is assigned.	<pre>private AlbumManager Manager
		{
		  get { return _manager; }
		  set
		  {
		    _manager = value;
		    AssignSelectDropDown();
		  }
		}</pre>

This is a good example using the `ToolStripControlHost` class, yet there are a few problems that might be worth fixing if we had a bit more space in this chapter. The drop-down strip keeps a reference to each image in the album, which for large photos or a large album can take up lots of memory. A better approach here might be to implement and use a `Thumbnail` property as described in the TRY IT! exercise at the end of chapter 13.

Another issue, and one more problematic to fix, is that the drop-down is really long for a really big album. It would be nice if the drop-down limited itself to only four or five images at a time, perhaps with a scroll bar to manage the list of images. This is not supported by the `ToolStrip` classes, but could be implemented as a borderless form containing an owner-drawn list box.

Once again, the point here was to illustrate how to host a control, which this example does quite nicely. This finishes our discussion on tool strips, as well as this chapter—not to mention part 2 of the book.

16.6 RECAP

We've come a long way from figure 1.1 way back in chapter 1, and have learned how to create Windows applications with a large variety of controls and behaviors.

In this chapter we looked at the `ToolStrip` and `ToolStripItem` classes. We created three different tool strips in our MyPhotos application, and used various tool strip items supported by the Windows Forms namespace, including standard, toggle, drop-down, and split buttons. Our toggle button example included code to dynamically change the image displayed on the button. We finished the chapter with a split button example utilizing the `ToolStripControlHost` class to host a `PictureBox` control within a tool strip.

Also along the way we examined the `ImageList` class to store and manage a collection of `Image` objects on behalf of a control or other object. We pointed out that Microsoft recommends using images in resource files for tool strips rather than from `ImageList` objects these days, but showed both approaches in the chapter so you can decide for yourself.

Two topics related to tool strips not covered here are layout engines and tool strip rendering. The `Control` class defines a `LayoutEngine` property that specifies a `LayoutEngine` object for arranging the control's children, and can be overridden to customize the layout of tool strip items within a tool strip. The `ToolStripRenderer` class is used to specify a style or theme for a tool strip container or individual tool strip. See the .NET documentation for detailed information and examples for these classes.

I encourage you to experiment with the controls and features discussed here and in earlier chapters in this book. The foundation presented so far is critical to developing and understanding Windows Forms applications, and will come in handy as we discuss the concepts presented in part 3.

PART 3

Advanced Windows Forms

If you have actually read this book from the beginning, then I applaud your fortitude and welcome you to the third and final part. For readers who jumped directly to this page, I encourage you to read the earlier chapters, as they build a foundation for much of the discussion that occurs in part 3. Of course, if you are browsing this book with the idea of buying it, then feel free to look around.

In part 3 we look at what might be considered advanced topics. If you have a firm, or at least decent, grasp of the material from part 2 of this book, then this section should be quite understandable.

Chapter 17 kicks off our discussion with the topic of custom controls. This chapter presents various ways to customize Windows Forms controls, and builds a `ScrollablePictureBox` class that allows scrolling of images within a `PictureBox` control.

Chapter 18, "Explorer interfaces and tree views," creates a new MyAlbumExplorer application as an example of an explorer-style interface. The `SplitContainer` and `TreeView` controls are discussed, and we build a custom tree view control to present and manage photo albums within the tree. Chapter 19 continues the explorer interface and discusses various aspects of list views. We incorporate a list view in our sample application to complete the MyAlbumExplorer application.

Chapter 20, "Multiple document interfaces," explores the support provided by the .NET Framework for multiple document interface (MDI) applications in Windows Forms. Here we return to our MyPhotos application from part 2 and convert it into an MDI application, using our `MainForm` class as the child window.

The topic of data binding is taken up in chapters 21 and 22. Chapter 21 presents data binding in general and the `DataGridView` class in particular. Data grid view styles, columns, rows, and cells are all examined over the course of this chapter. This discussion continues in chapter 22, "Two-way binding and binding sources," where the difference between complex and simple data binding is revealed. Chapter 22 discusses binding lists in the `IBindingList` interface and generic `BindingList<T>` class, and extends the `PhotoAlbum` class using these types. The `BindingSource` class, added in .NET 2.0, is shown and used to bind a set of simple controls to a `PhotoAlbum` data source.

We finish part 3 in chapter 23, "Odds and ends .NET." This chapter reviews various topics that should be of further interest, including printing, drag and drop, the `WebBrowser` control, application settings, and deployment. An example for each topic is provided using the MyPhotos MDI application built in chapter 20. The final section discusses deployment using both a setup package and the .NET 2.0 feature of ClickOnce deployment.

Following this last chapter are four appendices with some additional information on C#, an overview of .NET namespaces, a class hierarchy chart of the Windows Forms namespace, and resources for additional information on C# and the .NET Framework.

CHAPTER 17

Custom controls

To kick off the so-called advanced section of the book, we take a look at custom controls. A custom control is nothing more than a new class derived from an existing .NET control class. In a web application, such controls are sometimes called custom *server* controls since they run on a web server. In a Windows Forms application, they are called custom *client* controls. This book is all about Windows Forms, so we use the term *custom control* to mean a custom client control.

This chapter discusses some approaches to building custom controls, presents some classes provided by .NET intended to assist such efforts, and shows a few examples of exactly how this is done.

At a high level, a custom control is useful whenever you wish to encapsulate control functionality that is not explicitly provided by the Windows Forms namespace. Three distinct approaches are typically used when building custom controls. The first is to inherit from an existing Windows Forms control. This is useful when you wish to encapsulate some specific settings or extend the functionality of an existing control. We saw an example of this in chapter 7, where we encapsulated the settings required to turn a form into a dialog box as the `FormDialog` class in listing 7.4. We discuss this approach in more detail in section 17.1.

Another approach is to inherit directly from the `Control` class. This is appropriate when you need to provide a custom graphical interface for your control, or you wish to implement new functionality that is not available in the standard controls. Windows Forms provides some assistance in this area, which we discuss in section 17.2.

A final method for building custom controls is to make use of the `UserControl` class. This class is specifically designed to support the creation of a custom control from a composite of other controls. For example, you could imagine building a weather control that presents the temperature, wind speed, barometric pressure, and other information in a single control. This could be created by encapsulating a set of existing Windows Forms controls in a `UserControl` object. We discuss user controls in section 17.3.

17.1 EXTENDING EXISTING CONTROLS

One of the simplest ways to create a custom control is to inherit from an existing control. When an existing control provides most of the functionality you need, or when you simply wish to define a default behavior for a set of controls in your application, this is especially useful. For example, you might have an application with a number of multiline text boxes. To simplify the creation of these controls, you could define a `MultilineTextBox` class that adjusts the default properties of the `TextBox` class to enable multiple lines with vertical scrolling. Such a class is illustrated in listing 17.1.

Listing 17.1 MultilineTextBox class

```
public class MultiLineTextBox : TextBox
{
  public MultiLineTextBox()
  {
    Multiline = true;
    ScrollBars = ScrollBars.Vertical;
    WordWrap = true;
  }
}
```

The `MultilineTextBox` example is rather simplistic, although it is indeed a valid custom control. For a more full-featured example, this section illustrates a class that extends the `PictureBox` class to enable scrolling when the image is larger than the displayable area. As you may recall, this has been a problem in our MyPhotos application, as photographic images can be quite big, so it is not always possible to make the main application window large enough to show the entire image.

An example of the `ScrollablePictureBox` class created in this section is shown in figure 17.1. As you can see, a portion of our familiar goose image is displayed, with horizontal and vertical scroll bars that allow the user to scroll the image as desired.

Figure 17.1
This test application for the ScrollablePictureBox class allows us to load an image and dynamically alter the SizeMode property of the control.

17.1.1 Designing a scrollable picture box

Let's start with a design for our new control, beginning with the public interface. It is always a good idea to know what you are building before you actually build. For custom controls, as well as any new class, you should at least sketch out the public interface before you write any code.

For our class, we wish to build a picture box control that enables scrolling. We call the new class `ScrollablePictureBox`. At a minimum it seems reasonable to provide the public members shown in table 17.1

Table 17.1 ScrollablePictureBox class

This class is a picture box that allows scrolling. It inherits from the Windows Forms `PictureBox` class and adds the ability to scroll the image when the `SizeMode` property is set to `Normal` or `CenterImage` and the size of the image is larger than the client area of the control.		
Public Properties	AutoScroll	Gets or sets whether the picture box displays scroll bars as required.
Public Events	Scroll	Occurs when the image in the picture box is scrolled.

As you can see, our new class inherits most of its public functionality from the `PictureBox` class. We chose the name for the `AutoScroll` property based on the related property in the `ScrollableControl` class, and the name for the `Scroll` event based on the related event in the `ScrollBar` class, which we discuss in a moment.

The key to implementing this new control is the addition of scroll bar functionality. Fortunately for us, Windows Forms provides a `ScrollBar` class that encapsulates this concept; we just need to hook up a horizontal and vertical scroll bar as required. A summary of the `ScrollBar` class appears in .NET Table 17.2.

Notice how the `ScrollBar` class essentially manages a single value, encapsulated by the `Value` property. Other properties exist to determine the minimum and maximum setting for the value, and to define the amounts to add to or subtract from this value when the user moves the scroll bar up or down using the keyboard or mouse.

.NET Table 17.2 ScrollBar class

The `ScrollBar` class provides the base scrolling functionality for Windows Forms applications. This abstract class is part of the `System.Windows.Forms` namespace, and inherits from the `Control` class. To implement scrolling, use the derived classes: `HScrollBar` for a horizontal scroll bar and `VScrollBar` for a vertical scroll bar.

Public Properties	LargeChange	Gets or sets the amount to modify `Value` when the user pages the scroll bar up or down
	Maximum	Gets or sets the upper limit for the `Value` property
	Minimum	Gets or sets the lower limit for `Value`
	SmallChange	Gets or sets the amount to modify the `Value` property when the user clicks the arrow buttons at either end of the scroll bar
	Value	Gets or sets the numeric value that represents the current position of the scroll bar
Public Events	Scroll	Occurs when the scroll box has moved
	ValueChanged	Occurs when the `Value` property changes

The `Scroll` event is provided to perform an action whenever scrolling occurs. We discuss this event in more detail when we use it later in this chapter.

In our custom control, we employ the derived `HScrollBar` and `VScrollBar` classes to present a horizontal and vertical scroll bar within the picture box. These are illustrated in figure 17.2. I drew this figure in Visio to make sure it looked nice for the book, although I could just as easily have drawn it on paper. Aside from the two scroll bars required, the drawing highlights the fact that we need to account for a small square of empty space where the two scroll bars meet. This empty space is, in fact, one of the more interesting aspects of our new control.

Looking at figure 17.2, it appears that we can simply dock a horizontal scroll bar to the base of the picture box, and a vertical scroll bar to the right of the picture box.

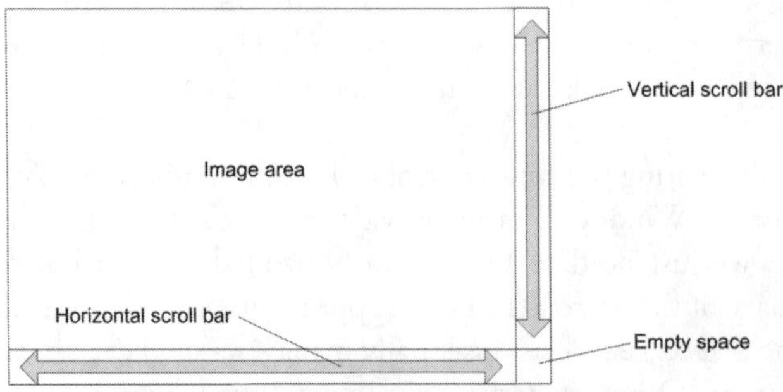

Figure 17.2 This figure highlights the four main areas required in the ScrollablePictureBox control.

This accounts for the two scroll bars, but not the required empty space, so this idea does not quite work. Instead, we can create a blank control to dock to the right of the picture box that in turn will contain the vertical scroll bar. The vertical scroll bar can then be positioned such that the base on the blank control is exposed, which draws the default control color in the required empty space.

With this in mind, let's forge ahead with our new control.

17.1.2 Creating a scrollable picture box

Now that we've agreed on a public interface and thought about an appropriate design, let's write some code. Conceptually, this control has nothing to do with our `Photograph` or `Album` classes and their related dialog boxes. Because of this, it might be worth creating a new library called MyControls that would hold this and other generic controls. A good idea, but let's stick with our existing MyPhotoControls project as an acceptable if not ideal location for the new control within the context of the book.

As we create this new control, we would also like to have some way to test it. It is often useful to create a small test application for new controls, so we do so here.

CREATE A SCROLLABLEPICTUREBOX CONTROL AND TEST APPLICATION

	Action	Result
1	Start a new ScrollablePictureBoxTest project as a new solution in Visual Studio.	Solution Explorer - Solution '... Solution 'ScrollablePictureBoxTest' MyPhotoControls ScrollablePictureBoxTest Properties References Program.cs TestForm.cs
2	Rename the default `Form1` class to "TestForm."	
3	Set the `Text` property for the `TestForm` form to "ScrollablePictureBox Test."	
4	Add the existing MyPhotoControls project to the solution.	

5	Add a new class called `ScrollablePictureBox` to the MyPhotoControls project.	`using System;`
		`using System.ComponentModel;`
		`using System.Drawing;`
		`using System.Windows.Forms;`
		
		`namespace Manning.MyPhotoControls`
		`{`
		`  public class ScrollablePictureBox : PictureBox`
		`  {`
		`  }`

6	Modify the new class to be public and inherit from the Windows Forms `PictureBox` class. Indicate that we are using the namespaces as shown.	

These steps create the test project and initial definition of the class. So far, the `ScrollablePictureBox` class is a custom control that behaves exactly as the `PictureBox` control. Although we have not implemented any functionality yet, this is a good time to finish our test program for the new control so we can test the functionality during our implementation.

A test application should allow a user to manipulate the control much like it might be manipulated in an actual program. For our purposes, the important aspects of the `PictureBox` control are probably the ability to load an image, the various display formats, and the behavior when the control is resized. So we create a quick program that allows these aspects of the control to be manipulated.

<table>
<tr><th colspan="3">FINISH THE SCROLLABLEPICTUREBOX TEST PROGRAM</th></tr>
<tr><th></th><th>Action</th><th>Result</th></tr>
<tr><td>7</td><td>In the TestForm.cs [Design] window, drop a button and combo box onto the form.
Settings
<table>
<tr><th>Control</th><th>Property</th><th>Value</th></tr>
<tr><td>Button</td><td>(Name)
Text</td><td>btnLoad
&Load</td></tr>
<tr><td>Combo Box</td><td>(Name)
Text</td><td>comboSizeMode
Normal</td></tr>
</table></td><td>ScrollablePictureBox Test
Load Normal</td></tr>
<tr><td>8</td><td>Add a scrollable picture box to the form.
How-to
Visual Studio automatically adds custom controls to the Toolbox. Locate the class in the toolbox and drag it onto the form.
Settings
<table>
<tr><th>Property</th><th>Value</th></tr>
<tr><td>(Name)</td><td>spbxImage</td></tr>
<tr><td>Anchor</td><td>Top, Left, Right, Bottom</td></tr>
<tr><td>BorderStyle</td><td>FixedSingle</td></tr>
</table></td><td></td></tr>
<tr><td>9</td><td>Set the values from the <code>PictureBoxSizeMode</code> enumeration as the values for the <code>Items</code> property in the <code>comboSizeMode</code> combo box.
How-to
Display the String Collection Editor from the Items entry in the Properties window.</td><td>String Collection Editor
Enter the strings in the collection (one per line):
AutoSize
CenterImage
Normal
StretchImage
Zoom</td></tr>
</table>

This defines the UI for our test application. We have a button to load a new image, a combo box to select the `SizeMode` property value, and our new `Scrollable-PictureBox` control as the subject of the test. All we need now is a couple of event handlers.

	Action	Result
DEFINE EVENT HANDLERS FOR THE SCROLLABLEPICTUREBOX TEST APPLICATION		

10	For the Load button, define a `Click` event handler to assign a chosen image to the scrollable picture box.	`private void btnLoad_Click(`
		`    object sender, EventArgs e)`
		`{`
		`  OpenFileDialog dlg = new OpenFileDialog();`
		`  if (dlg.ShowDialog() == DialogResult.OK)`
		`  {`
		`    spbxImage.Image`
		`        = Image.FromFile(dlg.FileName);`
		`  }`
		`}`

11	For the `ComboBox` control, define a `SelectedIndex-Changed` event handler to assign the image box's `Size-Mode` property to the enumeration value associated with the selected text.	`private void comboSizeMode_SelectedIndexChanged(`
		`    object sender, EventArgs e)`
		`{`
		`  if (comboSizeMode.Text.Length > 0)`
		`  {`
		`    this.spbxImage.SizeMode`
		`      = (PictureBoxSizeMode)`
		`        Enum.Parse(typeof(PictureBoxSizeMode),`
		`                   comboSizeMode.Text);`
		`  }`
		`}`

That's it. You can run this program to make sure that everything works properly. As we add functionality to our new control, this test program verifies that all features work as expected.

17.1.3 Implementing a scrollable picture box

The prior two sections designed and defined our new class, and built a test program to exercise this class. The next steps create the public interface and the desired structure for the class.

	Action	Result
DEFINE MEMBERS FOR THE SCROLLABLEPICTUREBOX CONTROL		

1	In the ScrollablePictureBox.cs file, define the public `AllowScrollBars` property.
	
	How-to
	Use a private boolean member to hold the assigned setting.
		`public class ScrollablePictureBox : PictureBox`
		`{`
		`  private bool _allowScrollBars = true;`
		
		`  public bool AllowScrollBars`
		`  {`
		`    get { return _allowScrollBars; }`
		`    set`
		`    {`
		`      if (_allowScrollBars != value)`
		`      {`
		`        // Force a redraw when value changes`
		`        _allowScrollBars = value;`
		`        Invalidate();`
		`      }`
		`    }`
		`  }`
		`}`

DEFINE MEMBERS FOR THE SCROLLABLEPICTUREBOX CONTROL *(CONTINUED)*		
	Action	**Result**

2	Define a public `Scroll` event and an overridable method to raise the event.	`public event ScrollEventHandler Scroll;`
		
		`protected virtual void OnScroll(`
		`    ScrollEventArgs e)`
		`{`
		`  if (Scroll != null)`
		`    Scroll(this, e);`
		`}`

3	Define some private members to hold the required scroll bars, as well as private properties to access these members.	`private HScrollBar _hbar = new HScrollBar();`
		`private VScrollBar _vbar = new VScrollBar();`
		`private Control _vbarContainer = new Control();`
		
		`private HScrollBar HBar {`
		`    get { return _hbar; } }`
		`private VScrollBar VBar {`
		`    get { return _vbar; } }`
		`private Control VContainer {`
		`    get { return _vbarContainer; } }`

4	Define a public constructor to initialize the scrolling members.
	How-to
	a. Dock the horizontal scroll bar on the bottom.
	b. Dock the vertical bar container on the right.
	c. Anchor the vertical scroll bar to all sides of its container, and set its height to exclude the height of the horizontal bar at the base of the box.
	d. For both scroll bars, establish a handler for the `Scroll` event.
		`public ScrollablePictureBox()`
		`{`
		`  // Initialize horizontal scroll bar`
		`  HBar.Visible = false;`
		`  HBar.Dock = DockStyle.Bottom;`
		`  HBar.Minimum = 0;`
		`  HBar.Maximum = 1000;`
		`  HBar.Scroll += HandleScroll;`
		
		`  // Initialize vertical scroll bar container`
		`  VContainer.Visible = false;`
		`  VContainer.Width = VBar.Width;`
		`  VContainer.Height = Height;`
		`  VContainer.Dock = DockStyle.Right;`
		
		`  // Initialize vertical scroll bar`
		`  VBar.Top = 0;`
		`  VBar.Left = 0;`
		`  VBar.Height = VContainer.Height - HBar.Height;`
		`  VBar.Anchor = AnchorStyles.Top`
		`      | AnchorStyles.Bottom`
		`      | AnchorStyles.Left`
		`      | AnchorStyles.Right;`
		`  VBar.Minimum = 0;`
		`  VBar.Maximum = 1000;`
		`  VBar.Scroll += HandleScroll;`

5	Add the vertical bar to the vertical container, and the horizontal bar and vertical container to the base picture box control.	`  VContainer.Controls.Add(VBar);`
		
		`  Controls.Add(HBar);`
		`  Controls.Add(VContainer);`

6	Also set the control to use double buffering.	`  DoubleBuffered = true;` `}`

7	Add a placeholder for the `HandleScroll` method that does nothing.	`private void HandleScroll(`
		`    object sender,   ScrollEventArgs e)`
		`{`
		`}`

Most of this code should make sense at this point in the book. The `Scroll` event implementation is worth a little more discussion. The `ScrollBar` class already provides a scroll event, with a related `ScrollEventArgs` handler argument to hold the event data. This is the exact information we need to provide to users of the `ScrollablePictureBox` control, so we reuse this event handler in our control. The properties provided by the `ScrollEventArgs` class are listed in .NET Table 17.3.

.NET Table 17.3 ScrollEventArgs class

The `ScrollEventArgs` class specifies the event data associated with the `Scroll` event. It is part of the `System.Windows.Forms` namespace and inherits from the `System.EventArgs` class.

Public Properties	NewValue	Gets or sets the new setting for the `Value` property
	OldValue	Gets the prior setting of the `Value` property
	ScrollOrientation	Gets the orientation of the scroll bar that raised the event
	Type	Gets the `ScrollEventType` enumeration value that indicates the reason the event occurred

The code for the `ScrollablePictureBox` class thus far defines the framework for the class. We have the scrolling controls defined and ready, so all we have to do is manipulate them correctly.

The `ScrollablePictureBox` class is coming along nicely. We have defined the pieces and appearance of the control; all that is left is to properly manage these aspects as the settings for the class are modified. We take a brief break from our implementation in the next section in order to discuss `Control`-based custom controls.

17.2 CONTROL-BASED CLASSES

The `Control` class is the basis for all Windows Forms controls. When an existing control does not define some desired graphical behavior, the best approach may be to inherit from the `Control` class directly. This provides the greatest amount of flexibility over the appearance and behavior of the control, while still utilizing the plethora of support built into the `Control` class.

This section presents a quick example of this idea, and summarizes some of the `Control` class members that you may find useful when building custom controls.

17.2.1 Creating a Control-based class

Let's look at an example. A common request is the creation of a round button. The Windows Forms classes do not support this directly, so this is a good candidate for a custom control class. Since no other class encapsulates the idea of a circular shape, we need to derive this new class from the `Control` class directly. Listing 17.2 contains one possible implementation of such a class.

Listing 17.2 RoundButton class

```
using System;
using System.Drawing;
using System.Drawing.Drawing2D;
using System.Windows.Forms;

namespace Manning.MyPhotoControls
{
  public class RoundButton : Control
  {
    private Pen _pen;
    private Brush _foreBrush;

    public RoundButton() { InitColorObjects(); }

    private void InitColorObjects()        <-- 1 Initializes drawing objects
    {
      if (_pen != null) _pen.Dispose();
      if (_foreBrush != null) _foreBrush.Dispose();

      _pen = new Pen(ControlPaint.DarkDark(BackColor), 2);
      _foreBrush = new SolidBrush(ForeColor);
    }

    protected override void OnPaint(PaintEventArgs e)
    {
      using (GraphicsPath path = new GraphicsPath())     | 2 Defines the
      {                                                  |   active region
        path.AddEllipse(ClientRectangle);
        Region = new Region(path);
      }

      Graphics g = e.Graphics;                    | 3 Paints the
      g.DrawEllipse(_pen, ClientRectangle);       |   button area

      if (Text.Length > 0)
      {
        StringFormat format = new StringFormat();
        format.Alignment = StringAlignment.Center;
        format.LineAlignment = StringAlignment.Center;
        if (Enabled)        <-- 4 Draws enabled or disabled text
        {
          g.DrawString(Text, Font, _foreBrush,
            new RectangleF(0, 0, ClientSize.Width, ClientSize.Height),
            format);
        }
        else
        {
          ControlPaint.DrawStringDisabled(g, Text, Font, BackColor,
            new RectangleF(0, 0, ClientSize.Width, ClientSize.Height),
            format);
        }
      }
    }
```

```
    protected override void OnBackColorChanged(EventArgs e)
    {
      base.OnBackColorChanged(e);
      InitColorObjects();
    }

    protected override void OnForeColorChanged(EventArgs e)
    {
      base.OnForeColorChanged(e);
      InitColorObjects();
    }

    protected override void OnTextChanged(EventArgs e)
    {
      base.OnTextChanged(e);
      Invalidate();
    }
  }
}
```

Refreshes colors when selections change ❺

The `RoundButton` class does not define any additional public properties, methods, or events other than those defined by the `Control` class. It uses the existing members to define a round button on a form.

The core of this implementation is the `OnPaint` method, which raises the `Paint` event. The `Paint` event occurs whenever all or a portion of the control must be redrawn. The event data for this event is defined by the `PaintEventArgs` class, which is shown in .NET Table 17.4. We should note that instances of our `RoundButton` custom control do not support the `Paint` event, since our `OnPaint` override never calls the base `OnPaint` method.

.NET Table 17.4 PaintEventArgs class

The `PaintEventArgs` class specifies the event data associated with the `Paint` event. It is part of the `System.Windows.Forms` namespace and inherits from the `System.EventArgs` class.

Public Properties	ClipRectangle	Gets the rectangular area of the control that requires repainting
	Graphics	Gets the `Graphics` object to use when painting the control

Let's examine the annotated portions of listing 17.2 in more detail:

❶ As you can see, the `InitColorObjects` method initializes the private pen and brush used to draw the control. This method is invoked from the constructor, and whenever one of the color properties is modified. Notice how the method disposes of any existing instances of these objects.

❷ In the `OnPaint` method, the first few lines define the active region for the control, as defined by the `Region` property. This is the collection of pixels where the control can draw graphical elements and receive events. In our case, we ensure that any controls "behind" our control paint the areas outside the ellipse, and that events such as `Click` are only received when the mouse is within the defined region. The `System.Drawing.Drawing2D` namespace supports two-dimensional and vector graphics functionality. The `GraphicsPath` class in this namespace specifies a connected series of lines and curves to form a 2D path. Here, we use this class to define our elliptical region.

3 Most custom controls have some sort of visual representation. For our control, the `Region` property defines the required elliptical area, and the `Control` class automatically draws the background color or image assigned to the control. We draw a two-pixel-wide border around this ellipse using a darker version of the background color.

4 There are a number of properties in the `Control` class that custom controls should support. We don't deal with all of them in this sample, but we do support the `Enabled` property. If the control is enabled, we use the `Graphics.DrawString` method to draw the text centered in the control with the foreground color. If the control is disabled, we use the `ControlPaint.DrawStringDisabled` method to draw the string. The `ControlPaint` class supports functionality required to paint common aspects of Windows Forms controls and their elements. The next section provides some additional examples of methods in this class.

5 You may have noticed throughout this book that many Windows Forms controls provide one or more `Changed` events. These typically occur when an associated property value changes. In our control, we need to refresh our color brushes whenever the background or foreground color properties are modified. We also force the control to redraw itself when the `Text` property changes.

If you wish, you can use this control in our ScrollablePictureBoxTest application in place of the existing Load button. To really see this control in action, I suggest modifying the `ScrollablePictureBox` control's `Dock` property to fill the entire form. We won't show the code for this, but the result of such a change is illustrated in figure 17.3.

Figure 17.3
This RoundButton class only paints the elliptical area representing the button.

TRY IT! As discussed in the next section, there are a number of aspects to the `Control` class that might be worth supporting in a custom control. If you are interested in exploring some of these, here are some suggestions:

- Override the `Dispose` method to ensure that the `Pen` and `Brush` objects are disposed when the control is disposed.
- Handle the `MouseHover` and `MouseLeave` events to alter the displayed border when the mouse is within the bounds of the control.
- Draw a focus rectangle around the text for the control whenever the `Focused` property is `true`. You can use the `DrawFocusRectangle` method in the `ControlPaint` class for this.

17.2.2 Common features of custom controls

Now that we have seen some examples of custom controls, this is a good place to review some common functionality you may require when creating a custom control. Rather than an extended discussion on this topic, we do this in tabular form. Table 17.5 provides a summary of various features that may be useful when creating custom controls. For each item, we provide a short description of the feature and a brief explanation of how to support it. Unless otherwise indicated, the properties, methods, and events mentioned in table 17.5 are part of the `Control` class.

Some of the items in table 17.5 may also be discussed elsewhere. Check the index at the back of the book to see if an example or other explanation is also provided for a topic. For detailed information, consult the Windows Forms documentation for the indicated classes or properties.

Table 17.5 A summary of possible functionality in custom controls

Feature	Description	How to achieve
Background image	Displays an image in the background of the control.	The `BackgroundImage` and `BackgroundImageLayout` properties define the image and its layout. If possible, use the built-in support in the `Control` class. Otherwise, draw the image as part of the `OnPaint` method.
Borders	Defines a border for the control.	Some Windows Forms controls support Win32-style borders. For newer controls, use the `Border3DStyle` enumeration to specify the style, and the `ControlPaint.DrawBorder3D` method to draw the border.
Cursor	Defines a custom cursor within the control.	Set the `Cursor` property.
Custom graphics	Draws a custom visual representation for the control.	Override the `OnPaint` method and use the `Graphics` property to achieve the desired effect.

Table 17.5 A summary of possible functionality in custom controls *(continued)*

Feature	Description	How to achieve
Double buffering	Allows graphical data for the control to be written to an internal buffer before writing it to the display surface. This can reduce or eliminate flickering on the control.	Set the protected `Control.DoubleBuffered` property to `true`. This property is new as of .NET 2.0.
Events	Indicates that some action has occurred.	For existing events, override the "On" method associated with the event. To define a new event, you need four things: an event declaration to define the event name, an event data class that derives from `EventArgs`, an event handler delegate that ends with `EventHandler`, and a protected method that raises the event with an "On" prefix. In the `ScrollablePictureBox` example, the `Scroll` event defines its event data in the `ScrollEventArgs` class, with delegate `ScrollEventHandler`. The protected method `OnScroll` raises the event.
Focus	Manages input focus for the control.	The `TabStop` property indicates whether the user can use the Tab key to give focus to the control. The `CanFocus` property indicates whether the control can receive focus. Use the protected `SetStyle` method to assign the `ControlStyles.Selectable` style to indicate whether the control can receive input focus. Indicate a control has focus by drawing a dotted rectangle within the control. The `DrawFocusRectangle` method in the `ControlPaint` class can do this for you. Perform custom actions when the control receives focus by handling the `GotFocus` and `LostFocus` events.
Image & Text	Allows images and/or text to appear in the control.	Define an `Image` property to allow your control to display an image in place of or in addition to text. To be consistent with Windows Forms controls, you might consider `DisplayStyle`, `ImageAlign`, `TextAlign`, or `TextImageRelation` properties as well.
Mouse over	Modifies the display of a control when the mouse is over it.	Use the `MouseEnter` and `MouseLeave` events whenever the mouse position is within the bounds of the control. Alternatively, use the `MouseHover` event if you prefer a delayed visual effect. The `MouseHoverTime` property in the `SystemInformation` class defines the hover time.
Preserving state	Preserves the state of the control across restarts of the containing application.	Support the `IPersistComponentSettings` interface to store and retrieve application settings on behalf of the control.

Table 17.5 A summary of possible functionality in custom controls *(continued)*

Feature	Description	How to achieve
Redrawing	Redraws the control when its position or size changes, or when it becomes exposed on the desktop.	The `Paint` event occurs whenever redrawing is required. Use the `Invalidate` method to force a redraw of a control. Override the `OnResize` method to customize resize behavior. To indicate that the entire control should be redrawn whenever it is resized, set the `RedrawResize` property to `true`.
Responding to changes	Alters the control when a property or other setting changes.	If possible, use an available `Changed` event to respond to the change. For example, the `TextChanged` event occurs whenever the `Text` property is modified. When defining your own properties, consider whether a corresponding change event is appropriate. In situations where no changed event is available, such as the lack of `ImageChanged` events in any Windows Forms control, define a new version of the property using the `new` keyword.
Scrolling	Enables scrolling within the control, or scrolls a control within its parent container.	When possible, inherit from a class that derives from the `ScrollableControl` class, such as `UserControl`, so scrolling is built in. To build custom scrolling, use one of the `ScrollBar` classes. For a control that exists within a scrollable container, set the `AutoScrollOffset` property to define the location for this control in the `ScrollControl-IntoView` method.
Selection	Allows the control to be selected.	The `CanSelect` property indicates whether the control can be selected. This is `true` if the control can receive focus, if it is contained by another control, and if it and all its parent controls are visible and enabled. A control can visually indicate it is selected by changing its background or border.
Window region	Defines the bounds of the control where painting occurs and events are received.	Define the `Region` property to the appropriate collection of pixels. Note that the region for a control does not have to be contiguous.

17.3 THE SCROLLABLEPICTUREBOX CLASS

This section completes our `ScrollablePictureBox` implementation to demonstrate a few of the features listed in table 17.5. We look at three problems often encountered while creating a custom control: painting the control, modifying the control as it is resized, and handling changes to the properties for the control.

17.3.1 Painting the control

Many custom controls are oriented around a required graphical representation. This may be as basic as customizing the colors or as complex as arranging a collection of controls and graphical elements within the client area. Supporting such requirements typically involves the `Paint` and `Resize` events.

In our scrollable picture box, the goal is to paint a scrollable image within the client area. This is the heart and soul of this class, and therefore a good place to start our discussion.

<table>
<tr><th colspan="3">DRAW THE SCROLLABLE PICTURE BOX</th></tr>
<tr><th></th><th>Action</th><th>Result</th></tr>
<tr><td>1</td><td>In the ScrollablePictureBox.cs file, override the <code>OnPaint</code> method for the class.</td><td><pre>protected override void OnPaint(
    PaintEventArgs e)
{
  base.OnPaint(e);</pre></td></tr>
<tr><td>2</td><td>If an image is present and the scroll bars are visible, draw the image using the current <code>Graphics</code> object.</td><td><pre> if (Image != null
      && (HBar.Visible || VContainer.Visible))
    DrawImage(e.Graphics);
}</pre>Note: Reusing the existing <code>Graphics</code> object is extremely important here, to ensure that the base class's <code>OnPaint</code> method and our implementation draw onto the same surface.</td></tr>
<tr><td>3</td><td>Implement a <code>DrawImage</code> method to draw the appropriate portion of the image based on the current scroll bar settings.

How-to
a. Determine the target rectangle where the image should be drawn.
b. Determine the source rectangle to draw within the target.
c. If the image should be centered, adjust the target appropriately.
d. Draw the source portion of the image into the target area of the control.</td><td><pre>private void DrawImage(Graphics g)
{
  Rectangle targetRect = new Rectangle(0, 0,
    Math.Min(Right - VBar.Width, Image.Width),
    Math.Min(Bottom - HBar.Height,
             Image.Height));
  Rectangle sourceRect = new Rectangle(
    HBar.Value, VBar.Value,
    Math.Min(Right - VBar.Width, Image.Width),
    Math.Min(Bottom - HBar.Height,
             Image.Height));

  if (SizeMode
        == PictureBoxSizeMode.CenterImage)
  {
    Point p = new Point(0, 0);

    if (Right - VBar.Width > Image.Width)
      p.X = Math.Max((ClientSize.Width
                - targetRect.Width) / 2, 0);
    if (Bottom - HBar.Height > Image.Height)
      p.Y = Math.Max((ClientSize.Height
                - targetRect.Height) / 2, 0);

    targetRect.Offset(p);
  }
  g.DrawImage(Image, targetRect, sourceRect,
              GraphicsUnit.Pixel);
}</pre></td></tr>
</table>

The `OnPaint` and `DrawImage` methods define the painting behavior for the class. When both scroll bars are invisible, this behaves exactly like the base `PictureBox` class. Otherwise, the `DrawImage` code determines the portion of the assigned `Image` to draw and the area where this portion should appear, and uses the DrawImage method to map the source portion onto the target area.

The code for the DrawImage method uses some pixel mathematics to determine exactly which portion of the image should appear, and where this portion should be drawn. We do not walk through this code in detail, but you can work through the math if you wish. I had to update this code a couple of times while writing this chapter based on problems discovered while testing the control. The test program proved invaluable for this, and makes me fairly confident that the code here is correct. If you find a problem that I missed, of course, please let me know.

17.3.2 Resizing the control

Our painting code requires that the Visible properties associated with each scroll bar be set prior to drawing the control. We handle the initialization of these settings in the next section. Here, let's take a look at the situation where the control is resized.

As the control is resized, the width or height of the control most likely changes. As a result, we need to verify that scrolling is still required and redraw the image into the new client area.

The following steps make these changes.

UPDATE THE SCROLL BARS WHEN THE CONTROL IS RESIZED

	Action	Result

1	Override the `OnResize` method to handle the `Resize` event.	`protected override void OnResize(EventArgs e)`
		`{`
		`  base.OnResize(e);`

2	When scrolling is active, adjust each scroll bar and force the entire control to redraw.	`  // Force redraw when scrolling`
		`  if (ScrollingActive())`
		`  {`
		`    AdjustScrollBars();`
		`    Refresh();`
		`  }`
		`}`

3	Create a `ScrollingActive` method to determine whether either scroll bar is visible.	`private bool ScrollingActive()` `{`

4	Within this method, if no image is assigned, the scroll bars are disabled, or the `SizeMode` property is set to a nonscrolling value, then make both scroll bars invisible.	`  if (Image == null || AllowScrollBars == false`
		`    || (SizeMode`
		`        != PictureBoxSizeMode.CenterImage`
		`      && SizeMode`
		`          != PictureBoxSizeMode.Normal))`
		`  {`
		`    HBar.Visible = false;`
		`    VContainer.Visible = false;`
		`  }`

	UPDATE THE SCROLL BARS WHEN THE CONTROL IS RESIZED *(CONTINUED)*	
	Action	**Result**

5	Otherwise, make each scroll bar visible if only a portion of the image can be shown in the corresponding dimension.	`else`
		`{`
		`  // Show scroll bars if partial image shown`
		`  HBar.Visible = Image.Width`
		`      >= ClientSize.Width - VBar.Width;`
		`  VContainer.Visible = Image.Height`
		`      >= ClientSize.Height - HBar.Height;`
		`}`

6	Return `true` if either or both of the scroll bars are visible.	`  return (HBar.Visible || VContainer.Visible);` `}`
7	Create an `AdjustScroll-Bars` method to adjust the settings of each scroll bar.	`private void AdjustScrollBars()` `{`

8	Within this method, if the horizontal scroll bar is visible, assign the `Maximum`, `LargeChange`, and `SmallChange` properties for this scroll bar.	`  if (HBar.Visible)`
		`  {`
		`    int max = Image.Width - ClientSize.Width;`
		`    HBar.LargeChange = Math.Max(max / 10, 1);`
		`    HBar.SmallChange = Math.Max(max / 20, 1);`
		
		`    HBar.Maximum = max + HBar.LargeChange;`
		`    if (VBar.Visible)`
		`      HBar.Maximum += VBar.Width;`
		`  }`

9	If the vertical container is visible, then ensure the required small empty space appears at the base of the container when both scroll bars are shown.	`  if (VContainer.Visible)`
		`  {`
		`    if (HBar.Visible)`
		`      VBar.Height = Height - HBar.Height;`
		`    else`
		`      VBar.Height = Height;`

10	Also assign the `Maximum`, `LargeChange`, and `SmallChange` properties for the vertical scroll bar.	`    int max = Image.Height - ClientSize.Height;`
		`    VBar.LargeChange = Math.Max(max / 10, 1);`
		`    VBar.SmallChange = Math.Max(max / 20, 1);`
		
		`    VBar.Maximum = max + VBar.LargeChange;`
		`    if (HBar.Visible)`
		`      VBar.Maximum += HBar.Height;`
		`  }`
		`}`

11	Replace the blank `HandleScroll` event handler to update the image and invoke the `Scroll` event for the custom control.	`protected void HandleScroll(`
		`    object sender, ScrollEventArgs e)`
		`{`
		`  Refresh();`
		`  OnScroll(e);`
		`}`

In this code, we define a private `ScrollingActive` property to assign the `Visible` properties and return `true` if either scroll bar is visible. We use this when the form is resized to identify whether the scroll bars should be adjusted. The `AdjustScroll-Bars` method updates the scrolling properties for both scroll bars based on the visibility properties.

The final code in step 10 handles the Scroll event from either scroll bar. Since the size of the control cannot change in this case, we simply need to redraw the image based on the new settings. This code also raises the Scroll event for our custom control, in case a user wants to perform any actions when this occurs.

So, this is all well and good, but if you run this the scroll bar never appears. This is because the initial state of the control has no image, and therefore no scroll bar. To fix this, we need to refresh and otherwise adjust the control when the image or size mode property changes. This is our next topic.

17.3.3 Handling property changes

Our custom control does not yet handle changes to the image or display mode. The display mode changes whenever the SizeMode property is altered. The image changes when a new Image property setting is assigned.

When SizeMode changes, the PictureBox control raises the SizeModeChanged event. We can use this event to update our control appropriately.

When the Image property changes, the PictureBox control does not provide an ImageChanged event or any other indication that the image has been modified. In fact, such an event is curiously absent from the Windows Forms namespace. In this case, we need another way to intercept this change.

The following steps respond to both changes here. Use of the SizeModeChanged event is fairly straightforward. We discuss our code for handling the Image property following the table.

RESPOND TO CHANGES TO THE CONTROL'S PROPERTIES

	Action	Result

1	Override the OnSizeModeChanged method to handle the SizeModeChanged event.	`protected override void OnSizeModeChanged(`
		`    EventArgs e)`
		`{`
		`  base.OnSizeModeChanged(e);`
		`  ResetScrollBars();`
		`}`

2	Create a private ResetScrollBars method to reset the scroll bar values based on any new settings.	`private void ResetScrollBars()`
		`{`
		`  // Reset scroll values`
		`  HBar.Value = 0;`
		`  VBar.Value = 0;`

3	Within this method, adjust the scroll bars and, if the SizeMode setting is CenterImage, set the values such that the image is initially centered within the display area.	`  if (Image != null && ScrollingActive())`
		`  {`
		`    AdjustScrollBars();`
		`    if (SizeMode`
		`          == PictureBoxSizeMode.CenterImage)`
		`    {`
		`      HBar.Value = Math.Abs(Image.Width / 2`
		`                    - ClientSize.Width / 2);`
		`      VBar.Value = Math.Abs(Image.Height / 2`
		`                    - ClientSize.Height / 2);`
		`    }`
		`  }`
		`}`

	Action	Result
RESPOND TO CHANGES TO THE CONTROL'S PROPERTIES *(CONTINUED)*		
4	Implement a new `Image` property.	`public new Image Image` `{`
5	For the `get` accessor, simply return the base value.	`get { return base.Image; }`

6	For the `set` accessor, assign the base value and reset the scroll bar settings.	`set`
		`{`
		`base.Image = value;`
		`ResetScrollBars();`
		`}`
		`}`

As you can see, handling `SizeMode` changes is easily done through the use of the `SizeModeChanged` event. For the `Image` property, we create a new version of the property using the `new` keyword. Our implementation replaces the existing `Image` property in the base `PictureBox` class, and enforces our change behavior.

In light of this, you may wonder why the various `Changed` events are even provided. Why not simply allow derived classes to create new property implementations?

The reason is that a caller can bypass our new `Image` implementation by casting the object to the base class. You can see this by replacing our current `btnLoad_Click` method in the TestForm.cs file with the following implementation:

```
private void btnLoad_Click(object sender, EventArgs e)
{
  OpenFileDialog dlg = new OpenFileDialog();
  if (dlg.ShowDialog() == DialogResult.OK)
  {
    PictureBox pb = (PictureBox)spbxImage;
    pb.Image = Image.FromFile(dlg.FileName);
  }
}
```

This code calls the `PictureBox.Image` property directly, bypassing the new `Image` property in our `ScrollablePictureBox` class. As a result, with this implementation, the `ResetScrollBar` method is never called and scrolling may not work correctly when a new image is assigned.

Although it is unlikely a caller would bypass our new code on purpose, using a `Changed` method solves this potential problem, and is therefore preferred when possible.

This completes an initial implementation of the `ScrollablePictureBox` custom control. Run the test program to see this control in action. We use this control throughout the rest of the book in lieu of the `PictureBox` class in cases where the image might be larger than the control area.

We have discussed creating custom controls by deriving from an existing Windows Forms control and by building upon the `Control` class directly. The final approach we discuss is the creation of user controls.

17.4 USER CONTROLS

As you may recall, we discussed the `UserControl` class in chapter 14, with an example that created a calendar tab in our MyAlbumEditor application. We discuss the two common uses of this class: as a reusable control and to simplify or encapsulate the code for a portion of an application.

In this chapter we have learned that a custom control is simply a reusable control, so there is not a lot to discuss here. As a result, we move our discussion along to the use of custom controls within Visual Studio.

If you wish to experiment creating a `UserControl`-based custom control, I suggest the following classes:

- A `TextInput` class that encapsulates the notion of a `Label` control that precedes a `TextBox` control. This might `Dock` to the top of its container so that a series of these controls could be stacked within a `Panel` or other parent. Of course, the `TableLayoutPanel` class supports this notion as well, but this example is fairly straightforward to implement.
- An `AlbumDisplay` control that displays a `PhotoAlbum` class object within a `FlowLayoutPanel` object. This would automatically create a series of `PictureBox` instances to hold the thumbnails associated with each image in an album, and could be used in our MyPhotos application to display an entire album at once.

Due to space limitations, we cannot discuss the details of implementing these classes here. Instead, we move on to the use of custom controls in Visual Studio.

17.5 CUSTOM CONTROLS IN VISUAL STUDIO

So far we have focused almost exclusively on the code required to build a custom control, with little regard to how a programmer might make use of such a control in Visual Studio. In this section we look at the support provided for this purpose.

Way back in chapter 1 we discussed the concept of attributes. An attribute indicates that a particular setting is associated with a specific piece of code. We used the `AssemblyVersion` attribute to associate a version number with an assembly.

Attributes are provided throughout the .NET Framework for various purposes. The Component Model namespace in particular provides various attributes to indicate how a class and its members should be treated in a visual design environment such as Visual Studio. In this chapter we review a number of these attributes and demonstrate their use in our `ScrollablePictureBox` control.

Sometimes an attribute just isn't enough, and more detailed influence is desired over the behavior of a control in a designer window. The `System.Windows.Forms.Design` namespace defines various types that support design-time configuration and behavior for Windows Forms components. Covering this topic in detail is a bit beyond the scope of this chapter, but we do provide an overview and give some suggestions for further exploration of this namespace.

17.5.1 Customizing class behavior

Let's start with the properties typically used with custom control classes. Table 17.6 lists attributes commonly used to customize how a control appears within a design environment. Of course, for our purposes, the only design environment we discuss is Visual Studio provided by Microsoft, but other designers do indeed exist, so we use the generic terms *designer* and *design environment* to indicate this fact.

The attributes in table 17.6 are almost all part of the `System.ComponentModel` namespace. One exception is the `ToolboxBitmapAttribute` class, which is part of the `System.Drawing` namespace. The toolbox item attributes are a bit complex and beyond our current discussion. There is a decent example showing how to use the `ToolboxItemAttribute` class in the .NET documentation for the `ToolboxItem` class, so if you are interested in this attribute you might start there. We discuss designer classes in section 17.5.3, after which the `DesignerAttribute` and `DesignerCategoryAttribute` classes should take on a bit more meaning.

Table 17.6 Attributes for custom control classes

Attribute	Description
DefaultEventAttribute	Specifies the default event for the associated component class.
DefaultPropertyAttribute	Specifies the default property for the associated component class.
DesignerAttribute	Specifies the designer class associated with the component. See section 17.5.3.
DesignerCategoryAttribute	Specifies the category for the associated component's designer class.
HelpKeywordAttribute	Specifies the context keyword for the associated component class or a member of the class. This keyword can be used by a help system to provide context-sensitive help information.
ToolboxBitmapAttribute	Specifies the bitmap to display for the associated component in a visual design environment.
ToolboxItemAttribute	Specifies the `ToolboxItem` object to invoke when the associated component is dropped onto a design surface in a visual design environment.
ToolboxItemFilterAttribute	Specifies a filter that indicates when an associated `ToolboxItem` should be available in a particular design environment; or how an associated designer enables or disables items within its environment.

We can demonstrate the use of the other attributes by applying them to our `ScrollablePictureBox` control. The following steps specify these attributes for our custom control.

DEFINE CLASS ATTRIBUTES IN THE SCROLLABLEPICTUREBOX CLASS

	Action	Result

1	In the ScrollablePictureBox.cs file, use the `DefaultEvent` attribute to define the `Click` event as the default event for the class.	`. . .`
		`namespace Manning.MyPhotoControls`
		`{`
		`  [DefaultEvent("Click")]`

2	Define the `Image` property as the default property for the class.	`  [DefaultProperty("Image")]`
		`  public class ScrollablePictureBox : PictureBox`
		`  {`

These two attributes define the default event and property for our custom control. You may immediately notice one of the drawbacks of attributes: the need to use strings to identify a member of a class or assembly. Consequently, spelling is important as there are no compile time checks that the given event or property name actually exists.

Assigning a toolbox bitmap is similar, although we first need to create a bitmap object to use. We do this by creating an embedded bitmap resource in our project and associating it with the custom control class.

DEFINE CLASS ATTRIBUTES IN THE SCROLLABLEPICTUREBOX CLASS

	Action	Result
3	In the MyPhotoControls project, create a new bitmap file called ScrollablePictureBox.bmp, and set its Build Action to Embedded Resource.	Properties ScrollablePictureBox.bmp File Prop Build Action: Embedded Resource
4	Display the new bitmap object, set its properties as shown, and draw an appropriate bitmap image for the control. **Settings** **Property** / **Value** Colors / 256 Color Height / 16 Width / 16	ScrollablePictureBox.bmp* **Note:** I tried to draw an image similar to the image used for the `PictureBox` control with the addition of scroll bars. As already established, I am no artist. You can copy my image or make up your own.

DEFINE CLASS ATTRIBUTES IN THE SCROLLABLEPICTUREBOX CLASS		
	Action	**Result**

5	Define this new bitmap as the bitmap image to display within a visual design environment.	`. . .`
		`namespace Manning.MyPhotoControls`
		`{`
		`  [DefaultEvent("Click")]`
		`  [DefaultProperty("Image")]`
		`  [ToolboxBitmap(typeof(ScrollablePictureBox),`
		`                 "ScrollablePictureBox.bmp")]`
		`  public class ScrollablePictureBox : PictureBox`
		`  {`

You can test these new settings in Visual Studio after rebuilding the project with these new changes. Display the TestForm.cs [Design] window and verify the behavior for each attribute by performing the following actions:

- Select the `ScrollablePictureBox` control and display its properties. The Properties window appears with the default `Image` property selected.
- Double-click the `ScrollablePictureBox` control on the design surface. An event handler method for the default `Click` event is added to the `InitializeComponent` method, with the new handler displayed in the TestForm.cs file.
- Open the Toolbox window and examine the components displayed for the MyPhotoControls project. You should see the `ScrollablePictureBox` control with the new bitmap image displayed. In my case, this didn't actually work, and I'm still scratching my head over this one. Everything I know and read[1] says this should work, so I'm leaving this example in hopes that some clever reader will find the flaw in my logic…

This ends our discussion on customizing the behavior of the class itself. Let's move on to attributes that can be used with members of such a class.

17.5.2 Customizing class member behavior

The Component Model namespace provides attributes for use with the members of a custom control class as well. The more commonly used attributes are summarized in table 17.7. As you can see, many of these attributes are intended for the properties or events in a custom control, since they are most often manipulated within a visual designer such as Visual Studio.

The attributes in table 17.7 simply assign a specific setting to the associated class member. A design environment can ignore these values or use them as it wishes. In Visual Studio, these attributes alter how the property, event, or other member appears to the user. For example, a property or event only appears in the Properties

---

[1] There are some posts on this topic in the public.dotnet.framework.windowsforms discussion group, which is a good place to start if you want to investigate this further.

Table 17.7 Attributes for custom control properties and events

Attribute	Description
AmbientValueAttribute	Specifies the value to pass to an associated property to cause the property to assign its value based on an external source.
BrowsableAttribute	Specifies whether an associated property or event should appear in a Properties window for the associated component.
CategoryAttribute	Specifies the category group for an associated property or event. This name can be used in a design environment to group related properties together in a Properties window.
DefaultValueAttribute	Specifies the default value for an associated property.
DescriptionAttribute	Specifies a brief description for an associated property or event.
DesignOnlyAttribute	Specifies whether an associated property or event can only be set at design time. Typically, such properties only exist at design time and do not correspond to an actual property.
DisplayNameAttribute	Specifies a display name to use in place of the actual name for an associated property, event, or public void method that takes no arguments
EditorAttribute	Specifies the `UITypeEditor` class to use as the editor for an associated property. See section 17.5.3.
EditorBrowsableAttribute	Specifies whether an associated class member should be viewable within a visual editor. This is used by IntelliSense in Visual Studio to determine what to show as a user enters text.
LocalizableAttribute	Specifies whether an associated class member should be localized.
PasswordPropertyTextAttribute	Specifies that an associated member's text representation should be obscured in a Properties window using an asterisk or other special character.
ReadOnlyAttribute	Specifies whether an associated property should appear as read-only in a design environment.
RefreshPropertiesAttribute	Specifies whether and how a property grid should be updated when the value for an associated property has changed.
TypeConverterAttribute	Specifies the `TypeConverter` class that provides data conversion for an associated property. See section 17.5.3.

window for a custom control if its `BrowsableAttribute` setting is `true`, which is the default. Similarly, when manipulating a custom control, only members with an `EditorBrowsableAttribute` setting of `true` appears in the IntelliSense drop-down list.

As another example, the `LocalizableAttribute` indicates that a member should be localized. A designer can implement this behavior in any way it chooses. In Visual Studio, properties with a `true` setting for this attribute have their property value saved in a resource file. This allows these values to be modified for a locale without modifying any code.

The `DefaultValueAttribute` class is also worth a mention, as this attribute can be used to specify a default property value for a design environment, which may be different than the actual default value for the property. In the Properties window,

Visual Studio displays a property's value in bold type if it does not match this default setting, and supports the Reset menu to return a property's value to its assigned default.

The `AmbientValueAttribute` supports properties such as `BackColor` and `Font` in the `Control` class, which both inherit their values from the parent control by default. The ability for a control to retrieve its value from an external source is known as *ambience*. Listing 17.3 illustrates a `Directory` property that uses this attribute. The code in this listing assumes a `_directory` field exists, and causes Visual Studio to assign the value `"default"` when the property is reset in the Properties window, which in turn assigns the current user's MyDocuments folder path as the new property value. For `Color` properties such as `BackColor` and `ForeColor` in the `Control` class, the ambient value is typically set to the `Color.Empty` value.

Listing 17.3 Using the AmbientValueAttribute class

```
[AmbientValue("default")]
public string Directory
{
  get { return _directory; }
  set
  {
    if (value == "default")
      _directory = Environment.GetFolderPath(
              Environment.SpecialFolder.MyDocuments);
    else
      _directory = value;
  }
}
```

Let's take a look at some of these attributes in our `ScrollablePictureBox` class. The following steps assign various attributes to our custom control. A discussion of these changes follows the table.

DEFINE CLASS MEMBER ATTRIBUTES IN THE SCROLLABLEPICTUREBOX CLASS

	Action	Result

1	In the `Scrollable-PictureBox` class, define appropriate attributes for the `AllowScrollBars` property.
	
	Note: The `Browsable-Attribute` setting here is not really required, since it defaults to `true` when not specified.
		`. . .`
		`public class ScrollablePictureBox : PictureBox`
		`{`
		`  private bool _allowScrollBars = true;`
		
		`  [Browsable(true)]`
		`  [Category("Layout")]`
		`  [DefaultValue(true)]`
		`  [Description("Gets or sets whether the control"`
		`      + " can display scroll bars")]`
		`  public bool AllowScrollBars`
		`  {`
		`    . . .`
		`  }`

	Define class member attributes in the ScrollablePictureBox class *(continued)*	
	Action	**Result**

2	Define appropriate attributes for the `Scroll` event.	`[Category("Action")]`
		`[Description("Occurs when a scroll bar is"`
		`    + " shown and the image is scrolled")]`
		`public event ScrollEventHandler Scroll;`
		`. . .`
		`}`

Of course, in a class with a more extensive public interface, these attributes would need to be set for each property and event. In our case, we rather conveniently have a single property and single event, so the changes are not that extensive. To see these attributes in action, display the Properties window for the `ScrollablePictureBox` control in the TestForm.cs [Design] window. The result is shown in figure 17.4 when the properties are displayed by category rather than alphabetically.

TRY IT! Alter the attribute settings for the `AllowScrollBar` property to see how Visual Studio responds to each attribute, and try setting values for other attributes such as `DisplayName` and `ReadOnly` to see their effect. For a more interesting change, replace the `PictureBox` control in our MyPhotos application with the `ScrollablePictureBox` control. This corrects a problem we identified in part 2 where a large photograph displayed in Actual Size mode could be larger than the available screen space.

17.5.3 Customizing design time behavior

Of course, all these attributes can only take you so far. Sometimes you want to have finer control over exactly how your control behaves within Visual Studio. For example, the properties under the Design category shown in figure 17.4 do not represent actual properties, so some design-time logic must have told Visual Studio to display these values. Other design-specific behaviors for Windows Forms controls abound: the graphical editing provided for the `Dock` and `Anchor` properties; the Add Tab and Remove Tab context menu items that appear for the `TabControl` class; and the ability to add and edit tool strip items in the various `ToolStrip` classes.

Figure 17.4 The setting for the AllowScrollBars property here is in a normal font, indicating it is the default property value.

The complete details of such functionality are a bit beyond this book, so we instead lay out some of the fundamentals and direct you to some further sources of information. Table 17.8 provides a summary for this discussion, beginning with the `DesignMode` property that can be embedded directly into the code for a custom control.

Table 17.8 Approaches for customizing the design-time behavior of a custom control

Item	Description
DesignMode property	Gets whether the component is in design mode. In a custom control, this can be used to enable or disable specific behavior when the control is running within a visual designer.
TypeConverter class	Base class for defining a conversion of values between types. In custom controls, the `TypeConverterAttribute` class is used to define a conversion to and from a textual representation of an associated property. This class is part of the `System.ComponentModel` namespace.
UITypeEditor class	Base class for defining a user interface for representing and editing the values of objects of the supported data types. In a custom control, the `EditorAttribute` class is used to define an editor to utilize with an associated property. This class is part of the `System.Drawing.Design` namespace.
ControlDesigner class	This class is the foundation of the `System.Windows.Forms.Design` namespace, and is the base class for customizing the design-time behavior of classes that derive from the Windows Forms `Control` class. The `DesignerAttribute` class is used to associated a designer with a custom control.

The other three items in table 17.8 are classes. Let's start with the last of these: the `ControlDesigner` class. Designer classes may be nested within a custom control class to provided design-time behavior for the class, as in the following code excerpt:

```
[Designer(typeof(ScrollablePictureBox.ScrollablePictureBoxDesigner))]
public class ScrollablePictureBox : PictureBox
{
  private class ScrollablePictureBoxDesigner : ControlDesigner
  {
    // designer code goes here
  }
  . . .
}
```

The details of creating a good control designer could fill numerous chapters. If you are interested in this topic, I recommend that you start with the article "Writing Custom Designers for .NET Components," by Shawn Burke. You can find this article by searching the MSDN website. There are other samples and articles on this topic, but this article provides a good overview that will get you started.

The `ControlDesigner` class is part of the `System.Windows.Forms.Design` namespace. This namespace supports the design-time behavior of Windows Forms controls. Among the many classes in this namespace are a number of `UITypeEditor` classes. The `UITypeEditor` class allows a custom visual editor for a property to be built, such as the `AnchorEditor` and `DockEditor` classes in the Windows Forms Design namespace that support editing the `Anchor` and `Dock` properties in Visual Studio.

For example, listing 17.4 defines a `BaseDirectory` property that uses the `FolderNameEditor` class provided in the design namespace. A `FileNameEditor` class is also available.

Listing 17.4 Sample code using a UITypeEditor for a directory property

```
private string _directory;

[Editor(typeof(System.Windows.Forms.Design.FolderNameEditor),
        typeof(System.Drawing.Design.UITypeEditor))]
public string BaseDirectory
{
  get { return _directory; }
  set { _directory = value; }
}
```

If you'd like to see this property and editor in action, add the code for this property to your `ScrollablePictureBox` class, reference the System.Design.dll assembly, and recompile the test project.

For the `TypeConverter` class, this class provides conversion between two different types, such as between an object and a corresponding string representation. The .NET Framework provides a number of type converters for use with various types. One of these is the `ColorConverter` class in the `System.Drawing` namespace. Listing 17.5 shows how a `BaseColor` property might be defined that uses this converter to display its `Color` value as a string. This code also utilizes the `ColorEditor` class to support visual editing of the color, and the `Color.Empty` field as an ambient value for the property.

Listing 17.5 Sample code using a TypeConverter for a Color property

```
private Color _color;

[EditorAttribute(typeof(System.Drawing.Design.ColorEditor),
  typeof(System.Drawing.Design.UITypeEditor))]
[TypeConverter(typeof(System.Drawing.ColorConverter))]
[AmbientValue(typeof(Color), "Empty")]
public Color BaseColor
{
  get { return _color; }
  set
  {
    if (value == Color.Empty)
      _color = BackColor;       // use BackColor by default
    else
      _color = value;
  }
}
```

Once again you can drop this code into our `ScrollablePictureBox` class and reference the System.Drawing.Design.dll assembly to see the code in action. For a complete list of .NET type converters, display the derived classes from the `TypeConverter` class reference page in the .NET documentation.

17.6 RECAP

In this chapter we discussed the creation of custom Windows Forms controls. We covered three basic approaches: extending an existing Windows Forms control, deriving an entirely new control from the `Control` class, and deriving a composite control from the `UserControl` class. We presented the merits of each approach, and discussed various ways to accomplish various types of custom behavior. This included the `ControlPaint` class, which supports some standard functionality required by many custom controls.

Throughout this discussion we built a sample custom control: the `ScrollablePictureBox` class. This control extends the `PictureBox` control to provide scrolling when the displayed image is larger than the client area. As part of this implementation, we built a test application to verify that the control works as expected.

We completed our discussion with some more advanced customization techniques. This included the `UITypeEditor`, `TypeConverter`, and `ControlDesigner` classes. We showed some examples of how these classes might be used, and indicated some editor and conversion classes provided by the .NET Framework.

The next chapter incorporates our new `ScrollablePictureBox` control in a new application that introduces the idea of explorer interfaces.

CHAPTER 18

Explorer interfaces and tree views

In computer programming, a style is a way of doing something, whether it's how a control is docked or anchored to a form or how a Windows interface is laid out. In this chapter we look at a specific application interface style known as the explorer interface.

An interface style, for our purposes, is just a convention for how a graphical user interface presents information to a user. The .NET Framework supports a number of interface styles. We introduce three in this chapter: single document interfaces, multiple document interfaces, and explorer interfaces. Chapter 20 looks at multiple document interfaces in more detail. In this chapter our focus is on explorer interfaces.

This chapter presents the following concepts:

- Understanding various interface styles
- Dividing containers with the `SplitContainer` control
- Representing a hierarchy with the `TreeView` control
- Adding `TreeNode` objects to a tree view
- Building a custom tree view control

These topics are covered as we progress through the chapter, beginning with interface styles.

18.1 *INTERFACE STYLES*

Sometimes programmers don't worry about what style of interface they are building. They build a program that accomplishes some task, and that's the end of it. The layout of controls in an application is a function of what needs to be done.

This typically results in a dialog interface style, where a bunch of controls are laid out on a form to accomplish a specific task. This works fine for small or very focused applications, but can be difficult to extend into a full-fledged Windows application with millions of users.

An alternate approach is to begin with a style in mind, and work toward this style as the application grows. Of course, it is even more desirable to have the completed application fully designed, and then incrementally build this application over a series of iterations. This is desirable but not always possible. My approach is to at least have a vision in mind, if not on paper, and work toward this vision as the application grows.

In this section we discuss three common styles of Windows interfaces that cover a broad range of possible applications. A style, in this sense, is simply an approach for how information is presented to the user. We examine these approaches:

- Single document interfaces
- Explorer interfaces
- Multiple document interfaces

We discuss each style separately.

18.1.1 Single document interfaces

A single document interface (SDI) is an interface that displays a single document or other encapsulated data within a single form. Our MyPhotos application, shown in figure 18.1, displays a single photo album to the user, and is a good example of this style. The contents of two albums cannot be compared unless two copies of the program are running simultaneously.

Figure 18.1 Our single document interface displays one photo album at a time.

More generally, a single document interface presents a single concept in a single window to the user, be it a photo album, a paper document, a tax form, or some other concept. Single document interfaces typically provide a menu bar to open, save, and otherwise manipulate the concept; a status bar to summarize information related to the presented information; and one or more toolbars as an alternate way to manipulate the data.

18.1.2 Multiple document interfaces

A multiple document interface (MDI) is a logical extension of the single document interface style. MDI applications allow multiple views of one or more documents or other encapsulated data to be displayed at the same time. This permits alternate views of the same data, or separate instances of the same concept, within a single window. For example, a stock market MDI application might present different historical or graphical views of stock portfolios, each within its own separate window as part of a larger application. Alternately, such an application might display a single portfolio, with different views of the data in multiple windows.

In the traditional conception of this style, a single window acted as a container for other windows, where each contained window displayed a specific instance or view of a concept. Such an interface is shown in figure 18.2. More recently, well-known MDI applications such as Microsoft Word and Excel have taken the approach of displaying all of their windows directly on the desktop, each within a separate application window, while still preserving an MDI look and feel from the menu bar and other parts of the interface. This relatively new style, the multiple single document interface (MSDI), is consistent with the manner in which web browsers have historically worked.

Figure 18.2 Our multiple document interface displays a selected set of photo albums within a single window.

Also note that Visual Studio, while providing an MDI-like interface, uses more of a `TabControl` look and feel for the set of displayed windows, or what might be called a tabbed document interface (TDI). In this style, multiple sets of windows are displayed as horizontal or vertical groups of tabs. The Mozilla Firefox browser, available at www.mozilla.org/products/firefox, uses this approach rather well.

Both the MSDI and MTDI approaches can be created using the .NET Framework as an alternative to the traditional MDI interface, although there is no direct support for these newer styles. As a result, implementing such interfaces requires a bit more effort from the developer and is therefore a bit beyond the scope of this book.

For our purposes, a traditional MDI application provides the means to discuss and demonstrate the manner in which the .NET Framework supports such applications. In chapter 20, we convert the existing MyPhotos application into an MDI application, as shown here in figure 18.2. As you can see, this application incorporates the `Form` classes we created in part 2 of this book.

The reuse of our existing classes is possible because of the manner in which the `Form` class in general and MDI support in particular is integrated into the Windows Forms hierarchy. As we discussed in chapter 7, a `Form` object is a `Control` instance that happens to display an application window. For MDI applications, `Form` controls are contained by a parent `Form`. The contained forms can be resized and moved within their container, just like any other control within a container, and yet can still display menus, status bars, and other controls. The relationship between MDI parent and child forms is slightly different than the relationship between control containers and controls, as we see in a moment.

18.1.3 Explorer interfaces

In an explorer interface a hierarchy or other organization is imposed on a concept or set of concepts, with the hierarchy shown on one side and details related to a selected item shown in the main portion of the window. The classic example of this style is the Windows Explorer interface, which displays information about the data available on the computer, be it from disk, CD, network, or another source.

Explorer interfaces give an overview of the concept in question, and typically provide a tree control to allow the user to explorer the data at a high level or successive levels of detail. The user can select a specific item, or *node*, in the tree and see information about this item in the other portion of the interface, most commonly in the form of a list showing the selected item's contents.

In this chapter we start building the MyAlbumExplorer interface as an example of this style. The end result is shown in figure 18.3. The next section begins this discussion with an exploration of splitter controls and an introduction to the `TreeView` and `ListView` controls.

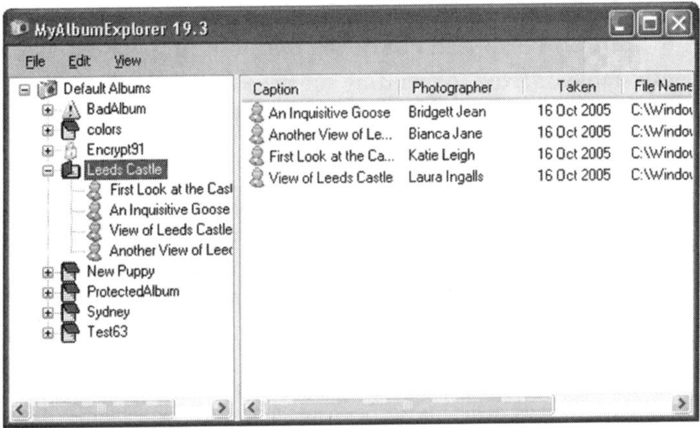

Figure 18.3 Our explorer interface allows a user to explore a collection of photo albums.

18.2 EXPLORER INTERFACES IN .NET

Now that we've reviewed the three main interface styles for Windows applications, let's take a look at the explorer interface in more detail. Part 1 of the book built a single document interface, and we examine multiple document interfaces in chapter 20.

We discuss the explorer interface style in this as well as the next chapter. This chapter focuses more on the interface itself, and the tree view and splitter controls commonly used for this interface. Chapter 19 elaborates on this discussion and examines the `ListView` control.

While building an explorer interface has always been possible in .NET, the release of .NET 2.0 made this task much easier. In the .NET 1.*x* releases, a `Splitter` class was provided that split a container into two distinct regions. The proper location of the splitter object was dependent on the order in which controls were added to the container, which could get rather confusing. This class is still available in .NET 2.0, but Microsoft no longer recommends its use.

Recognizing the error of their ways, the Windows Forms team has added the `SplitContainer` control. This class works much like the `JSplitPane` class in the Java Swing interface, for you Java aficionados out there. We discuss split containers in a moment.

Once a `SplitContainer` object is on a form, a `TreeView` control can be dropped into the left-hand side and a `ListView` control into the right-hand side. Explorer interfaces in Windows were never quite so easy.

We begin our discussion with the splitter controls.

18.2.1 The SplitContainer class

As already indicated, the `SplitContainer` class is the recommended mechanism for splitting a container into multiple sections. The members of this class are shown in .NET Table 18.1. As you can see, the `SplitContainer` class provides a number of properties to control the appearance of the two resulting panels. The size of each panel can be adjustable or fixed, depending on the `FixedPanel` and `IsSplitterFixed` properties described in the table. Panel-specific properties define a minimum size for each panel and allow either panel to be hidden from view.

.NET Table 18.1 SplitContainer class

New in 2.0 The `SplitContainer` class is a container control that provides two resizable panels separated by a movable bar. This control composes two panels, encapsulated as `SplitterPanel` objects, divided by a movable bar, or splitter, into a single control. This class is part of the `System.Windows.Forms` namespace, and inherits from the `ContainerControl` class.

The `SplitterPanel` class is a panel suitable for placing within a split container control. This class is part of the `System.Windows.Forms` namespace, and inherits from the `Panel` class.

Public Properties	*BorderStyle*	Gets or sets the border style applied to the panels within the control.
	FixedPanel	Gets or sets which panel, if any, cannot be resized.
	IsSplitterFixed	Gets or sets whether the splitter is movable.
	Orientation	Gets or sets the orientation of the panels and splitter within the control.
	Panel1	Gets the left or top panel in the container as a `SplitterPanel` instance. The `Panel2` property gets the right or bottom panel.
	Panel2Collapsed	Gets or sets whether the right or bottom panel is visible or hidden. The `Panel1Collapsed` property gets or sets whether the left or top panel is collapsed.
	Panel1MinSize	Gets or sets the minimum size for the left or top panel. The `Panel2MinSize` property affects the right or bottom panel.
	SplitterDistance	Gets or sets the distance, in pixels, of the splitter from the left or top edge of the form.
	SplitterIncrement	Gets or sets the smallest distance, in pixels, that the splitter will move.
	SplitterRectangle	Gets the location and size of the splitter relative to the container.
	SplitterWidth	Gets or sets the width of the splitter in pixels.
Public Events	*SplitterMoved*	Occurs after the splitter has moved.
	SplitterMoving	Occurs when the splitter is about to move.

The movable bar within a split container, called the *splitter*, is affected by properties that define its location and size within the container. The `SplitterIncrement` property allows a splitter to move in increments larger than one pixel. Additional tasks can be performed before or after a user moves the splitter by handling the `SplitterMoved` and `SplitterMoving` events.

Split containers can orient their panels in the horizontal or vertical direction, and can be nested to allow multiple display areas within a form. A quick example of these two concepts appears in listing 18.1, which creates the form shown in figure 18.4. This example displays a horizontal split container nested within the right panel of a vertical split container. Each panel assigns a different `BackColor` setting so the location of each splitter panel is immediately apparent.

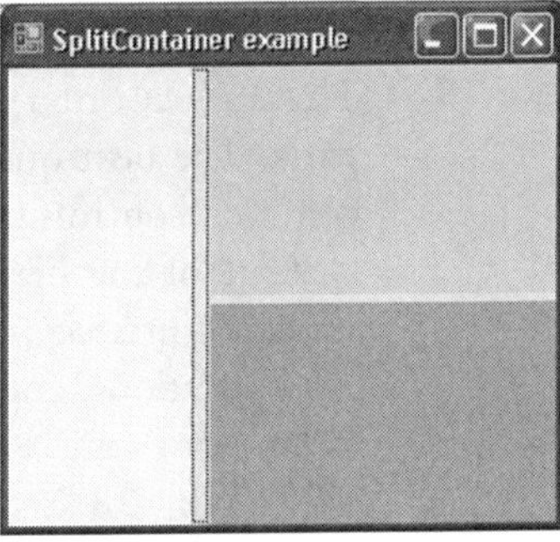

Figure 18.4 This sample application demonstrates nested SplitContainer controls.

Listing 18.1 Sample application using SplitContainer

```
using System;
using System.Drawing;
using System.Windows.Forms;

namespace SplitContainerExample
{
  static class SplitContainerProgram
  {
    [STAThread]
    static void Main()
    {
      Application.EnableVisualStyles();

      SplitContainer split2 = new SplitContainer();
      split2.Dock = DockStyle.Fill;
      split2.Orientation = Orientation.Horizontal;
      split2.Panel1.BackColor = Color.LightGray;
      split2.Panel2.BackColor = Color.DarkGray;

      // Create split1 container to hold split2 container
      SplitContainer split1 = new SplitContainer();
      split1.Dock = DockStyle.Fill;
      split1.Panel1.BackColor = Color.WhiteSmoke;
      split1.SplitterWidth = 10;
      split1.Panel2.Controls.Add(split2);

      // Create a form to hold split1 container
      Form f = new Form();
      f.Text = "SplitContainer example";
      f.Controls.Add(split1);

      // Display the form
      Application.Run(f);
    }
  }
}
```

18.2.2 The TreeView class

The `SplitContainer` class is great for dividing a form or other container into two parts. The next question, of course, is what to place in each part. One of the more common controls for the left side of a split form is the `TreeView` control.

One of the better-known examples of the `TreeView` control is the Windows Explorer interface, where the Folders view provides a tree of the devices, folders, network locations, and other information about the local computer environment. The Windows Forms `TreeView` class supports this functionality, and is summarized in .NET Table 18.2.

Each item in a tree view is called a *tree node*, or just a *node*. Tree nodes can contain additional nodes, called *child nodes*, to arbitrary levels in order to represent a hierarchy of objects in a single tree. Tree nodes at the top level of a tree view control are called *root nodes*. Figure 18.5 shows some of concepts and classes used with the Windows Forms `TreeView` control.

The members in .NET Table 18.2 are just some of the members defined by the `TreeView` class explicitly. As you can see, members are provided to manage the nodes in the tree, including the selection, drawing, and contents of each node. We use many of these members as we build our sample explorer application.

A short summary of some members not mentioned in .NET Table 18.2 is probably worthwhile. The nodes in the tree can be sorted alphabetically by setting the `Sorted` property to `true`, or a custom `IComparer` interface can be assigned to the `TreeViewNodeSorter` property to specify a custom sort for the nodes.

An additional set of properties defines how the nodes in the tree are laid out. The `Indent` property indicates how many pixels to indent each level in the tree, while the color, existence, and appearance of lines between nodes are affected by the `LineColor`, `ShowLines`, `ShowPlusMinus`, and `ShowRootLines` properties.

As shown in figure 17.5, each node in a tree view can display an icon next to the node label. The `ImageList` property defines the images to use for this purpose.

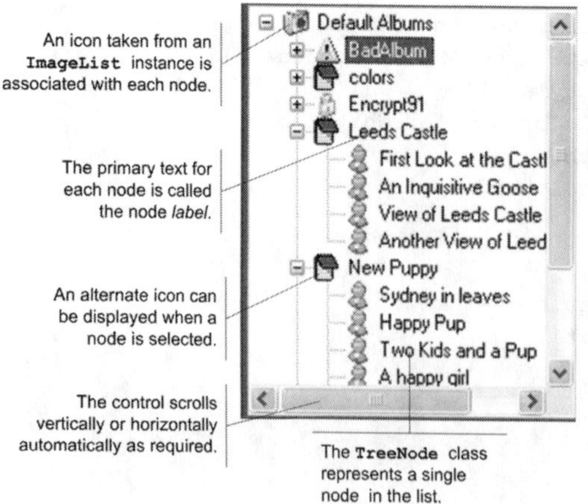
An icon taken from an ImageList instance is associated with each node.
The primary text for each node is called the node *label*.
An alternate icon can be displayed when a node is selected.
The control scrolls vertically or horizontally automatically as required.
The TreeNode class represents a single node in the list.
Default Albums
BadAlbum
colors
Encrypt91
Leeds Castle
First Look at the Castl
An Inquisitive Goose
View of Leeds Castle
Another View of Leed
New Puppy
Sydney in leaves
Happy Pup
Two Kids and a Pup
A happy girl

Figure 18.5
Icons in a tree view typically indicate additional information about each node. In this example a notebook indicates a valid album, a lock indicates an encrypted album, and an exclamation point indicates an album that could not be opened.

.NET Table 18.2 TreeView class

The `TreeView` class is a control that displays a collection of labeled items in a tree-style hierarchy. Typically an icon is displayed for each item in the collection to provide a graphical indication of the nature or purpose of the item. Items in a tree view are referred to as *nodes*, and each node is represented by a `TreeNode` class instance. The `TreeView` class is part of the `System.Windows.Forms` namespace, and inherits from the `Control` class.

Public Properties	BorderStyle	Gets or sets the border style for the tree view
	CheckBoxes	Gets or sets whether a check box appears next to each node
	DrawMode	Gets or sets the drawing mode for the tree view
	FullRowSelect	Gets or sets whether the selection of a node should span the width of the tree view
	HideSelection	Gets or sets whether the selected node is highlighted when the tree view loses focus
	HotTracking	Gets or sets whether a node label alters its appearance as the mouse passes over it
	ImageList	Gets or sets the image list that contains the images to use with the tree's nodes
	LabelEdit	Gets or sets whether node labels can be edited
	Nodes	Gets the tree's collection of `TreeNode` objects
	PathSeparator	Gets or sets the delimiter used for a tree node path
	SelectedNode	Gets or sets the selected tree node
	Sorted	Gets or sets whether nodes in the tree are sorted
	StateImageList	Gets or sets the image list used to indicate the state of each tree node
	TopNode	Gets or sets the first fully visible node in the tree
	VisibleCount	Gets the maximum number of nodes that can be fully visible in the tree
Public Methods	CollapseAll	Collapses all nodes in the tree
	ExpandAll	Expands all nodes in the tree
	GetNodeAt	Retrieves the tree node at the specified pixel location
	GetNodeCount	Returns the number of top-level nodes in the tree, or the total number of nodes in the entire tree
Public Events	AfterExpand	Occurs after a tree node has been expanded
	AfterLabelEdit	Occurs after a tree node label has been edited
	BeforeSelect	Occurs before a tree node is selected
	DrawNode	Occurs when a node should be drawn
	ItemDrag	Occurs when a user begins dragging a node
	NodeMouseClick	Occurs when a user clicks a tree node

Other image properties include the `ImageIndex` property to indicate the index of the default image and the `SelectedImageIndex` property to indicate the index of the default image for a selected node. The default images can alternately be specified by image name, using the `ImageKey` and `SelectedImageKey` properties, which we demonstrate in the next section.

A second set of images can also be displayed to represent the state of each node. The images for the state icons are defined by the `StateImageList` property. When the `CheckBoxes` property is `true` and state images are defined, the first two images in the `StateImageList` collection are used to indicate the unchecked and checked state, respectively.

One other set of members we should probably highlight consists of the `After` and `Before` events. A few of these are shown in .NET Table 18.2, but be aware that before and after events occur when a user clicks on node check boxes, expands or collapses nodes, edits node labels, or selects nodes.

18.2.3 Creating an explorer interface

So let's see a tree view in action. The following steps begin a new MyAlbumExplorer project for use in this and the next chapter, as well as show the creation of an explorer-style interface.

BEGIN THE MYALBUMEXPLORER APPLICATION

	Action	Result
1	Create a new Windows Application project called "MyAlbumExplorer."	
2	Rename the `Form1` class to "ExplorerForm." Set its `Size` to 450 by 300, and its `Text` to "Album Explorer."	
3	Add the MyPhotoAlbum and MyPhotoControls projects to the solution.	
4	Reference these two projects within the MyAlbumExplorer project.	
5	Set the version numbers in the AssemblyInfo.cs file (not shown) to 18.2 to match our section number.	

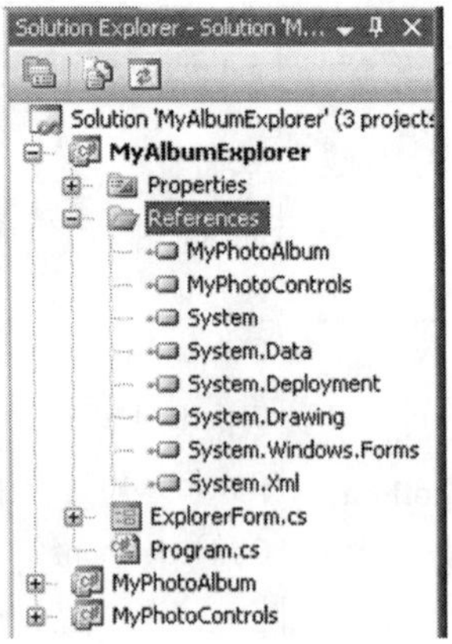

BEGIN THE MYALBUMEXPLORER APPLICATION *(CONTINUED)*

	Action	Result

6	In the ExplorerForm.cs source file, override the `OnLoad` method to display the version number in the title bar.	`protected override void OnLoad(EventArgs e)`
		`{`
		`  // Assign title bar`
		`  Version v = new Version(Application.`
		`                   ProductVersion);`
		`  this.Text = String.Format(`
		`      "MyAlbumExplorer {0:#}.{1:#}",`
		`      v.Major, v.Minor);`
		
		`  base.OnLoad(e);`
		`}`

7	Set the `Icon` property for the `ExplorerForm` form to the file "icons/WinXP/camera.ico" in the common image library.	camera.ico
8	Also set this icon as the Application icon in the MyAlbumExplorer project properties.	This icon displays in Windows operating system to represent the application. **Note:** We discussed icons for both forms and applications in chapter 15 in section 15.1.2.

This creates our new solution, with the version number displayed in the title bar and a new icon that represents our application. As you may recall, the common image library mentioned in step 7 is our shorthand for the graphics files provided with Visual Studio.

To turn this into an explorer interface, we need to split the display area into two sections, with a tree on the left and information about the selected tree node on the right. To do this, we need a `SplitContainer` and `TreeView` control, which we add here so they are available in the next section.

BEGIN THE MYALBUMEXPLORER APPLICATION

	Action	Result
9	Drag a `SplitContainer` control onto the form.	Album Explorer
10	Drag a `TreeView` control onto the left side of the split container. **Settings** **Property** / **Value** (Name): albumTree Dock: Fill ShowNodeToolTips: True	

When you add the split container, Visual Studio displays the text Panel1 and Panel2 on each `SplitterPanel` instance to make them easier to identify. Our application does not do very much yet, but it does work. The next section discusses how to populate this tree view with our album data.

18.3 TREE NODES

Each element in a tree view is called a tree view node, or simply a node. Tree views contain nodes, which in turn may contain other nodes, which may contain still other nodes, and so forth. Each node in the tree is represented by a `TreeNode` object. Nodes in a tree view can be created at design time in Visual Studio, or dynamically within application code.

This section presents the `TreeNode` class in detail and discusses how to use this class within an application.

18.3.1 The TreeNode class

The `TreeNode` class provides members for presenting and manipulating nodes within a tree view. A summary of these members is shown in .NET Table 18.3. The table focuses on members that are somewhat unique to the `TreeNode` class. The class also supports members similar to the Windows Forms `Control` class, such as the `BackColor`, `ContextMenuStrip`, `ForeColor`, `Parent`, `Tag`, and `Text` properties. Of these, only the `Text` property is shown in the table, since it defines the string that appears as the node's label.

In addition to the `ImageIndex` and `SelectedImageIndex` properties shown in .NET Table 18.3, there are other properties that define the images displayed next to the node. The available images are defined by the `ImageList` and `StateImageList` properties for the containing `TreeView` control. The `ImageKey` and `SelectedImageKey` properties can be used to specify an image by its name, or key, rather than its index. The `StateImageIndex` or `StateImageKey` property can be used to specify the image used to indicate the state of the node. These default and selected image properties apply when the associated `TreeView` property has an assigned `ImageList`; the state image properties only apply when a `StateImageList` instance is assigned to the tree.

Also worth a mention are the node navigation properties in the `TreeNode` class. The `NextNode` and `PrevNode` properties get the next or previous sibling node, at the same level as the current node. The `NextVisibleNode` and `PrevVisibleNode` properties get the next or previous child, sibling, or parent node that is visible in the tree.

.NET Table 18.3 TreeNode class

The `TreeNode` class is a marshaled object that represents an element, or node, within a `TreeView` control. A `TreeNode` object can contain other nodes to represent a hierarchy of objects within a tree view. Each `TreeNode` instance is contained by at most one `TreeView` or `TreeNode` object. This class is part of the `System.Windows.Forms` namespace, and inherits from the `System.MarshalByRefObject` class.

Public Properties	FirstNode	Gets the first node, if any, contained by this node.
	FullPath	Gets the path to this node, starting at the root node, using the tree's `PathSeparator` setting as a delimiter.
	ImageIndex	Gets or sets the index into the tree's image list of the default image for this node.
	IsEditing	Gets whether this node is currently being edited.
	IsExpanded	Gets whether the children of this node are displayed.
	IsSelected	Gets whether this node is currently selected.
	Level	Gets the zero-based depth of this node in the tree.
	NodeFont	Gets or sets the font used to display the node's label.
	Nodes	Gets the collection of nodes contained by this node.
	SelectedImage-Index	Gets or sets the index into the tree's image list of the image to display when this node is selected. The `Index` property gets or sets the index of the default image.
	Text	Gets or sets the label text to display for this node.
	ToolTipText	Gets or sets the tooltip for this node.
	TreeView	Gets the `TreeView` control containing this node.
Public Methods	Collapse	Ensures that no children of this node are displayed.
	ExpandAll	Expands all tree nodes contained by this node.
	Toggle	Toggles the tree node between the expanded or collapsed state, based on the `IsExpanded` setting.

18.3.2 Creating tree nodes

Now that we've reviewed the members of the `TreeNode` class, let's talk about how to create these objects. When a `TreeView` control is placed on a form within Visual Studio, you can add nodes to it within the designer or dynamically. The TreeNode Editor window, shown in figure 18.6, is available from the Properties window or the context menu for the `TreeView` control.

Programmatically, of course, tree nodes are created much like any other class. The `TreeNode` constructor has a number of overloads, and allows the caller to define the label, child nodes, or associated images.

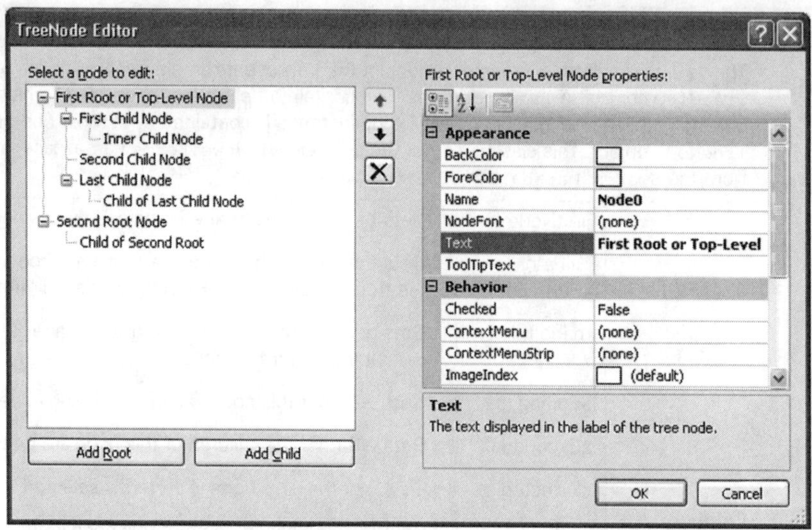

Figure 18.6 The TreeNode Editor in Visual Studio allows both root and child nodes to be created within the designer.

Listing 18.2 illustrates how our MyAlbumExplorer application can be extended to add tree nodes for each album in the default album directory. This code assumes that a `ScrollablePictureBox` control named `spbxPhoto` is docked to the right side of the split container, and that `BeforeSelect` and `AfterSelect` event handlers have been defined for the `TreeView` control. The application resulting from these changes is shown in figure 18.7.

Listing 18.2 Sample MyAlbumExplorer implementation that creates album and photograph nodes programmatically

```
. . .
using System.IO;
using Manning.MyPhotoAlbum;
using Manning.MyPhotoControls;

namespace MyAlbumExplorer
{
  public partial class ExplorerForm : Form
  {
    public ExplorerForm()
    {
      InitializeComponent();
    }

    private Photograph _priorPhoto = null;

    protected override void OnLoad(EventArgs e)
    {
      // Assign title bar
```

```
  Version v = new Version(Application.ProductVersion);
  this.Text = String.Format("MyAlbumExplorer {0:#}.{1:#}",
    v.Major, v.Minor);

  // Define nodes for the default albums
  albumTree.Nodes.Clear();
  string[] albums = Directory.GetFiles(
                      AlbumManager.DefaultPath, "*.abm");
  foreach (string file in albums)
  {
    string baseName = Path.GetFileNameWithoutExtension(file);
    try
    {
      // Define root album node
      PhotoAlbum album = AlbumStorage.ReadAlbum(file);

      string title = album.Title;
      if (String.IsNullOrEmpty(title))
        title = baseName;

      TreeNode node = albumTree.Nodes.Add(title);
      node.ToolTipText = file;

      foreach (Photograph p in album)
      {
        // Define child photograph node
        TreeNode child = node.Nodes.Add(p.Caption);
        child.ToolTipText = p.FileName;
        child.Tag = p;
      }
    }
    catch (AlbumStorageException)
    {
      // Unable to open album
      TreeNode node = albumTree.Nodes.Add(baseName);
      node.ToolTipText = "Unable to open album: " + file;
    }
  }

  base.OnLoad(e);
}

private void albumTree_BeforeSelect(object sender,
    TreeViewCancelEventArgs e)
{
  if (_priorPhoto != null)
  {
    spbxPhoto.Image = null;
    _priorPhoto.ReleaseImage();
    _priorPhoto = null;
  }
}

private void albumTree_AfterSelect(object sender,
    TreeViewEventArgs e)
```

1 Creates album node

2 Creates photograph node

3 Disposes of prior image

```
      {
        Photograph p = e.Node.Tag as Photograph;
        if (p != null)
          spbxPhoto.Image = p.Image;

        _priorPhoto = p;
      }
    }
  }
```

4 Assigns selected image

This code uses many of the concepts and ideas discussed in part 2 of the book. A few key points worth a mention are as follows.

1. When the form is loaded, a root node is created for each album in the default album directory. If available, the album's title is used as the node's label; otherwise the base file name of the album is used. Notice the `catch` block that handles `AlbumStorage-Exception` errors by creating a top-level node for the errant album. This exception occurs if the album is encrypted or if some other recognizable problem occurs.
2. When an album loads successfully, a child node is created for each photograph in the album. The node's `Tag` property is assigned to the associated `Photograph` object.
3. Since our application may display many images, we need to be careful not to leave too many resource-depleting bitmaps lying around. Our `BeforeSelect` event handler ensures that any photo previously displayed in the scrollable picture box is released before a new photo is selected.
4. The `AfterSelect` event handler looks to see if the selected node is tagged with a `Photograph` object. If so, then its image is displayed; otherwise the node is ignored. Our `ScrollablePictureBox` custom control handles any required scrolling automatically.

Before and after events in the `TreeView` class receive different event arguments. All after events receive a `TreeViewEventArgs` object, as shown in .NET Table 18.4. All before events receive a `TreeViewCancelEventArgs` object. The latter class provides the same `Action` and `Node` properties as the former class, and it inherits from

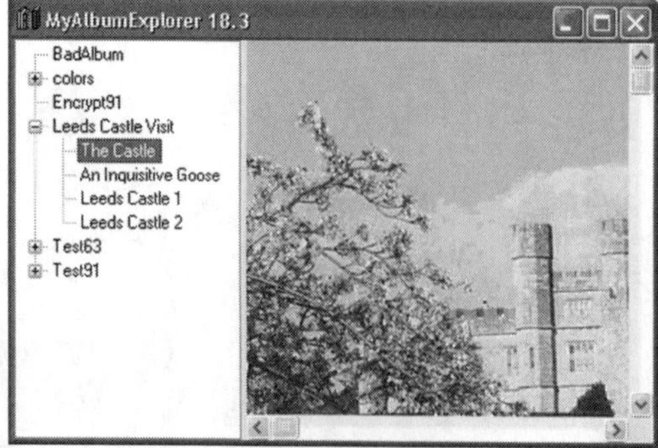

Figure 18.7
This application demonstrates the TreeView control used in conjunction with the ScrollablePictureBox custom control created in chapter 17.

the CancelEventArgs class to give the caller the option of canceling the event by assigning true to the Cancel property.

.NET Table 18.4 TreeViewEventArgs class

The TreeViewEventArgs class specifies the event data for events that occur after a tree view operation completes. This class is part of the System.Windows.Forms namespace, and inherits from the System.EventArgs class.

Public Properties	Action	Gets the TreeViewAction enumeration value representing the action that caused this event.
	Node	Gets the TreeNode object for the current operation.

The application in listing 18.2 is fine and works quite well. It can be extended to support all sorts of features and capabilities. A disadvantage of this approach is that all of the code to manipulate the TreeView and other controls is part of the ExplorerForm.cs file. As the application grows, this file gets larger and larger, and thus harder and harder to maintain.

An alternate approach is to encapsulate the tree view as custom controls. This would force us to encapsulate the logic for the customized control in a single file, providing better organization and simplifying reuse if desired. We finish this chapter by creating such a TreeView control for the purpose of displaying and manipulating album directories. This custom tree view is incorporated into the MyAlbumExplorer interface as part of our discussion.

TRY IT! Add the code in listing 18.2 to the ExplorerForm.cs file to get this application working in Visual Studio. There are many ways to improve this application. One addition you might try is to dock a ListBox control on the right side of the split container, and display the selected album's photographs in this list whenever an album node is selected. To do this, you need to assign the Visible property on both the ListBox and ScrollablePictureBox controls whenever a node is selected to ensure that only the desired control is visible.

18.4 CUSTOM TREE VIEWS

Like any control, the TreeView class can be customized in all sorts of ways to provide better, faster, and stronger functionality than what is provided in the base Windows Forms control. We discussed such customization in chapter 17, so we do not go through this again.

Sometimes it is useful to customize a control not so much for reuse or functionality purposes, but as a way to organize or otherwise encapsulate portions of a graphical interface. We introduced this idea in chapter 14, where we discussed the idea of defining UserControl classes to encapsulate a set of interfaces for an application, in that case a user control object that held a calendar showing dates when photographs were taken.

The `UserControl` example in chapter 14 represents this alternate reason to customize a control: to encapsulate a portion of an interface. This not only prevents the associated `Form` class from holding thousands of lines of user interface code, but also forces better encapsulation of the functionality required.

In this section we see how this idea is applied to the `TreeView` class. We create an `AlbumTreeView` custom control that displays one or more albums in a tree. This class is not strictly required, but places everything we need to display albums and photographs in our MyAlbumExplorer application in a single class.

18.4.1 Creating a custom tree view

To begin this great work, let's create the `AlbumTreeView` class and indicate the namespaces required. There is nothing new here.

HIDE THE TOOLBAR IN OUR CHILD FORM

	Action	Result

1	Add a new class to the MyAlbumExplorer project called AlbumTreeView.	`using System;`
		`using System.ComponentModel;`
		`using System.IO;`
		`using System.Windows.Forms;`

2	Indicate we will use the indicated `System` and `Manning` namespaces.	`using Manning.MyPhotoAlbum;`
		`using Manning.MyPhotoControls;`
		
		`namespace MyAlbumExplorer`
		`{`

3	Make the `AlbumTreeView` class internal and inherit from the `TreeView` class.	`  internal class AlbumTreeView : TreeView`
		`  {`
		`  }`
		`}`

This defines our new control class, which we fill in over the course of this section. We should create a test application for this new control to verify that these and subsequent changes work correctly. This might be a form that contains only the `AlbumTreeView` class and displays the albums in the default album directory.

To save time and space, we do not create such a test application here, but feel free to do this if you wish so you can verify our implementation as we go along. The rest of us must wait until the end of the chapter to see this control in action.

With our control defined, the next step is to define exactly what type of support we need to provide in the class.

18.4.2 Creating custom tree nodes

The goal of our tree view is to display albums. Albums appear in directories, and albums contain photographs. So in our tree, we should probably have three types of nodes: album directory nodes, album nodes, and photograph nodes. Rather than trying to manage these within the tree view control itself, we create a custom class for each type of node.

A custom `TreeNode` class, much like a custom `TreeView`, is quite useful to encapsulate the behavior required for a specific node as well as custom tasks that users may wish to perform against the node.

So, without further adieu, allow me to present the `AlbumDirectoryNode` class.

CREATE AN ALBUMDIRECTORYNODE CLASS

	Action	Result

1	In the MyAlbumExplorer project, create an internal class called `AlbumDirectoryNode`.
	Note: This could be a public class, but internal works fine for our purposes.
		`using System;`
		`using System.IO;`
		`using System.Windows.Forms;`
		
		`namespace MyAlbumExplorer`
		`{`
		`  internal class AlbumDirectoryNode : TreeNode`
		`  {`

2	Create a private field and public property for the directory represented by this node.	`private string _albumDir;`
		`public string AlbumDirectory`
		`    { get { return _albumDir; } }`

3	Define a constructor that accepts the name and directory for this node.	`public AlbumDirectoryNode(string name,`
		`    string albumDir) : base(name)`
		`{`
		`  if (albumDir == null)`
		`    throw new ArgumentNullException("albumDir");`
		`  if (!Directory.Exists(albumDir))`
		`    throw new ArgumentException(`
		`        "albumDir is not a valid directory");`

4	Assign the directory field to the given value, and create a fake child node in this node.	`_albumDir = albumDir;` `this.Nodes.Add("child");`

5	Also define both image keys for the node to use the name "AlbumDir."	`this.ImageKey = "AlbumDir";`
		`this.SelectedImageKey = "AlbumDir";`
		`}`

6	Define an `AlbumFiles` property that gets the collection of album files in the directory.	`public string[] AlbumFiles`
		`{`
		`  get { return Directory.GetFiles(`
		`          AlbumDirectory, "*.abm"); }`
		`}`

	Action	Result
	CREATE AN ALBUMDIRECTORYNODE CLASS *(CONTINUED)*	

7	Define a private field and public `AlbumNodes` property to retrieve the collection of album nodes for this directory node.	`private AlbumNode[] _albumNodes = null;`
		`public AlbumNode[] AlbumNodes`
		`{`
		`  get`
		`  {`
		`    CreateAlbumNodes();`
		`    return _albumNodes;`
		`  }`
		`}`

8	Define a `CreateAlbumNodes` method to create the album nodes, if necessary.	`public void CreateAlbumNodes()`
		`{`
		`  string[] files = AlbumFiles;`
		`  int count = files.Length;`

9	Replace the fake node with an `AlbumNode` for each album file in the directory.
	
	Note: This relies on the `AlbumNode` constructor, which we create in a moment.
		`  if (_albumNodes == null`
		`        || _albumNodes.Length != count)`
		`  {`
		`    Nodes.Clear();`
		`    _albumNodes = new AlbumNode[count];`
		`    for (int i = 0; i < count; i++)`
		`    {`
		`      // Add album node`
		`      string s = files[i];`
		`      string name`
		`        = Path.GetFileNameWithoutExtension(s);`
		`      _albumNodes[i] = new AlbumNode(name, s);`
		`    }`
		
		`    Nodes.AddRange(_albumNodes);`
		`  }`
		`}`
		`}`
		`}`

This code defines everything we need to manage an album directory node in our `TreeView` control. The constructor defines a fake child node to ensure that the `TreeView` control displays a plus (+) sign next to the node. When the user expands the node, our control will need to call the `CreateAlbumNodes` method to replace the fake node with the actual nodes for the album.

Also note that we assign an `ImageKey` value for the node. This has little meaning here, but becomes relevant later in the chapter when we incorporate our `AlbumTreeView` class into our application.

The other nodes are a bit more involved, so we create them in the next section.

18.4.3 Using interfaces with custom nodes

At times, especially in more complex applications, it is useful to share some base functionality among the various custom node classes. One approach for this is to define a base class, for example `BaseTreeNode`. All custom nodes inherit from the base class and override or otherwise inherit the base functionality as appropriate.

Another approach is to define an interface and have some or all of the custom node classes inherit this interface. We take the interface approach in our album and photograph nodes in order to refresh each node when the associated object changes. The following steps define an `IRefreshableNode` interface for this purpose and begin our implementation of the `AlbumNode` class.

CREATE AN ALBUMNODE CLASS

	Action	Result

1	Add a new internal interface in the project called `IRefreshableNode`, and define a single `RefreshNode` method within this interface.	<pre>namespace MyAlbumExplorer
		{
		  internal interface IRefreshableNode
		  {
		    void RefreshNode();
		  }
		}</pre>

2	Add a new internal class called `AlbumNode` to the project, and have it inherit from the `TreeNode` class and support the `IDisposable` and `IRefreshableNode` interfaces.	<pre>using System;
		using System.IO;
		using System.Windows.Forms;
		
		using Manning.MyPhotoAlbum;
		using Manning.MyPhotoControls;
		
		namespace MyAlbumExplorer
		{
		 internal class AlbumNode
		      : TreeNode, IDisposable, IRefreshableNode
		 {</pre>

3	Create private fields to hold the path and manager for the album, and a public `AlbumPath` property to retrieve the path.	<pre> private string _albumPath;
		  private AlbumManager _manager;
		
		  public string AlbumPath
		      { get { return _albumPath; } }</pre>

4	Define a constructor that accepts the name and album path for the new node.	<pre> public AlbumNode(string name, string albumPath)
		    : base(name)
		  {
		    if (albumPath == null)
		      throw new ArgumentNullException("albumPath");
		    if (!File.Exists(albumPath))
		      throw new ArgumentException(
		          "albumPath is not a valid path");
		
		    _manager = null;
		    _albumPath = Path.GetFullPath(albumPath);
		    this.Nodes.Add("child");</pre>

5	Set the image key for the node to "AlbumLock" if the album is encrypted. Otherwise use "Album" as the key, with "AlbumSelect" as the selected key name.	<pre> if (AlbumStorage.IsEncrypted(albumPath))
		    {
		      this.ImageKey = "AlbumLock";
		      this.SelectedImageKey = "AlbumLock";
		    }
		    else
		    {
		      this.ImageKey = "Album";
		      this.SelectedImageKey = "AlbumSelect";
		    }
		  }</pre>

CREATE AN ALBUMNODE CLASS *(CONTINUED)*		
	Action	**Result**

6	Implement a `GetManager` method to retrieve the manager for the node. Accept an `interactive` parameter to indicate whether to ask for the album password if necessary.	`public AlbumManager GetManager(bool interactive)`
		`{`
		`  if (_manager == null)`
		`  {`
		`    string path = AlbumPath;`
		`    string pwd = null;`
		
		`    try`
		`    {`

7	If the album is encrypted, allow the user to enter the password if running interactively.
	
	If not interactive, or the user cancels the password dialog box, abort the method by returning `null`.
		`      if (AlbumStorage.IsEncrypted(path))`
		`      {`
		`        DialogResult result = DialogResult.None;`
		`        if (interactive)`
		`        {`
		`          result = MessageBox.Show("The album "`
		`            + path + " is encrypted. "`
		`            + "Do you wish to open this album?",`
		`            "Encrypted Album",`
		`            MessageBoxButtons.YesNo,`
		`            MessageBoxIcon.Question,`
		`            MessageBoxDefaultButton.Button2);`
		`        }`
		
		`        if (result != DialogResult.Yes`
		`          || !AlbumController.CheckAlbumPassword(`
		`                                   path, ref pwd))`
		`          return null;  // cancelled`
		`      }`

8	If the manager is opened successfully, reset the default and selected image key settings.	`      _manager = new AlbumManager(path, pwd);`
		`      this.ImageKey = "Album";`
		`      this.SelectedImageKey = "AlbumSelect";`
		`    }`

9	If an `AlbumStorage` exception occurs, set the image keys to "AlbumError" and the manager to `null`.	`    catch (AlbumStorageException ex)`
		`    {`
		`      if (interactive)`
		`        MessageBox.Show("The album could not "`
		`          + "be opened [" + ex.Message + "]");`
		
		`      this.ImageKey = "AlbumError";`
		`      this.SelectedImageKey = "AlbumError";`
		`      _manager = null;`
		`    }`
		`  }`

10	When finished, return the resulting manager.	`  return _manager;` `}`

11	Implement a `GetAlbum` method to return the `PhotoAlbum` associated with the manager, if any.	`public PhotoAlbum GetAlbum(bool interactive)`
		`{`
		`  AlbumManager mgr = GetManager(interactive);`
		
		`  if (mgr == null)  return null;`
		`  else  return mgr.Album;`
		`}`

	Action	Result

12	Implement a `RemoveChildren` method to clean up any open images and clear the child nodes of the album node.	`public void RemoveChildren()`
		`{`
		`  AlbumManager mgr = GetManager(false);`
		`  if (mgr != null)`
		`  {`
		`    foreach (Photograph p in mgr.Album)`
		`      p.ReleaseImage();`
		`  }`
		
		`  Nodes.Clear();`
		`  Nodes.Add("child");`
		`}`

13	Implement the `IDisposable` interface to dispose of any manager created for this node.	`public void Dispose()`
		`{`
		`  if (_manager != null)`
		`    _manager.Album.Dispose();`
		`  _manager = null;`
		`}`

14	Implement the `IRefreshableNode` interface to refresh the `Text` property of the node, if necessary.	`public void RefreshNode()`
		`{`
		`  AlbumManager mgr = GetManager(false);`
		`  if (mgr != null && this.Text != mgr.ShortName)`
		`    this.Text = mgr.ShortName;`
		`}`

15	Define a `RenameAlbum` method to rename the path for the associated album to a given name.
	
	How-to
	Rely on a `RenameAlbum` method from the `AlbumManager` class, which does not yet exist. Display a message if an `ArgumentException` is thrown to indicate that the album name already exists.
		`public bool RenameAlbum(string newName)`
		`{`
		`  try`
		`  {`
		`    AlbumManager mgr = GetManager(false);`
		`    if (mgr == null)`
		`      _albumPath = AlbumManager.RenameAlbum(`
		`                        AlbumPath, newName);`
		`    else`
		`    {`
		`      mgr.RenameAlbum(newName);`
		`      _albumPath = mgr.FullName;`
		`    }`
		
		`    return true;`
		`  }`
		`  catch (ArgumentException)`
		`  {`
		`    MessageBox.Show("Unable to rename album. An "`
		`        + "album with that name already exists.");`
		`    return false;`
		`  }`
		`}`

CREATE AN ALBUMNODE CLASS *(CONTINUED)*		
	Action	**Result**

16	Define an `UpdatePath` method to modify the node when the path for the album is modified externally.	`public void UpdatePath(string newPath)`
		`{`
		`  if (!File.Exists(newPath))`
		`    throw new ArgumentException(`
		`        "newPath must be valid path");`
		
		`  AlbumManager mgr = GetManager(false);`
		`  if (mgr != null)`
		`  {`
		`    // Just pull new info from the manager`
		`    _albumPath = mgr.FullName;`
		`    Text = mgr.ShortName;`
		`  }`
		`  else`
		`  {`
		`    // use given path to update node`
		`    _albumPath = newPath;`
		`    Text = Path.GetFileNameWithoutExtension(`
		`                                      newPath);`
		`  }`
		`  }`
		` }`
		`}`

17	In the MyPhotoAlbum project, add a `RenameAlbum` method to the `AlbumManager` class that invokes a corresponding static method.	`public void RenameAlbum(string newName)`
		`{`
		`  _name = RenameAlbum(FullName, newName);`
		`}`

18	Implement a static `RenameAlbum` method that accepts an old and new filename for an album.	`public static string RenameAlbum(`
		`    string oldPath, string newName)`
		`{`
		`  string dir = Path.GetDirectoryName(oldPath);`
		`  string ext = Path.GetExtension(oldPath);`

19	Construct the new path and use the `File.Move` method to rename the file. Throw an `ArgumentException` if the new file already exists.	`  string newPath = dir + Path.`
		`      DirectorySeparatorChar + newName + ext;`
		
		`  if (File.Exists(newPath))`
		`  {`
		`    throw new ArgumentException(`
		`        "A file with the name "`
		`          + newPath + " already exists.");`
		`  }`
		
		`  // Presume no error is thrown here`
		`  File.Move(oldPath, newPath);`
		`  return newPath;`
		`}`

This defines our `AlbumNode` class, along with the methods that will prove useful as we develop our application. I am cheating here a bit, since I have already figured out what we need in the future from this class. In practice, a core class is typically defined and extended to support additional functionality as required by the application.

The PhotoNode class to represent photograph nodes is defined in a similar manner.

CREATE A PHOTONODE CLASS

	Action	Result

20	In the MyAlbumExplorer project, define an internal PhotoNode class.	`using System;`
		`using System.IO;`
		`using System.Windows.Forms;`
		`using Manning.MyPhotoAlbum;`
		
		`namespace MyAlbumExplorer`
		`{`
		` internal class PhotoNode`
		`     : TreeNode, IRefreshableNode`
		`  {`

21	Define a private field and public Photograph property to hold the photo associated with this node.	`private Photograph _photo;`
		`public Photograph Photograph`
		`    { get { return _photo; } }`

22	Define a constructor that accepts the Photograph to associate with the new node. Use the caption for the node's text, and the image key "Photo."	`public PhotoNode(Photograph photo) : base()`
		`{`
		`  if (photo == null)`
		`    throw new ArgumentNullException("photo");`
		
		`  _photo = photo;`
		`  Text = photo.Caption;`
		`  ImageKey = "Photo";`
		`  SelectedImageKey = "Photo";`
		`}`

23	Implement the IRefresh-ableNode interface to reset the node's text to the photo-graph's caption.	`public void RefreshNode()`
		`{`
		`  Text = Photograph.Caption;`
		`}`
		`}`
		`}`

As you can see, our PhotoNode class provides external access to the Photograph associated with the node. This completes our three TreeNode classes for use within our custom tree view. With these available, we are ready to continue our AlbumTreeView implementation.

18.4.4 Expanding and collapsing tree nodes

Let's begin with the creation of nodes in the tree. As mentioned earlier in the chapter, the TreeView class defines before and after events for a number of actions, including the expansion and contraction of tree nodes. We can employ these methods to dynamically add child nodes to our tree view.

The following steps display our three types of nodes in the tree, using the AlbumDirectoryNode class as the top-level node.

<table>
<tr><th colspan="3">DYNAMICALLY EXPAND AND COLLAPSE NODES</th></tr>
<tr><th></th><th>Action</th><th>Result</th></tr>
<tr><td>1</td><td>Define a new <code>AddAlbum-Directory</code> method in the <code>AlbumTreeView</code> class that adds a new directory node to the tree.</td><td><pre>
public AlbumDirectoryNode AddAlbumDirectory(
    string name, string albumDir)
{
  // Create a new top-level node
  AlbumDirectoryNode node
      = new AlbumDirectoryNode(name, albumDir);
  this.Nodes.Add(node);
  return node;
}
</pre></td></tr>
<tr><td>2</td><td>Override the <code>OnBeforeExpand</code> method to add the appropriate child nodes before a node is expanded.</td><td><pre>
protected override void OnBeforeExpand(
    TreeViewCancelEventArgs e)
{
  base.OnBeforeExpand(e);

  if (e.Node is AlbumDirectoryNode)
    ExpandAlbumDirectory(
        e.Node as AlbumDirectoryNode);
  else if (e.Node is AlbumNode)
    ExpandAlbum(e.Node as AlbumNode);
}
</pre></td></tr>
<tr><td>3</td><td>Implement an <code>ExpandAlbum-Directory</code> method to ensure the album nodes are created before the directory node expands.

How-to
Use the <code>BeginUpdate</code> and <code>EndUpdate</code> methods to disable drawing of the tree.</td><td><pre>
private void ExpandAlbumDirectory(
    AlbumDirectoryNode node)
{
  // Add a node per album
  BeginUpdate();
  try
  {
    // Make sure the album nodes exist
    node.CreateAlbumNodes();
  }
  finally { EndUpdate(); }
}
</pre></td></tr>
<tr><td>4</td><td>Implement an <code>ExpandAlbum</code> method to ensure the photo nodes are created before the album node expands.</td><td><pre>
private void ExpandAlbum(AlbumNode node)
{
  AlbumManager mgr = node.GetManager(true);
  if (mgr != null)
  {
    BeginUpdate();
    try
    {
      node.Nodes.Clear();
      foreach (Photograph p in mgr.Album)
      {
        PhotoNode newNode = new PhotoNode(p);
        node.Nodes.Add(newNode);
      }
    }
    finally { EndUpdate(); }
  }
}
</pre></td></tr>
</table>

	Action	Result
	DYNAMICALLY EXPAND AND COLLAPSE NODES *(CONTINUED)*	

5	Override the `OnAfter-Collapse` method to clean up child nodes after a tree node has been collapsed.	`protected override void OnAfterCollapse(`
		`    TreeViewEventArgs e)`
		`{`
		`  // Leave album directory nodes intact`
		`  // Clean up album nodes`
		`  if (e.Node is AlbumNode)`
		`    CollapseAlbum(e.Node as AlbumNode);`
		
		`  base.OnAfterCollapse(e);`
		`}`

6	Implement a `CollapseAlbum` method that removes the children from a given album node.	`private void CollapseAlbum(AlbumNode node)`
		`{`
		`  node.RemoveChildren();`
		`}`

This enables our tree view to internally expand and collapse the nodes, independent of the application it appears in. Child nodes are only created as they are needed, and `PhotoNode` objects are removed whenever their parent node is collapsed.

Two other features worth supporting in our tree view are selection and editing.

18.4.5 Selecting and editing tree nodes

As we have seen in other collection controls, the `TreeView` control allows a user to select a node in the control using either the keyboard or the mouse. The `BeforeSelect` and `AfterSelect` events are provided to process this action, and the events receive the `TreeViewCancelEventArgs` and `TreeViewEventArgs` classes discussed in the prior section.

In our custom tree view, we do not need to modify the selection behavior, but we do want to enable users of our control to select specific nodes. To support this, we provide two methods to aid in such efforts.

	Action	Result
	SUPPORT NODE SELECTION	

1	In the `AlbumTreeView` class, define a `SelectChild` method. Implement this method to select the `PhotoNode` within a given album node that is associated with a given photograph.	`public void SelectChild(`
		`  AlbumNode node, Photograph photo)`
		`{`
		`  foreach (TreeNode n in node.Nodes)`
		`  {`
		`    PhotoNode pNode = n as PhotoNode;`
		`    if (pNode != null`
		`        && pNode.Photograph == photo)`
		`    {`
		`      SelectedNode = n;`
		`      break;`
		`    }`
		`  }`
		`}`

	SUPPORT NODE SELECTION *(CONTINUED)*	
	Action	**Result**

2	Define an alternate `SelectChild` method to select an `AlbumNode` within a given album directory node that has a given album path.	<pre>public void SelectChild(
		  AlbumDirectoryNode node, string albumPath)
		{
		  foreach (TreeNode n in node.Nodes)
		  {
		    AlbumNode aNode = n as AlbumNode;
		    if (aNode != null
		        && String.Equals(aNode.AlbumPath,
		             albumPath, StringComparison.
		                 InvariantCultureIgnoreCase))
		    {
		      SelectedNode = n;
		      break;
		    }
		  }
		}</pre>

Another feature of tree views is the ability to edit the node text associated with a node. An edit can be issued programmatically using the `TreeNode.BeginEdit` method. The `BeforeLabelEdit` and `AfterLabelEdit` events that occur during editing both receive the `NodeLabelEditEventArgs` class, detailed in .NET Table 18.5.

.NET Table 18.5 NodeLabelEditEventArgs class

The `NodeLabelEditEventArgs` class specifies the event data for events that occur before and after a tree node edit operation takes place. This class is part of the `System.Windows.Forms` namespace, and inherits from the `System.EventArgs` class.

Public Properties	CancelEdit	Gets or sets whether the operation should be canceled. This can be set before or after the node is edited.
	Label	Gets the new text to assign to the node's label.
	Node	Gets the `TreeNode` object being edited.

Editing is typically used to rename the file name or some property associated with a node in the tree. In our case, we rename the album filename or the photo caption text. We do not permit album directories to be edited. The following steps implement the required editing logic.

	SUPPORT NODE EDITS	
	Action	**Result**

3	Override the `OnAfterLabelEdit` method in the `AlbumTreeView` class.	<pre>protected override void OnAfterLabelEdit(
		    NodeLabelEditEventArgs e)
		{</pre>

	Support node edits *(continued)*	
	Action	**Result**

4	If the edit is blank or was aborted, cancel the operation.	`if (String.IsNullOrEmpty(e.Label))`
		`{`
		`  e.CancelEdit = true;`
		`  return;`
		`}`

5	If the node is an album node, rename the underlying album path.	`if (e.Node is AlbumNode)`
		`{`
		`  // Rename the underlying album`
		`  AlbumNode node = e.Node as AlbumNode;`
		`  e.CancelEdit = !node.RenameAlbum(e.Label);`
		`}`

6	If the node is a photo node, modify the caption of the associated `Photograph` instance	`else if (e.Node is PhotoNode)`
		`{`
		`  // Modify the photo caption`
		`  PhotoNode node = e.Node as PhotoNode;`
		`  node.Photograph.Caption = e.Label;`
		`  SaveAlbumChanges();`
		`}`
		`}`

7	Also override the `OnKeyDown` method to edit the current node when the F2 key is pressed.	`protected override void OnKeyDown(KeyEventArgs e)`
		`{`
		`  if (e.KeyCode == Keys.F2)`
		`  {`
		`    if (SelectedNode != null)`
		`      SelectedNode.BeginEdit();`
		`    e.Handled = true;`
		`  }`
		`}`

In addition to handling a node edit appropriately, this code handles the F2 key to initiate an edit of the selected node. This matches the behavior in Windows Explorer and other applications, and seems appropriate here as well. We discussed keyboard events in chapter 10.

To round out our new control, we also add a few methods that will prove useful as we integrate this control into our MyAlbumExplorer application.

	Define some supporting methods	
	Action	**Result**

8	Define a method in the `AlbumTreeView` class that refreshes the current node using the `IRefreshableNode` interface.	`public void RefreshNode()`
		`{`
		`  IRefreshableNode refresh`
		`      = SelectedNode as IRefreshableNode;`
		
		`  if (refresh != null)`
		`    refresh.RefreshNode();`
		`}`

	Define some supporting methods (continued)	
	Action	**Result**

9	Define another method to save any changes associated with the current node. Within this method, determine the album to save.	`internal void SaveAlbumChanges()`
		`{`
		`  // Find the album to save`
		`  AlbumNode aNode = SelectedNode as AlbumNode;`
		`  if (aNode == null)`
		`  {`
		`    PhotoNode pNode = SelectedNode as PhotoNode;`
		`    if (pNode != null)`
		`      aNode = pNode.Parent as AlbumNode;`
		`  }`

10	If an album is found, then save the changes if an `AlbumManager` is available for the album.	`  if (aNode != null)`
		`  {`
		`    AlbumManager mgr = aNode.GetManager(true);`
		`    if (mgr.Album.HasChanged)`
		`    {`
		`      // Save data and update node`
		`      mgr.Save();`
		`      aNode.RefreshNode();`

11	Also update any photo nodes if the album node is expanded.	`      if (aNode.IsExpanded)`
		`      {`
		`        // Update photographs, as necessary`
		`        foreach (PhotoNode pNode in aNode.Nodes)`
		`        {`
		`          // Assumes no photos added / deleted`
		`          pNode.RefreshNode();`
		`        }`
		`      }`
		`    }`
		`  }`
		`}`

12	Define a `FindAlbumNode` method to locate the album node associated with the current album directory.	`internal AlbumNode FindAlbumNode(string path)`
		`{`
		`  AlbumDirectoryNode dirNode`
		`    = SelectedNode as AlbumDirectoryNode;`
		`  if (dirNode != null)`
		`  {`
		`    foreach (AlbumNode node in dirNode.AlbumNodes)`
		`    {`
		`      if (String.Equals(node.AlbumPath, path,`
		`          StringComparison.`
		`              InvariantCultureIgnoreCase))`
		`        return node;`
		`    }`
		`  }`
		
		`  return null;`
		`}`

	Action	Result
DEFINE SOME SUPPORTING METHODS *(CONTINUED)*		

13	Finally, define a `FindPhotoNode` method to locate the photo node associated with the current album.	`internal PhotoNode FindPhotoNode(Photograph photo)`
		`{`
		`  AlbumNode albumNode = SelectedNode as AlbumNode;`
		`  if (albumNode != null)`
		`  {`
		`    albumNode.Expand();`
		`    foreach (PhotoNode node in albumNode.Nodes)`
		`    {`
		`      if (node.Photograph == photo)`
		`        return node;`
		`    }`
		`  }`
		
		`  return null;`
		`}`

This completes our `AlbumTreeView` control. The next step is to employ it within an application. The bulk of this work is done in the next chapter. Even so, we would be remiss if we didn't show at least a little example here, so we finish out the chapter with this.

18.4.6 Integrating a custom tree view control

As you may have noticed, our tree view control never did provide a set of images to display. Instead we defined `ImageKey` property settings for each node. This allows an external application to dictate what images are displayed by defining the appropriate image names. Ideally, our `AlbumTreeView` control would provide some written documentation that explains all this. For our purposes, we simply demonstrate this in the following steps.

	Action	Result
USE THE ALBUMTREEVIEW CONTROL IN OUR EXPLORER APPLICATION		
1	In the ExplorerForm.cs [Design] window of the MyAlbumExplorer project, add an `ImageList` called "imageListSmall" to the designer.	The new image list is shown in the component tray.

<table>
<tr><th colspan="3">USE THE ALBUMTREEVIEW CONTROL IN OUR EXPLORER APPLICATION (CONTINUED)</th></tr>
<tr><th></th><th>Action</th><th>Result</th></tr>
<tr><td>2</td><td>Add the following set of images to the image list. These all come from the icons folder in the common image library.
Settings
<table>
<tr><th>#</th><th>File</th><th>Name</th></tr>
<tr><td>0</td><td>icons / WinXP / users.ico</td><td>Photo</td></tr>
<tr><td>1</td><td>icons / Win9x / NOTE03.ICO</td><td>Album</td></tr>
<tr><td>2</td><td>icons / Win9x / NOTE04.ICO</td><td>AlbumSelect</td></tr>
<tr><td>3</td><td>icons / WinXP / warning.ico</td><td>AlbumError</td></tr>
<tr><td>4</td><td>icons / WinXP / security.ico</td><td>AlbumLock</td></tr>
<tr><td>5</td><td>icons / WinXP / camera.ico</td><td>AlbumDir</td></tr>
</table></td><td>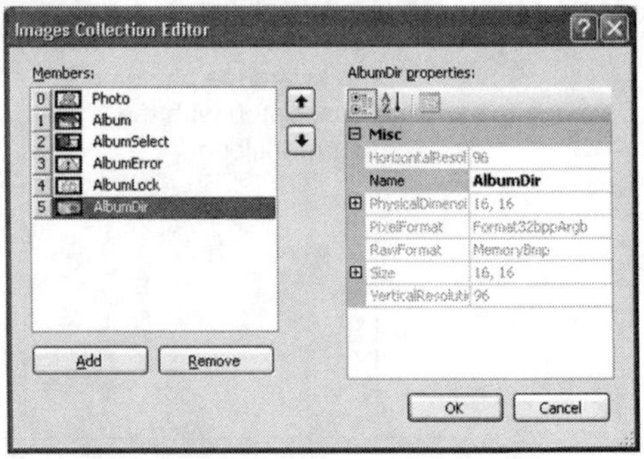

Note: The Name here is the <code>Name</code> property assigned to each image, which defaults to the base filename. This allows us to use the <code>ImageKey</code> property value to specify the image to display in our tree.</td></tr>
<tr><td>3</td><td>Also add a second image list to the form, and add the same set of images to the list.
Settings
<table>
<tr><th>Property</th><th>Value</th></tr>
<tr><td>(Name)</td><td>imageListLarge</td></tr>
<tr><td>ImageSize</td><td>32, 32</td></tr>
</table></td><td>The new image list is shown in the component tray. The <code>ImageSize</code> property setting ensures that we use the larger image from each icon.
Note: Set the <code>ImageSize</code> property first to establish the size before adding the icons. This ensures the properly sized image within each icon is placed in the list.</td></tr>
<tr><td>4</td><td>Replace the existing <code>TreeView</code> control with an <code>AlbumTreeView</code> control.
Settings
<table>
<tr><th>Property</th><th>Value</th></tr>
<tr><td>(Name)</td><td>atvAlbumTree</td></tr>
<tr><td>Dock</td><td>Fill</td></tr>
<tr><td>HideSelection</td><td>False</td></tr>
<tr><td>ImageList</td><td>imageListSmall</td></tr>
<tr><td>LabelEdit</td><td>True</td></tr>
</table></td><td>The window looks much the same, except that the tree view control is now our custom tree view rather than the standard tree view.</td></tr>
<tr><td>5</td><td>In the ExplorerForm.cs file, indicate we are using the <code>System.IO</code> and <code>Manning</code> namespaces.</td><td><pre>using System.IO;

using Manning.MyPhotoAlbum;
using Manning.MyPhotoControls;</pre></td></tr>
</table>

Use the AlbumTreeView control in our Explorer application *(continued)*

	Action	Result
6	In the override of the `OnLoad` method, add an album directory node for the default album folder location.	see code below

```
protected override void OnLoad(. . .)
{
  . . .
  atvAlbumTree.Nodes.Clear();
  atvAlbumTree.AddAlbumDirectory(
      "Default Albums",
      AlbumManager.DefaultPath);

  base.OnLoad(e);
}
```

At this point, we have a fully functional `AlbumTreeView` control on our form. Once we add the top-level directory node, our custom control handles the rest by allowing album and photograph nodes to appear as required.

The images we use for our image lists are perhaps not the best images we could wish for, but they serve our purposes here. This is where a good graphics artist would be useful.

We can round out our little example by dropping a `ScrollablePictureBox` control on the right side of the form to display a selected photograph.

Use the AlbumTreeView control in our Explorer application

	Action	Result
7	In the `ExplorerForm` designer window, drag a `ScrollablePictureBox` control to the right side of the split container.	
8	Add a private field to the `ExplorerForm` class that holds the current photo.	see code below
9	Handle the `BeforeSelect` event for the tree view control, and release any photograph currently displayed in the picture box.	see code below

Step 7 settings:

Property	Value
(Name)	spbxPhoto
Dock	Fill
SizeMode	Zoom

Step 8 result:

```
public partial class ExplorerForm : Form
{
  . . .
  private Photograph _currentPhoto = null;
```

Step 9 result:

```
private void atvAlbumTree_BeforeSelect(
  object sender,
  TreeViewCancelEventArgs e)
{
  if (_currentPhoto != null)
  {
    spbxPhoto.Image = null;
    _currentPhoto.ReleaseImage();
    _currentPhoto = null;
  }
}
```

	Action	Result
USE THE ALBUMTREEVIEW CONTROL IN OUR EXPLORER APPLICATION *(CONTINUED)*		

10	Handle the `AfterSelect` event to display the photo if the current node is a `PhotoNode` instance.	`private void atvAlbumTree_AfterSelect(`
		`  object sender, TreeViewEventArgs e)`
		`{`
		`  if (e.Node is PhotoNode)`
		`    DisplayPhoto(e.Node as PhotoNode);`
		`}`

11	Implement a `DisplayPhoto` method to display the image for a given photo node in the scrollable picture box.	`private void DisplayPhoto(`
		`  PhotoNode photoNode)`
		`{`
		`  _currentPhoto = photoNode.Photograph;`
		`  spbxPhoto.Image = _currentPhoto.Image;`
		`}`

This completes our example. The code used to display a photograph here is much like the code we presented in listing 18.2, so we won't discuss it again. Compile and run the application to see our custom tree view in action.

18.5 RECAP

In this rather long chapter, we presented the concept of interface styles and discussed the tree view control. We reviewed three common interface styles: single document interfaces (SDI), explorer interfaces, and multiple document interfaces (MDI).

This chapter focused on the explorer interface style. The `SplitContainer` class neatly divides a container such as a form or panel into two parts. We created a new MyAlbumExplorer application utilizing this control as an example of an explorer interface.

The bulk of the chapter examined tree view controls. The `TreeView` class displays a hierarchy of nodes, each represented by a `TreeNode` class instance.

We also built a custom tree view control for displaying photo albums, with a custom `TreeNode` for each of our three types of nodes. Our custom control manipulated these nodes to provide the appropriate functionality. We finished the chapter by employing this control in our MyAlbumExplorer application.

The next chapter continues this example by presenting the `ListView` control and illustrating its use within our sample explorer interface.

CHAPTER 19

List views

The `ListView` class often goes hand in hand with the `TreeView` class discussed in the previous chapter. Chapter 18 examined the most common control on the left side of an explorer interface, so this chapter continues this discussion with the most common control on the right side of such an interface. This includes the following topics:

- Understanding the `ListView` class
- Creating list views and list view items
- Defining and populating list view columns
- Populating list view columns with list view subitems
- Customizing sort behavior in a list view
- Selecting and editing list view items
- Activating list view items

As part of our discussion, we extend the MyAlbumExplorer application from chapter 18 to include a list view item so we can demonstrate each topic in the context of an application. As you might guess, our list view displays the contents of the item selected in our tree view control.

The discussion is divided into three parts. We describe some fundamental aspects of list views, present how list view columns are created and manipulated, and finish with some common features of the list view control.

19.1 LIST VIEW FUNDAMENTALS

In many ways, a list view is simply a more glamorous version of a list box. Conceptually both controls present a scrollable list of items to the user. The `ListBox` class stores a collection of `object` instances, while the `ListView` class contains a collection of `ListViewItem` instances, which in turn contains a collection of `ListViewSubItem` objects. There is, in fact, no relation from a class hierarchy perspective.

Another difference between the controls is how their contents are displayed. The `ListBox` control displays a string associated with each object by default, and supports an owner-drawn style to display other formats. The `ListView` control displays its items in a variety of formats defined by the `View` enumeration.

This section introduces the `ListView` class and some essential concepts required to use and understand this control.

19.1.1 The ListView class

Organizing a collection of objects is a common task in any application. The `ListView` class, as shown in .NET Table 19.1, provides one option for organizing a related set of items. As you can see, the `ListView` class provides a wide variety of features. Most of our .NET Tables provide a fairly complete overview of their classes. The `ListView` class is one for which a review of the complete list of members in the .NET documentation might be worthwhile, as cutting the table down to fit on a single page was difficult.

We discuss and show examples for many aspects of list views in this chapter, but an overview of some of the more interesting features is probably warranted.

List views support what we have seen from other list constructs. The items are stored in a collection, can optionally have check boxes, and support features such as selection, sorting, and owner draw. When the `HoverSelection` property is `true`, an item is selected when the mouse hovers over it.

Like the `TreeView` control, list views can display a state icon for each item, with the images defined by the `StateImageList` property. Also as for tree views, state images specify alternate check box images when the `CheckBoxes` property is `true`.

Figure 19.1 shows various features and classes available in the `ListView` control, including the ability to display information in columns. Sorting by column can be enabled as well, as we see in section 19.2.

.NET Table 19.1 ListView class

The `ListView` class is a control that displays a collection of labeled items as a list. Typically an icon is displayed for each item in the collection to provide a graphical indication of the nature or purpose of each item. The `View` enumeration defines the different ways the list can appear, with the `Details` view allowing additional items to appear in multiple columns within the control. This class is part of the `System.Windows.Forms` namespace, and inherits from the `Control` class.

Public Properties	Activation	Gets or sets how an item is activated by the user.
	Columns	Gets the `ColumnHeader` components for the list. The `HeaderStyle` property gets or sets the column style.
	Items	Gets the collection of items in the list.
	LabelEdit	Gets or sets whether the user can edit item labels.
	LabelWrap	Gets or sets whether item labels wrap their text as required.
	LargeImageList	Gets or sets the `ImageList` to use when displaying large icons. The `SmallImageList` property applies to small icons.
	ListViewItemSorter	Gets or sets the comparer to use when sorting list items.
	MultiSelect	Gets or sets whether multiple list items can be selected.
	OwnerDraw	Gets or sets whether list items are custom drawn.
	SelectedItems	Gets the collection of items selected in the list.
	Sorting	Gets or sets if and how items in the list are sorted.
	View	Gets or sets the current display style for the list control.
	VirtualMode	Gets or sets whether items are stored internally or retrieved dynamically using the `RetrieveVirtualItem` event.
Public Methods	Clear	Removes all items and columns from the list view.
	EnsureVisible	Ensures an item is visible, scrolling it into view if necessary.
Public Events	AfterLabelEdit	Occurs after an item label has been edited.
	ColumnClick	Occurs when the user clicks a column header.
	DrawItem	Occurs when `OwnerDraw` is `true` and a list item must be drawn.
	ItemActivate	Occurs when an item is activated.
	ItemDrag	Occurs when a user begins dragging an item in the list.
	SelectedIndexChanged	Occurs when the selection state of an item changes.

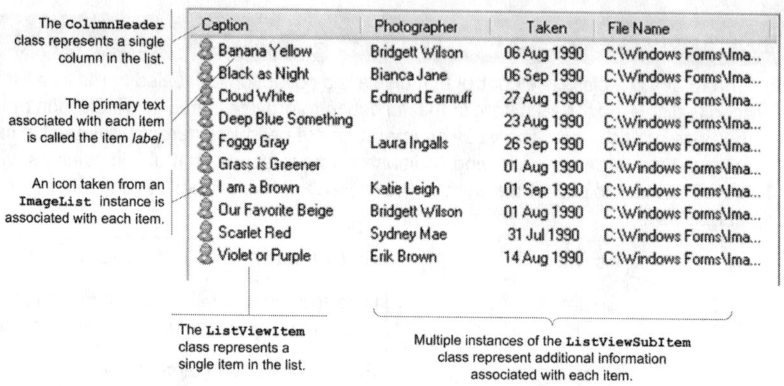

Figure 19.1 This graphic highlights some classes and terms used with the ListView control.

As you might expect, the items in a list view can also be custom drawn by setting the `OwnerDraw` property to `true`. When this occurs, the `DrawItem` event occurs whenever an item must be drawn, with event data defined by the `DrawListViewItemEventArgs` class. In addition, the `DrawSubItem` event occurs when a list subitem must be drawn and the `DrawColumnHeader` event occurs when a column header must be drawn. Subitems and column headers are demonstrated in section 19.2.

The custom drawing of list items is new in .NET 2.0, but is somewhat similar to other custom drawing we have seen, especially the owner-drawn list boxes described in chapter 13. Because of this, and to conserve chapter space, we won't demonstrate owner-drawn list views here. If you are interested in this topic, read through section 13.4 first before checking out the examples available in the .NET documentation.

Two other features worth a mention are automatic grouping and virtual items. Grouping enables the control to automatically display items in groups. The `Groups` property gets the collection of `ListViewGroup` objects that define the categories of items in the control. The `ShowGroups` property gets or sets whether items are actually displayed in groups. The heading, layout, and items for each group are defined by a `ListViewGroup` instance.

Virtual items are extremely useful, if not required, when displaying very large lists. By default, a `ListView` holds the entire collection of items in memory at all times. This is rather wasteful when displaying a large list, so this feature allows an application to provide list items dynamically as they are required by the control. An example of this is shown in section 19.4.

19.1.2 Creating a list view

Well, talk is cheap, so we should probably show this class in action. The MyAlbumExplorer project is just aching for a `ListView` control on the right side of the split panel, so the following steps do just this.

<table>
<tr><th colspan="3">ADD A MENU AND LIST VIEW TO THE MYALBUMEXPLORER APPLICATION</th></tr>
<tr><th></th><th>Action</th><th>Result</th></tr>
<tr><td>1</td><td>In the MyAlbumExplorer solution, add a <code>ListView</code> control to the right side of the <code>SplitContainer</code> in the ExplorerForm.cs [Design] window.

Settings
<table>
<tr><th>Property</th><th>Value</th></tr>
<tr><td>(Name)</td><td>lvAlbumList</td></tr>
<tr><td>Dock</td><td>Fill</td></tr>
<tr><td>FullRowSelect</td><td>True</td></tr>
<tr><td>LableEdit</td><td>True</td></tr>
<tr><td>LargeImageList</td><td>imageListLarge</td></tr>
<tr><td>SmallImageList</td><td>imageListSmall</td></tr>
</table></td><td>The new list view control fills the right-hand panel of the split container control.

Note: The <code>FullRowSelect</code> and <code>LabelEdit</code> properties used here are discussed later in the chapter when we populate list view columns and edit label text.</td></tr>
<tr><td>2</td><td>Also drop a <code>MenuStrip</code> control onto the title bar of the form, and add the following top-level menus.

Settings
<table>
<tr><th>Menu</th><th>Property</th><th>Value</th></tr>
<tr><td>File</td><td>(Name)
Text</td><td>menuFile
&File</td></tr>
<tr><td>Edit</td><td>(Name)
Text</td><td>menuEdit
&Edit</td></tr>
<tr><td>View</td><td>(Name)
Text</td><td>menuView
&View</td></tr>
</table></td><td>Note: If you drop the menu strip within the form, it might end up within the split container control. Dropping on the title bar ensures that the new strip is associated with the form itself.</td></tr>
</table>

ADD A MENU AND LIST VIEW TO THE MYALBUMEXPLORER APPLICATION *(CONTINUED)*

<table>
<tr><th></th><th>Action</th><th>Result</th></tr>
<tr><td>3</td><td>Within the View menu, create five menu items.

Settings
<table>
<tr><th>Menu</th><th>Property</th><th>Value</th></tr>
<tr><td>Large Icons</td><td>(Name)
Tag
Text</td><td>menuViewLarge
LargeIcon
Lar&ge Icons</td></tr>
<tr><td>Small Icons</td><td>(Name)
Tag
Text</td><td>menuViewSmall
SmallIcon
S&mall Icons</td></tr>
<tr><td>List</td><td>(Name)
Tag
Text</td><td>menuViewList
List
&List</td></tr>
<tr><td>Details</td><td>(Name)
Tag
Text</td><td>menuViewDetails
Details
&Details</td></tr>
<tr><td>Tiles</td><td>(Name)
Tag
Text</td><td>menuViewTiles
Tile
&Tiles</td></tr>
</table></td><td>Note: These values match those defined by the <code>View</code> enumeration, which is used to define a list view's display style. The <code>Tiles</code> value is only available on Windows XP and 2003 or later platforms. If you are using Windows 2000, you can leave this option off if you wish, or use the <code>System.Environment.OSVersion</code> property to enable or disable this method in the form's OnLoad method.</td></tr>
<tr><td>4</td><td>Within the File menu, add an Exit menu item along with an appropriate <code>Click</code> event handler.

Settings
<table>
<tr><th>Property</th><th>Value</th></tr>
<tr><td>(Name)</td><td>menuFileExit</td></tr>
<tr><td>Text</td><td>E&xit</td></tr>
</table></td><td><code>private void menuFileExit_Click(</code>
<code>   object sender, EventArgs e)</code>
<code>{</code>
<code> Close();</code>
<code>}</code></td></tr>
</table>

The View menu items created here allow us to switch between the various display styles offered by the `ListView` class. Since we already know all about menu objects, we may as well set up the appropriate event handlers here. The `ListView.View` property takes its values from the `View` enumeration, as shown in .NET Table 19.2.

.NET Table 19.2 View enumeration

The `View` enumeration specifies the display styles for the contents of the `ListView` control. This enumeration is part of the `System.Windows.Forms` namespace.

Enumeration Values	Details	Items are arranged in columns with headers, with one item per line, and subitem information shown in additional columns.
	LargeIcon	Each item appears as a large icon with a label below it.
	List	Items are arranged as small icons, in columns with no headers, and with the labels on the right.
	SmallIcon	Each item appears as a small icon with a label at the right.
	Tile	Each item appears as a large icon with item and subitem information on the right. On operating systems prior to Windows XP and 2003, this setting is ignored and `LargeIcon` is used instead.

The approach we use for setting the `View` property is similar to the menu item code we presented in chapter 4. As a result, this code is shown with little explanation.

HANDLE THE VIEW MENU ITEMS

	Action	Result

5	Add a `DropDownOpening` event handler for the View menu.	`private void menuView_DropDownOpening(`
		`    object sender, EventArgs e)`
		`{`

6	Implement this handler to check or uncheck each menu item as appropriate.	`  View v = lvAlbumList.View;`
		`  menuViewLarge.Checked = (v == View.LargeIcon);`
		`  menuViewSmall.Checked = (v == View.SmallIcon);`
		`  menuViewList.Checked = (v == View.List);`
		`  menuViewDetails.Checked = (v == View.Details);`
		`  menuViewTiles.Checked = (v == View.Tile);`
		`}`

7	Also add a `DropDown-ItemClicked` event handler for the View menu.	`private void menuView_DropDownItemClicked(`
		`  object sender, ToolStripItemClickedEventArgs e)`
		`{`

8	Implement this handler to assign the list's `View` property to the value associated with the clicked menu item.	`  ToolStripItem item = e.ClickedItem;`
		`  string enumVal = item.Tag as string;`
		`  if (enumVal != null)`
		`  {`
		`    lvAlbumList.View = (View)`
		`        Enum.Parse(typeof(View), enumVal);`
		`  }`
		`}`

Our program should still compile and run. The `ListView` control is lacking any meaningful contents, so let's tackle this topic next.

19.1.3 Populating a list view

As already indicated, a `ListView` control contains a collection of `ListViewItem` objects. The `ListViewItem` class inherits directly from the `System.Object` class, so all painting and other management of list items is performed by the `ListView` class itself. Having the parent `ListView` class paint the contained item objects is consistent with other container controls we have seen. This includes the `ListBox` control containing a collection of object instances as well as the `ToolStrip` control containing `ToolStripItem` instances.

The `ListViewItem` class is presented in .NET Table 19.3. These members are fairly straightforward, so we won't go into additional detail beyond what is shown in

.NET Table 19.3 ListViewItem class

The `ListViewItem` class represents an item within a `ListView` control. It is part of the `System.Windows.Forms` namespace, and supports the `ICloneable` and `ISerializable` interfaces.

Public Properties	Bounds	Gets the bounding rectangle of the item, including any displayed subitems.
	Focused	Gets or sets whether the item has the focus within the containing list view control.
	Font	Gets or sets the `Font` for any text display by the item.
	ForeColor	Gets or sets the foreground `Color` for the item.
	Group	Gets or sets the group assignment for this item.
	ImageKey	Gets or sets the name of the image to display for this item.
	Index	Gets the current position of the item within the list view.
	ListView	Gets the `ListView` control that contains this item.
	Selected	Gets or sets whether the item is selected in the list view.
	SubItems	Gets the collection of list view subitems assigned to this item. The item itself is the first element in this collection.
	Tag	Gets or sets the `object` associated with this item.
	Text	Gets or sets the text string, or item label, for this item.
	ToolTipText	Gets or sets the tooltip for this item.
	UseItemStyleForSubItems	Gets or sets whether the style properties for the item are used for all its subitems.
Public Methods	BeginEdit	Initiates an edit of this item's label.
	Clone	Creates an identical copy of this item.
	EnsureVisible	Ensures an item is visible, scrolling the view as necessary.
	GetSubItemAt	Returns the subitem of this item at the given coordinates.
	Remove	Removes the item from the containing view.

the table. As you can see, a number of these members, such as the `ForeColor` and `Tag` properties, duplicate functionality provided by the `Control` class.

As our application already contains a populated `AlbumTreeView` control, our `ListView` should probably display the contents of the selected node in the tree. When an album directory node is selected, the list should display the albums in the associated directory; and when an album node is selected, the list should display the photographs in the associated album.

The following steps implement the logic required.

POPULATE THE LIST VIEW CONTROL		
	Action	**Result**

1	In the ExplorerForm.cs [Design] window, rewrite the `AfterSelect` event handler to update the list view control.	`private void atvAlbumTree_AfterSelect(. . .)`
		`{`
		`  try`
		`  {`
		`    lvAlbumList.BeginUpdate();`
		`    lvAlbumList.Clear();`

2	If an album directory node is selected, display the list of albums; if an album node is selected, display the list of photographs; if a photograph node is selected, invoke the existing `DisplayPhoto` method.	`    if (e.Node is AlbumDirectoryNode)`
		`      ListAlbumData(e.Node`
		`           as AlbumDirectoryNode);`
		`    else if (e.Node is AlbumNode)`
		`      ListPhotoData(e.Node as AlbumNode);`
		`    else if (e.Node is PhotoNode)`
		`      DisplayPhoto(e.Node as PhotoNode);`
		`    else`
		`      throw new ArgumentException(`
		`                 "Unrecognized node");`

3	Complete the update within a `finally` block to guarantee our `EndUpdate` method is called.	`  }`
		`  finally`
		`  {`
		`    lvAlbumList.EndUpdate();`
		`  }`
		`}`

4	Update the `DisplayPhoto` method to show the picture box and hide the list view.	`private void DisplayPhoto(PhotoNode photoNode)`
		`{`
		`  spbxPhoto.Visible = true;`
		`  lvAlbumList.Visible = false;`
		`  . . .`
		`}`

5	Implement a private member and property in the class to indicate whether we are showing album items in the list.	`private bool _showingAlbums = true;`
		`private bool ShowingAlbums`
		`{`
		`  get { return _showingAlbums; }`
		`  set { _showingAlbums = value; }`
		`}`

6	Implement a `ListAlbumData` method that hides the picture box, makes the list view visible, and shows the available albums.	`private void ListAlbumData(`
		`    AlbumDirectoryNode dirNode)`
		`{`
		`  // Show albums in list view`
		`  spbxPhoto.Visible = false;`
		`  lvAlbumList.Visible = true;`
		`  ShowingAlbums = true;`

	POPULATE THE LIST VIEW CONTROL *(CONTINUED)*	
	Action	**Result**

7	Within this method, add a list view item for each album in the directory.	`// Add the albums for given node`
		`foreach (AlbumNode aNode`
		`        in dirNode.AlbumNodes)`
		`{`

8	For each item, use the base album file name as the label, and the album node's image.	`  string text`
		`    = Path.GetFileNameWithoutExtension(`
		`        aNode.AlbumPath);`
		`  ListViewItem item`
		`    = lvAlbumList.Items.Add(text);`
		`  item.ImageKey = aNode.ImageKey;`
		`}`
		`}`

9	Implement a `ListPhotoData` method that hides the picture box, makes the list view visible, and shows any available photographs in the album.	`private void ListPhotoData(AlbumNode albumNode)`
		`{`
		`  // Show photographs in list view`
		`  spbxPhoto.Visible = false;`
		`  lvAlbumList.Visible = true;`
		`  ShowingAlbums = false;`
		
		`  // Add the photos for given node`
		`  AlbumManager mgr= albumNode.GetManager(true);`
		`  if (mgr != null)`
		`  {`

10	Create a list item for each photo, using the caption as the label, and the Photo image.	`    foreach (Photograph p in mgr.Album)`
		`    {`
		`      ListViewItem item`
		`        = new ListViewItem(p.Caption, "Photo");`
		`      lvAlbumList.Items.Add(item);`
		`    }`
		`  }`
		`}`

This code leverages our custom `AlbumTreeView` control code in that it checks the `Type` of the selected node and fills the `ListView` control accordingly. The `ListAlbumData` method is called to display photo album items, while the `ListPhotoData` is called to display photograph items.

A `ListViewItem` object can be created directly or as part of the collection. Step 7 illustrates creating an item and adding it to the collection in a single call. The `Text` property for the item is initialized as the `ListViewItem` is created.

```
ListViewItem item = lvAlbumList.Items.Add(text);
```

An alternate way to create an item is shown in step 9, where the items are created using the `ListViewItem` constructor followed by an explicit `Add` to the collection:

```
ListViewItem item = new ListViewItem(p.Caption, "Photo");
lvAlbumList.Items.Add(item);
```

This version of the constructor assigns the `Text` and `ImageKey` properties as part of the call. The new item is then added to the collection.

Compile and run this program to see list view at work. Our `AlbumTreeView` control does the bulk of the work here, so we were able to populate the list view without writing too many lines of code. If you experiment with the different View menu items, you will quickly notice that the `Details` view does not display anything.

The `Details` view requires that one or more columns exist for the list. Since we have not created any, no contents appear in this view. The use of columns is our next topic.

19.2 LIST VIEW COLUMNS

As we've the seen, the `Details` view is not very exciting without a column or two available. The use of columns allows additional information about each item to be presented in the list. Typically, a list view should support a column view of the data, to enable detailed information about each item to appear—not strictly required, of course, but a good standard to follow.

In our application, for example, we might show each album's title or the number of photographs in the album. Figure 19.2 illustrates the application we build over the course of this section, with the available albums shown in the list view.

The figure illustrates the fact that each column displays a header and each item defines the text for each column. In this section we discuss the classes supporting columns, and extend our MyAlbumExplorer application to include columns for both album and photo data. We also examine how to enable the common Windows feature of sorting a column when the user clicks on the header.

19.2.1 Defining column headers

The columns for a list view are held by the `Columns` property. This property holds an instance of the `ListView.ColumnHeaderCollection` class, which in turn

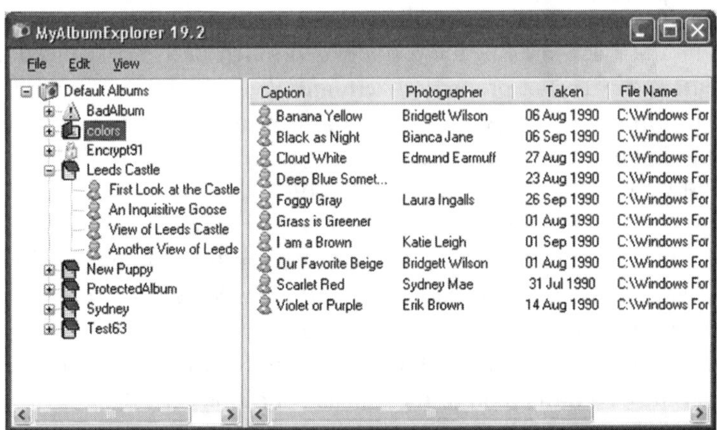

Figure 19.2 Our ListView uses the same icons employed in the AlbumTreeView control.

contains a collection of ColumnHeader objects. An overview of the ColumnHeader class is present in .NET Table 19.4.

.NET Table 19.4 ColumnHeader class

The ColumnHeader class represents a single column in a ListView control. These columns appear when the View property for the control is set to Details, and they display the subitems associated with each item in the view. The ColumnHeader class is part of the System.Windows.Forms namespace. It is derived from the System.ComponentModel.Component class, and supports the ICloneable interface.

Public Properties	*DisplayIndex*	Gets the relative display order for this column.
	ImageIndex	Gets or sets the index for the image to display in this column's header.
	ImageList	Gets the image list used for column images. This is the SmallImageList value for the containing list view.
	Index	Gets the location of this column within the view's Columns collection.
	ListView	Gets the list view control containing this column header.
	Tag	Gets or sets an object to associate with this column.
	Text	Gets or sets the text to display in the column header.
	TextAlign	Gets or sets the horizontal alignment of both the text in the header and the subitems displayed in the column.
	Width	Gets or sets the width of the header in pixels.
Public Methods	*AutoResize*	Resizes the width of the column as indicated by the given ColumnHeaderAutoResizeStyle value.
	Clone	Creates an identical copy of the column header. This new header is not contained in any list view control.

Columns in a list view are filled and populated much like other collections we have seen. The DisplayIndex property determines the order for each column relative to the other columns in the view. Each column can optionally display an image in its header by assigning the ImageIndex or ImageKey property, with the images taken from the list view's SmallImageList property.

In many applications, the columns displayed changes to reflect the information appropriate to the selected item. In our application, for example, we likely want to show different columns for PhotoAlbum data than for Photograph data. In support of this notion, all columns in a ListView control are removed whenever the ListView.Clear method is called. Of course, to remove only the items from a list, you can call the Clear method in the Items collection directly.

As you might expect by now, list view columns can be created directly in Visual Studio or programmatically. In Visual Studio, clicking the ellipsis (…) button associated with the Columns property brings up the familiar Collection Editor window.

Table 19.5 Columns to display in the MyAlbumExplorer application

Displayed Items	Text	Description
Albums	Name	Base filename of the album file
	Title	Title for the album
	Size	Number of `Photograph` objects in the album
Photographs	Caption	Caption for the photo
	Photographer	Photographer for the photo
	Taken	Date the photograph was taken
	File Name	Fully qualified image file name for the photo

You can experiment with this window if you wish. For our purposes, we create columns dynamically to allow us to switch between the album and photograph columns as required.

The following steps add the code to create the columns shown in table 19.5 for each type of data. We use a couple of different versions of the `Add` method on the collection to define the name, width, and alignment of each column. The alignment defaults to `Left`, so we only specify this setting when required.

CREATE COLUMN HEADERS FOR EACH TYPE OF DATA

	Action	Result

1	Modify the `ListAlbumData` method to create the columns to show when album information is displayed.	`private void ListAlbumData(. . .)`
		`{`
		`  // Show albums in list view`
		`  . . .`
		`  // Presume list cleared, so recreate columns`
		`  lvAlbumList.Columns.Add("Name", 80);`
		`  lvAlbumList.Columns.Add("Title", 120);`
		`  lvAlbumList.Columns.Add("Size", 40,`
		`      HorizontalAlignment.Center);`
		
		`  // Add the albums for given node`
		`  . . .`
		`}`

2	Modify the `ListPhotoData` method to create the columns to show when photographic information is displayed.
	
	Note: We could alternately create a `ColumnHeader-Collection` for each set of columns, and assign the correct collection as needed. We didn't do this here for simplicity.
		`private void ListPhotoData(AlbumNode albumNode)`
		`{`
		`  // Show photographs in list view`
		`  . . .`
		`  // Presume contents cleared, so recreate columns`
		`  lvAlbumList.Columns.Add("Caption", 120);`
		`  lvAlbumList.Columns.Add("Photographer", 100);`
		`  lvAlbumList.Columns.Add("Taken", 80,`
		`      HorizontalAlignment.Center);`
		`  lvAlbumList.Columns.Add("File Name", 200);`
		
		`  // Add the photos for given node`
		`  . . .`
		`}`

If you execute this application, the columns now appear when the `Details` view is displayed. The first column is the `ListViewItem` itself; the other columns need to be added explicitly. This is the subject of the next section.

19.2.2 Populating list view columns

The columns in the `Details` view contain both the item label and the text associated with each subitem of the item. The first column, by default, always contains the item label, with the subsequent columns showing the contents of the list item's `SubItems` property. The `SubItems` property contains a collection of `ListViewSubItem` objects. This class is only valid within the `ListViewItem` class, so the fully qualified class name within the Windows Forms namespace is `ListViewItem.ListViewSubItem`.

A summary of this class appears in .NET Table 19.6. As you can see, the members of this class allow the text and style for each subitem to be specified, along with the standard `Bounds`, `Name`, and `Tag` properties. You may recall that the `ListView-Item` class defines the `UseItemStyleForSubItems` property. When this property is `true`, the subitem properties for font and color are ignored and the associated item properties are used instead. When `UseItemStileForSubItems is false`, the explicit settings for each subitem are applied, with the item's properties used only if the corresponding subitem property is `null`.

As for most collections we have seen, subitems can be created using the `Add` method on the collection, or by initializing a new `ListViewItem.ListViewSub-Item` instance directly and then adding it to the collection. The set of subitems can also be created when the `ListViewItem` itself is initialized, as a few of the `List-ViewItem` constructors allow both the item and its subitems to be specified.

.NET Table 19.6 ListViewItem.ListViewSubItem class

The `ListViewSubItem` class represents a property or other value associated with a `ListViewItem` object. A `ListViewSubItem` appears in a `ListView` control when the control's `View` property is set to `Details` or `Tile` and a column is configured for the subitem. The set of `ListViewSubItem` objects associated with an item is defined by the `SubItems` property in the `ListViewItem` object.

This class is defined within the `ListViewItem` class, and is therefore part of the `System.Windows.Forms` namespace.

Public Properties	BackColor	Gets or sets the background `Color` for this subitem
	Bounds	Gets the bounding rectangle for this subitem
	Font	Gets or sets the `Font` for this subitem
	ForeColor	Gets or sets the foreground `Color` for this subitem
	Name	Gets or sets the name assigned to this subitem
	Tag	Gets or sets an `object` to associate with this subitem
	Text	Gets or sets the text string for this subitem
Public Methods	ResetStyle	Restores the style settings for this subitem to their default values

We see this in our code, where we use two different approaches for creating the required subitems. We have already created the columns for our list view, so the following steps only need to update the `LoadAlbumData` and `LoadPhotoData` methods to add the required subitems.

ADD THE PHOTOGRAPH SUBITEMS TO THE LIST

	Action	Result

1	Modify the `LoadAlbumData` method to add the subitems for each item, based on the `AlbumManager` associated with each node.
	
	Note: Since we open multiple albums here, we get the manager noninteractively.
		<pre>private void ListAlbumData(. . .)
		{
		  . . .
		  // Add the albums for given node
		  foreach (AlbumNode aNode in dirNode.AlbumNodes)
		  {
		    string text = . . .;
		    ListViewItem item =. . .Items.Add(text);
		
		    AlbumManager mgr = aNode.GetManager(false);
		    item.ImageKey = aNode.ImageKey;
		    AssignSubItems(item, aNode.AlbumPath, mgr);
		  }
		}</pre>

2	Implement an `AssignSubItems` method for albums that clears the current subitems and resets the item `Text` property.	<pre>private void AssignSubItems(ListViewItem item,
		    string path, AlbumManager mgr)
		{
		  item.SubItems.Clear();
		  item.Text = Path.
		      GetFileNameWithoutExtension(path);
		
		  ListViewItem.ListViewSubItem subitem;</pre>

3	When the manager is `null`, set the subitems to appropriate defaults.	<pre> if (mgr == null)
		  {
		    item.Tag = path;
		    item.SubItems.Add("");
		    subitem = item.SubItems.Add("?");
		    subitem.Tag = 999;
		  }</pre>

4	When a manager exists, create the required subitems using the associated album.	<pre> else
		  {
		    PhotoAlbum album = mgr.Album;
		    int count = album.Count;
		
		    item.Tag = mgr;
		    item.SubItems.Add(album.Title);
		    subitem = item.SubItems.Add(
		                    count.ToString());
		    subitem.Tag = count;
		  }
		}</pre>
		Note: We assign the associated album manager to the `Tag` property here so we can reference it later. In the prior step, we assigned the album path the `Tag` property if the album could not be opened.

This creates the subitems for the album view. The album item is added directly to the list's `Items` collection, and each subitem is added directly to the item's `SubItems` collection in the AssignSubItems method. In steps 3 and 4, we use the Tag property for our objects to record various information we need later in the chapter. The item's Tag property holds the path to the album or the AlbumManager itself. The Size column's subitem holds the actual integer value for the entry in the subitem's Tag property.

We could alternately derive classes from the ListViewItem and ListViewSubItem classes to encapsulate additional information as required, just as we extended the TreeNode class in chapter 18 for a similar purpose. Here we elect to take the shortcut of stuffing our values into the appropriate Tag entries. Both approaches work just fine, although deriving a class is generally more robust and easier to maintain.

We add the subitems for the photo view in a similar manner.

ADD THE PHOTO ALBUM SUBITEMS TO THE LIST

	Action	Result

5	Modify the LoadPhotoData method to create the required subitems for each photograph.	`private void ListPhotoData(AlbumNode albumNode)`
		`{`
		`  . . .`
		`  // Add the photos for given node`
		`  AlbumManager mgr = albumNode.GetManager(true);`
		`  if (mgr != null)`
		`  {`
		`    foreach (Photograph p in mgr.Album)`
		`    {`
		`      ListViewItem item = new . . .;`
		`      **AssignSubItems(item, p);**`
		`      lvAlbumList.Items.Add(item);`
		`    }`
		`  }`
		`}`

6	Implement an AssignSubItems method for photos that clears the current subitems and resets the item properties.	`private void AssignSubItems(`
		`    ListViewItem item, Photograph photo)`
		`{`
		`  item.SubItems.Clear();`
		`  item.Text = photo.Caption;`
		`  item.Tag = photo;`

7	Create the required subitems using the given photograph.	`  ListViewItem.ListViewSubItem subitem;`
		`  item.SubItems.Add(photo.Photographer);`
		`  subitem = item.SubItems.Add(`
		`      photo.DateTaken.ToString("dd MMM yyyy"));`
		`  subitem.Tag = photo.DateTaken;`
		`  item.SubItems.Add(photo.FileName);`
		`}`

Compile and run this code to ensure that it works. Display the Details view to display the new column information. Notice how a horizontal scroll bar automatically appears when the columns are wider than the application window. The width of each column can be adjusted by clicking the vertical line between two columns and dragging it to the left or right.

Congratulations, you have just completed the implementation of your first list view! Your life may never be the same. Before you go off and celebrate, there is one other topic related to columns that is worth some discussion.

TRY IT! The `Tile` value for the `View` enumeration displays the list items as a set of tiles. The large icon is shown with each item's subitems displayed on the right. You can alter the contents of the tiles by changing the columns assigned in the list view. This setting works fine, but the tiles use a default size that is a bit small when the contents of an album are shown. Modify the `LoadAlbumData` and `LoadPhotoData` methods to alter the list view's `TileSize` property dynamically, based on the number of columns assigned to the list. To do this, use the `Font.Height` setting to calculate an appropriate tile size based on the height of the font assigned to the form.

19.2.3 Sorting list view columns

It is typical in applications employing a list view control to sort the contents of the `Details` view whenever a column title is clicked. The first time the title is clicked, the items are sorted based on the column's contents in *ascending* order, or a to z order for strings; and a second click sorts in *descending*, or z to a, order. Supporting this behavior in your applications depends on your own circumstance. Many Windows users expect such behavior, and may find it odd if it is not provided. In this section we look at how to implement column sorting, using our MyAlbumExplorer application as an example.

The `ListView` class provides three members of particular importance when you wish to sort a column in the `Details` view:

- The `Sorting` property defines how the items are initially sorted. This is a `SortOrder` enumeration value, one of `None` for no sorting, `Ascending`, or `Descending`. The default is `None`, which is why our application currently displays items in the order they were added to the list.
- The `ColumnClick` event occurs when a column is clicked. This is used to modify the control's sorting behavior as appropriate for the selected column. Event handlers for this event receive a `ColumnClickEventArgs` parameter that contains a `Column` property indicating the column header clicked by the user.
- The `ListViewItemSorter` property defines the `IComparer` interface used to compare two `ListViewItem` objects in the list. The `IComparer` interface is presented in .NET Table 19.7. When the `ListViewItemSorter` property is assigned, the `Sort` method is called automatically.

We use each of these members to define sorting behavior in our application. To do this, we first define a class supporting the `IComparer` interface, and then use this class to implement a `ColumnClick` event handler.

To sort a ListView control's contents, the comparison must compare two ListViewItem objects and return an appropriate value depending on how the

.NET Table 19.7 IComparer interface

The IComparer interface defines an interface for comparing two objects, and is part of the System.Collections namespace. This namespace also provides two implementations of this interface for comparing string objects. The Comparer class supports case-sensitive comparisons, while the CaseInsensitiveComparer class supports case-insensitive comparisons. Both of these classes provide a static DefaultInvariant member that returns an initialized instance of the class for the invariant culture.

Public Methods	Compare	Returns an integer value indicating the equality relationship between two object instances. The value returned is less than zero, zero, or greater than zero, corresponding to whether the first object is less than, equal to, or greater than the second, respectively.

application wishes to sort its items. The ListView object itself defines the current sorting order based on the Sorting property value. Typically, an application tracks how items should be sorted as part of an IComparer implementation.

We can see this with an example in our MyAlbumExplorer application, using the not-so-creative name MyListViewComparer for a comparison class. The following steps define this class.

DEFINE A COMPARER CLASS FOR THE LIST VIEW

	Action	Result

1	Create a new MyListViewComparer class in the MyAlbumExplorer project, and adjust the using declarations as indicated.	`using System;`
		`using System.Collections;`
		`using System.Windows.Forms;`
		
		`namespace MyAlbumExplorer`
		`{`

2	Define the class as internal.	`internal class MyListViewComparer : IComparer` `{`

3	Define a private ListView field property to hold the list view associated with the comparer.	`// ListView to sort`
		`private ListView _listView;`
		
		`private ListView ListView`
		`{ get { return _listView; } }`

4	Define a private field to hold the column to sort, and a public SortColumn property so the caller can assign this column.	`// Track the current sorting column`
		`private int _sortColumn;`
		
		`public int SortColumn`
		`{`
		`get { return _sortColumn; }`
		`set { _sortColumn = value; }`
		`}`

	DEFINE A COMPARER CLASS FOR THE LIST VIEW *(CONTINUED)*	
	Action	**Result**

5	In the constructor, require that the caller provide the `ListView` that holds the items to compare.	`// Public constructor requires ListView`
		`public MyListViewComparer(ListView lv)`
		`{`
		`  _listView = lv;`
		`  _sortColumn = 0;`
		`}`

6	Define the `Compare` method required by the `IComparer` interface.	`public int Compare(object x, object y)` `{`

7	In this method, convert the two objects into list view items.	`  // Throws exception if not list items`
		`  ListViewItem item1 = (ListViewItem)x;`
		`  ListViewItem item2 = (ListViewItem)y;`

8	Swap the two items if the current sorting order is descending.
	
	Note: We could handle the sort order as part of each comparison, but swapping the items up front seems easier.
		`  // Swap items if descending order`
		`  if (ListView.Sorting`
		`          == SortOrder.Descending)`
		`  {`
		`    ListViewItem temp = item1;`
		`    item1 = item2;`
		`    item2 = temp;`
		`  }`

9	Handle the case where the current view is not `Details`.
	
	Note: When assigned to a `ListView`, the comparer is called whenever the items must be sorted, regardless of the current view.
		`  // Handle non-column case`
		`  if (ListView.View != View.Details)`
		`  {`
		`    return CaseInsensitiveComparer.`
		`        DefaultInvariant.`
		`        Compare(item1.Text, item2.Text);`
		`  }`

10	Otherwise, retrieve the subitems to compare and call a `CompareSubItems` method to perform the comparison.	`  // Get the subitems to compare`
		`  ListViewItem.ListViewSubItem sub1`
		`      = item1.SubItems[SortColumn];`
		`  ListViewItem.ListViewSubItem sub2`
		`      = item2.SubItems[SortColumn];`
		
		`  return CompareSubItems(sub1, sub2);`
		`}`

11	Implement a `CompareSubItems` method to compare the subitems as strings if the `Tag` property is not assigned.	`private static int CompareSubItems(`
		`  ListViewItem.ListViewSubItem sub1,`
		`  ListViewItem.ListViewSubItem sub2)`
		`{`
		`  if (sub1.Tag == null || sub2.Tag == null)`
		`  {`
		`    // Compare as strings`
		`    return CaseInsensitiveComparer.`
		`      DefaultInvariant.Compare(`
		`        sub1.Text,`
		`        sub2.Text);`
		`  }`

DEFINE A COMPARER CLASS FOR THE LIST VIEW *(CONTINUED)*		
	Action	**Result**

12	Otherwise, if the two subitems are integers, compare the values using the integer `CompareTo` method.	`else if (sub1.Tag is Int32)`
		`{`
		`  // Compare as integers`
		`  int x1 = (Int32)sub1.Tag;`
		`  int x2 = (Int32)sub2.Tag;`
		
		`  return x1.CompareTo(x2);`
		`}`

13	Otherwise, if the two subitems are dates, compare the values using the date-time `CompareTo` method.	`else if (sub1.Tag is DateTime)`
		`{`
		`  // Compare as dates`
		`  DateTime x1 = (DateTime)sub1.Tag;`
		`  DateTime x2 = (DateTime)sub2.Tag;`
		
		`  return x1.CompareTo(x2);`
		`}`

14	For all other data types, throw an exception indicating the items were not recognized.	`throw new ArgumentException("Unable to "`
		`  + "compare ListViewItem instances");`
		`  }`
		` }`
		`}`

We leverage the fact here that we assigned the actual value of each subitem to the `Tag` property for all nonstring columns. Knowing this, we sort the items based on the `Type` of the first item. We only handle integer and date-time types in our code, as these are the only types required for our sample. Additional types could be added in a similar manner.

To hook this comparer to our actual form, we create an instance of the `MyListViewComparer` class in our `ExplorerForm` class and assign it as the comparer for our list. We use the `Sort` method to force the list to re-sort whenever the settings change. This continues our previous steps.

IMPLEMENT SORTING WHEN A COLUMN IS CLICKED		
	Action	**Result**

15	In the ExplorerForm.cs file, define a private variable to hold the comparer class for the form.	`private MyListViewComparer _comparer;`
		`private MyListViewComparer MyComparer`
		`    { get { return _comparer; } }`

16	Create this comparer in the `OnLoad` method.	`protected override void OnLoad(EventArgs e)`
		`{`
		`  . . .`
		`  _comparer = new MyListViewComparer(`
		`                    lvAlbumList);`
		`  lvAlbumList.ListViewItemSorter = MyComparer;`
		`  . . .`
		`}`

	IMPLEMENT SORTING WHEN A COLUMN IS CLICKED *(CONTINUED)*	
	Action	**Result**

17	Handle the `ColumnClick` event for the `lvAlbumList` list view.	`private void lvAlbumList_ColumnClick(`
		`    object sender, ColumnClickEventArgs e)`
		`{`

18	If the current column is the sort column, then switch the sorting style between ascending and descending.	`  if (e.Column == MyComparer.SortColumn)`
		`  {`
		`    // Switch the sort order for this column`
		`    if (lvAlbumList.Sorting`
		`            == SortOrder.Ascending)`
		`      lvAlbumList.Sorting = SortOrder.Descending;`
		`    else`
		`      lvAlbumList.Sorting = SortOrder.Ascending;`
		`  }`

19	Otherwise, assign the clicked column as the sort column and use ascending as the sorting style.	`  else`
		`  {`
		`    // Define new sort column and order`
		`    MyComparer.SortColumn = e.Column;`
		`    lvAlbumList.Sorting = SortOrder.Ascending;`
		`  }`

20	Either way, re-sort the list at the end of the handler.	`  lvAlbumList.Sort();` `}`

Our comparison class implements sorting on behalf of the view based on the current settings. The `ColumnClick` event handler adjusts the sort settings for the given column, and assigns the comparer to ensure the items are re-sorted. Together, these changes ensure that the list is sorted based on the column clicked by the user.

Compile and run to verify that this sorting works as advertised. You may notice that if you sort the last column in the photograph display, and then switch to an album display, an error occurs because the current sort column index is greater than the number of columns.

We can fix this problem by resetting the sort values whenever new data is displayed. This makes use of the `ShowingAlbums` property we added in our `ExplorerForm` class to identify when sorting should be reset.

	RESET SORT SETTINGS WHEN REQUIRED	
	Action	**Result**

21	In the `AfterSelect` event handler for the tree view control, note the type of data currently shown.	`private void atvAlbumTree_AfterSelect(`
		`    object sender, TreeViewEventArgs e)`
		`{`
		`  try`
		`  {`
		`    **bool oldShowingAlbums = ShowingAlbums;**`
		`    lvAlbumList.BeginUpdate();`
		`    . . .`

RESET SORT SETTINGS WHEN REQUIRED *(CONTINUED)*		
	Action	**Result**

22	When the type of data shown changes, reset the sort settings.	`else`
		`  throw new ArgumentException(. . .);`
		
		`if (lvAlbumList.Visible`
		`    && ShowingAlbums != oldShowingAlbums)`
		`{`
		`  // Columns changed, so reset sorting`
		`  MyComparer.SortColumn = 0;`
		`  lvAlbumList.Sorting = SortOrder.Ascending;`
		`}`
		`}`
		`finally`
		`  . . .`
		`}`

Twenty-two steps in one section. That might be a record. This completes our discussion of columns and sorting. Our `ListView` control now displays both album and photo items in a variety of views, and sorts the columns for both types of data when the `Details` view is shown.

TRY IT! The `AllowColumnReorder` property indicates that users may rearrange columns by clicking and dragging them with the mouse. Set this property to `true` to see how this works. What happens when you sort a column after reordering the columns? Note that the `ColumnClick` event does not occur during a drag, even though the user must click and then release the column header.

19.3 LIST VIEW FEATURES

Our discussion so far has focused on how to display items in a list view. We have examined the `ListView` control itself, and the classes for items, subitems, and columns. In this section we look at how to manipulate specific items within the list. These features allow an application to interact with displayed items to alter their appearance, properties, or some other aspect. We look at the following topics:

- Viewing the properties associated with a selected item
- Editing the label of an item
- Taking an action when a user double-clicks an item

The first two topics cover familiar ground, in that we have seen selection and editing of items in other chapters. The final topic is related to something called item activation.

19.3.1 Selecting items

Like the `ListBox` control, a list view can support single item or multi-item selection. The `MultiSelect` property gets or sets a boolean value that indicates whether multiple selection is enabled. Much like the list box control, the collection of items selected in a list view is available via the `SelectedItems` and `Selected-Indices` properties.

Since we looked at multiple selection in chapter 11, we stick with single selection in this chapter. As an example, we add a Properties menu to our application that displays the properties dialog box for the selected item. Figure 19.3 illustrates this new behavior for a selected album.

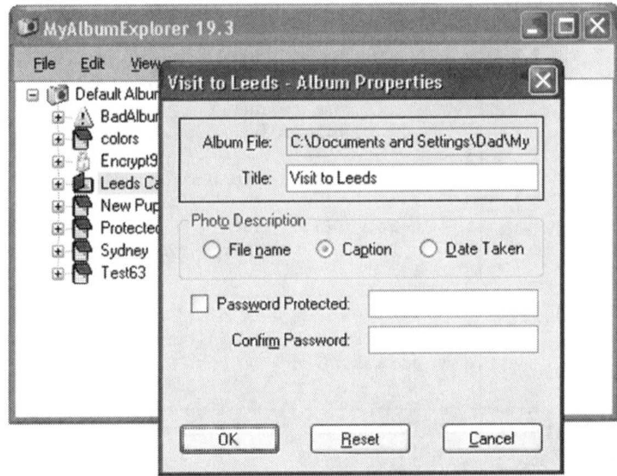

Figure 19.3 The Properties menu displays the appropriate dialog box for the selected tree node or list view item.

In our code, we must account for both the tree view and list view controls, in that we should probably display the properties dialog box for the selected item in whichever control has the focus. The following steps add the new menu and implement a `Click` event handler to enable this behavior.

ADD A MENU TO DISPLAY ALBUM PROPERTIES		
	Action	**Result**
1	In the ExplorerForm.cs [Design] window, add a Properties menu under the Edit menu. **Settings** **Property** / **Value** (Name): menuEdit-Properties Text: &Properties...	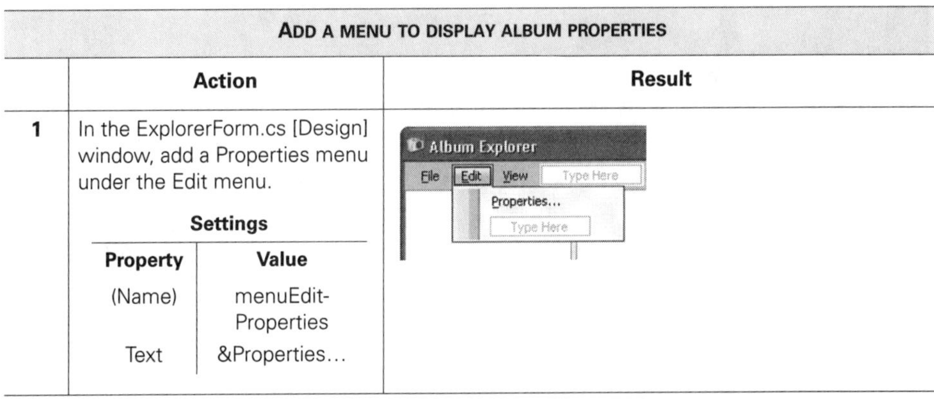

	ADD A MENU TO DISPLAY ALBUM PROPERTIES *(CONTINUED)*	
	Action	**Result**

2	Add a `Click` event handler for this menu to display the property dialog box for the selected item or node.	<pre>private void menuEditProperties_Click(
		    object sender, EventArgs e)
		{
		  // Note: picture box cannot receive focus
		  if (lvAlbumList.Focused)
		    DisplayListItemProperties();
		  else if (atvAlbumTree.Focused)
		    DisplayTreeNodeProperties();
		}</pre>

3	Implement a `DisplayTree-NodeProperties` method to display the properties dialog box for the selected tree node.	<pre>private void DisplayTreeNodeProperties()
		{
		  TreeNode node = atvAlbumTree.SelectedNode;
		  if (node is AlbumNode)
		  {
		    AlbumNode aNode = (AlbumNode) node;
		    AlbumManager mgr = aNode.GetManager(true);
		    if (mgr != null)
		      DisplayAlbumProperties(mgr);
		  }
		  else if (node is PhotoNode)
		  {
		    PhotoNode pNode = (PhotoNode)node;
		    DisplayPhotoProperties(pNode.Photograph);
		  }</pre>

4	At the end of this method, save any changes made to the photograph or album.	<pre> // Preserve and display any changes
		  atvAlbumTree.SaveAlbumChanges();
		  atvAlbumTree.RefreshNode();
		}</pre>

5	Implement a `DisplayList-ItemProperties` method to display the properties dialog box for the selected list view item, if any.
	
	How-to
	Use the `Tag` property to display the appropriate dialog box, and save any changes made by the user.
		<pre>private void DisplayListItemProperties()
		{
		  if (lvAlbumList.SelectedItems.Count == 1)
		  {
		    ListViewItem item
		        = lvAlbumList.SelectedItems[0];
		    if (item.Tag is AlbumManager)
		    {
		      AlbumManager mgr = (AlbumManager)item.Tag;
		      DisplayAlbumProperties(mgr);
		      AssignSubItems(item, mgr.FullName, mgr);
		
		      if (mgr.Album.HasChanged)
		        mgr.Save();
		    }</pre>

6	When displaying a photo dialog box, save any changes by saving the album node that caused this photo item to display.	<pre> else if (item.Tag is Photograph)
		    {
		      Photograph photo = (Photograph)item.Tag;
		      DisplayPhotoProperties(photo);
		
		      if (photo.HasChanged)
		      {
		        AssignSubItems(item, photo);
		        atvAlbumTree.SaveAlbumChanges();
		      }
		    }</pre>

	Add a menu to display album properties *(continued)*	
	Action	**Result**

7	If the `Tag` property for the item is not recognized, display an appropriate dialog box.	<pre> else
		      MessageBox.Show("The properties for this"
		          + " item cannot be displayed.");
		  }
		}</pre>**Note:** Here and throughout the rest of the book, we use the simplest form of the `MessageBox` dialog box. Feel free to use an alternate form if you prefer, as discussed in chapter 7.

8	Implement a `DisplayAlbum-Properties` method to display the properties dialog box for an album.	<pre>private void DisplayAlbumProperties(
		    AlbumManager mgr)
		{
		  using (AlbumEditDialog dlg
		            = new AlbumEditDialog(mgr))
		  {
		    dlg.ShowDialog();
		  }
		}</pre>

9	Implement a `DisplayPhoto-Properties` method to display the properties dialog box for a photograph.	<pre>private void DisplayPhotoProperties(
		    Photograph photo)
		{
		  using (PhotoEditDialog dlg
		            = new PhotoEditDialog(photo))
		  {
		    dlg.ShowDialog();
		  }
		}</pre>

This code is slightly involved, so we break it up into a number of methods to encapsulate and reuse the logic required. In the `Click` event handler for our Properties menu, we determine whether the `TreeView` or the `ListView` has focus, and invoke the corresponding method accordingly. The actual dialog boxes are broken out into additional methods so we can reuse the `DisplayAlbumProperties` and `DisplayPhotoProperties` methods in our display methods for each control.

The remainder of this code is fairly self-explanatory. In our `ListView` control, the `Tag` property records the object associated with the current item, which might be an `AlbumManager`, a `Photograph`, or the `string` path to an invalid or encrypted album. This works well in our application since we only display two kinds of items. In a more complex application this approach might be problematic.

An alternative tactic, of course, is to derive a new class from the `ListViewItem` or `ListViewSubItem` class for each type of object displayed. For applications with many kinds of items, this allows each item class to encapsulate operations specific to its object. In some cases, it may also be beneficial to create a base item class functionally common to all custom items.

As we have mentioned more than once, it is often good practice to encapsulate items in this fashion. Aside from the organizational and maintenance benefits, it reduces the size of your main `Form` class, which in our application is starting to get a bit large.

19.3.2 Editing item labels

Another feature worth examining is the ability to edit item labels. Editing an item label in place is one of the advantages the `ListView` class has over `ListBox` objects. In our application we use this feature to allow a user to edit the album name or photograph caption, much like we enabled this feature in our `AlbumTreeView` class.

Label editing is disabled by default, and turned on by setting the `LabelEdit` property to `true`. An actual edit of an item is initiated by the `ListViewItem.BeginEdit` method. Much like the `TreeView` control, the `ListView` control receives two events during the editing process: the `BeforeLabelEdit` event occurs before the edit process begins, while the `AfterLabelEdit` event occurs when the user completes the edit by pressing the Enter key or clicking outside of the edit area. Event handlers for both events receive the `LabelEditEventArgs` class as their event handler. The members of this class are shown in .NET Table 19.8.

.NET Table 19.8 LabelEditEventArgs class

The `LabelEditEventArgs` class specifies the event arguments for the `BeforeLabelEdit` and `AfterLabelEdit` events in the `ListView` class. This class is part of the `System.Windows.Forms` namespace, and inherits from the `System.EventArgs` class.

Public Properties	CancelEdit	Gets or sets whether the edit operation should be canceled. This can be set before or after the item is edited.
	Item	Gets the zero-based index of the item to be edited.
	Label	Gets the new text to assign to the label of the indicated item.

In our application, we allow an item to be edited in two ways. The first is through a Label menu under the top-level Edit menu, and the second is by selecting an item and pressing the F2 key. This second mechanism matches the keyboard shortcut supported by Windows Explorer and our `AlbumTreeView` control, so it seems appropriate here.

The code changes required are given in the following steps.

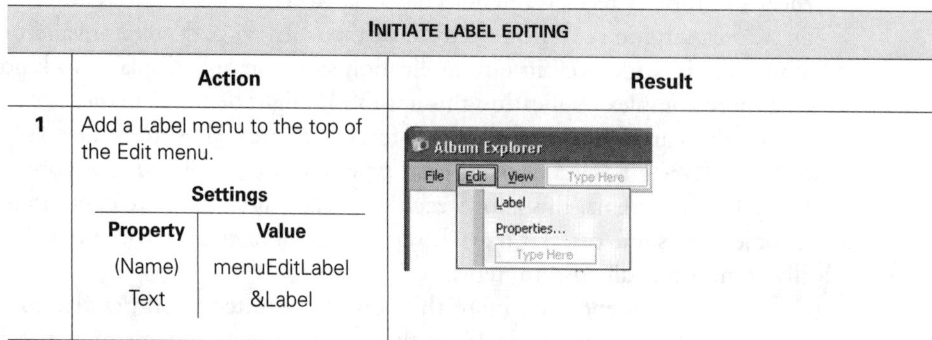

INITIATE LABEL EDITING

	Action	Result
1	Add a Label menu to the top of the Edit menu. **Settings** **Property** / **Value** (Name): menuEditLabel Text: &Label	(screenshot)

INITIATE LABEL EDITING *(CONTINUED)*		
	Action	**Result**

2	Handle the `DropDownOpening` event for the Edit menu to enable and set the `Text` of our menu appropriately.	<pre>private void menuEdit_DropDownOpening(
		    object sender, EventArgs e)
		{
		  menuEditLabel.Enabled = true;
		  if (lvAlbumList.Focused)
		    menuEditLabel.Text = "Captio&n";
		  else if (atvAlbumTree.Focused)
		    menuEditLabel.Text = "&Name";
		  else
		    menuEditLabel.Enabled = false;
		}</pre>

3	Add a `Click` event handler for the new menu.	<pre>private void menuEditLabel_Click
		    (object sender, EventArgs e)
		{</pre>

4	Within this handler, if an item is selected, edit the item.	<pre> if (lvAlbumList.Focused)
		  {
		    if (lvAlbumList.FocusedItem != null)
		      lvAlbumList.FocusedItem.BeginEdit();
		  }
		  else if (atvAlbumTree.Focused)
		  {
		    if (atvAlbumTree.SelectedNode != null)
		      atvAlbumTree.SelectedNode.BeginEdit();
		  }
		}</pre>

5	Also add a `KeyDown` event handler for the `ListView` control that edits the item with focus when the F2 key is pressed.	<pre>private void lvAlbumList_KeyDown(
		    object sender, KeyEventArgs e)
		{
		  if (e.KeyCode == Keys.F2)
		  {
		    if (lvAlbumList.FocusedItem != null)
		      lvAlbumList.FocusedItem.BeginEdit();
		    e.Handled = true;
		  }
		}</pre>

That's all it takes to edit our items. The actual work of interacting with the user is handled by the framework. This code allows a user to initiate an edit; the next step is to process the completed edit of an item.

As you may recall, our `AlbumTreeView` control handles editing internally, so here we need to handle our list view control. An `AfterLabelEdit` event handler is well suited for this purpose. There is also a `BeforeLabelEdit` event that is useful for selectively permitting an edit or altering an item before the edit begins. In a production environment, we would probably handle both events. The `BeginLabelEdit` event handler would ensure the item is valid and can be edited by the user. The `AfterLabelEdit` event handler would update the item appropriately.

In our code, we take the easy way out and only handle the `AfterLabelEdit` event. This means a user may edit an album only to find that the changes cannot be saved, which may not be the best interface from a usability perspective but suffices for our example.

PROCESS A LABEL EDIT		
	Action	**Result**

6	Add an `AfterLabelEdit` event handler for the `ListView` control.	`private void lvAlbumList_AfterLabelEdit`
		`    (object sender, LabelEditEventArgs e)`
		`{`

7	If the user canceled the edit, then we are finished.
	
	Note: For example, if the Esc key is pressed during editing, this handler is invoked with a `null` label.
		`  if (String.IsNullOrEmpty(e.Label))`
		`  {`
		`    e.CancelEdit = true;`
		`    return;`
		`  }`

8	In this handler, locate the item to be edited.	`  ListViewItem item = lvAlbumList.Items[e.Item];`

9	If the item is a photograph, modify the caption of the photo, and save the modified album.	`  if (item.Tag is Photograph)`
		`  {`
		`    Photograph photo = (Photograph)item.Tag;`
		`    photo.Caption = e.Label;`
		`    if (photo.HasChanged)`
		`      atvAlbumTree.SaveAlbumChanges();`
		`  }`

10	Otherwise, use the new label to rename the album associated with the item.	`  else`
		`  {`
		`    RenameAlbum(item, e.Label);`
		`  }`
		`}`

11	Implement a `RenameAlbum` method that tries to rename the given album to the new name.	`private void RenameAlbum(`
		`    ListViewItem item, string newName)`
		`{`
		`  try`
		`  {`
		`    string oldPath = null;`
		`    string newPath = null;`

12	If the item is associated with an `AlbumManager`, use this class to rename the album.	`    if (item.Tag is AlbumManager)`
		`    {`
		`      AlbumManager mgr = (AlbumManager)item.Tag;`
		`      oldPath = mgr.FullName;`
		`      mgr.RenameAlbum(newName);`
		`      newPath = mgr.FullName;`
		`    }`

13	If the item is associated with an album path string, then use the static `RenameAlbum` to rename the album.	`    else if (item.Tag is string)`
		`    {`
		`      // Presume tag is album path`
		`      oldPath = (string)item.Tag;`
		`      newPath = AlbumManager.RenameAlbum(`
		`                  oldPath, newName);`
		`      item.Tag = newPath;`
		`    }`

PROCESS A LABEL EDIT *(CONTINUED)*		
	Action	**Result**

14	If a path was found and renamed, then update the album node in the tree view if it is visible.	`if (oldPath != null)`
		`{`
		`  // Update the album node`
		`  AlbumNode aNode`
		`    = atvAlbumTree.FindAlbumNode(oldPath);`
		`  if (aNode != null)`
		`    aNode.UpdatePath(newPath);`
		`}`

15	If an argument exception occurs trying to rename the album, display a message box to this effect.	`}`
		`catch (ArgumentException aex)`
		`{`
		`  MessageBox.Show("Unable to rename album. ["`
		`    + aex.Message + "]");`
		`}`
		`}`

This relies on the `Tag` property of the item to identify what type of item has been modified. For photograph items we alter the caption and save the modified album. For albums, we use the `RenameAlbum` method created in chapter 18 to rename the album file path.

Our application now supports displaying item properties and editing item labels. The last feature we discuss is item activation.

19.3.3 Activating items

As you might expect, item activation is the means by which an item is displayed or otherwise activated by the control. Normally, activation is just a fancy way to say double-click. In our `ListBox` class in chapter 10, we activated an item in the list by handling the `DoubleClick` event and displaying the properties dialog box associated with the item. Such behavior is activation.

The reason for the fancy term is that the `ListView` class allows a few different activation styles. The `Activation` property holds an `ItemActivation` enumeration value that determines the type of activation supported. The possible values for this enumeration are shown in .NET Table 19.9. Note that the `OneClick` style is

.NET Table 19.9 ItemActivation enumeration

The `ItemActivation` enumeration specifies the type of activation supported by a control. This enumeration is part of the `System.Windows.Forms` namespace.

Enumeration Values	OneClick	A single click activates an item. The cursor appears as a hand pointer, and the item text changes color as the mouse pointer passes over the item.
	Standard	A double-click activates an item.
	TwoClick	A double-click activates an item, plus the item text changes color as the mouse pointer passes over the item.

similar to an HTML link in a web browser. In our program, we stick with standard activation.

Regardless of how items are activated, an `ItemActivate` event occurs whenever an item is activated. The event handler for this event receives a standard `System.EventArgs` parameter, so the activated item must be obtained from the `SelectedItems` collection.

The activation behavior for our MyAlbumExplorer application displays the contents of the activated item. For an album this consists of the photographs in the album; for a photograph this is the photographic image itself. Our tree view already does this: a selected album node displays the photographs while a selected photo node displays the image. So the task for our code is to find the desired node and select it.

<table>
<tr><th colspan="3">HANDLE THE ITEMACTIVATE EVENT</th></tr>
<tr><th></th><th>Action</th><th>Result</th></tr>
<tr><td>1</td><td>Add an <code>ItemActivate</code> event handler to the <code>ListView</code> control.</td><td><pre>private void lvAlbumList_ItemActivate(
    object sender, EventArgs e)
{</pre></td></tr>
<tr><td>2</td><td>Implement this method to find the item to activate.</td><td><pre> // ListViewItem is visible and selected
  ListViewItem item
      = lvAlbumList.SelectedItems[0];</pre></td></tr>
<tr><td>3</td><td>If albums are shown, then locate the album node associated with the activated album item.</td><td><pre> TreeNode node = null;
  if (ShowingAlbums)
  {
    string albumPath;
    AlbumManager mgr = item.Tag as AlbumManager;
    if (mgr == null)
      albumPath = item.Tag as string;
    else
      albumPath = mgr.FullName;

    if (albumPath != null)
      node = atvAlbumTree.
                 FindAlbumNode(albumPath);
  }</pre></td></tr>
<tr><td>4</td><td>Otherwise, locate the photo node associated with the activated photo item.</td><td><pre> else
  {
    Photograph photo = item.Tag as Photograph;
    if (photo != null)
      node = atvAlbumTree.FindPhotoNode(photo);
  }</pre></td></tr>
<tr><td>5</td><td>In either case, if a node was found, select this node in the tree view control.</td><td><pre> if (node != null)
    atvAlbumTree.SelectedNode = node;
}</pre></td></tr>
</table>

Our `TreeView` makes the activation logic quite simple; when a new tree view node is selected, our code for the `BeforeSelect` and `AfterSelect` events fires and updates the application appropriately. Try activating an album when the associated album directory node is collapsed and expanded to make sure this works correctly in both cases.

This completes our MyAlbumExplorer application discussion. The following Try It! offers some ways to further explore the `ListView` control. Before we leave this chapter completely, a brief example using virtual items is provided.

TRY IT! There are, of course, many ways to extend the MyAlbumExplorer application code. Here are some ideas you can pursue if you are interested:

- Add a new File menu called Add that prompts the user for a new directory path and adds it as a new album directory node.
- The `ColumnHeader` class can display an icon in the column heading, as defined by the `ImageList` or `ImageKey` property and taken from the list view's `SmallImageList` collection. Add appropriate up and down arrow icons to the end of this image list, and use these to indicate the column that is currently sorted, as well as the sort order of the column.
- Add a new View menu item called Thumbnails. Set the `OwnerDraw` property of the `ListItem` to `true` for this menu item, and `false` for the existing menu items. Handle the `DrawItem` event to draw a `LargeIcon` style of view that displays the actual image associated with each photo rather than the associated icon. Use the `Graphics` instance provided to draw the image and caption for the photograph. The `DrawListViewItemEventArgs` class provides some useful properties and methods for this task, such as the `State` property to determine if the item is selected or has focus and the `DrawFocusRectangle` method to draw a focus rectangle.

19.4 VIRTUAL ITEMS

One of the new features added to the `ListView` control for .NET 2.0 is support for virtual items. Prior to 2.0, a list view always held its entire contents in memory at all times. This is fine in the majority of cases, but fails miserably when displaying a huge database or other very large list of items.

As a quick example, consider the application shown in figure 19.4. A user can select a number from one to a billion, and the list view displays a list of numbers from zero to one less than the selected number, with each number shown in string rather than numeric form.

This application is contrived, of course, but illustrates the idea of having too many entries to display at once within the list. By setting the `VirtualMode` property to `true`, a list view invokes the `RetrieveVirtualItem` event to obtain each item in the list.

The critical code to implement this application is shown in listing 19.1.

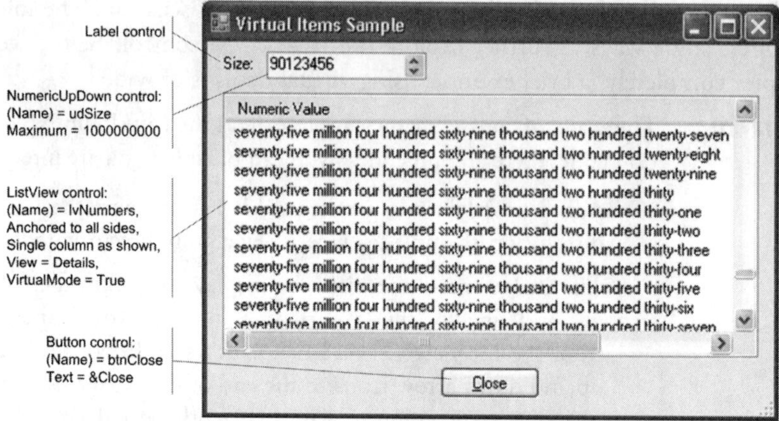

Figure 19.4 This graphic provides the types and settings used for each control on the form so you can create this form yourself if you wish.

Listing 19.1 Sample ListView application using virtual items

```
using System;
using System.Windows.Forms;

namespace ListViewSample
{
  public partial class ListViewForm : Form
  {
    public ListViewForm()
    {
      InitializeComponent();
    }

    // Strings for numbers from zero to nineteen
    string[] ones = { "zero", "one", "two", "three",
        . . ., "seventeen", "eighteen", "nineteen" };

    // Strings for numbers by tens from zero to ninety
    string[] tens = { "zero", "ten", "twenty",
        . . ., "sixty", "seventy", "eighty", "ninety" };

    private void lvNumbers_RetrieveVirtualItem(object sender,
        RetrieveVirtualItemEventArgs e)
    {
      int x = e.ItemIndex;

      string numString = NumericString(x);
      ListViewItem item = new ListViewItem(numString);
      e.Item = item;
    }

    private string NumericString(int x)
    {
```

1 Converts given index to numeric string

```
        if (x < 20)
          return ones[x];
        else if (x < 100)
        {
          int n = x % 10;
          x = x / 10;

          if (n == 0) return tens[x];
          else return tens[x] + "-" + ones[n];
        }
        else if (x < 1000)
        {
          string result = NumericString(x / 100) + " hundred ";
          return result + NumericString(x % 100);
        }
        else if (x < 1000000)
        {
          string result = NumericString(x / 1000) + " thousand ";
          return result + NumericString(x % 1000);
        }
        else if (x < 1000000000)
        {
          string result = NumericString(x / 1000000) + " million ";
          return result + NumericString(x % 1000000);
        }
        else
          return "number too big";
      }

      private void nudSize_ValueChanged(object sender, EventArgs e)
      {
        lvNumbers.VirtualListSize = (int)nudSize.Value;    <-- 2 Modifies the virtual size of the list
      }

      private void btnClose_Click(object sender, EventArgs e)
      {
        Close();
      }
    }
  }
```

Two points to highlight in this code are as follows:

1. When a virtual item is required, the `NumericString` method converts the desired index into a numeric string. The `RetrieveVirtualItem` event handler receives a `RetrieveVirtualItemEventArgs` instance that provides the required item index and receives the item to display.
2. When the user changes the number in the `NumericUpDown` control, the `VirtualListSize` property for the list is altered to define the new virtual size of the list.

When a list is in virtual mode, the following events are also available to permit more detailed management of the list. We do not use these events here, but in more complex scenarios they can be very useful.

- `CacheVirtualItems`: Occurs when the range of items required in the list changes. An event handler can cache or otherwise make the required data available to the application.
- `SearchForVirtualItem`: Occurs when a search occurs on a virtual list. An event handler can use the given criteria to locate the desired item in the virtual list.
- `VirtualItemsSelectionRangeChanged`: Occurs when items are selected or deselected in a virtual list. An event handler can alter the application appropriately based on the change.

19.5 RECAP

This chapter discussed the `ListView` control in detail, and extended the MyAlbumExplorer interface built in chapter 18 to include such a control. We began with our typical overview of the control, and added a list view to our MyAlbumExplorer application to create a traditional explorer interface.

We populated the list view with the contents of the selected tree node, either albums or photographs. Over the course of the chapter we supported all of the various view styles provided by the `ListView` control. This required columns for the details view and subitems for the detail and tiles view. We examined the `ListViewItem` class to represent list items, and the `ListViewItem.ListViewSubItem` class to hold the subitems for each item.

We also built a custom `IComparer` class to support column sorting within the list. We then reviewed some common features of list views, namely item selection, label editing, and item activation.

We finished the chapter with an example of the virtual items feature added as part of the .NET 2.0 release. Virtual items allow an application to display a huge list of items without keeping all of the item data in memory at once.

Chapters 18 and 19 have shown an example of an explorer interface, so it seems appropriate to make the next chapter discuss another interface style: the multiple document interface, or MDI.

CHAPTER 20

Multiple document interfaces

In the previous two chapters, we discussed the `ListView` and `TreeView` classes, which present a collection of objects within a single list or tree control. They are especially useful when creating an explorer-style interface such as our MyAlbumExplorer application, or the common Windows Explorer application. In chapter 18 we briefly discussed another kind of interface: the multiple document interface, or MDI (pronounced *em-dee-eye*).

An MDI application presents a collection of forms within a single application window. This style has fallen out of favor in recent years in lieu of more recent styles that are thought to be more useful. This includes the multiple single document interface style employed by Microsoft Word, and the multiple tabbed documents interface style employed by the Firefox web browser and Visual Studio. These styles were discussed in chapter 18 so we won't go into these again here.

The MDI style is still useful in some situations, and is worth understanding from a programming perspective before more complex interface styles are attempted. So we spend this chapter looking at this style and extending our MyPhotos application with this capability. This involves the following discussion areas:

- Creating an MDI container window
- Converting an SDI application into an MDI application
- Merging menu and tool strips into a single merged strip
- Using MDI-related members of various control classes
- Managing child windows in an MDI application

These topics are covered as we progress through the chapter, beginning with the creation of MDI container forms.

20.1 MDI FORMS

An MDI application requires a parent window to hold the multiple child windows for the application. In .NET, the `Form` class we know and love includes support for this kind of window, called an MDI container window. A MDI container in .NET appears with a special background color to indicate that it can hold multiple child windows. These child windows are themselves `Form` objects as well.

In this section we convert our existing MyPhotos application into an MDI application. This initial work is not as difficult as you might think. We need one `Form` to act as the top-level container, and the ability to create other forms as children within this container. We do this via the following three tasks:

1. Create a new parent form for the application to act as the MDI container.
2. Add a menu bar and New menu item to create MDI child forms.
3. Update our `Main` method to create the parent form.

Figure 20.1 In this window, the menu display is very strange. We explain and address these issues in section 20.2.

For our MyPhotos application, of course, other work is required to clean up the behavior of our application. These steps get us going, and subsequent sections deal with the additional changes. Figure 20.1 shows our application at the end of this section. Note in particular the two File menus. We address this issue in the next section while discussing merged menus.

20.1.1 Creating an MDI container

An MDI container form is created much like any other form. Such a form is often referred to as a parent form, since it acts as the parent for one or more MDI child forms. The details for this task are shown in the following steps.

CREATE A NEW FORM AS AN MDI CONTAINER

	Action	Result
1	In the MyPhotos solutions, add a new Windows Form to the MyPhotos project called `ParentForm`, and set its properties as follows. **Settings** **Property** / **Value** (Name) / ParentForm IsMdiContainer / True Size / 600, 400	ParentForm
2	Set the icon property for this form to the "icons/WinXP/camera.ico" file in the common image library.	

The big difference between this new `ParentForm` and other forms we have seen is the use of the `IsMdiContainer` property. Setting this property to `true` indicates that this is an MDI container, which causes the form to use an alternate background color. This color is the `System.AppWorkspace` color, which is typically a darker version of the `System.Control` color. This and other MDI-related members of the `Form` class are shown in table 20.1.

The background in an MDI container is a hidden `MdiClient` control. This control cannot be manipulated in code since it is not exposed by the `Form` class. The `MdiClient` control contains any MDI child forms, and is always last in the z-order. As a result, any controls added to the form appear in front of this background, and therefore in front of any MDI children. Typically, controls added to an MDI container are docked to one edge of the parent form.

With respect to table 20.1, note that the behavior of desktop-related actions within MDI child forms is modified. The Minimize and Maximize title bar buttons,

Table 20.1 Public members of the Form class related to MDI applications

	Name	Description	See section
Properties	ActiveMdiChild	Gets the MDI child window that is currently active.	20.2.3
	IsMdiChild	Gets whether the form is an MDI child.	20.1.2
	IsMdiContainer	Gets whether the form is an MDI container form.	20.1.1
	MdiChildren	Gets the set of MDI children contained by this form as an array of `Form` objects.	20.3.3
	MdiParent	Gets or sets the MDI container for this form. If set, then this form is an MDI child form.	20.1.2
Methods	LayoutMdi	Arranges the MDI children within this form using a given layout style.	20.4.1
Events	MdiChildActivate	Occurs when an MDI child form is activated or deactivated within an MDI application. Note that MDI children do not receive the `Activated` and `Deactivate` events.	20.3.1

for example, work within the MDI container form, rather than on the desktop itself. We see this and other MDI-specific behavior later in the chapter.

The code generated for our ParentForm class is much like other forms we have seen in this book. The properties for the form are assigned in the ParentForm.Designer.cs file as part of the `InitializeComponent` method generated by Visual Studio.

With the parent form created, we turn our attention to child forms.

20.1.2 Creating an MDI child

With our MDI container in place, we can add the infrastructure required to generate our MDI child forms. This consists of a menu bar and a New menu item. Fortunately, we already have our `MainForm` class available to act as the child form.

The following steps show how to create a child form in our application. As part of this task, we add the requisite Exit menu item as well.

ADD THE ABILITY TO CREATE CHILD FORMS

	Action	Result
1	Drag a `MenuStrip` object onto the form in the ParentForm.cs [Design] window, and create a top-level File menu containing the three menu items as shown. (See Settings below.)	ParentForm File Type Here New Ctrl+N Exit Type Here

2	Add a `Click` event handler for the Exit menu item to close the form.	`private void menuFileExit_Click(`
		`  object sender, EventArgs e)`
		`{`
		`  Close();`
		`}`

3	Add a `Click` event handler for the New menu item that creates a new `MainForm` object as a child of the MDI container.	`private void menuFileNew_Click`
		`  (object sender, EventArgs e)`
		`{`
		`  CreateMdiChild(new MainForm());`
		`}`

4	Define a `CreateMdiChild` method that accepts a `Form` and makes it an MDI child of the parent form.	`private void CreateMdiChild(`
		`    Form child)`
		`{`
		`  child.MdiParent = this;`
		`  child.Show();`
		`}`

Settings (step 1)

Menu	Property	Value
File	(Name)	menuFile
	Text	&File
New	(Name)	menuFileNew
	ShortcutKeys	Ctrl+N
	Text	&New
separator		
Exit	(Name)	menuFileExit
	Text	E&xit

That's all it takes to create a child form. You have almost created your first MDI application.

If you compile and run this code, the MyPhotos application runs exactly as before. This is because the `Main` method in the `Program` class is still the entry point for the application, and it displays the `MainForm` object using the `Application.Run` method. To fix this, we need to display the `ParentForm` class in the entry point for the application. This is our next subject.

20.1.3 Updating the entry point

The entry point is the initial code executed by our application. The basic task here is to modify the `Program.Main` method to create and display a new `ParentForm` object rather than a new MainForm instance. There are three approaches for how we might do this.

The simplest means would be to modify the Main method directly. The new code would create our MDI form rather than the MainForm class, with the following line:

```
Application.Run(new ParentForm());
```

Although this code would do exactly what we want, a drawback is that we could no longer compile the application as the single-document interface we finished in chapter 16. To preserve this ability, another approach would be to create a completely separate Main method. For example, we could create an MdiProgram class that defines a Main method to kick off our MDI application. In this approach, we would also need to assign this method as the Startup Object for the project. This can be done in the Application tab of the project properties window, or using the /main switch of the C# compiler on the command line.

This second approach works fine, though if we ever wished to perform multiple steps in our entry point method, we might need to maintain this code in two separate places. To avoid this potential drawback, we opt for a third approach that updates the existing Main method to create either our new MDI application or the existing SDI application. The following steps perform this task.

<table>
<tr><th colspan="3">UPDATE THE ENTRY POINT TO CREATE PARENTFORM</th></tr>
<tr><th></th><th>Action</th><th>Result</th></tr>
<tr><td>1</td><td>In the Program.cs code window, update the Main method to conditionally allow either form to be created and displayed.
How-to
Use a #if directive with the compilation symbol AS_MDI_APP.</td><td><pre>. . .
  static class Program
  {
    . . .
    [STAThread]
    static void Main()
    {
      Application.EnableVisualStyles();
      Application.SetCompatibleText…(false);
#if AS_MDI_APP
      Application.Run(new ParentForm());
#else
      Application.Run(new MainForm());
#endif
    }
  }</pre></td></tr>
<tr><td>2</td><td>In the Build tab of the MyPhotos project properties window, define the conditional compilation symbol AS_MDI_APP.
Note: The graphics in the Build tab may vary depending on the IDE version you are running.</td><td>Application
Build*
Build Events
Debug
Resources
Settings
Configuration: Active (Debug) Platform: Ac
General
Conditional compilation symbols: AS_MDI_APP
Define DEBUG constant
Define TRACE constant
Platform target: Any CPU</td></tr>
</table>

The application is now ready. The compilation symbol AS_MDI_APP causes the compiler to include the code that creates a new `ParentForm` instance, and ignores the code that creates a `MainForm` instance. We could also have set the `IsMdiApp` symbol using the `#define` keyword directly in our Program.cs code, but we chose to do this in the project properties instead. Visual Studio uses the `/define` switch to define any project symbols when compiling the project.

Another approach would be to use the Visual Studio Configuration Manager to define solution configurations for both the MDI and SDI applications. By default, every solution has a Debug and Release configuration to permit different settings when building the solution for debugging than for release. The Debug configuration typically defines the DEBUG and TRACE symbols for use in code, much the way we use the AS_MDI_APP symbol here.

Run the application to verify that the `ParentForm` window appears and the New menu item can be used to create `MainForm` objects as child windows. If you explore this new application, you may find some rather peculiar behavior for some of the controls. We discuss and address these issues throughout the remainder of this chapter.

TRY IT! We do not discuss the ins and outs of Visual Studio configurations in this book. Configurations are not available in Visual C# Express, but should be present in the various Visual Studio editions. If your edition supports this feature, you should see a Configuration Manager menu item under the Build menu. Select this item to display the Configuration Manager window, and create two new configurations for the SDI and MDI styles as a way to gain some insight into this feature of Visual Studio. Compile the application with both configurations to verify that you can see our familiar SDI application as well as our new MDI application.

Among the odd features you may notice in the MDI version of this application is the menu bar. In particular, there are two File menus when a `MainForm` window is displayed. Adjusting this behavior is our next topic.

20.2 MERGED MENUS

By definition, an MDI application permits multiple windows to be displayed. Each child window may be the same or different, and each may display different information about one or more objects. It would be nice if the menu items for the application could be customized depending on which child window is displayed. This is of course possible, and is the subject of this section.

As an example, consider a car-buying application that permits users to search for, display, and purchase used cars. As an MDI application, this might display a photograph of the car in one window, standard features and warranty information in another window, and optional packages and pricing information in a third window. Clearly the set of menus and the contents of each menu should differ depending on which style window is currently active. For instance, menus for the photograph window might permit different colors to be viewed or the image to be rotated or otherwise altered. These concepts make no sense for the other windows, and should not be accessible when these windows are active.

While our application is not quite so ambitious, we do have the problem of our File menu, since both the `ParentForm` and the `MainForm` class contain this menu. Once we make the two File menus merge, we also have to deal with the contents of these menus, to ensure the items appear in an appropriate order.

The `ToolStrip` and `ToolStripItem` classes define properties that indicate whether and how tool strips are merged together. Theses are available to the menu-related classes as well, where some other MDI-related properties are available. Table 20.2 provides a list of these properties and a short description of each.[1]

Table 20.2 Tool strip and item properties used in MDI applications

Class	Property name	Description	See section
ToolStrip	AllowMerge	Gets or sets whether multiple strips can be combined into a single strip. Defaults to `true` in menu strips.	20.3.1
MenuStrip	MdiWindowListItem	Gets or sets the `ToolStripMenuItem` object within this strip that displays the list of MDI child forms on the associated form object.	20.4.2
ToolStripItem	MergeAction	Gets or sets how child menus are merged with parent menus.	20.2.1
	MergeIndex	Gets or sets the relative position of the menu item when it is merged with another menu.	20.2.2
ToolStripMenuItem	IsMdiWindowListItem	Gets whether this menu item displays the list of MDI child forms for the associated form.	20.4.2

In MDI applications, an MDI container form automatically merges the assigned menu for the active child form with the `MenuStrip` object assigned to its `MainMenuStrip` property. Since this merging occurs automatically, this section focuses on how menus are merged together, and makes the appropriate changes in our MDI application to merge the two File menus together. First we discuss the various ways to merge two menus, followed by the mechanism for establishing the order of merged menu items.

---

1 We should probably note here that the Win32 menu classes also provide this capability. The `Menu` class provides a `MergeMenu` method, and the `MenuItem` class provides `MergeOrder` and `MergeType` properties that work in the same spirit as the `MergeAction` and `MergeIndex` properties discussed in this chapter.

20.2.1 Assigning merge actions

As indicated in table 20.2, the `ToolStripItem` class contains two properties that control how two menus are merged. This section discusses the `MergeAction` property that controls exactly how the two menus are merged. Later we look at the `MergeIndex` property that controls the final position of a merged item.

The `MergeAction` property gets or sets a `MergeAction` enumeration value, specifying how this item should be merged into a target tool strip. The values in this enumeration are described in .NET Table 20.3. Programmatically, the default is `MatchOnly`, but Visual Studio assigns `MergeAction.Append` as the default `MergeAction` property value.

.NET Table 20.3 MergeAction enumeration

New in 2.0 The `MergeAction` enumeration specifies the actions that can be taken when combining `ToolStripItem` objects on a tool strip. This enumeration is part of the `System.Windows.Forms` namespace.

Enumeration Values	*Append*	Appends item to the end of the merged collection, regardless of any match or index setting.
	Insert	Inserts the item into the target's collection immediately preceding the matching item, or at the assigned merge index.
	MatchOnly	A match is required, but the source item is not included in the target collection. Children of the source item become children of the matched item, subject to their merge property settings.
	Remove	Removes the matching item from the collection.
	Replace	Replaces the matching item with the source item. The original item's drop-down items are not shown in the new item.

This explains why our existing application has two File menus. Since the `Append` value adds the menu regardless of any match, all of the menus in our child form are simply added to the parent menu collection.

We can fix this by modifying the `MergeAction` property for the child form.

Merge the parent and child File menus		
	Action	**Result**
1	In the MainForm.cs [Design] window, set the `MergeAction` property of the File menu to `MatchOnly`.	The two File menus now merge into a single menu in the application as shown in the graphic. The `MainForm` File menu items exhibit the default merge behavior, which is `Append`.

Compile and run the application, and open a client form in the parent window to see the merged menu as shown in the prior step. The two menus are merged, but duplicates exist and the contents are not exactly in an acceptable order. This is because each item within the child form's File menu is appended to the target File menu in the parent. The existing items appear first, followed by the items from the child form.

We can fix this, of course, but first a brief aside.

TRY IT! Modify the `MergeAction` property for `MainForm` File menu to each of the `MergeAction` enumeration values. Run the application with each setting to view the resulting behavior first-hand.

Also modify the `Text` property for the File menu in the `ParentForm` class to "Fickle." Run the application to see what happens.

Back in our sample app, we have two problems with the merged File menu. The first is that we have two versions of the New and Exit menu items, and the second is that the order of the merged menu is a bit of a mess.

We address these two problems together as part of a discussion on the `MergeIndex` property.

20.2.2 Assigning merge indexes

So far we have merged our two File menus into a single menu. The next step is to clean up the contents of this menu. This involves setting the appropriate `MergeAction` for each menu, and using the `MergeIndex` property to establish the order of the items within the merged menu. The `MergeIndex` property contains the zero-based position for merging and placing the item within the merged menu. If multiple items are assigned the same index, they appear one after another in the merged menu, beginning at the indicated position. By default, `MergeIndex` is set to -1 to indicate that the menu item is not assigned a preset position.

Before we start making changes to our existing menus, let's step back a moment and consider how our File menu should appear when we are finished. Table 20.4 shows a reasonable File menu structure for our MDI application when our MainForm window is the active child. This table includes the position, description, and implementation notes for each command.

Table 20.4 Contents of the merged File menu in our MDI application

Menu item	Position	Description	Implementation Notes
New	0	Opens a new album in a new MDI child window	Same as existing New menu item in the ParentForm class. The New item in the MainForm class should be hidden.
Open	1	Opens an existing album file in a new MDI child window	This should be processed by the ParentForm class in order to create a new child window. The Open menu item in the MainForm class should be hidden.
Close	2	Closes the active child	Similar to the MainForm Exit menu item.
separator	3		
Save	4	Saves the album in the active MDI child window	Same as existing Save menu item in the MainForm class
Save As	5	Saves the album in the active child under a new name	Same as existing Save As menu item in the MainForm class.
separator	6		
Print	7	Prints the image in the active MDI child window	Same as existing Print menu item in the MainForm class (see chapter 23).
Print Preview	8	Shows a preview for a print of the image in the active child	Same as existing Print Preview menu item in the MainForm class (see chapter 23).
separator	9		
Exit	10	Closes all child windows as well as the MDI container form	Same as existing Exit menu item in the ParentForm class.

This details how the merged menu should look. There is still the question of the menu structure in the ParentForm and MainForm classes. This is detailed in the following steps. It is important to keep in mind that the ParentForm class defines the target menu where the final File menu is assembled. The MergeAction and MergeIndex properties are defined in the MenuStrip control within the MainForm class.

	Assign the merge action and index for our File menu items	
	Action	**Result**
1	In the ParentForm.cs [Design] window, add an Open and Close menu item to the existing File menu as shown in the graphic. **Settings** <table><tr><th>Menu</th><th>Property</th><th>Value</th></tr><tr><td rowspan="3">Open</td><td>(Name)</td><td>menuFileOpen</td></tr><tr><td>ShortcutKeys</td><td>Ctrl+O</td></tr><tr><td>Text</td><td>&Open</td></tr><tr><td rowspan="3">Close</td><td>(Name)</td><td>menuFileClose</td></tr><tr><td>ShortcutKeys</td><td>Ctrl+F4</td></tr><tr><td>Text</td><td>&Close</td></tr></table>	ParentForm File Type Here New Ctrl+N Open Ctrl+O Close Ctrl+F4 Exit Type Here
2	In the File menu for the MainForm.cs [Design] window, update the merge settings for the items in this menu. **Settings** <table><tr><th>Menu</th><th>MergeAction</th><th>MergeIndex</th></tr><tr><td>New</td><td>MatchOnly</td><td>0</td></tr><tr><td>Open</td><td>MatchOnly</td><td>1</td></tr><tr><td>*separator*</td><td>Replace</td><td>3</td></tr><tr><td>Save</td><td>Insert</td><td>4</td></tr><tr><td>Save As</td><td>Insert</td><td>5</td></tr><tr><td>*separator*</td><td>Insert</td><td>6</td></tr><tr><td>Print</td><td>Insert</td><td>7</td></tr><tr><td>Print Preview</td><td>Insert</td><td>8</td></tr><tr><td>*separator*</td><td>Insert</td><td>9</td></tr><tr><td>Exit</td><td>MatchOnly</td><td>10</td></tr></table>	MyPhotos File Edit View Help New Ctrl+N Open Ctrl+O Save Ctrl+S Save As Print Ctrl+P Print Preview Exit Type Here

With these settings, the New, Open, and Exit menu items in the `MainForm` class match and are replaced by those in the `ParentForm` class. The first separator in the `MainForm` class replaces the one in the `ParentForm` class. Between these menus, the remaining `MainForm` menu items are inserted at the indicated positions.

If you run our application at this point, you may notice that the menu in our `MainForm` class still displays the remnants of our original File menu. Since we do not want this menu to appear, we hide it when the `Form` is an MDI child.

HIDE THE MENU IN OUR MDI CHILD FORM		
	Action	**Result**

3	In the MainForm.cs code window, modify the `OnLoad` method to hide the `MenuStrip` control and display any assigned album when the form is an MDI child form.	`protected override void OnLoad(EventArgs e)`
		`{`
		`  . . .`
		`  // Adjust form if MDI child`
		`  if (IsMdiChild)`
		`  {`
		`    menuStrip1.Visible = false;`
		`    DisplayAlbum();`
		`  }`
		
		`  base.OnLoad(e);`
		`}`

Compile and run the application to verify that our changes produce the appropriate menu structure. Create a new MDI child window and display the File menu. The items should appear as laid out in table 20.4.

Of course, the Open and Close menu items in our `ParentForm` class are not implemented, and the `Toolbar` control in our child window still provides access to the now hidden New and Open menu items in the `MainForm` class.

We deal with our toolbar shortly. First, let's discuss our new menus.

20.2.3 Opening and closing child forms

The Open menu item in the parent form should work much like the now hidden Open menu item from the `MainForm` class. Similarly, the Close menu item should work much like the now hidden Exit menu item. The code required here is nothing new, so let's get to it.

IMPLEMENT HANDLERS FOR OPEN AND CLOSE MENUS		
	ACTION	**RESULT**
1	Indicate that we use the Manning namespaces in the `ParentForm` class.	`using Manning.MyPhotoAlbum;` `using Manning.MyPhotoControls;`

2	Add a `Click` handler for the Open menu item that opens an album in a new MDI child window.	`private void menuFileOpen_Click(`
		`    object sender, EventArgs e)`
		`{`
		`  OpenAlbum();`
		`}`

	IMPLEMENT HANDLERS FOR OPEN AND CLOSE MENUS *(CONTINUED)*	
	ACTION	**RESULT**

3	Define an `OpenAlbum` method that uses the `AlbumController` class to allow the user to select an album to open.	`private void OpenAlbum()`
		`{`
		`  string path = null;`
		`  string pwd = null;`
		`  if (AlbumController.OpenAlbumDialog(`
		`                        ref path, ref pwd))`
		`  {`
		`    try`
		`    {`
		`      CreateMdiChild(new MainForm(path, pwd));`
		`    }`

4	If an album storage exception occurs, indicate that the album cannot be opened.	`    catch (AlbumStorageException aex)`
		`    {`
		`      MessageBox.Show(this,`
		`      "Unable to open album " + path`
		`      + "\n [" + aex.Message + "]",`
		`      "Open Album Error",`
		`      MessageBoxButtons.OK,`
		`      MessageBoxIcon.Error);`
		`    }`
		`  }`
		`}`

5	Add a `Click` handler for the Close menu item.	`private void menuFileClose_Click(`
		`    object sender, EventArgs e)`
		`{`

6	Within this handler, use the `ActiveMdiChild` property to identify and close the active child window.	`  if (ActiveMdiChild != null)`
		`    ActiveMdiChild.Close();`
		`}`

7	Since the Close menu item requires an active child, handle the `DropDownOpening` event for the File menu to only enable this item when appropriate.	`private void menuFile_DropDownOpening(`
		`    object sender, EventArgs e)`
		`{`
		`  menuFileClose.Enabled`
		`    = (this.ActiveMdiChild != null);`
		`}`

The Open menu item handler allows the user to create an MDI child window using the selected album file. This code requires a new constructor for the `MainForm` class, namely one that accepts an album file path and password.

The Close menu item handler uses the `ActiveMdiChild` property of the `ParentForm` class, which returns the `Form` object representing the active child window, or `null` if no child is currently active. We also use the `ActiveMdiChild` property to enable the Close menu item only when an MDI child window is active.

For our new `MainForm` constructor, it would be nice if we could make use of the existing constructor code already present in our default constructor. We can do this by invoking the default constructor explicitly, as illustrated in the following steps.

CREATE A MAINFORM CONSTRUCTOR THAT ACCEPTS AN ALBUM FILE		
	Action	**Result**
8	In the MainForm.cs file, create a new constructor that accepts the path and password for an album.	`public MainForm(string path, string pwd)`
9	Invoke the default constructor within our new constructor.	`    : this()` `{`

10	Within this constructor, create an `AlbumManager` with the given parameters.	`  // Caller must deal with any exception`
		`  Manager = new AlbumManager(path, pwd);`
		`}`

These changes permit the `ParentForm` class to create a new child window containing an open album, and to close an active child window when desired. Compile and run the application to verify that this all works as expected. The File menu from our two classes is now fully merged, and all menus are fully implemented.

As can be seen from this discussion, the ability to merge menus provides a powerful mechanism for controlling the menu bar in MDI applications. They permit the placement of menu items and control over which class, the parent or child, processes each item. While we only merged two File menus here, you may find in your own MDI applications that additional menus must be merged. The principles and methods for doing this are identical to those utilized here.

With our menus completed, the next item in the development of our MDI application is to tidy up other parts of the interface, such as the toolbar and the pixel data dialog box. This cleanup is our next topic.

20.3 MDI CHILDREN

Our MDI application is coming along nicely. We have a parent form that contains `MainForm` class instances as child forms. Each form displays a new or existing album, and the menu bars have been integrated to present a logical set of choices to the user. Additional members of the `Form` class are related to the creation of MDI applications. This section examines a few of these members as we correct some issues in the MyPhotos MDI application we have built thus far.

If you have experimented with the interface created in the previous section, you may have found the following issues that do not behave as you might expect:

- The toolbar control: The toolbar on the child form gives access to the New and Open menu in the `MainForm` class, which we are trying not to expose in the MDI version of our application.
- The pixel data form: This dialog box appears separately from the MDI application, rather than as a child form within it. In addition, when multiple album windows are open, each window opens its own separate `PixelDialog` form, which gets rather confusing.

- Opening multiple albums: If you open the same album twice, you end up with two windows showing the same album. Aside from the errors that can occur from having two instances operate on different versions of the same album simultaneously, it seems a bit strange to permit two copies of the same file to open in the same parent window.

We address each of these items separately, and present and make use of MDI-related members of the `Form` class as required.

20.3.1 Merging tool strips

The main tool strip in our `MainForm` class was designed to interact with the form's menu bar, which is now hidden. As a result, this tool strip is no longer appropriate for our purposes. A simple solution to this problem might simply hide this tool strip when the `MainForm` object is an MDI child form, and create a more appropriate toolbar in the `ParentForm` class.

Although this would work just fine, it seems a shame to give up the tool strip items we created in our `MainForm` class. We were able to reuse our menu items in the parent, so why can't we reuse our tool strip items? The merge functionality, as you may have noticed, is defined by the `ToolStrip` class. While menus in MDI applications are merged automatically, you can merge other kinds of tool strips using the `ToolStripManager` class. Let's see this by modifying our MDI application to merge the main tool strip in our child form with a new strip in the parent. The result of this change appears in figure 20.2.

Figure 20.2 The main tool strip in the MainForm class has been merged into the parent form. The Dialogs and Images tool strips still appear in the child.

The ToolStripManager class is summarized in .NET Table 20.5. As you can see, this class lets you control the default painting, or rendering, behavior of tool strips, and provides methods to inquire about keyboard shortcuts, merge two tool strips, and preserve or restore tool strip layout information.

The LoadSettings and SaveSettings methods provide an automated means to persist and restore user modifications to the tool strips on a form. They allow an application to preserve user changes made to the docking of strips in a ToolStripPanel or the ordering of items when the AllowItemReorder property is enabled. These methods use the built-in settings engine provided by Windows Forms that is discussed in chapter 23.

In our application, we'd like to merge the tool strip in our child into a tool strip located in the parent. This code uses a number of concepts from part 2 as well as the merge properties we just discussed for menu strips.

.NET Table 20.5 ToolStripManager class

New in 2.0 The ToolStripManager class provides static members for querying and controlling tool strip objects in an application. This class is part of the System.Windows.Forms namespace.

Public Static Properties	*Renderer*	Gets or sets the default ToolStripRender applied to all tool strips in the application
	RenderMode	Gets or sets the default painting style applied to all tool strips in the application
	VisualStylesEnabled	Gets or sets whether tool strips are rendered using visual style information called themes
Public Static Methods	*FindToolStrip*	Returns the ToolStrip with the given name in the application
	IsShortcutDefined	Returns whether the given shortcut key is utilized by any tool strip in the application
	IsValidShortcut	Returns whether the given key combination is a valid shortcut key
	LoadSettings	Restores the tool strip settings for a form
	Merge	Merges a given tool strip into a target tool strip
	RevertMerge	Undoes a prior merge of two tool strips
	SaveSettings	Saves the tool strip settings for a form, using the fully qualified name or a given name as the settings key
Public Static Events	*RendererChanged*	Occurs when the Renderer property is modified

<table>
<tr><th colspan="3">MERGE TOOL STRIPS IN THE PARENT FORM</th></tr>
<tr><th></th><th>Action</th><th>Result</th></tr>
<tr><td>1</td><td>Add a new `ToolStrip` control to the `ParentForm` class named `toolStripParent` containing two tool strip buttons. These buttons will correspond to the parent's New and Open menu items.

Settings<table><tr><th>Button</th><th>Property</th><th>Value</th></tr><tr><td>First</td><td>(Name)
Text</td><td>tsbNew
New Album</td></tr><tr><td>Second</td><td>(Name)
Text</td><td>tsbOpen
Open Album</td></tr></table></td><td>Note: You might be tempted to add a `ToolStripContainer` control here, to allow the strip to float among the sides of the parent form. That's a good idea, but it doesn't work in MDI applications, as the central panel in this container would obscure the MDI surface where all child forms are displayed.</td></tr>
<tr><td>2</td><td>In the ParentForm.cs file, override the `OnLoad` method,</td><td>`protected override void OnLoad(`
`    EventArgs e)`
`{`</td></tr>
<tr><td>3</td><td>Within this method, load the resources for the `MainForm` class.</td><td>`  ComponentResourceManager resources`
`    = new ComponentResourceManager(`
`          typeof(MainForm));`</td></tr>
<tr><td>4</td><td>Assign the images for the New and Open menu items as well as the tool strip buttons using the corresponding resources from the `MainForm` class.</td><td>`  Image newImage = (Image) resources.`
`     GetObject("menuFileNew.Image");`
`  Image openImage = (Image) resources.`
`     GetObject("menuFileOpen.Image");`
`  menuFileNew.Image = newImage;`
`  menuFileOpen.Image = openImage;`
`  tsbNew.Image = newImage;`
`  tsbOpen.Image = openImage;`

`  base.OnLoad(e);`
`}`</td></tr>
<tr><td>5</td><td>Add a `Click` handler for the New button that mimics the New menu item.</td><td>`private void tsbNew_Click(`
`    object sender, EventArgs e)`
`{`
`  CreateMdiChild(new MainForm());`
`}`</td></tr>
<tr><td>6</td><td>Add a `Click` handler for the Open button that mimics the Open menu item.</td><td>`private void tsbOpen_Click(`
`    object sender, EventArgs e)`
`{`
`  OpenAlbum();`
`}`</td></tr>
<tr><td>7</td><td>Override the `OnMdiChildActivate` method.</td><td>`protected override void`
`    OnMdiChildActivate(EventArgs e)`
`{`</td></tr>
</table>

	Merge tool strips in the parent form *(continued)*	
	Action	**Result**

8	Within this method, if the active child is a `MainForm` instance, then merge the child's main tool strip with the parent's tool strip.
	
	Note: The `MainToolStrip` property used here is defined in step 10 later in this section.
		<pre> ToolStripManager.RevertMerge(
		      toolStripParent);
		
		  MainForm f = ActiveMdiChild as MainForm;
		  if (f != null)
		  {
		    ToolStripManager.Merge(
		        f.MainToolStrip,
		        toolStripParent.Name);
		    toolStripParent.ImageList
		      = f.MainToolStrip.ImageList;
		  }
		
		  base.OnMdiChildActivate(e);
		}</pre>

This completes the changes required in the `ParentForm` class. We create a new `ToolStrip` with buttons for the New and Open menu items. Since we have similar buttons in our `MainForm` class, we simply load the existing resources for the `MainForm` type and apply their images to the menu items and our new tool strip buttons.

The actual merge is performed whenever a `MainForm` child is activated. The `MdiChildActivate` event occurs whenever a child form is activated. The code merges the main `ToolStrip` in the `MainForm` class into the new `ToolStrip` created in the `ParentForm` class.

There are two versions of the `ToolStripManager.Merge` method. The one used here requires two of the same kind of strips, such as two `MenuStrip` objects or, in this case, two `ToolStrip` objects. The first parameter is the source `ToolStrip`, while the second is the name of the target tool strip.

As you can see, our code first invokes the `RevertMerge` method to undo any existing merge on the target tool strip. After the merge is performed, the code assigns the `ImageList` for the source tool strip to the parent tool strip, to ensure that any image list images appear in the merged tool strip. This is a limitation of using image lists with tool strips–merged tool strip items take their images from the target tool strip's image list rather than the original image list in the source tool strip.

If you try to run this code, you will see a compiler error. The `MainToolStrip` property is not yet defined in the `MainForm` class. The changes required in our `MainForm` class are detailed next.

SET UP CHILD FORM'S TOOL STRIP TO BE MERGED		
	Action	**Result**

9	In the MainForm.cs file, modify the `OnLoad` method to hide the main tool strip when displayed as an MDI child.	`protected override void OnLoad(`
		`    EventArgs e)`
		`{`
		`  . . .`
		`  // Adjust form if MDI child`
		`  if (this.IsMdiChild)`
		`  {`
		`    menuStrip1.Visible = false;`
		`    toolStripMain.Visible = false;`
		`    DisplayAlbum();`
		`  }`
		
		`  base.OnLoad(e);`
		`}`

10	Define an internal `MainToolStrip` property that gets the main tool strip instance.	`internal ToolStrip MainToolStrip`
		`{`
		`  get { return toolStripMain; }`
		`}`

11	In the MainForm.cs [Design] window, assign the merge settings for the New and Open tool strip buttons in the main tool strip. **Settings** **Button** / **MergeAction** / **MergeIndex** tsbNew / MatchOnly / 0 tsbOpen / MatchOnly / 1	Properties tsbOpen System.Windows.Forms.To Image: System.Dr ImageAlign: MiddleCenter ImageScaling: SizeToFit ImageTranspare: Magenta Margin: 0, 1, 0, 2 MergeAction: **MatchOnly** MergeIndex: **1** Modifiers: Private Overflow: AsNeeded
12	Also set the `AllowMerge` property for the `toolStripDialogs` and `toolStripImages` tool strips to `false`.	This ensures that these other tool strips are not merged into the parent form.

That's it. The child's tool strip is hidden when displayed as an MDI child form, and the contents of this strip are set to merge into the parent. The result is that the parent's New and Open tool strip buttons remain in the merged strip, with the remaining items from the child's strip appended to the end of the tool strip in the parent.

20.3.2 Displaying pixel data

The `PixelDialog` form is another area where our MDI application does not behave as we might wish. Right now, every child has a separate pixel dialog box, and these dialog boxes are independent of the parent form. To integrate this additional form into our MDI application, it would be nice if a single `PixelDialog` was used for all child album windows, and if this dialog box was an MDI child window. Just for fun, we should also preserve our ability to run the MyPhotos application as an SDI where only a single album can be displayed.

Figure 20.3 The PixelDialog form here is partially obscured to prove that it really is an MDI child form. Also notice that the menu and tool strips do not display any child items, since the PixelDialog form does not employ a menu or tool strip.

This section makes the changes required for these features, the result of which appears in figure 20.3. These changes require the following tasks:

- Create a `PixelDialog` instance that can be shared by all `MainForm` instances.
- Provide a means to display this dialog box as an MDI child form.
- Access this global instance from the `MainForm` class instances.
- Ensure this dialog box is always associated with any active `MainForm` window.

This may seem like a daunting task for a single section. In fact, our application is well prepared for these changes. Pulling out my soapbox for a moment, the real test of a program's architecture is not its ability to work as designed, but rather its ability to perform tasks for which it was not designed. The coding techniques we have used throughout this book are valuable in any application to accommodate future requirements. These techniques include encapsulating tasks into separate methods, sketching a user interface design or enumerating the steps required before writing any code, and building reusable libraries and methods where possible.

As a result, our code is well prepared for new changes such as those made in this section, since we have consistently tried to use good coding practices and not duplicate our tasks in multiple places. While perhaps not always successful, I believe we have done a reasonable job.

In the PixelDialog form, for example, we were careful to only update this form in the UpdatePixelData method of the MainForm class. Similarly, the only location where the PixelDialog form is created right now is in the Click event handler for the menuPixelData object. Such organization occasionally requires a little extra work, or in our case a few more pages, but this effort often pays off as the code is maintained and updated in the future.

Enough of my soapbox here. Let's return to the topic at hand, and make our changes in the order shown in the prior list, beginning with a global PixelDialog instance. For this we provide a static property in the PixelDialog class that returns a shared form.

CREATE A SHARED PIXELDIALOG INSTANCE

	Action	Result
1	In the PixelDialog class of the MyPhotoControls project, create static members to hold the shared instance and an MDI parent form, if any.	`static private Form SharedMdiParent= null;` `static private PixelDialog SharedInstance;`

2	Create a public property to get or set the MDI container form to associate with the class.	`static public Form GlobalMdiParent`
		`{`
		`  get { return SharedMdiParent; }`
		`  set { SharedMdiParent = value; }`
		`}`

3	Create a public property to retrieve the shared form.
	How-to
	If the current SharedInstance value is invalid, create a new instance of the Form.
		`static public PixelDialog GlobalInstance`
		`{`
		`  get`
		`  {`
		`    if (SharedInstance == null`
		`            || SharedInstance.IsDisposed)`
		`    {`
		`      SharedInstance = new PixelDialog();`
		`      SharedInstance.MdiParent`
		`        = GlobalMdiParent;`
		`      SharedInstance.Visible = false;`
		`    }`
		
		`    return SharedInstance;`
		`  }`
		`}`

The GlobalInstance property allows all child MainForm instances to access the same PixelDialog form. Recall that our PixelDialog form is disposed whenever the user clicks the Close button. For this reason, this property re-creates the dialog box whenever it is null or disposed.[2]

[2] You may notice that there is a potential concurrency issue here if the GlobalInstance property is invoked simultaneously by two callers. In .NET, as in other environments, Windows applications invoke their UI operations in a single-threaded fashion, so this concurrency problem cannot occur.

The GlobalMdiParent property enables this dialog box to act as an MDI child, since our ParentForm class can establish itself as the MDI container for the dialog box.

SET THE MDI PARENT FOR THE GLOBAL PIXELDIALOG FORM		
	Action	**Result**

4	In the ParentForm.cs code window, modify the OnLoad method to assign this form as the MDI parent for the global PixelDialog form.	`protected override void OnLoad(EventArgs e)`
		`{`
		`  . . .`
		`  // Assign MDI parent for all pixel forms`
		`  PixelDialog.GlobalMdiParent = this;`
		
		`  base.OnLoad(e);`
		`}`

With this change, as the parent is initially displayed the global MDI parent is assigned for all PixelDialog forms. This ensures the global instance assigns our ParentForm object as the MDI parent. With this in place, we are ready to access the global instance from the MainForm class. As mentioned earlier, right now the dialog box is created only in the menuPixelData_Click method, so this is the only place we need to call our new property.

ACCESS THE GLOBAL PIXELDIALOG FROM THE MAINFORM CLASS		
	Action	**Result**

5	In the MainForm.cs code window, modify the menuPixelData_Click method to create the PixelDialog instance using the new GlobalInstance property.	`private void menuPixelData_Click(`
		`  object sender, System.EventArgs e)`
		`{`
		`  if (PixelForm == null || PixelForm.IsDisposed)`
		`  {`
		`    PixelForm = **PixelDialog.GlobalInstance**;`
		`    PixelForm.Owner = this;`
		`  }`
		
		`  PixelForm.Show();`
		`  . . .`
		`}`

This change simply retrieves the global dialog box rather than creating a new instance. You can compile and run this if you like. The code works fine until a second MDI child window is added. When this occurs, the PixelDialog form is not associated with this window and no longer updates appropriately.

There are a couple ways to fix this problem. Since all mouse movement in each window is processed by the pbxPhoto_MouseMove event handler in the MainForm class, which in turn calls the UpdatePixelDialog method, we can fix this by associating any existing PixelDialog form with the new window at the start of our update method.

The following steps make this change to our application.

ENSURE ANY EXISTING PIXELDIALOG FORM IS ASSIGNED TO NEW CHILD INSTANCES		
	Action	**Result**

6	Modify the `UpdatePixelData` method to assign the `PixelForm` property at the beginning of the method.	`protected void UpdatePixelData(int xPos, yPos)`
		`{`
		  `if (IsMdiChild)`
		    `PixelForm = PixelDialog.GlobalInstance;`
		
		  `if (PixelForm != null && PixelForm.Visible)`
		  `. . .`
		`}`

This guarantees that a child form picks up the global `PixelDialog` form as needed. Of course, this change also causes the dialog box to be created even when it is not used. Such a change might not be appropriate in a large application with multiple utility forms such as our pixel dialog box. For our purposes, it should be okay.

The final problem we have is our Pixel Data tool strip button. Back in chapter 16, we ensured this button was properly pressed by overriding the `OnActivated` method. Unfortunately, the `Activated` and `Deactivate` events do not occur in MDI child forms. As a result, an alternate solution is required. The answer is to use the `Enter` and `Leave` events instead, since these do occur in MDI children. Our final step in this section makes this change.

ENSURE ANY EXISTING PIXELDIALOG FORM IS ASSIGNED TO NEW CHILD INSTANCES		
	Action	**Result**

7	In the `MainForm` class, override the `OnEnter` method to assign the Pixel Data button's pressed state appropriately.	`protected override void OnEnter(EventArgs e)`
		`{`
		  `if (IsMdiChild)`
		    `UpdatePixelButton(`
		        `PixelDialog.GlobalInstance.Visible);`
		
		  `base.OnEnter(e);`
		`}`

Compile and run the program to verify that our new code works. Also realize that all of our changes are consistent with our non-MDI application. When a single `MainForm` instance is present, all of our `PixelDialog` code works as we originally intended in chapter 7. You can test this by modifying the MyPhotos project settings to compile without the `AS_MDI_APP` symbol defined.

The `PixelDialog` form is now integrated into our MDI application. The next task we identified is to ensure that we do not open multiple windows for the same album file.

20.3.3 Opening an album twice

Looking at our current code for the parent's Open menu item, a new child window is always created to contain the selected album. This is fine when the selected album has not been previously opened by the user. In the case where a `MainForm` window already exists for the album, it would be more appropriate to simply bring the existing window to the front of the z-order.

This can be done by searching through the list of child windows for one that displays the selected album. The `MdiChildren` property in the `Form` class retrieves an array of child forms in the application, and can be used to find a matching form.

This property is useful whenever a specific form is desired, as we do here. It can also be used to see if any child forms are present in an MDI application or to obtain the number of MDI child forms, although checking the `ActiveMdiChild` property is typically a more efficient mechanism for the former task.

When searching for a child form, keep in mind the fact that forms other than the desired form might be displayed. In our case, we are looking for the `MainForm` class. The following steps detail a solution with this fact in mind.

<table>
<tr><th colspan="3">HANDLE AN ATTEMPT TO OPEN A DISPLAYED ALBUM</th></tr>
<tr><th></th><th>Action</th><th>Result</th></tr>
<tr><td>1</td><td>In the <code>MainForm</code> class, add a public <code>AlbumPath</code> property to retrieve the path to the displayed album.</td><td><pre>public string AlbumPath
{
  get { return Manager.FullName; }
}</pre></td></tr>
<tr><td>2</td><td>In the ParentForm.cs file, modify the <code>OpenAlbum</code> method to loop through the MDI child forms before creating a new window.</td><td><pre>private void OpenAlbum()
{
  string path = null;
  string pwd = null;
  if (AlbumController.OpenAlbumDialog(. . .))
  {
    try
    {
      foreach (Form f in MdiChildren)
      {</pre></td></tr>
<tr><td>3</td><td>For each form, if it is a <code>MainForm</code> instance with the selected path, display the existing child form for this album.</td><td><pre>   MainForm mf = f as MainForm;
        if (mf != null && mf.AlbumPath == path)
        {
          // Show existing child
          if (mf.WindowState
                == FormWindowState.Minimized)
            mf.WindowState
                = FormWindowState.Normal;
          mf.BringToFront();
          return;
        }
      }</pre></td></tr>
<tr><td>4</td><td>If no match is found, create a new child window for the selected album.</td><td><pre>   // Not found, so create a new child
      CreateMdiChild(new MainForm(path, pwd));
    }
    . . .</pre></td></tr>
</table>

This code uses some properties we have not seen before. When a matching child `Form` is found, the `WindowState` property is used to ensure the form is visible. For a top-level form, this property affects the display state on the desktop; for a child form, it affects the display state within the MDI container. The property takes its values from the `FormWindowState` enumeration, shown in .NET Table 20.6. In our code, we check to see if the MDI child is minimized, and if so return it to a `Normal` state.

.NET Table 20.6 FormWindowState enumeration

The `FormWindowState` enumeration specifies the possible display states for a `Form` on the desktop or within an MDI application. This enumeration is part of the `System.Windows.Forms` namespace.

Enumeration Values	Maximized	The form is maximized to fill the entire display area.
	Minimized	The form is minimized within the current display area.
	Normal	The form appears with its default size in the current display area.

Our code also uses the `BringToFront` method to display the form at the top of the z-order within the MDI container. This method is part of the `Control` class and can be used to adjust the z-order position of any Windows Forms control within its container. There is also a corresponding `SendToBack` method to place a control at the bottom of the z-order.

Compile and run the application. Open some new or existing albums, and then open the same album multiple times with its window in various states to verify that the proper behavior occurs.

This completes the three tasks we set out at the start of this section. We have added a toolbar to our parent form, turned the `PixelDialog` form into an MDI child when running as an MDI application, and ensured that an album can only appear once in our application.

As a final change, and to create a slightly more polished application, let's make one more addition here to place the current album in the title bar.

20.3.4 Updating the title bar

Typically, an MDI application updates its title bar to reflect the contents of the currently active child form. This provides good feedback to users, especially when the application is minimized and only appears in the task bar. In our case, we should probably also include the version number on the title bar, since this is our custom. The result of this change is shown in figure 20.4.

We could like to update the title bar whenever a new form is activated within the MDI container. The `MdiChildActivate` event we used to merge our tool strips in section 20.3.1 can be used for this purpose as well.

Figure 20.4 The title bar must handle the various kinds of child forms that our MDI application can display.

We should mention again that MDI child forms do not receive the `Activated` or `Deactivate` events. As a result, when converting from a single document interface to a multiple document interface, any tasks performed in these events must be handled via another mechanism. Sometimes the `MdiChildActivate` event can handle the work previously done in these events. Another option is to use the focus-related events, such as the `Enter` or `Leave` event, as we did in section 20.3.2.

Let's modify our `MdiChildActivate` event handler to update the title bar.

UPDATE THE TITLE BAR IN THE PARENT FORM		
	Action	**Result**

1	In the `MainForm` class, add an `AlbumTitle` property to retrieve the title of the current album.	`public string AlbumTitle`
		`{`
		`  get { return Manager.Album.Title; }`
		`}`

2	In the `ParentForm` class, implement a `SetTitleBar` method to update the title bar.	`protected void SetTitleBar()` `{`

3	Within this method, retrieve the version number for the application and assign local variables to hold the title bar format and name for the current child.	`  Version ver = new Version(`
		`      Application.ProductVersion);`
		`  string titleBarFormat`
		`      = "{0} - MyPhotos MDI {1:#}.{2:#}";`
		`  string childName = "Untitled";`

	UPDATE THE TITLE BAR IN THE PARENT FORM *(CONTINUED)*	
	Action	**Result**

4	Determine an appropriate name for the current child window.
	How-to
	Use the album title for `MainForm` instances, and the string "Pixel Data" for the `PixelDialog` form.
		<pre>MainForm mf = ActiveMdiChild as MainForm;
		if (mf != null && !String.
		            IsNullOrEmpty(mf.AlbumTitle))
		  childName = mf.AlbumTitle;
		else if (ActiveMdiChild is PixelDialog)
		  childName = "Pixel Data";</pre>

5	Assign the `Text` property of the parent form based on the determined information.	<pre>Text = String.Format(titleBarFormat,
		  childName, ver.Major, ver.Minor);
		}</pre>

6	Modify the `OnMdiChildActivate` method to assign the title bar.	<pre>protected override void OnMdiChildActivate(
		    EventArgs e)
		{
		  . . .
		  SetTitleBar();
		  base.OnMdiChildActivate(e);
		}</pre>

7	Also set the title bar when the form is first displayed, in the `OnLoad` method.	<pre>protected override void OnLoad(EventArgs e)
		{
		  . . .
		  SetTitleBar();
		  base.OnLoad(e);
		}</pre>

The text that appears in the title bar depends on which type of window is currently active. When no window, or an unrecognized window, is active, the title bar simply includes the version number.

Compile and run the application to see our title bar in action. The title bar for both parent and child forms is rather similar. Feel free to modify one or the other to make the title bars more unique. If you do this, make sure you consider the behavior of the `MainForm` class as both an SDI and MDI application.

Our final topic in this chapter is the addition of layout management for our MDI child forms.

20.4 MDI CHILD WINDOW MANAGEMENT

Ultimately, an MDI application is simply a collection of `Forms` displayed in a parent window. The .NET Framework provides some assistance in managing these forms within this parent. In this section we discuss child form layout and how to show the active forms in a menu. The `Form` class contains a `LayoutMdi` method for the former, while the `MenuStrip` class contains an `MdiWindowListItem` property for the latter. A new top-level Window menu, shown in figure 20.5, makes use of these constructs.

We begin with the automatic layout of MDI child forms.

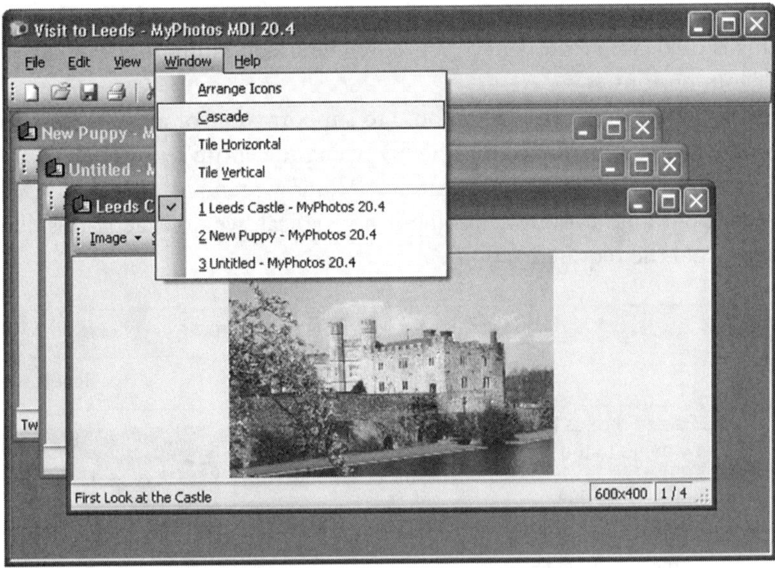

Figure 20.5 The Window menu permits the automatic layout of MDI child forms and provides a list of MDI children displayed within the container area.

20.4.1 Arranging MDI children

In an MDI application, as well as on the Windows desktop, a number of windows are created and strewn about in various locations. It would be nice if our application permitted automatic organization of the windows at the user's request. In theory at least, this allows the user to immediately see all open windows and select the desired one.

Such support is provided by the `LayoutMdi` method of the `Form` class. This method can be called from an MDI container form, and accepts an `MdiLayout` enumeration value specifying the type of layout to apply to the MDI container.

.NET Table 20.7 MdiLayout enumeration

The `MdiLayout enumeration` specifies the possible layout options for a set of MDI child forms. This is used in the `LayoutMdi` method of the `Form` class to automatically display a set of forms with the given layout mode. This class is part of the `System.Windows.Forms` namespace.

Enumeration Values	ArrangeIcons	The icons or minimized forms are arranged within the client window. This has no effect on child forms that are not minimized.
	Cascade	The child forms are displayed on top of each other in step fashion so that only the title bar of the hidden forms is visible.
	TileHorizontal	The client area is divided horizontally into equal sections and each open window is displayed in a section.
	TileVertical	The client area is divided vertically into equal sections and each open window is displayed in a section.

The `MdiLayout` enumeration is detailed in .NET Table 20.7. To demonstrate how this is used, we create a new Window menu containing options for each of the main layout options.

In your applications, you can choose to support some or all of these options. The various layout styles are useful for quickly seeing the entire set of open windows in an MDI application, and typically appear in a Window menu located on the MDI parent form. Since our application is nothing if not typical, we do exactly this. The following steps detail the required actions.

<table>
<tr><th colspan="3">ADD LAYOUT MENUS TO THE PARENT FORM</th></tr>
<tr><th></th><th>Action</th><th>Result</th></tr>
<tr><td>1</td><td>In the ParentForm.cs [Design] window, add a top-level Window menu to the form.

Settings
<table><tr><th>Property</th><th>Value</th></tr><tr><td>(Name)</td><td>menuWindow</td></tr><tr><td>Text</td><td>&Window</td></tr></table></td><td>ParentForm
File Window Type Here
Type Here</td></tr>
<tr><td>2</td><td>Add a menu item for each layout style.

Settings
<table><tr><th>Menu</th><th>Property</th><th>Value</th></tr><tr><td rowspan="4">Arrange</td><td>(Name)</td><td>menuWindowArrange</td></tr><tr><td>Text</td><td>&Window</td></tr><tr><td>Tag</td><td>ArrangeIcons</td></tr><tr><td>Text</td><td>&Arrange Icons</td></tr><tr><td rowspan="3">Cascade</td><td>(Name)</td><td>menuWindowCascade</td></tr><tr><td>Tag</td><td>Cascade</td></tr><tr><td>Text</td><td>&Cascade</td></tr><tr><td rowspan="3">Horizontal</td><td>(Name)</td><td>menuWindowHorizontal</td></tr><tr><td>Tag</td><td>TileHorizontal</td></tr><tr><td>Text</td><td>Tile &Horizontal</td></tr><tr><td rowspan="3">Vertical</td><td>(Name)</td><td>menuWindowVertical</td></tr><tr><td>Tag</td><td>TileVertical</td></tr><tr><td>Text</td><td>Tile &Vertical</td></tr></table></td><td>ParentForm
File Window Type Here
Arrange Icons
Cascade
Tile Horizontal
Tile Vertical
Type Here</td></tr>
</table>

ADD LAYOUT MENUS TO THE PARENT FORM *(CONTINUED)*		
	Action	**Result**
3	In the MainForm.cs [Design] window, modify the merge properties for the menu strip so the menus merge appropriately. **Settings** **Menu** / **MergeAction** / **MergeIndex** Edit / Insert / 1 View / Insert / 2 Help / Append / 4	These settings cause the Edit and View menus to be inserted between the File and Window menus. The Help menu remains appended to the end of the merged menu. Visit to Leeds - MyPhotos MDI 20.4 File Edit View Window Help

These changes establish the new Window menu and ensure that the existing `MainForm` menus merge appropriately with this menu. One `Click` event handler to go and we are ready to use our new menus.

HANDLE WINDOW MENU ITEM CLICK		
	Action	**Result**

4	Use Visual Studio to add a shared `Click` event handler called `menuWindowItem_Click` for all four Window menu items.	`private void menuWindowItem_Click(`
		`    object sender, EventArgs e)`
		`{`

5	Implement this handler to convert the item's `Tag` property to an `MdiLayout` enumeration value, and call the `LayoutMdi` method to arrange the child forms.	`  ToolStripItem item = sender as ToolStripItem;`
		`  if (item != null)`
		`  {`
		`    string enumVal = item.Tag as string;`
		`    if (enumVal != null)`
		`    {`
		`      LayoutMdi((MdiLayout) Enum.Parse(`
		`          typeof(MdiLayout), enumVal));`
		`    }`
		`  }`
		`}`

Four menu items, one method, and suddenly users can automatically arrange open windows according to the selected style. Compile, run, open a few windows, and be amazed.

The last topic for discussion is the `MdiWindowListItem` property.

20.4.2 Displaying an MDI child list menu

Most MDI applications provide a list of open child windows as part of the Window menu. This permits the user to quickly jump to an open window at the click of the mouse. The .NET folks at Microsoft were kind enough to provide a quick way to do this through the `MdiWindowListItem` property of the `MenuStrip` class.

When this property is set to an available `ToolStripMenuItem` object contained by the menu strip, the list of child forms is automatically added to the indicated menu. Figure 20.5 shows an example of this behavior using the Window menu in our `ParentForm` class. The list of forms appears below any existing menu items. The active child form within the container is automatically checked.

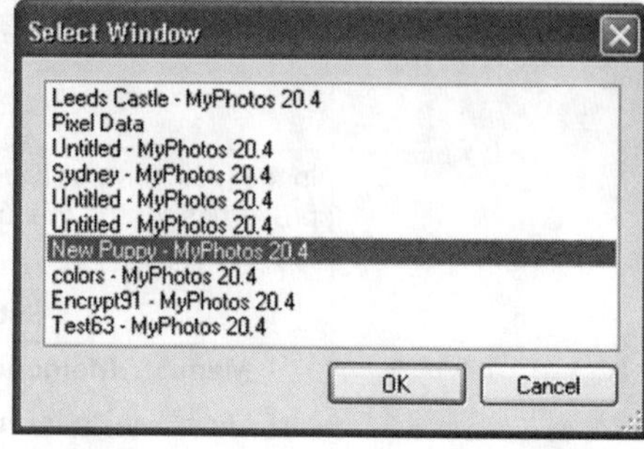

Figure 20.6 The Select Window dialog box displays all active MDI children, including our Pixel Dialog class.

Up to nine forms are displayed, with a More Windows menu item added if more than nine child forms exist. This additional menu is added as needed by Windows Forms, and displays a dialog box showing the list of all child forms. An example of the Select Window dialog box displayed by the More Windows menu item is shown in figure 20.6.

We can add this feature to our application simply by setting the `MdiWindowListItem` property for the Window menu. When displaying the window list, the .NET Framework automatically adds a separator item between any existing menu items and the window items.

ENABLE A LIST OF CHILD WINDOWS TO APPEAR

	Action	Result
1	In the ParentForm.cs [Design] window, set the `MdiWindowListItem` property of the `menuStrip1` control to the `menuWindow` menu item.	The MDI child windows are automatically inserted when the contents of this menu are displayed.

That's all it takes. Compile, run, and see it in action.

The related `IsMdiWindowListEntry` property exists in the `ToolStripMenuItem` class, and can be used to identify whether a menu item is automatically added as an MDI window list item. We have not used this property in our sample application.

Before we leave the topic of child form layout, it is also worth mentioning that child forms can be positioned manually using the standard members of the `Control` class such as the `Top`, `Width`, `Size`, and `Location` properties. This is not typically required, but it's worth mentioning.

This completes our MDI application discussion and sample application. As is our custom, a short recap of our accomplishments here rounds out the chapter.

TRY IT! Another menu item sometimes found in MDI applications is a Close All menu. Add such an item to the Window menu and implement it to close all open albums.

20.5 RECAP

In this chapter we converted the single document interface, or SDI, application created in part 2 of the book into a multiple document interface, or MDI, application. We accomplished this amazing feat by creating a new parent form window and using members of the `Form` class and other Windows Forms constructs.

We began by creating the `ParentForm` class to serve as our MDI container form, and used the existing `MainForm` class as our child form. We examined the `MergeAction` and `MergeIndex` properties of the `ToolStripItem` class to merge the menus of our parent and child forms into a single menu bar. We created a tool strip on our parent form and merged the main tool strip from our `MainForm` class into the parent form as well.

This created a reasonable MDI application, but we finished our discussion with some common MDI behavior and features. We integrated the `PixelDialog` form into the application and made it an MDI child form as well. We also illustrated the ability of the Windows Forms namespace to automatically insert a list of MDI child forms into a specified menu.

From MDI applications we move to the topic of data binding.

CHAPTER 21

Data binding

Data binding is a means for associating Windows Forms controls with one or more data sources. We saw a little of this concept in chapters 11 and 12 for list box and combo box controls. These controls provide the `DataSource` and `DataMember` properties for binding the list displayed by the control to a specific source of data.

In this chapter and the next, we explore data binding in more detail. While the discussion is focused on Windows Forms classes, many of the examples and discussions carry over to databases and the `System.Data` namespace where classes such as `DataSet` and `DataTable` are found.

Our discussion here is centered on the `DataGridView` class, which displays data in a tabular view. This class replaces the `DataGrid` control provided in prior versions of the Windows Forms namespace. Although the `DataGrid class` is retained for backward compatibility, the `DataGridView` control is the preferred mechanism for displaying tabular data as of the .NET 2.0 release.

To illustrate the `DataGridView` control, this chapter begins a new MyAlbum-Data application that is similar in spirit to the MyAlbumEditor application created in chapters 18 and 19. A `ComboBox` control will display a list of available albums, and the photographs in the selected album will appear on the remainder of the form. This new application is shown in figure 21.1 as it appears at the end of this chapter.

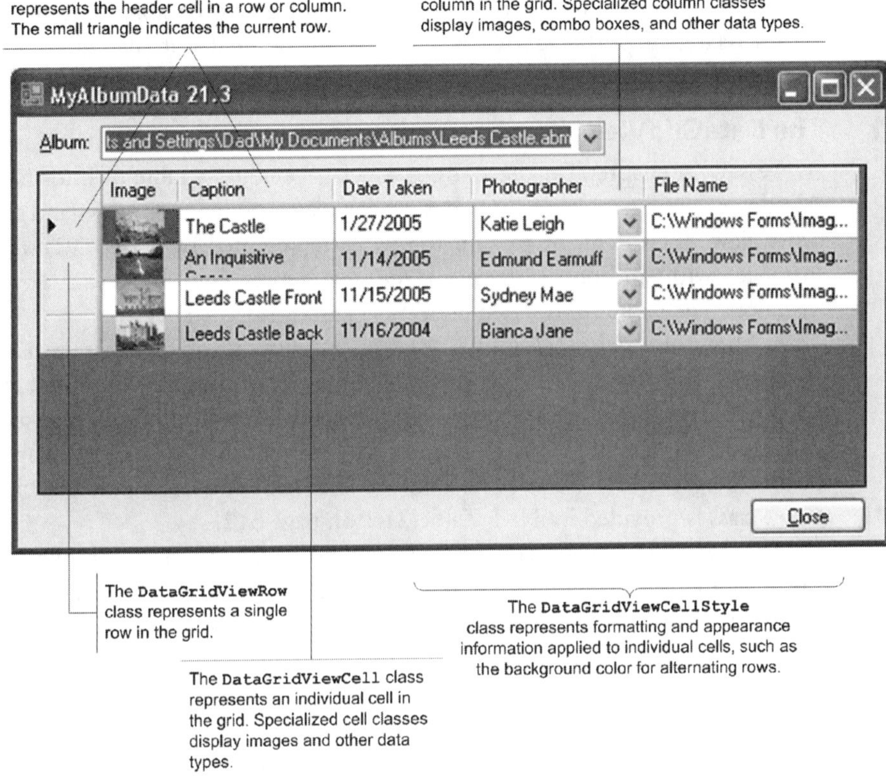
The DataGridViewHeaderCell class represents the header cell in a row or column. The small triangle indicates the current row.
The DataGridViewColumn class represents a column in the grid. Specialized column classes display images, combo boxes, and other data types.
MyAlbumData 21.3
Album:
ts and Settings\Dad\My Documents\Albums\Leeds Castle.abm
Image
Caption
Date Taken
Photographer
File Name
The Castle
1/27/2005
Katie Leigh
C:\Windows Forms\Imag...
An Inquisitive
11/14/2005
Edmund Earmuff
C:\Windows Forms\Imag...
Leeds Castle Front
11/15/2005
Sydney Mae
C:\Windows Forms\Imag...
Leeds Castle Back
11/16/2004
Bianca Jane
C:\Windows Forms\Imag...
Close
The DataGridViewRow class represents a single row in the grid.
The DataGridViewCellStyle class represents formatting and appearance information applied to individual cells, such as the background color for alternating rows.
The DataGridViewCell class represents an individual cell in the grid. Specialized cell classes display images and other data types.

Figure 21.1 This figure illustrates the key classes used with the DataGridView control.

In the next chapter we extend this application as we discuss data binding on individual Windows Forms controls. Chapter 22 also presents the `BindingSource` class, which encapsulates the use and manipulation of data sources.

21.1 DATA GRID VIEWS

A data grid view is just that: a grid in which data is displayed. The `DataGridView` class encapsulates this concept, allowing various collections of data to be displayed and manipulated by a user. The concept of data binding is central to the `DataGridView` class, as data is typically displayed in the control by binding an existing database table or collection class to the data grid view object.

As shown in figure 21.1, the `DataGridView` class displays data as a set of rows and columns. The grid in general represents a specific collection of data, and this case represents a `PhotoAlbum` instance. Each row, in turn, represents a specific item in the overall collection, and each column represents a specific field that can be assigned to each item. In our application, each row will represent a Photograph object, and each column a possible property of a photograph. Various terms and classes related to DataGridView controls are pointed out in figure 21.1 as they relate to our application.

21.1.1 The DataGridView class

As we saw in chapter 14, the ListView class presents a table of information. The Windows Forms namespace provides explicit classes to represent rows and columns in a list view. Each item, or row, in the list is represented by a ListViewItem class instance, with additional items in the row represented by ListViewSubItem instances. Each column is based on a ColumnHeader instance.

As shown by figure 21.1, the DataGridView class takes a somewhat different approach. The contents of the grid are contained in a single collection, such as an array, a photo album, or a database table. Classes exist to configure the style for the provided data, including colors, borders, column ordering, and other properties. We discuss details of these classes later in the chapter. An overview of the DataGridView class is provided in .NET Table 21.1 on page 612.

The DataGridView class may win the award for the most complicated class in the Windows Forms namespace. It has more members and is more flexible and customizable than most programmers realize. For this reason, .NET Table 21.1 is larger than usual in order to illustrate the breadth of this class. Even so, only a small portion of the available members are shown.

Many of the DataGridView class members are centered on displaying, manipulating, and managing cells, columns, and rows. For example, there are methods to begin, end, commit, and cancel edits to a specific cell, and a related set of events for processing these actions. There is also an EditMode property that defines what keyboard action, if any, initiates an edit of a cell.

Another set of members enable the display and management of errors that occur in external code on behalf of a cell or row in the grid. The DataError event allows exceptions that occur in such code to be intercepted by the control.

One other member worth a mention is the HitTest method. This works much like the MonthCalendar.HitTest method discussed in section 14.3. The method returns a DataGridView.HitTestInfo object that contains information about a given location.

21.1.2 Creating a data grid view

While the DataGridView class includes numerous members of every ilk, it is possible to create a very simple grid with only a few lines of code. We begin with such an application, and enhance it over the course of the chapter.

The following steps lay out the creation and initial layout of our new application.

CREATE THE MYALBUMDATA PROJECT

	Action	Result
1	Create a new project and solution in Visual Studio called MyAlbumData.	The new solution is shown in the Solution Explorer window, with the default Form1.cs [Design] window displayed.

2 — **Action:** Rename the Form1.cs file and related class file to the `DataForm` class and assign its settings as shown.

Settings

Property	Value
(Name)	DataForm
Size	450, 300
Text	MyAlbumData

Result: The settings are assigned in the `InitializeComponent` method of the DataForm.Designer.cs file.

```
//
// DataForm
//
this.AutoScaleDimensions = new
  System.Drawing.SizeF(6F, 13F);
this.AutoScaleMode = System.Windows.
        Forms.AutoScaleMode.Font;
this.ClientSize = new
  System.Drawing.Size(442, 266);
this.Name = "DataForm";
this.Text = "MyAlbumData";
```

3 — **Action:** Drag a `Label`, `ComboBox`, `DataGridView`, and `Button` control onto the form. Arrange these controls as shown in the graphic.

Settings

Control	Property	Value
Label	Text	&Album:
Combo box	(Name)	combo-Album
	Anchor	Top, Left, Right
	DropDown Width	500
DataGrid View	(Name)	gridPhoto-Album
	Anchor	Top, Bottom, Left, Right
Button	(Name)	btnClose
	Anchor	Bottom, Right
	Text	&Close

4 — **Action:** Create a `Click` event handler for the Close button to shut down the application.

Result:

```
private void btnClose_Click
    (object sender, EventArgs e)
{
  Close();
}
```

.NET Table 21.1 DataGridView class

New in 2.0 The `DataGridView` class is a control that displays a collection of data as a grid of rows and columns. The data displayed and the style in which it is presented is fully configurable. This class is part of the `System.Windows.Forms` namespace, and inherits from the `Control` class.

Public Properties	*AllowUserToAddRows*	Gets or sets whether the user is permitted to add rows to the grid. Similar properties allow a user to delete or resize rows, and order or resize columns.
	CellBorderStyle	Gets or sets the `DataGridViewCellBorderStyle` enumeration value representing the border style for cells. Other border style properties exist as well—if you can imagine it, there is probably a property for it.
	Columns	Gets the collection of columns in the grid. A series of `ColumnHeader` properties control the style, height, and visibility of column headers.
	CurrentCell	Gets or sets the current active cell.
	DataSource	Gets or sets the source of data for the grid. The `DataMember` property gets or sets the name of the list or table within this source to display.
	DefaultCellStyle	Gets or sets the `DataGridViewCellStyle` object to apply to the grid if no other style is set. Other cell style properties exist as well—if you can imagine it, there is probably a property for it.
	EditingControl	Gets the `Control` hosted by the current cell when the cell is in edit mode. The `EditPanel` property gets the `Panel` containing this control, and the `EditMode` property defines how edit mode is enabled.
	FirstDisplayedCell	Gets or sets the first visible cell of the grid.
	GridColor	Gets or sets the color of grid lines separating the cells in the grid.
	IsCurrentCellDirty	Gets whether the current cell has uncommitted changes. The `IsCurrentRowDirty` property gets whether the current row has uncommitted changes.
	IsCurrentCellInEditMode	Gets whether the current cell is in edit mode.
	Item	Gets or sets the cell located at an indicated row and column.
	MultiSelect	Gets or sets whether more than one cell, row, or column can be selected at a time.

.NET Table 21.1 DataGridView class *(continued)*

Public Properties *(continued)*	*RowTemplate*	Gets or sets a template for rows in the grid, which can be a custom `DataGridViewRow` object.
	SelectedCells	Gets the collection of cells selected in the grid. `SelectedColumns` and `SelectedRows` properties also exist.
	SelectionMode	Gets or sets how cells, columns, or rows are selected in the grid.
	VirtualMode	Gets or sets whether cell data management for the grid is customized (`true`) or handled internally by the class (`false`).
Public Methods	*AutoResizeColumn*	Adjusts the width of a column to fit its contents. Other `AutoResize` methods exist as well.
	BeginEdit	Puts the selected cell into edit mode.
	DisplayedRowCount	Returns the number of rows currently displayed.
	GetCellCount	Returns the number of cells satisfying a given filter.
	HitTest	Returns location information within the grid of a specified point on the screen.
	InvalidateCell	Forces the contents of a cell to be repainted. The `InvalidateColumn` and `InvalidateRow` methods also exist.
Public Events	*CellClick*	Occurs when any part of a cell is clicked.
	CellEnter	Occurs when a cell receives input focus. A `RowEnter` event also exists.
	CellMouseDown	Occurs when the user presses a mouse button within a cell.
	CellValueNeeded	Occurs when the `VirtualMode` property is `true` and a value is needed so the grid can format and display a cell.
	ColumnHeaderMouseClick	Occurs when a column header is clicked. A `RowHeaderMouseClick` event also exists.
	DataBindingComplete	Occurs when a data binding operation has finished.
	DataError	Occurs when an external data error occurs, or when an attempt to commit a data change fails.
	Scroll	Occurs when the user scrolls the data grid.
	Sorted	Occurs when a sort operation has completed.

Nothing new here. The application compiles, runs, and even has a convenient Close button. Let's move along.

21.1.3 Populating a data grid view

Our main window in the MyAlbumData application contains a combo box and a data grid. Our `ComboBox` will show the list of albums in the default album directory, while our `DataGridView` control will display the contents of the selected album. This section makes the changes required for this behavior. Section 21.2 looks at how this information can be customized within the grid.

Fortunately, our existing MyPhotoAlbum project can do most of the work here. The changes required are detailed in the following steps.

DISPLAY ALBUM DATA IN THE MYALBUMDATA APPLICATION

	Action	Result
1	In the Solution Explorer window, add the MyPhotoAlbum and MyPhotoControls projects to the solution and reference them within the MyAlbumData project.	Solution Explorer - Solution 'MyAlb... Solution 'MyAlbumData' (3 projects) MyAlbumData Properties References DataForm.cs DataForm.Designer.cs DataForm.resx Program.cs MyPhotoAlbum MyPhotoControls

2	At the top of the DataForm.cs file, indicate that we are using the two Manning and the `System.IO` namespaces.	`. . .`
		`using System.IO;`
		`. . .`
		`using Manning.MyPhotoAlbum;`
		`using Manning.MyPhotoControls;`

3	Define a private field and internal property to hold the `AlbumManager` for the class.	`public partial class DataForm : Form`
		`{`
		`  private AlbumManager _manager;`
		`  internal AlbumManager Manager`
		`      { get { return _manager; } }`

DISPLAY ALBUM DATA IN THE MYALBUMDATA APPLICATION *(CONTINUED)*

<table>
<tr><th></th><th>Action</th><th>Result</th></tr>
<tr><td>4</td><td>Override the <code>OnLoad</code> method to:
a. Show the version number in the title bar.
b. Initialize the manager field.
c. Set the album filenames to appear in the <code>ComboBox</code> control.
d. Open the current album.
Note: As in our other applications, we assume the version is set to the current section number, in this case 21.1.</td><td><pre>protected override void OnLoad(EventArgs e)
{
  Version ver = new Version(
                Application.ProductVersion);
  Text = String.Format("MyAlbumData "
    + "{0:#}.{1:#}", ver.Major, ver.Minor);

  _manager = new AlbumManager();

  comboAlbum.DataSource = Directory.GetFiles(
      AlbumManager.DefaultPath, "*.abm");
  OpenAlbum();
  SetDataSources();
}</pre>Note: We discussed the <code>DataSource</code> property here as an example of data binding in chapters 11 and 12. In this case, we bind the collection of objects for the <code>ComboBox</code> control to an array of directory strings.</td></tr>
<tr><td>5</td><td>Handle the <code>SelectionChangeCommitted</code> event on the <code>ComboBox</code> control to open the selected album and bind it to the grid.</td><td><pre>private void
  comboAlbum_SelectionChangeCommitted(
    object sender, EventArgs e)
{
  OpenAlbum();
  SetDataSources();
}</pre></td></tr>
<tr><td>6</td><td>Implement an <code>OpenAlbum</code> method to retrieve the string selected in the combo box, make sure a new album is selected, and close any existing album.</td><td><pre>private void OpenAlbum()
{
  string albumPath
    = comboAlbum.SelectedItem.ToString();

  if (Manager.FullName == albumPath)
    return;
  if (CloseAlbum() == false)
    return;</pre></td></tr>
<tr><td>7</td><td>Open the selected album file.</td><td><pre> try
  {
    _manager = new AlbumManager(albumPath);
  }</pre></td></tr>
<tr><td>8</td><td>If a known error occurs, reset the manager and display an appropriate dialog box.</td><td><pre> catch (AlbumStorageException aex)
  {
    _manager = new AlbumManager();
    MessageBox.Show("Unable to open album - "
        + aex.Message);
  }
}</pre></td></tr>
<tr><td>9</td><td>Implement the <code>CloseAlbum</code> method to dispose of any existing album, and return <code>true</code> for now to indicate the operation completed successfully.</td><td><pre>private bool CloseAlbum()
{
  if (Manager.Album != null)
    Manager.Album.Dispose();

  return true;
}</pre></td></tr>
</table>

	Display album data in the MyAlbumData application *(continued)*	
	Action	**Result**

10	Implement a `SetDataSources` method that assigns the current album as the data source for the data grid view.	`private void SetDataSources()`
		`{`
		`  gridPhotoAlbum.DataSource = Manager.Album;`
		`}`

This code opens the selected album and binds its contents to the grid. The result is that the collection of `Photograph` objects magically appears in the grid. As you can see, the grid determines the properties of our `Photograph` class automatically. These properties are then used as the columns in the grid, and each `Photograph` in the album is presented as a row in the grid. The result when this code is executed appears in figure 21.2.

The properties to display are determined using the `System.Reflection` namespace. We do not discuss this namespace in detail here. The members of this namespace allow .NET objects such as the `DataGridView` control to determine type and member information of an object at runtime. In this way our data grid can understand how the `PhotoAlbum` object is organized, and automatically create an appropriate grid structure.

Since the order of columns in the grid corresponds to the internal order of properties in the `PhotoAlbum` class, your columns might be ordered differently than those shown in figure 21.2. Properties that only provide a `get` access method are treated as read-only, while properties with both a `get` and `set` access method are modifiable. As a result the FileName and HasChanged columns are read-only, while the Photographer and Notes columns can be modified. We look at how to update the class with these changes shortly.

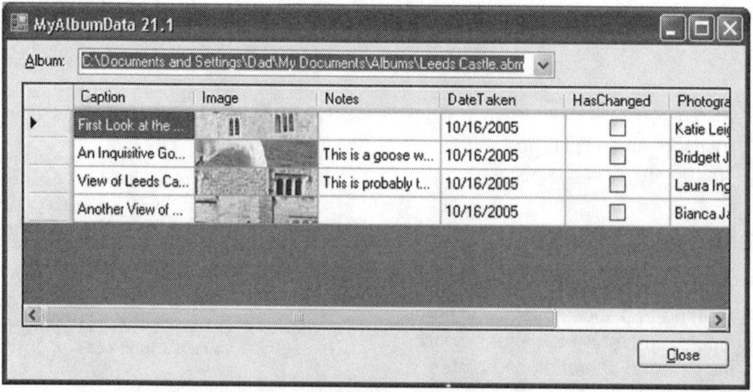

Figure 21.2 The DataGridView control adjusts each column based on the type of the corresponding property. The width and height of columns and rows can be adjusted using the mouse.

Back to our `DataSource` property, classes that wish to act as data sources must implement one or more interfaces to support this functionality. A summary of possible interfaces for this purpose is shown in table 21.2. For a more exhaustive list, see the topic *Interfaces Related to Data Binding* in the *Windows Forms Data Architecture* section of the .NET documentation.

Table 21.2 Interfaces related to data binding in the Windows Forms namespace

Interface	Usage	Notes
IList	A homogenous collection of objects. The first item in the list determines the type. The first property in that type is displayed as the only column when bound to a data grid.	This includes any simple array in C#, and all classes based on the `Array` object.
IListSource	The `GetList` method required by this interface returns an `IList` object that can be bound to a data source.	This is useful in classes that do not support `IList` but need to be bound to a data source. Examples include the `DataSet` and `DataTable` classes.
typed IList	A typed collection, such as our `PhotoAlbum` class. The type returned by the `Item` property is used as the assigned type, and all properties in this type can be displayed in a data grid. These can be bound to a data grid only at runtime.	Most notably, generic collections based on the Collection<T> class. This also includes classes derived from the `CollectionBase` class or classes with an indexer of a fixed type.
ITypedList	The `GetItemProperties` method required by this interface returns the properties used to bind data.	An object can support both the `IList` and `ITypedList` interface. When the `ITypedList` interface is not supported, the bindable properties are determined using reflection.
IList and IComponent	With both interfaces available, the class may appear in Visual Studio in the component tray and be bound to a data grid at design time.	As discussed in chapter 17, a component or control can be added to the Toolbox using the Customize entry in the Toolbox window's pop-up menu.
IBindingList	This interface permits two-way notification of changes, both from the control to the class and from the class to the control.	The generic binding list class supported by the BindingList<T> class is perhaps the simplest way to create collections with this feature.
IEditableObject	Classes implementing this interface are permitted to roll back, in a transaction-oriented manner, changes made to an object. **Note:** The term *transaction* indicates that a series of steps either fully completes or appears to never have happened. Aborting an operation partway through the required steps is said to *roll back*, or *undo*, the transaction.	As an example, the `DataRowView` class is a customized view of a row that supports transactional changes to the elements of the row.

Table 21.2 Interfaces related to data binding in the Windows Forms namespace *(continued)*

Interface	Usage	Notes
IDataErrorInfo	Objects implement the `Error` and `Item` properties to offer custom error information that controls can bind to.	The `DataRowView` class supports this interface as well in order to provide appropriate feedback to controls such as the `DataGridView` class when an error occurs.

For our purposes, we continue to use the typed `IList` interface supported by our `PhotoAlbum` class, and expand our functionality over the course of this chapter. The next section discusses various ways of customizing what appears in the grid.

21.2 COLUMNS AND ROWS

One of the obvious drawbacks of letting the `DataGridView` control generate the columns automatically is that we have no control over the selection and order of columns to appear in the grid. This is readily apparent in figure 21.2, where we see two image columns and the rather important `Caption` property is not visible. This section discusses how the contents of the grid view can be customized for a particular data source. We demonstrate some of these features by adjusting our application as shown in figure 21.3.

As we've already discussed, a `DataGridView` presents a collection of cells arranged into rows and columns. Each column is a `DataGridViewColumn` object that defines the style and contents for the column. When the `AutoGenerateColumns` property is `true`, the columns for the grid are generated whenever the `DataSource` or `DataMember` property value changes. After the columns are created, the

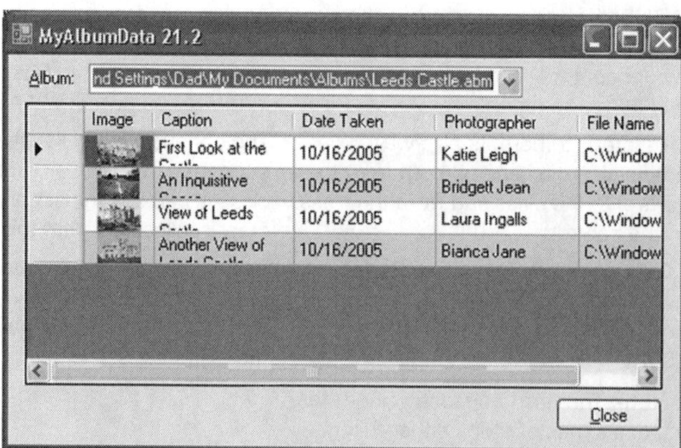

Figure 21.3 This grid view displays only certain properties of the Photograph class, and the size and content of each column has been customized compared with the application in the prior section.

columns are available in the Columns property and can be customized in the following manner:

- Columns can be hidden be setting their Visible property to false. This is useful to dynamically show or hide information in the grid depending on an application's state or settings.
- Columns can be added or removed using the Columns collection directly. For example, a column can be removed instead of hiding it when the contents of the column are never required.
- The order of columns can be adjusted by setting the DisplayIndex property of each column. The AllowUserToOrderColumns property can be set to permit users to adjust the order of columns manually.

Internally, at least in .NET 2.0, the columns are created as part of the internal OnPaint method, so you must wait until the control is painted before the columns can be adjusted. This might be problematic for properties that are dynamically created and consume resources. Our Image property in our Photograph class, for instance, would be created as a column even if we wanted to remove or otherwise adjust the column.

An alternative is to create columns explicitly, and set the AutoGenerateColumns property to false so the grid view will use the manually assigned columns rather than generating columns internally. In this case the resulting cells and rows can also be customized within the grid.

Such manual customization is the topic of this section, beginning with data grid view columns.

21.2.1 Creating columns

Columns in a DataGridView control are represented by the DataGridViewColumn class, as summarized in .NET Table 21.3. Columns are logical representations of cells that define how the column should appear and behave within the grid view. The actual cells displayed in the grid are stored in the Rows property of the grid, which holds a collection of DataGridViewRow objects. We talk more about rows shortly.

As you can see, the properties in .NET Table 21.3 relate more to the column itself than to the data it contains. Among the exceptions is the DataPropertyName property. This property defines how the data for the column binds to an assigned data source. If the data source is a collection, this property specifies the name of the property in the collection's objects to display in the column. For example, if our PhotoAlbum class is the data source, then the DataPropertyName value indicates the property from the Photograph class to display in the column.

When the grid is bound to a database object, such as the DataSet or DataTable class from the System.Data namespace, then DataPropertyName specifies the name of the column from the data source to display in the grid.

.NET Table 21.3 DataGridViewColumn class

The `DataGridViewColumn` class represents a vertical band of cells in a `DataGridView` control. It does not contain the actual cells in the grid view, but defines members to adjust the appearance and behavior of the column. This class is part of the `System.Windows.Forms` namespace, and inherits from the `DataGridViewBand` class.

Public Properties	AutoSizeMode	Gets or sets whether and how the column automatically adjusts its width within the grid.
	CellTemplate	Gets or sets the template used to create new cells for the column.
	CellType	Gets the actual type of the cell template.
	DataPropertyName	Gets or sets the property or data column name to bind to when displaying data from a data source in the column.
	DisplayIndex	Gets or sets the display order of the column relative to other columns.
	DividerWidth	Gets or sets the width of the column's right margin in pixels.
	HeaderCell	Gets or sets the cell that represents the column header.
	HeaderText	Gets or sets the text to display in the header cell. If not set, the value of the `Name` property is used.
	IsDataBound	Gets or sets whether the column is bound to a data source.
	MinimumWidth	Gets or sets the minimum width of the column in pixels.
	SortMode	Gets or sets whether and how the column is sorted.
	ToolTipText	Gets or sets the tooltip that displays when the mouse hovers over the column header.
	ValueType	Gets or sets the actual type of the values stored in the column's cells.
	Width	Gets or sets the current width of the column.

As you may have noticed, the `DataGridViewColumn` class does not specify how data is displayed in the column's cells. For this, we turn to the classes derived from the base column class. Table 21.4 contains the set of column classes based on the `DataGridViewColumn` class, along with the corresponding cell class used for cells shown in this column. A few of the additional properties defined by each column class are also shown in this table.

Table 21.4 Column classes derived from the DataGridColumn class

Column Class	Description	Properties
DataGridViewButtonColumn	Represents a column of buttons. Each cell is a `DataGridViewButtonCell` instance.	FlatStyle Text
DataGridViewCheckBoxColumn	Represents a column of check boxes. Each cell is a `DataGridViewCheckBoxCell` instance.	FalseValue FlatStyle TrueValue
DataGridViewComboBoxColumn	Represents a column of combo boxes. Each cell is a `DataGridViewComboBoxCell` instance.	DataSource DisplayStyle Sorted
DataGridViewImageColumn	Represents a column of images. Each cell is a `DataGridViewImageCell` instance.	Image ImageLayout
DataGridViewLinkColumn	Represents a column of clickable links, much like a hyperlink. Each cell is a `DataGridViewLinkCell` instance.	LinkBehavior LinkColor Text
DataGridViewTextBoxColumn	Represents a column of `TextBox` objects. Each cell is a `DataGridViewTextBoxCell` instance.	MaxInputLength

We can use some of these classes to customize the columns to appear in our MyAlbumData application. To ensure the new columns take effect before the grid control is drawn, we define the columns as part of the form's constructor.

CUSTOMIZE THE COLUMNS DISPLAYED IN THE DATAGRIDVIEW

	Action	Result

1	In the DataForm.cs code window, modify the constructor to invoke a `SetupGrid` method.	`public DataForm()`
		`{`
		`  InitializeComponent();`
		`  SetupGrid();`
		`}`

2	Implement this method to suspend layout of the grid and manually define the columns to display.	`private void SetupGrid()`
		`{`
		`  gridPhotoAlbum.SuspendLayout();`
		`  gridPhotoAlbum.AutoGenerateColumns = false;`
		`  gridPhotoAlbum.`
		`      AlternatingRowsDefaultCellStyle.`
		`          BackColor = Color.LightGray;`

3	Create an image column to hold the image associated with each photograph.
	
	Note: As in prior chapters, the existence of a `Thumbnail` property in the `Photograph` class would improve the performance of this code.
		`DataGridViewImageColumn thumbCol`
		`  = new DataGridViewImageColumn();`
		`thumbCol.DataPropertyName = "Image";`
		`thumbCol.ImageLayout`
		`  = DataGridViewImageCellLayout.Zoom;`
		`thumbCol.Name = "Image";`
		`thumbCol.Width = 50;`

CUSTOMIZE THE COLUMNS DISPLAYED IN THE DATAGRIDVIEW *(CONTINUED)*		
	Action	**Result**

4	Similarly, create text box columns to hold the caption, date taken, photographer, and filename associated with each photograph. Also set the cell style for the caption property to wrap its text.	`DataGridViewColumn captionCol`
		`  = new DataGridViewTextBoxColumn();`
		`captionCol.DataPropertyName = "Caption";`
		`captionCol.DefaultCellStyle.WrapMode`
		`  = DataGridViewTriState.True;`
		`captionCol.Name = "Caption";`
		
		`DataGridViewColumn takenCol`
		`  = new DataGridViewTextBoxColumn();`
		`takenCol.DataPropertyName = "DateTaken";`
		`takenCol.Name = "Date Taken";`
		
		`DataGridViewColumn pgCol`
		`  = new DataGridViewTextBoxColumn();`
		`pgCol.DataPropertyName = "Photographer";`
		`pgCol.Name = "Photographer";`
		
		`DataGridViewTextBoxColumn fileCol`
		`  = new DataGridViewTextBoxColumn();`
		`fileCol.DataPropertyName = "FileName";`
		`fileCol.Name = "File Name";`

5	Add these new columns to the collection of columns displayed in the grid.	`gridPhotoAlbum.Columns.AddRange(`
		`    new DataGridViewColumn[] {`
		`  thumbCol,`
		`  captionCol,`
		`  takenCol,`
		`  pgCol,`
		`  fileCol});`
		
		`gridPhotoAlbum.ResumeLayout();`
		`}`

This change causes the application to display only the properties referenced by the `DataPropertyName` settings for the columns. The five columns are defined and then added to the grid's `Columns` collection. We use the `ImageLayout` property of the `DataGridViewImageColumn` class to indicate that images should scale to fit within their cell.

You may also notice that we set a couple of image style properties here. We set the entire grid to use a different background color for alternating rows, and the caption column to wrap the text in each cell. These features appear in figure 21.3.

Cell styles are based on the `DataGridViewCellStyle` class, which is summarized in .NET Table 21.5. Styles can be set through various properties on the entire grid and for columns, rows, and finally the cell itself. As illustrated by our code, multiple style settings are merged together to determine the final style for each cell. We discuss the `DataGridViewCell` class in section 21.3, but it is worth mentioning here that this class defines an `InheritedStyle` property that holds the combined style settings for a cell. This property references a `DataGridViewCellStyle` instance, where the value for each setting is assigned to the first assigned value in the following properties:

- `DataGridViewCell.Style`—Cell style settings take precedence over all other style settings.
- `DataGridViewRow.DefaultCellStyle`—Row style settings are preferred over any column style settings.
- `DataGridView.AlternatingRowsDefaultCellStyle`—This style only applies to cells in every other row.
- `DataGridView.RowsDefaultCellStyle`—Default row styles also override any column settings.
- `DataGridViewColumn.DefaultCellStyle`—Column styles override any default style for the grid.
- `DataGridView.DefaultCellStyle`—Default style settings in the grid are used only if the corresponding setting is not set in any other style for the cell.

The settings in .NET Table 21.5 default to a "not set" value that causes the corresponding setting to be ignored when determining the `InheritedStyle` settings for a cell according the prior hierarchy. For example, the `Color` properties default to

.NET Table 21.5 DataGridViewCellStyle class

New in 2.0 The `DataGridViewCellStyle` class defines formatting and display settings that can be applied to cells within a `DataGridView` control. This class is part of the `System.Windows.Forms` namespace, and supports the `ICloneable` interface.

Public Properties	*Alignment*	Gets or sets the vertical and horizontal alignment for cell content.
	BackColor	Gets or sets the background color for a cell. The `ForeColor` property gets or sets the foreground color.
	DataSourceNullValue	Gets or sets the object stored in the data source when a `null` value is entered into the cell.
	Font	Gets or sets the `Font` to use for textual content in a cell.
	Format	Gets or sets the format string to apply to textual content in a cell. The `FormatProvider` property defines the `IFormatProvider` to utilize when formatting a cell.
	NullValue	Gets or sets the object to display when a cell has a value of `null` or `DBNull.Value`.
	SelectionForeColor	Gets or sets the foreground color for selected cells. The `SelectionBackColor` property gets or sets the background color for selected rows.
	Tag	Gets or sets an `object` to associate with this style.
	WrapMode	Gets or sets whether textual content in a cell uses multiple lines or is truncated when displayed.

Color.Empty, while the enumerations used for the Alignment and WrapMode properties include a NotSet value.

It is worth experimenting with the different style properties in the various classes to get a feel for what can and cannot be done in a grid view. We will not delve into the style class in more detail, but instead take a closer look at the combo box column type.

TRY IT! The DataGridView control provides a CellFormatting event that allows an application to alter the value for a cell before it is displayed. Add a new TextBox column that displays the size of the image associated with the photograph. Set the DataPropertyName for the column to "Image" and handle the CellFormatting event on the grid to convert the given image value for the cell to a string showing the width and height of the associated image.

21.2.2 Creating combo box columns

Now that we have customized our data grid view to show only the columns we are interested in, let's take a more in-depth look at some specific elements of the grid view control. In this section we take a quick look at the combo box column. In the next section we examine the row class.

As mentioned in table 21.4, the DataGridViewComboBoxColumn class represents a column where each cell contains a combo box, or, more specifically, each cell contains a DataGridViewComboBoxCell instance. A summary of the column class is shown in .NET Table 21.6.

.NET Table 21.6 DataGridViewComboBoxColumn class

New in 2.0 The DataGridViewComboBoxColumn class represents a data grid view column that displays a combo box in each cell. This class is part of the System.Windows.Forms namespace, and inherits from the DataGridViewColumn class.

Public Properties	*AutoComplete*	Gets or sets whether each cell in the column completes the entered text with the closest matching selection.
	DataSource	Gets or sets the object that provides selection data.
	DisplayMember	Gets or sets the property or column in the data source that holds the display string for the combo boxes. The ValueMember property gets or sets the property or column that holds the value for each list item.
	DisplayStyle	Gets or sets how the combo boxes appear when not in edit mode.
	DropDownWidth	Gets or sets the width of all drop-down lists.
	Items	Gets the object collection to use as selections for the combo boxes.
	MaxDropDownItems	Gets or sets the maximum number of drop-down items to display in the combo boxes.

As you can see, the members in the combo box column class are much like the standard `ComboBox` control. One major difference is that the properties in the table apply to the entire column in the grid. So, for example, when you set a data source for the column, every cell in the column will use this same data source as the set of drop-down items to display. In fact, each cell in such a column is a `DataGridView-ComboBoxCell` class. This cell class defines many of the same properties as the column class to allow each cell to customize its behavior and content. For example, the `DataGridViewComboBoxCell` class defines a `DataSource` property to set the source for selection items specific to the cell. When overriding a column setting such as the data source, the cell property should normally be defined after the column properties have been set.

We can use the infrastructure we set up while discussing the actual `ComboBox` control to turn our Photographer column into a combo box column. The following steps make this change.

CREATE A COMBO BOX COLUMN IN THE GRID VIEW

	Action	Result

1	Modify the `SetupGrid` method to create a combo box column for the photographer setting.	<pre>private void SetupGrid()
		{
		  . . .
		  DataGridViewComboBoxColumn pgCol
		      = new DataGridViewComboBoxColumn();</pre>

2	Configure the combo boxes so that auto-completion is on and all drop-down lists show no more than four items at a time.	<pre> **pgCol.AutoComplete = true;**
		  pgCol.DataPropertyName = "Photographer";
		  pgCol.MaxDropDownItems = 4;
		  pgCol.Name = "Photographer";
		  . . .
		}</pre>

3	Modify the `SetDataSources` method to assign the list of photographers for the album as the data source for the combo box column's drop-down lists.	<pre>private void SetDataSources()
		{
		  gridPhotoAlbum.DataSource = Manager.Album;
		  DataGridViewComboBoxColumn pgCol
		    = gridPhotoAlbum.Columns["Photographer"]
		        as DataGridViewComboBoxColumn;
		  if (pgCol != null)
		    pgCol.DataSource = Manager.Photographers;
		}</pre>

Compile and run the application to view the new column; this column is shown at the start of the next section in figure 21.4. Each cell in the column displays the current photographer assigned to the image, and displays a drop-down arrow where an alternate photographer can be selected. Our code enables automatic text completion within each cell, and restricts the maximum number of drop-down items to four.

If you experiment with the combo box cells, you will quickly realize that the grid view's combo box does not permit new items to be entered in the cell. The standard `ComboBox` control provides a `DropDownStyle` property for this purpose, but an equivalent setting is not available in the .NET 2.0 version of the `DataGridView-ComboBoxColumn` class. As a result, only existing photographers can be assigned to each image. The next section provides an alternative way to assign the photograph to work around this limitation.

TRY IT! The `DisplayStyle` property in the `DataGridViewComboBoxColumn` class defines how each cell appears when it is not being edited. This property takes its values from the `DataGridViewComboBoxDisplayStyle` enumeration. Alter the column to use each of the possible values in this enumeration to observe the different style settings available.

21.2.3 Understanding bands and rows

Now that we've spent all these pages talking about columns, you're probably asking yourself, "Well, sure, but what about rows in a grid?" Not to worry, now is the time to tackle this topic. Figure 21.4 shows the context menu we add next, in addition to the combo box column created in the prior section.

If you think about it, columns and rows are somewhat similar. A column is simply a vertical collection of cells, while a row is horizontal collection of cells. In the .NET Framework, this concept is encapsulated by the `DataGridViewBand` class, as summarized in .NET Table 21.7.

As you can see, the members of the `DataGridViewBand` class apply equally well to both rows and columns. For example, the `Frozen` property freezes a row or column so that it is always visible in the control. This is applied to the column header row by default to ensure that it remains visible while the rest of a grid's contents are scrolled by the user.

The `DataGridViewColumn` classes presume that all of the cells in the column display a similar user interface. A number of classes are provided to encapsulate the various column types you might wish to employ, and custom columns can be built to encapsulate other kinds of columns as desired. Building a custom column is not an easy task, and is certainly beyond our current discussion, but it can of course be done.

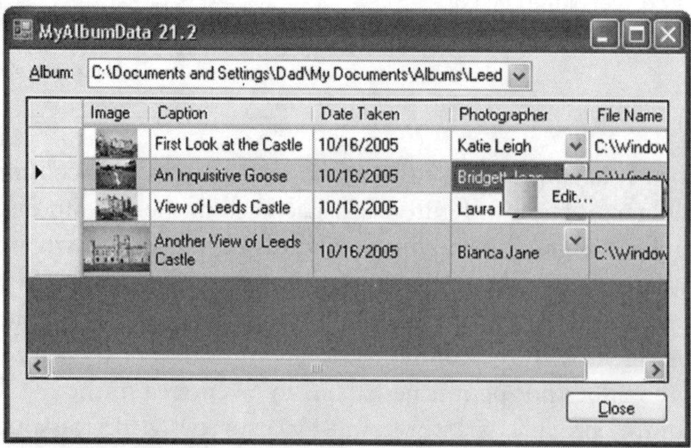

Figure 21.4 The "Another View" photograph row in this figure illustrates how the image column automatically resizes when the height of a row is modified.

.NET Table 21.7 DataGridViewBand class

New in 2.0 The `DataGridViewBand` class represents a linear collection of cells in a data grid view control. The `DataGridViewColumn` and `DataGridViewRow` classes derive from this base class. This class supports the `ICloneable` and `IDisposable` interfaces, is part of the `System.Windows.Forms` namespace, and inherits from the `DataGridViewElement` class.

Public Properties	*ContextMenuStrip*	Gets or sets the context menu strip for the band
	DefaultCellStyle	Gets or sets the default style applied to cells in this band
	Displayed	Gets whether the band is currently shown onscreen
	Frozen	Gets or sets whether the band moves when a user scrolls the associated `DataGridView` control
	Index	Gets the relative position of the band
	ReadOnly	Gets or sets whether the band's cells can be edited
	Resizeable	Gets or sets whether the band's cells can be resized
	Selected	Gets or sets whether the band is currently selected
Public Methods	*Clone*	Creates an exact copy of this band
	Dispose	Releases any resources used by the band

A row, on the other hand, holds a collection of cells of varying types. The first cell may be an image, the second a check box, the third a string, and so forth. A row holds all of the cells related to a specific object, typically a custom class or a database row. As a result, multiple row classes are not required. A single class, the `DataGridViewRow` class, can be used for all kinds of row configurations.

As shown in .NET Table 21.8, the `DataGridViewRow` class extends the `DataGridViewBand` class with properties and methods specific to rows in a grid. In particular, the class defines the `Cells` property that holds a `DataGridViewCellCollection` instance representing the collection of cells in the row. We discuss cells, or more specifically the `DataGridViewCell` class, in the next section.

We mentioned earlier in the chapter how the `DataGridView` control can support a wide range of grids, more than most programmers typically require. You are probably starting to see how this is true, with all the classes for columns, rows, bands, and other intricacies of this control.

Rather than cover every single detail of grid views, we continue to present this class in summary form, and allow you to experiment and investigate additional subtleties on your own. Here we show a brief example using the row class, by displaying a dynamic context menu associated with the current row.

.NET Table 21.8 DataGridViewRow class

New in 2.0 The `DataGridViewRow` class represents a horizontal band of cells in a data grid view control. Unlike the column class, the `DataGridViewRow` class contains the collection of cells in the row. This class is part of the `System.Windows.Forms` namespace, and inherits from the `DataGridViewBand` class.

Public Properties	*Cells*	Gets the collection of cells in this row as a `DataGridViewCellCollection` object
	DataBoundItem	Gets the object from the data source that populated this row
	ErrorText	Gets or sets the error text for row-level errors
	HeaderCell	Gets or sets the header cell for the row
	Height	Gets or sets the height for the row
	IsNewRow	Gets whether the row is a new or populated row
	MinimumHeight	Gets or sets the minimum height for the row
Public Methods	*CreateCells*	Resets the values of all cells in the row
	SetValues	Sets the values of all cells in the row

The following steps create and handle this context menu.

DISPLAY A CONTEXT MENU IN THE GRID

	Action	Result

1	Handle the `CellMouseDown` event in the grid view control.	`private void gridPhotoAlbum_CellMouseDown(`
		`    object sender,`
		`    DataGridViewCellMouseEventArgs e)`
		`{`

2	Within this handler, create a context menu to display at the current mouse position.	`  if (e.Button == MouseButtons.Right`
		`   && e.RowIndex >= 0 && e.ColumnIndex >= 0)`
		`  {`
		`    ContextMenuStrip menu`
		`        = new ContextMenuStrip();`
		`    ToolStripItem item`
		`        = menu.Items.Add("Edit...");`

3	Add a `Click` event handler for this menu called `editMenu_Click` and record the current row before displaying the menu at the current mouse position.	`    item.Tag`
		`        = gridPhotoAlbum.Rows[e.RowIndex];`
		`    item.Click`
		`        += new EventHandler(editMenu_Click);`
		
		`    menu.Show(MousePosition);`
		`  }`
		`}`

You may note, of course, that the `DataGridView` control, not to mention the `DataGridViewBand` class, supports a `ContextMenuStrip` property where a context menu can be specified in the designer. We could use this support if we wished, but it seems easier to create this menu dynamically.

We use the `CellMouseDown` event here as it supports both our current task and a cell-based task we illustrate in the next section. A number of row-based events are also available for data grid view controls, such as the `RowEnter` and `RowLeave` events, that are useful when you need to interact more directly with the rows in a grid. The `CellMouseDown` event used here receives the `DataGridViewCellMouseEventArgs` class as the event arguments. This class is based on the standard `MouseEventArgs` class and defines additional properties to retrieve the row and column index clicked by the user.

We still need to implement the `Click` handler for the Edit menu. The following steps also illustrate the Visual Studio's refactoring support for extracting a method from an existing set of code.

CREATE A COMBO BOX COLUMN IN THE GRID VIEW

	Action	Result

4	Extract a new `SetComboColumnDataSource` method from the lines in the `SetDataSources` method that assigns the data source for the grid's combo box column.
	How-to
	a. Highlight the lines in the `SetDataSources` method that assign the data source.
	b. Right-click this selection to display the context menu.
	c. Select the Extract Method item from the Refactor menu as shown in the graphic.
	d. Enter the new method name `SetComboColumnDataSource` into the Extract Method dialog box.
		The selection of the Extract Method item from step c of the action is illustrated here.
		After the new method name is specified, this action produces the following code.
		`private void SetDataSources()`
		`{`
		`  bsAlbum.DataSource = Manager.Album;`
		`  SetComboColumnDataSource();`
		`}`
		
		`private void SetComboColumnDataSource()`
		`{`
		`  DataGridViewComboBoxColumn pgCol`
		`    = gridPhotoAlbum.Columns["Photographer"]`
		`        as DataGridViewComboBoxColumn;`
		`  if (pgCol != null)`
		`    pgCol.DataSource = Manager.Photographers;`
		`}`

5	Create the `editMenu_Click` method to handle the Edit item in the context menu.	`private void editMenu_Click(`
		`    object sender, EventArgs e)`
		`{`

6	If the sender contains the `Point` structure we assigned, determine the row associated with the indicated row index.	`  ToolStripItem item`
		`      = sender as ToolStripItem;`
		`  if (item != null`
		`      && item.Tag is DataGridViewRow)`
		`  {`
		`    DataGridViewRow row`
		`        = item.Tag as DataGridViewRow;`

	Create a combo box column in the grid view *(continued)*	
	Action	**Result**

7	Display the `PhotoEditDialog` for the `Photograph` instance associated with this row.	`Photograph photo`
		`    = row.DataBoundItem as Photograph;`
		`using (PhotoEditDialog dlg`
		`        = new PhotoEditDialog(photo))`
		`{`

8	If the user modifies the photo, then update the data source for the combo box column, in case a new photographer was specified.	`if (dlg.ShowDialog() == DialogResult.OK`
		`    && photo.HasChanged)`
		`{`
		`  SetComboColumnDataSource();`
		`}`
		`}`
		`}`
		`}`

This change works around the problem with our combo box column, in that the user cannot enter a photographer that is not already specified in the album. These changes allow a user to right-click a row and edit all properties of an associated photograph.

This concludes our discussion of the column and row classes in the `DataGridView` control. Next up: the `DataGridViewCell` class.

21.3 Cells

We started this chapter with grids, moved on to rows and columns, and now arrive at cells. A *cell* is simply a single box within the grid. It can be a *header cell* for a row or column, or a *data cell* containing information on a specific object represented by the grid.

A cell is the smallest object within a `DataGridView` control. In many applications there is no need to manipulate individual cells, but if the need arises, the cell class is quite useful.

21.3.1 The DataGridViewCell class

Just like rows and columns share the idea of a linear collection of cells, called a *band*, cells share various properties with bands. Both cells and bands are *elements* of a data grid view. As such, both classes inherit from the `DataGridViewElement` class, as summarized in .NET Table 21.9.

As you can see, the `DataGridViewElement` class is not overly complex. The `State` property may be the most interesting member. It defines a bitwise combination of `DataGridViewElementStates` enumeration values representing the current user interface state of the element. The `DataGridViewElementStates` enumeration indicates information such as whether the element is currently displayed on screen; is frozen, read only, or resizable; whether it is selected; and if it is displayable within the grid. While these states are enforced by the user interface, they can be overridden programmatically.

.NET Table 21.9 DataGridViewElement class

New in 2.0 The `DataGridViewElement` class is the base class for the parts of a grid view. In particular, the `DataGridViewCell` and `DataGridViewBand` classes derive from this class. This class is part of the `System.Windows.Forms` namespace.

Public Properties	*DataGridView*	Gets the data grid view associated with this element.
	State	Gets the UI state of the element.
Protected Methods	*RaiseCellClick*	Raises the `DataGridView.CellClick` event. This is one of a number of protected methods that raise events in the associated `DataGridView` object.

The `DataGridViewCell` class defines a large number of properties and methods to define and manipulate cells in the `DataGridView` class. A summary of this class is shown in .NET Table 21.10, which should give you a sense of what is available. See the .NET documentation for the complete list. As you can see, many of these members are similar to members of other data grid view classes.

Let's move on to a brief example that makes use of this class.

21.3.2 Using the cell class

You may have noticed that a `DateTime`-oriented column is not provided for the `DataGridView` control. You can, of course, build such a column by constructing a custom column and cell class for this purpose. This example is, in fact, included in the .NET documentation under the heading *How to: Host Controls in Windows Forms DataGridView Cells*. If you are interested in this topic, this article is certainly worth reviewing.

Building a custom column is a bit more than we'd like to cover here, especially since an example is readily available in the existing documentation. As an alternative, we will modify our `CellMouseDown` event handler to display a calendar whenever the right button is clicked in the Date Taken column. The result is shown in figure 21.5.

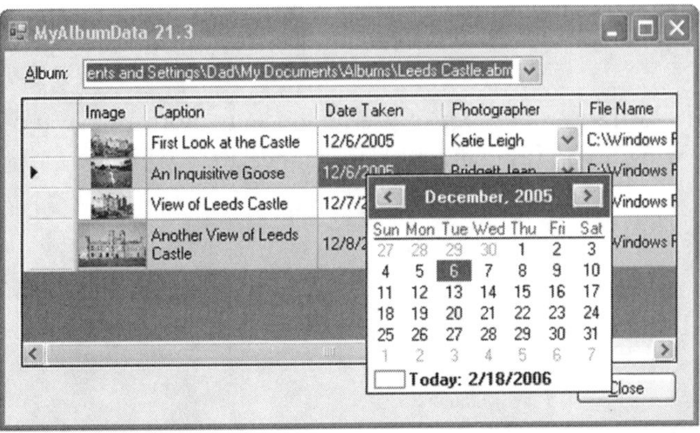

Figure 21.5 The pop-up calendar here is implemented as a borderless form that contains a panel and a month calendar control.

.NET Table 21.10 DataGridViewCell class

New in 2.0 The `DataGridViewCell` class represents an individual cell in a `DataGridView` control. The row and column index of this class identify the location of the cell within the grid. This class is part of the `System.Windows.Forms` namespace, inherits from the `DataGrid-ViewElement` class, and supports the `ICloneable` and `IDisposable` interfaces.

Public Properties	*ColumnIndex*	Gets the column index for this cell. The `RowIndex` property gets the row index.
	ContentBounds	Gets the bounds of the cell's content area.
	DefaultNewRowValue	Gets the default value for the cell in a newly created row.
	Displayed	Gets whether the cell is currently visible on screen.
	EditType	Gets the `Type` of the editing control hosted by the cell.
	ErrorIconBounds	Gets the bounds of the error icon for the cell.
	ErrorText	Gets or sets the text describing an error condition associated with the cell.
	IsInEditMode	Gets whether the cell is currently being edited.
	OwningColumn	Gets the column that contains this cell. The `OwningRow` property gets the cell's row.
	PreferredSize	Gets the rectangular area that can contain this cell.
	Style	Gets or sets the style for this cell.
	ToolTipText	Gets or sets the tooltip associated with this cell.
	Value	Gets the sets the value for this cell. The `ValueType` property gets or sets the data type for these values.
Public Methods	*Clone*	Creates an exact copy of this cell.
	InitializeEditingControl	Initializes the control used to edit the cell.
	PositionEditingControl	Sets the location and size of the editing control hosted by the cell.

The code for this illustrates a number of useful concepts, both in C# and Windows Forms. The following steps implement this change, after which we discuss some salient points.

SHOW A POP-UP CALENDAR WHEN THE DATE COLUMN IS CLICKED

	Action	Result

1	Rewrite the `CellMouseDown` event handler for the `gridPhotoAlbum` control to determine the row and cell clicked by the event.	private void gridPhotoAlbum_CellMouseDown(
		    . . .)
		{
		  if (e.Button == MouseButtons.Right
		    && e.RowIndex >= 0 && e.ColumnIndex >= 0)
		  {
		    DataGridViewRow row
		        = gridPhotoAlbum.Rows[e.RowIndex];
		    DataGridViewCell cell
		        = row.Cells[e.ColumnIndex];

2	If the Date Taken column is clicked, show a calendar drop-down.	int dateIndex = gridPhotoAlbum.Columns
		                    ["Date Taken"].Index;
		    if (dateIndex == e.ColumnIndex)
		      ShowCalendarDropdown(cell);

3	Otherwise, reuse the prior code to display the Edit menu in a context menu strip.	else
		    {
		      ContextMenuStrip menu = new . . .;
		      ToolStripItem item = . . .
		      item.Tag = gridPhotoAlbum.Rows[. . .];
		      item.Click += new EventHandler(. . .);
		      menu.Show(MousePosition);
		    }
		  }
		}

4	Implement the `ShowCalendar-Dropdown` method to determine the current value of the given cell.	private void ShowCalendarDropdown(
		    DataGridViewCell cell)
		{
		  DateTime current = (DateTime)cell.Value;

5	Create a month calendar, panel, and form control for use in this method.	MonthCalendar cal = new MonthCalendar();
		  Panel panel = new Panel();
		  Form f = new Form();

6	Configure the calendar control to select a single date, with the current date set to the value of the cell.	// Initialize calendar control
		  cal.MaxSelectionCount = 1;
		  cal.SetDate(current);
		  cal.DateSelected += new
		      DateRangeEventHandler(cal_DateSelected);

7	Configure the panel to be just large enough to contain the calendar and a border.	// Embed calendar within panel
		  panel.Width = cal.Width + 2;
		  panel.Height = cal.Height + 2;
		  panel.BorderStyle = BorderStyle.FixedSingle;
		  panel.Controls.Add(cal);

8	Configure the form to contain the panel, have no border, and appear at the current mouse position.	// Place panel in borderless form
		  f.FormBorderStyle = FormBorderStyle.None;
		  f.ShowInTaskbar = false;
		  f.Size = panel.Size;
		  f.Location = MousePosition;
		  f.StartPosition = FormStartPosition.Manual;
		  f.Controls.Add(panel);

9	When the form is deactivated, close the form.	f.Deactivate += delegate { f.Close(); };

	Action	Result
SHOW A POP-UP CALENDAR WHEN THE DATE COLUMN IS CLICKED *(CONTINUED)*		

10	As the form closes, set the cell's value to the selected date, if any.	`// Assign selected date during close`
		`f.FormClosing += delegate`
		`  {`
		`    if (cal.SelectionStart != current)`
		`      cell.Value = cal.SelectionStart;`
		`  };`

11	Finally, show the form on the screen.	`  f.Show();` `}`

12	Implement the `cal_DateSelected` event handler to close the associated form.	`void cal_DateSelected(`
		`    object sender, DateRangeEventArgs e)`
		`{`
		`  MonthCalendar cal = sender as MonthCalendar;`
		`  Form f = cal.FindForm();`
		`  f.Close();`
		`}`

This code dynamically creates a borderless form to hold the calendar, and updates the cell's value with any date selected by the user. Most of this code is straightforward, but the anonymous methods used here are worth a mention. Step 10, in particular, illustrates an anonymous method with hidden arguments. The code shown is short for the following code:

```
  . . .
  f.FormClosing += new FormClosingEventHandler(HiddenHandler);
  . . .

private void HiddenHandler(object sender, FormClosingEventArgs)
{
  if (cal.SelectionStart != current)
    cell.Value = cal.SelectionStart;
}
```

Even this code is not fully representative, as the `current` variable is local to the `ShowCalendarDropdown` method. So in addition to creating a hidden method similar to the prior code, the C# compiler automatically ensures that the value of the local `current` variable is available within this hidden handler.

This completes our discussion on data grid view cells. The last task here is the rather mundane task of saving any changes to the album.

21.3.3 Saving a modified album

So far we have bound a `PhotoAlbum` object to our `DataGridView` control and customized the columns and behavior of the resulting grid. At the moment, any changes made by the user to a displayed `PhotoAlbum` are discarded when a new album is selected or the application exits. This is not really desirable, so let's write some code to properly save changes made to the grid.

SAVE CHANGES MADE TO AN ALBUM		
	Action	**Result**

1	Rewrite the `CloseAlbum` method to ask the user if changes to an album should be saved.
	
	How-to
	Use the static `AskForSave` method in the `AlbumController` class.
		`private bool CloseAlbum()`
		`{`
		`  if (Manager.Album != null)`
		`  {`
		`    if (Manager.Album.HasChanged)`
		`    {`
		`      DialogResult result`
		`        = AlbumController.AskForSave(Manager);`

2	If the user cancels the request, return `false` to abort the operation.	`      if (result == DialogResult.Cancel)` `        return false;   // don't dispose`

3	Otherwise, save the album if requested and dispose of the album.	`      if (result == DialogResult.Yes)`
		`        Manager.Save();`
		`    }`
		
		`    Manager.Album.Dispose();`
		`  }`

4	Return `true` to indicate that the operation was successful.	`  return true;` `}`

5	Also override the `OnFormClosing` method for the form, to ensure that the album is saved as the application exits.	`protected override void OnFormClosing(`
		`    FormClosingEventArgs e)`
		`{`
		`  e.Cancel = !CloseAlbum();`
		`  base.OnFormClosing(e);`
		`}`

Ah, the joy of reusable code. Our efforts in part 2 to create a UI controller class, along with the features we built into the `AlbumManager` class, make this code rather straightforward. There's nothing to discuss here, so we may as well finish the chapter.

21.4 RECAP

In this chapter we investigated data binding while discussing the `DataGridView` class. We began with a new project, the MyAlbumData project, and created a form that displayed a selected album in a `DataGridView` control. We saw how to create and fill a data grid view, and how to customize the style used to display the contents of the data grid view control.

We then discussed the various `DataGridViewColumn` classes, and customized our grid to only display a selected set of columns. We took a closer look at the class that supports combo box cells, the `DataGridViewComboBoxColumn` class. We noted how the combo box that appears in a data grid view does not support all of the functionality in the standard `ComboBox` class.

Next up was the row class, suitably called `DataGridViewRow`. We created a dynamic context menu that allows the user to edit the `Photograph` object bound to the associated row. We reused our `PhotoEditDialog` class to do this.

The final section discussed cells, and in particular the `DataGridViewCell` class. This completed our review of the core `DataGridView` content classes, starting with the `DataGridViewElement` class, from which the cell and band classes derive. The row and column classes are based on the band class. We also indicated how custom columns are created, and showed a cell example using a borderless form to allow `DateTime` entries to be edited graphically.

As we mentioned in the chapter, the support provided by the `DataGridView` class is rather vast, and there are a number of additional features that are probably worth exploring but were beyond our available chapter space. I encourage you to experiment and explore this class to learn more about its capabilities.

The next chapter continues our look at classes related to data binding with a discussion of some key data binding interfaces and the `DataConnector` class.

CHAPTER 22

Two-way binding and binding sources

In chapter 21 we explored data binding and the data grid view control. The data binding covered in chapter 21 is called *complex data binding*, since the control binds to multiple objects in an array or other collection. Another kind of data binding, which we discuss in this chapter, is *simple data binding*, where a property is bound to a property of an element in a specified data source.

We will stick with our MyAlbumData project here, and extend the interface to support simple data binding within a tab control as an alternate way to view the selected album. More on this later in the chapter.

Before we discuss simple data binding, we look at a couple interfaces sometimes used when building data bound interfaces: the `IBindingList` and `IEditableObject` interfaces. Our existing data binding only occurs in one direction: the grid binds to the album data and updates the album with any changes made by the user.

In some situations the data may change independently of the user interface. For example, a help desk application may display a list of customers waiting on the phone. This list would most likely be stored in a database, and if there are multiple folks answering the phone, the list will change as each phone call is answered. In such an application, controls bound to this data should automatically update when the internal collection representing this data changes. Such two-way interaction between the data source and the bound controls is called *two-way binding*.

22.1 BINDING LISTS

The critical type for two-way binding is the `IBindingList` interface. This interface extends the `IList` interface discussed in chapter 5 to support more advance data binding scenarios required by some Windows Forms applications. The `DataView` class provided by the `System.Data` namespace supports this interface. As a result, in interfaces where the `DataSet` and `DataTable` classes are used as the source for data binding, you do not need to worry about this interface as it is inherently implemented on your behalf.

This interface becomes important if you wish to implement your own custom collection class, in the spirit of our `PhotoAlbum` class.[1] In this case, you may wish to implement the `IBindingList` interface as part of your base collection class or explicitly in your collection objects. As of the 2.0 release, the .NET Framework provides a generic `BindingList` class, which greatly assists such an effort.

We begin with the basics, of course, by discussing the `IBindingList` interface, before we move on to the generic `BindingList` class. Over the course of this discussion, we will upgrade our `PhotoAlbum` class as well.

22.1.1 The IBindingList interface

As we saw in chapter 5, the `IList` interface gives us pretty much everything we would want to manage a collection. The interface requires methods to add, insert, query, and remove items in a list. What is missing is the ability to edit and otherwise interact with an external class as the list is manipulated and modified. The `IBindingList` class, summarized in .NET Table 22.1, provides this support.

As you can see, the `IBindingList` interface provides members that allow an external class to add new entries in the list, sort the list, search the list, and receive notification that a list has changed. Classes like the `DataGridView` control employ such members to provide support for these activities.

For example, a grid can check the `AllowNew` property to see if a collection supports the addition of items via the `AddNew` method. If so, then the grid can add a new row by invoking this method. Similarly, the grid can use this interface to sort a column, search for a specific entry in a column, and update a row or the entire grid when a modification occurs.

---

[1] There is a good article by Paul Ballard on this topic in the August 2005 edition of MSDN Magazine, called "Give Your Everyday Custom Collections a Design-Time Makeover." The article covers both how to build custom collections and when you should consider using them.

.NET Table 22.1 IBindingList interface

The `IBindingList` interface extends the `IList` interface to support advanced data binding scenarios. This class is part of the `System.ComponentModel` namespace, and requires the `IList`, `ICollection`, and `IEnumerable` interfaces.

Properties	AllowEdit	Gets whether items in the list can be edited
	AllowNew	Gets whether items in the list can be added using the `AddNew` method
	AllowRemove	Gets whether items in the list can be removed using the `Remove` or `RemoveAt` methods
	IsSorted	Gets whether the list is sorted
	SortProperty	Gets the `PropertyDescriptor` object used for sorting
	SupportsChange-Notification	Gets whether a `ListChanged` event is raised when the list or an item in the list is modified
	SupportsSearching	Gets whether the list supports searching using the `Find` method
Methods	ApplySort	Sorts the list using a given property and direction
	RemoveSort	Removes any sort applied using the `ApplySort` method
Events	ListChanged	Occurs when the list or an item within the list has been modified

The `ListChanged` event is perhaps one of the more intriguing aspects of this interface. Handlers for this event receive a `ListChangedEventArgs` instance that identifies exactly what has changed. The members of this class are shown in .NET Table 22.2, which provides some insight into how a class such as the `DataGridView` control employs this event to updates its contents.

The `ListChangedType` property here returns a `ListChangedType` enumeration value that identifies what has changed. This is either an item that was added,

.NET Table 22.2 ListChangedEventArgs class

The `ListChangedEventArgs` class provides event data for the `ListChanged` event in classes that support the `IBindingList` interface. This class is part of the `System.ComponentModel` namespace, and inherits from the `System.EventArgs` class.

Public Properties	ListChangedType	Gets the kind of change applied
	NewIndex	Gets the index of the affected item
	OldIndex	Gets the prior index of an item that has been moved
	PropertyDescriptor	Gets the `PropertyDescriptor` instance for the property that was affected by this change

modified, deleted, or moved; a property that was added, modified, or deleted; or a large change that requires a complete refresh of the collection's data.

22.1.2 Creating a binding list

In the good old days of the .NET 1.*x* Framework, implementing the binding list interface took a bit of time and effort. With the advent of generics in .NET 2.0, a new generic `BindingList` class is provided that greatly eases the effort required. A summary of this class appears in .NET Table 22.3.

Since binding lists are by definition somewhat interactive with the collection, the `BindingList<T>` class cannot provide a complete implementation of the `IBindingList` interface. A series of protected virtual `Core` members provide the means for a derived collection to customize the behavior of the list. For example, the `AddingNewCore` method can be overridden to define the behavior of the `IBindingList.AddingNew` method.

The generic class also supports the `ICancelAddNew` and the `IRaiseItemChangedEvents` interfaces. The `ICancelAddNew` interface requires the `CancelNew` and `EndNew` methods to provide transactional behavior when new items are added to the list. The `IRaiseItemChangedEvents` interface allows a class to indicate whether it raises the `ListChanged` event when a property is modified.

As you may recall, our `PhotoAlbum` class implementation is based on the `Collection<T>` class. The class definition currently begins with the line

```
public class PhotoAlbum : Collection<Photograph>, IDisposable
```

.NET Table 22.3 BindingList<T> class

New in 2.0 The `BindingList<T>` class, new in .NET 2.0, provides a generic collection interface that supports advanced data binding. This class is part of the `System.ComponentModel` namespace, inherits from the `System.Collections.ObjectModel.Collection<T>` class, and supports the `IBindingList`, `ICancelAddNew`, and `IRaiseItemChangedEvents` interfaces. Members of the `IBindingList` interface are shown in .NET Table 22.1, and are therefore excluded from the following list of members.

Protected Properties	*IsSortedCore*	Gets whether the list is sorted
	SupportsSearchingCore	Gets whether the list supports searching
Public Methods	*CancelNew*	Discards a pending new item created with the `AddNew` method
	EndNew	Commits a pending new item to the collection
Protected Methods	*AddNewCore*	Adds a new item to the end of the collection
	OnAddingNew	Raises the `AddingNew` event
	OnListChanged	Raises the `ListChanged` event
Public Events	*AddingNew*	Occurs just before an item is added to the list

We can convert this class to support the `IBindingList` interface with the following simple change.

SAVE CHANGES MADE TO AN ALBUM		
	Action	**Result**
1	In the MyPhotoAlbum project, indicate that we are using the `ComponentModel` namespace.	`using System.ComponentModel;`
2	Modify the `PhotoAlbum` class to derive from the generic `BindingList<T>` class.	`public class PhotoAlbum` `    : BindingList<Photograph>, IDisposable`

This completes the bulk of the implementation. Our `PhotoAlbum` class now provides two-way binding. One feature that is not supported by default is the ability to raise the `ListChanged` event when an item in the collection is modified. This requires that the collection is somehow notified whenever an item in the collection, in this case a `Photograph` object, is modified.

We can enable this behavior by adding a `Modified` event that is invoked whenever a `Photograph` object changes.

ADD A MODIFIED EVENT TO THE PHOTOGRAPH CLASS		
	Action	**Result**
3	In the `Photograph` class, add a `Modified` event.	`public event EventHandler Modified;`

4	Add an `OnModified` method that raises this event.	`protected virtual void OnModified(EventArgs e)`
		`{`
		`  if (Modified != null)`
		`    Modified(this, e);`
		`}`

Assuming this event is actually invoked when a `Photograph` instance is altered, a containing class could receive this event and take appropriate action. One way to raise this event is to modify each property `set` accessor to invoke the event when the value changes. For example, listing 22.1 illustrates how the `Caption` property might invoke the `Modified` event when the caption changes.

As you might guess, we do not take the approach shown in listing 22.1. It is a good change and you are welcome to make it for this and other properties in your version of the class. We use an alternate approach as part of our discussion on the `IEditableObject` interface in the next section.

Listing 22.1 Sample Caption property that raises the Modified event

```
public string Caption
{
  get { return _caption; }
  set
  {
    if (_caption != value)
    {
      _caption = value;
      HasChanged = true;
      OnModified(EventArgs.Empty);
    }
  }
}
```

In the meantime, let's discuss how our PhotoAlbum class can receive this event now that it is based on the BindingList<T> class. We need to make sure that every change to the collection raises this event. Fortunately, we already know the methods where such actions can occur.

ADD A MODIFIED EVENT TO THE PHOTOGRAPH CLASS

	Action	Result

5	In the `PhotoAlbum` class, modify the `InsertItem` method to handle the `Modified` event for the given `Photograph`.	`protected override void InsertItem(`
		`    int index, Photograph item)`
		`{`
		`  `**`item.Modified += photo_Modified;`**
		`  base.InsertItem(index, item);`
		`  HasChanged = true;`
		`}`

6	Modify the `SetItem` method in a similar manner.	`protected override void SetItem(`
		`    int index, Photograph item)`
		`{`
		`  `**`item.Modified += photo_Modified;`**
		`  base.SetItem(index, item);`
		`  HasChanged = true;`
		`}`

7	Modify the `RemoveItem` method to remove the `Modified event` handler for the indicated photo.	`protected override void RemoveItem(int index)`
		`{`
		`  `**`Photograph p = Items[index];`**
		`  `**`p.Modified -= photo_Modified;`**
		`  base.RemoveItem(index);`
		
		`  p.ReleaseImage();`
		`  HasChanged = true;`
		`}`

	Add a Modified event to the Photograph class *(continued)*	
	Action	**Result**

8	Rewrite the `ClearItems` method to remove the event handler for all contained photos when the collection is cleared.	`protected override void ClearItems()`
		`{`
		`  if (Count > 0)`
		`  {`
		`    foreach (Photograph p in this)`
		`      p.Modified -= photo_Modified;`
		
		`    Dispose();`
		`    base.ClearItems();`
		`    HasChanged = true;`
		`  }`
		`}`

9	Implement the `photo_Modified` handler to raise the `ListChanged` event for the affected `Photograph` instance.
	How-to
	Convert the sender to a `Photograph` instance and use the `ResetItem` method to raise the `ListChanged` event.
		`private void photo_Modified(`
		`    object sender, EventArgs e)`
		`{`
		`  Photograph photo = sender as Photograph;`
		`  if (photo != null)`
		`  {`
		`    int index = IndexOf(photo);`
		`    ResetItem(index);`
		`  }`
		`}`

This prepares our `PhotoAlbum` class to raise the `ListChanged` event whenever a `Photograph` is added, removed, or modified. Controls that bind to an album, such as our `DataGridView` control, are able to refresh any displayed data as required.

All that remains to make this all work is the ability for our `Photograph` objects to invoke the `Modified` event appropriately. As already mentioned, we do this in the next section.

22.2 Editable objects

Editing an object can be a tricky endeavor. In our example, we have a single user, a single application, and a single `PhotoAlbum` object. We own the object, no one else can touch it, and life is good.

In the so-called real world, this is not always the case. A distributed application may have multiple users, all accessing the same set of data. If the data is stored in a database, then other programs or tools may also interact with this data. This can all get rather complicated rather quickly.

What we need is way to say, "This object is mine, so nobody touch it." When we are finished with the object we need to say, "Okay, I'm done." Or perhaps we might want to say, "Oops, never mind." For example, in a parts-management application, you would not want one user to request the last instance of a part at the same time another user requests the same part, without supplying a way to determine who actually gets it.

The IEditableObject interface enables this type of support in .NET objects. In this section we discuss this interface, when to use it, and how to incorporate it into our sample application.

22.2.1 The IEditableObject interface

As we have already seen, the editing of rows in our DataGridView control is handled directly using the discovered properties associated with our PhotoAlbum object. When the user changes a caption, the Caption property is called automatically by the grid to update the corresponding Photograph object with the new value. Similarly, when the photographer is changed, the Photographer property is called.

As discussed in the introduction, it would be good to coordinate these changes with other users or applications that may wish to interact with the same data. The IEditableObject interface, summarized in .NET Table 22.4, defines a mechanism for modifying an object in a transactional manner. This allows an application to obtain proper permission before modifying the object, and ensures that either all changes to an object are made or none of the changes are made. This is especially important in databases, where the fields of a row may be dependent on one another, or, as we have discussed, in multiuser environments.

The DataRowView class in the System.Data namespace supports the IEditableObject interface to ensure transactional update to the rows in a database. We are not building a database here, but we would like to update the PhotoAlbum object in a consistent manner. The IEditableObject interface provides a way for us to do this.

.NET Table 22.4 IEditableObject interface

The IEditableObject interface defines the ability to perform transactional operations on an object. This interface is used by various .NET classes such as the Windows Forms DataGridView control to track and enforce transactional behavior. This interface is part of the System.ComponentModel namespace.

Methods	BeginEdit	Initiates an edit operation on an object.
	CancelEdit	Discards any changes made since the last edit operation began. If the object was created with the IBindingList.AddNew method, it is discarded.
	EndEdit	Finalizes an edit operation. Any changes made since the last edit operation began are made permanent in the object. An object created with the IBindingList.AddNew method is made permanent in its container.

22.2.2 Creating an editable object

Looking at the Photograph class, there are four modifiable properties: Caption, Photographer, DateTaken, and Notes. These are the properties we need to consider in our IEditableObject implementation. Our implementation is not something you would present at a computer science convention, but it does illustrate some important aspects of editable objects.

With this excuse in mind, let's add support for the `IEditableObject` interface in our `Photograph` class.

<table>
<tr><th colspan="3">SUPPORT THE IEDITABLEOBJECT INTERFACE IN THE PHOTOGRAPH CLASS</th></tr>
<tr><th></th><th>Action</th><th>Result</th></tr>
<tr><td>1</td><td>In the Photograph.cs file, indicate that we use members of the <code>System.ComponentModel</code> namespace.</td><td><pre>using System.ComponentModel;</pre></td></tr>
<tr><td>2</td><td>Support the <code>IEditableObject</code> interface in the <code>Photograph</code> class.</td><td><pre>public class Photograph : IDisposable,
                          IFormattable,
                          IEditableObject
{</pre></td></tr>
<tr><td>3</td><td>Add an internal field to track when the object is in an editable state, and create an internal property with a private <code>set</code> accessor for this state.</td><td><pre> private bool _editing = false;
  internal bool Editing
  {
    get { return _editing; }
    private set { _editing = value; }
  }</pre></td></tr>
<tr><td>4</td><td>Add some fields to track the old values of the four modifiable properties.</td><td><pre> private string _savedCaption;
  private string _savedPhotographer;
  private DateTime _savedDateTaken;
  private string _savedNotes;</pre></td></tr>
<tr><td>5</td><td>Implement the <code>BeginEdit</code> method.

How-to
If editing is not already enabled, save the current values and enable editing.</td><td><pre> public void BeginEdit()
  {
    if (!Editing)
    {
      _savedCaption = Caption;
      _savedPhotographer = Photographer;
      _savedDateTaken = DateTaken;
      _savedNotes = Notes;
      Editing = true;
    }
  }</pre></td></tr>
<tr><td>6</td><td>Implement the <code>CancelEdit</code> method.

How-to
a. If editing is enabled, restore the saved values and disable editing.
b. Indicate that no changes have occurred, and raise the <code>Modified</code> event.</td><td><pre> public void CancelEdit()
  {
    if (Editing)
    {
      Caption = _savedCaption;
      Photographer = _savedPhotographer;
      DateTaken = _savedDateTaken;
      Notes = _savedNotes;
      Editing = false;

      HasChanged = false;
      OnModified(EventArgs.Empty);
    }
  }</pre></td></tr>
</table>

	SUPPORT THE IEDITABLEOBJECT INTERFACE IN THE PHOTOGRAPH CLASS *(CONTINUED)*	
	Action	**Result**

7	Implement the `EndEdit` method.
	How-to
	If editing is enabled, turn editing off and raise the modified event.
		`public void EndEdit()`
		`{`
		`  if (Editing)`
		`  {`
		`    Editing = false;`
		`    OnModified(EventArgs.Empty);`
		`  }`
		`}`

8	In the `AlbumStorage class, when a Photograph` is written, complete any active edit.	`static private void WritePhoto(`
		`    StreamWriter sw, Photograph p)`
		`{`
		`  **if (p.Editing)**`
		`    **p.EndEdit();**`
		
		`  sw.WriteLine(p.FileName);`
		`  . . .`
		`}`

These changes allow a class to begin, end, and abort an edit. Of course, our existing properties do not enforce the use of these methods. Ideally, we would also modify each property as shown for the `Caption` property in listing 22.2, where an exception is thrown if the `set` accessor is called without first calling `BeginEdit`.

Listing 22.2 Sample Caption property that enforces editing

```
public string Caption
{
  get { return _caption; }
  set
  {
    if (!Editing)
      throw new InvalidOperationException(
        "The object is not in an editable state");

    if (_caption != value)
    {
      _caption = value;
      HasChanged = true;
    }
  }
}
```

Of course, changing the `Photograph` properties as shown in listing 22.2 would break the applications we built in part 1 of this book. So, of course, we do not do this. Typically, ensuring that `BeginEdit` is always called before a class is modified is a good idea so you can enforce whatever synchronization or other coordination is required. Classes like the `DataRow` class in the `System.Data` namespace require that the `BeginEdit` method be called before its contents are modified.

The IEditableObject interface is now fully implemented, and our MyPhotoAlbum library is ready to go. We can test these changes in a couple ways. For the change we just made, the DataGridView class automatically detects that the IEditableObject interface is supported and uses it appropriately. You can see this by running the application, modifying a couple of values in the same row, and then hitting the Esc key to abort the change. The modified values will reset to their original settings.

For the IBindingList change, you can see the two-way binding in action by adding a new Test button next to the Close button within the application. The following code shows a sample Click handler that modifies the first Photograph in an album. Since our PhotoAlbum class now fully supports the IBindingList interface, the DataGridView automatically picks up the change and displays it in the grid.

```
private void btnTest_Click(object sender, EventArgs e)
{
  if (Manager.Album != null && Manager.Album.Count > 0)
  {
    Photograph p = Manager.Album[0];
    p.BeginEdit();
    p.Caption = "Test IBindingList";
    p.EndEdit();
  }
}
```

Now that we have a better understanding of the data binding support that collections can provide, let's get back to our user interface and talk about the binding source component.

22.3 SIMPLE DATA BINDING

As we mentioned in the introduction, binding data to a data grid view is referred to as *complex data binding*, since multiple values are bound to a single control. Complex data binding also refers to binding objects to a list control, such as a list box or combo box.

Simple data binding is used for binding single property values to a specific data source. This type of binding is supported by the Control class directly, and is therefore inherited by and available in all controls in the Windows Forms namespace. The concepts and techniques for so-called simple data binding are fairly identical to those we have already discussed for the DataGridView control.

In the .NET 1.*x* Framework, data binding was performed directly between Windows Forms controls and the desired data source. The Control class provided, and continues to provide, various properties and methods to help manage bound data in one control or a group of controls. Managing data binding with this support requires a rather explicit relationship between control and data, and a solid understanding of the various Control-based support.

During the design of the .NET 2.0 Framework, the Microsoft team realized that an indirect relationship would have some advantages. Controls would bind to an interim object, and this object would then manage the bound data. The goal was to simplify how data binding worked, especially for individual controls such as labels and text boxes.

The first attempt at this was the `DataContainer` class. The idea was to provide a container where bound controls could appear, much like the `Panel` control, and have all bound controls exist within this container—a fine idea, but it forced all controls to be somewhat grouped together.

Forcing bound controls to coexist was not really the goal, so the next attempt was a `Component` object that had no presence on the form other than to manage bound data. This control was called the `DataConnector` class, and it became the official solution. This class was later renamed to `BindingSource`.

This section discusses the result of this brief history, the `BindingSource` class, and how to use this class to support simple data binding within our MyAlbumData project.

22.3.1 The BindingSource class

A binding source is simply a source for bound data. It serves as a layer of indirection between controls and data sources. A binding source is somewhat transparent, in that it fills in as a `DataSource` object for a control. As a result, a `BindingSource` is used much like any other data source.

As shown in .NET Table 22.5, the `BindingSource` class supports the standard set of collection interfaces, including the `IBindingList` interface as well as the `IList`, `ICollection`, and `IEnumerable` interfaces. It also supports the `ICancelAddNew` interface we saw in chapter 21, to enable transactional additions of new members if supported by the underlying data source.

The specific `Type` for the underlying data source for a binding source is established in one of two ways. First, of course, the `DataSource` property can be assigned to a specific list or other object. The `BindingSource` then enforces the support inherent in the given source. As you may recall, table 21.2 in chapter 21 summarized the various interfaces that support such data binding.

A second way to fix the `Type` for a binding source is to add an item to the component using the `Add` method. This creates a strongly typed list for the `Type` associated with the assigned object.

In addition to standard collection and data binding support, the `BindingSource` class provides members for accessing and navigating the underlying data. The `Position` property sets the current index, with the `Current` property retrieving the item at this index, while the various `Move` methods navigate to the first, previous, next, or last item in the list.

A number of properties and methods also provide editing support for the list and its contained objects. This includes `EndEdit` and `CancelEdit` methods that invoke

.NET Table 22.5 BindingSource class

New in 2.0 The `BindingSource` class is a component that encapsulates a data source for a Windows `Form`. A binding source provides a layer of indirection between the controls on a `Form` and a data source. This class is part of the `System.Windows.Forms` namespace, inherits from the `Component` class, and supports the `IBindingList`, `ICancelAddNew`, and a number of other interfaces related to data binding. Because there are so many members of this class, properties and methods from the `IBindingList` and `ICancelAddNew` interfaces are excluded from the below set of members.

Public Properties	*CurrencyManager*	Gets the `CurrencyManager` for the data source
	Current	Gets the current item in the underlying list
	DataMember	Gets the specific list in the data source to bind to
	DataSource	Gets the data source for this binding source
	Item	Gets or sets the list element at a given index
	List	Gets the underlying list for the binding source
	Position	Gets or sets the index of the current item in the list
	RaiseList-ChangedEvents	Gets or sets whether `ListChanged` events should be raised
	Sort	Gets or sets how the underlying list should be sorted
Public Methods	*GetItemProperties*	Returns the collection of property descriptors for the items in the bound data source
	MoveFirst	Makes the first item in the data source the current item
	MoveNext	Increments the `Position` property to the next item
	RemoveCurrent	Removes the current item from the underlying list
	ResetBindings	Notifies any controls bound to this binding source to refresh their displayed values
	SuspendBinding	Prevents changes to the underlying list from simple-bound controls until `ResumeBinding` is called
Public Events	*BindingComplete*	Occurs when all clients have been bound to this binding source
	CurrentChanged	Occurs when the currently bound item changes

the corresponding calls on each item if the `IEditableObject` interface is supported by the underlying elements in the list.

To demonstrate the `BindingSource` class, we could simply alter the existing MyAlbumData project to utilize a `BindingSource` object rather than assigning the grid's `DataSource` property to the current album explicitly. This would not be very exciting, nor would it result in much of an example.

To really see the power of this class, we need to use it in conjunction with simple data binding. We set about building this example in the next section.

22.3.2 Altering the MyAlbumData application

Before we talk about the details of simple data binding, let's whip through some changes to our MyAlbumData application in preparation for this discussion. The change we make is to place our existing `DataGridView` control within a `TabPage` object, and add a new tab to display the `Photograph` information for an album one photo at a time. Figure 22.1 shows the modified application we build in this and the next few sections.

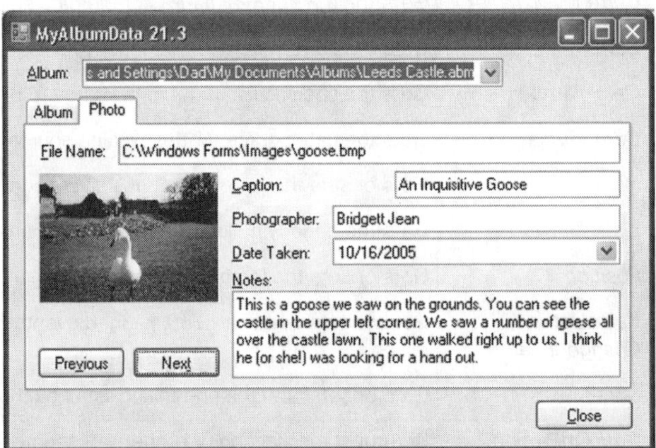

Figure 22.1 The controls on the Photo tab shown here are bound to their corresponding values in a Photograph object.

In this section we simply move our existing `DataGridView` control into an Album tab and create a Photo tab containing the controls shown in the figure. The following steps implement this change.

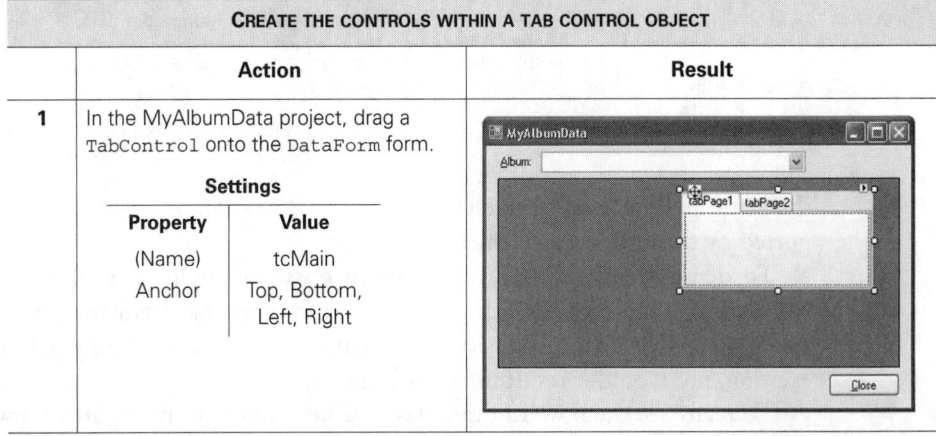

CREATE THE CONTROLS WITHIN A TAB CONTROL OBJECT		
	Action	**Result**
1	In the MyAlbumData project, drag a `TabControl` onto the `DataForm` form. **Settings** **Property** / **Value** (Name): tcMain Anchor: Top, Bottom, Left, Right	(screenshot: MyAlbumData form with Album, tabPage1, tabPage2, Close)

	CREATE THE CONTROLS WITHIN A TAB CONTROL OBJECT *(CONTINUED)*	
	Action	**Result**
2	Dock the `DataGridView` control to fill the first tab page; alter the `TabControl` to fill the bulk of the form. **Settings** **Page** / **Property** / **Value** First: (Name) = pageAlbum; Text = Album Second: (Name) = pagePhoto; Text = Photo	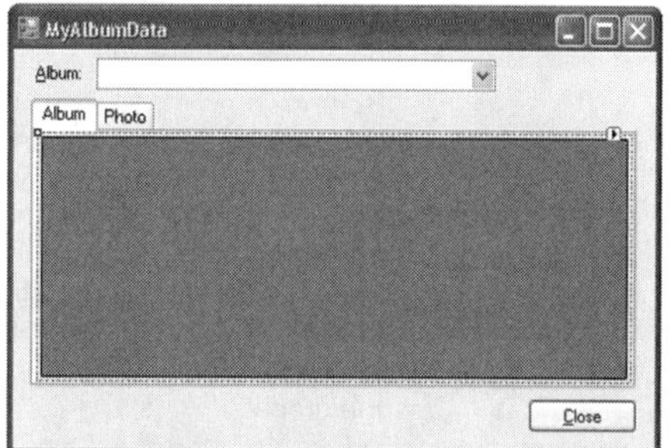
3	Create and position the controls for the Photo tab page as shown in the graphic. Set the `Text` property for each `Label` control as in the graphic, and the properties of the `TextBox` controls as follows: **Settings** **TextBox** / **Property** / **Value** FileName: (Name) = txtFileName; ReadOnly = True Caption: (Name) = txtCaption Photo-grapher: (Name) = txtPhoto-grapher Notes: (Name) = txtNotes; Multiline = True	The graphic here is the result of the changes in both this and the subsequent step. 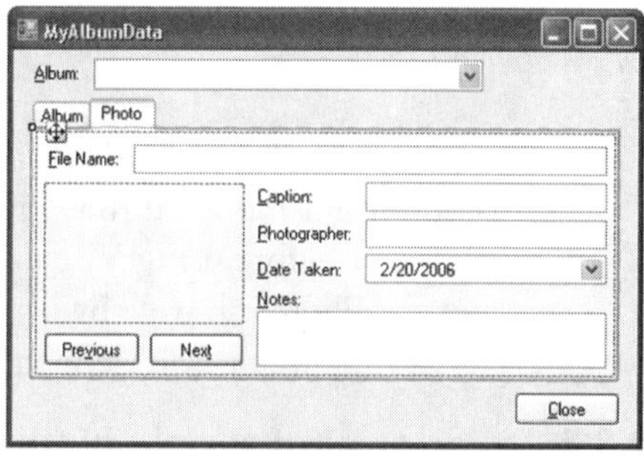
4	Assign properties of the other controls as follows: **Settings** **Control** / **Property** / **Value** Picture-Box: (Name) = pbxPhoto; SizeMode = Zoom Previous Button: (Name) = btnPrevious; Text = Pre&vious Next Button: (Name) = btnNext; Text = Nex&t DateTime Picker: (Name) = dtpDate-Taken; Format = Short	We set our keyboard mnemonics carefully here so a unique character is used for each control. The mnemonics for the `Label` controls are shown in the previous graphic.

CREATE THE CONTROLS WITHIN A TAB CONTROL OBJECT *(CONTINUED)*		
	Action	**Result**
5	Set the `Anchor` property for each control to an appropriate value. **How-to** You can assign this property for multiple controls by selecting a group of controls and assigning the `Anchor` value accordingly.	Generally, controls should be anchored to their closest edges. The key question is which controls you wish to grow as the form is expanded. In my project I set the anchor for the `PictureBox` control to all four sides so it can expand along with the form.
6	Assign the tab order for the controls within the Photo tab page as shown in the graphic.	

That took a bit of work. As we mentioned earlier in the book, you can reduce the amount of time spent drawing forms in Visual Studio by sketching out your controls on paper before using Visual Studio. While not illustrated in these pages, I sketched out the Photo tab page by hand before creating this page in Visual Studio.

With our controls defined, we are ready for our data binding discussion.

22.3.3 Performing simple binding

In complex data binding, a control provides a `DataSource` and `DataMember` property, and binds to the data found in the assigned source. Simple data binding, contrary to its name, is a bit more complicated. The idea is to bind a single property of a control to a single value of a bound item, where the item is a member of a defined data source.

Figure 22.2 illustrates the relationship between simple data binding and a data source. The data source is a collection of items, represented in the figure by the `DataGridView` showing a `PhotoAlbum` instance. The data source, in this case our album, holds items of a specific type, in this case `Photograph` instances.

Each control on a `Form` defines a binding between one of its properties and a specific property of the items held by the data source. For example, the `PictureBox` control defines a binding for its `Image` property, bound to the `Image` property in the `Photograph` class.

To support simple data binding, Windows Forms provides classes and members for each aspect of the binding illustrated in figure 22.2. The data source is the bound collection, database table, or `BindingSource` instance. The arrows between the controls and the data source is a `Binding` class instance, which we discuss momentarily. The `BindingManagerBase` class provides the glue between the bindings and

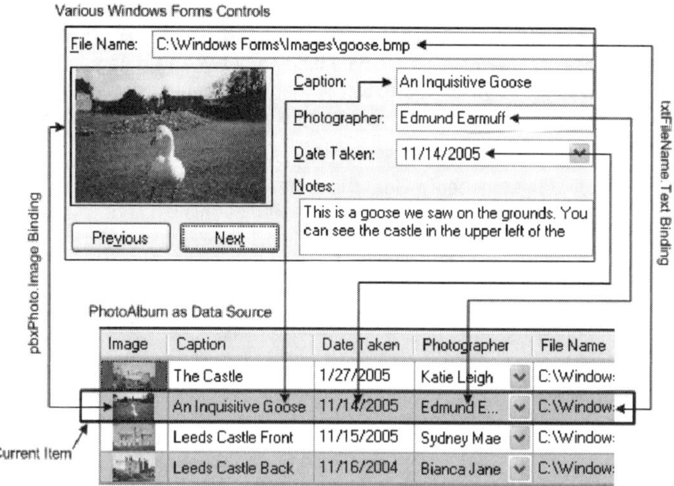

Figure 22.2 This graphic illustrates simple data binding between various controls and a current item within a data source.

the data source, synchronizing each binding with the current item selected from the data source. We discuss the `BindingManagerBase` class in the next section.

As shown in .NET Table 22.6, the `Binding` class represents a simple binding from a control's property to data. The constructor for this class indicates the property name and data source to bind to. Typically, the `DataBindings` property for a control is used for this purpose, so that the associated `Control` object is defined in the same statement. This property is of type `ControlBindingsCollection` collection. The signature to add a new `Binding` is as follows:

```
ControlBindingsCollection.Add(string propertyName,
                              object DataSource,
                              string DataMember);
```

The `Binding` class serves as a vehicle for customizing how the binding occurs. An `IFormatProvider` can be assigned with an associated format string to automatically format a value before it is assigned to the control property. Of special note are the `Format` and `Parse` events, which allow an application to customize how values are translated between the data source and the control.

For example, JPEG images allow an embedded caption to be stored within the image data. An application might wish to bind the `Text` property of a `TextBox` control to a JPEG image, in order to display or update the caption associated with the image. The `Format` and `Parse` events enable this to occur, since the `Format` event can be used to extract the caption text from the image and push it to the control, and the `Parse` event can be used to update the bound image with a new caption.

.NET Table 22.6 Binding class

The `Binding` class represents a simple data binding between a data source entry and a property of a Windows Form control. The `Binding` instances defined for a specific control are contained by its `DataBindings` property. This class is part of the `System.Windows.Forms` namespace.

Public Properties	BindingManagerBase	Gets the `BindingManagerBase` class instance for the data source used by this binding.
	BindingMemberInfo	Gets the `BindingMemberInfo` structure containing information about the data member used by this binding.
	Control	Gets the control that is the subject of this binding.
	ControlUpdateMode	Gets or sets when data source changes are propagated to the bound property.
	DataSource	Gets the data source used by this binding, taken from the corresponding value passed to the `Binding` constructor.
	DataSourceNullValue	Gets or sets the object to assign when the value from the data source is `null`.
	DataSourceUpdateMode	Gets or sets when changes to the bound property are propagated to the data source.
	FormatInfo	Gets or sets the format provider that provides custom formatting for this binding. The `FormatString` property gets or sets the formatting string for this provider.
	IsBinding	Gets whether this binding is currently active.
	PropertyName	Gets or sets the property name of the control that is the subject of this binding. This is taken from the corresponding value passed to the `Binding` constructor.
Public Events	*BindingComplete*	Occurs when a binding operation has completed.
	Format	Occurs when the value from the data source must be assigned to the bound control property.
	Parse	Occurs when the value from the control property must be assigned to a data source entry.

We can see this in our example by establishing bindings to our controls in the Photo tab. The following steps illustrate using a `BindingSource` object as the data source as well as establishing simple data bindings for our Photo controls.

BIND THE PHOTO TAB CONTROLS TO PROPERTIES IN THE PHOTOGRAPH CLASS

	Action	Result
1	Add a `BindingSource` component called `bsAlbum` to the `DataForm` designer window.	The component appears below the form in the component tray.

	Bind the Photo tab controls to properties in the Photograph class *(continued)*	
	Action	**Result**

2	In the `OnLoad` event, call a new `SetBindings` method to assign the required data bindings.	`protected override void OnLoad(EventArgs e)`
		`{`
		`  . . .`
		`  **SetBindings();**`
		`  OpenAlbum();`
		`  SetDataSources();`
		`}`

3	Implement a `SetBindings` method that sets the data source for the `DataGridView` control to the new binding source object.	`private void SetBindings()`
		`{`
		`  // Bindings for Album tab`
		`  gridPhotoAlbum.DataSource = bsAlbum;`

4	Also assign data bindings for the controls on the Photo tab page.	`  // Bindings data for Photo tab`
		`  txtFileName.DataBindings.`
		`      Add("Text", bsAlbum, "FileName");`
		`  txtCaption.DataBindings.`
		`      Add("Text", bsAlbum, "Caption");`
		`  txtPhotographer.DataBindings.`
		`     Add("Text", bsAlbum, "Photographer");`
		`  dtpDateTaken.DataBindings.`
		`      Add("Value", bsAlbum, "DateTaken");`
		
		`  txtNotes.DataBindings.`
		`      Add("Text", bsAlbum, "Notes");`
		`  pbxPhoto.DataBindings.`
		`      Add("Image", bsAlbum, "Image");`
		`}`

5	In the `SetDataSources` method, replace the line assigning the `DataGridView` data source with a statement that assigns the data source for the `BindingSource` instead.	`private void SetDataSources()`
		`{`
		`  **bsAlbum.DataSource = Manager.Album;**`
		`  SetComboColumnDataSource();`
		`}`

The controls are now bound to the appropriate properties of the `Photograph` items contained by the `PhotoAlbum` instance. Take, for example, the `DateTimePicker` control. We bind the `Value` property of this control to the `DateTaken` property of the active `Photograph` object in the data source with the following code:

```
dtpDateTaken.DataBindings.Add("Value", bsAlbum, "DateTaken");
```

We could create the `Binding` object explicitly with the subsequent code, but using the `DataBindings` collection is probably simpler.

```
Binding theBind = new Binding("Value", bsAlbum, "DateTaken");
dtpDateTaken.DataBindings.Add(theBind);
```

Note that the `Photograph.DateTaken` property is a `DateTime` value, which happens to match the type of the `DateTimePicker.Value` property. In fact, the type of all our bindings, including the `Image` property for the `PictureBox` control, matches the bound property in the `Photograph` object. The .NET Framework attempts to convert between the binding value and the bound value, but in our case conversion is not necessary. As we mentioned earlier, the Format and Parse events can handle the conversion explicitly if required.

It is worth mentioning once again that any property of a control can be bound. For example, we could add a MatteColor property to our Photograph object, and bind the background color, the BackColor property, of the PictureBox or even the TabPage itself to this color. We don't do this here, and I should probably caution you not to get too carried away with such features both in your data and in your applications. In some situations, such as a picture frame ordering interface, this type of feature could be very useful.

This code compiles and runs, with the result similar to figure 22.1. Notice how the BindingSource class handles changes to the data source automatically when an alternate album is selected.

All that is left here is to enable the Next and Previous buttons to work correctly. Before we do, it is also worth mentioning that Visual Studio provides direct graphical support for data binding when using a database or other class that supports both the IList and IComponent interfaces. In particular, the values from a database can be bound to a control during design time using the (DataBindings) setting in the Properties window. This is beyond the scope of this book, but worth keeping in mind as you develop more complex applications.

22.3.4 Updating data bound controls

Prior to the advent of the BindingSource class, the binding of controls to data involved various Windows Forms classes and Control properties. These classes are still part of the 2.0 framework, and correspond to the work performed by the .NET Framework on behalf of bound controls: tracking and managing data sources; and tracking and managing data bindings. A summary of these is shown in table 22.7. The table also shows how these activities are supported by the Control and BindingSource classes.

We have already seen how the Binding class represents a specific binding between a control property and a data source item. This works much the same regardless of whether a BindingSource is used, although the BindingSource provides more flexibility in altering and updating the data source associated with the controls.

When it comes to managing and tracking data sources, the situation is quite different. The BindingManagerBase class works fine, and was the only solution in the 1.*x* framework. The BindingContext class holds a collection of BindingManagerBase objects, and the Control.BindingContext property holds the binding context for the control.

A summary of the BindingManagerBase class appears in .NET Table 22.8. In a running application, an instance of this class is created for each active data source, and this instance is stored in the BindingContext instance associated with the Control object. Normally, the BindingContext created for the Form object is used,

Table 22.7 **Activities related to managing Windows Forms data binding**

Activity	Class	Control support	BindingSource support
Tacking the data sources bound to controls.	BindingContext	`BindingContext` property	Does not apply, since each `BindingSource` binds to a single data source
Managing a specific data source.	BindingManagerBase	`BindingContext` property, which contains a collection of `BindingManagerBase` objects	Usually handled explicitly through members like `Current` and `MoveNext`
Managing the data bindings for a control.	ControlBindingsCollection	`DataBindings` property	Not applicable
Managing a specific binding	Binding	`DataBindings` property, which contains a collection of `Binding` objects	Not applicable

although a `BindingContext` can be attached to any Control. For example, a `BindingContext` can be created for a `GroupBox`, `Panel`, or other parent control to contain the data sources for all controls within the container.

As you can see from the table, the `BindingSource` class provides many of the same members as the `BindingManagerBase` class. This is by design, of course, since a binding source is intended to be used instead of a `BindingManagerBase` instance.

As implied by the table 22.7, one difference between `BindingManagerBase` and `BindingSource` is that a `BindingContext` object is used to access the base class associated with a specific data source. Listing 22.3 illustrates how these classes might be used to implement `Click` event handlers for our Next and Previous buttons.

Listing 22.3 Next and Previous Click handlers using ButtonManagerBase

```
private void btnNext_Click(object sender, EventArgs e)
{
  BindingManagerBase bm = BindingContext[bsAlbum];      <-- 1 Gets manager for data source
  if ((bm != null) && (bm.Position < bm.Count - 1))
    bm.Position ++;
}

private void btnPrevious_Click(object sender, EventArgs e)
{
  BindingManagerBase bm = BindingContext[_album];
  if ((bm != null) && (bm.Position > 0))      2 Displays previous item in data source
    bm.Position --;
}
```

Some brief comments on the annotated code in the listing are in order:

1. The `BindingContext` property contains a collection of `BindingManagerBase` objects indexed by data source. Since our data source is actually a `BindingSource` instance, we look up the base class using this data source. In situations where a `BindingSource` instance is not used, the `DataSet`, collection, or other data source object should be provided.
2. In this code, we wish to move to the previous item in the list. This is accomplished using the `Position` property, although we check to ensure that the base class is valid and we are not at the start of the list.

.NET Table 22.8 BindingManagerBase class

The `BindingManagerBase` class represents a data source bound to one or more Windows Forms controls. This class enables synchronization of all controls with a property bound to the associated data source, and is part of the `System.Windows.Forms` namespace.

This class is abstract and cannot be instantiated. The `CurrencyManager` class is used for all data sources that support the `IList` interface, while the `PropertyManager` class is used for all single-value data sources. Also note that most of the members listed here are abstract as well, and must be overridden by a derived class.

Public Properties	Bindings	Gets the collection of bindings for this object.
	Count	Gets the number of items managed by this object.
	Current	Gets the current item in the associated data source.
	IsBinding-Suspended	Gets or sets whether binding is suspended.
	Position	Gets or sets the index of the current item.
Public Methods	AddNew	Adds a new item of the appropriate type to the associated data source.
	EndCurrentEdit	Completes the current edit, if any, for the associated data source. The `CancelCurrentEdit` method cancels the current edit.
	GetItemProperties	Retrieves the collection of `PropertyDescriptor` objects from the associated data source.
	RemoveAt	Deletes the item at the specified index from the associated data source.
	SuspendBinding	Suspends data binding for the data source. The `ResumeBinding` method resumes binding.
Public Events	*BindingComplete*	Occurs when a binding operation has completed.
	CurrentChanged	Occurs when the `Current` property changes.
	DataError	Occurs when an `Exception` is silently handled by this class.
	PositionChanged	Occurs when the `Position` property changes.

As you can see from listing 22.3, the `BindingManagerBase` class works quite well, although it might be considered a little complicated. In our sample application, we can use the members of the `BindingSource` class, which greatly simplifies this code.

HANDLE THE CLICK EVENTS FOR THE NEXT AND PREVIOUS BUTTONS		
	Action	**Result**

1	Handle the `Click` handler for the Next button to move to the next item in the binding source.	`private void btnNext_Click(`
		`    object sender, EventArgs e)`
		`{`
		`  bsAlbum.MoveNext();`
		`}`

2	Handle the `Click` handler for the Previous button to move to the prior item in the binding source.	`private void btnPrevious_Click(`
		`    object sender, EventArgs e)`
		`{`
		`  bsAlbum.MovePrevious();`
		`}`

3	Also handle the `CurrentChanged` event for the `BindingSource` component to enable or disable the Next and Previous buttons appropriately.	`private void bsAlbum_CurrentChanged(`
		`    object sender, EventArgs e)`
		`{`
		`  btnNext.Enabled = (bsAlbum.Position`
		`                  < bsAlbum.Count - 1);`
		`  btnPrevious.Enabled`
		`      = (bsAlbum.Position > 0);`
		`}`

This change allows the user to move forward and backward within the selected album. As you can see, the `Move` methods in the `BindingSource` class do all the work for us, including when we are at the start or end of the list.

We also use the `CurrentChanged` event in this code to disable the Next button when at the end of the list and the Previous button when at the start of the list. This is not strictly required, of course, but makes for a nicer user interface.

We should also point out that the `BindingManagerBase` class does not provide a method to update, or refresh, the controls bound to the associated data source. This is because some binding managers, notably the `PropertyManager`, have no need for this functionality. The refresh behavior is only required when a data source contains multiple instances. In this case, the binding manager is a `CurrencyManager` class instance. A summary of this class appears in .NET Table 22.9.

As you can see, the `Refresh` method forces an update of the bound controls. Once again our `BindingSource` class provides an equivalent solution, this time in the `ResetBindings` method. More importantly, in our application, since our `PhotoAlbum` class supports the `IBindingList` interface the `BindingSource` automatically detects changes to the underlying data and updates the bound controls. If a data source is used that does not support such two-way binding, these update methods are quite useful.

Access to the currency manager for a data source is not usually required, as the `BindingSource` component provides much of the same functionality. In the rare

.NET Table 22.9 CurrencyManager class

The `CurrencyManager` class represents a binding manager associated with a data source supporting the `IList` interface. This class is part of the `System.Windows.Forms` namespace, and inherits from the `BindingManagerBase` class. See .NET Table 22.8 for the members inherited from the base class.

Public Methods	Refresh	Forces a repopulation of all bound controls for a data source that does not support notification when the underlying data changes.
Public Events	ItemChanged	Occurs when an item in the associated data source is altered. This only occurs if the data source supports two-way notification, such as the `IBindingList` interface.
	MetaDataChanged	Occurs when the metadata of the underlying list has been altered.

situation where the `CurrencyManager` is required, the `BindingSource` class provides a `CurrencyManager` property for this purpose.

TRY IT! There is a problem in our application that occurs when the selected album is invalid. When this occurs, the controls on the Photo tab raise an exception because the data source is empty and the controls cannot bind to a `Photograph` object.

Fix this by adding a `ClearBindings` method that clears the existing values displayed and removes the assigned data bindings. Call this method whenever an album fails to load, and call the `SetBindings` method to reset the bindings when a non-empty data source exists.

22.3.5 Binding navigators

There is one other control added for the .NET 2.0 release that we should mention here. This is the `BindingNavigator` control, summarized in .NET Table 22.10. A binding navigator is a tool strip that supports navigation of a data source bound to an associated binding source.

The `BindingNavigator` control mimics the navigation functionality provided by the `BindingSource` component. This class was originally called the `DataNavigator` control, but was renamed when the `DataConnector` class was renamed to `BindingSource`.

The user interface provided by the `BindingNavigator` control can be customized or augmented as desired. We won't go into any further detail on this class, other than to present the code in listing 22.4 that creates the application shown in figure 22.3.

The application in listing 22.4 is not a complete application in some aspects, so feel free to augment or otherwise modify the code in the listing to improve this application.

.NET Table 22.10 BindingNavigator class

New in 2.0 The `BindingNavigator` class is a tool strip that allows navigation of an associated collection or database object. A binding navigator holds an associated `BindingSource` object, and presents a set of tool strip items that allows a user to navigate the associated data source. This class is part of the `System.Windows.Forms` namespace, and inherits from the `ToolStrip` class. See .NET Table 16.1 for the members inherited from the base class.

Public Properties	*AddNewItem*	Gets or sets the `ToolStripItem` associated with the Add New functionality.
	BindingSource	Gets or sets the `BindingSource` component.
	CountItem	Gets or sets the `ToolStripItem` that represents the total number of items in the associated binding source. The `PositionItem` property gets or sets the item that shows the current position in the binding source.
	MoveNextItem	Gets or sets the `ToolStripItem` associated with the Move Next functionality.
Public Methods	*AddStandardItems*	Adds the standard set of tool strip items to the navigation control.
Public Events	*RefreshItems*	Occurs when the navigator's interface should be updated to reflect the state of the underlying binding source.

Figure 22.3 In the BindingNavigator control here, the Delete button is available since images can be deleted from an album. The Add New button is disabled as no mechanism is provided to add new photographs to the album.

Listing 22.4 Sample application using the BindingNavigator control

```
using System;
using System.IO;
using System.Windows.Forms;
using Manning.MyPhotoAlbum;
using Manning.MyPhotoControls;

namespace BindingNavigatorSample
{
  static class Program
  {
    [STAThread]
    static void Main()
    {
      Application.EnableVisualStyles();
      Application.Run(new MyForm());
    }
  }

  public class MyForm : Form
  {
    private ComboBox _combo = new ComboBox();
    private ScrollablePictureBox _scrollBox = new ScrollablePictureBox();
    private BindingSource _source = new BindingSource();

    public MyForm()
    {
      Text = "BindingNavigator Sample";

      _combo.DataSource = Directory.GetFiles(
        AlbumManager.DefaultPath, "*.abm");
      _combo.Dock = DockStyle.Top;
      _combo.SelectionChangeCommitted
          += new EventHandler(combo_SelectionChangeCommitted);

      _scrollBox.BorderStyle = BorderStyle.Fixed3D;
      _scrollBox.Dock = DockStyle.Fill;

      BindingNavigator nav = new BindingNavigator(_source);
      nav.Dock = DockStyle.Bottom;

      Controls.AddRange(new Control[] { _scrollBox, _combo, nav });
    }

    protected override void OnLoad(EventArgs e)
    {
      OpenAlbum();
      base.OnLoad(e);
    }

    private void combo_SelectionChangeCommitted(object sender, EventArgs e)
    {
      OpenAlbum();
    }
```

```
    private void OpenAlbum()
    {
      string path = _combo.SelectedItem.ToString();

      try
      {
        AlbumManager am = new AlbumManager(path);

        _source.DataSource = am.Album;
        if (_scrollBox.DataBindings.Count == 0)
          _scrollBox.DataBindings.Add("Image", _source, "Image");
      }
      catch (AlbumStorageException)
      {
        _scrollBox.DataBindings.Clear();
        MessageBox.Show("Unable to open album");
      }
    }
  }
}
```

22.4 RECAP

In this chapter we continued our discussion on data binding begun in chapter 21 by extending our MyAlbumData application to support the individual display of the properties in the current photograph. This involved discussing two-way data binding and so-called simple data binding.

We began with a discussion on binding lists, including the `IBindingList` interface and the `BindingList<T>` generic class. We converted our `PhotoAlbum` class, which enabled our `DataGridView` control to update its displayed values automatically whenever the underlying album data source is modified.

The `IEditableObject` interface was next, providing a way to support transactional updates to our bound data. We implemented this interface in our `Photograph` class to track and save any changes made by a user.

Binding to data grid views is referred to as complex data binding. We also examined simple data binding, used to bind a single property of a control to a value in a data source. We moved our existing grid into a `TabPage` control, and created a second page to hold a set of controls related to the properties of the `Photograph` class. The `BindingSource` class provided a mechanism to manage our album data source, and we bound various properties of our Windows Forms controls to properties of the active `Photograph` in our binding source.

The `BindingSource` class is new in version 2.0 of the .NET Framework, so we also contrasted the data binding support provided via that `Control` class, which was available in version 1.*x*, with the support in the `BindingSource` class. This showed how many of the members provided by the `BindingManagerBase` and `CurrencyManager` classes are supported by the `BindingSource` class directly.

We completed the chapter with a quick look at the `BindingNavigator` control, which provides a visual interface for navigating an underlying data source.

It is probably worth noting that while the examples in this chapter did not use the `System.Data` namespace, the binding of data grid views and controls to database objects was discussed along the way in order to provide some insight into how such binding might be performed.

The final chapter of this book covers various topics that may be of additional interest or that never quite fit into previous chapters.

CHAPTER 23

Odds and ends .NET

In this last chapter of the book, it seems appropriate to mention a number of topics worthy of further exploration. This chapter presents various concepts that might be of interest to you as you build and deploy Windows Forms applications. Since the details of each topic could fill all or most of a chapter, we simply provide a brief explanation and quick example for each subject. These examples should point you in the right direction as you expand your knowledge of .NET in general and Windows Forms in particular.

We take a quick look at five topics:

- Printing data, including setting up your page and using print preview
- Performing drag-and-drop, both into and out of Windows Forms applications
- Browsing web pages using the `WebBrowser` control
- Managing application settings with the `ApplicationSettingsBase` class
- Installing applications, including setup projects and ClickOnce deployment

For no particular reason, these topics are presented in the same order as they are listed. We begin with printing from Windows Forms applications.

23.1 PRINTING

Printing in Windows Forms is supported by the `System.Drawing.Printing` namespace in addition to Windows Forms constructs. In this section we add printing support to the MyPhotos MDI application built in chapter 20. The classes commonly used to support printing are shown in table 23.1. As you can see, this consists of a `PrintDocument` class that oversees the print process, and three dialog classes to provide required user interaction.

Table 23.1 Classes used for printing in Windows Forms applications

Class	Description
PrintDocument	A reusable component used to send output to the printer. The `PrintPage` event occurs when print data should be sent to the printer device.
PrintDialog	A common dialog box that offers options related to printing.
PrintPreviewDialog	A form that contains a `PrintPreviewControl` object for presenting how a document will look when it is printed on a specific printer device.
PageSetupDialog	A common dialog box that permits a user to alter the page settings associated with a print document.

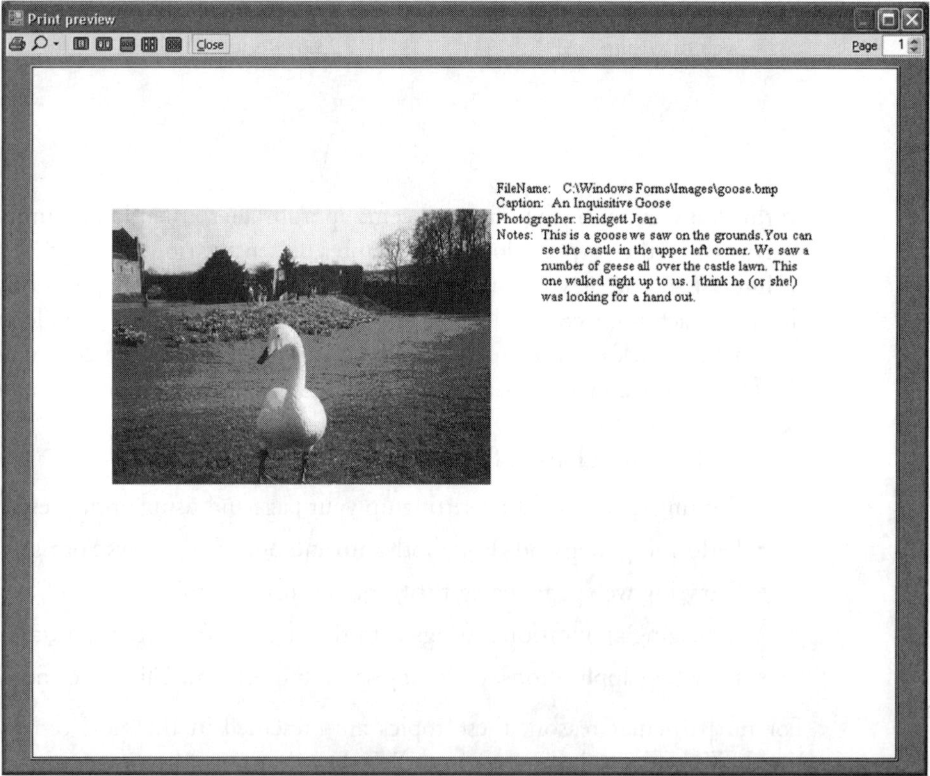

Figure 23.1 The text on this page is drawn to the right of the image. Long strings, such as the Notes setting, are formatted to fit within the available page margins.

Our example uses each of these four classes to support printing of an individual photograph. Figure 23.1 shows the print preview dialog box for one of our images.

While our example may not be the prettiest image-printing application, it does demonstrate some important principles, such as page margins and text wrapping. We present the changes in two parts: the first part illustrates how to use the print dialog boxes to initiate printing in an application; the second part shows the actual work in sending data to the selected printer.

23.1.1 Using the print classes

As you may recall, our MDI application defines a `ParentForm` class as the parent MDI container, with the `MainForm` class from part 2 of the book as the child form. For this example, we create a separate `PrintSupport` class to encapsulate the required printing tasks. Way back in chapter 6 we added the Print and Print Preview menu items as part of the standard menus supported by the `MenuStrip` class.

Here, we add one more menu item to allow the user to customize the page setup.

<table>
<tr><th colspan="3">MODIFY PARENT FORM TO SUPPORT PRINT MENUS</th></tr>
<tr><th></th><th>Action</th><th>Result</th></tr>
<tr><td>1</td><td>In the MainForm.cs [Design] window of the MyPhotos project, add a Page Setup menu just above the existing Print menu.

Settings<table><tr><th>Property</th><th>Value</th></tr><tr><td>(Name)</td><td>menuFilePageSetup</td></tr><tr><td>MergeAction</td><td>Insert</td></tr><tr><td>MergeIndex</td><td>7</td></tr></table></td><td></td></tr>
<tr><td>2</td><td>Increment by 1 each of the <code>MergeIndex</code> settings for the subsequent menus so the child menu merges with the parent File menu properly.</td><td>The four menus items below the Page Setup item in the prior graphic are updated.</td></tr>
</table>

Since we want to print at the application level, it might make more sense to have these menus in our `ParentForm` class, rather than `MainForm` as we do here. An advantage of our approach, of course, is that our final solution works for both our MDI and SDI applications.

On the other hand, we do not want printing objects in every child window. To avoid this, let's create a static `PrintSupport` class that encapsulates the required code.

<table>
<tr><th colspan="3">HANDLE PRINT-RELATED MENUS IN THE PARENT FORM</th></tr>
<tr><th></th><th>Action</th><th>Result</th></tr>
<tr><td>3</td><td>Create a new static <code>PrintSupport</code> class that depends on the <code>System</code>, <code>Windows.Forms</code>, <code>Drawing</code>, <code>Drawing.Printing</code>, and <code>Manning.MyPhotoAlbum</code> namespaces.</td><td><pre>using System;
using System.Windows.Forms;
using System.Drawing;
using System.Drawing.Printing;
using Manning.MyPhotoAlbum;

namespace MyPhotos
{
 static class PrintSupport
 {</pre></td></tr>
<tr><td>4</td><td>Create a static <code>PrintDocument</code> field and property in this class.</td><td><pre> static private PrintDocument _printDoc;
  static private PrintDocument Document
      { get { return _printDoc; } }</pre></td></tr>
<tr><td>5</td><td>Initialize the print document in a static constructor, adding a handler for the <code>PrintPage</code> event.</td><td><pre> static PrintSupport()
  {
    _printDoc = new PrintDocument();
    _printDoc.PrintPage += printDoc_PrintPage;
  }</pre></td></tr>
<tr><td>6</td><td>Still in the <code>PrintSupport</code> class, add a <code>PageSetup</code> method that displays a setup dialog box for the print document.</td><td><pre> static public void PageSetup()
  {
    PageSetupDialog dlg = new PageSetupDialog();
    dlg.Document = Document;
    dlg.ShowDialog();
  }</pre></td></tr>
<tr><td>7</td><td>Add a <code>PrintPreview</code> method that displays a print preview dialog box for the print document.</td><td><pre> static public void PrintPreview()
  {
    PrintPreviewDialog dlg
        = new PrintPreviewDialog();
    dlg.Document = Document;
    dlg.ShowDialog();
  }</pre></td></tr>
<tr><td>8</td><td>Add a <code>Print</code> method that displays a print dialog box and sends the document to the selected printer.</td><td><pre> static public void Print()
  {
    PrintDialog dlg = new PrintDialog();
    dlg.Document = Document;
    if (dlg.ShowDialog() == DialogResult.OK)
      Document.Print();
  }
 }
}</pre></td></tr>
<tr><td>9</td><td>Back in the <code>MainForm</code> class, add a <code>Click</code> event handler for the Page Setup menu that calls the corresponding <code>PrintSupport</code> method.</td><td><pre> private void menuFilePrintPreview_Click(
      object sender, EventArgs e)
  {
    PrintSupport.PrintPreview();
  }</pre></td></tr>
<tr><td>10</td><td>Add similar <code>Click</code> event handlers for the Print Preview and Print menus.</td><td><pre> private void menuFilePrint_Click(
      object sender, EventArgs e)
  {
    PrintSupport.Print();
  }

  private void menuFilePageSetup_Click(
      object sender, EventArgs e)
  {
    PrintSupport.PageSetup();
  }</pre></td></tr>
</table>

These event handlers establish the required interaction with the user in order to print the current photograph. If you wish to test these dialog boxes, add the following temporary implementation for the `printDoc_PrintPage` handler and run the application:

```
static void printDoc_PrintPage(object sender,
                               PrintPageEventArgs e)
{
  MessageBox.Show("Printing...");
}
```

When you are ready, move on to the next section to see the actual print logic.

23.1.2 Drawing a print page

The prior section established our interaction with the user, so our task here is to implement the actual printing of a page. When a page is ready to print, the `PrintPage` event is raised to kick off the required logic.

This event is of type `PrintPageEventHandler`, with handlers receiving a `PrintPageEventArgs` instance. The members defined in the event data class are shown in .NET Table 23.2.

As you can see, the event data provides everything necessary to print a single page. The `HasMorePages` property should be set to `true` if additional pages are required. In this case, the `PrintPage` event recurs for each additional page. It is up to the application to track which page is next and any data that might be required for these pages. Our `PrintSupport` class encapsulates the printing logic we need for our application, including printing a selected photograph. This class needs to retrieve the current photo from the `MainForm` class, after which it can draw the photograph using the provided `Graphics` object, and use a private `PrintTextString` method to draw the individual properties for the photograph.

.NET Table 23.2 PrintPageEventArgs class

The `PrintPageEventArgs` class specifies the event data required for the `PrintArgs` event in the `PrintDocument` class. This class is part of the `System.Drawing.Printing` namespace, and inherits from the `System.EventArgs` class.

Public Properties	Cancel	Gets or sets whether the print job should be canceled
	Graphics	Gets the `Graphics` object to use for painting the page
	HasMorePages	Gets or sets whether an additional page should be printed after the current one
	MarginBounds	Gets the printable area of the page, which is the rectangle within the margins of the page
	PageBounds	Gets the page area, which is the rectangle representing the entire page
	PageSettings	Gets the `PageSettings` object representing the settings for the current page

IMPLEMENT THE PRINTPAGE HANDLER

<table>
<tr><th></th><th>Action</th><th>Result</th></tr>
<tr><td>1</td><td>In the <code>MainForm</code> class, modify the <code>Manager</code> property to be internal so our <code>PrintSupport</code> class can access it.</td><td><pre>private AlbumManager _manager;
internal AlbumManager Manager
{
  get { return _manager; }
  set { . . . }
}</pre></td></tr>
<tr><td>2</td><td>In the <code>PrintSupport</code> class, define the static <code>printDoc_PrintPage</code> method.</td><td><pre>static void printDoc_PrintPage(
    object sender, PrintPageEventArgs e)
{</pre></td></tr>
<tr><td>3</td><td>Retrieve the form created for the application, or the active child form if this is an MDI application.</td><td><pre> Form f = Application.OpenForms[0];
  if (f != null && f.IsMdiContainer)
    f = f.ActiveMdiChild;</pre></td></tr>
<tr><td>4</td><td>Get the current photograph displayed by this form.</td><td><pre> MainForm mf = f as MainForm;
  Photograph photo = null;
  if (mf != null && mf.Manager != null)
    photo = mf.Manager.Current;</pre></td></tr>
<tr><td>5</td><td>If a current photo does not exist, then cancel the operation. Otherwise, call a <code>PrintPhoto</code> method to print the photo.</td><td><pre> if (photo == null)
    e.Cancel = true; // nothing to print
  else
    PrintPhoto(photo, e);
}</pre></td></tr>
<tr><td>6</td><td>Create a static <code>PrintPhoto</code> method to arrange a given photograph on the given graphics, and create some shortcuts for the margins of the page and the <code>Graphics</code> object.</td><td><pre>static private void PrintPhoto(
    Photograph photo, PrintPageEventArgs e)
{
  // Establish some useful shortcuts
  float leftMargin = e.MarginBounds.Left;
  float rightMargin = e.MarginBounds.Right;
  float topMargin = e.MarginBounds.Top;
  float bottomMargin = e.MarginBounds.Bottom;
  float printableWidth = e.MarginBounds.Width;
  float printableHeight
          = e.MarginBounds.Height;
  Graphics g = e.Graphics;</pre></td></tr>
<tr><td>7</td><td>Create a <code>Font</code> object to use when printing text.
How-to
a. Use 12-point Times New Roman.
b. Use the <code>GetHeight</code> method to determine the height of a line of text.
c. Use the <code>MeasureString</code> method to determine the width of a space.</td><td><pre> // Define the Font to use for text
  Font printFont
    = new Font("Times New Roman", 12);
  float fontHeight = printFont.GetHeight(g);
  float spaceWidth = g.MeasureString(" ",
                          printFont).Width;</pre></td></tr>
</table>

	Action	Result
IMPLEMENT THE PRINTPAGE HANDLER *(CONTINUED)*		

8	Determine the correct length so that the image can be drawn into a box that is 75 percent of the shortest side of the page.
	
	Note: This logic accounts for both landscape and portrait page orientation. The `xPos` and `yPos` variables represent where the first line of text should be drawn.
		`// Draw image in box 75% of shortest edge`
		`float imageBoxLength;`
		`float xPos = leftMargin;`
		`float yPos = topMargin + fontHeight;`
		`if (printableWidth < printableHeight)`
		`{`
		`  imageBoxLength = printableWidth * 75/100;`
		`  yPos += imageBoxLength;`
		`}`
		`else`
		`{`
		`  imageBoxLength = printableHeight * 75/100;`
		`  xPos += imageBoxLength + spaceWidth;`
		`}`

9	Draw the image into a box of the determined size.
	
	How-to
	Use the `ScaleToFit` method created in chapter 7 to determine where the image should be drawn.
		`// Draw image at start of the page`
		`Rectangle imageBox = new Rectangle(`
		`    (int)leftMargin + 1,`
		`    (int)topMargin + 1,`
		`    (int)imageBoxLength,`
		`    (int)imageBoxLength);`
		`Rectangle targetBox = ImageUtility.`
		`        ScaleToFit(photo.Image, imageBox);`
		`g.DrawImage(photo.Image, targetBox);`

10	Determine the `RectangleF` object where all text should be drawn.	`// Determine rectangle for text`
		`RectangleF printArea`
		`  = new RectangleF(xPos, yPos,`
		`          rightMargin - xPos,`
		`          bottomMargin - yPos);`

11	Print the filename, caption, photographer, and notes properties for the photograph onto the page.
	
	How-to
	Use a yet-to-be-written `PrintTextString` method.
		`PrintTextString(g, printFont,`
		`    "FileName:", photo.FileName,`
		`    ref printArea);`
		`PrintTextString(g, printFont,`
		`    "Caption:", photo.Caption,`
		`    ref printArea);`
		`PrintTextString(g, printFont,`
		`    "Photographer:", photo.Photographer,`
		`    ref printArea);`
		`PrintTextString(g, printFont,`
		`    "Notes:", photo.Notes,`
		`    ref printArea);`
		`}`

The `PrintTextString` method is implemented in the subsequent steps. Our implementation prints the given string across multiple lines, if necessary, by drawing each word in the text string separately. Also note that the `printArea` variable is passed by reference. This is required so we can modify the printable area for subsequent text strings from the `PrintTextString` method. The `printArea` variable is a `RectangleF` structure, so as a value type it would normally be passed by value.

One feature of our implementation is its ability to wrap a long `Caption` or `Notes` setting to appear on multiple lines. The `Graphics.DrawString` method does this automatically when drawing a string into a rectangle. In our case, we do not know in advance how big a rectangle to use for each string, so we do not take advantage of this feature. Our approach performs word wrapping manually.

IMPLEMENT THE PRINTTEXTSTRING METHOD		
	Action	**Result**

12	Add a static `PrintTextString` method to the `PrintSupport` class.	`static private void PrintTextString(`
		`    Graphics g,`
		`    Font printFont,`
		`    string name,`
		`    string text,`
		`    ref RectangleF printArea)`
		`{`

13	Create some local variables for the margins of the printable area.	`  // Establish some useful shortcuts`
		`  float leftMargin = printArea.Left;`
		`  float rightMargin = printArea.Right;`
		`  float topMargin = printArea.Top;`
		`  float bottomMargin = printArea.Bottom;`

14	Also determine the height of the font and the coordinates where text strings should be drawn.	`  float fontHeight = printFont.GetHeight(g);`
		`  float xPos = printArea.Left;`
		`  float yPos = topMargin + fontHeight;`

15	Find the width of a space and the name for the text string.	`  float spaceWidth = g.MeasureString(" ",`
		`    printFont).Width;`
		`  float nameWidth`
		`    = g.MeasureString(name, printFont).Width;`

16	If this name does not fit in the printable area, then abort the operation.	`  if (!printArea.Contains(xPos + nameWidth,`
		`                         yPos))`
		`  {`
		`    // Does not fit, so abort`
		`    throw new ApplicationException(`
		`        "Print name does not fit");`
		`  }`

17	Otherwise, draw the name on the page and adjust the left margin to occur after this string.	`  g.DrawString(name, printFont,`
		`     Brushes.Black, new PointF(xPos, yPos));`
		`  leftMargin += nameWidth + spaceWidth;`
		`  xPos = leftMargin;`

18	Divide the text string into individual words, and iterate over these words.	`  // Draw text, use multi-lines if necessary`
		`  string[] words`
		`    = text.Split(" \r\t\n\0".ToCharArray());`
		`  foreach (string word in words)`
		`  {`

19	Determine the width of the next word.	`    float wordWidth = g.MeasureString(`
		`        word, printFont).Width;`
		`    if (wordWidth == 0.0)`
		`      continue;`

20	If the size of this word takes it past the right margin, then adjust the drawing coordinates to start a new line.	`    if (xPos + wordWidth > rightMargin)`
		`    {`
		`      // Start a new line`
		`      xPos = leftMargin;`
		`      yPos += fontHeight;`
		`      if (yPos > bottomMargin)`
		`      {`
		`        // no more page, abort foreach loop`
		`        break;`
		`      }`
		`    }`

	Action	Result
IMPLEMENT THE PRINTTEXTSTRING METHOD *(CONTINUED)*		

21	Draw this word at the current position, and adjust the x-coordinate appropriately.	`g.DrawString(word, printFont,`
		`    Brushes.Black,`
		`    new PointF(xPos, yPos));`
		`  xPos += wordWidth;`
		`}`

22	When finished drawing the text, adjust the printable area to exclude the area just drawn.	`// Adjust print area based on drawn text`
		`printArea.Y = yPos;`
		`printArea.Height = bottomMargin - yPos;`
		`}`

When you test this code, make sure it works properly when printing with both landscape and portrait orientation. The page setup dialog box can be used to alter the orientation, as well as the margins on the page.

23.2 DRAG-AND-DROP

Let's turn our attention away from printing and toward *drag-and-drop*. This refers to dragging an object from one location to another, and can occur within an application or between applications. Typically, a drag-and-drop operation is begun by clicking an object with the mouse pointer; holding down the mouse button while moving, or *dragging*, the object to a new location; and dropping the object at the new location by releasing the mouse button.

This topic can get fairly complicated, so we show a rather basic example supporting the following types of drag-and-drop operations. These are shown in the context of our MyPhotos application, of course.

- Dragging a file from the Windows file system into an application
- Dragging an image from within an application to an external location
- Dragging an image to a text editor to display associated text information
- Dragging an image between two child forms within an MDI application

Support for drag-and-drop is built into the Windows Forms `Control` class, as indicated in table 23.3.

At a high level, a drag-and-drop operation performs the series of actions listed here. These actions are illustrated in the subsequent sections. The source and target of the operation may be within the same application or in separate applications.

1 A source control initiates drag-and-drop, typically within a `MouseDown` event handler, when the `DoDragDrop` method is called. One or more data objects and associated formats are provided as part of invoking this method.

2 The user drags the object to a target control that has its `AllowDrop` property set to `true`. By default, all controls disable this operation.

3 As the mouse enters the target control, the `DragEnter` event occurs to permit the target to identify whether the data can be recognized by this control. This permits the operating system to display an appropriate mouse cursor for the user.
4 If the data is recognized, the `DragOver` event occurs as the user moves the drag-and-drop object within the control.
5 If the object is dragged out of the control, the `DragLeave` event occurs.
6 If the user releases the object within the target control, the `DragDrop` event occurs to permit the control to receive the data.
7 The result of the operation is returned by the `DoDragDrop` method called on the original source control.

Table 23.3 Members of the Control class related to drag-and-drop

Public Properties	AllowDrop	Gets or sets whether the control permits drag-and-drop operations within its boundaries.
Public Methods	DoDragDrop	Initiates a drag-and-drop operation from within the control. This is typically called from a `MouseDown` event handler.
Public Events	GiveFeedback	Occurs during drag-and-drop to allow the initiator to provide feedback when a valid drop target is encountered.
	DragDrop	Occurs when a dragged object is released within the control.
	DragEnter	Occurs when a dragged object enters the control.
	DragLeave	Occurs when a dragged object exits the control.
	DragOver	Occurs when a dragged object moves within the control.
	QueryContinueDrag	Occurs during drag-and-drop to allow the initiator to indicate whether the operation should continue.

We divide our example into two sections. First, we begin a drag-and-drop operation from within the `PictureBox` control of our `MainForm` class. Next, we receive external drag-and-drop operations within this same control.

23.2.1 Initiating drag-and-drop

The key to beginning a drag-and-drop operation is the `DoDragDrop` method. This method defines the data for the operation and the kind of operation permitted.

```
public DragDropEffects DoDragDrop(object data,
                                  DragDropEffects allowedEffects);
```

While the `data` parameter can be any data, the `DataObject` class provides a standard mechanism for safely transferring data between applications. The `DragDropEffects` enumeration permits different kinds of drag-and-drop operations to be supported as an or'd set of flags. For example, the `Move`, `Copy`, and `Link` values permit an object to be moved, copied, or linked from the original data source to the drop target.

The DoDragDrop method does not return until the drag-and-drop operation is complete. The return value indicates what effect was performed by the operation. The QueryContinueDrag event in the Control class can be used to keep tabs on the operation. This event occurs periodically during drag-and-drop and can be used to cancel the operation or to modify the application window as required.

In our application, we simply begin the operation and let the .NET Framework take care of the rest. We provide two types of data formats using the DataObject class: the FileDrop format recognized by the Windows file system and applications such as Microsoft Paint; and the Text format recognized by word processors and other text-oriented programs.

BEGIN A DRAG-AND-DROP OPERATION

	Action	Result

1	In the MainForm [Design] window, handle the `MouseDown` event handler for the `PictureBox` control.	`private void pbxPhoto_MouseDown`
		`  (object sender, MouseEventArgs e)`
		`{`

2	Check to see if a photograph is available for drag-and-drop.	`// Prepare image for drag-and-drop`
		`Photograph photo = Manager.Current;`
		
		`if (photo != null)`
		`{`

3	Create a `DataObject` instance to define the type of data provided by this application.	`// Create object for encapsulating data` `DataObject data = new DataObject();`

4	Associate a string array containing the photo's file path as the `FileDrop` data format when dragging the photograph to a new location.	`// Construct string array for FileDrop`
		`string[] fileArray = new string[1];`
		`fileArray[0] = photo.FileName;`
		`data.SetData(DataFormats.FileDrop,`
		`        fileArray);`
		
		Note: The `DataFormats` class encapsulates various formats for use in drag-and-drop operations. The `FileDrop` format used here expects a `string` array as the data type to allow multiple files to be specified at once.

5	Also assign a `Text` format using the `Caption` property of the photograph as the associated data.	`// Use the caption for the text format`
		`data.SetData(DataFormats.Text,`
		`        photo.Caption);`

6	Call the `DoDragDrop` method with the constructed data object to initiate a drag-and-drop `Copy` operation.	`// Initiate drag-and-drop`
		`pbxPhoto.DoDragDrop(data,`
		`      DragDropEffects.Copy);`
		`  }`
		`}`

This code begins a drag-and-drop operation that can be received by any other application on the computer. Other applications look at the provided data formats to identify whether they can accept the dragged data. We look at how to do this next.

Figure 23.2 The FileDrop format used here to drag an image into Microsoft Paint is a common method for transferring files between applications.

Of course, in applications that can receive multiple formats, the result they receive depends on which format they prefer. Most word processing applications look for the `Text` format first, and would therefore receive the `Caption` property of our photo, rather than the associated file object.

Compile and run the application. Display an album and click on the image. Hold the mouse and drag it to a new location. Figure 23.2 shows the result of dragging one of our favorite images from the MyPhotos application into a Microsoft Paint application window. The Paint application opens the given file and displays a copy of the image in its main window. Also try dragging an image into WordPad or some other word processor to see how the caption string appears.

This completes the first part of our example: initiating a drag-and-drop operation. The next section handles the receipt of such an operation.

23.2.2 Receiving drag-and-drop

Regardless of where a drag-and-drop operation originates, an application, or more specifically a control, can elect to handle the incoming data. The `DragEnter` and `DragDrop` events receive such operations, with the `DragEventArgs` class as their event parameter. A summary of these event arguments appears in .NET Table 23.4.

.NET Table 23.4 DragEventArgs class

The DragEventArgs class specifies the event data for drag-and-drop events, such as DragEnter, DragOver, and DragDrop. This class is part of the System.Windows.Forms namespace, and inherits from the System.EventArgs class.

Public Properties	AllowedEffect	Gets the drag-and-drop operations permitted by the source of the drag event
	Data	Gets the IDataObject interface that holds the data and data formats associated with the event
	Effect	Gets or sets the drag-and-drop operations permitted by the target of the drag event
	KeyState	Gets the current state of the Shift, Ctrl, and Alt keys
	X	Gets the x-coordinate of the current mouse pointer position
	Y	Gets the y-coordinate of the current mouse pointer position

In our example, we recognize the FileDrop format in the MainForm window to receive files dragged from the file system or from other MainForm windows. The steps required are as follows.

HANDLE DRAG-AND-DROP IN THE MAINFORM WINDOW

	Action	Result
1	In the OnLoad method of the MainForm class, set the AllowDrop property on the PictureBox control to true.	Drop operations are now permitted. **Note:** The PictureBox class hides the AllowDrop property so it does not appear in the design window or IntelliSense. It still works if we set it manually as we do here.

2	Handle the DragEnter event within the picture box control.	`private void pbxPhoto_DragEnter(`
		`    object sender, DragEventArgs e)`
		`{`

3	If the data associated with the event supports the FileDrop data format, then support the Copy drag-and-drop effect in the control. **How-to** Use the GetDataPresent method from the IDataObject interface.	`  // Allow file drops only`
		`  if (e.Data.GetDataPresent(`
		`               DataFormats.FileDrop))`
		`    e.Effect = DragDropEffects.Copy;`

4	Otherwise, indicate that the current drag-and-drop data is not accepted by this control.	`  else`
		`    e.Effect = DragDropEffects.None;`
		`}`

5	Add a DragDrop event handler for the picture box.	`private void pbxPhoto_DragDrop(`
		`    object sender, DragEventArgs e)`
		`{`

	Handle drag-and-drop in the MainForm window *(continued)*	
	Action	**Result**

6	In this handler:
	a. Retrieve the data in `FileDrop` format associated with the event.
	b. Convert this to an `Array` instance.
	c. For each `object` in the array, convert the `object` to a `string`.
		`// Get the object data for the drop`
		`object obj = e.Data.GetData(`
		`    DataFormats.FileDrop);`
		`Array files = obj as Array;`
		
		`int index = -1;`
		`foreach (object o in files)`
		`{`
		`  string s = o as string;`

7	If a string is found, then:
	a. Create a new `Photograph` object using this string.
	b. See if the `Photograph` is already in the current album.
	c. If not, then add the new photo to the album.
		`  if (s != null)`
		`  {`
		`    Photograph photo`
		`        = new Photograph(s);`
		
		`    // Add the file (if not present)`
		`    index`
		`      = Manager.Album.IndexOf(photo);`
		`    if (index < 0)`
		`    {`
		`      Manager.Album.Add(photo);`
		`      index = Manager.Album.Count - 1;`
		`    }`
		`  }`
		`}`

8	If a `Photograph` was found in the `foreach` loop, display the associated photo within the album.	`if (index >= 0)`
		`{`
		`  Manager.Index = index;`
		`  DisplayAlbum();`
		`}`
		`}`

This completes our handling of drag-and-drop. Compile and run the program to see this in action. Display two different albums in separate `MainForm` windows. You should be able to perform the following drag-and-drop operations:

- Find an image file in Windows Explorer. Drag this file into an album window. The image is added to the album and displayed in the form.
- Find an image file in Windows Explorer that is already in an album. Drag this file into the album. The existing `Photograph` object is displayed in the window.
- Highlight a set of files in Windows Explorer. Drag these files into an album window. Each file is added to the window if not already present. The last file added is displayed in the window.
- Click an image displayed in one album window and drag it to a second album window. The image is added to the second album if it is not already present, and displayed in the target window's picture box.

We should mention here that the `ListView` and `TreeView` classes support per-item dragging via the `ItemDrag` event. The `ItemDrag` event occurs when the user begins dragging an item in the list or tree. Typically, the event handler for the `ItemDrag` event calls the `DoDragDrop` method as we did in this section, with the `object` associated with a specific list item or tree node as the source of the operation. For example, we could modify our MyAlbumExplorer interface to permit photographs to be reordered within the `ListView` control, or dragged into a new album in the `TreeView` control.

TRY IT! Modify the MyAlbumExplorer application to support drag-and-drop within the `ListView` control when photographs are displayed to allow a user to reorder an album.

23.3 WEB BROWSING

Moving right along, an important feature in some applications is the ability to browse the Internet. In the .NET 1.*x* releases, this was possible in Windows Forms but took a bit of work, using the `AxHost` class to wrap the ActiveX Web control. In .NET 2.0, the addition of the `WebBrowser` control has made this task rather straightforward.

To illustrate this, we host a browser control within an About Box dialog box for our MyPhotos application. This may seem slightly unorthodox, but it creates an interesting example while presenting the topic at hand.

To do this, we create an `AboutBox` form to display information about the application. As shown in figure 23.3, this `Form` includes a `LinkLabel` instance, which we have not used very often in the book. We could just as easily use a button here, but a link is more in line with our "Web" feel. When the user clicks the "Click to close window" label, the window closes as we have seen with a Close button in previous examples. When the user clicks the "Click for book's website" label, a hidden panel appears that displays the website for the book you are reading. This is shown in figure 23.4, where the title bar of the form reflects the current web page, and the link label now allows the user to hide the web browser. Of course, connecting to the website presumes you have an active connection to the Internet available.

We divide our discussion into three sections. First we create the form required; then we take a quick peek at the actual control; and finally we use this control to display a web page as in the figure.

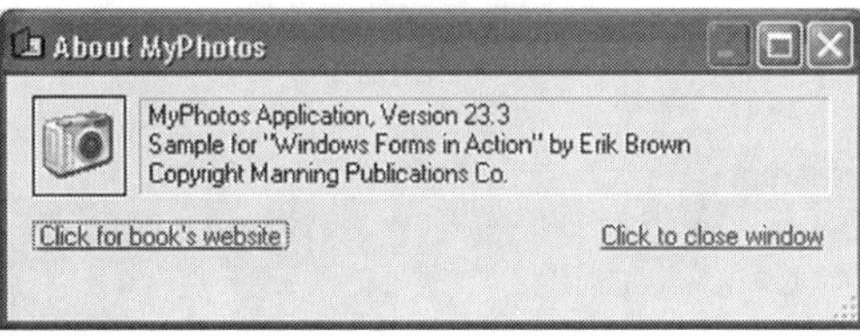

Figure 23.3 This form uses a Label control to display the application Icon and LinkLabel controls rather than Buttons to initiate user actions.

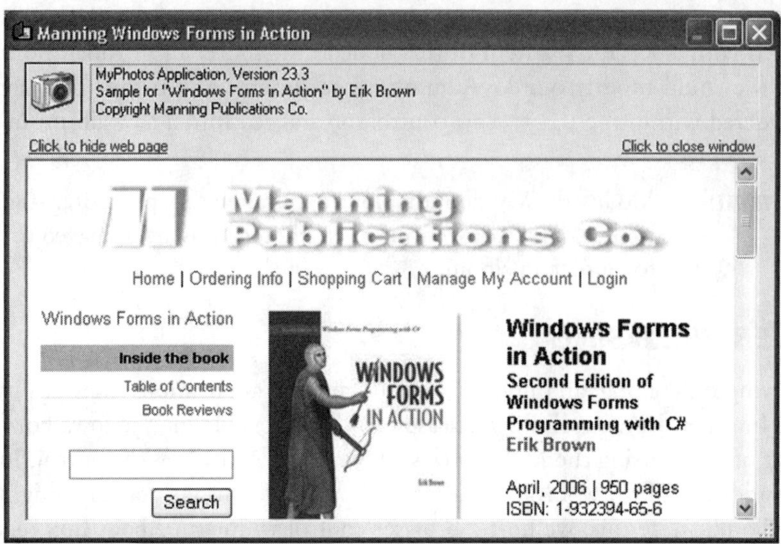

Figure 23.4 The embedded web page in this window supports link navigation, keyboard shortcuts, and other standard browser actions.

23.3.1 Creating an about box

An about box typically identifies version and other information about the application. The following steps create a `Form` for this purpose.

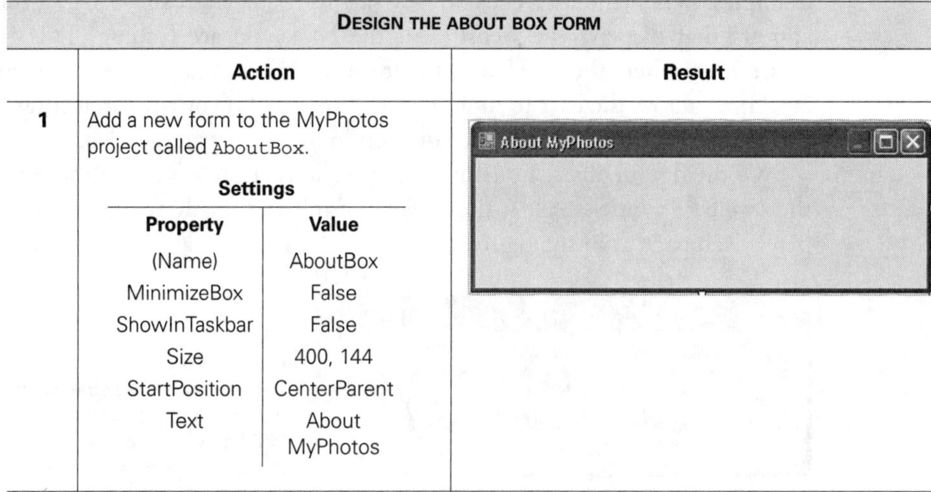

DESIGN THE ABOUT BOX FORM

	Action	Result
1	Add a new form to the MyPhotos project called `AboutBox`. **Settings** **Property** / **Value** (Name) / AboutBox MinimizeBox / False ShowInTaskbar / False Size / 400, 144 StartPosition / CenterParent Text / About MyPhotos	About MyPhotos

<table>
<tr><th colspan="3">DESIGN THE ABOUT BOX FORM (CONTINUED)</th></tr>
<tr><th></th><th>Action</th><th>Result</th></tr>
<tr><td>2</td><td>Drag an <code>ImageList</code> onto the form named <code>imageIcons</code>. Set its <code>ImageSize</code> to 32, 32, and add the following icons from the common image library:
• icons/Win9x/NOTE04.ICO
• icons/WinXP/camera.ico</td><td>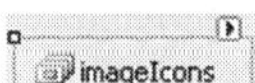
</td></tr>
<tr><td>3</td><td>Add two labels to hold the icon and textual information for the form.
<table>
<tr><th colspan="3">Settings</th></tr>
<tr><th>Control</th><th>Property</th><th>Value</th></tr>
<tr><td rowspan="6">Icon Label</td><td>(Name)</td><td>lblIcon</td></tr>
<tr><td>AutoSize</td><td>False</td></tr>
<tr><td>BorderStyle</td><td>FixedSingle</td></tr>
<tr><td>ImageList</td><td>imageIcons</td></tr>
<tr><td>ImageIndex</td><td>0</td></tr>
<tr><td>Text</td><td></td></tr>
<tr><td rowspan="5">Text Label</td><td>(Name)</td><td>lblAboutText</td></tr>
<tr><td>Anchor</td><td>Top, Left, Right</td></tr>
<tr><td>AutoSize</td><td>False</td></tr>
<tr><td>BorderStyle</td><td>Fixed3D</td></tr>
<tr><td>Text</td><td>MyPhotos</td></tr>
</table></td><td>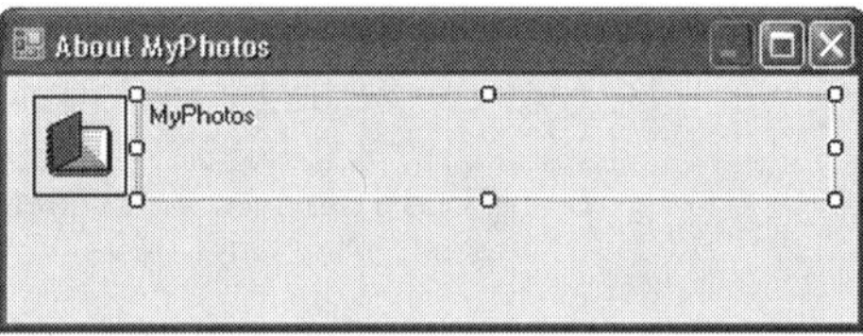

Note: Size and position these labels as in this graphic.</td></tr>
<tr><td>4</td><td>Add two <code>LinkLabel</code> controls to represent the two actions the user can take.
<table>
<tr><th colspan="3">Settings</th></tr>
<tr><th>Control</th><th>Property</th><th>Value</th></tr>
<tr><td rowspan="2">Site Link</td><td>(Name)</td><td>lnkWebSite</td></tr>
<tr><td>Text</td><td>Click for book's website</td></tr>
<tr><td rowspan="3">Close Link</td><td>(Name)</td><td>lnkClose</td></tr>
<tr><td>Anchor</td><td>Top, Right</td></tr>
<tr><td>Text</td><td>Click to close window</td></tr>
</table></td><td>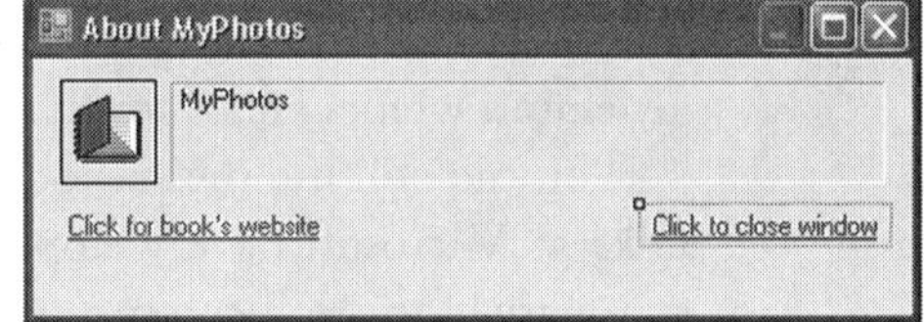
</td></tr>
</table>

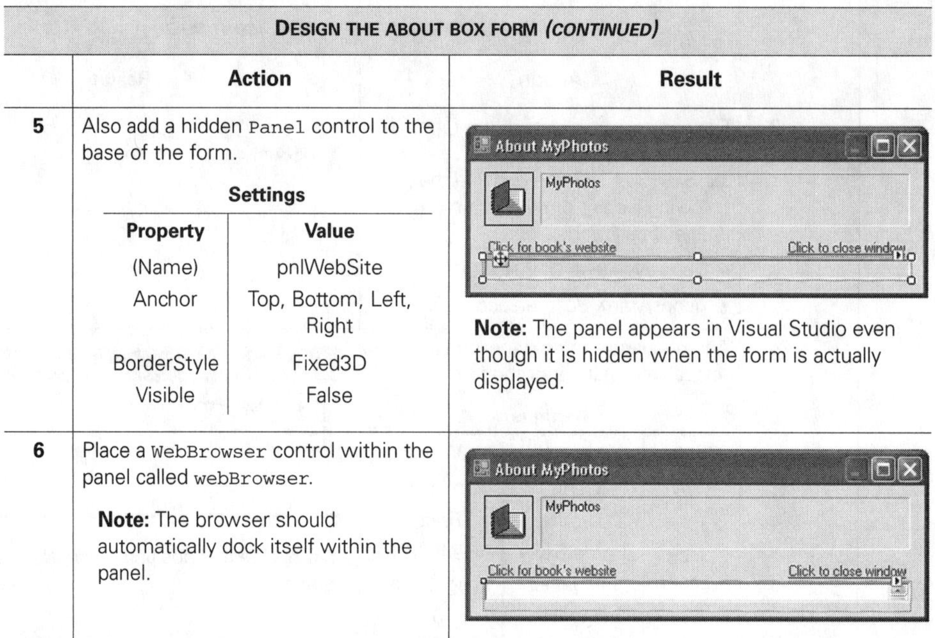

DESIGN THE ABOUT BOX FORM *(CONTINUED)*

	Action	Result
5	Also add a hidden `Panel` control to the base of the form. **Settings** **Property** / **Value** (Name): pnlWebSite Anchor: Top, Bottom, Left, Right BorderStyle: Fixed3D Visible: False	About MyPhotos / MyPhotos / Click for book's website / Click to close window **Note:** The panel appears in Visual Studio even though it is hidden when the form is actually displayed.
6	Place a `WebBrowser` control within the panel called `webBrowser`. **Note:** The browser should automatically dock itself within the panel.	About MyPhotos / MyPhotos / Click for book's website / Click to close window

This completes the layout of our `AboutBox` form. We already have the About menu item within our Help menu, so we simply need to wire this up and make it work. Before we do this, let's take a quick look at the `WebBrowser` control.

23.3.2 The WebBrowser class

As mentioned at the start of this section, in .NET 1.*x* you had to leverage the `AxHost` class to create a usable browser control for a Windows Forms application. The Windows Forms ActiveX Control Importer program, called `aximp`, was used to generate a wrapper class for the Web Browser library `shdocvw.doc`.

You can still use the `AxHost` class for this purpose, but as of .NET 2.0 the good folks at Microsoft have wrapped the browser control to make it easily available. A summary of the `WebBrowser` class is shown in .NET Table 23.5. As you can see, this class is built on the `WebBrowserBase` class, defined by Microsoft to wrap the Internet Explorer ActiveX browser control internally. This base class provides an `ActiveXInstance` property to retrieve the underlying ActiveX browser control.

The table highlights some key members of the `WebBrowser` control. Additional members are available to manage the encryption, title, status, and other data for the control. To see an example employing this class, read the next section.

.NET Table 23.5 WebBrowser class

New in 2.0 The `WebBrowser` class is a web browsing class that supports the display and navigation of web pages within a Windows Forms application. This class is part of the `System.Windows.Forms` namespace, and inherits from the `WebBrowserBase` class.

Public Properties	*AllowNavigation*	Gets or sets whether the user can navigate to other pages from the initial page
	CanGoBack	Gets whether a previous page in the navigation history is available
	Document	Gets an `HtmlDocument` instance representing the currently displayed page
	IsBusy	Gets whether the browser is currently loading a document
	Url	Gets or sets the URL for the current document
	Version	Gets the version of Internet Explorer installed
Public Methods	*GoForward*	Navigates to the next page in the navigation history, if available
	GoHome	Navigates to the home page of the current user
	GoSearch	Navigates to the search page of the current user
	Navigate	Loads an indicated document into the browser
	Print	Prints the current document in the browser
	Stop	Cancels any pending navigation and stops all dynamic elements, such as sound or animations
Public Events	*DocumentCompleted*	Occurs when the browser has finished loading a document
	Navigating	Occurs before the browser navigates to a new document

23.3.3 Browse to a web site

We defined a user interface for the `AboutBox` form earlier in this section. Here we implement the actual logic required by our form. The following steps begin this process by describing the changes required for our two label controls.

HANDLE THE LABEL CONTROLS

	Action	Result
1	In the `AboutBox` class, create two constants for the two types of icons in our image list.	`private const int SDI_ICON = 0;` `private const int MDI_ICON = 1;`

<table>
<tr><th colspan="3">HANDLE THE LABEL CONTROLS (CONTINUED)</th></tr>
<tr><th></th><th>Action</th><th>Result</th></tr>
<tr><td>2</td><td>Implement a public <code>IsMdiApplication</code> property to allow a caller to define whether this is an MDI application.

How-to
Define a <code>set</code> accessor that assigns the <code>ImageIndex</code> property for the icon label based on the given <code>value</code> setting.</td><td><pre>
public bool IsMdiApplication
{
  set
  {
    if (value)
      lblIcon.ImageIndex = MDI_ICON;
    else
      lblIcon.ImageIndex = SDI_ICON;
  }
}
</pre></td></tr>
<tr><td>3</td><td>Implement a public <code>AboutText</code> property to get or set the <code>Text</code> property for the <code>lblAboutText</code> control.</td><td><pre>
public string AboutText
{
  get { return lblAboutText.Text; }
  set { lblAboutText.Text = value; }
}
</pre></td></tr>
<tr><td>4</td><td>In the MainForm.cs [Design] window, add a <code>Click</code> handler for the About menu.</td><td><pre>
private void menuHelpAbout_Click(
    object sender, EventArgs e)
{
</pre></td></tr>
<tr><td>5</td><td>Implement this handler to create an <code>AboutBox</code> form and assign whether it is an MDI application.</td><td><pre>
  using (AboutBox dlg = new AboutBox())
  {
    dlg.IsMdiApplication = IsMdiChild;
</pre></td></tr>
<tr><td>6</td><td>Set the <code>AboutText</code> property as shown in the code, and the <code>Owner</code> and <code>Icon</code> properties to match the current form.</td><td><pre>
    dlg.AboutText = String.Format(
      "MyPhotos Application, Version {0}\n"
      + "Sample for \"Windows Forms in "
      + "Action\" by Erik Brown\n"
      + "Copyright Manning Publications Co.",
      Application.ProductVersion);
    dlg.Owner = this;
    dlg.Icon = this.Icon;
</pre></td></tr>
<tr><td>7</td><td>Show the form as a modal dialog box.</td><td><pre>
    dlg.ShowDialog();
  }
}
</pre></td></tr>
</table>

These changes configure the label controls with the appropriate icon and textual information. All that remains is for us to define the behavior of the `LinkLabel` controls. Note that the `LinkClicked` event for this class employs the `LinkLabelLinkClickedEventArgs` object as its event parameter. The `LinkLabel` class provides a `Links` property that defines one or more links, as a collection of `LinkLabel.Link` objects, within the single link label control. This permits multiple links to be specified within a single control instance, with the `LinkLabelLinkClickedEventArgs` object indicating the specific link clicked by the user.

Our application is not so grand, so our `LinkLabel` controls use the entire text string as their single link. Let's continue the previous steps and see how to display a website within our form.

	Action	Result
HANDLE THE LINKLABEL CONTROLS		

8	In the AboutBox.cs [Design] window, handle the `LinkClicked` event for the `lnkClose` link label to close the associated form.	`private void lnkClose_LinkClicked(`
		`  object sender, LinkLabelLinkClickedEventArgs e)`
		`{`
		`  Close();`
		`}`

9	Add a `LinkLabel` event handler for the `linkWebSite` control.	`private void lnkWebSite_LinkClicked(`
		`  object sender, LinkLabelLinkClickedEventArgs e)`
		`{`

10	In this handler, reverse the value of the panel's `Visible` property.	`  pnlWebSite.Visible = !pnlWebSite.Visible;`

11	If the panel is now visible, display the book's website and adjust the link text and form size as shown.	`  if (pnlWebSite.Visible)`
		`  {`
		`    webBrowser.Url = new Uri(`
		`        "http://www.manning.com/eebrown2");`
		`    lnkWebSite.Text = "Click to hide web page";`
		`    Size = new Size(600, 400);`
		`  }`

12	Otherwise, reset the controls and the form to their original settings.	`  else`
		`  {`
		`   lnkWebSite.Text = "Click for book's web site";`
		`    Size = new Size(400, 144);`
		`    Text = "About MyPhotos";`
		`  }`
		`}`

13	Handle the `Document-Completed` event for the browser control to set the form's title to match the browser document's title.	`private void webBrowser_DocumentCompleted(`
		`    object sender,`
		`    WebBrowserDocumentCompletedEventArgs e)`
		`{`
		`  Text = webBrowser.DocumentTitle;`
		`}`

This completes our implementation. Compile and run to view the `AboutBox` dialog box in all its glory. When viewing a web page within our application, note that the user can follow links on the page but cannot navigate to an arbitrary web address. This is very different than using a web browser such as Internet Explorer directly, where the user has full control over which pages are displayed.

One drawback of our application is that the Help menu only appears if a child `MainForm` window is active. This suffices for our example, but might not be the best approach in a production application. Feel free to fix this problem in your application.

As you can tell, there is much more to the `WebBrowser` control than shown here. The `Uri` class used in step 11 is part of the `System` namespace and encapsulates a uniform resource locator (URI) object. Other classes, such as the `HtmlDocument` class mentioned in .NET Table 23.5, also exist. The .NET documentation includes an article called "How To: Add Web Browser Capabilities to a Windows Forms Application," which may provide additional insight into the use of the control.

The final two sections cover features related to the configuration and management of applications. First we examine application settings, and then finish our discussion with deployment.

23.4 APPLICATION SETTINGS

In more complex Windows Forms applications, there is often a need to manage one or more settings on behalf of each user or group of users. For example, a music service might wish to save a user's account name, or track each user's preferred genre. Such settings are not associated with a particular song or playlist, but instead are specific to the application and user.

As of version 2.0 of the .NET Framework, direct support for such settings is provided by the `System.Configuration` namespace, and exposed for easy access in Visual Studio. This section implements two examples: first we persist the location of the `ParentForm` window on the desktop; and later we persist the active album a user is viewing when they close the application. Between these examples we examine the classes that support these features.

23.4.1 Storing the Location setting

When using a computer, users often size and position their applications in a certain manner. As a result, it is a nice usability feature when an application saves and restores such settings each time a program is run. This is a subtle feature that some users may not recognize unless it is missing.

In our MyPhotos MDI application, we can use the application settings support in Visual Studio to restore the location of the window each time it is run. This is done with the following steps.

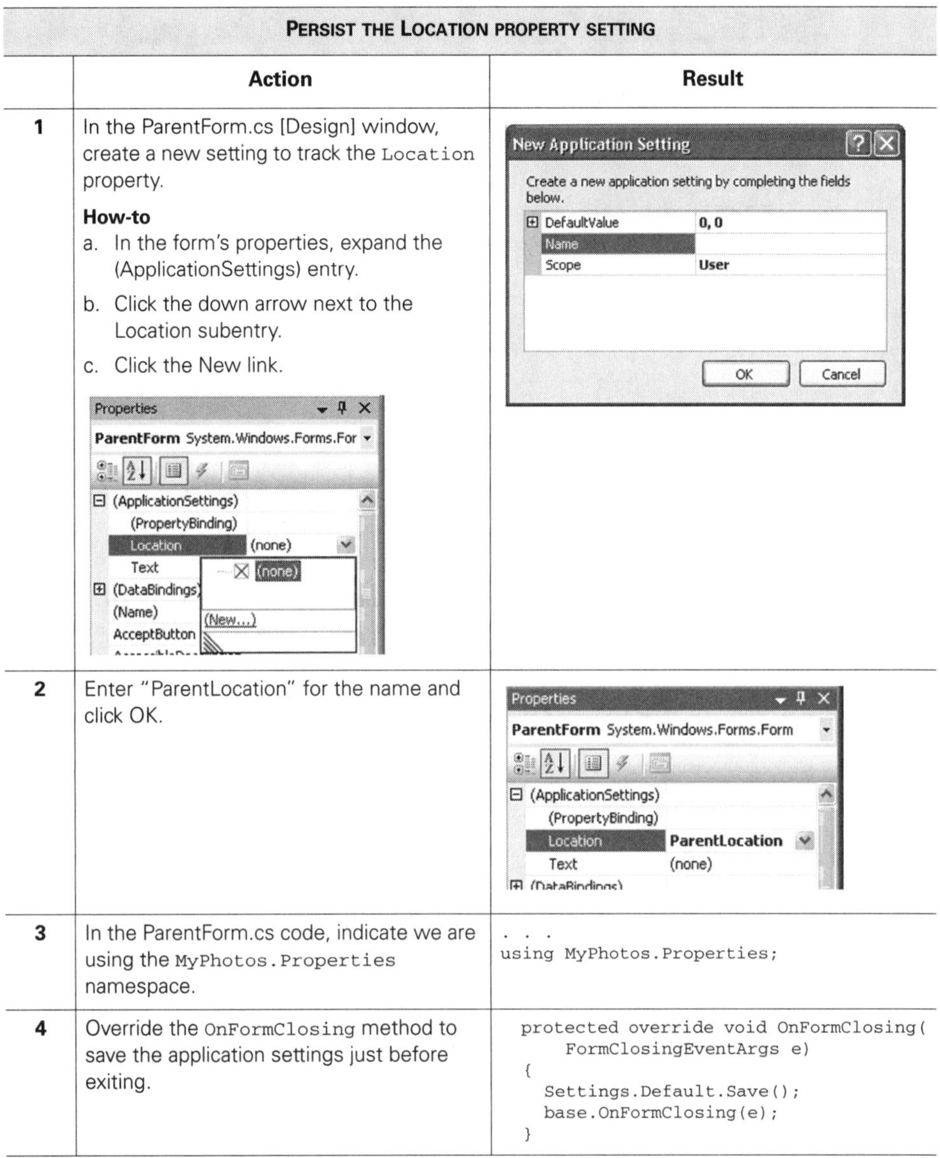

PERSIST THE LOCATION PROPERTY SETTING

	Action	Result
1	In the ParentForm.cs [Design] window, create a new setting to track the `Location` property. **How-to** a. In the form's properties, expand the (ApplicationSettings) entry. b. Click the down arrow next to the Location subentry. c. Click the New link.	
2	Enter "ParentLocation" for the name and click OK.	
3	In the ParentForm.cs code, indicate we are using the `MyPhotos.Properties` namespace.	`. . .` `using MyPhotos.Properties;`

4	Override the `OnFormClosing` method to save the application settings just before exiting.	`protected override void OnFormClosing(`
		`    FormClosingEventArgs e)`
		`{`
		`  Settings.Default.Save();`
		`  base.OnFormClosing(e);`
		`}`

So what have we done here? Windows Forms projects include a Settings.settings entry within the Properties section in Solution Explorer. You can double-click this to bring up the Settings editor, but more interesting is the generated Settings.Designer.cs file beneath this entry. Listing 23.1 shows the contents of this file, with the beginning comments of the file omitted.

Listing 23.1 The generated Settings.Designer.cs file

```
. . .
namespace MyPhotos.Properties {

  [global::System.Runtime.
       CompilerServices.CompilerGeneratedAttribute()]
  [global::System.CodeDom.Compiler.GeneratedCodeAttribute(
       "Microsoft.VisualStudio.Editors.SettingsDesigner.
            SettingsSingleFileGenerator", "8.0.0.0")]
  internal sealed partial class Settings
   : global::System.Configuration.ApplicationSettingsBase {

    private static Settings defaultInstance = ((Settings)(global::
      System.Configuration.ApplicationSettingsBase.Synchronized(
          new Settings())));

    public static Settings Default {                    ❶ Defines Default property
      get { return defaultInstance; }
    }

    [global::System.Configuration.UserScopedSettingAttribute()]
    [global::System.Diagnostics.DebuggerNonUserCodeAttribute()]
    [global::System.Configuration.
         DefaultSettingValueAttribute("0, 0")]
    public global::System.Drawing.Point ParentLocation {    ❷ Defines
      get {                                                   ParentLocation
        return ((global::System.Drawing.Point)                setting
                    (this["ParentLocation"]));
      }
      set { this["ParentLocation"] = value; }
    }
  }
}
```

As you can see in this code, the file defines a `Settings` class as part of the `MyPhotos.Properties` namespace. This class provides a standard interface for all application settings defined in the project. Let's look at the annotated portions of listing 23.1 in more detail.

❶ The static `Default` property provides access to the global `Settings` instance. This includes the defined settings as well as the members inherited from the base `ApplicationSettingsBase` class. This base class is summarized in .NET Table 23.6, and manages the persistence and lookup of the assigned settings.

❷ Settings classes ultimately define a collection of property names and values. Properties are defined and accessed using the indexer on the `ApplicationSettingsBase` class, as in the `this["ParentLocation"]` in our code. In our case, the retrieved object is cast to a `Point` structure to correspond to the type for the `ParentLocation` property.

Although application settings classes can be defined manually, the interface in Visual Studio covers most situations. By default, defined settings are persisted using the `LocalFileSettingsProvider` class, which stores values as XML files in the `LocalApplicationData` directory as defined in the `Environment.SpecialFolder` enumeration discussed in chapter 6.

.NET Table 23.6 ApplicationSettingsBase class

New in 2.0 The `ApplicationSettingsBase` class is an abstract settings class that supports the creation of settings wrapper classes in Windows Forms applications. This class is part of the `System.Configuration` namespace, and inherits from the `System.Configuration.SettingsBase` class.

Public Properties	*Item* (overridden from SettingsBase)	Gets or sets the value of the specified settings property
	Properties (overridden from SettingsBase)	Gets the collection of `SettingsProperty` objects in the current settings class
	Providers (overridden from SettingsBase)	Gets the collection of `SettingsProvider` objects used to store configuration data
Public Methods	*Reload*	Refreshes the settings property values
	Reset	Restores all settings to their default values
	Save (overridden from SettingsBase)	Stores all settings property values to persistent storage
Public Events	*PropertyChanged*	Occurs after the value of a setting has changed
	SettingChanging	Occurs before the value of a setting is changed
	SettingsLoaded	Occurs after settings are retrieved from storage
	SettingsSaving	Occurs before values are saved to the data store

Looking back at listing 23.1, there are a number of attributes employed, both to define the file as generated code and configure the `ParentLocation` setting. The two setting attributes assigned are the `UserScopedSettingAttribute` and `DefaultSettingValueAttribute` classes, both part of the `System.Configuration` namespace. The latter attribute assigns the default value for the setting, used as the initial value and in methods such as `Reset`.

Each setting property can also apply to the entire application or be specific for each user. A property is specific to the current user if the `UserScopedSettingAttribute` is applied, and defines a common value for all users if the `ApplicationScopedSettingAttribute` class is applied. A `ConfigurationErrorsException` is thrown if both attributes are applied to the same setting property.

TRY IT! Modify the application settings to persist the size of the `ParentForm` window in addition to the location. This can be done by defining a setting for the `ClientSize` property. Click the small ... button next to the (PropertyBinding) entry beneath the (ApplicationSettings) entry in the Properties window to do this. This displays the list of application settings for the control, and allows additional settings to be defined.

23.4.2 Defining a custom setting

As discussed in the prior section, settings can apply to the entire application or only the current user. Now that we've seen how to persist a property of a form, let's define a custom setting property to persist something unique to our MyPhotos application.

Let's save the most recent album viewed by the user, and reload this album during application startup. The steps required for this change are as follows.

<table>
<tr><th colspan="3">PERSIST THE LAST ALBUM VIEWED BY A USER</th></tr>
<tr><th></th><th>Action</th><th>Result</th></tr>
<tr><td>1</td><td>Create a new <code>LastAlbumPath</code> setting property in the MyPhotos project.

How-to
a. In the Solution Explorer window, double-click the Settings.settings entry.
b. In the Settings.settings window, enter the new name LastAlbumPath.
c. Set Type to string and Scope to User.</td><td>Settings.settings | ParentForm.cs [Design] | AssemblyInfo.cs
Synchronize | View Code
Application settings allow you to store and retrieve property settings and other information for your application dynamically. For example, the application can save a user's color preferences, then retrieve them the next time it runs. Learn more about application settings...

Name | Type | Scope | Value
ParentLocation | System.Dra... | User | 0, 0
LastAlbumPath | string | User |
*</td></tr>
<tr><td>2</td><td>In the <code>ParentForm</code> class, modify the <code>OnMdiChildActivate</code> method to save the path each time an album window becomes active.</td><td><pre>protected override void OnMdiChildActivate(
    EventArgs e)
{
  . . .
  MainForm f = ActiveMdiChild as MainForm;
  if (f != null)
  {
    . . .
    Settings.Default.LastAlbumPath
        = f.AlbumPath;
  }
  . . .
}</pre></td></tr>
</table>

PERSIST THE LAST ALBUM VIEWED BY A USER *(CONTINUED)*		
	Action	**Result**

3	In the `OnLoad` method, display a `MainForm` child window with the last album path whenever the `LastAlbumPath` setting is non-empty and the associated album is not encrypted.	`protected override void OnLoad(EventArgs e)`
		`{`
		`  . . .`
		`  // Re-load last active album`
		`  string name`
		`      = Settings.Default.LastAlbumPath;`
		`  if (!string.IsNullOrEmpty(name)`
		`    && !AlbumStorage.IsEncrypted(name))`
		`  {`
		`    CreateMdiChild(new MainForm(name, null));`
		`  }`
		
		`  base.OnLoad(e);`
		`}`

Look at the Settings.Designer.cs file to view the code generated for this new setting. A new `LastAlbumPath` property is defined, much like the `ParentLocation` property was defined in the previous section.

```
[global::System.Configuration.UserScopedSettingAttribute()]
[global::System.Diagnostics.DebuggerNonUserCodeAttribute()]
[global::System.Configuration.DefaultSettingValueAttribute("")]
public string LastAlbumPath {
  get {
    return ((string)(this["LastAlbumPath"]));
  }
  set {
    this["LastAlbumPath"] = value;
  }
}
```

This completes our discussion on application settings. Of course, if you wish to give users control over their settings, you can build a dialog box where application settings can be examined and modified.

The final topic in this chapter is deployment.

TRY IT! Modify the MyPhotos application to persist the specific photograph viewed by the user in the last displayed album. This is slightly more complicated than you may expect, since the photograph displayed is controlled by the `MainForm` class rather than `ParentForm`. Make sure you account for possible error scenarios as well, such as when the last photograph is in a new album that is not saved.

23.5 DEPLOYMENT

After all the code we've written building the MyPhotos application, it somehow seems fitting to end our discussions with a section on how to deploy this application to other computers. As you would expect, .NET defines multiple mechanisms for deploying applications, and provides a number of classes to support such efforts.

This section walks through two deployment methods. The first creates a traditional setup file that can be copied and otherwise transported to other computers for installation. The second is the new ClickOnce deployment offered as of the .NET 2.0 release.

23.5.1 Creating a setup project

A setup file is an executable that installs an application on a computer. The advantage of having such a file is its flexibility. You can store it on a server, email it to your friends, or distribute it on a CD or other media to anyone in the world.

The .NET Framework defines setup projects for the creation of such files. The following steps use the Setup Wizard to create such a project for our application.

Setup projects are not supported in Visual C# Express, so if you are using this edition you will not be able to create a setup project here. If you have one of the Visual Studio editions, then you should be fine. Visual C# Express does support ClickOnce deployment, as described in the next section.

CREATE A SETUP PROJECT FOR THE MYPHOTOS APPLICATION

	Action	Result
1	Under the File menu, select New Project from the Add menu item to add a new project to the solution.	The Add New Project dialog box appears.
2	Create a new MyPhotosSetup project based on the Setup Wizard template. **How-to** a. In the Project types area, expand Other Project Types and select Setup and Deployment. b. Select the Setup Wizard template. Setup Wizard c. Enter "MyPhotosSetup" as the Name for the project. d. Click OK to create the project.	The Setup Project Wizard appears.

CREATE A SETUP PROJECT FOR THE MYPHOTOS APPLICATION *(CONTINUED)*

	Action	Result
3	Configure the setup project to install the MyPhotos executable file. **How-to** a. Click Next. b. In step 2 of 5, click Next to create a project for installing a Windows application. c. In step 3 of 5, click the check box for the "Primary output from MyPhotos" entry to include the MyPhotos executable in the new project. d. Click Next. e. In step 4 of 5, click Next to include no additional files. f. In step 5 of 5, click Finish.	The new project appears in the Solution Explorer window.

This defines a setup project called MyPhotosSetup that installs the executable created by the MyPhotos project on target machines. There are a number of views of a setup project supported by Visual Studio that define how data is installed onto a target machine. The File System view shown in figure 23.5 appears by default. This view defines where installation files appear on the target machine. By default directories for the application folder, the user's desktop, and the user's Programs menu are defined. A number of other folders are available as well, which you can see if you right-click the File System on Target Machine heading in Visual Studio and expand the Add Special Folder submenu.

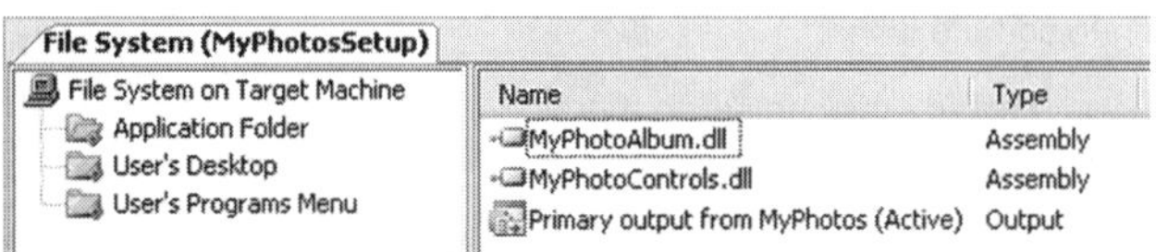

Figure 23.5 This figure indicates the files to install in the application folder, including the primary output, or MyPhotos.exe program, from the MyPhotos project.

To control additional aspects of the resulting setup program, you need to display the other views available. This is done by right-clicking the MyPhotosSetup project and expanding the View submenu. Besides the File System view, you should see the following:

- Registry: Windows Registry entries to add or modify on the target machine.
- File Types: File types to install on the target machine. In our MyPhotos application, for example, we could install the .abm file type for album files.
- User Interface: Controls the flow of the setup windows during installation. The default screens can be modified, and new screens can be added.
- Custom Actions: Additional actions to perform during installation. Generally these are classes that have the `RunInstaller` attribute assigned and derive from the `Installer` class in the `System.Configuration.Install` namespace. For example, the `PerformanceCounterInstaller` class installs performance counters on the target machine.
- Launch Conditions: Conditions that must be met before the installation can occur—for example, a required Registry or file entry, or a required program. By default, the installer is configured to verify that the .NET Framework is installed on the target machine.

Our somewhat modest installation program simply places a shortcut on the user's program menu that invokes our MyPhotos application. The following steps complete our project.

DEFINE THE FILE SYSTEM LAYOUT FOR OUR SETUP PROJECT		
	Action	**Result**
4	In the File System view for the MyPhotosSetup project, add the common library file icons\Win- XP\camera.ico to the application folder directory. **How-to** a. Right-click the Application Folder and select File from the Add menu. b. Locate and select the icon. c. Click Open to add the icon.	The camera.ico file is displayed as part of the Application Folder in the File System view.
5	Add a Windows Forms in Action folder to the user's Programs menu. **How-to** a. Right click the User's Programs Menu and select Folder from the Add menu. b. Enter the name for the folder.	File System (MyPhotosSetup) File System on Target Machine Application Folder User's Desktop User's Programs Menu Windows Forms in Action

DEFINE THE FILE SYSTEM LAYOUT FOR OUR SETUP PROJECT *(CONTINUED)*		
	Action	**Result**
6	Within the Windows Forms in Action folder, add a shortcut to the MyPhotos executable. **How-to** a. Display the empty contents of the new folder. b. Right-click on the blank contents and select Create New Shortcut. c. In the dialog box, double-click the Application Folder item. d. Select Primary Output from MyPhotos. e. Click OK to add the shortcut.	The new shortcut appears in the folder, with the name "Shortcut to Primary output from MyPhotos (Active)."
7	Modify the properties associated with this shortcut. You have to click Browse to assign the Icon entry. **Settings** **Property** / **Value** (Name) / MyPhotos Icon / Camera.ico	Name / Type MyPhotos / Shortcut
8	Set the Manufacturer for the setup project to Manning. **How-to** a. Select the MyPhotosSetup project name in the Solution Explorer window. b. Display the Properties window. c. Set the Manufacturer entry to "Manning."	Properties MyPhotosSetup Deployment Project Localization / English (United S Manufacturer / Manning ManufacturerUrl

This completes our setup project. The final step here assigns the Manufacturer for the project, which is used as part of the deployment directory path within the Program Files folder.

By default, since it sometimes takes a while, setup projects are not built when the solution is built. To build the project, right-click the MyPhotosSetup project and select Build. You can install the program from here as well, assuming the setup project has been built, by selecting Install from the same menu. Alternately, you can navigate to the setup project's directory and copy the installation files to another computer or other location. The initial screen of our installation is shown in figure 23.6.

When you have finished experimenting with this project, make sure you uninstall the program from your computer before moving to the ClickOnce deployment described in the next section.

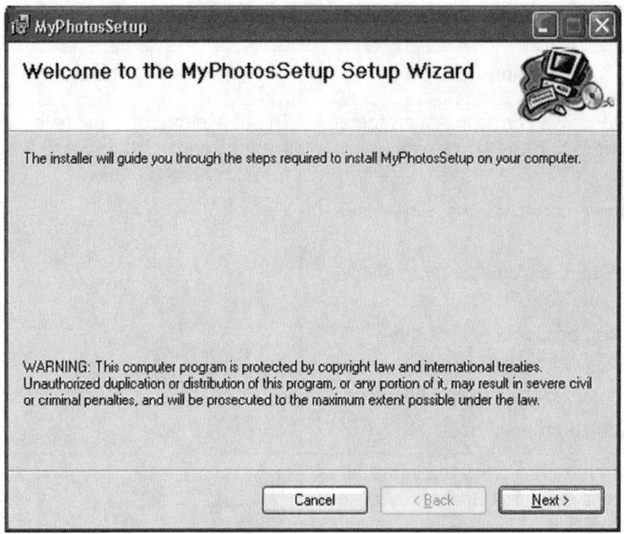

Figure 23.6 The dialog boxes used for a .NET installation program are defined by the User Interface view of the setup project.

23.5.2 Publishing a ClickOnce application

While setup projects are quite flexible and can install pretty much any configuration on the target machine, they are also limited in their ability to manage ongoing updates and changes to the associated application. It is certainly possible to build update installations, and distribute these to users no matter where they are. The administration of such an ongoing effort can be problematic, and you have no guarantee that all of your users will actually install the upgrade on their computer.

For this reason, application development in recent years, especially for large business applications, has focused on web applications rather than Windows applications. A web application requires no installation on a user's computer, and any changes are immediately available to the entire user community. Further, the user is forced to always use the latest version of the application, since the old web application is normally replaced with every release.

From a Microsoft perspective, this brings into question the utility of having a fancy operating system available. If all you need is a web browser to run applications, then why buy a Windows-enabled PC, and why upgrade to the latest version of the Windows operating system? Not a good business situation for Microsoft.

In addition, of course, a local desktop application has a number of advantages over web-based applications. Most of the UI management is computed locally, rather than on a server machine, and Windows Forms supports a much richer user experience than your typical web application. Caching, error handling, and user feedback are easier to manage locally than from a remote server. Common tasks such as printing and file management are also simpler when running on the local machine rather than over a network.

As a result, one of the design goals for the Window Forms team during the development of .NET 2.0 was to create a deployment solution for Windows Forms applications that matches the simplicity and benefits of deploying web applications. The result is ClickOnce deployment.

On the surface, ClickOnce is a rather simple concept. You can install a Windows Forms application over the Internet, simplifying the deployment and synchronization of the application for all of its users. Our example illustrates this simplicity, but indicates areas where the deployment can be extended to include richer functionality. We should also note that ClickOnce requires an available Internet Information Services (IIS) Web Server. Our example assumes you have an IIS Server running locally on your development machine.

The following steps perform a ClickOnce deployment for our MyPhotos application.

DEPLOY THE APPLICATION USING CLICKONCE

	Action	Result
1	Set the Install Mode for the project so that the application is available only while the user is online. **How-to** a. Display the Properties window for the MyPhotos project. b. Display the Publish tab. c. Under Install Mode and Settings, select "The application is available online only."	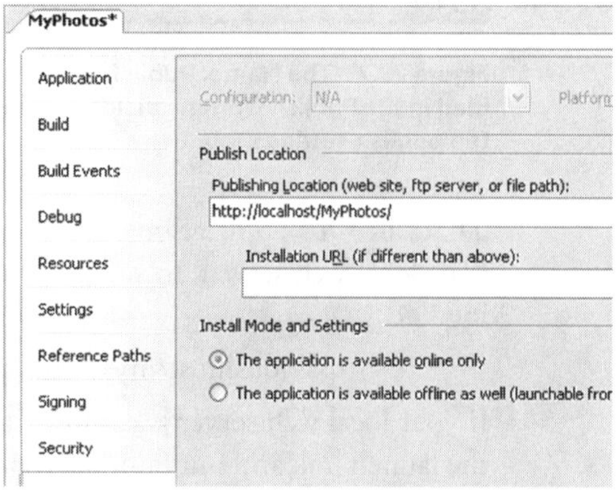 MyPhotos* Application Build Build Events Debug Resources Settings Reference Paths Signing Security Configuration: N/A Platform Publish Location Publishing Location (web site, ftp server, or file path): http://localhost/MyPhotos/ Installation URL (if different than above): Install Mode and Settings The application is available online only The application is available offline as well (launchable fror
2	Also set the Publish Version for the application to 23.5.0.0, and set the revision number so it is never incremented.	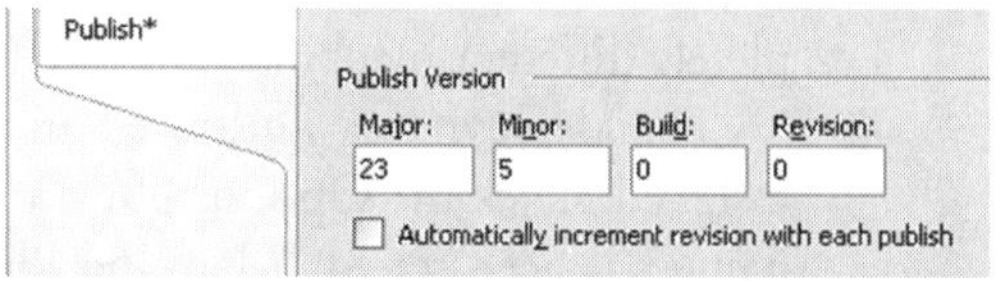 Publish* Publish Version Major: 23 Minor: 5 Build: 0 Revision: 0 Automatically increment revision with each publish
3	Click the Publish Now button to publish the application to the local web server.	When the task completes, the project is published to the configured location, which should be the default http://localhost/MyPhotos.

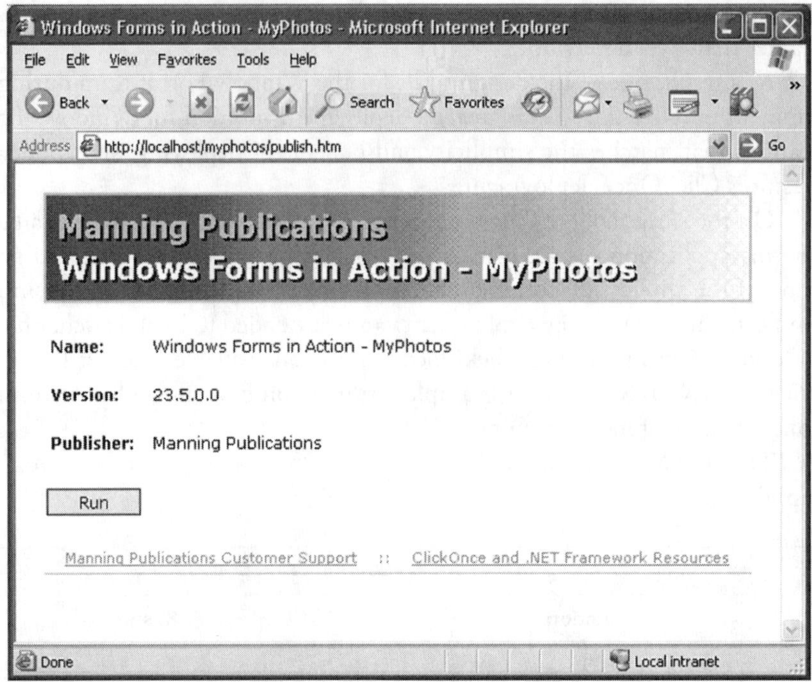

Figure 23.7 The Name, Publisher, web page file, and other settings can be modified in the Publish Options dialog box available by clicking the Options button on the publish settings tab.

That's it. Our application is now published and available to anyone with access to your local web server. To see this, open Internet Explorer and navigate to the following URL:

http://localhost/myphotos/publish.htm

If your local web server is running, a page much like figure 23.7 should appear. Click the launch link and our familiar application appears on the local desktop. This is more impressive, of course, when published to a remote server and downloaded on a completely different machine. The steps to do this are basically the same as shown here.

The deployment illustrated in figure 23.7 has some of the optional settings assigned. Click the Options button to view these settings. In the figure, the publisher name has been set to "Manning Publications" and the product name to "Windows Forms in Action – MyPhotos."

There are a large number of additional settings here, of course. Here are a few changes you can make to explore some of the available options.

- An application can be published via the Publish Wizard button instead of the Publish Now button. This is available on the Publish tab, or by selecting the Publish item from the Build menu.

- When the user launches the application, the deployment framework verifies that the user has the most recent version. This is done by comparing the local version number with the version number on the server. Modify the title bar for the MainForm application and republish the project without changing the version. When you click the launch link, the new version will not be downloaded. Republish with a new version number and this will suddenly work. To avoid this problem, check the "Automatically increment revision with each publish" check box.
- The Install Mode on the Publish tab controls whether the application is only available online or can be accessed when the user is not connected to the Internet. Make the application available offline and republish. A shortcut is placed in the Start menu to access the application. Even so, the application automatically checks the server for updates each time it is run, to ensure that the user always has the most recent version.
- The Security tab defines the permissions expected by the application. By default an application expects full trust, meaning that it can do anything the user can do locally. This is quite different than a web page, which is constrained by the permissions defined for the user. To see this, display the Security tab and make the application partial trust. Set the FileDialogPermission to Exclude. Publish and run the application, and an exception occurs when you try to open a file dialog window.
- The Signing tab allows a certificate to be associated with the installation. This is useful to ensure that users only install authorized versions of the software. You can simulate this by creating a test certificate for your application.

This completes our discussion of ClickOnce deployment. As indicated, our example is rather straightforward to show how easy it is to deploy an application to remote users via a web server. More information on ClickOnce deployment is available online. See appendix D for a list of websites you might wish to explore for this and other Windows Forms topics.

In keeping with tradition, we provide a final recap of our discussion.

23.6 Recap

This chapter presented an overview of various topics in Windows Forms application development. Each topic was discussed rather briefly, and demonstrated with an example that extended the MyPhotos MDI application built in chapter 20.

The specific topics covered included printing from an application, dragging and dropping objects on the desktop, using the `WebBrowser` control, managing application settings, and deploying applications. On the final topic, we deployed our application using first a standard setup program and then the ClickOnce deployment feature.

If you have read this book from cover to cover, then congratulations. Regardless of how you came to this sentence, the appendices include some reference material on C# and .NET namespaces, as well as class hierarchy charts and a list of recommended websites.

I hope you have enjoyed reading this book as much (or more!) than I have enjoyed writing it. Good luck with your programming endeavors. May your code always compile and applications never fail.

A P P E N D I X   A

C# primer

This appendix provides an introduction and reference to the C# programming language. If you are looking for a detailed description of C#, a number of resources listed in the bibliography provide this kind of coverage. If you are familiar with object-oriented programming or with C-based languages such as C++ or Java, then this appendix should get you started and serve as a quick reference for terms and keywords you encounter in this book and elsewhere.

You may also discover that many of the terms and keywords presented here are discussed in detail in the text. If you are interested in further discussion or examples for a topic, consult the index at the back of the book.

This appendix approaches C# in a somewhat formal manner. We discuss the following topics:

- Organization of a C# program
- Types and type members available in the language
- Elements of the language, including built-in types, operators, and keywords
- Special features of C#, such as arrays and automated documentation

A.1 C# PROGRAMS

A C# program consists of a collection of *source files* where each source file is an ordered sequence of Unicode characters. Typically, each source file corresponds to a single file in the file system. A program is *compiled* into a set of computer instructions known as an *assembly.* The .NET Framework interprets or otherwise executes an assembly to perform the instructions given in the original program.

A.1.1 Assemblies

Assemblies are containers for types, and are used to package and deploy compiled C# programs. An assembly may contain one or more types, the instructions to implement these types, and references to other assemblies. While not strictly required, an assembly is normally a single file in a file system. For example, the System.Windows.Forms.dll file is the assembly for the `System.Windows.Forms` namespace.

There are two kinds of assemblies: *applications* and *libraries.* An application is an assembly that has a *main entry point* and usually has an .exe extension. Applications are used to perform a specific task or tasks on behalf of a computer user. The main entry point of an application is the initial instruction to execute in the program.

A library is an assembly that does not have a main entry point and usually has a .dll extension. Libraries are used to encapsulate one or more types for use when building other assemblies.

A.1.2 Namespaces

Logically, the source files in a C# program contain a collection of *namespaces.* Each namespace defines a scope, or *declaration space,* in which a set of zero or more *type declarations* and zero or more nested namespaces are defined. The possible type declarations are classes, structures, interfaces, enumerations, and delegates. Each type declaration is assigned a *name* that is unique within its declaration space, in this case within the defined namespace. It is an error for two type declarations to have the same name within the same namespace.

All type declarations are assigned to a namespace. If a specific namespace is not specified, then the type is assigned to the *default namespace,* also called the *global namespace.*

A namespace is declared in the following manner:[1]

```
namespace <name>
{
  <nested-namespaces>opt
  <type-declarations>
}
```

---

[1] We use the convention here and in other syntax examples where items in angle brackets < > are filled in by the programmer. An optional item will include an "opt" subscript following the item.

The <name> here can be a single identifier, or a series of identifiers separated by periods. Nested namespaces are declared in the same way as non-nested namespaces. The various kinds of type declarations each have their own syntax, and are described next.

A.2 TYPES

A type is classified as either a *value type* or a *reference type*. These correspond to whether the type stores the actual data, or value, for the type, or whether the type simply stores a reference to the actual data.

Value types include simple built-in types such as `int` and `char`, enumerations, and structures. A value type contains its data. For example, an `int` type assigned to the number 5 stores this number directly. Thus, two different value types contain separate copies of the data and, therefore, modifying one of these types has no effect on the other.

Reference types, on the other hand, contain a reference to their data. Examples include the `string` type and all Windows Forms controls. A `string` type assigned to the string "Hello" stores a reference to a section of memory where the characters H-e-l-l-o are actually stored. The area of memory reserved for reference types is called the *heap*, and is managed internally by the .NET Framework. Thus, two different reference types can point to the same physical data. As a result, the modification of one reference type can affect another reference type. Reference types include classes, interfaces, delegates, and arrays.

Table A.1 illustrates the differences between these two kinds of types. In the table, the assignment of `v2 = v1` copies the contents of `v1` into `v2`. As a result, changing the value of `v1.vData` has no effect on the value stored by `v2`. In the reference column, the assignment of `r2 = r1` causes both objects to refer to the same data. Here, changing the value of `r1.rData` also affects the value seen by `r2`. Note that all value types in the .NET Framework implicitly inherit from the `System.ValueType` class. This class overrides the methods inherited from the `System.Object` class with more appropriate implementations for value types.

Table A.1 A comparison of value and reference types

	Value type	Reference type

Declaration	`struct ValInt {`
	`  public int vData;`
	`}`
		`class RefInt {`
		`  public int rData;`
		`}`

Usage	`ValInt v1, v2;`
	`v1.vData = 5;`
	`v2 = v1;`
	`v1.vData = 7`
		`RefInt r1, r2;`
		`r1.rData = 5;`
		`r2 = r1;`
		`r1.rData = 7;`

Result	Value of `v2.vData` is still 5.	Value of `r2.rData` is now 7.

Back to the topic at hand, a type is specified with a type declaration as part of a namespace, or within the default namespace. The possible type declarations are classes, structures, interfaces, enumerations, and delegates.

A.2.1 Classes

A *class* is a reference type that defines a new data abstraction. Each class is composed of one or more *members* that define the contents, operations, and behavior supported by instances of the class.

A `class` is declared using the class keyword in the following manner:

```
<modifiers>opt class <identifier> : <base>opt <interfaces>opt
{
  <class-members>
}
```

where

- `<modifiers>` is optional, and is an accessibility level as defined in table A.2 or one of the keywords `new`, `abstract`, `static`, `partial`, or `sealed`. If unspecified, a class is assigned the default accessibility level of the containing declarative scope. Multiple complementary modifiers may be specified.
- `<identifier>` is the unique name to assign to the class.
- `<base>` is optional, and defines a single base class for the new class.
- `<interfaces>` is optional, and specifies one or more interface types which this class supports. If both `<base>` and `<interfaces>` are omitted, then the colon (:) is also omitted.
- `<class-members>` are the members of the class. The possible members of a class are constants, fields, methods, properties, events, indexers, operators, constructors, and nested type declarations. Nested type declarations are simply other types defined to exist within the declarative scope defined by the class. The other kinds of members are discussed in the subsequent sections.

Every member of a class, and in fact every member of any type, has a defined *accessibility* associated with it. The accessibility of a member controls which regions of a program may make use of that member. The five levels of accessibility are shown in table A.2.

Table A.2 The possible accessibility levels for C# types

Accessibility level	Meaning
public	Any type in any assembly can access the member.
protected	Any derived type in any assembly can access the member.
internal	Any type in the same assembly can access the member.
protected internal	Any derived type in the same assembly can access the member.
private	Only the containing type can access the member.

These accessibility levels are used to declare nested types as well as other members. The default accessibility level of top-level types is `internal`. Within a class declaration, the default accessibility level is `private`. The default value of a class instance is `null`.

Two new features added to the C# language for .NET 2.0 are partial classes and static classes. Partial classes allow a single type to be split into multiple files, and are discussed in chapter 2. Static classes provide a mechanism for declaring that all members of the class are static.

The various kinds of class members other than nested types are described in the following sections. All class members support an optional modifier. If the modifier is not specified, the member is assigned the default accessibility level of the containing declarative scope. Multiple complementary modifiers may also be specified.

Constants

A *constant* is an unchangeable value that can be computed at compile time. A constant is declared using the const keyword in the following manner:

```
<modifiers>opt const <type> <constant-name> = <value> ;
```

where

- `<modifiers>` is optional, either an accessibility level or the `new` keyword.
- `<type>` is any value type.
- `<constant-name>` is the unique name for the constant.
- `<value>` is the fixed value to assign to the constant.

Here are a few examples of constant declarations:

```
const int DaysPerYear = 365;

// The constant value here is calculated by the compiler.
const double AlmostPi = 22.0 / 7.0;

// A constant taken from a public enumeration.
public enum Weekday = { Sun, Mon, Tue, Wed, Thu, Fri, Sat };
protected const Weekday FirstDayOfWeek = Sun;
```

Fields

A *field* is a variable value that can be modified at runtime. A field is declared in the following manner:

```
<modifiers>opt <type> <field-name> = <initial-value>opt ;
```

where

- `<modifiers>` is optional, either an accessibility level or one of the keywords `new`, `readonly`, `static`, or `volatile`.
- `<type>` is any valid type.

- <field-name> is the unique name for the field.
- <initial-value> is the value to initially assign to the field. This value may be modified by the program at runtime.

Here are a few examples of field declarations:

```
public readonly string _defaultDir = @"C:\My Documents\Albums";
private PhotoAlbum _album;

// Possible fields in a Fraction class
public class Fraction
{
  private long _num;
  private long _den;
  . . .
}
```

Methods

A *method* is a member that implements an operation or action that can be performed by a class or other object. For example, in a Fraction class, a method could be used to add two fractions together or compute the inverse of a fraction. A method may return a result, and can optionally accept one or more parameters that are used to perform the implemented action. A method is declared in the following manner:

```
<modifiers>opt <return-type> <member-name> ( <parameters>opt )
{
  <statements>opt
}
```

where

- <modifiers> is optional, either an accessibility level or one of the keywords new, static, virtual, sealed, override, abstract, or extern.
- <return-type> is either a valid type or the void keyword. When a type is specified, the return keyword is used to return an instance of this type as the result of the method.
- <member-name> is the unique name for the method.
- <parameters> is optional. When specified, each parameter provides a type and an identifier, with possible modifiers out and ref. The params keyword may be used as the final parameter to indicate an array of values of a given type.
- <statements> is optional and indicates one or more statements specifying the computer instructions for performing the defined action.

Here are a few examples of method declarations that might be provided as part of a Fraction class:

```
// public method
public void Add(Fraction b)
```

```
{
  this._den = this._den * b._den;
  this._num = (this._num * b._den) + (b._num * this._den);
}

// protected method with ref parameter
protected void Invert(ref Fraction a)
{
  Fraction f = new Fraction(a._den, a._num);
  a = f;
}

// static method with return type and params parameter
public static Fraction AddMultiple(params Fractions[] fracts)
{
  Fraction a = new Fraction(1, 1);
  foreach (Fraction f in fracts)
  {
    a.Add(f);
  }

  return a;
}
```

Properties

A *property* is a member that provides access to a characteristic of a class or other object. For example, in a `Fraction` class, a property might provide the numerator of the fraction, or the floating-point value of the fraction. A property provides *accessors* that specify the operations to perform when its value is read or written. A property may support both read and write accessors, called `get` and `set`, respectively, or be read-only or write-only. A property is declared in the following manner:

```
<modifiers>opt <type> <member-name>
{
  <property-accessors>
}
```

where

- `<modifiers>` is optional, either an accessibility level or one of the keywords `new`, `static`, `virtual`, `sealed`, `override`, `abstract`, or `extern`.
- `<type>` is the type for the property.
- `<member-name>` is the unique name for the property.
- `<property-accessors>` is one or both of the `get` and `set` accessors. Each accessor consists of its accessor type, either `get` or `set`, and the block of statements defining the programming instructions for this accessor. In the `get` accessor, the type of the property must be returned using the `return` keyword. In the `set` accessor, an implicit parameter called `value` is used to represent the instance of the specified type provided by the caller.

Note that properties are declared much like methods, except that properties do not use parentheses and cannot have explicit parameters. A few examples of property declarations that might be used within a `Fraction` class are as follows:

```
public long Numerator
{
  get { return this._num; }
  set { this._num = value; }
}

public long Denominator
{
  get { return this._den; }
  set
  {
    if (value == 0)
      throw new DivideByZeroException("Denominator cannot be zero");

    this._den = value;
  }
}

// a read-only property
protected double Value
{
  get { return ((double)this._num / (double)this._den); }
}
```

Events

An *event* is a member that enables a class or other object to provide notifications. An instance of a class can associate one or more methods, known as *event handlers*, with specific events in order to receive such notifications. An event is declared using the `event` keyword. Like properties, an event can declare *accessors* to specify how event handlers are added to or removed from the event. Such accessors are optional, resulting in the following forms for an event declaration:

```
<modifiers>opt event <delegate-type> <member-name> ;

<modifiers>opt event <delegate-type> <member-name>
{
  <event-accessors>
}
```

where

- `<modifiers>` is optional, either an accessibility level or one of the keywords `new`, `static`, `virtual`, `sealed`, `override`, `abstract`, or `extern`.
- `<delegate-type>` is the delegate on which this event is based.
- `<member-name>` is the unique name for the property.

- `<event-accessors>`, when specified, must provide both the `add` and `remove` accessor. These accessors define how a given method is added to and removed from the event. In both accessors, an implicit parameter called `value` is used to represent the specified method.

Outside of the type where an event is defined, only the += and −= operators are permitted in order to add and remove methods, respectively. Methods are added to events as delegate instances based on the delegate type for the event. The following code shows how a `DivideByZero` event might be implemented within a `Fraction` class:

```
// public class for event data
public class DivideByZeroArgs
{
  . . .
}

public delegate void DivideByZeroHandler(object sender,
                                         DivideByZeroArgs e);

public class Fraction
{
  . . .
  // Declare the DivideByZero event for this class
  public event DivideByZeroHandler DivideByZero;

  // Declare a method to invoke the event
  public virtual void OnDivideByZero(DivideByZeroArgs e)
  {
    if (DivideByZero == null)
    {
      // No handlers, so raise exception
      throw new DivideByZeroException("Divide by zero");
    }
    else
      DivideByZero(this, e);  // call event handlers
  }

  // Declare property that can invoke event
  public long Denominator
  {
    get { return this._den; }
    set
    {
      if (value == 0)
      {
        DivideByZeroArgs args = new DivideByZeroArgs(..);
        OnDivideByZero(this, args);
        // Do something based on event handler
      }
      else
        this._den = value;
    }
  }
```

Indexers

An *indexer* is a member that enables an object to be treated as an array. Elements in the "array" are referenced using square brackets. An indexer employs the `this` keyword as part of its declaration, which typically looks like this:

```
<modifiers>opt <type> this [ <parameters> ]
{
  <accessors>
}
```

where

- `<modifiers>` is optional, either an accessibility level or one of the keywords `new`, `virtual`, `sealed`, `override`, or `abstract`.
- `<type>` is the type returned by this indexer. This usually corresponds to the type of objects contained by the containing class.
- `<parameters>` are the parameters for the indexer. The format corresponds to that of a method, except that at least one parameter is required, and `ref` and `out` parameters are not permitted.
- `<accessors>` provide the block of statements associated with reading and writing indexer elements. These are identical to the accessors used for properties.

The following code shows a `PartsOfOne` class that provides the fractions between 0 and 1, inclusive, that divide an object into an equal number of parts. An indexer is used to return the nth `Fraction` object. For example, `PartsOfOne(3)` will return the fractions for zero (as 0 over 3), one-third, two-thirds, and one (as 3 over 3).

```
public class PartsOfOne
{
  private ulong _parts;

  PartsOfOne(ulong parts)
  {
    _parts = parts;
  }

  // Indexer to return nth part as a Fraction between 0 and 1
  public Fraction this[ulong n]
  {
    if (n < 0 || n > _parts)
      throw new IndexOutOfRangeException();

    return new Fraction(n, _parts);
  }
}
```

Operators

An *operator* is a member that defines the meaning of an expression operator as applied to an instance of an object. There are three types of operators. A *unary operator* applies to a single type, a *binary operator* applies to two types, and a *conversion operator* converts an object from one type to another. The corresponding three operator types all use the `operator` keyword, and are formatted as follows:

```
<modifiers> <type> operator <unary-op> (<parameter>)
{
  <statements>
}

<modifiers> <type> operator <binary-op> (<parameter>, <parameter>)
{
  <statements>
}

<modifiers> <conv-kind> operator <type> (<parameter>)
{
  <statements>
}
```

where

- `<modifiers>` must be one of the keywords `public`, `static`, or `extern`.
- `<type>` is the type returned by the operator.
- `<unary-op>` is a unary operator: `+ - ! ~ ++ -- true false`
- `<binary-op>` is a binary operator: `+ - * / % & | ^ << >> == != > < >= <=`
- `<conv-kind>` is the kind of conversion, either `implicit` or `explicit`. An implicit conversion is invoked automatically by the compiler, such as from `int` to `long`. An explicit conversion requires an explicit cast, such as from `int to byte`.
- `<parameter>` is a type and identifier to accept in the conversion.
- `<statements>` is the block of statements associated with the operator. This block must return a value of the specified type.

The following code shows an example of unary, binary, and conversion operator declaration for a `Fraction` class:

```
// Unary operator for the negative operation
public Fraction operator -(Fraction a)
{
  return new Fraction(-a.Numerator, a.Denominator);
}

// Binary operator for the addition operation
public Fraction operator +(Fraction a, Fraction b)
{
  int den = a.Denominator * b.Denominator;
  int num = (a.Numerator * b.Denominator)
            + (b.Numerator * a.Denominator);
  return new Fraction(num, den);
}
```

```
// Explicit conversion from Fraction to double
static explicit operator double(Fraction a)
{
  return ((double)a.Numerator / (double)a.Denominator);
}
```

Constructor

A *constructor* is a member that initializes a class or an instance of a class or other object. There are two types of constructors. A *static constructor* performs onetime initialization for an object, while an *instance constructor* initializes a specific instance of an object. Static constructors cannot be invoked explicitly and are executed, at most, once in a program after any static fields have been initialized and before any static class members are referenced or instances of the class created. Instance constructors are executed as an object is created. The *default constructor* for a class is an instance constructor with no parameters. By default, if no instance constructors are provided, a class has an implicit instance constructor that takes no arguments.

Constructors are declared as follows, with static constructors declared using the `static` keyword:

```
static <identifier>()
{
  <statements>
}

<modifiers> <identifier> (<parameters>opt) <initializer>opt
{
  <statements>
}
```

where

- `<identifier>` is the name of the type for which the constructor is defined.
- `<modifiers>` is optional, and must be an accessibility level or `extern`.
- `<parameters>` is optional, and specifies one or more parameters for the constructor. These are identical to method parameters.
- `<initializer>` is optional, and specifies another instance constructor to invoke before this instance constructor is executed. This has the form `base(<args>)` or `this(<args>)`, where `<args>` specifics zero or more arguments for the constructor to invoke. The `base` keyword form invokes an instance constructor in the base class, while the `this` keyword form invokes another instance constructor in the same object.
- `<statements>` is the block of statements associated with the constructor.

The following code shows some examples of constructors as might be provided for a `Fraction` class:

```
public class Fraction
{
  private static readonly int Unit;

  // This a lame example of a static constructor
  static Fraction()
  {
    Unit = 1;
  }

  private long _num;
  private long _den;

  // Instance constructors
  public Fraction(long top, long bottom)
  {
    _num = top;
    _den = bottom;
  }

  public Fraction(long number) : this(number, 1)
  {
  }
  . . .
}
```

Destructor

A *destructor* is a member that implements the actions required to destroy an instance of a class. The destructor for a class is invoked any time after the instance is no longer accessible by any code. Any destructors for inherited classes are invoked at this time as well. A destructor is declared as follows:

```
~ <identifier>()
{
  <statements>
}
```

where

- `<identifier>` is the name of the class for which the destructor is defined.
- `<statements>` is the block of statements associated with the destructor.

In many, if not most, situations, a destructor is not required. When a `Dispose` method is required to clean up non-memory resources, a destructor should normally be provided to call the `Dispose` method in the event a program fails to do so explicitly.

For a `Fraction` class, a destructor is most likely not required. However, in order to give an example, a destructor for this class might be concocted as follows:

```
public class Fraction : IDisposable
{
  private long _num;
  private long _den;
```

```
        . . .

        // Destructor
        ~Fraction()
        {
          Dispose()
        }

        // Dispose method (suppresses finalizer)
        public Dispose()
        {
          // release some system resource (file, connection, etc.)
          GC.SuppressFinalize(this);
        }
    }
```

Most of the time, a destructor should be avoided, as the garbage collector (GC) requires two passes to clean up a class with a destructor. When required, resources should be cleaned up in a `Dispose` method, and the second GC pass can be avoided by calling the `SuppressFinalize` method on the `GC` class.

A.2.2 Structures

A *structure* is a value type that defines a new data abstraction. Structures are very similar to classes, except that classes are allocated on the heap while structures are allocated in place, either on the stack or within the type that declares them. Structures also cannot be inherited, nor can they inherit from other classes. The default value of a structure instance is the value obtained by setting each value type member to its default value and all reference types to `null`.

A structure is declared using the `struct` keyword with the following form:

```
<modifiers>opt struct <identifier> : <interfaces>opt
{
  <struct-members>
}
```

where

- `<modifiers>` is optional, and must be an accessibility level or `new`.
- `<identifier>` is the unique name to assign to the structure.
- `<interfaces>` is optional, and specifies one or more supported interface types. If `<interfaces>` is omitted, then the colon (:) is also omitted.
- `<struct-members>` are the members of the structure. Structures contain the same kinds of members as classes. One difference is that a default constructor for structures is provided automatically, and cannot be explicitly specified.

Structures are appropriate for short-lived or small objects where local allocation is beneficial. The `Fraction` class used in examples throughout this appendix might be a good candidate for a structure. Here is an example of a PageRef structure that stores a range of page numbers:

```
public struct PageRef
{
  private int _startPage;
  private int _endPage;

  // Declarations of members to manipulate pages
}
```

A.2.3 Interfaces

An *interface* is a reference type that defines a contract consisting of a set of members. A class or structure supports an interface by specifying the interface in its specification and adhering to the defined contract. This is done by providing implementations of each interface member within the class or structure. An instance of an interface type cannot be explicitly declared, although an instance of a class or structure may be cast to an interface type.

An interface is declared using the interface keyword in the following manner:

```
<modifiers>opt interface <identifier> : <interfaces>opt
{
  <interface-members>
}
```

where

- <modifiers> is optional, and must be an accessibility level or new.
- <identifier> is the unique name to assign to the interface. By convention, all interface identifiers begin with a capital I.
- <interfaces> is optional, and specifies one or more interface types required to support this interface. If omitted, the colon (:) is also omitted.
- <interface-members> are the members required in order to support this interface. The possible members of an interface are methods, properties, events, and indexers, except that an implementation is not provided nor is an accessibility level defined.

Here is an example of an IBookDisplay interface that might be provided to indicate how a book is displayed in a Windows Forms Panel control:

```
interface IBookDisplay
{
  // Interface properties must indicate which accessors to support
  int ReadingRate { get; set; }

  void BeginDisplay(Panel displayPanel);
  void NextPage();
  void EndDisplay();

  Page this[int pageNum];
```

```
}

// Class that supports the IBookDisplay interface
public class PhotoAlbum : CollectionBase, IBookDisplay
{
  // Implementation of IBookDisplay
  // interface and other members
}
```

A.2.4 Enumerations

An *enumeration* is a value type that defines a related group of symbolic constants, and is quite similar to enumeration types in C. The default value of an enumeration instance is the value obtained by casting the number 0 to the enumeration type. All enumeration types implicitly inherit from the `System.Enum` class in the .NET Framework. This class provides a standard set of methods that may be used when manipulating enumerations.

An enumeration is declared using the `enum` keyword in the following manner:

```
<modifiers>opt enum <identifier> : <int-type>opt
{
  <enum-members>
}
```

where

- `<modifiers>` is optional, and must be an accessibility level or `new`.
- `<identifier>` is the unique name to assign to the enumeration.
- `<int-type>` is optional, and specifies a built-in integer type to represent the declared enumeration values, one of `byte`, `sbyte`, `short`, `ushort`, `int`, `uint`, `long`, or `ulong`. If not specified, the colon is omitted and the `int` type is used. Note that the possible values for an enumeration are not limited to its explicitly declared members. Any valid value of the underlying type is a valid value for the enumeration.
- `<enum-members>` are the members of this enumeration. Each member is written as `<identifier>` or as `<identifier> = <int-value>`. Multiple members are separated by commas and each member has an assigned constant integer value. The default assigned value for the first member is 0, and the default value for subsequent members is one greater than the value assigned to the previous member.

Here are a few examples of enumerations:

```
// Days of week (values 0 to 6)
enum DaysOfWeek1 = { Sun, Mon, Tue, Wed, Thu, Fri, Sat }

// Days of week as unsigned short types (values 1 to 7)
enum DaysOfWeek2 : ushort = { Sunday = 1, Monday, Tuesday,
                              Wednesday, Thursday, Friday, Saturday }
```

```
// Multiples of 10 enumeration
enum TensTable =
{
  Ten = 10, Twenty = 20, Thirty = 30, Forty = 40, Fifty = 50,
  Sixty = 60, Seventy = 70, Eighty = 80, Ninety = 90
}
```

A.2.5 Delegates

A *delegate* is a reference type that encapsulates one or more methods. A delegate is created with a defined method signature, and any method in any class or structure that adheres to this defined signature may be assigned to the delegate. Each method assigned to a delegate is referred to as a *callable entity.*

In the .NET Framework, a delegate is a class implicitly derived from the `System.Delegate` class. Since a delegate is implicitly a class, its default value is `null`.

Delegates are declared and used somewhat like function pointers in C++, except that delegates encapsulate both an object instance and a method. This encapsulation of the object as well as the method permits delegates to refer to both static and instance methods. The declaration of a delegate requires the `delegate` keyword employed in the following manner:

```
    <modifiers>opt delegate <return-type> <identifier> ( <parameters>opt
)
```

where

- `<modifiers>` is optional, and must be an accessibility level or `new`.
- `<return-type>` is the return type for the delegate.
- `<identifier>` is the unique name to assign to the delegate.
- `<parameters>` is optional, and indicates the parameters for the delegate, in the same manner as parameters for a class method.

A few examples of delegates are given here. Delegates are also used to create events in the prior discussion of events.

```
protected delegate int FindIndex(string name);
public delegate void EventHandler(object sender, EventArgs e);
public delegate Photograph ReadDelegate(StreamReader sr);
```

The definition of a method to use with a delegate can be explicit or implicit. An implicit definition is called an *anonymous method.* This concept is discussed in detail in chapter 13.

A.3 LANGUAGE ELEMENTS

This section presents the built-in types, operators, and keywords of C# in tabular form. The tables present a brief description of each item. The following aspects of the C# language are presented:

- Built-in types
- Operators
- Keywords

A.3.1 Built-in types

Table A.3 summarizes the types built into C#. These types, as well as all user-defined types in C#, implicitly inherit from the `object` class, which also appears in this table. The table provides a short description of each type, along with each type's default value and the class used to represent the type in the .NET Framework. In C# source files written for the framework, the type and the .NET class are interchangeable.

Table A.3 The built-in C# types

Type	Description	Default value	.NET class
bool	A boolean value	`false`	System.Boolean
byte	An unsigned 8-bit integer	`(byte)0`	System.Byte
char	A 16-bit Unicode character	`'\0'`	System.Char
decimal	A 128-bit decimal value	`0.0m`	System.Decimal
double	A 64-bit floating point value	`0.0d`	System.Double
float	A 32-bit floating point value	`0.0f`	System.Single
int	A 32-bit integer	`0`	System.Int32
long	A 64-bit integer	`0L`	System.Int64
object	Any object. The ultimate base class of any type.	`null`	System.Object
sbyte	An 8-bit integer	`(sbyte)0`	System.SByte
short	A 16-bit integer	`0`	System.Int16
string	A reference type of a collection of char types	`null`	System.String
uint	An unsigned 32-bit integer	`0u`	System.UInt32
ulong	An unsigned 64-bit integer	`(ulong)0`	System.UInt64
ushort	An unsigned 32-bit integer	`(ushort)0`	System.UInt16

A.3.2 Operators

Many of the operators in C# are taken from C++ and have identical meanings. Table A.4 summarizes the operators available as they relate to the built-in types. Most of these operators may be overridden for user-defined types. Keyword operators such as `true`, `new`, and `is` are not shown in this table. These are summarized in the table of keywords provided in the next section.

Table A.4 Operators available in C#

<table>
<tr><th>Category</th><th>Operators</th><th>Examples</th></tr>
<tr><td>Arithmetic</td><td>+ - * / %</td><td><code>int num = -12;
int age = days / 365;
int onesPlace = number % 10;</code></td></tr>
<tr><td>Logical (boolean and bitwise)</td><td>& | ^ ! ~ && ||</td><td><code>bool isTrue = ! false;
int choices = gates & openSet;</code></td></tr>
<tr><td>String concatenation</td><td>+</td><td><code>string hi = "Hello " + "World!";</code></td></tr>
<tr><td>Increment, decrement</td><td>++ –</td><td><code>index ++;</code></td></tr>
<tr><td>Shift</td><td><< >></td><td><code>long kilobyte = 1 << 10;</code></td></tr>
<tr><td>Relational</td><td>== != > < <= >=</td><td><code>bool isDigit = (x >= 0) && (x <
10);</code></td></tr>
<tr><td>Assignment</td><td>= += -= *= /= %= &= |=
^= <<= >>=</td><td><code>int byFives += 5;</code></td></tr>
<tr><td>Member access</td><td>.</td><td><code>return myString.ToLower();</code></td></tr>
<tr><td>Indexing</td><td>[]</td><td><code>Photograph first = _album[0];</code></td></tr>
<tr><td>Cast</td><td>()</td><td><code>short num = (short)7;
Photograph photo = (Photograph)
obj;</code></td></tr>
<tr><td>Conditional</td><td>?:</td><td><code>int size
  = (list == null) ? 0 :
list.Count;</code></td></tr>
<tr><td>Delegates</td><td>+ - += -=</td><td><code>photo.Display += new

DisplayHandler(photo_Display);</code></td></tr>
<tr><td>Indirection and Address (in unsafe code only)</td><td>* -> {} &</td><td><code>int num = 11;
int* pnum = #</code></td></tr>
</table>

A.3.3 Keywords

This section presents a complete list of all keywords used by C#, along with a description and example of each keyword. These keywords are reserved words that have special meanings to the C# compiler, and should not normally be used as identifiers in your programs. To use a reserved keyword as an identifier, prefix the string with an at-sign (`@`) character. For example, while `class` is a reserved keyword, `@class` is a valid identifier.

The keywords related to C# types are discussed in detail in table A.5. Many of these keywords also appear elsewhere in the book. Check the index for other sections of the book where these keywords are discussed.

Table A.5 Keywords used in C# programs

Keyword	Description	Example

abstract	Indicates that a class cannot be instantiated and is intended as a base for other classes.	`// Define an abstract class`
		`public abstract class Person`
		`{`
		`  // Define abstract members`
		`  public abstract string Address;`
		`  public abstract Point GetHomeCoord();`
		`  . . .`
		`}`

	Within an abstract class, indicates that a property or method has no implementation and must be overridden in a derived class.	
as	Converts an expression to a given type. On an error, returns the value `null`.	`object obj = lstPhotos.SelectedItem;` `Photograph photo = obj as Photograph;`
base	Represents the base class from within a derived class.	*See example for* `override` *keyword.*
bool	Denotes a boolean type, with possible values `true` and `false`.	`bool result = photo.IsValidImage();` `bool isExample = true;`

break	Terminates the enclosing loop or conditional construct. Execution resumes after the terminated construct.	`foreach (Photograph p in _album)`
		`{`
		`  if (p == myPhoto)`
		`    break;`
		`}`

byte	Denotes an unsigned 8-bit integer value, with values 0 to 255.	`char c = 'y';` `byte b = Convert.ToByte(c);`
case	Identifies a possible expression within a `switch` statement.	*See example for* `switch` *keyword.*
catch	Identifies a type of exception to handle in a try-catch statement.	*See example for* `try` *keyword.*
char	Denotes a Unicode 16-bit character value.	`char response = ReadResponse();` `char yes = 'y', no = 'n';`

checked	Performs integer overflow checking on the given statement. If an overflow occurs, an exception is raised. By default, all integer expressions are checked.	`try`
		`{`
		`  y = checked(a/b + c);`
		`}`
		`catch (System.OverflowException e)`
		`{`
		`  . . .`
		`}`

class	Defines a new data abstraction, or data type, along with a set of members that interact with this type. Classes are represented as reference types. A class can inherit from at most one other class and from multiple interfaces.	*See examples for* `const` *and* `override` *keywords.*

Table A.5 Keywords used in C# programs *(continued)*

<table>
<tr><th>Keyword</th><th>Description</th><th>Example</th></tr>
<tr><td>const</td><td>Indicates that a field or variable cannot be modified. The value for a constant must be assigned as part of the declaration.</td><td><pre><code>public class BookReference
{
  // Must be assigned here
  protected int timeout = 30;
  protected const string defaultURL
      = "www.manning.com/eebrown2";

  // Assigned here or in constructor
  public readonly string bookURL;

  BookReference(string name, string url)
  {
    if (url == null)
      bookURL = defaultURL;
    else
      bookURL = url;
    . . .
  }
}</code></pre></td></tr>
<tr><td>continue</td><td>Passes control to the next iteration of the enclosing loop.</td><td><pre><code>for (int x = 0;
     x < Contractors.Count;
     x++)
{
  if (Contractors[x].IsSalaried)
    continue;

  // Determine hourly pay
}</code></pre></td></tr>
<tr><td>decimal</td><td>Denotes a decimal number with up to roughly 28 significant digits. Stored as a 128-bit data value. Use the suffix m or M to denote a numeric value as a <code>decimal</code> type.</td><td><pre><code>decimal circumference;
decimal radius = 7m;
decimal pi = 3.1415;
circumference = 2m * pi * radius;</code></pre></td></tr>
<tr><td>default</td><td>In a switch block, identifies the statement to execute if none of the given constant expressions match the given expression.</td><td>See example for <code>switch</code> keyword.</td></tr>
<tr><td>delegate</td><td>Defines a reference type that encapsulates a method with a specific signature.</td><td><pre><code>// Define the ReadDelegate delegate
public delegate Photograph
    ReadDelegate(StreamReader sr);</code></pre></td></tr>
<tr><td>do</td><td>Executes a statement or block one or more times until a specified <code>while</code> expression evaluates to <code>false</code>.</td><td><pre><code>do
{
  name = reader.ReadLine();
  if (name != null)
    // Make use of the name
} while (name != null);</code></pre></td></tr>
<tr><td>double</td><td>Denotes a 64-bit floating-point value. By default, all nonintegral numbers are treated as values of this type. Use the d or D suffix to denote a numeric value as a <code>double</code> type.</td><td><pre><code>double circumference;
double radius = 7d;
double pi = 3.1415;
circumference = 2d * pi * radius;</code></pre></td></tr>
<tr><td>else</td><td>In an <code>if</code> statement, the statement to execute if the expression returns <code>false</code>.</td><td>See example for <code>if</code> keyword.</td></tr>
<tr><td>enum</td><td>Denotes an enumeration, or enumerated type, consisting of a defined set of constants each assigned a value from a given integral type.</td><td><pre><code>enum WeekDays= { Sun, Mon, Tue, Wed,
                 Thu, Fri, Say };</code></pre></td></tr>
</table>

Table A.5 Keywords used in C# programs *(continued)*

Keyword	Description	Example

event	Defines a handler abstraction in which to define a set of methods that should be invoked when a specific incident, or event, occurs. Methods are added or removed to an event with the += and -= operators.	`class Photograph`
		`{`
		`  public event ReadDelegate LoadPhoto;`
		`  . . .`
		`}`

explicit	Declares that a type conversion must be invoked with a cast. Omitting the cast results in a compile-time error.	`public static explicit`
		`    operator Photograph(string s)`
		`{`
		`  // code to convert from string`
		`}`

extern	Modifies a class member declaration to indicate that the member is implemented outside the current class file.	`class Photograph`
		`{`
		`  public extern void Draw(Graphics g);`
		`  . . .`
		`}`

false	As an operator in user-defined types, defines the meaning of "false" for instances of that type.	`public static bool`
		`    operator false(MyType x)`
		`{`
		`  // Return whether MyType is "false"`
		`}`

	As a literal, the boolean value of false.	`bool isChapter = false;`
finally	Indicates a block of code that executes regardless of whether an exception occurs in the preceding `try` block.	*See example for `try` keyword.*

fixed	In unsafe code, prevents relocation of a variable by the garbage collector.	`// In unsafe code, pin current photo`
		`fixed (Photograph photo = CurrentPhoto)`
		`{`
		`  // Perform unsafe operations`
		`}`
		`// CurrentPhoto no longer pinned`

float	Denotes a 32-bit floating-point value. Use the f or F suffix to denote a numeric value as a `float` type.	`float circumference;`
		`float radius = 7f;`
		`float pi = 3.1415f;`
		`circumference = 2f * pi * radius;`

for	Executes a statement or block repeatedly as long as a given expression evaluates to `true`.	`public bool FindPhoto(string name,`
		`                      out int index)`
		`{`
		`  for (int x = 0; x < this.Count; x++)`
		`  {`
		`    if (this[x].Name == name)`
		`    {`
		`      index = x;  // assign out param`
		`      return true;`
		`    }`
		`  }`
		
		`  return false;`
		`}`

foreach	Executes a statement or block using every element in an array or collection, if any.	`foreach (Photograph p in CurrentAlbum)`
		`{`
		`  // Do something with each Photograph`
		`}`

Table A.5 Keywords used in C# programs *(continued)*

Keyword	Description	Example

goto	Transfers program control directly to a labeled statement.
	Note: The use of this keyword is generally discouraged.
		`do`
		`{`
		`// Do something`
		`if (unable to continue)`
		`goto CleanUp;`
		
		`// Do something else`
		`} while (` *`some expression`* `);`
		
		`CleanUp:`
		`f.Close();`

	In a `switch` statement, transfers control to a given case label or to the default label.	`switch (version)`
		`{`
		`case 67:`
		`photo = Photograph.ReadVer67(s);`
		`goto default;`
		
		`case 77:`
		`. . .`
		`default:`
		`Photograph.ReadGlobalData(s);`
		`break;`
		`}`

if	A control statement in which a statement is executed only if a given expression evaluates to `true`.	`if (_album.Count > 0)`
		`DisplayPhotos(_album);`
		`else`
		`statusBar.Text = "Album is empty";`

implicit	Declares that a type conversion should be invoked automatically by the compiler as required.	`public static implicit`
		`operator Photograph(Bitmap img)`
		`{`
		`// code to convert from Bitmap`
		`}`

in	In a `foreach` block, separates the identifier from the expression.	*See example for* `foreach` *keyword.*

int	Denotes a 32-bit integer value. Integer values are treated as `int` by default. Note that there is no implicit conversion from floating point values to `int`.	`int apprxCircum`
		`int radius = 7;`
		`int pi = 31415;`
		`apprxCircum = 2 * pi * radius / 10000);`

interface	Defines a new data abstraction, or data type, in which all members are implicitly abstract. A class or structure can inherit from multiple interfaces.	`interface IBookDisplay`
		`{`
		`// Declaration of interface members`
		`}`

internal	Access modifier for types and type members that indicates the identifier is only accessible by objects within the same assembly.	*See example for* `private` *keyword.*

is	Identifies whether a given expression can be converted, or cast, to a given type.	`object obj = lstPhotos.SelectedItem;`
		`if (obj is Photograph)`
		`{`
		`Photograph photo = (Photograph) obj;`
		`. . .`
		`}`

Table A.5 Keywords used in C# programs *(continued)*

<table>
<tr><th>Keyword</th><th>Description</th><th>Example</th></tr>
<tr><td>lock</td><td>Marks a statement block as a critical section, ensuring that only one thread can execute the statement block at a time.</td><td><pre>public void SortPhotos(bool ascending)
{
  lock (this) {
  {
    . . .
  }
}</pre></td></tr>
<tr><td>long</td><td>Denotes a 64-bit integer value. Use the <code>L</code> suffix to denote an integer value as a <code>long</code> type. The <code>l</code> suffix may also be used, but is easily confused with the number 1 and is not recommended.</td><td><pre>long apprxCircum
long radius = (long)7;
long pi = (long) 314159265;
apprxCircum
    = 2L * pi * radius / 100000000L);</pre></td></tr>
<tr><td>namespace</td><td>Declares a scope for organizing code and naming types and members. If no namespace is defined, an object is part of the unnamed, or global, namespace.</td><td><pre>namespace MyPhotoAlbum
{
  class MyClass { . . . }
}</pre></td></tr>
<tr><td>new</td><td>As an operator, creates an object and invokes its constructor. Value types are created in place, while reference types are created on the heap.

As a modifier, explicitly hides a member inherited from a derived class. This is typically used to give a new meaning or purpose to an identifier.</td><td><pre>int index = new int();
string s;
Photograph photo = new Photograph(s);

s = new string();</pre><pre>public MainForm : Form
{
  . . .
  protected new void OnLoad(EventArgs e)
  {
    . . .
  }
}</pre></td></tr>
<tr><td>null</td><td>Literal that represents an uninitialized state, often referred to as a null reference. This is the default value for all reference types.</td><td><pre>Photograph photo = _album.CurrentPhoto;
if (photo != null)
{
  // Do something with photograph
}</pre></td></tr>
<tr><td>object</td><td>The base class of all types in C#. Any value of any type can be assigned to variables of type <code>object</code>.</td><td><pre>object o1 = 7;
object o2 = new string("hear me roar!");
object o3 = _album.CurrentPhoto;</pre></td></tr>
<tr><td>operator</td><td>Declares the behavior of an operator when used with a specific type, such as a class or structure. Three kinds of operators are supported: unary operators, binary operators, and conversion operators.</td><td><pre>public static Complex operator -(Complex x)
{
  return new Complex(-x.Real, -x.Imgn);
}

public static Complex
    operator +(Complex x, Complex y)
{
  return new Complex(x.Real + y.Real,
                     x.Imgn + y.Imgn);
}</pre></td></tr>
<tr><td>out</td><td>Indicates that any changes made to a method parameter should be reflected in the variable when control returns to the caller. A variable used as an <code>out</code> method parameter may be uninitialized.</td><td>See example for <code>for</code> keyword.</td></tr>
</table>

Table A.5 Keywords used in C# programs *(continued)*

Keyword	Description	Example

override	Explicitly replaces a member inherited from a derived class. This is typically used to provide a more appropriate implementation of an inherited member in the current type.	public class BaseClass
		{
		  . . .
		  public virtual void Clear()
		  {
		    // Base implementation of Clear
		  }
		}
		
		public class DerivedClass : BaseClass
		{
		  . . .
		  public override void Clear()
		  {
		    // Override implementation of Clear
		    base.Clear();
		  }
		}

params	Indicates that a method will receive a set of parameters. This can occur only once and at the end of the list of parameters.	public void AddRange
		    (params Photograph[] photos)
		{
		  foreach (Photograph p in photos)
		  {
		    _album.Add(p);
		  }
		}

private	Access modifier for types and type members that indicates the object or member is accessible only to the type in which it is defined.	public class PhotoAlbum : CollectionBase
		{
		  // only available within this class
		  private int _defaultPhotoIndex;
		
		  // Only available in this assembly
		  internal bool IsDisplayed
		  {
		    . . .
		  }

protected	Access modifier for types and type members that indicates the object or member is only accessible by the containing type or by types derived from the containing type.	// available to any derived class
		  protected void TurnPage()
		  {
		    . . .
		  }

public	Access modifier for types and type members that indicates the object or member is accessible by any type.	// available to any type
		  public Photogram CurrentPhoto
		  {
		    . . .
		  }
		}

readonly	Indicates that a field cannot be assigned except in the declaration of the field or the constructor of the containing type.	*See example for* const *keyword.*

ref	Indicates that any changes made to a method parameter should be reflected in the variable when control returns to the caller. Unlike the out keyword, a variable used as a ref method parameter must be initialized.	// Locate photo after given index
		public bool FindPhotoAfter
		    (string name, ref int index)
		{
		  . . .
		}

Table A.5 Keywords used in C# programs *(continued)*

Keyword	Description	Example
return	Terminates execution of the containing method and passes control and the result of the method back to the caller.	*See example for* `for` *keyword.*
sbyte	Denotes a signed 8-bit integer value from –128 to 127. An explicit cast is required to convert an integer value to a `sbyte` type.	`sbyte sb = 'y';` `sbyte sb = (sbyte)5; e`

sealed	Indicates that a class cannot be inherited. A `sealed` class cannot also be `abstract`. Note that `struct` types are implicitly `sealed`.	`public sealed class SecurePerson : Person`
		`{`
		`  . . .`
		`}`

short	Denotes a 16-bit integer value from –32,768 to 32,768. An explicit cast is required to convert an integer value to a `short` type.	`short apprxCircum`
		`short radius = (short)7;`
		`short pi = (short) 314;`
		`apprxCircum`
		`    = (short)(2 * pi * radius / 100);`

sizeof	Determines the size in bytes of a value type.	`int size1 = sizeof(long);`
		`int size2 = sizeof(Rectangle);`
		`int size3 = sizeof(Complex);`

stackalloc	In unsafe code, allocates a block of memory on the stack and returns a pointer to this block. This memory is not subject to garbage collection and is valid only within the method in which it is defined.	`public unsafe void QuickSort()`
		`{`
		`  Photograph* photos`
		`      = stackalloc Photograph[Count];`
		
		`  // Sort album using local memory`
		`}`

static	Declares a member that is associated with the type itself rather than with each instance of that type.	`private string _defaultDir`
		`    = @"C:\My Documents\Albums";`
		
		`public static string DefaultAlbumDir`
		`{`
		`  get { return _defaultDir; }`
		`  set { _defaultDir = value; }`
		`}`

string	Object representing a set of Unicode characters. While string is a reference type, the equality operators == and != are defined to compare values rather than references.	`string s = null;`
		`string defaultAlbum = "myAlbum";`
		`string _defaultDir`
		`    = @"C:\My Documents\Albums";`

struct	Defines a new data abstraction, or data type, along with a set of members that interact with this type. Structures are represented as value types, and are implicitly sealed.	`struct Complex`
		`{`
		`  double real;`
		`  double imaginary;`
		`}`

switch	Executes one of a given set of statements based on the constant value of a given expression. If a match for the current value is not found, then a `default` statement can optionally be executed.	`switch (version)`
		`{`
		`  case 67:`
		`    photo = Photograph.ReadVersion67(s);`
		`    break;`
		
		`  default:`
		`    throw ApplicationException(`
		`      "Unrecognized album version");`
		`}`

this	Represents the current instance for which a method is called. Static member functions cannot employ the `this` keyword.	*See example for* `for` *keyword.*

Table A.5 Keywords used in C# programs *(continued)*

Keyword	Description	Example
throw	Raises a new exception, or re-raises a caught exception.	*See example for* `switch` *keyword.*

true	As in operator in user-defined types, defines the meaning of "true" for instances of that type.	`public static bool`
		`operator true(MyType x)`
		`{`
		`// Return whether MyType is "true"`
		`}`

	As a literal, the boolean value of true.	`bool isAppendix = true;`

try	Begins a block in which exceptions may be handled, depending on the attached catch clauses.	`// Open a file`
		`FileStream fs = new FileStream(...);`
		
		`try {`
		`// Do something with open file`
		`}`
		`catch (IOException ex) {`
		`// Handle caught exception`
		`}`
		`finally {`
		`fs.Close(); // ensure file closure`
		`}`

typeof	Obtains the `System.Type` object for a given type. Use the `Object.GetType` method to obtain the type instance for an expression.	`Type t = typeof(Photograph);`

uint	Denotes an unsigned 32-bit integer value. Use the u or U suffix to denote an integer value as a `uint` type.	`uint apprxCircum`
		`uint radius = 7u, pi = 314159;`
		`apprxCircum = 2u * pi * radius / 100000u;`

ulong	Denotes an unsigned 64-bit integer value. When using the `L` suffix to denote a long integer or the `U` suffix to denote an unsigned integer, the value is considered ulong if it is beyond the range of the `long` or `uint` type, respectively.	`ulong apprxCircum`
		`ulong radius = 7L;`
		`ulong pi = 31415926535`
		`apprxCircum`
		`= 2 * pi * radius / 10000000000L);`

unchecked	Suppresses integer overflow checking on the given statement. If an overflow occurs, the result is truncated. By default, all integer expressions are checked.	`long bigPrime = 9876543211;`
		`long notSoBigNum`
		`= unchecked(bigPrime * bigPrime);`

unsafe	Indicates an unmanaged region of code, in which pointers are permitted and normal runtime verification is disabled.	*See example for* `stackalloc` *keyword.*

ushort	Denotes an unsigned 16-bit integer value. A cast is required to convert an `int` or `uint` value to `ushort`.	`ushort apprxCircum`
		`ushort radius = (ushort)7;`
		`ushort pi = (ushort)314;`
		`apprxCircum = (ushort)2`
		`* pi * radius / (ushort)100;`

using	As a directive, indicates either a namespace from which types do not have to be fully qualified; or a shortcut, or alias, for a given class or namespace name.	`using System.Windows.Forms;`
		`using App = Application;`
		
		`public void Main() {`
		`Form f = new MainForm();`
		`App.Run(f);`
		`}`

Table A.5 Keywords used in C# programs *(continued)*

Keyword	Description	Example

	As a statement, defines a scope for a given expression or type. At the end of this scope, the given object is disposed.	`using (OpenFileDialog dlg`
		`        = new OpenFileDialog())`
		`{`
		`  // Do something with dlg`
		`}`

virtual	Declares that a method or property member may be overridden in a derived class. At runtime, the override of a type member is always invoked.	*See example for* `override` *keyword.*

volatile	Indicates that a field may be modified in a program at any time, such as by the operating system or in another thread.	`// Read/Write x anew for each line.`
		`volatile double x = 70.0;`
		`int num = x;`
		`x = x * Sqrt(x);`

void	Indicates that a method does not return a value.	*See examples for* `override` *and* `protected` *keywords.*

while	As a statement, executes a statement or block of statements until a given expression is `false`.	`Photograph p = _album.FirstPhoto;`
		`while (p != null)`
		`{`
		`  // Do something with Photograph`
		`  p = _album.NextPhoto;`
		`}`

	In a `do-while` loop, specifies the condition that will terminate the loop.	*See example for* `do` *keyword.*

yield	Allows a simplified way to implement an iterator, such as the `IEnumerable` interface for `foreach` support. A method employs the `yield return` statement to return a sequence of results to a caller.	`public class Sample {`
		` . . .`
		` // Implementing the enumerable pattern`
		` public IEnumerable MyIterator(int x, int y)`
		` {`
		`   for (int i=x; i<=y; i++)`
		`      yield return i;`
		` }`
		` . . .`
		`}`
		
		`  // Code somewhere using this iterator`
		`  Sample s = new Sample();`
		`  foreach (int n in s.SampleIterator(1, 10))`
		`      System.Console.WriteLine(n);`
		`  . . .`

A.4 SPECIAL FEATURES

This section presents some noteworthy features of the C# language. These topics did not fit in previous sections of this appendix, but are important concepts for programming in the language. The topics covered are exceptions, arrays, generics, the Main entry point, boxing, and documentation.

Readers more familiar with C# will realize that some features have been omitted from this appendix and the book in general. These include attributes, reflection, and the preprocessor. These features, while important, were considered beyond the scope of this book, and are not required in many Windows Forms applications. The brief discussions that do occur for these and other topics are listed in the index.

A.4.1 Exceptions

An *exception* is a type of error. Exceptions provide a uniform type-safe mechanism for handling system level and application level error conditions. In the .NET Framework, all exceptions inherit from the `System.Exception` class. Even system-level errors such as divide-by-zero and `null` references have well-defined exception classes.

If a program or block of code ignores exceptions, then exceptions are considered *unhandled.* By default, an unhandled exception immediately stops execution of a program.[2] This ensures code that ignores exceptions does not continue processing when an error occurs. Code that does not ignore exceptions is said to *handle* exceptions, and must indicate the specific set of exception classes that are handled by the code. An exception is said to be *handled* or *caught* if a block of code can continue processing after an exception occurs. Code that generates an exception is said to *throw* the exception.

The `try` keyword is used to indicate a block of code that handles exceptions. The `catch` keyword indicates which exceptions to explicitly handle. The `finally` keyword is used to indicate code that should be executed regardless of whether an exception occurs.

Code that handles one or more exceptions in this manner uses the following format:

```
try
  <try-block>
<catch-blocks>opt
<finally-block>opt
```

where

- `<try-block>` is the set of statements, enclosed in braces.
- `<catch-blocks>` is optional, and consists of one or more *catch blocks* as defined below.
- `<finally-block>` is optional, and consists of the `finally` keyword followed by the set of statements, enclosed in braces.

The format of a `try` block allows for one or more catch blocks, also called *catch clauses*, to define which exceptions to process. These are specified with the `catch` keyword in the following manner:

```
catch <exception>opt
  <catch-block>
```

---

[2] Well, most of the time. If an unhandled exception occurs during the execution of a static constructor, then a `TypeInitializationException` is thrown rather than the program exiting. In this case, the original exception is included as the *inner exception* of the new exception.

where

- <exception> is optional, and indicates the exception this block handles. This must be a class enclosed in parenthesis with an optional identifier that the block will use to reference this exception. If no class is provided, then all exceptions are handled by the block.
- <catch-block> is the set of statements, enclosed in braces.

For example, one use for exceptions is to handle unexpected conversion errors, such as converting a string to an integer. Table A.6 contrasts two ways of handling such an exception.

Table A.6 Comparison of two approaches for catching a format exception

<table>
<tr>
<td><pre>// A string theString requires conversion
int version = 0;
try
{
  version = Convert.ToInt32(theString);
}
catch
{
  version = 0;
}</pre></td>
<td><pre>// A string theString requires conversion
int version = 0;
try
{
  version = Convert.ToInt32(theString);
}
catch (FormatException)
{
  version = 0;
}</pre></td>
</tr>
<tr>
<td>If any exception occurs while converting the string to an int, then the catch clause will set version to 0. For example, if the theString variable is null, an ArgumentException will occur, and version will still be set to 0. This is not a recommended approach, as an unexpected system exception would be caught and ignored here as well.</td>
<td>The catch clause will set version to 0 only if a FormatException exception occurs while converting the string to an int. Any other exception is unhandled and will exit the program if not handled by another catch clause in the call stack. This is the recommended approach, since the exceptions to handle are explicitly indicated.</td>
</tr>
</table>

When an exception occurs in a program that satisfies more than one catch block within the same try block, the first matching block is executed. For this reason, the more distinct exceptions should appear first in the list of catch blocks. As an example, consider the IOException class, which is thrown when an unexpected I/O error occurs. This class derives from the Exception class. The following code shows how an exception block might be written to handle exceptions that might occur while reading a file:

```
// Open some file system object
FileStream f = new FileStream(...);

try
{
  //Code that makes use of FileStream object
}
catch (IOException ioex)
{
   // Code that handles an IOException
   // This code can use the "ioex" variable to reference the exception
```

```
}
catch (Exception ex)
{
  // Code that handles any other exception
}
```

Additional examples of exceptions appear throughout the book.

A.4.2 Arrays

An *array* is a reference type consisting of a collection of variables, all of the same type. Arrays are built into C# and may be one-dimensional or multidimensional. Each dimension of an array has an associated integral length. In the .NET Framework, the `System.Array` class serves as the base class for all array objects. More information on the `Array` and related `ArrayList` class can be found in chapter 5.

A standard array for any type is constructed using square brackets in the following manner:

```
<type> [ <dimension>opt ]
```

where

- `<type>` is the type of objects in the array.
- `<dimension>` is zero or more commas indicating the array's dimensions.

Note that multiple square brackets may be specified to have variable length array elements. An example of this is shown below. To reference a value in an array, square brackets are again used, with an integer expression from zero (0) to one less than the length of the array. If an array index is outside of the valid range of the array, an `IndexOutOfRangeException` exception is thrown.

Some examples of arrays and additional comments on the use of arrays are given below. Note that the `Length` property from the `System.Array` class determines the number of elements in an array, and the `foreach` keyword can be used on all arrays to enumerate the contained elements.

```
// an uninitialized array defaults to null
int[] a;

// This array contains 4 int values, which default to 0
// The valid indexes are b[0], b[1], b[2], b[3]
int[] b = new int[4];

// An array can be initialized directly or with the new keyword
// evens.Length will return 6
// foreach (int p in primes) iterates through the elements in primes
int[] evens = { 2, 4, 6, 8, 10, 12 };
int[] primes = new int[] {2, 3, 5, 7, 11, 101, 9876543211 };

// This example shows a 2 by 2 string array
// Here, names[0,0] = "Katie" and names[1,1] = "Bianca"
string[,] names = { { "Katie", "Sydney" }, { "Laura", "Bianca"} };
```

```
// This example shows an array of arrays.
// Here, x[0] is an int array of length three with values 1, 2, 3.
// Also, x[1][1] = 12 and x[2][4] = 25.
// Attempting to reference x[3] or x[1][2] will throw an exception
int[][] x = { { 1, 2, 3 }, { 11, 12 }, { 21, 22, 23, 24, 25} };
```

A.4.3 Generics

Generic types are new to C# in the 2.0 version of the framework. These types are discussed in chapter 5, so we do not repeat the discussion here.

A.4.4 Main

A program has to start somewhere. In C and C++ programs, the global procedure `main` is the defined starting point for the program. This starting point is referred to as the *entry point* for the program.

In C#, a program must define a static method called `Main` to serve as the entry point. The method must have one of the following signatures.

```
static void Main()
static void Main(string[] args)
static int Main()
static int Main(string[] args)
```

A program will return a value if the `Main` method returns a value. A program can receive command-line arguments by specifying an array of `string` objects as the only parameter to the `Main` method.

If two or more classes in a program contain a `Main` method, the `/main` switch must be used with the C# compiler to specify which method to consider the entry point for the program.

A.4.5 Boxing

By definition, the `object` class is a reference type. It also serves as the ultimate base class for all types, including built-in types. As a result, value types such as `int` and `bool` can be used wherever an object instance is required. For example, the `ArrayList` class represents a dynamically sized array, and includes an `Add` method to add an object to the array. This method is declared as follows:

```
public virtual int Add(object value);
```

Within the `Add` method, a reference type is expected. So what happens when a value type is passed into this method? Clearly, some mechanism for dealing with value types is required here.

This mechanism is called *boxing*. Boxing implicitly copies the data in a value type into an `object` instance allocated on the heap. For example:

```
// Boxing of bool value
object obj = true;

// Boxing of an int type.
```

```
ArrayList list = new ArrayList();
int x = 32768;
list.Add(x);
```

A boxed value is converted back into a value type through a process called *unboxing*. Conceptually, boxing and unboxing happens automatically and the programmer can remain blissfully unaware of this concept. Boxed values can be treated as their unboxed equivalents. For example:

```
int n = 5;
object obj = 123;
if (obj is int)
  n = (int) obj;
```

These statements are perfectly legal, and result in the value of `123` for the variable `n`. The reason boxing is important is because of the performance implications involved. The boxing and unboxing of values takes time, and this can seriously impact the performance of an application.

Note in particular that boxing occurs when a structure, which is a value type, is cast to an interface, which is a reference type. For this reason, care should be taken when creating structures that support one or more interfaces. In such a situation, the performance implications of boxing might warrant using a class instead of a structure.

A.4.6 Documentation

A final topic worth mentioning in this appendix is that of automated documentation. C# recommends a set of XML-style tags that can be used in comments and extracted by compilers. Such comments must begin with a triple-slash (`///`) and can occur before the declaration of most types and type members.

The C# compiler supports the `/doc` switch to generate the XML documentation file. Details on this process and the resulting output are available in the .NET documentation.

Table A.7 provides a summary of the tags that are currently recognized by the compiler.. Check the index for a reference to additional discussion and an example with the `<summary>` tag in chapter 5.

Table A.7 Recommended tags for C# documentation comments

Tag	Purpose
<c>	Specifies text that should be marked as code.
<code>	Specifies multiple lines that should be marked as code.
<example>	Documents an example of a type or method.
<exception>	Specifies documentation for an exception class.
<include>	Includes an external file to include in the documentation.
<list>	Specifies a list of items within another tag. This supports bulleted lists, numbered lists, and tables.
<para>	Starts a new paragraph within another tag.

Table A.7 Recommended tags for C# documentation comments *(continued)*

Tag	Purpose
<param>	Documents a parameter within a method or other construct.
<paramref>	Specifies text that should be marked as a parameter.
<permission>	Documents the accessibility level of a member.
<remarks>	Documents general comments about a type or type member.
<returns>	Documents the return value of a method.
<see>	Specifies a link in running text to another member or field accessible from the current file.
<seealso>	Specifies a link in a See Also section to another member of field accessible form the current file.
<summary>	Documents a short description of the member or type.
<typeparam>	Documents a type parameter within a method or other construct.
<typeparamref>	Specifies text that should be marked as a type parameter.
<value>	Documents the value that a property represents.

A P P E N D I X B

.NET namespaces

This appendix provides an overview of some of the `System` namespaces provided by Microsoft in the .NET Framework, and discusses their relationship to Windows Forms applications. For a complete list of namespaces in .NET, of course, see the .NET Framework Class Library documentation.

The `System` namespace contains the commonly used types[1] required by .NET programs and libraries, as well as services such as data type conversion, environment management, and mathematical operations. In particular, most of the classes mentioned in appendix A that implement core functionality such as the built-in types, enumerations, and delegates are included in this namespace. Members of this namespace are discussed throughout the book as they are used in the sample programs.

---

[1] The word *type* is used in the C# sense here, as defined in appendix A. More generally, a type can be a class, structure, interface, enumeration, or a delegate. By definition, a namespace defines one or more types.

The remainder of this appendix discusses specific namespaces under the System umbrella. Each section discusses a separate namespace, arranged in alphabetical order.

For additional information on these and other namespaces in .NET, see the resources listed in appendix D and in the bibliography.

B.1 SYSTEM.COLLECTIONS

The System.Collections namespace defines various types required to manipulate collections of objects, including lists, queues, stacks, hash tables, and dictionaries. An exception is the Array class, which is part of the System namespace, since this class provides core functionality defined by the C# language.

The System.Collections.Generic and System.Collections.ObjectModel namespaces were added in .NET 2.0 to support generic collection classes and interfaces for use with the framework.

Members of the collections namespaces are discussed throughout the book, and in particular in chapter 5, where the PhotoAlbum class is built as a collection of Photograph objects. Chapter 5 provides details on generics, with the System.Collections.Generic namespace summarized in .NET Table 5.7.

B.2 SYSTEM.COMPONENTMODEL

This namespace defines various types that specify the runtime and design-time behavior of components and controls. In particular, the Component and Container classes and their corresponding interfaces are defined in this namespace.

The Component class is introduced in chapter 3 as the base class for much of the functionality in the Windows Forms namespace. Members of this namespace are also critical for data binding support, discussed in chapters 21 and 22.

B.3 SYSTEM.DATA

The System.Data namespace defines classes and other types that constitute the ADO.NET architecture. This architecture enables the manipulation and management of data from multiple data sources, including both local and remote databases with connected or disconnected interaction.

Although this namespace is not discussed in the book, chapters 21 and 22 provide some details on using databases with the data binding interface supported by Windows Forms, and in particular with the Windows.Forms.DataGrid control.

See the bibliography for references to additional information on this namespace.

B.4 SYSTEM.DRAWING

This namespace defines basic functionality in the graphical device interface (GDI) architecture. This includes the Graphics class for drawing to a device, the Pen class for drawing lines and curves, and the `Brush` class used to fill the interiors of shapes. It also includes the `Point`, `Size`, `Rectangle`, and other structures used for positioning and sizing Windows Forms controls within a container.

The `System.Drawing.Design` namespace provides design-time support for user interface logic and drawing. Some discussion of the classes in this namespace occurs in chapter 17 on custom controls.

The `System.Drawing.Printing` namespace provides print-related classes and other types. Printing is discussed in chapter 23.

An overview of the `System.Drawing` namespace is provided in .NET Table 13.5. Members of this namespace are used to create owner-drawn tab pages and list boxes, also discussed in chapter 13.

B.5 SYSTEM.GLOBALIZATION

The `System.Globalization` namespace defines locale-related information, such as the formatting of dates, times, currency, and numbers.

A number of Windows Forms controls include some sort of formatting property that can be used to specify formatting information. Chapter 12 discusses numeric formatting, while chapter 14 discusses data and time formatting. Also check the index for the various control classes where `Format` and `FormatInfo` members are defined.

Another key part of this namespace is the culture functionality. A new feature in .NET 2.0 is the ability to define custom cultures. Chapters 12 and 14 provide some examples using these classes during their formatting discussions.

B.6 SYSTEM.IO

This namespace defines types for performing synchronous and asynchronous reading and writing of data streams and files. It also defines types for interacting with the file system, such as the `Directory`, `File`, and `Path` classes.

The various `Stream` classes are introduced in chapter 6 in order to read and write album files for the MyPhotos application. Members for interacting with the file system are discussed here as well.

B.7 SYSTEM.NET

The `System.Net` namespace defines types for common Internet protocols such as HTTP and local file management, including the abstract `WebRequest` and `WebResponse` classes. The related `System.Net.Sockets` namespace defines a managed implementation of the Windows Sockets interface.

These interfaces can be very useful in Windows Forms applications for interacting with remote servers and services, and for building custom communication interfaces between one or more applications. In Windows Forms applications, it is common to create a specific thread responsible for external communication of this kind, rather than performing such communication as part of a user interface thread. See the discussion on the `System.Threading` namespace later in this appendix for more information on threading.

Since the examples in this book are designed to be standalone applications, neither of these namespaces is discussed in the book.

B.8 SYSTEM.REFLECTION

This namespace defines a managed view of loaded types and their members, including classes and their methods, properties, and events. It supports the ability to dynamically create new types and invoke existing types and their members. For example, the classes in this namespace can be used to query the classes in an assembly and invoke specific properties and methods within that assembly.

Windows Forms controls use this namespace internally to query and interact with various types of objects. Listing 14.1 in chapter 14 provides an example that uses reflection to dynamically alter the value of a user-selected property in a `DateTimePicker` control. Reflection is also briefly discussed in chapter 17.

B.9 SYSTEM.RESOURCES

The `System.Resources` namespace defines types that permit programs to create, store, and manage resources used by an application. Resources can be stored in a loaded assembly or in a satellite assembly that is external to the application. In particular, this namespace is used to manage culture-specific resources for an application, and is used for localization of applications.

Localization is the process of building an interface that can be used in multiple cultures and languages. Typically, it involves placing strings, images, and other culture-specific resources into a resource file, and loading such resources dynamically at runtime. This resource file can then be translated into another language or based on another culture to generate alternate resource files. These alternate files can then be used with the same program assembly to execute the program in the corresponding language or culture.

For example, while the applications in this book were written for a U.S. English user, we might want to support users that understand Canadian French, or Mexican Spanish. Placing our original strings and other constructs in a separate resource file would allow us to do just this.

If you are interested in writing an application targeted at multiple cultures, it is worth your time to understand this process before you begin. It can be quite difficult to localize an existing program, rather than building in such support from the start.

Resources are generally discussed in chapter 15, which should serve as a good primer if you wish to understand localization. The .NET documentation provides some sample programs that illustrate localization, as do many of the references provided later in the book.

B.10 SYSTEM.SECURITY

This namespace defines the common language runtime security system, including security permissions for code and assemblies. The `SecurityManager` class in this namespace is the main access point for classes interacting with the security system.

Some aspects of the security namespace are discussed in chapter 10, where a number of classes from the `System.Security.Cryptography` namespace are employed in an example showing how to securely encode an album file.

B.11 SYSTEM.THREADING

The `System.Threading` namespace defines the types that enable multithreaded programming, including the `Thread` class and synchronization primitives such as the `Monitor` and `Mutex` classes. A *thread* is a sequence of execution corresponding to a defined set of computer instructions. All C# programs in .NET begin with a `Main` method, running in what is called the *main thread*. This main thread may create, or *spawn*, additional threads as required. Each thread performs a defined task or set of tasks. At a basic level, multiple threads simply permit a program to do multiple things at once.

Generally speaking, threads are either *interface threads* or *worker threads*. An interface thread is a thread that interacts with the user in some fashion. The main thread in a Windows Forms program is typically an interface thread, and the `Application.Run` method introduced in chapter 1 is used to start a message loop on this thread that receives operating system messages and converts them into .NET events, which in turn invoke event handlers registered with the program.

A worker thread is a thread that performs some kind of analysis or other work on behalf of a program, and typically is hidden from a user. For example, a worker thread might receive stock price information from a remote server that a user interface thread displays in a `ListView` control.

Threads are created using the `Thread` class, with a `ThreadStart` delegate specifying the method or other program code that should be executed within the thread. The trick with multithreaded programming isn't the ability to have multiple threads; it is the synchronization, or co-existence, of these threads that causes difficulties. For this reason, synchronization constructs such as *locking* have evolved to control the interaction between multiple threads, and to make sure that different threads do not access the same portion of memory, databases, or other shared data at the same time.

As we focused on the Windows Forms namespace in this book, our examples did not include multiple threads of control. Section 14.4 in chapter 14 shows how the `ProgressBar` control and `BackgroundWorkerThread` class can be used to perform asynchronous tasks. This section includes a brief discussion on threading.

B.12 SYSTEM.WEB

This namespace defines types and additional namespaces for interacting with Web browsers and servers over the Internet. It contains the `System.Web.Services` namespace used when building web services, and the `System.Web.UI` namespace for building user interfaces in web applications.

As this book is all about building Windows-based applications, it does not discuss these namespaces.

B.13 SYSTEM.WINDOWS.FORMS

The `System.Windows.Forms` namespace defines types for building Windows-based applications. The `Control` class in this namespace is the basis for the user interface objects defined here.

The related `System.Windows.Forms.Design` namespace is used to provide design-time support for Windows Forms controls, most notably for integrating custom controls into Visual Studio. The design namespace permits custom controls to define their behavior in the Toolbox and Properties windows, and manage their appearance when displayed in the Windows Forms Designer window.

The Windows Forms namespace is, of course, the topic of this book, with custom controls discussed in chapter 17.

B.14 SYSTEM.XML

This namespace defines types in support of various Extensible Markup Language (XML) standards, including XML 1.0 and XSD schemas. The XML standards were based on an older Standards Generalized Markup Language (SGML) originally developed as a generalized solution for formatting documentation. Pure SGML proved a bit problematic for communication over networks, most notably the Internet, so XML was designed as a restricted form of SGML to overcome these difficulties.

XML is a great way to specify data in a generalized manner for use with the `DataSet` class in the `System.Data` namespace, and for interacting with remote applications and databases.

APPENDIX C

Visual index

This appendix presents a visual index of the Windows Forms namespace as covered in this book, as well as some of the other .NET types discussed in the text. These are organized into sections in order to fit neatly on these pages. Sections C.1 through C.10 present class hierarchy diagrams, while sections C.11 through C.13 present tables showing enumeration, event argument, and interface types.

The figures on the subsequent pages have the following features:

- Classes in the Windows Forms namespace are gray.
- Classes from other namespaces are white.
- Classes presented or discussed in the book indicate the table, figure, or other location where more information can be found. Also consult the index for alternate places in the text where the class may be discussed.

An overview of this appendix is illustrated in the following diagram.

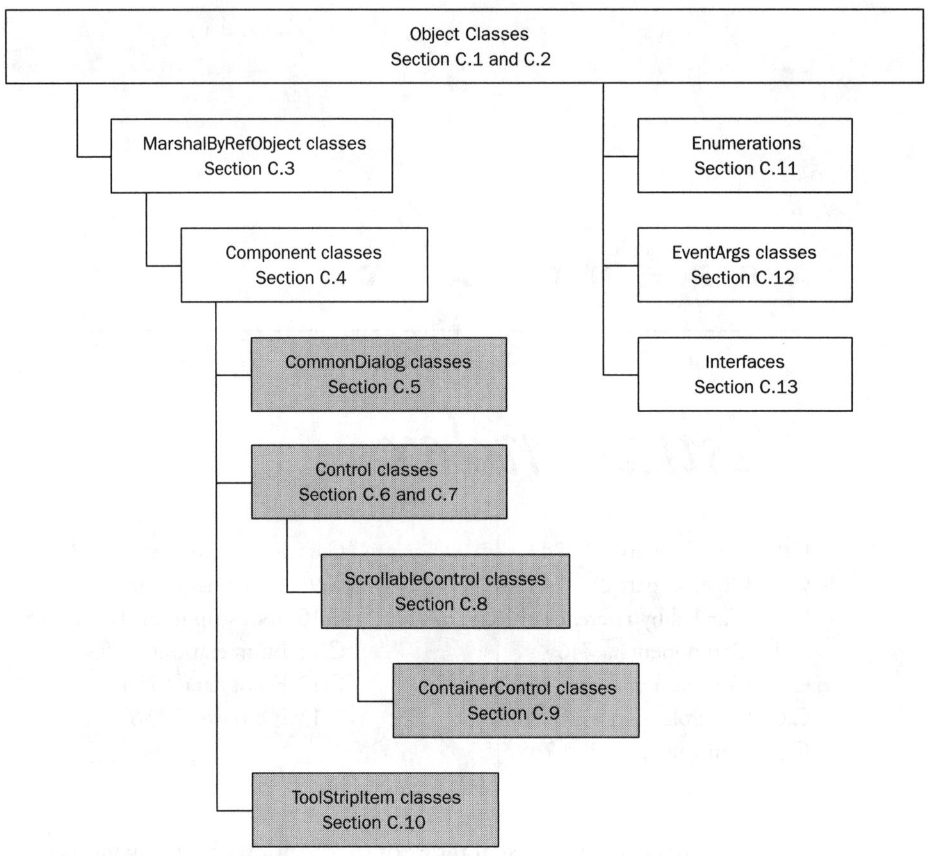

Most of the classes in the Windows Forms namespace appear in these diagrams. Internal and private classes are omitted, of course, as are many of the collection classes that support the components and controls in the namespace. Classes that are no longer recommended, such as most of the `DataGrid`-related classes and the `Menu` subclasses, have been omitted as well. Due to space constraints, some of the more specialized classes are also excluded.

In addition, classes that represent individual or special aspects of a control may not be shown here. For example, the `DataGridViewCell` and `DataGridViewColumn` classes are included, but the cell and column types such as the `DataGridViewCheckBoxColumn` and `DataGridViewCheckBoxCell` classes are not.

C.1 Objects (part 1)

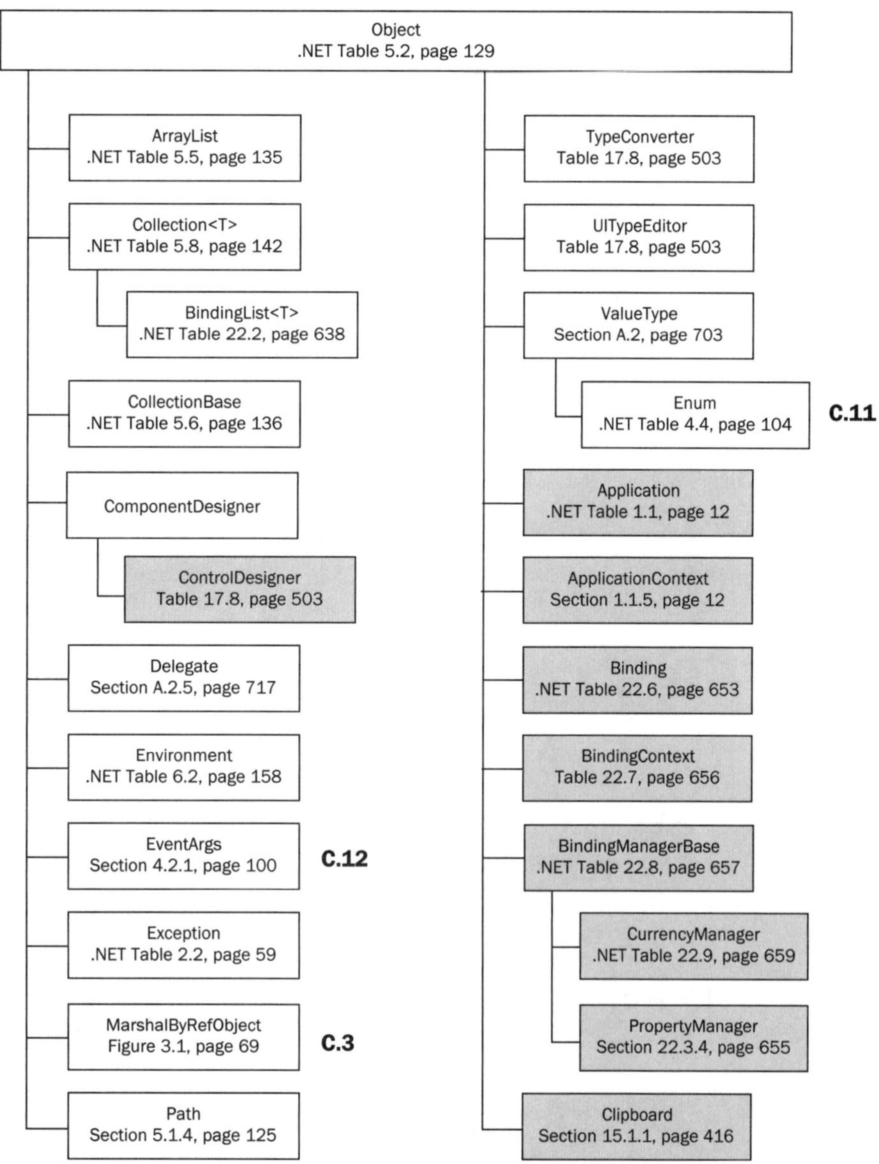

Figure C.1 The Object class is the base class of all types in the .NET Framework.

C.2 OBJECTS (PART 2)

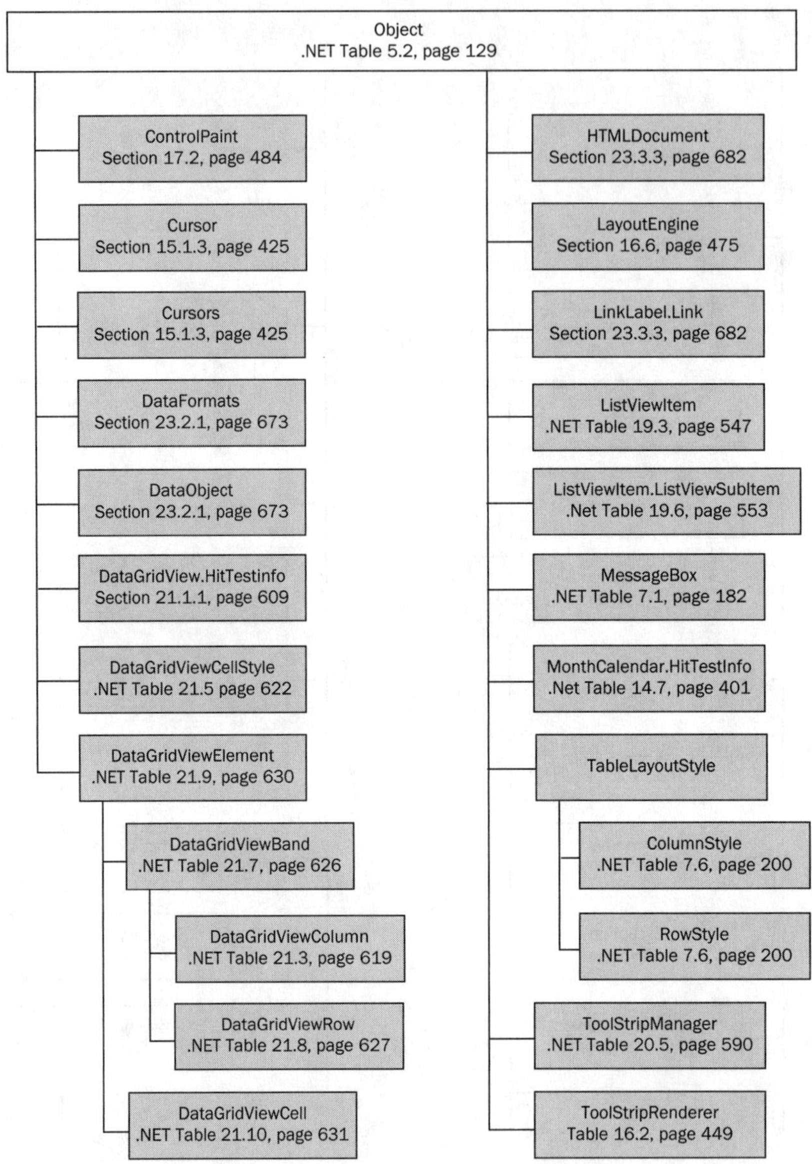

Figure C.2 This and the preceding figure show object classes that appear in the book.

C.3 MARSHAL BY REFERENCE OBJECTS

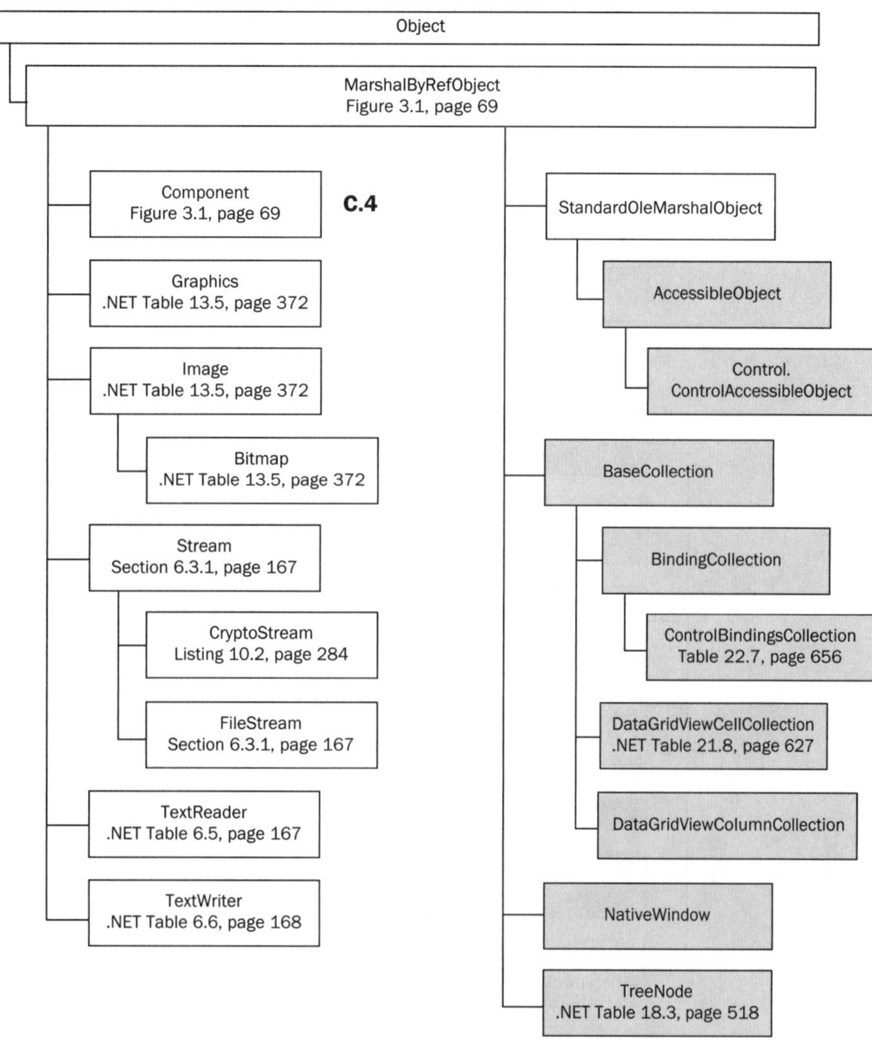

Figure C.3 The MarshalByRefObject class represents an object that must be marshaled by reference.

C.4 COMPONENTS

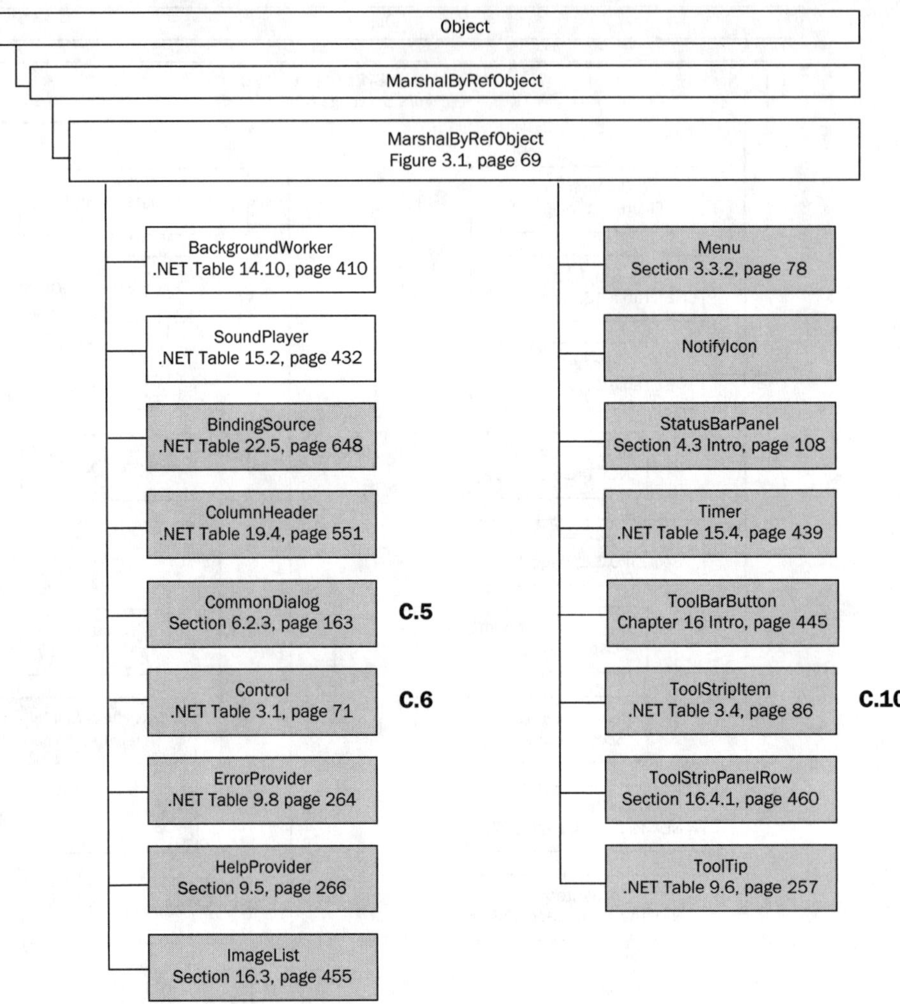

Figure C.4 The Component class represents a marshaled by reference object that can exist within a container.

C.5 COMMON DIALOGS

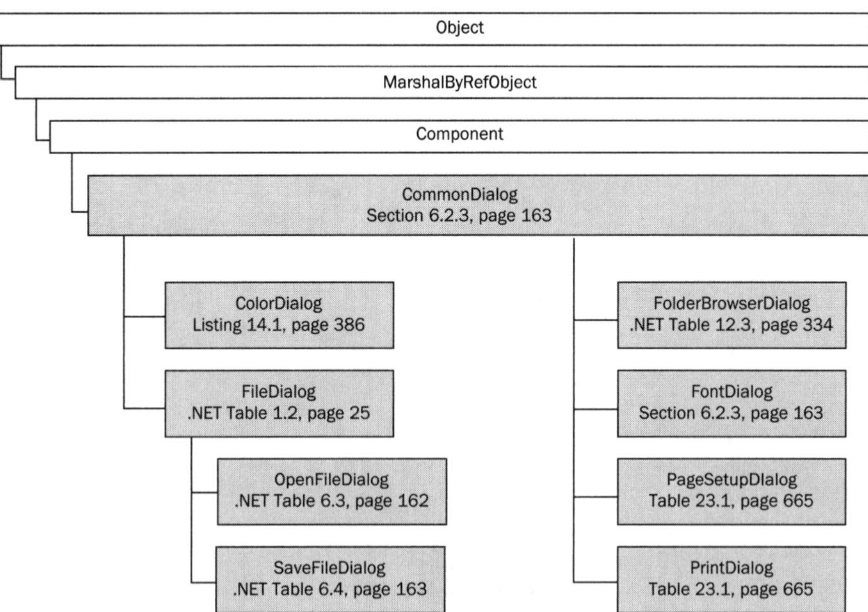

Figure C.5 The CommonDialog class represents a component that provides a standard interface for functionality required by Windows Forms applications.

C.6 CONTROLS (PART 1)

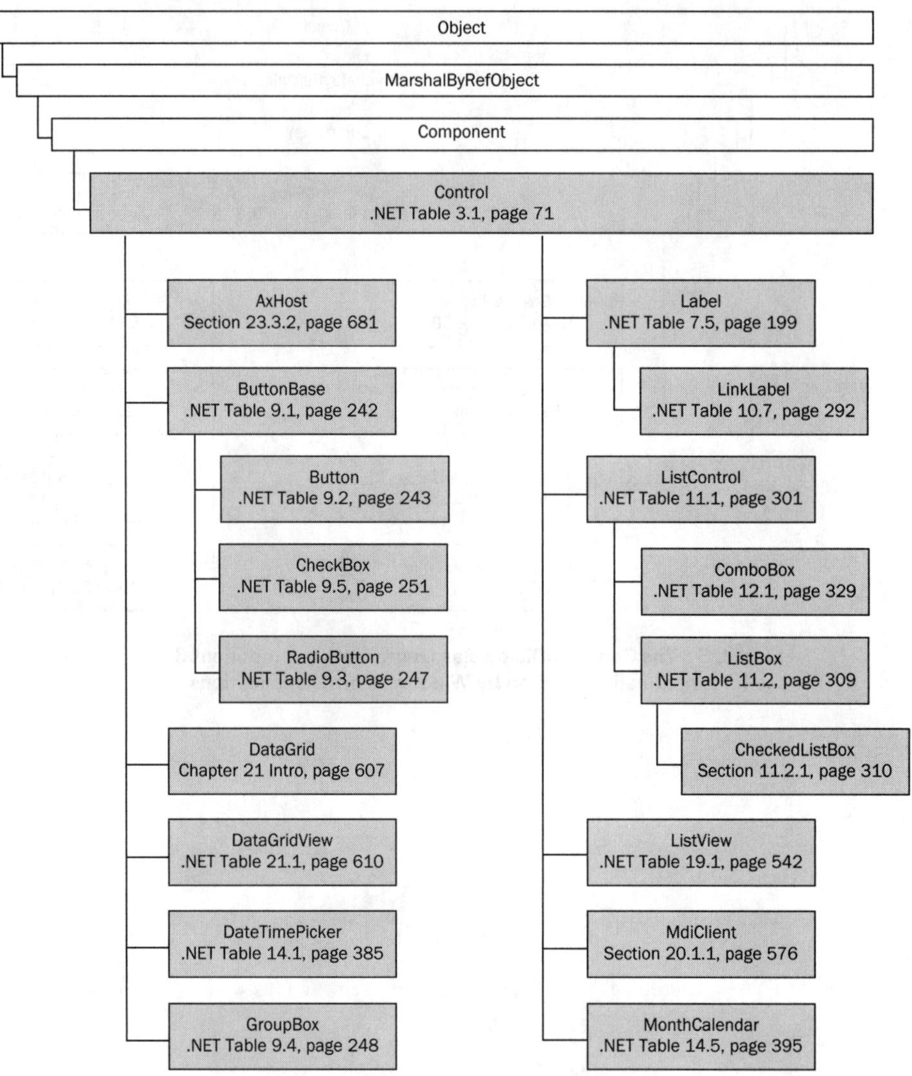

Figure C.6 The Windows Forms Control class represents a component with a visual representation on the Windows desktop.

C.7 CONTROLS (PART 2)

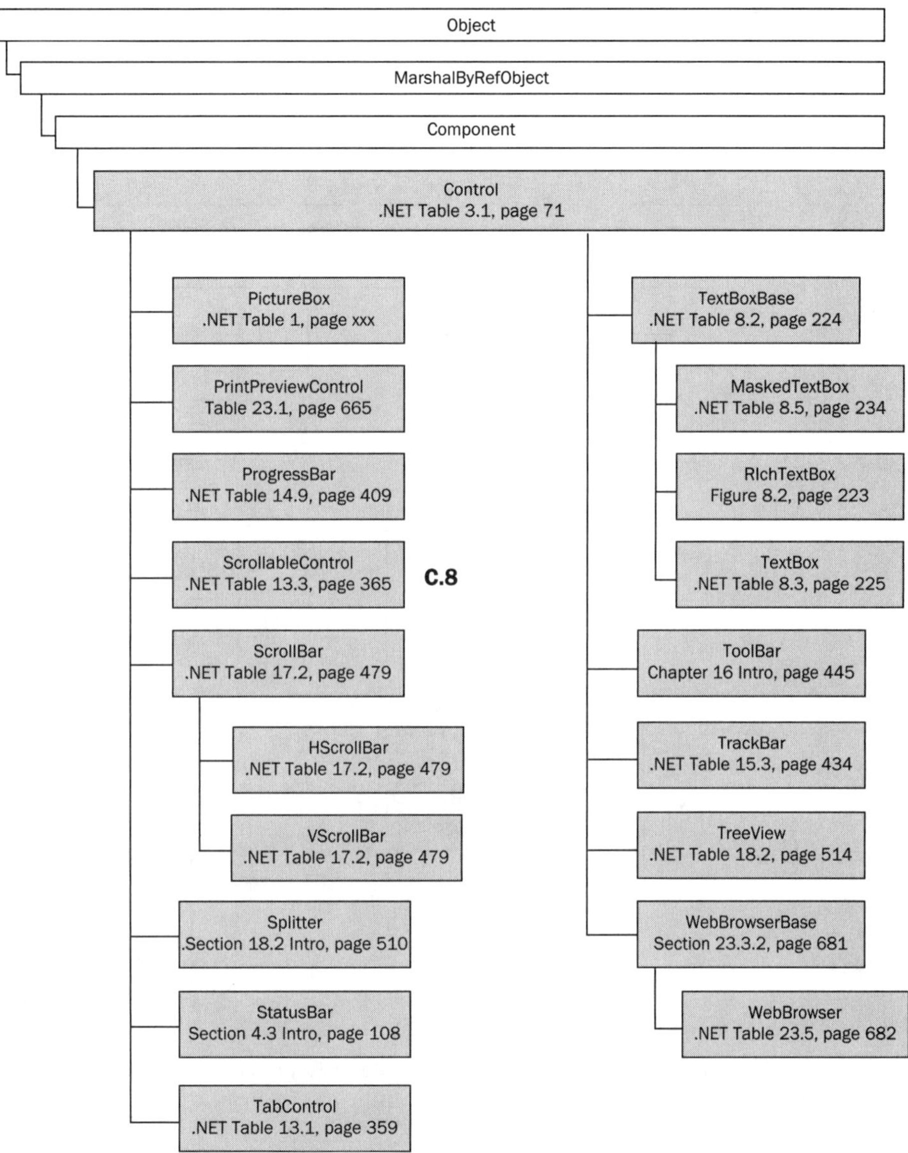

Figure C.7 This and the preceding figure show control classes in the Windows Forms namespace.

C.8 Scrollable controls

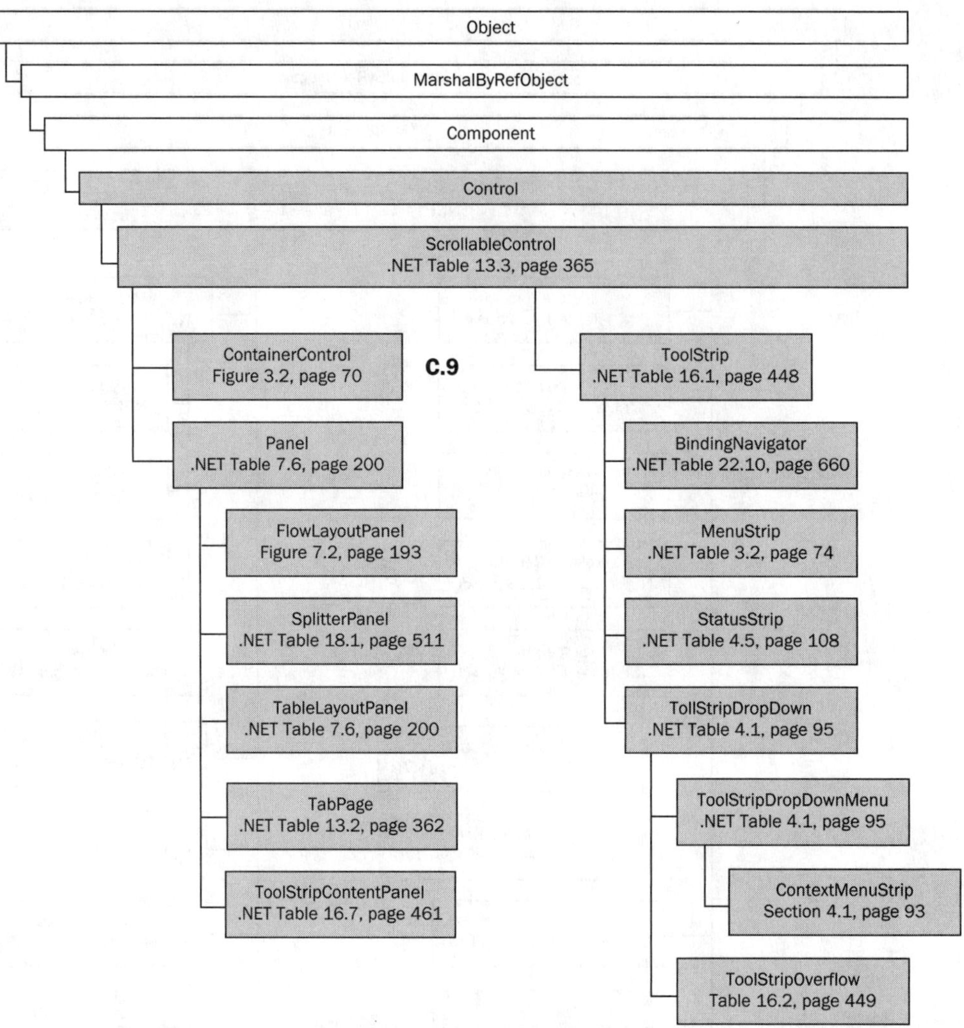

Figure C.8 The ScrollableControl class is a Windows Forms control that supports automated scrolling.

C.9 CONTAINER CONTROLS

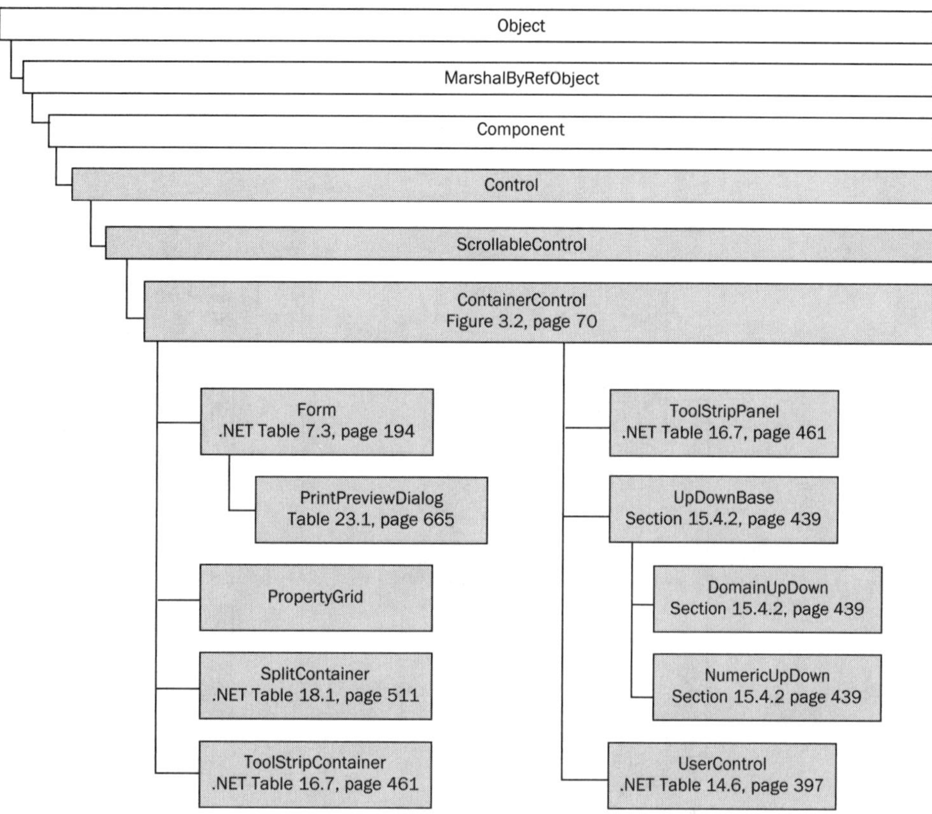

Figure C.9 The ContainerControl class is a scrollable control that provides a logical boundary for a contained collection of controls.

C.10 Tool strip item classes

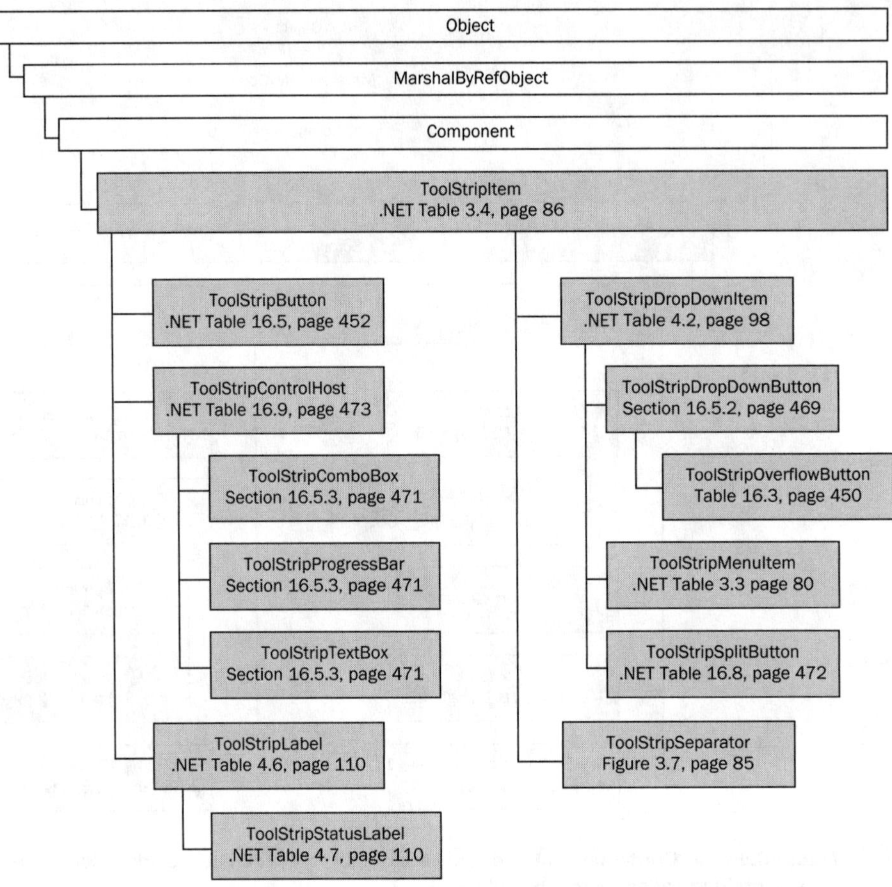

Figure C.10 The ToolStripItem class is a component that can exist within a tool strip.

C.11 ENUMERATIONS

The `Enum` structure is the base for all enumerations in .NET, and is described in .NET Table 4.4 on page 104. The following table provides a quick reference for the enumerations discussed in the book. If you wish to define your own enumerations, see section A.2.4 in appendix A on page 716. In the table, many of the references simply mention the enumeration in an appropriate context or use it in an example. The Values column indicates whether the enumeration values associated with each entry are also discussed at the indicated reference.

Enumeration	Reference	Values	Page
AnchorStyles	.NET Table 1.3	y	29
AutoCompleteMode	.NET Table 12.4	y	342
AutoCompleteSource	.NET Table 12.5	y	344
Border3DStyle	Section 4.3.2		109
BorderStyle	Section 2.2.3		46
CharacterCasing	.NET Table 8.3		225
CheckState	.NET Table 9.5	y	251
CipherMode	.NET Table 10.6		283
ColumnHeaderAutoResizeStyle	.NET Table 19.4		551
ComboBoxStyle	.NET Table 12.2	y	331
ContentAlignment	Section 8.2.2	y	225
ControlStyles	Table 17.5		488
CryptoStreamMode	.NET Table 10.6	y	283
DataGridViewCellBorderStyle	.NET Table 21.1		610
DataGridViewComboBoxDisplayStyle	Section 21.2.2		623
DataGridViewElementStates	Section 21.3.1		629
DateTimePickerFormat	.NET Table 14.4	y	393
DialogResult	.NET Table 7.2	y	185
DockStyle	.NET Table 1.4	y	31
DragDropEffects	Section 23.2.1		673
DrawItemState	Section 13.3.1		370
DrawMode	.NET Table 13.6	y	377
ErrorBlinkStyle	.NET Table 9.8		264
ErrorIconAlignment	.NET Table 9.8		264
FlatStyle	.NET Table 7.5		199
FormBorderStyle	Table 7.4		195

Enumeration	Reference	Values	Page
FormWindowState	.NET Table 20.6	y	599
HorizontalAlignment	Section 8.2.2	y	225
ItemActivation	.NET Table 19.9	y	568
Keys	Listing 3.3		82
LeftRightAlignment	.NET Table 14.1		385
LinkBehavior	.NET Table 4.6		110
MaskFormat	.NET Table 8.5		234
MdiLayout	.NET Table 20.7	y	602
MergeAction	.NET Table 20.3	y	582
MessageBoxButtons	.NET Table 7.1	y	182
MessageBoxDefaultButton	.NET Table 7.1	y	182
MessageBoxIcon	.NET Table 7.1	y	182
MessageBoxOptions	.NET Table 7.1	y	182
MonthCalendar.HitArea	.NET Table 14.8		402
MouseButtons	.NET Table 10.5		275
PaddingMode	.NET Table 10.6		283
PictureBoxSizeMode	.NET Table 4.3	y	101
ProgressBarStyle	Section 14.4.2	y	408
ScrollEventType	.NET Table 17.3		484
SelectionMode	.NET Table 11.3	y	318
SortOrder	Section 19.2.3	y	556
SpecialFolder	Listing 6.2		156
StringComparison	Section 5.2.2		128
StringFormatFlags	Listing 13.3		373
TabAlignment	Listing 13.4		376
TabDrawMode	Section 13.3.1	y	370
TableLayoutPanelCellBorderStyle	.NET Table 7.6		200
TableLayoutPanelGrowStyle	.NET Table 7.6		200
TextImageRelation	.NET Table 9.1		242
ToolStripDropDownCloseReason	.NET Table 4.1		95
ToolStripDropDownDirection	.NET Table 4.2		98
ToolStripItemDisplayStyle	.NET Table 3.4		86
ToolStripItemOverflow	Section 16.2.3		454
ToolStripLayoutStyle	.NET Table 16.1		448

Enumeration	Reference	Values	Page
ToolStripTextDirection	.NET Table 16.1		448
TreeViewAction	.NET Table 18.4		522
View	.NET Table 19.2	y	546

C.12 EVENT DATA

The `System.EventArgs` class is the base for classes that contain event data. The following table provides a quick reference for event classes discussed in the book. If you wish to define your own event, see the Events entry in table 17.5 on page 488.

EventArgs class	Reference	Page
CancelEventArgs	Section 7.2.2	190
ColumnClickEventArgs	Section 19.2.3	556
DataGridViewCellMouseEventArgs	Section 21.2.3	625
DateRangeEventArgs	Section 21.3.2	630
DoWorkEventArgs	Section 14.4.3	410
DragEventArgs	.NET Table 23.4	676
DrawItemEventArgs	.NET Table 13.4	370
DrawListViewItemEventArgs	Section 19.1.1	541
DrawToolTipEventArgs	Section 9.4.2	258
FormClosedEventArgs	Section 16.5.1	465
FormClosingEventArgs	Section 7.2.2	190
KeyEventArgs	.NET Table 10.2	271
KeyPressEventArgs	.NET Table 8.4	232
LabelEditEventArgs	.NET Table 19.8	565
LinkLabelLinkClickedEventArgs	Section 23.3.3	682
ListChangedEventArgs	.NET Table 22.2	638
MeasureItemEventArgs	.NET Table 13.7	378
MouseEventArgs	.NET Table 10.5	275
NodeLabelEditEventArgs	.NET Table 18.5	533
PaintEventArgs	.NET Table 17.4	486
PrintPageEventArgs	.NET Table 23.2	668
ProgressChangedEventArgs	Section 14.4.3	410
RetrieveVirtualItemEventArgs	Section 19.4	570
ScrollEventArgs	.NET Table 17.3	484

EventArgs class	Reference	Page
ToolStripItemClickedEventArgs	Listing 4.1	103
TreeViewCancelEventArgs	Section 18.3.2	518
TreeViewEventArgs	.NET Table 18.4	522
TypeValidationEventArgs	.NET Table 8.7	237
WebBrowserDocumentCompletedEventArgs	Section 23.3.3	682

C.13 INTERFACES

The term *interface* is described in section 5.3 on page 131. The following table provides a quick reference for the interfaces discussed in the book. If you wish to define your own interfaces, see section A.2.3 in appendix A on page 715.

Interface	Reference	Page
IBindingList	.NET Table 22.1	638
IButtonControl	Section 9.1.1	241
ICancelAddNew	Section 22.1.2	639
ICollection	Table 5.3	132
ICollection<T>	.NET Table 5.7	141
IComparer	.NET Table 19.7	557
IComponent	Figure 3.1	69
ICryptoTransform	.NET Table 10.6	283
ICustomFormatter	.NET Table 12.6	346
IDataErrorInfo	Table 21.2	616
IDataObject	Section 23.2.2	675
IDisposable	.NET Table 5.9	145
IEditableObject	.NET Table 22.4	643
IEnumerable	Table 5.3	132
IEnumerable<T>	.NET Table 5.7	141
IEnumerator	Table 5.3	132
IExtenderProvider	.NET Table 9.7	261
IFormatProvider	.NET Table 12.6	346
IFormattable	.NET Table 12.6	346
IList	Table 5.3	132
IList<T>	.NET Table 5.7	141

Interface	Reference	Page
IListSource	Table 21.2	616
IMessageFilter	.NET Table 1.1	12
IPersistComponentSettings	Table 17.5	488
IRaiseItemChangedEvents	Section 22.1.2	639
ISupportInitialize	Listing 2.4	50
ITypedList	Table 21.2	616

APPENDIX D

For more information

This appendix lists additional sources of information about the .NET Framework. The Internet sites listed here were valid as of February 20, 2006. The sites are listed without prejudice. You can make your own judgment on which ones most closely match your needs.

Microsoft sites

msdn.microsoft.com (Microsoft Developer Network)
msdn2.microsoft.com (online documentation)
www.asp.net
www.gotdotnet.com
www.windowsforms.net

Internet resources

www.4guysfromrolla.com
www.aewnet.com
www.csharphelp.com
www.csharp-station.com
www.codeguru.com
www.codeproject.com
www.c-sharpcorner.com
www.developerfusion.co.uk
www.devx.com

www.dotnet247.com
www.dotnetjunkies.com
www.dotnetwire.com
www.devdex.com
www.error-bank.com
www.only4gurus.com
www.mastercsharp.com
www.mono-project.com
www.sharptoolbox.com
www.syncfusion.com/faq/windowsforms
www.vscodeswap.com

Magazines

Dr. Dobbs Journal: www.ddj.com
MSDN Magazine: msdn.microsoft.com/msdnmag
.NET Programmer's Journal: dotnet.sys-con.com
Software Development: www.sdmagazine.com
Visual Studio Magazine: www.ftponline.com/vsm
Web Services Journal: webservices.sys-con.com

Newsgroups

Many of the sites in the prior list support discussion forums of one kind or another. Microsoft provides various Windows Forms forums that are available from the www.windowsforms.net site by clicking the Forums tab. The following newsgroups are available from the msnews.microsoft.com server, and can be viewed in Outlook Express or from sites such as groups.google.com.

microsoft.public.dotnet.framework.sdk
microsoft.public.dotnet.framework.windowsforms
microsoft.public.dotnet.framework.windowsforms.controls
microsoft.public.dotnet.framework.windowsforms.databinding
microsoft.public.dotnet.framework.windowsforms.designtime
microsoft.public.dotnet.languages.csharp

bibliography

Microsoft .NET Framework

Archor, Tom. *Inside C#, Second Edition*, Redmond, WA: Microsoft Press, 2003.

Grimes, Fergal. *Microsoft .NET for Programmers,* Greenwich, CT: Manning Publications, 2002.

Gunnerson, Eric. *A Programmer's Introduction to C#, Second Edition*, Berkeley, CA: Apress, 2001.

Liberty, Jesse. *Programming C#: Building .NET Applications with C#,* Sebastopol, CA: O'Reilly & Associates, 2005.

Rammer, Ingo and Szpuszta, Mario. *Advanced .NET Remoting, Second Edition*, Berkeley, CA: Apress, 2005.

Richter, Jeffery. *Applied Microsoft .NET Framework Programming,* Richmond, WA: Microsoft Press, 2002.

Troelsen, Andrew. *Pro C# 2005 and the .NET 2.0 Platform, Third Edition*, Berkeley, CA: Apress, 2005.

Related languages and environments

Flanagan, David. *Java in a Nutshell, Fourth Edition*, Sebastopol, CA: O'Reilly & Associates, 2002.

Kernighan, Brian W. and Ritchie, Dennis M. *The C Programming Language, Second Edition*, Prentice Hall, 1988.

Liskov, B., Atkinson, et al. *CLU Reference Manual,* Harrisonburg, VA: Springer-Verlag, 1984.

Prosise, Jeff. *Programming Windows 95 with MFC,* Redmond, WA: Microsoft Press, 1996.

Robinson, Matthew and Vorobiev, Pavel. *Swing, Second Edition*, Greenwich, CT: Manning Publications, 2003.

Stroustrup, Bjarne. *The C++ Programming Language, Third Edition*, Reading, MA: Addison-Wesley, 1997.

Software development and user interface design

Brooks, Jr., Frederick P. *The Mythical Man-Month: Essays on Software Engineering, 20th Anniversary Edition*, Reading, MA: Addison-Wesley, 1995.

Fowler, Martin. *Refactoring: Improving the Design of Existing Code*, Reading, MA: Addison-Wesley, 1999.

Fowler, Martin. *Patterns of Enterprise Application Architecture*, Reading, MA: Addison-Wesley, 2002.

Gamma, Erich et al. *Design Patterns: Elements of Reusable Object-Oriented Software*, Reading, MA: Addison-Wesley, 1995.

Kelly, Tom. *The Art of Innovation: Lessons in Creativity from IDEO, America's Leading Design Firm*, New York, NY: Doubleday, 2001.

Microsoft Corporation, *Enterprise Solution Patterns Using Microsoft .Net: Version 2.0 : Patterns & Practices*, Redmond, WA: Microsoft Press, 2003.[1]

Norman, Donald A. *The Design of Everyday Things*, New York, NY: Basic Books, 2002.

Shalloway, Alan and Trott, James, *Design Patterns Explained: A New Perspective on Object-Oriented Design (2nd Edition)*, Reading, MA: Addison-Wesley, 2004.

Schneiderman, Ben. *Designing the User Interface, Strategies for Effective Human-Computer Interaction (4th Edition)*, Reading, MA: Addison-Wesley, 2004.

---

1 This text is also available online at http://msdn.microsoft.com/library/en-us/dnpatterns/html/esp.asp.

index

Symbols

Numerics

A

B

C

D

E

F

J

K

L

M

N

O

P

S

T

U

V

W

X

Y

Z